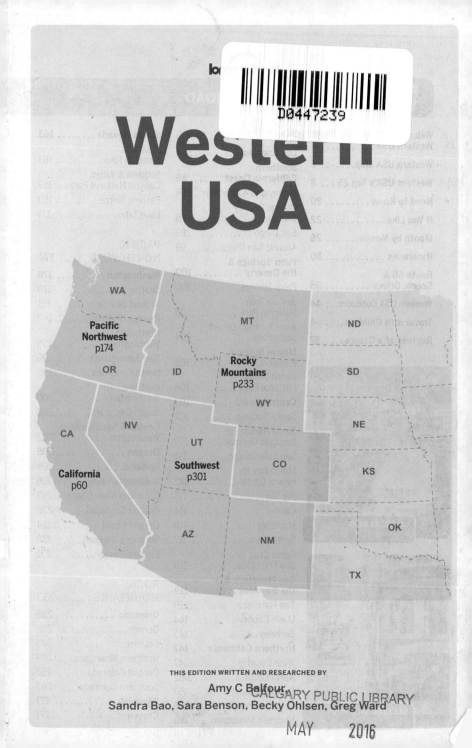

Western USA

Pacific Northwest
p174

Rocky Mountains
p233

Southwest
p301

California
p60

WA

MT

ND

OR

ID

SD

WY

NV

NE

CA

UT

CO

KS

AZ

NM

OK

TX

THIS EDITION WRITTEN AND RESEARCHED BY

Amy C Balfour

Sandra Bao, Sara Benson, Becky Ohlsen, Greg Ward

Contents

MITCHELL FUNK / GETTY IMAGES ©

LAS VEGAS P306

WOOWOO LEE / GETTY IMAGES ©

SAN FRANCISCO P119

Contents

UNDERSTAND

SURVIVAL GUIDE

SPECIAL FEATURES

Welcome to Western USA

Landscapes and legends draw adventurers to the West, where a good day includes locavore dining, vineyard wine-sipping, cowboy history and outdoor fun.

Great Outdoors

When it comes to scenery in the West, the hyperbole is usually on point. Awesome. Epic. Once-in-a-lifetime. But what gives Western views extra punch? The sounds of adventure – whoosh! splash! clink! – rippling across the landscape. Surfers, kayakers and beachcombers flock to the Western coastline, which stretches north from the sunny shores of San Diego to the bluffs of central California and on to the rocky beaches of Oregon and Washington. Red rocks, gorges and prickly-pear deserts lure hikers and cyclists to the Southwest, where the biggest wonder is the 277-mile Grand Canyon. Meanwhile, in the Rockies, skiing, ice climbing and mountain-biking never looked so pretty or sounded so fun.

Regional Food & Wine

Regional specialties are as diverse as the landscapes. One commonality? Chefs and consumers alike are focusing on fresh and locally grown food, a locavore trend that started in the West. This eco-consciousness has also been embraced by wine producers, who are increasingly implementing organic and biodynamic growing principles. And speaking of winemaking, Napa and Sonoma now share the spotlight with Washington, Oregon, central California and Arizona.

Urban Oases

Western cities have distinct personalities. In California there's the hey-bro friendliness of San Diego, the Hollywood flash of Los Angeles and the bohemian cool of San Francisco. Further north in Seattle, cutting-edge joins homegrown, often over a cup of joe. Cosmopolitan chic meets plucky frontier spirit in Denver, while patio preening and spa pampering give Phoenix a strangely compelling spoiled-girl vibe. And then there's Las Vegas, a glitzy neon playground where you can get hitched in the Elvis Chapel, spend your honeymoon in Paris and then bet the mortgage – all in the very same weekend.

Hands-On History

Museums? Save 'em for later. First you'll want to climb a ladder into a cliff dwelling, poke around the ruins of a Pony Express station, or simply join the congregation inside a 1700s Spanish mission. What else is there to explore in the West? Crumbling forts. Abandoned mining towns. A former Titan Missile silo. Wander historic sites like these for up-close and evocative links to the region's not-so-long-ago past.

Why I Love Western USA

By Amy C Balfour, Writer

There's a new adventure or awesome view after every bend in the trail. My first glimpse of the Grand Canyon (not including a first look as a toddler) came after a mad dash from my car to Mather Point during a cross-country road trip. I've been hooked on the West ever since. I subsequently spent seven years in Los Angeles, using the city as a launchpad for exploring Western beaches, deserts, mountains and some truly glorious national parks, not to mention lots of great restaurants. The West is a special place, worth an extended visit.

For more about our writers, see page 480

Above: Falls at Havasu Canyon (p344)

Western USA

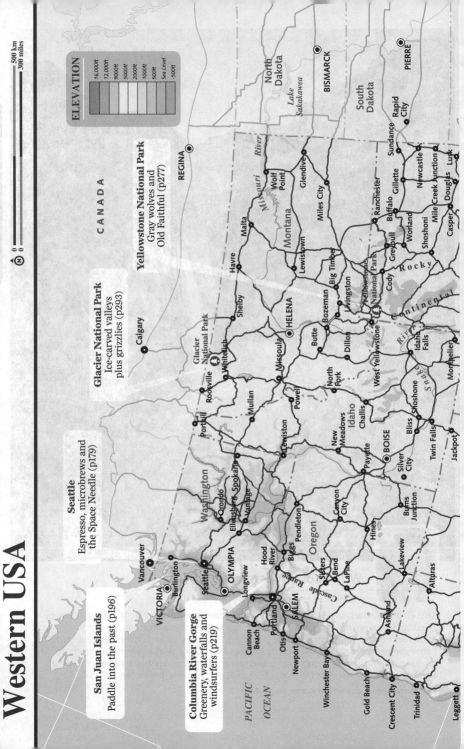

San Juan Islands (p196)
Paddle into the past

Seattle
Espresso, microbrews and the Space Needle (p179)

Columbia River Gorge
Greenery, waterfalls and windsurfers (p219)

Glacier National Park
Ice-carved valleys plus grizzlies (p293)

Yellowstone National Park
Gray wolves and Old Faithful (p277)

ELEVATION
16,000ft
12,000ft
9000ft
5000ft
2000ft
1000ft
500ft
Sea Level
-500ft

500 km
300 miles

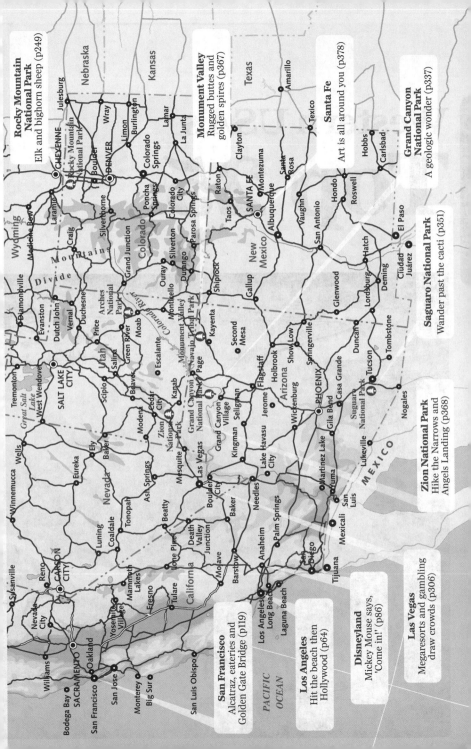

Western USA's
Top 25

Yellowstone National Park

1 This grand park recently celebrated its 125th anniversary. What makes Yellowstone (p277) so enduring? Geologic wonders for one thing, from geysers and hot springs to fumaroles and mud pots. There's also Mt Washburn, an impressive central peak with inspiring views from its summit. Add in a towering waterfall, a historic inn and an abundance of bison, elk, moose and bears, and you've described perfection. The famous gray wolves, restored in 1995, recently numbered about 95 in the park. Finally, America's first park has the one-and-only Old Faithful, a beloved geyser still blowing its top for appreciative crowds. Grand Prismatic Spring (p278)

San Francisco

2 Change is afoot in this boom-and-bust city, currently enjoying a very high-profile boom. Amid the growth, the fog and the clatter of old-fashioned trams, the diverse neighborhoods of San Francisco (p119) invite long days of wandering, with great indie shops, world-class restaurants and bohemian nightlife. Highlights include peering into the cells at Alcatraz, strolling across the Golden Gate Bridge and dining inside the Ferry Building. And you must take at least one ride on the trolley. How cool is San Francisco? Trust us – turn that first corner to a stunning waterfront view, and you'll be hooked. Golden Gate Bridge (p130)

IGNACIO PALACIOS / GETTY IMAGES ©

JOE DANIEL PRICE / GETTY IMAGES ©

Grand Canyon National Park

3 The sheer immensity of the canyon (p337) is what grabs you at first – a two-billion-year-old rip across the landscape that reveals the earth's geologic secrets with commanding authority. But it's Mother Nature's artistic touches, from sun-dappled ridges and crimson buttes to lush oases and a ribbon-like river, that hold your attention and demand your return. To explore the canyon, take your pick of adventures: hiking, biking, rafting or mule riding. Or simply grab a seat along the Rim Trail and watch the canyon change colors before you.

Las Vegas

4 Just when you think you've got a handle on the West – majestic, soul-nourishing – here comes Vegas (p306). Beneath the neon lights of the Strip, it puts on a dazzling show: dancing fountains, a spewing volcano, the Eiffel Tower. But it saves its most dangerous charms for the gambling dens – seductive lairs where the fresh-pumped air and bright colors share one goal: separating you from your money. Step away if you can for fine restaurants, Cirque du Soleil, Slotzilla and the Mob Museum. The Venetian (p312)

STEPHEN YELVERTON PHOTOGRAPHY / GETTY IMAGES ©

SYLVAIN SONNET / GETTY IMAGES ©

THOMAS WINZ / GETTY IMAGES ©

OLEG KORSHAKOV / GETTY IMAGES ©

ANTHONY PIDGEON / GETTY IMAGES ©

Pacific Coast Highways

5 A drive along America's western coastline is road tripping at its finest. In California, Hwy 1 (also called the Pacific Coast Highway, or PCH; p37), Hwy 101 and I-5 pass sea cliffs, idiosyncratic beach towns and a few major cities: laid-back San Diego, rocker LA and beatnik San Francisco. North of the redwoods, Hwy 101 swoops into Oregon for windswept capes, rocky tide pools and, for *Twilight* fans, Ecola State Park, the stand-in for werewolf haven La Push, Washington. Cross the Columbia River into Washington for wet-and-wild Olympic National Park. Pacific Coast Highway near Big Sur

Los Angeles

6 A perpetual influx of dreamers, go-getters and hustlers gives this shiny coastal city (p64) an energetic buzz. Learn the tricks of movie-making during a studio tour. Bliss out to acoustically perfect symphony sounds in the Walt Disney Concert Hall. Wander gardens and galleries at the hilltop Getty Museum. And stargazing? Take in the big picture at the revamped Griffith Observatory or look for stylish, earthbound 'stars' at the Grove. Ready for your close-up darling? You will be – an hour on the beach guarantees that sun-kissed LA glow. Walt Disney Concert Hall (p67), designed by Frank Gehry

Portland

7 Is the dream of the '90s alive in Portland (p205)? The characters in the award-winning indie series *Portlandia* sure think so, and their satiric skits make it clear that this city is a quirky but loveable place. It's as friendly as a big town, and home to a mix of students, artists, cyclists, hipsters, young families, old hippies, eco-freaks and everything in between. There's great food, awesome music and culture aplenty, plus it's as sustainable as you can get. Come visit, but be careful – like everyone else, you might just want to move here!

Yosemite National Park

8 Meander through wildflower-strewn meadows in valleys carved by glaciers, avalanches and earthquakes, whose hard work makes everything look bigger here: thunderous waterfalls that tumble over sheer cliffs, enormous granite domes, ancient groves of giant sequoias, the planet's biggest trees. For the most sublime views, perch at Glacier Point (p164) on a full-moon night or drive the high country's dizzying Tioga Rd in summer.

Route 66

9 As you step up to the counter at the Snow-Cap Drive In at Seligman, Arizona, you know a prank is coming – a squirt of fake mustard, perhaps, or ridiculously incorrect change. Though it's all a bit hokey, you'd be disappointed if the owner forgot to 'get you.' It's these down-home touches that make the 'Mother Road' (p35) – which crosses California, Arizona and New Mexico – so memorable. Begging burros, the Wigwam Motel, the neon signs of Tucumcari – a squirt of fake mustard beats a mass-consumption McBurger every time.

INGRAM PUBLISHING / GETTY IMAGES ©

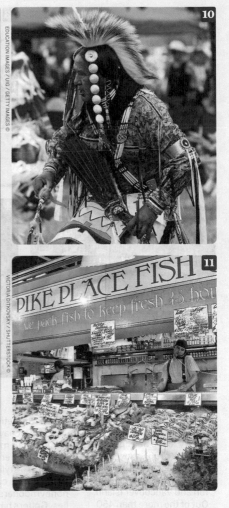

Native American History & Culture

10 The Southwest is home to a fascinating array of Native American sites. To learn about America's earliest inhabitants, climb into the ancient cliff-top homes of Ancestral Puebloans at Mesa Verde National Park in Colorado (p267), or study petroglyphs in Sedona (p332). For living cultures, visit Arizona's Navajo and Hopi nations. As you'll discover here and in regional museums, many designs have religious significance. The baskets, rugs and jewelry crafted today often put a fresh spin on the ancient traditions.

Seattle

11 A cutting-edge Pacific Rim city with an uncanny habit of turning locally hatched ideas into global brands, Seattle (p179) has earned its place in the pantheon of 'great' US metropolises with a world-renowned music scene, an obsessive coffee culture and a penchant for internet-driven innovation. But, while Seattle's trendsetters rush to unearth the next big thing, city traditionalists guard its soul with distinct urban neighborhoods, a home-grown food culture, and arguably the nation's finest public market, Pike Place. Pike Place Market (p179)

San Juan Islands

12 Go back in time by hopping on a ferry to the San Juan Islands (p196), a low-key archipelago north of Puget Sound between Washington and Vancouver Island. Out of the more than 450 'islands' (most are only rocky promontories), only about 60 are inhabited and just four are regularly served by ferries. Nature is the main influence here and each island has its own personality, both geographic and cultural. What can you do here? Start with cycling, kayaking and spotting orcas – then just sit back and relax. Sailboats near Orcas Island (p197)

Phoenix

13 Sometimes you just have to ask, 'What about me?'. Phoenix (p323) answers that question with a stylish grin. Posh resorts cater to honeymooners and families. Golfers have their pick of more than 200 golf courses. Other refined distractions range from luxurious spas and weekly art walks to top-notch museums, spotlight relaxation, Native American arts and crafts, and musical instruments. Add in patio-dining, chichi shopping and an average of 211 sunny days per year, and it's easy to condone a bit of selfishness. Golf course, Scottsdale (p325)

Disneyland & Disney California Adventure

14 Inside Disneyland (p86), beloved cartoon characters waltz down Main Street, U.S.A, Space Mountain rockets through the darkness, and fireworks explode over Sleeping Beauty Castle. And yes, those Audio-Animatronics dolls are still singing 'it's a small world'. Next door, Disney California Adventure showcases the best of the state with a recreated Hollywood back lot, a coastal boardwalk and a patio that's perfect for sipping California wine. The most impressive aspect of both parks? The amazing attention to detail.

Boulder

15 Tucked up against its signature Flatirons (p245), Boulder has a sweet location and a progressive soul, which has attracted a groovy bag of entrepreneurs, hippies and hard-bodies. Packs of cyclists ride the Boulder Creek Bike Path, which links to an abundance of city and county parks purchased through a popular Open Space tax. The pedestrian-only Pearl St Mall is lively, especially at night, when students from the University of Colorado and Naropa University mingle and flirt. In many ways Boulder, not Denver, is the state's tourist hub. Flatirons (p245)

Columbia River Gorge

16 Carved by the mighty Columbia as the Cascades were uplifted, the Columbia River Gorge (p219) is a geologic marvel. With Washington State on its north side and Oregon on its south, the state-dividing gorge offers countless waterfalls and spectacular hikes, as well as an agricultural bounty of apples, pears and cherries. If you're into windsurfing or kiteboarding, head to the sporty town of Hood River, ground zero for these extreme sports. Whether you're a hiker, apple lover or adrenaline junkie, the gorge delivers.

FJONOVAJ / GETTY IMAGES ©

DANITA DELIMONT / GETTY IMAGES ©

17

18

SAM CHRYSANTHOU / GETTY IMAGES ©

KYLIE MCLAUGHLIN / GETTY IMAGES ©

Navajo Nation

17 'May I walk in beauty' is the final line of a famous Navajo prayer. Beauty takes many forms on the Navajos' sprawling reservation (p345), but makes its most famous appearance at Monument Valley, a cluster of rugged buttes and towers. Beauty swoops in on the wings of birds at Canyon de Chelly, a valley where farmers till the land near age-old cliff dwellings. Elsewhere, beauty is in the connections, from the docent explaining Navajo clans, to the guide sharing photography tips in the flickering light of Antelope Canyon. Monument Valley (p367)

Santa Fe & Taos

18 Santa Fe (p378) is an old city with a very young soul. On Friday nights, art lovers flock to Canyon Rd to gab with artists, sip wine and explore more than 80 galleries. Art and history partner up in style within the city's consortium of museums, and the food and the shopping are first rate, too. With that turquoise sky as a backdrop, the experience is darn near sublime. Artists also converge in gallery-filled Taos (p386) but the vibe is quirkier, with ski bums, off-the-grid Earthshippers and a few celebs keeping things offbeat. Santa Fe

California Wine Country

19 The Golden State is home to more than 100 wine regions. The rolling vineyards of Napa (p147), Sonoma (p149) and the Russian River Valley (p150) lure travelers north from San Francisco. Sample a world-class Cabernet in chichi Napa, enjoy a picnic in laid-back Sonoma, or cap off an outdoor adventure with a complex Pinot Noir near the Russian River. Further south, day trippers head to the lovely vineyards clustered east of Santa Barbara (p110), a bucolic area made famous by the 2004 wine-centric movie *Sideways*. Napa Valley (p147)

Mountain Towns

20 Another thing the West does well? Mountain towns, where outdoorsy types drop in from the trail and the slopes to savor the microbrews. Many of the best double as gateways to the country's finest national parks. Our favorite? Flagstaff (p334), which sits ruggedly on the Colorado Plateau in northern Arizona. Highlights include a thriving ale trail, innovative farm-to-table eateries, an observatory and Route 66's awesome Museum Club. And we almost forgot to mention the Grand Canyon, just 80 miles north. Museum Club (p336)

Rocky Mountain National Park

21 From behind the row of RVs growling along Trail Ridge Rd, Rocky Mountain National Park (p249) can look a bit overrun. But with hiking boots laced and the trail unfurling beneath your feet, the park's majestic, untamed splendor becomes unforgettably personal. From epic outings on the Longs Peak Trail to family-friendly romps to Calypso Falls, there's something here for people of every ability and ambition. With just the slightest effort, you'll feel like you have the place to yourself. Longs Peak

The Deserts

22 The human-like saguaro cactus is one of the West's most enduring symbols. A denizen of the Sonoran Desert, it's a survivor in a landscape that's harsh, but also strangely beautiful. Four deserts – the Sonoran, Mojave, Chihuahuan and Great Basin – stretch across the Southwest and California. Each is home to an array of well-adapted reptiles, mammals and plants. It's this thriving diversity that makes a stroll through the desert a one-of-a-kind experience – try it at Saguaro National Park (p351). Sonoran Desert

ETHAN WELTY / GETTY IMAGES ©

THOMAS ROCHE / GETTY IMAGES ©

MICHELE FALZONE / GETTY IMAGES ©

JORDAN SIEMENS / GETTY IMAGES ©

TVERDOHLIB / GETTY IMAGES ©

Zion & Bryce Canyon National Parks

23 Towering red rocks hide graceful waterfalls, narrow slot canyons and hanging gardens in Zion National Park (p370). This lush wonderland lies in the shadow of Angels Landing, which is the lofty terminus of the Angels Landing Trail – one of the great North American day hikes. Photographers and view hounds should scoot north to Bryce Canyon National Park (p369), where golden-red rock spires shimmer like trees in a magical forest of stone – a hypnotic, Tolkienesque place. Zion National Park

Glacier National Park

24 Yep, the rumors are true. The namesake attractions at Glacier National Park (p293) are melting away. There were 150 glaciers in the area in 1850; today there are 25. But even without the giant ice cubes, Montana's sprawling national park is worthy of an in-depth visit. Road warriors can maneuver the thrilling 50-mile Going-to-the-Sun Road; wildlife-watchers can scan for elk, wolves and grizzly (but hopefully not too close); and hikers have 700 miles of trails, trees and flora – including mosses, mushrooms and wildflowers – to explore.

Microbreweries

25 Microbreweries (p423) are a specialty of the West, and you'll find at least one good one in outdoorsy towns from Missoula to Moab. Though usually closely identified with their home towns, these popular watering holes share a few commonalities: boisterous beer sippers, deep-flavored brews with locally inspired names, and cavernous drinking rooms that smell of sweat and adventure. Hiking, biking or climbing near Boulder? Relax post-adventure with a Pearl Street Porter at Mountain Sun Pub & Brewery (p248).

Need to Know

For more information, see Survival Guide (p439)

Currency
US dollar ($)

Language
English

Visas
Visitors from Canada, the UK, Australia, New Zealand, Japan and many EU countries do not need visas for less than 90 days, with ESTA approval. Other nations, see travel.state.gov.

Money
ATMs widely available. Credit cards normally required for hotel reservations and car rentals.

Cell Phones
GSM multiband models will work in the USA. Coverage can be spotty in remote or mountainous areas.

Time
The 11 states follow either Mountain Standard Time (GMT/UTC minus seven hours) or Pacific Standard Time (GMT/UTC minus eight hours). For more information see p448.

When to Go

Seattle
GO Jun–Sep

San Francisco
GO May–Oct

Salt Lake City
GO Jan–Dec

Denver
GO May–Aug

Las Vegas
GO Jan–Dec

Los Angeles
GO Apr–Oct

Phoenix
GO Oct–May

Desert climate
Dry climate
Warm to hot summers, mild winters
Mild summers, cold winters

High Season
(Jun–Aug; Sep–Apr)

➡ Busiest season; sunny days and higher accommodation prices.

➡ Clouds may blanket the southern coast during May and June.

➡ Mountain high season January to March; deserts September to April.

Shoulder (Apr & May; Sep & Oct)

➡ Crowds and prices drop along the coast and in the mountains.

➡ A good time to visit national parks, with milder temperatures.

➡ Blooming spring flowers; fiery autumn colors.

Low Season
(Nov–Mar)

➡ Accommodation rates drop by the coast.

➡ Dark, wintery days, with snowfall in the north and heavier rains.

Websites

American Southwest (www. americansouthwest.net) Parks and landscapes.

Lonely Planet (www.lonely planet.com/usa) Destination info, bookings and forums.

National Park Service (www. nps.gov) Information on national parks and monuments.

Recreation.gov (www.recreation. gov) Camping reservations on federally managed lands.

Roadside America (www.road sideamerica.com) Find 'uniquely odd tourist attractions.'

Important Numbers

To call any regular number, dial the area code, followed by the seven-digit number.

USA country code	☑1
International access code	☑011
Emergency	☑911
National Sexual Assault Hotline	☑800-656-4673
Directory assistance	☑411
Statewide road conditions	☑511

Exchange Rates

Australia	A$1	$0.72
Canada	C$1	$0.75
Europe	€1	$1.06
China	Y10	$1.56
Japan	¥100	$0.81
Mexico	MXN10	$0.60
New Zealand	NZ$1	$0.66
UK	£1	$1.51

For current exchange rates see www.xe.com.

Daily Costs

Budget: Less than $100

➡ Campgrounds and hostel dorms: $12–45

➡ Free activities (beach, park concerts): $0

➡ Food at farmers markets, taquerias, street vendors: $3–12

➡ Bus, subway: $0–5

Midrange: $100–200

➡ Mom-and-pop motels, low-priced chains: $70–120

➡ Museums, national and state parks: $5–25

➡ Diners, good local restaurants: $12–35

➡ Car rental per day, excluding insurance and gas: from $30

Top End: More than $200

➡ B&Bs, boutique hotels, resorts: from $190

➡ Meal in top restaurant, excluding wine: $25-55

➡ Hiring an outdoor outfitter; going to a top show: from $80

➡ Convertible rental per day: from $70

Opening Hours

Opening hours vary throughout the year, with many attractions and visitor centers open longer hours in high season. We've provided high-season hours.

Banks 8:30am–4:30pm Monday to Thursday, to 5:30pm Friday (some 9am–noon Saturday)

Bars 5pm–midnight Sunday to Thursday, to 2am Friday and Saturday

Cafes 7:30am–8pm

Restaurants 11am–2:30pm and 5pm–9pm; many Utah restaurants are closed on Sunday

Stores 10am–6pm Monday to Saturday, noon–5pm Sunday

Arriving in Western USA

Denver International Airport (p245) Check the airport website (www.flydenver.com) for details about the new hotel and transit center set to open in early 2016. The project includes a commuter rail system linking to downtown Denver, a 35-minute ride. Taxis cost $56 to downtown Denver and $89 to Boulder.

Los Angeles International Airport (p85) Taxis cost about $46 to downtown; door-to-door shuttles from $16 for shared ride; free Shuttle G to Metro Rail Green Line Aviation Station and free Shuttle C to the Metro Bus Center; FlyAway bus to downtown LA is $8.

Seattle-Tacoma International Airport (p190) Light-rail trains run regularly from the 4th floor of the parking garage to downtown from 5am to 1am Monday to Saturday and 6am to midnight on Sunday ($2.25 to $3); taxis are available on the 3rd floor of the parking garage and cost $46 to downtown.

Getting Around

Car The best option for travelers who leave urban areas to explore national parks and more remote areas. Drive on the right.

Train Amtrak can be slow due to frequent delays, but trains are a convenient option for travel along the Pacific Coast. Cross-country routes to Chicago run from the San Francisco area and Los Angeles.

Bus Cheaper and slower than trains; can be a good option for travel to cities not serviced by Amtrak.

For much more on **getting around**, see p453 ➡

If You Like...

Geology

Grand Canyon A 277-mile river cuts through two-billion-year-old rocks, whose layered geological secrets are revealed within a mile-high stack. (p337)

Yellowstone National Park Massive geysers, rainbow-colored thermal pools and a supervolcano base – this 3472-sq-mile national park puts on a dazzling show. (p277)

Arches National Park Drive, hike or bike past sandstone arches, windows, fins and a precariously balanced rock. (p365)

White Sands National Monument The white and chalky gypsum dunes here are mesmerizing. (p394)

Carlsbad Caverns A 1.25-mile trail descends to the Big Room – a veritable underground cathedral concealed in a massive cave system. (p396)

Chiricahua National Monument A rugged wonderland of rock chiseled by rain and wind into pinnacles, bridges and balanced rocks. (p353)

Volcanoes The earth's shifting crust formed powerful volcanoes in Washington. Hike around Mt Rainier or visit Mt St Helens to learn about its mighty 1980 eruption. (p202)

Old West Sites

The Southwest, particularly Arizona and New Mexico, is your best bet if you want to walk in the footsteps of cowboys and gunslingers at sites within a day's drive of each other.

Lincoln Billy the Kid's old stomping – and shooting – grounds during the Lincoln County War. (p395)

Tombstone Famous for the gunfight at the OK Corral, this dusty town is also home to Boot Hill Graveyard and the Bird Cage Theater. (p352)

Whiskey Row A block of Victorian-era saloons in downtown Prescott has survived fires, filmmakers and tourists. (p331)

Pony Express stations Rte 50 across Nevada, known as the Loneliest Road, traces the route of the Pony Express; several crumbling changing stations line the highway. (p321)

Virginia City Site of the Comstock Lode silver strike, this hard-charging mining town gained notoriety in Mark Twain's semi-autobiographical book *Roughing It*. (p321)

Steam train Channel the Old West on the steam-driven train that's chugged between Durango and Silverton for 125 years. (p269)

Life-List Thrills

Half Dome Hold tight to steel cables while scrambling to the summit of Yosemite's most recognizable rock. (p163)

Raft the Grand Canyon The Colorado River roars through the depths of the Big Ditch for 277 miles. (p342)

Carlsbad Caverns The elevator drops the length of the Empire State Building in less than one minute. (p396)

Angels Landing Sheer drops flank the whip-thin trail to the top of Angels Landing in Zion National Park. (p370)

Stratosphere Leap from the top of a 110-story casino. In Las Vegas of course. (p312)

Audrey Headframe Park Stand on the clear panel covering the 1910ft deep mineshaft in Jerome, AZ. Look down. (p332)

Film & TV Locations

Los Angeles Hollywood was born here, and iconic celluloid sites beckon from Mulholland Dr to Malibu. (p64)

Monument Valley Stride John Wayne tall beneath the iconic red monoliths that starred in seven of the Duke's westerns. (p367)

Las Vegas Bad boys and their hijinks brought Sin City back to the big screen in *Ocean's Eleven* and *The Hangover*. (p306)

Moab & around The directors of *Thelma & Louise* and *127 Hours* shot their most dramatic scenes in nearby parks. (p364)

Albuquerque Tax incentives lure production companies. The city is the backdrop for the TV series *Better Call Saul* and predecessor *Breaking Bad*. (p372)

Fabulous Food

San Francisco Temptations await: real-deal taquerias and trattorias, top-notch Vietnamese, magnificent farmers markets and trailblazing chefs. (p136)

Chez Panisse Chef Alice Waters revolutionized California cuisine in the '70s with Bay Area locavarian cooking. (p146)

Food trucks LA sparked the mobile gourmet revolution, but the food truck craze also thrives in San Francisco (p137) and Portland (p212).

Green chiles The chiles grown in the town of Hatch are the pride of New Mexico. This spicy accompaniment is slathered over enchiladas, layered onto cheeseburgers and celebrated at the Hatch Chile Festival. (p28)

Las Vegas Great food is never a gamble in Sin City, with famous chefs, decadent buffets and flavor-rich Asian restaurants. (p312)

Emerging Wine Regions

Verde Valley wine country Home to an up-and-coming Arizona wine trail that winds through Cottonwood, Jerome and Cornville. (p332)

Top: Foodie heaven at the Ferry Building (p120), San Francisco
Bottom: Durango & Silverton Narrow Gauge Railroad (p269), Colorado

Willamette Valley Outside Portland, OR, this fertile region produces some of the tastiest Pinot Noir on the planet. (p216)

Walla Walla Washington's hot wine-growing region, with its namesake town as a very pretty centerpiece. (p203)

Santa Barbara Wine Country Large-scale winemaking since the 1980s, and the climate is perfect for Pinots near the coast and further inland. (p110)

Hiking

Grand Canyon Rim to Rim Earn bragging rights on this classic 17-mile trek on the South Kaibab and North Kaibab Trails between the Grand Canyon's south and north rims. (p337)

Red Rock Country Hike to vortexes in Sedona, hoodoos in Bryce Canyon, and slender spans in Arches (p365) and Canyonlands National Parks (p366).

Rocky Mountain National Park Longs Peak gets all the buzz but there are several loop trails best done in two or three nights; wildlife sightings are the norm. (p249)

Wonderland Trail Circumnavigate Mt Rainier's lofty peak – it's 93 miles of spectacular nature. (p202)

Palm Springs & the Deserts Discover hidden palm-tree oases, stroll across salt flats or take a guided walk through Native American canyons. (p100)

Los Angeles Urban hiking at its best, with mountaintop trails overlooking the coast and the celeb-favored Runyon Canyon. (p77)

Highline Trail This stunner in Glacier National Park passes bighorn sheep, mountain wildflowers and snow-capped peaks, with a side-hike to glacier views. (p293)

National Parks

Theodore Roosevelt once said that camping in Yellowstone was like lying in a vast and beautiful cathedral. Similar high praise can be applied to all of the great parks of the West – unique in their details but bound by their grandeur.

Yellowstone National Park The nation's first park is a stunner: lakes, waterfalls, mountains, wildlife galore and a cauldron of geysers and springs. (p277)

Grand Canyon National Park Two billion years of geologic history? Yeah, yeah, that's cool, but have you seen that view? (p337)

Glacier National Park Come for the glaciers, stay for the Going-to-the-Sun Road, grand old lodges and free-range animals. (p293)

Yosemite National Park Flanked by El Capitan and Half Dome, Yosemite Valley is indeed cathedral-like, but the lush Sierra Nevada backcountry will have you singing hallelujah, too. (p163)

Southern Utah There's too much red-rock goodness in Utah to narrow it down to one fave. Arches (p365), Canyonlands (p366), Bryce (p369), Zion (p370) and Capitol Reef (p368) – see 'em all!

Offbeat Stuff

Route 66 This two-lane ode to Americana is dotted with wacky roadside attractions, especially in western Arizona. (p35)

Burning Man Festival A temporary city in the Nevada desert attracts more than 66,000 people for a week of self-expression and blowing sand. (p320)

Roswell Did a UFO crash outside Roswell, New Mexico, in 1947? Museums and a UFO festival explore whether the truth is out there. (p396)

Seattle's public sculptures In Fremont, look for a car-eating troll, a human-faced dog, and folks waiting, and waiting, for the train. (p183)

Venice Boardwalk Gawk at the human zoo, which includes chainsaw-jugglers, medical marijuana 'clinicians' and Speedo-clad snake-charmers. (p73)

Frozen Dead Guy Days Celebrates a cryogenically frozen Norwegian, kept cold in Nederland, CO, for more than 20 years. (p27)

The Loneliest Road A singing sand dune and a scraggly Shoe Tree are quirky distractions on Hwy 50 in Nevada. (p321)

Mini Time Machine Museum of Miniatures The exhibits get small, very small, at this whimsical museum in Tucson, Arizona. (p348)

Historic Sites

Dinosaur National Monument Touch a 150-million-year-old fossil at one of the largest dinosaur fossil beds in North America. (p363)

Mesa Verde Climb to cliff dwellings that housed Ancestral Puebloans more than 700 years ago. (p267)

Manzanar National Historic Site This WWII Japanese American internment camp interprets a painful chapter of the USA's collective past. (p169)

Little Bighorn Battlefield National Monument Native American battlefields where General George Custer made his famous 'last stand' against the Lakota Sioux. (p289)

Balboa Park (p92), San Diego

Los Alamos The community that arose on this lonely mesa southwest of Santa Fe was top secret during WWII – a necessity for the scientists developing the atomic bomb. (p385)

Museums

Getty Center & Villa Art museums as beautiful as their ocean views in west LA and Malibu. (p73)

Los Angeles County Museum of Art More than 150,000 works of art spanning the ages and crossing all borders. (p72)

California Academy of Sciences SF's natural-history museum breathes 'green' in its eco-certified design, with a four-story rainforest and living roof. (p131)

Balboa Park Museum-hop in San Diego's favorite park where you can dive into top-notch art, history and science exhibitions. (p92)

Heard Museum Highlights the history and culture of Southwestern tribes. (p323)

EMP Museum Enjoy a little fantasy, a little sci-fi and a lot of rock 'n' roll at the Experience Music Project in Seattle. (p183)

Spas & Resorts

Truth or Consequences Built over hot springs beside the Rio Grande, pools bubble with soothing, hydro-healing warmth. (p391)

Ojo Caliente Mineral Springs Resort & Spa Four types of mineral water soothe guests in pools at this 145-year-old resort north of Santa Fe. (p386)

Phoenix & Scottsdale Honeymooners, families, golfers – there's a resort for all travelers within a few miles of Camelback Rd. (p327)

Las Vegas Mandalay Bay, Cosmopolitan and other top hotels offer lavish resort amenities. (p311)

Sheraton Wild Horse Pass Resort & Spa On the Gila Indian Reservation, this resort embraces its Native American heritage with style. (p328)

Month by Month

January

Skiers and snowboarders descend on lofty ski resorts. Palm Springs and southern deserts welcome travelers seeking warmer climes and saguaro-dotted landscapes.

⚡ Tournament of Roses

This famous New Year's Day parade (www.tournamentofroses.com) of flower-festooned floats, marching bands and prancing equestrians draws about 700,000 spectators to Pasadena, CA, before the Rose Bowl college football game.

☆ Sundance Film Festival

Park City, UT, unfurls the red carpet for indie filmmakers, actors and moviegoers who flock to the mountain town in late January for a week of cutting-edge films (www.sundance.org/festival).

☆ Cowboy Poetry

Wranglers and ropers gather in Elvo, NV, for a week of poetry readings and folklore performances (www.westernfolklife.org). Started in 1985, this event has inspired cowboy poetry readings across the region.

February

It's the height of ski season, but there are plenty of distractions for those not swooshing down the slopes – low-desert wildflowers bloom, whales migrate off the California coast, and dude ranches saddle up in southern Arizona.

⚡ Carnival in Colorado

Mardi Gras meets the mountains in Breckenridge (www.gobreck.com/events/mardi-gras), where folks celebrate with a street party, live jazz and, well, fire dancers.

⚡ Tucson Gem & Mineral Show

At the largest mineral and gem show in the US (www.tgms.org/calendar), held the second full weekend in February, about 250 dealers sell jewelry, fossils, crafts and lots of rocks. Lecture seminars and a silent auction round out the weekend.

☆ Oregon Shakespeare Festival

In Ashland, tens of thousands of theater fans party with the Bard at this nine-month festival (that's right!) that kicks off in February and features world-class plays and Elizabethan drama (p229; www.osfashland.org).

March

Ah spring, when a young man's fancy turns to thoughts of...beer! Jet skis! Parties! March is spring-break season, when hordes of college students converge on Arizona's lakes. Families ski or visit parks in warmer climes.

🏃 Spring Whale-Watching Week

Gray whales migrate along the Pacific Coast (p50).

Around Oregon's Depoe Bay, it's semi-organized, with docents and special viewpoints. The northward migration happens through June.

☆ Cactus League

Major league baseball fans head to southern Arizona in March and early April for the preseason Cactus League (www.cactusleague. com), when some of the best pro teams play ball in Phoenix and Tucson.

🎉 Frozen Dead Guy Days

Celebrate a cryogenically frozen town mascot, 'Grandpa Bredo,' in Nederland, CO, with coffin races, ice turkey bowling, a polar plunge and copious beer drinking (http://frozen deadguydays.org).

April

Wildflowers bloom in California's high deserts while migrating birds swoop into nature preserves in southern Arizona. For ski resorts, it's shoulder season, meaning slightly lower room prices (except Easter weekend).

☆ Coachella Music & Arts Festival

Indie rock bands, cult DJs, superstar rappers and pop divas converge outside Palm Springs for this musical extravaganza (www. coachella.com), now held on two consecutive long weekends in mid-April.

☆ Gathering of Nations

More than 3000 Native American dancers and singers from the US and Canada compete in this powwow (www.gathering ofnations.com) in late April in Albuquerque, NM. There's also an Indian market with more than 800 artists and craftspeople.

May

A great time to visit most national parks, which are ready for the summer crush but with children still in school the masses don't show until Memorial Day weekend, the last weekend of the month.

🎉 Cinco de Mayo

Celebrate the victory of Mexican forces over the French army at the Battle of Puebla on May 5, 1862, with margaritas, music and merriment. Denver, Los Angeles and San Diego do it in style. (p238)

🏃 Bay to Breakers

Tens of thousands run costumed, naked and/or clutching beer from Embarcadero to Ocean Beach in San Francisco on the third Sunday in May. The race dates from 1912. (p132)

🎉 Boulder Creek Festival

Start the summer in the Rockies on Memorial Day weekend with food, drink, music, a rubber duck race and glorious sunshine. It closes with Bolder Boulder, a 10km race celebrated by screaming crowds. (p246)

☆ Sasquatch!

Indie music fans converge at the outdoor Gorge Amphitheater in George, WA, near the Columbia River Gorge, for live music on Memorial Day weekend (www. sasquatchfestival.com).

June

High season begins for most of the West. Rugged passes are open, rivers are thick with snowmelt and mountain wildflowers bloom. There may be gray fog (June gloom) over southern California beaches.

🎉 Pride Month

California's LGBTQ pride celebrations occur throughout June, with costumed parades, coming-out parties, live music and more. The biggest, bawdiest celebrations are in Los Angeles (http://lapride.org) and San Francisco. (p132)

☆ Telluride Bluegrass Festival

In mid-June, join 'Festivarians' for the high lonesome sounds of bluegrass in the mountain-flanked beauty of Telluride, CO. (p265)

July

Vacationers head to beaches, theme parks, mountain resorts, and state and national parks. Broiling desert parks are best avoided.

☆ Aspen Music Festival

From early July to mid-August, top-tier classical performers put on spectacular shows (www.aspenmusicfestival.com) while students from orchestras led by sought-after conductors bring street corners to life with smaller groups.

🎆 Independence Day

Across the West, communities celebrate America's birth with rodeos, music festivals, parades and fireworks on July 4.

🎆 Comic-Con International

'Nerd Prom' is the alt-nation's biggest annual convention (www.comic-con.org) of comic-book geeks, sci-fi and animation lovers, and pop-culture memorabilia collectors. Held in San Diego in mid-July.

☆ Cheyenne Froniter Days

Celebrate the American cowboy with roping, riding and a parade at this 115-year-old Wyoming rodeo (www.cfdrodeo.com).

🍺 Oregon Brewers Festival

During this fun beer festival (www.oregonbrewfest.com) in Portland, about 85,000 microbrew lovers eat, drink and whoop it up on the banks of the Willamette River. Held the last full weekend in July.

August

Learn about Native American culture at art fairs, markets and ceremonial gatherings across the Southwest.

Rodeos are popular in Colorado and Arizona.

🏃 Sturgis Motorcycle Rally

This convivial gathering of motorcycle fanatics (www.sturgismotorcyclerally.com) celebrated its 75th birthday in 2015. Get your motor running in southern South Dakota in early August.

🎆 Old Spanish Days Fiesta

A celebration of early rancho culture with parades, a rodeo, crafts exhibits and shows (www.oldspanishdays-fiesta.org) in Santa Barbara in early August.

👁 Perseids

Peaking in mid-August, these annual meteor showers are the best time to catch shooting stars with your naked eye or a digital camera. Try http://darksky.org for info. For optimal viewing, head into the southern deserts.

👁 Santa Fe Indian Market

Santa Fe's most famous festival is held the third week of August on the historic plaza where more than 1100 artists from about 220 tribes and pueblos exhibit. (p381)

September

Summer's last hurrah is the Labor Day holiday weekend. It's a particularly nice time to visit the Pacific Northwest, where nights are cool and days are reliably sunny. Fall colors begin to appear in the Rockies.

🍴 Hatch Chile Festival

On Labor Day weekend, join hot-pepper lovers in Hatch, NM, for a parade, a mariachi competition and numerous chile-eating contests (www.hatchchilefest.com).

☆ Burning Man

Outdoor celebration of self-expression known for elaborate art displays, an easygoing barter system, blowing sand and the final burning of the man. This temporary city rises in the Nevada desert the week before Labor Day. (p320)

🍺 Great American Beer Festival

This three-day celebration of beer in Denver in late September or early October is so popular it always sells out in advance, with 700 US breweries getting in on the sudsy action. More than 3500 beers available. (p238)

☆ Bumbershoot

In early September, Seattle's biggest arts and cultural event (www.bumbershoot.com) hosts hundreds of musicians, artists, comedians, writers and theater troupes on various stages.

October

Shimmering aspens lure road-trippers to Colorado and northern New Mexico for the annual fall show. Watch for ghouls, ghosts and hard-partying maniacs as Halloween, on October 31, approaches.

✿ International Balloon Fiesta

Look to the skies in early October for the world's biggest gathering of hot-air balloons in Albuquerque, NM. (p374)

◉ Sedona Arts Festival

This fine-art show (www.sedonaartsfestival.org) overflows with jewelry, ceramics, glass and sculptures in early October when 125 artists exhibit their works at Sedona's Red Rock High School.

☆ Litquake

Author readings, discussions and literary events (www.litquake.org) such as the legendary pub crawl in San Francisco in mid-October.

✿ Halloween Carnaval

Hundreds of thousands of costumed revelers come out to play in LA's West Hollywood LGBTQ neighborhood for all-day partying, dancing, kids' activities and live entertainment (www.weho.org/visitors/events-in-the-city/halloween-carnaval).

November

Temperatures drop across the West. Most coastal areas, deserts and parks are less busy, with the exception of the Thanksgiving holiday. Ski season begins.

✿ Día de los Muertos

Mexican communities honor dead ancestors on November 2 with costumed parades, sugar skulls, graveyard picnics, candlelight processions and fabulous altars.

⬤ Wine Country Thanksgiving

More than 160 wineries in the Willamette Valley (www.willamettewines.co) open their doors to the public for three days in late November.

⛷ Yellowstone Ski Festival

Thanksgiving week celebration at West Yellowstone (http://yellowstoneskifestival.squarespace.com) is a great time for ski buffs and newcomers alike. Highlights include ski clinics and races. Nordic skiing kicks off around this time, too.

December

'Tis the season for nativity scenes, holiday light shows and other celebrations of Christmas. The merriment continues through New Year's Eve. Expect crowds and higher prices at ski resorts.

✿ Holiday Light Displays

Communities decorate boats, parks and shopping malls with twinkling lights. In California, watch colorful boat parades in Newport Beach and San Diego, or check out illuminated displays in LA's Griffith Park Zoo. The Desert Botanical Gardens are aglow in Phoenix, as is the Tlaquepaque Arts & Crafts Village in Sedona.

✿ Snow Daze

Vail, CO, marks the opening of the mountain with a week-long festival (www.vail.com/events/snow-daze.aspx) featuring an expo village, parties and plenty of big-name live performances.

Itineraries

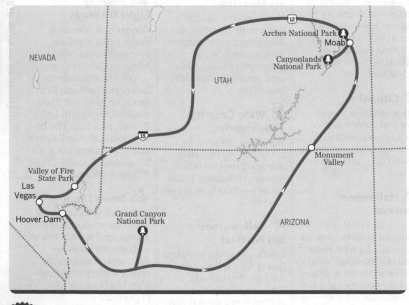

Rolling Through Red Rocks

Cameras get a workout on this tour, which spotlights the most iconic sites in the Southwest. You'll loop past the region's most famous city, its biggest canyon and its most breathtaking red-rock scenery.

Start in **Las Vegas** and spend a few days traveling the world on the Strip. Partied out? Head east to swoop past the **Hoover Dam**, then say hello to the **Grand Canyon National Park**. You'll want a couple of days to explore America's most famous park. For a once-in-a-lifetime experience, descend from the South Rim into the chasm on a mule and spend the night at Phantom Ranch on the canyon floor. From the Grand Canyon head northeast to **Monument Valley**, with scenery straight out of a Hollywood western, to the national parks in Utah's southeast corner – they're some of the most visually stunning in the country. Hike the shape-shifting slot canyons of **Canyonlands National Park**, mountain bike slickrock outside **Moab** or take a photo of Balanced Rock in **Arches National Park**. Drive west on one of the most spectacular stretches of pavement, Hwy 12, until it hooks up with I-15. Swing south to for a sunset meditation at **Valley of Fire State Park**, before heading back to Las Vegas.

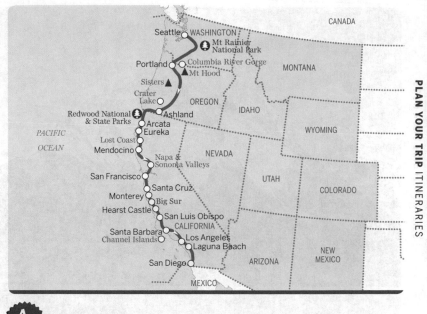

4 WEEKS Wandering along the West Coast

Hug a tree, surf a wave and taste the fresh deliciousness of west coast fare on this nature lover's trip which ribbons from Seattle to San Diego.

Kick off with fresh-roasted coffee in java-loving **Seattle** and check out the city's sprawling food markets, microbreweries and waterfront. Heading south, visit **Mt Rainier National Park**, where superb hiking trails and relaxing inns nestle beneath the snow-covered peak. Continue to the cutting-edge city of **Portland**, known for its sprawling parks, eco-minded residents and progressive urbanism – plus food carts, coffeehouse culture and great nightlife. Wonder at waterfalls and indulge in fresh road-side produce with a scenic drive east along the **Columbia River Gorge**, then turn south and make for **Mt Hood** for winter skiing or summer hiking. Further adventures await at the **Sisters**, a trio of 10,000ft peaks, and the striking blue waters of **Crater Lake**. Catch a Shakespearian play in sunny **Ashland**, then trade the mountains for the foggy coast. Enter California via Hwy 199 and stroll through the magnificent old-growth forests in **Redwood National & State Parks**.

Hug the coast as it meanders south through funky **Arcata** and seaside **Eureka**, lose yourself on the **Lost Coast**, and catch Hwy 1 through quaint **Mendocino**, where the scenic headlands and rugged shoreline make for a requisite wander. For wine tasting with a photogenic backdrop, travel inland to the rolling vineyards of the **Napa & Sonoma Valleys**, then continue south to romantically hilly, ever free-spirited **San Francisco**. Return to scenic Hwy 1 through surf-loving **Santa Cruz**, stately bayfront **Monterey** and beatnik-flavored **Big Sur**. In no time, you'll reach the surreal **Hearst Castle** and laid-back, collegiate **San Luis Obispo**. Roll into Mediterranean-esque **Santa Barbara** for shopping and wine tasting then hop aboard a ferry in Ventura to the wildlife-rich **Channel Islands**. The pull from **Los Angeles** is strong. Go ahead – indulge your fantasies of Hollywood then stroll the rugged hills of Griffith Park, followed by cruise through LA's palm-lined neighborhoods. After racking up a few sins in the City of Angels, move south to wander the bluffs of **Laguna Beach** then cruise into picture-perfect **San Diego**.

Top: Grand Teton
National Park (p284),
Wyoming

Bottom: Silverton
(p267), Colorado

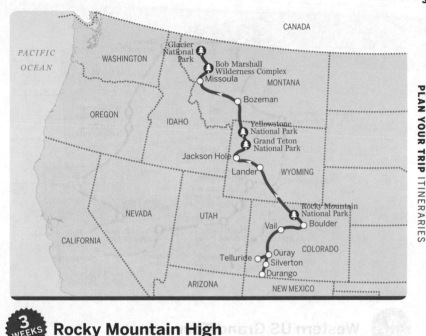

3 WEEKS Rocky Mountain High

Pack your bathing suit, mountain bike and hiking boots for this high-altitude cruise atop the Continental Divide; from here, rivers flow toward the west on one side and toward the east on the other.

Spend your first two days enjoying craft beers and single-track mountain-biking trails in **Durango**, a fine mountain town. From here, take the Million Dollar Hwy (Hwy 550) north through the San Juan Mountain range, sightseeing in **Silverton** and dipping into hot springs in **Ouray**. Take a side trip to **Telluride** for a festival – there's one almost every weekend in summer. From Montrose, drive east on Hwy 50 before continuing to Hwy 24 north. Finish your first week in style with an overnight stay in ritzy **Vail**.

Enjoy kayaking, rock climbing and people-watching in high-energy **Boulder** then twist up to **Rocky Mountain National Park** to hike and horseback ride. While here, drive the thrilling Trail Ridge Rd through alpine vistas. Continue north on I-25. In Wyoming, take I-80 west to Hwy 287; follow this highway to **Lander** for rock climbing.

Continue north to **Jackson Hole**, another fun gateway town. Anchored by a central park surrounded by chic stores and cowboy bars, it's a good place to relax, catch a rodeo or spend the night before rafting the Snake River. From here, it's an easy glide north into **Grand Teton National Park**, a scenic spot for a lazy lake day and a mountain stroll. Next up is mighty **Yellowstone National Park**, where geysers, bison and hiking are highlights.

Start your last week with a drive on the gorgeous Beartooth Hwy, following it into Montana then hooking onto I-90 west to **Bozeman** and **Missoula**; both are good places to stock up before the final push. Serious nature awaits in the **Bob Marshall Wilderness Complex**, while **Glacier National Park** is a place to visit now – there are still some 25 glaciers hanging tight, but they may not be there for long. Scan for wildlife on a hike, then end with a drive on the stunning Going-to-the-Sun Road.

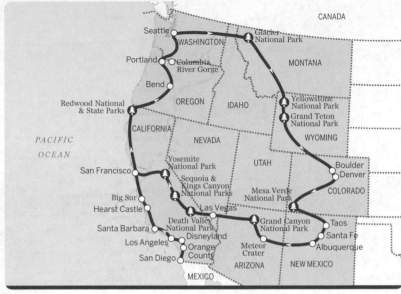

Western US Grand Tour
4 WEEKS

This lasso loop corrals the best of the west as it rolls north along the California coast, cruises through the lush landscapes of the Pacific Northwest, the alpine villages of the Rockies and the glowing red-rock beauty of the Southwest, with a final swing back into California for a hit-parade tour of the state's national parks.

From sunny **San Diego**, follow Hwy 1 north through the surf-loving coastal villages of **Orange County**, detouring to **Disneyland** before driving into shiny **Los Angeles**. Continue up the coast on scenic Hwy 1, stopping to shop and sample wine in glossy **Santa Barbara**. Gawk at gawdy **Hearst Castle** then continue north through woodsy **Big Sur**. Dine and shop then wander through Alcatraz in bohemian **San Francisco**. Return to Hwy 1 for the quirky towns dotting the northern California coast.

View the big trees in **Redwood National & State Parks** and continue into Oregon, taking time for outdoor fun in **Bend**. Soak in the greenery traveling west along the **Columbia River Gorge**, then spend a few days savoring brews and views in **Portland**. Zip up the Space Needle in **Seattle** and drive east into wide-open Montana, heading for the outdoor wonders of **Glacier National Park**. Continue south into **Yellowstone National Park** where Old Faithful blasts regularly beside its namesake lodge, and sightseers brake for buffalo. Swoosh below majestic peaks in **Grand Teton National Park** before swinging southeast through Wyoming's vast cowboy plains.

In Colorado, breathe deep in outdoorsy **Boulder** then embrace the charms of city life in bustling **Denver**. The mining towns of the San Juan Mountains are next, followed by **Mesa Verde National Park**. Just south in New Mexico, artist meccas **Taos** and **Santa Fe** are fab stops for one-of-a-kind gifts. Slurp green chile stew in **Albuquerque** and follow Route 66 west into Arizona, stopping at **Meteor Crater** before detouring north for **Grand Canyon National Park**. Continue west to **Las Vegas**, then drive into central California for **Death Valley National Park**, and **Sequoia & Kings Canyon National Parks**, concluding with **Yosemite National Park**. Complete the loop with a glass of California wine in San Francisco.

Route 66 & Scenic Drives

Underground minerals drew prospectors and adventurers to the West in the 19th and 20th centuries. Today, the allure is in the above-ground treasures: the stunning drives. From desert backroads and coastal highways to mountain-hugging thrill rides to the iconic Mother Road, the West is chock-full of picturesque byways and backroads.

Route 66

A wigwam motel. A meteor crater. Begging burros. And a solar-powered Ferris wheel overlooking the Pacific Ocean. Hmm, looks like 'Get your kitsch on Route 66' might be a better slogan for the scrubby stretch of Mother Road running through California, Arizona and New Mexico. It's a bit off-the-beaten path, but folks along the way will be very glad you're here.

Why Go

History, scenery and the open road. This alluring combination is what makes a Route 66 road trip so enjoyable. Navigators should note that I-40 and Route 66 overlap through much of New Mexico and Arizona.

In New Mexico, the neon signs of Tucumcari are a fun-loving welcome to the West. They also set the mood for adventure – the right mood to have before dropping into the scuba-ready Blue Hole in Santa Rosa. Fuel up on lip-smacking green chile stew at Frontier in Albuquerque then grab a snooze at the 1937 El Rancho motel (p378) – John Wayne slept here! – in Gallup.

In Arizona, swoop off the highway for a grand drive through Petrified Forest National Park (p347). First up? Sweeping views of the Painted Desert. Trade

Road-Trip Necessities

Top Tips

A prepared road-tripper is a happy road-tripper, especially in the West, with its lonely roads and unpredictable weather.

Pack a spare tire and tool kit (eg jack, jumper cables, ice scraper), as well as emergency equipment in your vehicle; if you're renting a car, consider buying a roadside safety kit.

Bring good maps, especially if you're touring away from highways; don't depend on GPS units as they may not work in remote areas.

Carry extra water. You may need it if the car breaks down in the desert.

Fill up the tank regularly; gas stations can be few and far between in the West.

Always carry your license and proof of insurance.

Best Roadside Dining

Turquoise Room (p346), Route 66, Winslow, AZ

Hell's Backbone Grill (p368), Highway 12, Boulder, UT

Asylum Restaurant (p332), Highway 89/89A, Jerome, AZ

Frontier (p375), Route 66, Albuquerque, NM

Santa Barbara Shellfish Co (p109), Pacific Coast Highway, Santa Barbara, CA

Scenic Drives

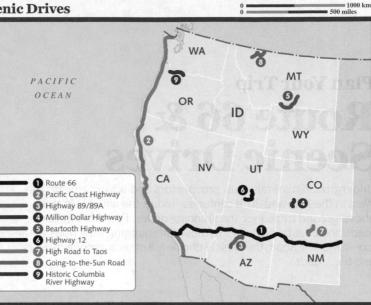

0		1000 km
0		500 miles

PACIFIC
OCEAN

WA
OR
ID
MT
WY
NV
UT
CA
CO
AZ
NM

- **1** Route 66
- **2** Pacific Coast Highway
- **3** Highway 89/89A
- **4** Million Dollar Highway
- **5** Beartooth Highway
- **6** Highway 12
- **7** High Road to Taos
- **8** Going-to-the-Sun Road
- **9** Historic Columbia River Highway

panoramas for close-up views in the southern section of the park, where fossilized 225-million-year-old logs are clustered beside the main park road. You can snooze in a concrete tipi in Holbrook, west of the park. Next stop is the 'Take It Easy' town of Winslow. Snap a photo of the famous corner then savor a spectacular dinner in the Turquoise Room (p35) at La Posada Hotel. Meteor Crater (p336), east of Flagstaff, is a mighty big hole in the ground – and a good place to slow down and catch your breath. From here, Route 66 parallels the train tracks into energetic Flagstaff, passing the wonderful Museum Club (p336), a cabin-like roadhouse where everyone's having fun or is about to. Next up is Williams, a railroad town lined with courtyard motels and brimming with small-town charm.

Seligman is a quirky little village that greets travelers with retro motels, a roadkill cafe and a squirt of fake mustard at the Snow-Cap Drive In. Burma Shave signs share funny advice on the way to Grand Canyon Caverns, where you'll be lured 21 stories underground for a tour or possibly an overnight stay. From here, highlights include an eclectic general store in Hackberry, the Route 66 museum (p347) in Kingman and hay-loving burros in sun-baked Oatman.

Things stay sun-baked in California as the Mother Road swoops into the Mojave Desert and passes ghost towns heralded by lonesome railroad markers. In Victorville, the Brian Burger comes with a spicy kick at Emma Jean's Holland Burger Café (www.hollandburger.com). The vibe kicks up in stylish Pasadena before the road's final push to the Pacific. At the Santa Monica Pier (p73), hop on the solar-powered Ferris wheel and celebrate your journey with a panoramic sunset view.

When to Go

The best time to travel Route 66 is from May to September, when the weather is warm and you'll be able to take advantage of more outdoor activities.

The Route

This journey starts in Tucumcari, NM, then continues west through Arizona and California, roughly paralleling I-40 all the way to Barstow, CA. After Barstow, Route 66 south passes through San Bernardino on the I-15 before cutting west and heading

HISTORY OF ROUTE 66

Launched in 1926, Route 66 would ultimately stretch from Chicago to Los Angeles, linking a ribbon of small towns and country byways as it rolled across eight states. The road gained notoriety during the Great Depression, when migrant farmers followed it west from the Dust Bowl across the Great Plains. The nickname 'The Mother Road' first appeared in John Steinbeck's novel about the era, *The Grapes of Wrath*. Things got a little more fun after WWII, when newfound prosperity prompted Americans to get behind the wheel and explore. Nat King Cole recorded 'Get Your Kicks on Route 66' in 1946, which added to the road's allure. But just as things got going, the Feds rolled out the interstate system, which eventually caused the Mother Road's demise. The very last town on Route 66 to be bypassed by an interstate was Arizona's Williams, in 1984.

into Pasadena. Follow I-110 to Santa Monica Blvd west to seaside Santa Monica.

Time & Mileage

Time: You might be able to do this trip in two or three days if you rush, but plan for six and enjoy the drive.

Mileage: About 1250 miles, depending on segments driven.

Pacific Coast Highway

Slip on your sunglasses, roll down the window and crank up your favorite song about the road. The highways connecting Canada and Mexico on the West Coast were made for driving, and the ridiculously scenic Pacific Coast Hwy (PCH) is the king of them all.

Why Go

This epic West Coast journey, which rolls through California, Oregon and Washington, takes in cosmopolitan cities, surf towns and charming coastal enclaves ripe for exploration. For many travelers, the biggest draw is the magnificent scenery: wild and remote beaches, cliff-top views overlooking crashing waves, rolling hills, and lush forests thick with redwoods and eucalyptus trees. But the route is not loved only for its looks. It's also got personality, offering beside-the-highway adventures for surfers, kayakers, scuba divers and hikers.

Highlights? Let's start with the cities. Coastal highways connect the dots between some of the West Coast's most striking municipalities, starting with surf-loving San Diego in Southern California

and moving north through hedonistic Los Angeles and offbeat San Francisco. Way up north, take a worthwhile detour to artsy and alternative-minded Seattle, Washington.

If you want to bypass urban areas, it's easy to stick to the places in between. In southern California, PCH rolls past the almost-too-perfect beaches of California's Orange County ('the OC') and Santa Barbara (the 'American Riviera'). Further north, Hwy 1 passes wacky Santa Cruz, a university town and surfers' paradise, then redwood forests along the Big Sur coast and north of Mendocino. Hwy 1 cruises past the sand dunes, seaside resorts and fishing villages of coastal Oregon; and finally, the wild lands of Washington's Olympic Peninsula, with its primeval rainforest and bucolic San Juan Islands, served by coastal ferries.

When to Go

There's no bad time of year to drive the route, although northern climes will be rainier and snowier during winter. Peak travel season is June through August, which isn't always the best time as many stretches of the coast are socked in by fog during early summer (locals call it 'June Gloom'). The shoulder seasons before Memorial Day (ie April and May) and after Labor Day (ie September and October) can be ideal, with sunny days, crisply cool nights and fewer crowds.

The Route

Highways stretch nearly 1500 miles from border to border – that is, from Tijuana, Mexico, to British Columbia, Canada. In California, the coastal route jumps between I-5, Hwy 101 and Hwy 1 (when in doubt, just hug the coast) before committing to Hwy 101 in Oregon and Washington.

Time & Mileage

Time: No stopping? Give yourself four days because traffic and two-lane roads will slow you down; to fully enjoy the sights, allow 10 to 14 days.

Mileage: About 1500 miles.

Highway 89/89A: Wickenburg to Oak Creek Canyon

Hwy 89 and its sidekick Hwy 89A cross some of the most scenic and distinct regions in Arizona. The route described here travels north over the Weaver and Mingus mountains before rolling into Sedona and Oak Creek Canyon.

Why Go

This is our favorite drive in Arizona. It may not be the prettiest or the wildest, but there's a palpable sense of the Old West infusing the trip, like you've slipped through the swinging doors of history. But the route's not stuck in the 19th century, far from it. Weekend art walks, a burgeoning wine trail, stylish indie-owned shops and restaurants all add some 21st-century sparkle.

For those interested in cowboy history, Wickenburg and its dude ranches are a good place to spend some time. Hwy 89 leaves town via Hwy 93 and soon tackles the Weaver Mountains, climbing 2500ft in 4 miles. The road levels out at mountain-topping Yarnell, site of a devastating fire in the summer of 2013, then passes grassy buttes and grazing cattle in the Peeples Valley. From here, one highlight is Prescott's infamous Whiskey Row, home of the historic Palace Saloon. Thumb Butte is a hard-to-miss landmark west of downtown, and you'll pass the unusual boulders of Granite Dells on your way out of town.

Follow Hwy 89A to Jerome and hold on tight. This serpentine section of road brooks no distraction, clinging tight to the side of Mingus Mountain. If you dare, glance east for stunning views of the Verde Valley. The zigzagging reaches epic propor-

tions in Jerome, a former mining town cleaved into the side of Cleopatra Hill. Pull over for art galleries, tasting rooms, quirky inns and an unusually high number of ghosts. Stand over a 1910ft-long mining shaft at Audrey Headframe Park then visit the mining museum at Jerome State Historic Park next door.

Hwy 89A drops through another mining town, Clarkdale, on its way to Old Town Cottonwood. On the way to Sedona, detour to wineries on Page Springs Rd or loop into town via the Cathedral Rock, passing Red Rock Loop Rd. Sedona is made for rejuvenation, a pretty place to commune with a vortex, dine on a fine meal or shop for art and Navajo rugs. This trip ends with a cannonball into Oak Creek Canyon where the namesake creek sparkles with riparian lushness in the shadows of a towering red-rock corridor.

When to Go

This route is best traveled in spring, summer and fall to avoid winter snow – although you might see a few flakes in the mountains in April! In the dead of summer, you won't want to linger in low-lying, toasty Wickenburg.

The Route

From Wickenburg, follow Hwy 93 to Hwy 89 then drive north to Prescott. North of town, pick up Hwy 89A, following it to Sedona.

Time & Mileage

Time: This route can be driven in a half-day, but we recommend two to three days for maximum enjoyment.

Mileage: 134 miles.

Million Dollar Highway

Stretching between Ouray and Silverton in southern Colorado is one of the most gorgeous alpine drives in the US. Part of the 236-mile San Juan Skyway, this section of US 550 is known as the Million Dollar Hwy because the road, they say, is filled with ore.

Why Go

Twenty-five miles of smooth, buttery pavement twists over three mountain passes, serving up views of Victorian homes, snow-capped peaks, mineshaft headframes and a gorge lined with rock. But the allure isn't just the beauty part of the thrill is the driving. Hairpin turns, occasional rock slides and narrow, mountain-hugging pavement flips this route from a Sunday-afternoon drive to a NASCAR-worthy adventure.

Charming Ouray sits at nearly 7800ft, surrounded by lofty peaks. It also fronts the Uncompahgre Gorge, a steep, rocky canyon famous for its ice climbing. While here, take a hike or soak in the town's hot springs. From Ouray, the Million Dollar Hwy – completed in 1884 after three years of construction – hugs the side of the gorge, twisting past old mines that pock the mountainsides. Stay vigilant for the masochistic, spandex-clad cyclists pumping over the passes on the ribbon-thin road. In Silverton, step away from the car and enjoy the aspen-covered mountains or watch the steam-powered Durango & Silverton Narrow Gauge Railroad (p269) chug into town.

When to Go

Summer is the best time to visit. In winter, the highest pass sometimes closes and at other times you may need chains. You might even see snow on the ground in summer, though it likely won't be on the road.

MILLION DOLLAR HIGHWAY DETOUR

The drive between Ouray and Telluride is 50 miles – if you take the paved route. If you're feeling adventurous and have a 4WD (don't try it otherwise), consider the unpaved 16-mile road over Imogene Pass. On this old mining road you'll cross streams, alpine meadows and one of the state's highest passes. You'll also pass an old mine. We should mention one thing: this 'short cut' takes three hours. Still game?

The Route

From Ouray, follow Hwy 550 south to Silverton.

Time & Mileage

Time: The drive can be done in a few hours, but give yourself a day to see the sights.

Mileage: 25 miles.

Beartooth Highway

Depending on who's talking, the sky-high Beartooth Hwy is either the best way to get to Yellowstone, the most exciting motorcycle ride in the West or the most scenic highway in America. Not bad choices.

Why Go

Sometimes you just want to find a place so beautiful that it'll make you pull over, leave your car, beat your chest (or shake out your hair) and yell 'Yeah!' In the West, that place is the Beartooth Hwy.

From Red Lodge, Montana, this adventurous drive ascends Rock Creek Canyon's glaciated valley via a series of spaghetti-loop switchbacks, gaining an amazing 5000ft in elevation in just a few miles. Pull off at Rock Creek Vista Point Overlook for a short, wheelchair-accessible walk to superb views. The road continues up onto the high plateau, past 'Mae West Curve' and into Wyoming.

Twin Lakes has views of the cirque as well as the ski lift that carries the daring to an extreme spring ski run. After a series of switchbacks, look northwest for the Hellroaring Plateau and the jagged Bears Tooth (11,612ft). The route, flanked by alpine tundra, crests at the Beartooth Pass West Summit, the highest point at 10,947ft. Fifteen-foot snowbanks may linger here as late as June (sometimes even July).

After passing more lakes, the road descends past Beartooth Butte, a huge lump of the sedimentary rock that once covered the Beartooths. The highway drops to several excellent fishing areas on the Clark's Fork, then re-enters Montana, reaching Cooke City via Colter Pass (8066ft). The northeast entrance of Yellowstone is 4 miles from Cooke City.

Top: Apache Trail (p43), Arizona

Bottom: Pacific Coast Highway (p37), California

When to Go

To add some hiking to your driving, visit in August. That's when the weather's typically the best for outdoor adventure.

The Route

From Red Lodge, follow Hwy 212 west – crossing into and out of Wyoming – to Cooke City, MT.

Time & Mileage

Time: It's hard to zip through the twisty Beartooth Hwy; allow at least an afternoon or morning to drive it.

Mileage: 68 miles.

Highway 12

Arguably Utah's most diverse and stunning route, Hwy 12 winds through a remote and rugged canyon land, linking several national and state parks – and several fantastic restaurants – in the state's red-rock center.

Why Go

With crimson canyons, sprawling deserts, thick forests and lofty peaks calling out for exploration, Hwy 12 in remote southern Utah works well for adventurous explorers. The trip kicks off at Bryce Canyon National Park where the eye-catching gold-and-crimson spires set the stage for the color-infused journey to come.

Traveling east, the first highlight is Kodachrome Basin State Park (http://stateparks.utah.gov/parks/kodachrome-basin), home to petrified geysers and dozens of red, pink and white sandstone chimneys – some nearly 170ft tall. Pass through tiny Escalante and then, 8 miles down the road, pull over for the view at Head of the Rocks Overlook, atop the Aquarius Plateau. From here you'll lord over giant mesas, towering domes, deep canyons and undulating slickrock, all unfurling in an explosion of color.

The adjacent Grand Staircase-Escalante National Monument (p369) is the largest park in the Southwest at nearly 1.9 million acres. The Lower Calf Creek Recreation Area, inside the park and beside Hwy 12, holds a picnic area and a pleasant campground. It's also the start of a popular 6-mile round-trip hike to the impressive 126ft Lower Calf Creek Falls. The razor-thin Hogback Ridge, between Escalante and Boulder, is pretty stunning, too.

The best section of the drive? Many consider it to be the switchbacks and petrified sand dunes between Boulder and Torrey. But it's not just about the views. In Boulder, treat your taste buds to a locally sourced meal at Hell's Backbone Grill (p368), followed by homemade pie at the Burr Trail Grill & Outpost, or enjoy a flavor-packed Southwestern dish at Cafe Diablo (p368) further north in Torrey.

When to Go

For the best weather and driving conditions – especially over 11,000ft Boulder Mountain – drive Hwy 12 between May and October.

The Route

From US Hwy 89 in Utah, follow Hwy 12 east to Bryce Canyon National Park. The road takes a northerly turn at Kodachrome Basin State Park then continues to Torrey.

Time & Mileage

Time: Although the route could be driven in a few hours, two to three days will allow for a bit of exploration.

Mileage: 124 miles.

High Road to Taos

This picturesque byway (www.newmexico.org/high-road-to-taos-trail) in northern New Mexico links Santa Fe to Taos, rippling through a series of adobe villages and mountain-flanked vistas in and around the Truchas Peaks.

Why Go

Santa Fe and Taos are well-known artists' communities, lovely places brimming with galleries, studios and museums. Two cities this stunning should be linked by an aesthetically pleasing byway, and the mountainous High Road to Taos obliges.

From Santa Fe follow Hwy 84/285 north. Exit onto Hwy 503 toward Nambe, where you can hike to waterfalls or simply meditate by the namesake lake. From here, the road leads north to picturesque

Chimayo. Abandoned crutches line the wall in El Santuario de Chimayo (p385), also known as 'The Lourdes of America.' In 1816 this two-towered adobe chapel was built over a spot said to have miraculous healing powers. Take some time to wander through the community, and admire the fine weaving and woodcarving in family-run galleries.

Near Truchas, a village of galleries and century-old adobes, you'll find the High Road Marketplace (www.highroadmarket place.com). This cooperative on SR 676 sells a variety of artworks by area artists. Original paintings and carvings remain in good condition up Hwy 76 inside the Church of San José de Gracia (www.nps. gov/nr/travel/amsw/sw43.htm), considered one of the finest surviving 18th-century churches in the USA. Next is Picuris Pueblo (www.picurispueblo.org), once one of the most powerful pueblos in the region. This ride ends at Penasco, a gateway to the Pecos Wilderness, which is also home to the engagingly experimental Penasco Theatre (www.penascotheatre.org). From here, follow Hwys 75 and 518 into Taos.

When to Go

The high season is summer, but spring can be a nice time to see blooming flowers. Fall presents a show of colorful leaves. With mountains on the route, winter is not the best time to visit.

The Route

From Santa Fe, take 84/285 west to Pojoaque and turn right on Hwy 503, toward Nambe. From Hwy 503, take Hwy 76 to Hwy 75, then drive into Taos on Hwy 518.

Time & Mileage

Time: Without stopping, this drive should take about a half day, but give yourself a full day if you want to shop and explore.

Mileage: 85 miles.

Going-to-the-Sun Road

A strong contender for the most spectacular drive in America, the 53-mile Going-to-the-Sun Road is the only paved road through Glacier National Park in Montana.

Why Go

Glaciers! Grizzlies! Yep, the Going-to-the-Sun Road (p293) inspires superlatives and exclamation points. But the accolades are deserved. The road, completed in 1933, crosses a ruggedly beautiful alpine landscape, twisting and turning over a lofty Continental Divide that's usually blanketed in snow.

From the park's west entrance, the road skirts the shimmering Lake McDonald. Ahead, the looming Garden Wall forms the 9000ft spine of the Continental Divide and separates the west side of the park from the east side. The road crosses the divide at Logan Pass (6880ft). From here, the 7.6-mile Highline Trail (one way) traces the park's mountainous backbone, with views of glaciated valleys, sawtooth peaks, wildflowers and wildlife. And the wildlife you might see? Mountain goats. Bighorn sheep. Moose. Maybe even a grizzly bear or an elusive wolverine. After Logan Pass, the road passes Jackson Glacier Overlook, where you can bear witness to one of the park's melting monoliths. Experts say that at current global temperatures, all of the park's glaciers will be gone by 2030, so now is the time to visit.

When to Go

This snow-attracting route opens late and closes early, and is typically drivable between mid-June and mid-September. In 2011, due to an unusually heavy snowpack, the road didn't completely open until July 13.

GOING-TO-THE-SUN ROAD: A LEGEND AND A LANDMARK

Going-to-the-Sun Road was named after Going-to-the-Sun Mountain. According to legend – or a story concocted in the 1880s – a deity of the Blackfeet Tribe once taught tribal members to hunt. After the lesson, he left an image of himself on the mountain as inspiration before he ascended to the sun. Today, the road is a National Historic Landmark and a National Civil Engineering Landmark, the only road in the country to hold both designations.

MORE SCENIC DRIVES

Hungry for more road trips? Here are a few more good ones.

Turquoise Trail, NM This back route between Tijeras, near Albuquerque, and Santa Fe was a major trade route for several thousand years. Today it rolls past art galleries, shops (with turquoise jewelry) and a mining museum. From I-40, follow Hwy 14 north to I-25. Also see www.turquoisetrail.org.

Apache Trail, AZ This isn't your grandmother's Sunday-afternoon drive – unless your grandmother likes 45 miles of rabid road. From Apache Junction east of Phoenix, follow Hwy 88 past a kid-friendly ghost town, the wildflowers of Lost Dutchman State Park and three Salt River lakes. In the middle of it all? A snarling dirt section that drops 1000-plus feet in less than 3 miles. Hold tight!

The Loneliest Road Hwy 50 slices across the white-hot belly of Nevada, stretching from Fallon east to Great Basin National Park and the Utah state line. This remote highway unfurls past a singing sand dune, Pony Express stations and mining towns. A burger at Middlegate Station is a tasty pit stop.

Eastern Sierra Scenic Byway, CA From Topaz Lake, follow Hwy 395 south along the eastern flank of the mighty Sierra Nevada, ending at Little Lake. The region holds 14,000ft peaks, ice-blue lakes, pine forests, desert basins and hot springs.

The Route

From the west entrance of Glacier National Park, follow the Going-to-the-Sun Road east to St Mary.

Time & Mileage

Time: It varies depending on conditions, but plan to spend at least a half-day on the drive.

Mileage: 53 miles.

Historic Columbia River Highway

Lush foliage and trailblazing history are highlights on US 30, a carefully planned byway that ribbons alongside the Columbia River Gorge east of Portland, Oregon.

Why Go

Just how many waterfalls can one scenic highway hold? Quite a few if that road is the Historic Columbia River Hwy. The original route – completed in 1922 – connected Portland to The Dalles. The first paved road in the Pacific Northwest, it was carefully planned, built with the pleasure of driving in mind rather than speed. Viewpoints were carefully selected, and stone walls and arching bridges stylishly complement the gorgeous scenery.

Also notable is the history. Lewis and Clark traveled this route as they pushed toward the Pacific Ocean in 1805. Fifty years later, Oregon Trail pioneers ended their cross-country trek with a harrowing final push through the gorge's treacherous waters. Today, although sections of the original byway have been closed, or replaced by US 84, much of US 30 is still open for driving and some closed portions can be traversed by hiking or cycling.

One roadside highlight is the Portland Women's Forum Park, which provides one of the best views of the gorge. Just east, the 1916 Vista House, honoring the Oregon Trail pioneers, holds a visitor center. It's perched on Crown Point, a good viewpoint. And don't miss Multnomah Falls, Oregon's tallest waterfall at 642ft.

When to Go

Waterfalls are at their peak February to May, while summer is great for hiking.

The Route

To reach the historic highway, take exit 17, 28 or 35 off I-84 east of Portland. The western section of the original highway ends at Multnomah Falls. From here hop onto I-84 and continue east to exit 69 at Mosier where you can return to Hwy 30.

Time & Mileage

Time: One day.

Mileage: 100 miles.

Plan Your Trip
Western USA Outdoors

Whether you're a newbie hiker, a weekend warrior or an ironman (or maiden), the West has an outdoor activity for you. The best part? A stunning landscape as your backdrop. Scan for hummingbirds, paddle rapids, bounce over slickrock trails, swoosh down powdery slopes, surf curling waves or hike into the world's most famous canyon.

Best Outdoors

Ultimate Outdoor Experiences

Rafting the Colorado River through the Grand Canyon, AZ

Hiking to the summit of Half Dome, Yosemite National Park, CA

Cycling in Maroon Bells, Aspen, CO

Rock climbing in Joshua Tree National Park, CA

Scrambling to Angels Landing, Zion National Park, UT

Skiing in Vail, CO

Kayaking the San Juan Islands, WA

Glacier spotting in Glacier National Park, MT

Best Wildlife Watching

Bears: Glacier National Park, MT

Elk, bison and gray wolves: Yellowstone National Park, WY

Birds: Patagonia-Sonoita Creek Preserve, AZ

Whales and dolphins: Monterey Bay, CA

Camping

Campers are absolutely spoiled for choice in the West. Pitch a tent beside alpine lakes and streams in Colorado, sleep under saguaro cacti in southern Arizona or snooze on gorgeous strands of California sand.

Campground Types & Amenities

Primitive campsites Usually have fire pits, picnic tables and access to drinking water and vault toilets; most common in national forests (USFS) and on Bureau of Land Management (BLM) land.

Developed campgrounds Typically found in state and national parks, with more amenities, including flush toilets, barbecue grills and occasionally hot showers and a coin-op laundry.

RV (recreational vehicle) hookups and dump stations Available at many privately owned campgrounds, but only a few public-lands campgrounds.

Private campgrounds Cater mainly to RVers and offer hot showers, swimming pools, wi-fi and family camping cabins; tent sites may be few and uninviting.

Walk-in (environmental) sites Providing more peace and privacy; a few public-lands campgrounds reserve these for long-distance hikers and cyclists.

WESTERN US NATIONAL PARKS

PARK	FEATURES	ACTIVITIES	BEST TIME
Arches (p365)	more than 2000 sandstone arches	scenic drives, day hikes	spring-fall
Bryce Canyon (p369)	brilliantly colored, eroded hoodoos	day & backcountry hikes, horseback riding	spring-fall
Canyonlands (p366)	epic Southwestern canyons, mesas, and buttes	scenic viewpoints, backcountry hikes, white-water rafting	spring-fall
Carlsbad Caverns (p396)	extensive underground cave system; free-tail bat colony	cave tours, backcountry hikes	spring-fall
Death Valley (p106)	hot, dramatic desert & unique ecology	scenic drives, day hikes	spring
Glacier (p293)	impressive glaciated landscape; mountain goats	day & backcountry hikes, scenic drives	summer
Grand Canyon (p337)	spectacular 277-mile-long, 1-mile-deep river canyon	day & backcountry hikes, mule trips, river running	spring-fall
Grand Teton (p284)	towering granite peaks; moose, bison, wolves	day & backcountry hikes, rock climbing, fishing	spring-fall
Mesa Verde (p267)	preserved Ancestral Puebloan cliff dwellings, historic sites, mesas and canyons	short hikes	spring-fall
Olympic (p192)	temperate rainforests, alpine meadows, Mt Olympus	day & backcountry hikes	spring-fall
Petrified Forest (p347)	fossilized trees, petroglyphs, Painted Desert scenery	day hikes	spring-fall
Redwood (p155)	virgin redwood forest, world's tallest trees; elk	day & backcountry hikes	spring-fall
Rocky Mountain (p249)	stunning peaks, alpine tundra, the Continental Divide; elk, bighorn sheep, moose, beavers	day & backcountry hikes, cross-country skiing	summer-fall
Saguaro (p351)	giant saguaro cactus, desert scenery	day & backcountry hikes	spring-fall
Sequoia & Kings Canyon (p167)	sequoia redwood groves, granite canyon	day & backcountry hikes, cross-country skiing	summer-fall
Yellowstone (p277)	geysers & geothermal pools, impressive canyon; prolific wildlife	day & backcountry hikes, cycling, cross-country skiing	year-round
Yosemite (p163)	sheer granite-walled valley, waterfalls, alpine meadows	day & backcountry hikes, rock climbing, skiing	year-round
Zion (p370)	immense red-rock canyon, Virgin River	day & backcountry hikes, canyoneering	spring-fall

Rates & Reservations

Many public and private campgrounds accept reservations for all or some of their sites, while a few are strictly first-come, first-served. Overnight rates range from free for the most primitive campsites to $50 or more for pull-through RV sites with full hookups.

Top: White-water rafting (p49), Colorado River

Bottom: Angels Landing Trail, Zion National Park (p370)

These agencies let you search for campground locations and amenities; check availability and reserve campsites online:

Recreation.gov (www.recreation.gov) Camping and cabin reservations for national parks, national forests, BLM land etc.

ReserveAmerica (www.reserveamerica.com) Reservations for state parks, regional parks and some private campgrounds across North America. See website for phone numbers by state.

Kampgrounds of America (KOA; www.koa.com) Chain of reliable but more expensive private campgrounds with full facilities, including for RVs.

Hiking & Trekking

Good hiking trails are abundant in the West. Fitness is a priority throughout the region, and most metropolitan areas have at least one large park with trails. National parks and monuments are ideal for both short and long hikes. If you're hankering for nights in the wilderness beneath star-filled skies, however, plan on securing a backcountry permit in advance, especially in places like the Grand Canyon – spaces are limited, particularly during summer.

Hiking Resources

Wilderness Survival, by Gregory Davenport, is easily the best book on surviving nearly every contingency. Useful websites:

American Hiking Society (www.americanhiking. org) Links to local hiking clubs and 'volunteer vacations' building trails.

Backpacker (www.backpacker.com) Premier national magazine for backpackers, from novices to experts.

TOP TRAILS IN THE WEST

Ask 10 people for their top trail recommendations throughout the West and no two answers will be alike. The country is so varied and distances so enormous, there's little consensus. That said, you can't go wrong with the following all-star sampler.

South Kaibab/North Kaibab Trail, Grand Canyon, AZ (p340) A multiday cross-canyon tramp down to the Colorado River and back up to the rim.

Longs Peak Trail, Rocky Mountain National Park, CO (p249) This very popular 15-mile round-trip hike leads to the bouldery summit of Longs Peak (14,259ft) and its views of snow-capped summits.

Angels Landing, Zion National Park, UT (p370) After a heart-pounding scramble over a narrow, precipice-flanked strip of rock, the reward is a sweeping view of Zion Canyon. It's a 5.4-mile round-trip hike.

Mt Washburn Trail, Yellowstone National Park, WY (p281) From Dunraven Pass, this wildflower-lined trail climbs 3 miles to expansive views from the summit of Mt Washburn (10,243ft). Look for bighorn sheep.

Pacific Crest Trail (PCT; www.pcta.org) Follows the spines of the Cascades and Sierra Nevada, traipsing 2650 miles from Canada to Mexico, passing through six of North America's seven ecozones.

Half Dome, Yosemite National Park, CA (p163) Strenuous, but the Yosemite Valley views and sense of accomplishment are worth it. Park permit required.

Enchanted Valley Trail, Olympic National Park, WA (p192) Mountain views, roaming wildlife and lush rainforests – all on a 13-mile out-and-back trail.

Great Northern Traverse, Glacier National Park, MT (p293) A 58-mile haul that cuts through grizzly country and crosses the Continental Divide.

The Big Loop, Chiricahua National Monument, AZ (p353) A 9.5-mile hike along several trails that wind past an 'army' of wondrous rock pillars in southeastern Arizona once used as a hideout by Apache warriors.

Tahoe Rim Trail, Lake Tahoe, CA (p171) This 165-mile all-purpose trail circumnavigates the lake from high above, affording glistening Sierra views.

Rails-to-Trails Conservancy (www.railstotrails.org) Converts abandoned railroad corridors into hiking and biking trails; publishes free trail reviews at www.traillink.com.

Survive Outdoors (www.surviveoutdoors.com) Dispenses safety and first-aid tips, plus helpful photos of dangerous critters.

Fees & Wilderness Permits

➡ State parks typically charge a daily entrance fee of $5 to $15; there's often a reduced fee, or no charge, if you walk or bike into these parks.

➡ National park entry averages $10 to $25 per vehicle for seven consecutive days; some national parks are free. Check the national park website for dates for Free Entrance Days (www.nps.gov/findapark/feefreeparks.htm).

➡ For unlimited admission to national parks, national forests and other federal recreation lands for one year, buy an 'America the Beautiful' pass ($80).

➡ Often required for overnight backpackers and extended day hikes, wilderness permits are issued at ranger stations and park visitor centers. Daily quotas may be in effect during peak periods, usually late spring through early fall.

➡ Some wilderness permits may be reserved ahead of time, and very popular trails (eg Half Dome, Mt Whitney) may sell out several months in advance.

➡ To hike in the forest surrounding Sedona, AZ, you'll need to buy a Red Rock Pass ($5 per day, $15 per week). Passes can be purchased at USFS ranger stations, kiosks (at some trailheads) and the Sedona Chamber of Commerce (p334). National Park interagency passes are accepted in lieu of the Red Rock Pass.

Cycling

The popularity of cycling is growing by the day in the USA, with cities adding more cycle lanes and becoming more bike-friendly. An increasing number of greenways traverse urban areas and the countryside. You'll find diehard enthusiasts in every town, and numerous outfitters offer guided trips for all levels and durations.

MAD FOR MOUNTAIN BIKING

Mountain-biking enthusiasts will find trail nirvana in Crested Butte, CO, Moab, UT, Bend, OR, Ketchum, ID and Marin, CA, the latter being where Gary Fisher and Co bunny-hopped the sport forward by careening down the rocky flanks of Mt Tamalpais on home-rigged bikes. For info about trails and gear, check out Bicycling magazine (www.bicycling.com/mountain-bike) or IMBA (www.imba.com/destinations). Great destinations include the following:

Kokopelli's Trail, UT (www.blm.gov) One of the premier mountain-biking trails in the Southwest stretches 142 miles on mountainous terrain between Loma, CO, and Moab, UT. Other nearby options include the 206-mile, hut-to-hut ride between Telluride, CO, and Moab, UT, and the shorter but very challenging 38-mile ride from Aspen to Crested Butte – an equally stunning route.

Sun Top Loop, WA (www.visitrainier.com) A 22-mile ride with challenging climbs and superb views of Mt Rainier and surrounding peaks on the western slopes of Washington's Cascade Mountains.

Downieville Downhill, Downieville, CA (www.sierracountychamber.com) Not for the faint of heart, this piney trail, located near its namesake Sierra foothill town in Tahoe National Forest, skirts river-hugging cliffs, passes through old-growth forest and drops 4200ft in under 14 miles.

McKenzie River Trail, Willamette National Forest, OR (www.fs.usda.gov/activity/willamette/recreation) Twenty-five miles of blissful single-track winding through deep forests and volcanic formations. The town of McKenzie is about 50 miles east of Eugene.

Porcupine Rim, Moab, UT (www.blm.gov/ut) A 30-mile loop from town, this venerable high-desert romp features stunning views and hairy downhills. It's a difficult trail. Be prepared and bring lots of water.

Many states offer social multiday rides, such as Ride the Rockies (www.ridetherockies.com) in Colorado. For a fee, you can join the peloton on a scenic, well-supported route; your gear is ferried ahead to that night's camping spot.

In Colorado, Aspen's Maroon Bells is a top cycling spot. Another standout ride is Arizona's Mt Lemmon (www.fs.usda.gov/main/coronado), a thigh-zinging, 28-mile climb from the Sonoran Desert floor to the 9157ft summit. You can also rent bikes on the South Rim of the Grand Canyon at Grand Canyon National Park (p337). Ride to Hermit's Rest on the park's Hermit Rd and the ever-lengthening Greenway Trail (www.nps.gov/grca/planyourvisit/bicycling.htm).

Top Cycling Towns

San Francisco, CA A pedal over the Golden Gate Bridge lands you in the stunningly beautiful, and stunningly hilly, Marin Headlands.

Boulder, CO Outdoors-loving town with loads of great biking paths, including the 16-mile Boulder Creek Trail.

Portland, OR A trove of great cycling (on- and off-road) in the Pacific Northwest.

Surfing

The best surf in the continental USA breaks off the coast of California. There are loads of options – from the funky and low-key Santa Cruz (p117) to San Francisco's Ocean Beach (p130) – a tough spot to learn! – or bohemian Bolinas, 30 miles north. South, you'll find strong swells and Santa Ana winds in San Diego (p96), La Jolla (p95), Malibu (p73) and Santa Barbara (p108, all of which sport warmer waters, fewer sharks of the great white variety and a saucy SoCal beach scene; the best conditions are from September to November. Along the coast of Oregon and Washington are miles of crowd-free beaches and pockets of surfing communities.

Top California Surf Spots

Huntington Beach (aka Surf City, USA) is the quintessential surf capital, with perpetual sun and a 'perfect' break,

particularly during winter when the winds are calm.

Huntington Beach, Orange County (p88) Surfer central is a great place to take in the scene – and some lessons.

Oceanside Beach, Oceanside One of SoCal's prettiest beaches boasts one of the world's most consistent surf breaks in summer. It's a family-friendly spot.

Rincon, Santa Barbara Arguably one of the planet's top surfing spots; nearly every major surf champion on the globe has taken Rincon for a ride.

Steamer Lane and Pleasure Point, Santa Cruz There are 11 world-class breaks, including the point breaks over rock bottoms, at these two sweet spots.

Swami's, Encinitas Located below Seacliff Roadside Park, this popular surfing beach has multiple breaks guaranteeing you some fantastic waves.

Surfing Resources

Surfline (www.surfline.com) Browse the comprehensive atlas, live webcams and surf reports for the lowdown from San Diego to Maverick's.

Surfer (www.surfermag.com) Orange County–based magazine website with travel reports, gear reviews, newsy blogs and videos.

Surfrider (www.surfrider.org) Enlightened surfers can join up with this nonprofit organization that aims to protect the coastal environment.

White-Water Rafting

There's no shortage of scenic and spectacular rafting in the West. In California, both the Tuolumne and American Rivers surge with moderate-to-extreme rapids, while in Idaho the Middle Fork of the Salmon River (p299) has it all: abundant wildlife, thrilling rapids, a rich history, waterfalls and hot springs. The North Fork of the Owyhee – which snakes from the high plateau of southwest Oregon to the rangelands of Idaho – is rightfully popular and features towering hoodoos. North of Moab, UT, look for wildlife on an easy float on the Colorado River (p342) or ramp it up several notches with a thrilling romp through class V rapids and the

WHALE-WATCHING

Gray and humpback whales have the longest migrations of any mammal in the world – more than 5000 miles from the Arctic to Mexico, and back again. In the Pacific Northwest, most pass through from November to February (southbound) and March to June (northbound). Gray whales can be spotted off the California coast from December to April, while blue, humpback and sperm whales pass by in summer and fall. Bring binoculars! Top spots include:

Depoe Bay and Newport, OR (p227) Good whale-watching; tour boats.

Long Beach and Westport, WA (p74) Scan from shore.

Puget Sound and San Juan Islands, WA (p196) Resident pods of orca.

Klamath River Overlook, CA (p162) Watch for whales from bluffs.

Point Reyes Lighthouse, CA (p145) Gray whales pass by in December and January.

Monterey, CA (p116) Whales can be spotted year-round.

Channel Islands National Park, CA (p109) Take a cruise or peer through the telescope on the visitor center tower.

Point Loma, CA Cabrillo National Monument (p95) The best place in San Diego to watch gray-whale migration from January to March.

red rocks of Canyonlands National Park (p366).

To book a spot on the Colorado River through the Grand Canyon (p342), the quintessential river trip, make reservations at least a year in advance. And if you're not after white-knuckle rapids, fret not – many rivers have sections suitable for peaceful float trips or innertube drifts that you can enjoy with a cold beer in hand.

Kayaking & Canoeing

For exploring flatwater (no rapids or surf), opt for a kayak or canoe. For big lakes and the sea coast use a sea kayak. Be aware that kayaks are not always suitable for carrying bulky gear.

For scenic sea kayaking, you can push into the surf just about anywhere off the California coast. Popular spots include La Jolla (p95) as well as the coastal state parks just north of Santa Barbara (p107). In the Pacific Northwest, you can enjoy world-class kayaking in and around the San Juan Islands (p196), the Olympic Peninsula (p192) and Puget Sound. There's a full-moon paddle in Sausalito's Richardson Bay, CA. Sea-kayak rentals average $32 to $40 for two hours. Reputable outfitters will make sure you're aware of the tide

schedule and wind conditions of your proposed route.

White-water kayaking is also popular in the Pacific Northwest, where water tumbles down from the ice-capped volcanoes. Look for bald eagles on the Upper Sgakit River or slip through remote wilderness canyons on the Klickitat River. Close to Portland, try the Clackamas and the North Santiam. For urban white-water kayaking, you can't beat Colorado. Look for white-water parks in Boulder (p245) and Denver (p235).

Kayaking & Canoeing Resources

American Canoe Association (www.americancanoe.org) Organization supporting and providing information about canoeing and kayaking.

American Whitewater (www.americanwhitewater.org) Advocacy group for responsible recreation works to preserve America's wild rivers.

Canoe & Kayak (www.canoekayak.com) Special-interest magazine for paddlers.

Kayak Online (www.kayakonline.com) Advice for buying gear and helpful links to kayaking manufacturers, schools and associations.

Skiing & Other Winter Sports

There are ski resorts in every western state, including Arizona. Colorado has some of the best skiing in the region, although California and Utah are both top-notch destinations for the alpine experience. The ski season typically runs from mid-December to April, though some resorts have longer seasons. In summer, many resorts offer mountain biking and hiking courtesy of chair lifts. Ski packages (including airfares, hotels and lift tickets) are easy to find through resorts, travel agencies and online travel booking sites; these packages can be a good deal if your main goal is to ski.

Wherever you ski, it won't come cheap. Find the best deals by going midweek, purchasing multiday tickets, heading to lesser-known 'sibling' resorts, like Alpine Meadows (www.squawalpine.com) near Lake Tahoe, or checking out mountains that cater to locals including Santa Fe Ski Area (www.skisantafe.com) and Colorado's Wolf Creek (www.wolfcreekski.com).

Top Ski Resorts

➡ For snow, altitude and attitude: Vail, CO (p255); Squaw Valley, CA (p172); Aspen, CO (p257).

➡ For an unfussy scene and steep vertical chutes: Alta, UT (p360); Telluride, CO (p265); Jackson, WY (p275); Taos, NM (p388).

Snowboarding

On powdered slopes across the USA, snowboarding has become as popular as downhill skiing – all thanks to snow-surfing pioneer Jake Burton Carpenter, who set up a workshop in his Vermont garage and began to build snowboards in the mid-1970s. Snowboarders flock almost everywhere out West, including Sun Valley (p298), Tahoe (p171) and Taos (p388). For a fix during the summer months, head to Oregon's Mt Hood area (p220), where several resorts offer snowboard camps.

Cross-Country Skiing & Snowshoeing

Most downhill ski resorts have cross-country (Nordic) ski trails. In winter, popular areas of national parks, national forests and city parks often have cross-country ski and snowshoe trails, and ice-skating rinks.

You'll find superb trail networks for Nordic skiers and snowshoers in California's Royal Gorge (p172), North America's largest Nordic ski area, and Washington's sublime and crowd-free Methow Valley (p200). Backcountry passionistas will be happily rewarded throughout the Sierra Nevada (p163), with its many ski-in huts. There are 60 miles of trails around five ski-in huts in the San Juan Mountains (www.sanjuanhuts.com) in Colorado; the 10th Mountain Division Association (www.huts.org) manages more than two-dozen huts in the Rockies. The South Rim of the Grand Canyon (p337) and the surrounding Kaibab National Forest (p339) are pretty spots for wintery exploring.

Ski & Snowboard Resources

Cross-Country Ski Areas Association (www.xcski.org) Comprehensive information and gear guides for cross-country skiing and snowshoeing across North America.

Cross Country Skier (www.crosscountryskier.com) Magazine with Nordic-skiing news stories and destination articles.

Powder (www.powdermag.com) Online version of *Powder* magazine for skiers.

Ski Resorts Guide (www.skiresortsguide.com) Comprehensive guide to resorts, with lodging info and more.

SkiNet (www.skinet.com) Online versions of *Ski* and *Skiing* magazines.

SnoCountry Mountain Reports (www.snocountry.com) Snow reports for North America, as well as events, news and resort links.

Rock Climbing & Canyoneering

In California, rock hounds test their mettle on the big walls, granite domes and boulders of world-class Yosemite National Park (p165), where the climbing season lasts from April to October. Climbers also flock to Joshua Tree National Park (p103), an otherworldly shrine in southern California's sun-scorched desert. There, amid

AND LET'S NOT FORGET...

ACTIVITY	WHERE?	WHAT?	MORE INFORMATION
Horseback riding	Southern Arizona dude ranches, AZ	Old West country (most ranches close in summer due to the heat)	www.azdra.com
	Grand Canyon South Rim, AZ	Low-key trips through Kaibab National Forest; campfire rides	www.apachestables.com
	Santa Fe, NM	Kids' rides; sunset rides	www.bishopslodge.com
	Telluride, CO	All-season rides in the hills	www.ridewithroudy.com
	Durango, CO	Day rides and overnight camping in Weminiuche Wilderness	www.vallecitolakeoutfitter.com
	Yosemite National Park, CA	Rides in Yosemite Valley, Tuolumne Meadows and near Wawona	www.yosemitepark.com
	Florence, OR	Romantic beach rides	www.oregonhorsebackriding.com
Diving	Blue Hole near Santa Rosa, NM	81ft-deep artesian well; blue water leads into a 131ft-long submerged cavern	www.santarosanm.org
	La Jolla Underwater Park, CA	Beginner friendly; snorkelers enjoy nearby La Jolla Cove	www.sandiego.gov/lifeguards/beaches
	Channel Islands National Park, CA	Kelp forests, sea caves off coastal islands	www.nps.gov/chis
	Point Lobos State Reserve, CA	Fantastic shore diving; shallow reefs, caves, sea lions, seals, otters	www.pointlobos.org
	Puget Sound, WA	Clear water, diverse marine life (including giant octopus!)	www.underwatersports.com
Hot-air ballooning	Sedona, AZ	Float above red-rock country; picnic with bubbly	www.northernlightballoon.com
	Napa Wine Country, CA	Colorful balloons float over vineyards	www.balloonrides.com; www.napavalleyballoons.com

craggy monoliths and the country's oldest trees, they make their pilgrimage on 8000 routes, tackling sheer vertical, sharp edges and bountiful cracks. For beginners, outdoor outfitters at both parks offer guided climbs and instruction.

In Zion National Park (p370) in Utah, multiday canyoneering classes teach the fine art of going *down:* rappelling off sheer sandstone cliffs into glorious red-rock canyons filled with trees. Some of the sportier pitches are made in dry suits, down the flanks of roaring waterfalls into ice-cold pools.

For ice climbing, try Ouray Ice Park (p263) in Ouray, off the Million Dollar

Highway in southwest Colorado. Inside a narrow slot canyon, 200ft walls and waterfalls are frozen in thick sheets.

Other great climbing spots:

Grand Teton National Park, WY (p284) Good for climbers of all levels: beginners can take basic climbing courses and the more experienced can join two-day expeditions up to the top of Grand Teton itself; a 13,770ft peak with majestic views.

City of Rocks National Reserve, ID (p393) More than 500 routes up wind-scoured granite and pinnacles 60 stories tall.

Bishop, CA (p169) This sleepy town in the Eastern Sierra is the gateway to excellent climbing in the nearby Owens River Gorge and Buttermilk Hills.

Red Rock Canyon, NV (p317) Ten miles west of Las Vegas is some of the world's finest sandstone climbing.

Rocky Mountain National Park, CO (p249) Offers alpine climbing near Boulder.

Flatirons, CO (p246) Also near Boulder, has fine multipitch ascents.

Climbing & Canyoneering Resources

American Canyoneering Association (www.canyoneering.net) An online canyons database with links to courses, local climbing groups and more.

Climbing (www.climbing.com) Cutting-edge rock-climbing news and information since 1970.

SuperTopo (www.supertopo.com) One-stop shop for rock-climbing guidebooks, downloadable topo maps and route descriptions.

Plan Your Trip

Travel with Children

The West is a top choice for adventure-loving families, with superb attractions for all ages: amusement parks, zoos, science museums, unique campsites, hikes in wilderness reserves, boogie-board surfing at the beach and bike rides through scenic forests. Most national and state parks offer kid-focused programs (junior ranger activities and the like).

Best Regions for Kids

Grand Canyon & Southern Arizona

Hike into the Grand Canyon, splash in Oak Creek and ponder the saguaro cacti outside Tucson. Water parks, dude ranches and ghost towns should also keep kids entertained.

Los Angeles & Southern California

See celebrity handprints in Hollywood, ogle the La Brea tar pits, take a studio tour in Burbank and hit the beach in Santa Monica. Orange County and San Diego have theme parks galore.

Colorado

The whole state is kid-friendly: museums in Denver, outdoor fun in the Rockies, rafting near Buena Vista and Salida, and ski resorts everywhere.

Western USA for Kids

To find family-oriented sights and activities, accommodations, restaurants and entertainment in our coverage, just look for the child-friendly icon (⬛).

Dining with Children

The US restaurant industry seems built on family-style service: children are not just accepted almost everywhere, they are usually encouraged by special children's menus with smaller portions and lower prices. In some restaurants children under a certain age even eat for free. Restaurants usually provide high chairs and booster seats. Some may also offer children crayons and puzzles.

Restaurants without children's menus don't necessarily discourage kids, though higher-end restaurants might; however, even at the nicer places, if you arrive early, you can usually eat without too much stress. You can ask if the kitchen will make a smaller order of a dish (check price), or if they will split a normal-size main dish between two plates for the kids.

Accommodations

Motels and hotels typically have rooms with two beds, which are ideal for families.

Some also have roll-away beds or cribs that can be brought into the room for an extra charge (these are usually portable cribs, which may not work for all children). Many hotels have adjoining doors between rooms. Some offer 'kids stay free' programs, for children up to 12 or sometimes 18 years old. Many B&Bs don't allow children; ask when reserving. Most resorts are kid friendly and many offer children's programs, but ask when booking, as a few cater only to adults.

Babysitting

Resort hotels may have on-call babysitting services; otherwise, ask the front-desk staff or concierge to help you make arrangements. Always ask if babysitters are licensed and bonded, what they charge per hour per child, whether there's a minimum fee, and if they charge extra for transportation or meals. Most tourist bureaus list local resources for child care, plus recreation facilities, medical services and so on.

Discounts for Children

Child concessions often apply for tours, admission fees and transport, with some discounts as high as 50% off the adult rate. However, the definition of 'child' can vary

from under 12 to under 16 years. Some sights also have discount rates for families. Most attractions give free admission to children under two years.

Children's Highlights
Outdoor Adventure

Yellowstone National Park Watch powerful geysers, spy on wildlife and take magnificent hikes. (p277)

Grand Canyon National Park Gaze across one of the earth's great wonders, followed by a hike, a ranger talk and biking. (p337)

Olympic National Park Explore the wild and pristine wilderness of one of the world's few temperate rainforests. (p192)

Oak Creek Canyon Swoosh over red rocks at Slide Rock State Park in Arizona. (p331)

Theme Parks

Disneyland It's the attention to detail that amazes most at Mickey Mouse's enchantingly imagined Disneyland, in the middle of Orange County, California. (p86)

Legoland Younger kids will get a kick out of the Lego-built statues and low-key rides scattered across this amusement park in Carlsbad, CA. (p100)

Universal Studios Hollywood movie-themed action rides, special-effects shows and a studio back-lot tram tour in Los Angeles. (p72)

Aquariums & Zoos

Arizona-Sonora Desert Museum Coyotes, cacti and docent demonstrations are highlights at this indoor/outdoor repository of flora and fauna in Tucson. (p348)

Monterey Bay Aquarium Observe denizens of the deep next door to the California central coast's biggest marine sanctuary. (p115)

Aquarium of the Pacific High-tech aquarium at Long Beach houses critters from balmy Baja California to the chilly north Pacific, plus a shark lagoon. (p75)

San Diego Zoo This sprawling zoo is home to creatures great and small, with more than 3700 animals. (p93)

ON THE ROAD & IN THE AIR

➡ Many public toilets have a baby-changing table (sometimes in men's toilets, too), and gender-neutral 'family' facilities appear in airports.

➡ Car-rental agencies should be able to provide an appropriate child seat, since these are required in every state, but you need to request it when booking and expect to pay around $13 more per day.

➡ Domestic airlines don't charge for children under two years. Those two or over must have a seat, and discounts are unlikely. Very rarely, some resort areas (like Disneyland) offer a 'kids fly free' promotion. Currently, children from two to 12 years enjoy 50% off the lowest Amtrak rail fare when they travel alongside a fare-paying adult.

Rainy-Day Activities

LA Museums See stars (the real ones) at LA's Griffith Observatory (p71), dinosaur bones at the Natural History Museum of LA (p69) and the Page Museum (p72) at the La Brea Tar Pits, then get hands-on at the amusing California Science Center (p70).

SF Museums San Francisco's Bay Area is a mind-bending classroom for kids, especially at the interactive Exploratorium (p120) ✔ and eco-friendly California Academy of Science (p131).

Pacific Science Center Fascinating, hands-on exhibits at this center in Seattle, plus an IMAX theater, planetarium and laser shows. (p187)

New Mexico Museum of Natural History & Science Check out the Hall of Jurassic Supergiants in Albuquerque. (p394)

Mini Time Machine Museum of Miniatures You may not get many rainy days in Tucson, but when the monsoon season arrives this museum of tiny but intricate houses and scenes is a mesmerizing place to explore. (p348)

Planning

Consider the weather and the crowds when planning a Western US family getaway. The peak travel season is from June to August, when schools are out and the weather is warmest. Expect high prices and abundant crowds – meaning long lines at amusement and water parks, fully booked resort areas, and heavy traffic on the roads; reserve well in advance for popular destinations. The same holds true for winter resorts (eg the Rockies, Lake Tahoe) during the high season of January to March.

What to Pack

➡ Bring lots of sunscreen, especially if you'll be spending a lot of time outside.

➡ For hiking, you'll need a front baby carrier (for children under one) or a backpack (for children up to about four years old) with a built-in shade top. These can be purchased or rented from outfitters throughout the region.

➡ Older kids need sturdy shoes and, for playing in streams, water sandals.

➡ To minimize concerns about bed configurations, it's a good idea to bring a portable crib for infants and sleeping bags for older children.

➡ Towels for playing in water between destinations.

➡ Rain gear.

➡ A snuggly fleece or heavy sweater (even in summer, desert nights can be cold).

➡ Sun hats (especially if you are camping).

➡ Bug repellent.

Resources for Families

Travel with Children For all-round information and advice, check out Lonely Planet's guide.

Kids in the Wild: A Family Guide to Outdoor Recreation (Cindy Ross and Todd Gladfelter) For outdoor advice.

A Trailside Guide: Parents' Guide to Hiking & Camping (Alice Cary)

Family Travel Files (www.thefamilytravelfiles. com) Offers ready-made vacation ideas, destination profiles and travel suggestions by age range.

Kids.gov The eclectic, enormous national resource, where you can download songs and activities and follow links to kid-focused information from big-name museums like the Smithsonian and MOMA.

Regions at a Glance

What image springs to mind when someone mentions the West? A saguaro cactus, or maybe the Grand Canyon? Either would be accurate – for Arizona. But the West holds so much more. Sun-kissed beaches in California. Lush forests in the Pacific Northwest. Leafy single-track trails in the Rockies. Crimson buttes and crumbly hoodoos in Utah. There's a landscape for every mood and adventure.

Cultural travelers can explore Native American sites in Arizona and New Mexico. There's upscale shopping, fine dining and big-city bustle in Los Angeles, Phoenix, San Francisco and Seattle. Are you a history buff? Visit Mormon settlements in Utah, Spanish missions in California or Old West towns just about everywhere. Ready to let loose? Two words: Las Vegas.

California

Beaches
Outdoor Adventure
Food & Wine

Gorgeous Shores

With more than 1100 miles of coastline, California rules the sands: you'll find rugged, pristine beaches in the north and people-packed beauties in the south, with great surfing, sea kayaking or beach-walking all along the coast.

Wild Playgrounds

Swoosh down snowy slopes, raft on white-water rivers, kayak beside coastal islands, hike past waterfalls and climb boulders in the desert. The problem isn't choice in California, it's finding enough time to do it all.

Nature's Bounty

Fertile fields, talented chefs and an insatiable appetite for the new make California a major culinary destination. Browse local food markets, sample Pinot and Chardonnay beside lush vineyards, and dine on farm-to-table fare.

p60

Pacific Northwest

Cycling
Food & Wine
National Parks

Pedal Power

Bicycle on paved, rolling roads in the tranquil San Juan Islands, cruise the bluff-dotted Oregon coast along Hwy 101 or pedal the streets of Portland, a city that embraces two-wheeled travel with loads of bike lanes, costumed theme rides and handcrafted bike shows.

Locavores & Oenophiles

No longer 'Up and coming,' the food scene has arrived and smudged up its apron in the Pacific Northwest. In Portland and Seattle, chefs blend fish caught in local waters with vegetables harvested in the Eden-like valleys surrounding the Columbia River. Washington's wine is second only to California's.

Classic Parks

The Northwest has four national parks, including three classics dating from the turn of the 20th century – Olympic, Mount Rainier and Crater Lake. The newest is North Cascades, established in 1968.

p174

Rocky Mountains

Outdoor Adventure
Western Culture
Dramatic Landscapes

Rugged Fun

Adrenaline junkie? Hit the Rockies, a world-class skiing, hiking and cycling destination. Everyone is welcome, with hundreds of races and group rides, and an incredible infrastructure of parks, trails and adventure huts.

Modern Cowboys

Once sporting Stetson cowboy hats and prairie dresses, today's freedom-loving Rocky folk are more often spotted in lycra, with a mountain bike hitched nearby, sipping a microbrew or latte at a sunny outdoor cafe. Hard playing and slow living still rule.

Alpine Wonderland

The snow-covered Rocky Mountains are pure majesty. With chiseled peaks, clear rivers and red-rock contours, the Rockies contain some of the world's most famous parks, and bucketloads of clean mountain air.

p233

Southwest

Natural Scenery
Native Cultures
Food

Red-Rock Country

The Southwest is famous for the jaw-dropping Grand Canyon, the dramatic red buttes of Monument Valley, the crimson arches of Moab and the fiery buttes of Sedona – just a few of many geographic wonders in and around the spectacular national parks and forests.

Pueblos & Reservations

Visiting the Hopi and Navajo Nations or one of the 19 New Mexico pueblos is a fine introduction to America's first inhabitants. This is your best bet for appreciating, and purchasing, native-made crafts.

Good Eats

Try chile-slathered chicken enchiladas in New Mexico, a messy Sonoran hotdog in Tucson or a hearty steak just about anywhere in the region. In Vegas, stretch your fat pants and your budget at one of the extravagant buffets. For gourmands, off-the-Strip restaurants offer the most intriguing epicurean experiences.

p301

On the Road

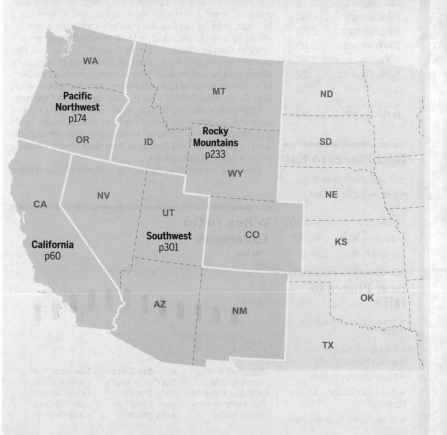

California

Best Places to Eat

➡ Chez Panisse (p146)

➡ Oxbow Public Market (p148)

➡ State Bird Provisions (p139)

➡ George's at the Cove (p98)

➡ Bestia (p80)

Best Places to Hike

➡ Yosemite National Park (p163)

➡ Sequoia & Kings Canyon National Parks (p167)

➡ Marin County (p144)

➡ Redwood National & State Parks (p155)

➡ Death Valley National Park (p106)

Why Go?

With bohemian spirit and high-tech savvy, not to mention a die-hard passion for the good life – whether that means cracking open a bottle of old-vine Zinfandel, climbing a 14,000ft peak or surfing the Pacific – California soars beyond any expectations sold on Hollywood's silver screens.

More than anything, California is iconic. It was here that the hurly-burly gold rush kicked off in the mid-19th century, where poet-naturalist John Muir rhapsodized about the Sierra Nevada's 'range of light,' and where Jack Kerouac and the Beat Generation defined what it really means to hit the road.

California's multicultural melting pot has been cookin' since this bountiful promised land was staked out by Spain and Mexico. Today, waves of immigrants from around the world still look to find their own American dream on these palm-studded Pacific shores.

Come see the future in the making here in the Golden State.

When to Go

Los Angeles

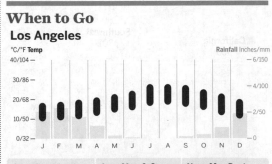

Jun–Aug Mostly sunny weather, occasional coastal fog; summer vacation crowds.

Apr–May & Sep–Oct Cooler nights, many cloudless days; travel bargains galore.

Nov–Mar Peak tourism at mountain ski resorts and in SoCal's warm deserts.

History

By the time European explorers arrived in the 16th century, more than 100,000 indigenous people called this land we now call California home. Spanish conquistadors combed through what they named Alta (Upper) California in search of a fabled 'city of gold,' but they left the territory virtually alone after failing to find it. Not until the Mission Period (1769–1833) did Spain make a serious attempt to settle the land, establishing 21 Catholic missions – many founded by Franciscan priest Junípero Serra – and presidios (military forts) to deter the British and Russians.

After winning independence from Spain in 1821, Mexico briefly ruled California, but got trounced by the fledgling United States in the Mexican-American War (1846–48). The discovery of gold just weeks before the Treaty of Guadalupe Hidalgo was signed saw the territory's nonindigenous population quintuple to 93,000 by 1850, when California became the 31st US state. Thousands of imported Chinese laborers helped complete the transcontinental railroad in 1869, which opened up markets and further spurred migration to the Golden State.

The 1906 San Francisco earthquake was barely a hiccup as California continued to grow exponentially in size, diversity and importance. Mexican immigrants streamed in during the 1910–20 Mexican Revolution, and again during WWII, to fill labor shortages. Military-driven industries developed during wartime, while anti-Asian sentiments led to the unjust internment of many Japanese Americans, including at Manzanar in the Eastern Sierra.

California has long been a social pioneer thanks to its size, confluence of wealth, diversity of immigration and technological innovation. Since the early 20th century, Hollywood has mesmerized the world with its cinematic dreams. Meanwhile, San Francisco reacted against the banal complacency of post-WWII suburbia with Beat poetry in the 1950s, hippie free love in the '60s and gay pride in the '70s.

California is not a finished work. Today's issues revolve around growth. In a state that has an economy bigger than Canada's and is the headquarters for cutting-edge industries, from space probes to biotechnology to Silicon Valley, the question of how to manage a burgeoning human population – with accompanying traffic gridlock, scarce affordable housing and the sky-high cost of living – is challenging.

Meanwhile, prisons are overflowing, state parks are underfunded and the conundrum of illegal immigration from Mexico, which fills a critical cheap labor shortage (especially in agriculture), vexes the state. Most worrying is California's extreme, years-long drought that shows no signs of abating, affecting farmers and urban dwellers alike with water shortages. In response, Governor Jerry Brown officially declared a state of emergency and instituted strict water-conservation measures statewide.

CALIFORNIA IN...

One Week

California in a nutshell: start in beachy **Los Angeles**, detouring to **Disneyland**. Head up the breezy Central Coast, stopping in **Santa Barbara** and **Big Sur**, before getting a dose of big-city culture in **San Francisco**. Head inland to nature's temple, **Yosemite National Park**, then zip back to LA.

Two Weeks

Follow the one-week itinerary above, but at a saner pace. Add jaunts to NorCal's **Wine Country**; **Lake Tahoe**, perched high in the Sierra Nevada; the bodacious beaches of **Orange County** and laid-back **San Diego**; or **Joshua Tree National Park**, near the chic desert resort of **Palm Springs**.

One Month

Do everything described above, and more. From San Francisco, head up the foggy North Coast, starting in Marin County at **Point Reyes National Seashore**. Stroll Victorian-era **Mendocino** and **Eureka**, find yourself on the **Lost Coast** and ramble through fern-filled **Redwood National & State Parks**. Inland, snap a postcard-perfect photo of **Mt Shasta**, drive through **Lassen Volcanic National Park** and ramble in California's historic **Gold Country**. Trace the backbone of the **Eastern Sierra** before winding down into otherworldly **Death Valley National Park**.

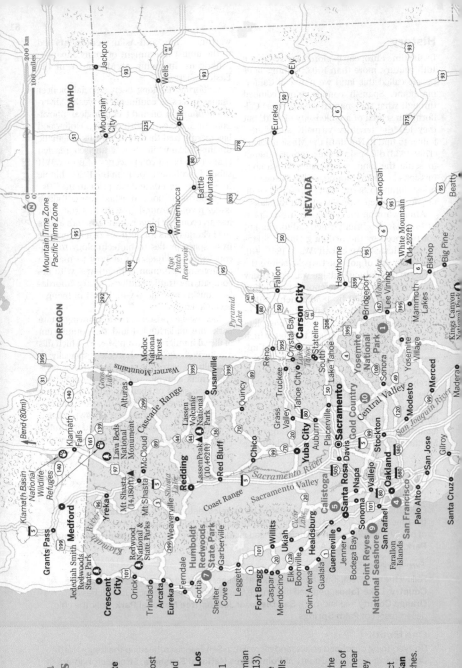

California Highlights

1 Chasing waterfalls and climbing granite domes in **Yosemite National Park** (p163).

2 Making the most of multicultural neighborhoods and Hollywood's red-carpet nightlife in **Los Angeles** (p64).

3 Cruising Hwy 1 atop sculpted sea cliffs on the bohemian **Big Sur** coast (p113).

4 Riding a cable car up dizzying hills in foggy, always fabulous **San Francisco** (p119).

5 Wallowing in the volcanic mud baths of **Calistoga** (p147) near famous Napa Valley vineyards.

6 Surfing perfect waves off sunny **San Diego** (p89) beaches.

7 Craning your neck at the world's tallest trees along the Avenue of the Giants in **Humboldt Redwoods State Park** (p154).

8 Trekking across sand dunes and uncovering Old West ghost towns in **Death Valley National Park** (p106).

9 Spotting whales, elephant seals and tule elk at wind-blown **Point Reyes National Seashore** (p145).

10 Dipping into swimming holes and panning like a forty-niner prospector in **Gold Country** (p158).

CALIFORNIA FACTS

Nickname Golden State

State motto Eureka ('I Have Found It')

Population 38.8 million

Area 155,779 sq miles

Capital city Sacramento (population 479,686)

Other cities Los Angeles (population 3,884,307), San Diego (population 1,355,896), San Francisco (population 837,442)

Sales tax 7.5%

Birthplace of Author John Steinbeck (1902–68), photographer Ansel Adams (1902–84), US president Richard Nixon (1913–94), pop-culture icon Marilyn Monroe (1926–62)

Home of The highest and lowest points in the contiguous US (Mt Whitney, Death Valley), world's oldest, tallest and biggest living trees (ancient bristlecone pines, coast redwoods and giant sequoias, respectively)

Politics Majority Democrat, minority Republican, one in five Californians vote independent

Famous for Disneyland, earthquakes, Hollywood, hippies, Silicon Valley, surfing

Kitschiest souvenir 'Mystery Spot' bumper sticker

Driving distances Los Angeles to San Francisco 380 miles, San Francisco to Yosemite Valley 190 miles

Local Culture

Currently the world's seventh-largest economy, California is a state of extremes, where grinding poverty shares urban corridors with fabulous wealth. Waves of immigrants keep arriving, and neighborhoods are often miniversions of their homelands. Tolerance for others is the social norm, but so is intolerance, which you'll encounter if you smoke or drive on freeways during rush hour.

Untraditional and unconventional attitudes define California, a trendsetter by nature. Think of the state as the USA's most futuristic social laboratory. If technology identifies a new useful gadget, Silicon Valley will build it at light speed. If postmodern celebrities, bizarrely famous for the mere fact of being famous, make a fashion statement or get thrown in jail, the nation pays attention. Arguably no other state has as big of an effect on how the rest of Americans work, play, eat and, yes, recycle.

LOS ANGELES

LA County represents the nation in extremes. Its people are among America's richest and poorest, most established and newest arrivals, most refined and roughest, most beautiful and most botoxed, most erudite and most airheaded. Even the landscape is a microcosm of the USA, from cinematic beaches to snow-dusted mountains, skyscrapers to suburban sprawl and even wilderness where mountain lions prowl.

If you think you've already got LA figured out – celebutantes, smog, traffic, bikini babes and pop-star wannabes – think again. LA is best defined by simple life-affirming moments: a cracked-ice, jazz-age cocktail after midnight, a hike high into the sagebrush of Griffith Park, a pink-washed sunset over a Venice Beach drum circle, or simply tracking down the perfect taco.

With Hollywood and Downtown LA both undergoing an urban renaissance, the city's art, music, food and fashion scenes are all in high gear. Chances are, the more you explore, the more you'll love 'La-La Land.'

History

The hunter-gatherer existence of the area's Gabrieleño and Chumash peoples ended with the arrival of Spanish missionaries and colonists in the late 18th century. Spain's first civilian settlement, El Pueblo de Nuestra Señora la Reina de Los Ángeles del Río de Porciúncula, remained an isolated farming outpost for decades after its founding in 1781. The city wasn't officially incorporated until 1850.

LA's population repeatedly swelled after the collapse of the California gold rush, the arrival of the transcontinental railroad, the growth of the citrus industry, the discovery of oil, the launch of the port of LA, the birth of the movie industry and the opening of the California Aqueduct. After WWII, the city's population doubled from nearly two million in 1950 to almost four million today.

◉ Sights

A dozen miles inland from the Pacific, Downtown LA combines history and high-brow arts and culture. Hip-again Hollywood awaits northwest of Downtown, while urban-designer chic and gay pride rule West Hollywood. South of WeHo, Museum Row is Mid-City's main draw. Further west are ritzy Beverly Hills, Westwood near the University of California, Los Angeles (UCLA) campus and West LA. Beach towns include kid-friendly Santa Monica, boho Venice, star-powered Malibu and busy Long Beach. Leafy Pasadena lies northeast of Downtown.

◉ Downtown

For decades, LA's historic core and main business and government district emptied out on nights and weekends. No more. Crowds fill fine-arts performance and pop-entertainment venues, and young professionals and artists have moved into lofts, bringing bars, restaurants and art galleries. Downtown is most easily explored on foot, combined with short Metro Rail and DASH minibus rides. Parking lots are cheapest around Little Tokyo and Chinatown.

◉ El Pueblo de Los Angeles & Around

Compact, colorful and car free, this historic district immerses you in LA's Spanish-Mexican roots. Its spine is festive **Olvera St** (Map p68; www.calleolvera.com; 🚶), where you can snap up handmade folkloric trinkets, then chomp on tacos and sugar-sprinkled churros.

'New' **Chinatown** (Map p68; www.chinatown-la.com) is about a half mile north along Broadway and Hill St, crammed with dim-sum parlors, herbal apothecaries, curio shops and Chung King Rd's edgy art galleries.

La Plaza de Cultura y Artes   MUSEUM
(Map p68; ☎213-542-6200; www.lapca.org; 501 N Main St; ⊙noon-5pm Mon, Wed & Thu, to 6pm Fri-Sun) **FREE** This museum chronicles the Mexican-American experience in Los Angeles, from the Mexican-American War when the border crossed the original pueblo, to the Zoot Suit Riots to Cesar Chavez and the Chicana movement.

Avila Adobe   MUSEUM
(Map p68; ☎213-628-1274; http://elpueblo.lacity.org; Olvera St; ⊙9am-4pm) **FREE** The oldest surviving house in LA was built in 1818 by a wealthy ranchero and one-time LA mayor, and later became a boarding house and (restaurant. Restored and furnished in heavy

---

LOS ANGELES IN...

Distances are ginormous in LA, so allow extra time for traffic and don't try to pack too much into a day.

One Day

Fuel up for the day at the **Original Farmers Market**, then go star-searching on the **Hollywood Walk of Fame** along Hollywood Blvd. Up your chances of spotting actual celebs by hitting the fashion-forward boutiques on paparazzi-infested **Robertson Boulevard**, or get a dose of nature at **Griffith Park**. Then drive west to the lofty **Getty Center** or head out to the **Venice Boardwalk** to see the seaside sideshow. Catch a Pacific sunset in **Santa Monica**.

Two Days

Explore rapidly evolving Downtown LA. Dig up the city's roots at **El Pueblo de Los Angeles**, then catapult to the future at dramatic **Walt Disney Concert Hall** topping Grand Ave's **Cultural Corridor**. Walk off lunch ambling between Downtown's historic buildings, **Arts District** galleries and **Little Tokyo**. At South Park's glitzy **LA Live** entertainment center, romp through the multimedia **Grammy Museum**, then join real-life celebs cheering on the LA Lakers next door at the **Staples Center**. After dark, hit the dance floor at clubs in **Hollywood**.

Greater Los Angeles

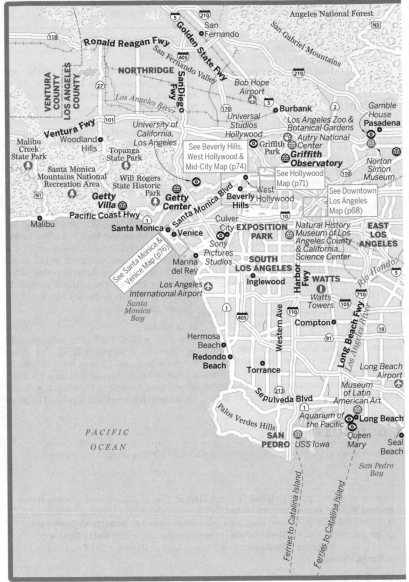

oak, it's open for self-guided tours and provides a look at life in the early 19th century.

Union Station   LANDMARK
(Map p68; www.amtrak.com; 800 N Alameda St; P)
Built on the site of LA's original Chinatown,
the station opened in 1939 as America's last grand rail station. It's a glamorous exercise in Mission Revival style with art-deco accents. The marble-floored main hall, with cathedral ceilings, original leather chairs and grand chandeliers, is breathtaking.

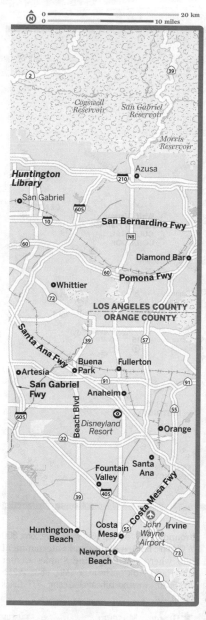

0 ————————— 20 km
0 ————————— 10 miles

Civic Center & Cultural Corridor

★ **Walt Disney Concert Hall** BUILDING
(Map p68; ☑ info 213-972-7211, tickets 323-850-2000; www.laphil.org; 111 S Grand Ave; ☺ guided

tours usually noon & 1pm Tue-Sat; Ⓟ) FREE A molten blend of steel, music and psychedelic architecture, this iconic concert venue is the home base of the Los Angeles Philharmonic, but has also hosted contemporary bands such as Phoenix and classic jazz men like Sonny Rollins. Frank Gehry pulled out all the stops: the building is a gravity-defying sculpture of heaving and billowing stainless steel.

Museum of Contemporary Art MUSEUM
(MOCA; Map p68; ☑ 213-626-6222; www.moca.org; 250 S Grand Ave; adult/child $12/free, 5-8pm Thu free; ☺ 11am-5pm Mon & Fri, to 8pm Thu, to 6pm Sat & Sun) A collection that arcs from the 1940s to the present and includes works by Mark Rothko, Dan Flavin, Joseph Cornell and other big-shot contemporary artists is housed in a postmodern building by Arata Isozaki. Galleries are below ground, yet sky-lit bright.

Cathedral of Our Lady of the Angels CHURCH
(Map p68; ☑ 213-680-5200; www.olacathedral.org; 555 W Temple St; ☺ 6:30am-6pm Mon-Fri, from 9am Sat, from 7am Sun; Ⓟ) FREE José Rafael Moneo mixed Gothic proportions with contemporary design for his 2002 Cathedral of Our Lady of the Angels, which exudes a calming serenity achieved by soft light filtering through its alabaster panes. Wall-sized tapestries as detailed as a Michelangelo fresco festoon the main nave.

City Hall LANDMARK
(Map p68; ☑ 213-978-1995; www.lacity.org; 200 N Spring St; ☺ 9am-5pm Mon-Fri) FREE Until 1966 no LA building stood taller than the 1928 City Hall, which appeared in the *Superman* TV series and 1953 sci-fi thriller *War of the Worlds*. On clear days you'll have views of the city, the mountains and several decades of Downtown growth from the observation deck.

Little Tokyo

Little Tokyo swirls with shopping arcades, Buddhist temples, traditional gardens, authentic sushi bars and noodle shops, and a provocative branch of **MOCA** (Map p68; ☑ 213-626-6222; www.moca.org; 152 N Central Ave; adult/child/student 12yr & under $12/free/7; ☺ 11am-5pm Mon & Fri, to 8pm Thu, to 6pm Sat & Sun).

Japanese American National Museum MUSEUM
(Map p68; ☑ 213-625-0414; www.janm.org; 100 N Central Ave; adult/child $9/5; ☺ 11am-5pm Tue-Wed & Fri-Sun, noon-8pm Thu) A great first

Downtown Los Angeles

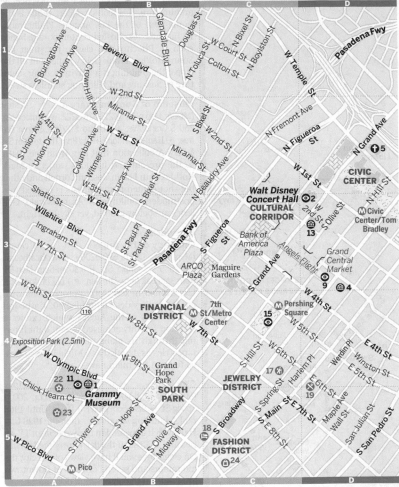

stop in Little Tokyo, this is the country's first museum dedicated to the Japanese immigrant experience. You'll be moved by galleries dealing with the painful chapter of the WWII internment camps. Afterward relax in the tranquil garden, and browse the well-stocked gift shop. Admission is free on Thursdays from 5pm to 8pm, and all day on the third Thursday of each month.

◎ South Park

South Park isn't actually a park but an emerging Downtown LA neighborhood

around **LA Live** (Map p68; www.lalive.com; 800 W Olympic Blvd), a dining and entertainment hub where you'll find the Staples Center (p83) and **Nokia Theatre** (Map p68; ☎213-763-6030; www.nokiatheatrelive.com; 777 Chick Hearn Ct).

★ Grammy Museum   MUSEUM

(Map p68; ☎213-765-6800; www.grammymuseum.org; 800 W Olympic Blvd; adult/child $13/11, after 6pm $8; ◎11:30am-7:30pm Mon-Fri, from 10am Sat & Sun; ⊕) It's the highlight of LA Live. Music lovers will get lost in interactive exhibits, which define, differentiate and link

musical genres, while live footage strobes. You can glimpse such things as Guns N' Roses' bass drum, Lester Young's tenor sax, Yo Yo Ma's cello and Michael's glove (though exhibits and collections do rotate).

◎ Exposition Park & Around

Just south of the University of Southern California (USC) campus, this park has a full day's worth of kid-friendly museums. Outdoor landmarks include the **Rose Garden** (www.laparks.org; 701 State Dr; ◎9am-sunset Mar 16–Dec 31) FREE and the **Los Angeles Me**morial Coliseum, site of the 1932 and 1984 Summer Olympic Games.

Parking costs around $10. From Downtown, take the Metro Expo Line or DASH minibus F.

Natural History Museum of Los Angeles   MUSEUM
(☑213-763-3466; www.nhm.org; 900 Exposition Blvd; adult/child/student & senior $12/5/9; ◎9:30am-5pm; 🔁) Dinos to diamonds, bears to beetles, hissing roaches to African elephants – this museum will take you around the world and back, across millions of years in time. It's all housed in a beautiful 1913 Spanish Renaissance–style building that

stood in for Columbia University in the first Toby McGuire *Spider-Man* movie – yup, this was where Peter Parker was bitten by the radioactive arachnid.

California Science Center
MUSEUM

(🗹 film schedule 213-744-2109, info 323-724-3623; www.californiasciencecenter.org; 700 Exposition Park Dr; IMAX movie adult/child $8.25/5; ⊙ 10am-5pm; 🖩) **FREE** A simulated earthquake, baby chicks hatching and a giant techno-doll named Tess bring out the kid in all of us at this multimedia museum with plenty of buttons to push, lights to switch on and knobs to pull. Don't miss seeing the space shuttle *Endeavour*, which requires a timed-ticket reservation (fee $2)

Watts Towers
LANDMARK

(🗹 213-847-4646; www.wattstowers.us; 1761-1765 E 107th St; adult/child under 13yr/child 13-17yr & senior $7/free/$3; ⊙ 11am-3pm Fri, 10:30am-3pm Sat, 12:30-3pm Sun; 🅿) The fabulous Watts Towers rank among the world's greatest monuments of folk art. In 1921 Italian immigrant Simon Rodia set out 'to make something big' and then spent 33 years cobbling together this whimsical free-form sculpture from a motley assortment of found objects, from green 7-Up bottles to sea shells, and rocks to pottery.

👁 Hollywood

Just as aging movie stars get the occasional face-lift, so has Hollywood. While it still hasn't recaptured its mid-20th-century 'Golden Age' glamour, its contemporary seediness is disappearing. The **Hollywood Walk of Fame** (Map p71; www.walkoffame.com; Hollywood Blvd) honors more than 2400 celebrities with stars embedded in the sidewalk.

The Metro Red Line stops beneath **Hollywood & Highland** (Map p71; www.hollywood andhighland.com; 6801 Hollywood Blvd; ⊙ 10am-10pm Mon-Sat, to 7pm Sun) **FREE**, a multistory mall with nicely framed views of the hillside **Hollywood Sign**, erected in 1923 as an advertisement for a land development called Hollywoodland. Two-hour validated mall parking costs $2 (daily maximum $15).

TCL Chinese Theatre
LANDMARK

(Map p71; 🗹 323-463-9576; www.tclchinese theatres.com; 6925 Hollywood Blvd; tours & movie tickets adult/child/senior $13.50/6.50/11.50) Ever wondered what it's like to be in George Clooney's shoes? Just find his footprints in the forecourt of this world-famous movie palace. The exotic pagoda theater – complete with temple bells and stone heaven dogs from China – has shown movies since 1927 when Cecil B DeMille's *The King of Kings* first flickered across the screen.

Hollywood Museum
MUSEUM

(Map p71; 🗹 323-464-7776; www.thehollywoodmuseum.com; 1660 N Highland Ave; adult/child $15/5; ⊙ 10am-5pm Wed-Sun) We quite like this musty temple to the stars, crammed with kitsch posters, costumes and rotating props. The museum is housed inside the handsome 1914 art-deco Max Factor Building, where the make-up pioneer once worked his magic on Marilyn Monroe and Judy Garland.

Dolby Theatre
THEATER

(Map p71; www.dolbytheatre.com; 6801 Hollywood Blvd; tours adult/child, senior & student $19/15; ⊙ 10:30am-4pm) The Academy Awards are handed out at the Dolby Theatre, which has

---

HISTORIC DOWNTOWN LOS ANGELES

At the center of Downtown's historic district, **Pershing Square** (Map p68; www.laparks. org; 532 S Olive St) was LA's first public park (1866). Now encircled by high-rises, the park exhibits public art and hosts summer concerts and outdoor movie nights.

Nearby, some of LA's turn-of-the-last century architecture remains as it once was. Pop into the 1893 **Bradbury Building** (Map p68; www.laconservancy.org; 304 S Broadway; ⊙ lobby usually 9am-5pm), the dazzling galleried atrium of which has had a cameo in several hit movies, including *Blade Runner*, *(500) Days of Summer* and *The Artist*.

In the early 20th century, Broadway was a glamorous shopping and theater strip, where megastars like Charlie Chaplin leapt from limos to attend premieres at lavish movie palaces. Some – such as the 1927 **United Artists Theatre** (Map p68; 🗹 213-623-3233; www.acehotel.com/losangeles/theatre; 929 S Broadway) – have been restored and once again host film screenings and live shows. Otherwise, take a weekend walking tour (reservations advised) with the **Los Angeles Conservancy** (🗹 info 213-430-4219, reservations 213-623-2489; www.laconservancy.org; adult/child $10/5).

Hollywood

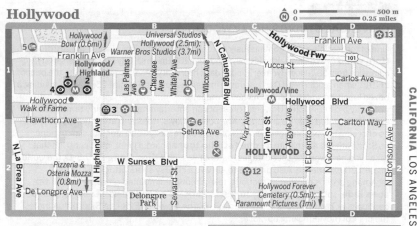

also hosted the American Idol finale, the ESPY awards, the Miss USA pageant and a recent Neil Young residency. On the tour you get to sniff around the auditorium, admire a VIP room and see an Oscar statuette up close.

Hollywood Forever Cemetery CEMETERY
(☑ 323-469-1181; www.hollywoodforever.com; 6000 Santa Monica Blvd; ◷ 8am-5pm; ℙ) Next to Paramount, Hollywood Forever boasts lavish landscaping, over-the-top tombstones, epic mausoleums and a roll call of departed superstars. Residents include Cecil B DeMille, Rudolph Valentino, femme fatale Jayne Mansfield and punk-rock icons Johnny and Dee Dee Ramone. For a full list of residents, pick up a map ($5) at the flower shop (open from 9am to 5pm).

◉ Griffith Park

America's largest urban **park** (☑ 323-913-4688; www.laparks.org/dos/parks/griffithpk; 4730 Crystal Springs Dr; ◷ 5am-10:30pm, trails sunrise-sunset; ℙ ♿) **FREE** is five times the size of New York's Central Park, with an outdoor theater, zoo, observatory, museum, merrygo-round, antique and miniature trains, children's playgrounds, golf, tennis and over 50 miles of hiking paths, including to the original *Batman* TV series cave.

★Griffith Observatory MUSEUM
(☑ 213-473-0800; www.griffithobservatory.org; 2800 E Observatory Rd; planetarium shows adult/child $7/3; ◷ noon-10pm Tue-Fri, from 10am Sat & Sun; ℙ ♿) **FREE** This landmark 1935 observatory opens a window onto the universe

Hollywood

◉ Sights
1 Dolby Theatre A1
  Egyptian Theatre .... (see 11)
2 Hollywood & Highland A1
3 Hollywood Museum B1
4 TCL Chinese Theatre A1

◆ Activities, Courses & Tours
  TMZ Tours .... (see 4)

◉ Sleeping
5 Magic Castle Hotel A1
6 USA Hostels Hollywood B2
7 Vibe Hotel D1

⊗ Eating
8 Life Food Organic C2

◉ Drinking & Nightlife
9 Musso & Frank Grill B1
10 No Vacancy B1

✦ Entertainment
11 American Cinematheque B1
12 Arclight Cinemas C2
13 Upright Citizens Brigade
   Theatre D1

❶ Information
  Hollywood Visitor
  Information Center .... (see 2)

from its perch on the southern slopes of Mt Hollywood. Its planetarium boasts the world's most advanced star projector. Astronomical touch displays cover the evolution of the telescope and the ultraviolet x-rays used to map our solar system. We loved the camera obscura on the main floor.

DON'T MISS

UNIVERSAL STUDIOS HOLLYWOOD

One of the world's oldest continuously operating movie studios, **Universal Studios Hollywood** (www.universalstudioshollywood.com; 100 Universal City Plaza, Universal City; admission from $87, under 3yr free; ☺ open daily, hours vary; P ⊞) first opened to the public in 1915, when studio head Carl Laemmle invited visitors at a quaint 25¢ each (including a boxed lunch) to watch silent films being made.

Nearly a century later, Universal presents an entertaining mix of fairly tame – and sometimes dated – thrills, including live-action shows, rides and attractions. The chances of seeing any action, however, let alone a real-life Hollywood star, are slim to none.

Start with the 45-minute narrated **studio tour** aboard a giant, multicar tram that takes you past working soundstages, outdoor sets and **King Kong 360 3-D**, the world's biggest 3D experience. Also prepare to survive a cheesy shark attack à la *Jaws*.

Among dozens of other attractions, take a motion-simulated romp on **The Simpsons Ride**, splash down among **Jurassic Park – The Ride** dinosaurs or fight off Decepticons in **Transformers: The Ride 3-D**. The **Special Effects Stage** illuminates the craft of movie-making up close.

Self-parking costs from $17 (after 3pm from $10). Free park shuttle buses connect with the Metro Red Line.

Los Angeles Zoo & Botanical Gardens ZOO (☎ 323-644-4200; www.lazoo.org; 5333 Zoo Dr; adult/child/senior $18/13/15; ☺ 10am-5pm, closed Christmas; P ⊞) The Los Angeles Zoo, with its 1100 finned, feathered and furry friends from over 250 species, rarely fails to enthrall the little ones. What began in 1912 as a refuge for retired circus animals now brings in over a million visitors each year.

Autry National Center MUSEUM (☎ 323-667-2000; www.autrynationalcenter.org; 4700 Western Heritage Way; adult/child/senior & student $10/4/6, 2nd Tue each month free; ☺ 10am-4pm Tue-Fri, to 5pm Sat & Sun; P) Want to know how the West was really won? Then mosey over to this excellent museum – its exhibits on the good, the bad and the ugly of America's westward expansion rope in even the most reluctant cowpokes. Kids can pan for gold and explore a stagecoach. Year-round gallery talks, symposia, film screenings and other cultural events spur the intellect.

◉ West Hollywood & Mid-City

In WeHo, rainbow flags fly proudly over Santa Monica Blvd, while celebs keep gossip rags happy by misbehaving at clubs on the fabled **Sunset Strip**. Boutiques along Robertson Blvd and Melrose Ave purvey sassy and ultrachic fashions for Hollywood royalty and celebutantes. WeHo's also a hotbed of cutting-edge interior design, fashion and art, particularly in the **West Hollywood Design District** (http://westhollywooddesigndistrict.com). Further south, some of LA's best museums line Mid-City's **Museum Row** along Wilshire Blvd east of Fairfax Ave.

★**Los Angeles County Museum of Art** MUSEUM (LACMA; Map p74; ☎ 323-857-6000; www.lacma.org; 5905 Wilshire Blvd; adult/child $15/free; ☺ 11am-5pm Mon, Tue & Thu, to 9pm Fri, 10am-7pm Sat & Sun; P) LA's premier art museum, LACMA's galleries are stuffed with all the major players – Rembrandt, Cézanne, Magritte, Mary Cassat, Ansel Adams, to name a few – plus several millennia worth of ceramics from China, woodblock prints from Japan, pre-Columbian art, and ancient sculpture from Greece, Rome and Egypt.

Page Museum & La Brea Tar Pits MUSEUM (Map p74; www.tarpits.org; 5801 Wilshire Blvd; adult/child/student & senior $12/5/9, 1st Tue of month Sep-Jun free; ☺ 9:30am-5pm; P ⊞) Mammoths and saber-toothed cats used to roam LA's savannah in prehistoric times. We know this because of an archaeological trove of skulls and bones unearthed at La Brea Tar Pits, one of the world's most fecund and famous fossil sites.

◉ Beverly Hills & the Westside

The mere mention of Beverly Hills conjures images of Maseratis, manicured mansions and megarich moguls. Take a saunter along pricey, pretentious **Rodeo Drive**, a three-block ribbon where sample-size fembots browse for fashions from international houses of couture. **Via Rodeo** is a cobbled lane lined with outdoor cafes for primo people-watching.

Several municipal lots and garages in downtown Beverly Hills offer two hours of free parking.

★**Getty Center**   MUSEUM
(☑310-440-7300; www.getty.edu; 1200 Getty Center Dr, off I-405 Fwy; ⊙10am-5:30pm Tue-Fri & Sun, to 9pm Sat; **P**) **FREE** In its billion-dollar, in-the-clouds perch, high above the city grit and grime, the Getty Center presents triple delights: a stellar art collection (everything from Renaissance artists to David Hockney), Richard Meier's cutting-edge architecture, and the visual splendor of seasonally changing gardens. Admission is free, but parking is $15 ($10 after 5pm).

Paley Center for Media   MUSEUM
(Map p74; ☑310-786-1000; www.paleycenter.org; 465 N Beverly Dr; suggested donation adult/child $10/5; ⊙noon-5pm Wed-Sun; **P**) The main lure here is the mind-boggling archive of TV and radio broadcasts dating to 1918. The Beatles' US debut on the *Ed Sullivan Show*? The moon landing? The *All In The Family* pilot? All here. Plus, two theaters for screenings and discussions with the casts of shows such as the great *Key & Peele* and *How I Met Your Mother*.

Hammer Museum   MUSEUM
(http://hammer.ucla.edu; 10899 Wilshire Blvd; ⊙11am-8pm Tue-Fri, to 5pm Sat & Sun) **FREE** Once a vanity project of the late oil tycoon Armand Hammer, his eponymous museum has become a widely respected art space. Selections from Hammer's personal collection include relatively minor works by Monet, Van Gogh and Mary Cassat, but the museum really shines when it comes to cutting-edge contemporary exhibits featuring local, under-represented and controversial artists. Best of all, it's free.

⊙ Malibu

Hugging 27 spectacular miles of the Pacific Coast Hwy, Malibu has long been synonymous with surfing and Hollywood stars, but it actually looks far less posh than glossy tabloids make it sound. Still, it has been celebrity central since the 1930s. Many A-listers have homes here, and can sometimes be spotted shopping at the villagelike **Malibu Country Mart** (www.malibucountrymart.com; 3835 Cross Creek Rd).

One of Malibu's natural treasures is mountainous **Malibu Creek State Park** (www.parks.ca.gov; Las Virgenes/Malibu Canyon Rd), a popular movie and TV filming location with hiking trails galore (parking $12). A string of famous beaches include aptly named **Surfrider** near Malibu Pier, secretive **El Matador**, family fave **Zuma Beach** and wilder **Point Dume** (beach parking $3 to $12.50).

★**Getty Villa**   MUSEUM
(☑310-430-7300; www.getty.edu; 17985 Pacific Coast Hwy; ⊙10am-5pm Wed-Mon; **P**) **FREE** Although self-described as the Getty Villa Malibu, this famous museum in a replica 1st-century Roman villa is actually in Pacific Palisades. It's a stunning 64-acre showcase for exquisite Greek, Roman and Etruscan antiquities amassed by oil tycoon J Paul Getty. Admission requires a timed ticket, reservable online; parking costs $15.

⊙ Santa Monica

The belle by the beach mixes urban cool with a laid-back vibe. Tourists, teens and street performers throng car-free, chain-store-lined **Third Street Promenade**. For more local flavor, shop posh **Montana Avenue** or eclectic **Main Street**, backbone of the neighborhood once nicknamed 'Dogtown,' the birthplace of skateboard culture.

There's free 90-minute parking in most public garages downtown.

Santa Monica Pier   LANDMARK
(Map p76; ☑310-458-8900; www.santamonicapier.org; ⊛) Once the very end of the mythical Route 66, and still the object of a tourist love affair, the Santa Monica Pier dates back to 1908, and is the city's most compelling landmark. There are arcades, carnival games, a vintage carousel, a Ferris wheel, a roller coaster and an aquarium, and the pier comes alive with free concerts (Twilight Dance Series) and outdoor movies in the summertime.

⊙ Venice

The **Venice Boardwalk** (Ocean Front Walk) is a freak show, a human zoo, a wacky carnival and an essential LA experience. This cauldron of counterculture is the place to get your hair braided and a qigong back massage, or pick up a Rastafarian-colored knit beret. Encounters with bodybuilders, a Speedo-clad snake charmer or a

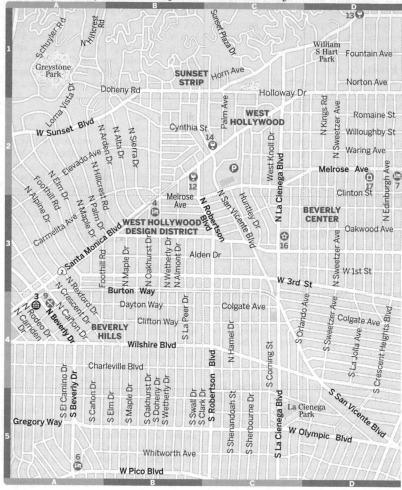

roller-skating Sikh minstrel are possible, especially on sunny afternoons.

To escape the hubbub, meander inland to the **Venice Canals**, a vestige of Venice's early days when Italian gondoliers poled tourists along artificial waterways. Funky, hipper-than-ever **Abbot Kinney Blvd** is a palm-lined mile of restaurants, cafes, art galleries and eclectic shops selling vintage furniture and handmade fashions.

There's street parking near Abbot Kinney Blvd. Beach parking lots cost $4 to $18.

Long Beach

Long Beach stretches along LA County's southern flank, harboring the world's third-busiest container port after Singapore and Hong Kong. Its industrial edge has been worn smooth downtown – **Pine Ave** is chockablock with restaurants and bars – and along the restyled waterfront.

The Metro Blue Line connects Downtown LA with Long Beach in under an hour. **Passport** (www.lbtransit.com) minibuses shuttle around major tourist sights for free.

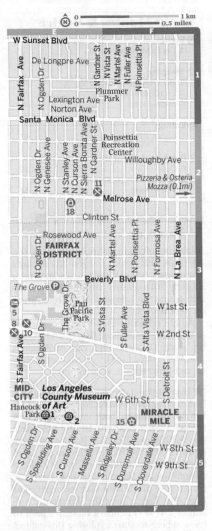

Aquarium of the Pacific   AQUARIUM
(📞tickets 562-590-3100; www.aquariumofpacific.org; 100 Aquarium Way; adult/child/senior $29/15/26; ⊙9am-6pm; 👣) Long Beach's most mesmerizing experience, the Aquarium of the Pacific is a vast, high-tech indoor ocean where sharks dart, jellyfish dance and sea lions frolic. More than 12,000 creatures inhabit four re-created habitats: the bays and lagoons of Baja California, the frigid northern Pacific, the coral reefs of the tropics, and local kelp forests. Parking costs $8.

Queen Mary   BOAT
(www.queenmary.com; 1126 Queens Hwy; tours adult/child from $26/15; ⊙10am-6:30pm; 🅿) Long Beach's 'flagship' attraction is this grand and supposedly haunted British luxury liner. Larger and more luxurious than even the *Titanic*, she transported royals, dignitaries, immigrants, WWII troops and vacationers between 1936 and 1966. Sure, it's a tourist trap, but study the memorabilia, and you may envision dapper gents escorting ladies in gowns to the art-deco lounge for cocktails or to the sumptuous Grand Salon for dinner.

USS Iowa   MUSEUM, MEMORIAL
(📞877-446-9261; www.pacificbattleship.com; 250 S Harbor Blvd, Berth 87; adult/child $18/10; ⊙10am-5pm, from 9am Jun-Aug; 🅿) Step onto the gangway and take a self-guided audio tour of this retired Pacific battleship, which transported Franklin D Roosevelt (FDR) and General Douglas MacArthur during WWII and saw action in the Cold War and beyond. Hourly parking is $1.

Santa Monica & Venice

◎ Pasadena

Below the lofty San Gabriel Mountains, this city drips with wealth and gentility, feeling a world apart from urban LA. It's known for its early 20th-century arts-and-crafts architecture and the Tournament of Roses Parade on New Year's Day.

Amble on foot around the shops, cafes, bars and restaurants of **Old Town Pasadena**, along Colorado Blvd east of Pasadena Ave. Metro Gold Line trains connect Pasadena and Downtown LA (20 minutes).

★**Huntington Library** MUSEUM, GARDENS
(📞626-405-2100; www.huntington.org; 1151 Oxford Rd, San Marino; adult weekday/weekend & holidays $23/25, child $10, 1st Thu each month free; ⊙10:30am-4:30pm Wed-Mon Jun-Aug, noon-4:30pm Mon & Wed-Fri, from 10:30am Sat, Sun & holidays Sep-May; P) Unwind in the Zen-like tranquillity of a Japanese garden. Study the jaunty pose of Thomas Gainsborough's *The Blue Boy*. Linger over the illuminated vellum of a 1455 Gutenberg Bible. It's hard to know where to start exploring this genteel country estate, the legacy of railroad tycoon Henry Huntington, and one of the most delightful and inspirational spots in LA.

Advance tickets are required for free day admission.

Gamble House ARCHITECTURE
(📞info 626-793-3334, tickets 800-979-3370; www.gamblehouse.org; 4 Westmoreland Pl, Pasadena; tours adult/child $15/free; ⊙tours noon-3pm Thu-Sun, gift shop 10am-5pm Tue-Sat, 11:30am-5pm Sun; P) It's the exquisite attention to detail that impresses most at the Gamble House,

Museum of Latin American Art MUSEUM
(www.molaa.org; 628 Alamitos Ave; adult/child/senior & student $9/free/6, Sun free; ⊙11am-5pm Wed, Thu, Sat & Sun, to 9pm Fri; P) This gem of a museum presents a rare survey of Latin American art created since 1945. Cecilia Míguez' whimsical bronze statuettes, Eduardo Kingman's wrenching portraits of indigenous people and Arnaldo Roche Rabel's intensely spiritual abstracts are among the many outstanding pieces in the permanent collection.

a 1908 masterpiece of arts-and-crafts architecture built by Charles and Henry Greene for Procter & Gamble–heir David Gamble. The entire home is a work of art, its foundation, furniture and fixtures all united by a common design and theme inspired by its Southern California environs.

Norton Simon Museum   MUSEUM
(www.nortonsimon.org; 411 W Colorado Blvd, Pasadena; adult/child $10/free; ☺noon-5pm Mon, Wed & Thu, 11am-8pm Fri-Sat; P) Rodin's *The Thinker* is only a mind-teasing overture to the full symphony of art in store at this exquisite museum. Norton Simon (1907–93) was an entrepreneur with a Midas touch and a passion for art who parlayed his millions into a respectable collection of Western art and Asian sculpture.

🏃 Activities

Cycling & In-line Skating
Get scenic exercise pedaling or skating along the paved **South Bay Bicycle Trail**, which parallels the beach for most of the 22 miles between Santa Monica and Pacific Palisades. Rental shops are plentiful in busy beach towns. Warning: it's crowded on weekends.

Hiking
Turn on your celeb radar while strutting it with the hot bods along **Runyon Canyon Park** above Hollywood. **Griffith Park** is also laced with trails. For longer rambles, head to the Santa Monica Mountains, where **Will Rogers State Historic Park**, **Topanga State Park** and **Malibu Creek State Park** are all excellent gateways to beautiful terrain (parking $8 to $12).

Swimming & Surfing
Top beaches for swimming are Malibu's **Leo Carrillo State Park**, **Santa Monica State Beach** and the South Bay's **Hermosa Beach**. Malibu's **Surfrider Beach** is a legendary surfing spot. Parking rates vary seasonally.

'Endless summer' is, sorry to report, a myth; much of the year you'll want a wet suit in the Pacific. Water temperatures become tolerable by June and peak just under 70°F (21°C) in August. Water quality varies; check the 'Beach Report Card' at http://brc.healthebay.org.

☞ Tours

★ Esotouric   BUS TOUR
(☎323-223-2767; www.esotouric.com; tours $58) Discover LA's lurid and fascinating underbelly on these offbeat, insightful and entertaining walking and bus tours themed around famous crime sites (Black Dahlia anyone?), literary lions (Chandler to Bukowski) and more.

Dearly Departed   BUS TOUR
(☎855-600-3323; www.dearlydepartedtours.com; tours $48-75) This long-running, occasionally creepy, frequently hilarious tour will clue you in on where celebs kicked the bucket, George Michael dropped his trousers, Hugh Grant received certain services and the Charles Manson gang murdered Sharon Tate. Not for kids.

TMZ Tours   BUS TOUR
(Map p71; ☎855-486-9868; www.tmz.com/tour; 6925 Hollywood Blvd; adult/child $55/45; ☺approx 10 tours daily) Cut the shame, do you really want to spot celebrities, glimpse their homes, and gawk and laugh at their dirt? Join this

---

WORTH A TRIP

TOURING MOVIE & TV STUDIOS

Half the fun of visiting Hollywood is hoping you'll see stars. Up the odds by joining the studio audience of a sitcom or game show, which usually tape between August and March. For free tickets, check with **Audiences Unlimited** (☎818-260-0041; www.tvtickets.com).

For an authentic behind-the-scenes look, take a shuttle tour of **Warner Bros Studios** (☎877-492-8687, 818-972-8687; www.wbstudiotour.com; 3400 W Riverside Dr, Burbank; tours from $54; ☺8:15am-4pm Mon-Sat, hours vary Sun) or **Paramount Pictures** (☎323-956-1777; www.paramountstudiotour.com; 5555 Melrose Ave; tours from $53; ☺tours 9:30am-2pm Mon-Fri, hours vary Sat & Sun), or a walking tour of **Sony Pictures Studios** (☎310-244-8687; www.sonypicturesstudiostours.com; 10202 W Washington Blvd; tour $38; ☺tours usually 9:30am, 10:30am, 1:30pm & 2:30pm Mon-Fri). All of these tours show you around soundstages and backlots (outdoor sets), and inside wardrobe and make-up departments. Reservations are required (minimum-age requirements apply); bring photo ID.

LOS ANGELES FOR CHILDREN

Keeping kids happy is child's play in LA. The sprawling Los Angeles Zoo (p72) in family-friendly Griffith Park (p71) is a sure bet. Dino-fans will dig the La Brea Tar Pits (p72) and the Natural History Museum (p69), while budding scientists crowd the Griffith Observatory (p71) and California Science Center (p70). For under-the-sea creatures, head to the Aquarium of the Pacific (p75) in Long Beach. The amusement park at Santa Monica Pier (p73) is fun for all ages. Activities for younger kids are more limited at tween/teen-oriented Universal Studios Hollywood (p72). In neighboring Orange County, Disneyland (p86) and Knott's Berry Farm (p87) are ever-popular theme parks.

branded tour imagined by the papparazzi made famous. Tours are two hours long, and you will likely meet some of the TMZ stars and perhaps even celebrity guests on the bus!

Festivals & Events

Monthly street fairs for art-gallery-hopping, shopping and food truck meet-ups include **Downtown Art Walk** (Map p68; www.downtownartwalk.org; ⊙ noon-9pm 2nd Thu of month) FREE and Venice's **First Friday** (www.abbotkinney1stfridays.com) events.

Rose Parade PARADE
(www.tournamentofroses.com; ⊙ Jan) This cavalcade of flower-festooned floats snakes through Pasadena on New Year's Day. Get close-ups during postparade viewing at Victory Park. Avoid traffic and take the Metro Rail Gold Line to Memorial Park.

Academy Awards FILM
(www.oscars.org; ⊙ Feb-Mar) Ogle your favorite film stars from the Dolby Theatre's red-carpet-adjacent bleachers. Apply in September for one of 600 lucky spots. Held in late February or early March.

West Hollywood
Halloween Carnaval CARNIVAL
(www.visitwesthollywood.com; ⊙ Oct) This rambunctious street fair brings 350,000 revelers – many in over-the-top and/or X-rated costumes – out for a day of dancing, dishing and dating on Halloween.

🛏 Sleeping

For seaside life, base yourself in Santa Monica, Venice or Long Beach. Cool-hunters and party people will be happiest in Hollywood or WeHo; culture-vultures, in Downtown LA. Prices do not include lodging taxes (12% to 14%).

🛏 Downtown

Ace Hotel HOTEL $$$
(Map p68; ☎ 213-623-3233; www.acehotel.com/losangeles; 929 S Broadway Ave; r/ste from $250/400) Either lovingly cool, a bit too hip or a touch self-conscious depending upon your purview, there is no denying that Downtown's newest hotel opened to universal acclaim. And the minds behind it care deeply about their product. Some rooms are cubby-box small, but the 'medium' rooms are doable.

🛏 Hollywood

USA Hostels Hollywood HOSTEL $
(Map p71; ☎ 323-462-3777; www.usahostels.com; 1624 Schrader Blvd; dm $30-40, r without bath $81-104; ❋ @ �🛜) This sociable hostel puts you within steps of the Hollywood party circuit. Private rooms are a bit cramped, but making new friends is easy during staff-organized barbecues, comedy nights and $25 all-you-can-drink limo tours. Freebies include a cook-your-own-pancake breakfast. It has cushy lounge seating on the front porch and free beach shuttles too.

Vibe Hotel HOSTEL $
(Map p71; ☎ 323-469-8600; www.vibehotel.com; 5920 Hollywood Blvd; dm $22-25, r $85-95; P @ �🛜) A funky motel turned hostel with both coed and female-only dorms, each with a flat-screen TV and kitchenette, and several recently redone private rooms that sleep three. You'll share space with a happening international crowd.

Magic Castle Hotel HOTEL $$
(Map p71; ☎ 323-851-0800; http://magiccastlehotel.com; 7025 Franklin Ave; r from $174; P ❋ @ 🛜 ❄ 👪) Walls at this perennial pleaser are a bit thin, but otherwise it's a charming base of operations with large, modern rooms, exceptional staff and a petite courtyard pool where days start with fresh pastries and gourmet coffee. Enquire about access to the Magic Castle, a fabled members-only magic club in an adjacent Victorian mansion. Parking costs $11.

West Hollywood & Mid-City

Pali Hotel BOUTIQUE HOTEL **$$**
(Map p74; ☑ 323-272-4588; www.pali-hotel.com; 7950 Melrose Ave; r from $179; P@🛜) We love the rustic wood-panelled exterior, the polished-concrete floor in the lobby, the Thai massage spa (just $35 for 30 minutes), and the 32 contemporary rooms with two-tone paint jobs, wall-mounted, flat-screen TV, and enough room for a sofa. Some have terraces. Terrific all-around value.

Farmer's Daughter Hotel MOTEL **$$**
(Map p74; ☑ 323-937-3930; www.farmersdaughter-hotel.com; 115 S Fairfax Ave; r from $209; P✱@🛜☷) Denim bedspreads and rocking chairs lend this flirty motel a farmhouse vibe. Long before the renovation, a young Charlize Theron stayed here with mom when they were hunting for a Hollywood career. Adventurous lovers should ask about the No Tell Room, which has mirrored headboards and another mirror on the ceiling.

Beverly Hills

Beverly Terrace Hotel HOTEL **$$**
(Map p74; ☑ 310-274-8141; www.hotelbeverlyterrace.com; 469 N Doheny Dr; r from $199; P🛜) This older, but high-value, Euro-style property dances on the border with West Hollywood and puts you close to the Santa Monica Blvd fun zone. Rooms aren't huge but are decorated in Mid-Century Modern style with soothing greens, crisp blues and bright reds. The rooftop sundeck is blessed with beautiful views of the Hollywood Hills. Parking is $12.

★**Mr C** HOTEL **$$$**
(Map p74; ☑ 877-334-5623; www.mrchotels.com; 1224 Beverwil Dr; r from $320) This long-standing tower hotel has been redesigned by the Cipriani brothers, who have been so involved in their passion project, they've designed everything down to the furniture in the rooms. Rooms on even floors offer white decor, odd floors are brown, and both varieties include marble baths, leather sofas and lounges. North-facing rooms have spectacular views.

Santa Monica

HI Los Angeles-Santa Monica HOSTEL **$**
(Map p76; ☑ 310-393-9913; www.hilosangeles.org; 1436 2nd St; dm $38-49, r without bath $99-159; ✱@🛜) Near the beach and Promenade, this hostel has an enviable location on the cheap. Its 200 beds in single-sex dorms and bed-in-a-box doubles with shared bathrooms are clean and safe, and there are plenty of public spaces to lounge and surf, but those looking to party are better off in Venice or Hollywood.

Sea Shore Motel MOTEL **$$**
(Map p76; ☑ 310-392-2787; www.seashoremotel.com; 2637 Main St; r from $140; P✱🛜) These friendly, family-run lodgings put you just a Frisbee toss from the beach on happening Main St (expect some street noise). The tiled rooms are basic, but families can stretch out comfortably in the modern suites with kitchen and balcony in a nearby building.

Shore Hotel HOTEL **$$$**
(Map p76; ☑ 310-458-1515; www.shorehotel.com; 1515 Ocean Ave; r from $309) 🏊 Massive and modern with clean lines, this is one of the newest hotels on Ocean Ave, and the only gold LEED-certified hotel in Santa Monica, which means it has a reasonably light footprint. Case in point: the lovely back garden is seeded with drought-tolerant plants. The wood-and-glass rooms each have private terraces.

Long Beach

Dockside Boat & Bed B&B **$$**
(☑ 562-436-3111; www.boatandbed.com; Rainbow Harbor, Dock 5, 330 S Pine Ave; r from $175; P🛜) Get rocked to sleep by the waves aboard your own private yacht with retro '70s charm, galley kitchen and high-tech entertainment center. Boats are moored right along the newly expanded waterfront fun zone in downtown Long Beach, so expect some noise. Breakfast is delivered to your vessel.

Pasadena

★**Bissell House B&B** B&B **$$**
(☑ 626-441-3535; www.bissellhouse.com; 201 S Orange Grove Ave, South Pasadena; r $159-259; P🛜☷) Antiques, hardwood floors and a crackling fireplace make this secluded Victorian B&B on 'Millionaire's Row' a bastion of warmth and romance. The hedge-framed garden feels like a sanctuary, and there's a pool for cooling off on hot summer days. The Prince Albert room has gorgeous wallpaper and a claw-foot tub. All seven rooms have private baths.

✗ Eating

With some 140 nationalities living in LA, ethnic neighborhoods for foodies to explore abound, including Downtown LA's Little Tokyo and Chinatown; Mid-City's Koreatown; Thai Town, east of Hollywood; East LA's Boyle Heights for Mexican flavors; and the Westside's Little Osaka for Japanese kitchens.

✗ Downtown

For cheap, fast meals-on-the-go, graze the international food stalls of the historic **Grand Central Market** (Map p68; www.grand-centralmarket.com; 317 S Broadway; ⊗8am-6pm Sun-Wed, to 9pm Thu-Sat).

Cole's   SANDWICHES $
(Map p68; www.213nightlife.com/colesfrenchdip; 118 E 6th St; sandwiches $6-9; ⊗11am-10pm Sun-Wed, to midnight Thu, to 1am Fri & Sat) A funky old basement tavern known for originating the French Dip sandwich way back in 1908, when those things cost a nickel. You know the drill: French bread piled with sliced lamb, beef, turkey, pork or pastrami, dipped once or twice in au jus.

Sushi Gen   JAPANESE $$
(Map p68; ☎213-617-0552; www.sushigen.org; 422 E 2nd St; sushi $11-21; ⊗11:15am-2pm & 5:30-9:45pm) Come early to grab a table, and know that it doesn't do the ubercreative 'look at me' kind of rolls. In this Japanese classic sushi spot, seven chefs stand behind the blonde wood bar, carving thick slabs of melt-in-your-mouth salmon, buttery toro and a wonderful Japanese snapper, among other staples. Their sashimi special at lunch ($18) is a steal.

★Bestia   ITALIAN $$$
(☎213-514-5724; http://bestiala.com; 2121 7th Pl; dishes $10-29; ⊗5-11pm Sun-Thu, to midnight Fri & Sat) The most sought-after reservation in town can be found at this new and splashy Italian kitchen in the Arts District. The antipasti ranges from crispy lamb pancetta to sea urchin crudo to veal tartare crostino. Did we mention the lamb's heart? Yeah, you may have to leave the vegan at home.

✗ Hollywood & Griffith Park

★Yuca's   MEXICAN $
(☎323-662-1214; www.yucasla.com; 2056 Hillhurst Ave; items $4-10; ⊗11am-6pm Mon-Sat) Loca-

tion, location, location...is definitely not what lures people to this parking-lot snack shack. It's the tacos! And the *tortas,* burritos and other Mexican faves that earned the Herrera family the coveted James Beard Award in 2005.

Life Food Organic   RAW $
(Map p71; www.lifefoodorganic.com; 1507 N Cahuenga Ave; dishes $4-14; ⊗7:30am-9pm) ✔ This place serves the healthiest fast food around. Have a chocolate shake made with almond milk, a veggie chili burger with a sesame seaweed salad on the side and a chocolate cream pie for dessert. None of it cooked! You can dine in, but most take it away.

Pizzeria & Osteria Mozza   ITALIAN $$$
(☎323-297-0100; www.mozza-la.com; 6602 Melrose Ave; pizzas $11-19, dinner mains $27-38; ⊗pizzeria noon-midnight daily, osteria 5:30-11pm Mon-Fri, 5-11pm Sat, 5-10pm Sun) Osteria Mozza is all about fine cuisine crafted from market-fresh, seasonal ingredients; but being a Mario Batali joint, you can expect adventure (squid-ink *chitarra freddi* with Dungeness crab, sea urchin and jalapeno) and consistent excellence. Reservations are recommended.

✗ West Hollywood & Mid-City

Original Farmers Market   MARKET $
(Map p74; www.farmersmarketla.com; 6333 W 3rd St; mains $6-12; ⊗9am-9pm Mon-Fri, to 8pm Sat, 10am-7pm Sun; ℗♿) The Farmers Market is a great spot for a casual meal any time of day, especially if the rug rats are tagging along. There are lots of options here, from gumbo to Singapore-style noodles to tacos.

Pingtung   ASIAN $
(Map p74; ☎323-866-1866; www.pingtungla.com; 7455 Melrose Ave; dishes $6-12; ⊗11:30am-10pm Sun-Thu, to 11pm Fri & Sat; 🕏) Our new favorite place to eat on Melrose is this Pan-Asian market cafe where the dim sum (wild crab dumplings), seaweed and green papaya salads, and rice bowls piled with curried chicken and BBQ beef are all worthy of praise. It has an inviting back patio with ample seating, wi-fi and good beer on tap.

★Mercado   MEXICAN $$
(Map p74; ☎323-944-0947; www.mercadorestaurant.com; 7910 W 3rd St; dishes $9-26; ⊗5-10pm Mon-Wed, to 11pm Thu & Fri, 11am-3pm & 4-11pm Sat, 11am-3pm & 4-10pm Sun) Terrific *nuovo-*

Mexican food served in white-washed brick environs, with dangling bird-cage chandeliers and a terrific marble tequila bar. The slow-cooked *carnitas* (braised pork) melt in your mouth. It also spit-roasts beef, grills sweet corn, and folds tasty tacos and enchiladas. The *hora feliz* (happy hour) is among the best in the city.

Nate 'n Al DELI $$
(Map p74; ☑310-274-0101; www.natenal.com; 414 N Beverly Dr; dishes $7-13; ⊗7am-9pm; ▣) Dapper seniors, chatty girlfriends, busy execs and even Larry King have kept this New York–style nosh spot busy since 1945. The huge menu brims with corned beef, lox and other old-school favorites, but we're partial to the pastrami, made fresh on-site.

✖ Santa Monica & Venice

Lemonade CALIFORNIAN $
(http://lemonadela.com; 1661 Abbot Kinney Blvd; meals $8-13; ⊗11am-9pm) The first incarnation of an imaginative, local market cafe with a lineup of tasty salads (watermelon radish and chili or tamarind pork and spicy carrots), and stockpots bubbling with lamb and stewed figs or miso-braised short ribs. It has six kinds of lemonade augmented with blueberries and mint or watermelon and rosemary. Yummy sweets too.

Abbot's Pizza Company PIZZA $
(Map p76; ☑310-396-7334; www.abbotspizzaco.com; 1407 Abbot Kinney Blvd; slices $3-5, pizzas $12-29; ⊗11am-11pm Sun-Thu, to midnight Fri & Sat; ▣) Join the flip-flop crowd at this shoe-box-sized pizza kitchen for habit-forming bagel-crust pies tastily decorated with tequila-lime chicken, portobello mushrooms, goat's cheese and other gourmet morsels served up at tummy-grumbling speed.

Father's Office PUB FOOD $$
(☑310-736-2224; www.fathersoffice.com; 1018 Montana Ave; dishes $5-15; ⊗5-10pm Mon-Wed, 5-11pm Thu, 4-11pm Fri, noon-11pm Sat, noon-10pm Sun) This elbow-to-elbow gastropub is famous for its burger: a dry-aged-beef number dressed in smoky bacon, sweet caramelized onion and an ingenious combo of Gruyère and blue cheese. Pair it with fries served in a mini shopping cart and a mug of handcrafted brew chosen from the three dozen on tap. No substitutions tolerated.

✖ Long Beach

Pier 76 SEAFOOD $$
(☑562-983-1776; www.pier76fishgrill.com; 95 Pine Ave; mains $8-19; ⊗11am-9pm) A terrific, affordable seafood house in downtown Long Beach. Step to the counter and order yellowtail, salmon, trout, mahimahi or halibut glazed and grilled, and served with two sides. The fries and kale salad are both good. It has fish tacos, sandwiches, poke and ceviche, too. It even has a $19 lobster.

✖ Pasadena

Ración SPANISH $$$
(☑626-396-3090; www.racionrestaurant.com; 119 W Green St; dishes $5-45; ⊗6-10pm Mon, 11:30am-3pm & 6-10pm Tue-Thu, to 11pm Fri & Sat, 5:30-10pm Sun) This Basque-inspired restaurant offers tapas such as duck sausage, stuffed squid, beer-braised octopus and seared prawns in salsa verde. It house-cures yellowfin tuna in anchovy vinegrette, and offers *raciones* (larger plates) ranging from a wild market fish with heirloom beans to slow-braised lamb belly.

♟ Drinking & Nightlife

Hollywood has been legendary sipping territory since before the Rat Pack days. Creative cocktails are the order of the day at reinvented watering holes in Downtown LA and edgier neighborhoods. Beachside bars run the gamut from surfer dives to candlelit cocktail lounges.

To confirm all your preconceived prejudices about LA, look no further than a velvet-roped nightclub in Hollywood. Come armed with a hot bod or a fat wallet to impress the bouncers.

★ No Vacancy BAR
(Map p71; ☑323-465-1902; www.novacancyla.com; 1727 N Hudson Ave; ⊗8pm-2am) An old, shingled Victorian has been converted into LA's hottest night out. Even the entrance is theatrical: you'll follow a rickety staircase into a narrow hall and enter the room of a would-be madame, dressed in fishnet and brimming with hospitality, who will soon press a button to reveal another staircase down into the living room and out into a courtyard.

Bar Marmont BAR
(Map p74; ☎323-650-0575; www.chateaumar-mont.com/barmarmont.php; 8171 Sunset Blvd; ⊙6pm-2am) Elegant, but not stuck up; been around, yet still cherished. With high ceilings, molded walls and terrific martinis, the famous, and wish-they-weres, still flock here. If you time it right you might see Tom Yorke, or perhaps Lindsay Lohan? Come midweek. Weekends are for amateurs.

Angel City Brewery BREWERY
(Map p68; ☎213-622-1261; www.angelcitybrewery.com; 216 S Alameda St; ⊙4-10pm Mon-Wed, to midnight Thu & Fri, noon-midnight Sat, noon-10pm Sun) This wonderful microbrewer of fine beers and ales is the only one of its kind in Downtown LA. Located on the edge of the Arts District, it runs tours on weekends, but you can always stop by its Public House to drink beer, listen to occasional live music and patronize the food trucks that descend with welcome flavor.

Copa d'Oro BAR
(Map p76; www.copadoro.com; 217 Broadway; ⊙5:30pm-midnight Mon-Wed, to 2am Thu-Sat) The cocktail menu was created by the talented Vincenzo Marianella – a man who knows his spirits, and has trained his team to concoct addictive cocktails from a well of top-end spirits and a produce bin of fresh herbs, fruits, juices and a few veggies too. The rock tunes and the smooth, dark ambience don't hurt.

Tiki-Ti BAR
(☎323-669-9381; www.tiki-ti.com; 4427 W Sunset Blvd; ⊙4pm-2am Wed-Sat) This garage-sized tropical tavern packs in grizzled old-timers and young cuties for sweet and wickedly strong drinks (try a Rae's Mistake, named for the bar's founder). The under-the-sea decor is surreal. Cash only.

Townhouse & Delmonte Speakeasy BAR
(Map p76; www.townhousevenice.com; 52 Windward Ave; ⊙5pm-2am Mon-Thu, noon-2am Fri-Sun) Upstairs is a cool, dark and perfectly dingy bar with pool tables, booths and good booze. Downstairs is the speakeasy, where DJs spin pop, funk and electronic music, comics take the mic, and jazz players set up and jam. It's a reliably good time almost any night.

Musso & Frank Grill BAR
(Map p71; www.mussoandfrankgrill.com; 6667 Hollywood Blvd) Hollywood history hangs in the thick air at Musso & Frank Grill, Tinseltown's oldest eatery (since 1919). Charlie Chaplin used to knock back vodka gimlets at the bar and Raymond Chandler penned scripts in the high-backed booths.

☆ Entertainment

For discounted and half-price tickets, check **Goldstar** (www.goldstar.com) or **LA Stage Tix** (www.lastagetix.com), the latter strictly for theater.

GAY & LESBIAN LA

'Boystown,' along Santa Monica Blvd in West Hollywood (WeHo), is gay ground zero, where dozens of high-energy bars, cafes, restaurants, gyms and clubs are found. The diverse crowd in Silver Lake is all-inclusive, from leather-and-Levi's bars to hipster haunts. Venice and Long Beach have neighborly scenes.

Out & About (www.outandabout-tours.com) Leads weekend walking tours of the city's lesbi-gay cultural landmarks. The festival season kicks off in May with **Long Beach Pride** (http://longbeachpride.com) and continues with WeHo's **LA Pride** (http://lapride.org) in June.

Abbey (Map p74; www.abbeyfoodandbar.com; 692 N Robertson Blvd; mains $9-13; ⊙11am-2am Mon-Thu, from 10am Fri, from 9am Sat & Sun) At WeHo's definitive gay bar and restaurant, take your pick of preening on an outdoor patio, in a chill lounge or on the dance floor, and enjoy flavored martinis. A dozen other bars and nightclubs are a short stumble away.

Micky's (Map p74; www.mickys.com; 8857 Santa Monica Blvd; ⊙5pm-2am Sun-Thu, to 4am Fri & Sat) A two-story, quintessential WeHo dance club, with go-go boys, expensive drinks, attitude and plenty of eye candy. Check online for special events.

Akbar (www.akbarsilverlake.com; 4356 W Sunset Blvd; ⊙4pm-2am) Killer jukebox, casbah-style atmosphere and a Silver Lake crowd that's been known to change from hour to hour – gay, straight or just hip, but not too-hip-for-you.

★**Hollywood Bowl** CONCERT VENUE
(☎323-850-2000; www.hollywoodbowl.com; 2301 N Highland Ave; rehearsals free, performance costs vary; ☺Jun-Sep) Summers in LA just wouldn't be the same without this chill spot for music under the stars, from symphonies to big-name acts such as Baaba Maal, Sigur Ros, Radiohead and Paul McCartney. A huge natural amphitheater, the Hollywood Bowl has been around since 1922 and has great sound.

★**Upright Citizens Brigade Theatre** COMEDY
(Map p71; ☎323-908-8702; http://franklin.ucb-theatre.com; 5919 Franklin Ave; tickets $5-10) Founded in New York by *Saturday Night Life* alums Amy Poehler and Ian Roberts along with Matt Besser and Matt Walsh, this sketch-comedy group cloned itself in Hollywood in 2005 and is arguably the best improv theater in town.

Dodger Stadium BASEBALL
(☎866-363-4377; www.dodgers.com; 1000 Elysian Park Ave; ☺Apr-Sep) Few clubs can match the Dodgers when it comes to history (Jackie Robinson, Sandy Koufax, Kirk Gibson, and Vin Scully), success and fan loyalty. The club's newest owners bought the organization for roughly two billion dollars, an American team-sports record.

Staples Center BASKETBALL
(Map p68; ☎213-742-7340; www.staplescenter.com; 1111 S Figueroa St; ⊕) The **LA Lakers** (☎213-742-7340; www.nba.com/lakers; tickets $50-250) were down on their luck as of this writing, but the NBA's most successful organization still packs all 19,000 seats on a regular basis. Floor seats, like those filled by the ubiquitous Jack Nicholson, cost in excess of $5000 per game.

Largo at the Coronet LIVE MUSIC, PERFORMING ARTS
(Map p74; ☎310-855-0530; www.largo-la.com; 366 N La Cienega Blvd) Ever since its early days on Fairfax Ave, Largo has been progenitor of high-minded pop culture (it nurtured Zach Galifinakis to stardom). Now part of the Coronet Theatre complex, it features edgy comedy, such as Sarah Silverman and Jon Hodgman, and nourishing night music from Brad Meldau and his jazz piano to Andrew Bird's acoustic ballads.

Arclight Cinemas CINEMA
(Map p71; ☎323-464-1478; www.arclightcinemas.com; 6360 W Sunset Blvd; tickets $14-16)

Assigned seats and exceptional celeb-sighting potential make this 14-screen multiplex the best around. If your taste dovetails with its schedule, the awesome 1963 geodesic Cinerama Dome is a must. Bonuses: age 21-plus screenings where you can booze it up, and Q&As with directors, writers and actors. Parking is $3 for four hours.

El Rey LIVE MUSIC
(Map p74; www.theelrey.com; 5515 Wilshire Blvd; cover varies) An old art-deco dance hall decked out in red velvet and chandeliers and flaunting an awesome sound system and excellent sightlines. Although it can hold 800 people, it feels quite small. Performance-wise, it's popular with indie acts such as Black Joe Lewis and the Honeybears, and the rockers who love them.

American Cinematheque CINEMA
(Map p71; www.americancinematheque.com; 6712 Hollywood Blvd; adult/senior & student $11/9) A nonprofit screening tributes, retrospectives and foreign films in the **Egyptian Theatre** (Map p71; www.egyptiantheatre.com; 6712 Hollywood Blvd). Directors, screenwriters and actors often swing by for postshow Q&As.

Kirk Douglas Theatre THEATER
(www.centertheatergroup.org; 9820 Washington Blvd) An old-timey movie house has been recast as a 300-seat theater, thanks to a major cash infusion from the Douglas family. Since its opening in 2004, it has become an integral part of Culver City's growing arts scene. It's primarily a showcase for terrific new plays by local playwrights.

★**Echo** LIVE MUSIC
(www.attheecho.com; 1822 W Sunset Blvd; cover varies) Eastsiders hungry for an eclectic alchemy of sounds pack this funky-town dive that's basically a sweaty bar with a stage and a smoking patio. It books indie bands, and also has regular club nights. Its Funky Sole party every Saturday is always a blast.

🛍 Shopping

Although Beverly Hills' Rodeo Drive is the most iconic shopping strip in LA, the city abounds with other options for retail therapy. Fashionistas and their paparazzi piranhas flock to Mid-City's Robertson Blvd. You also might spot celebs shopping on nearby 3rd St. Unusual and unique local boutiques line Main St in Santa Monica, Venice's Abbot Kinney Blvd and Sunset Blvd in Silver Lake.

Fashion District
FASHION

(Map p68; www.fashiondistrict.org) Fashion Institute of Design & Merchandising (FIDM) graduates often go on to launch their own brands or work for established labels in this 90-block nirvana for shopaholics. Bounded by Main and Wall Sts and 7th St and Pico Blvd, the district's prices are lowest in bazaar-like Santee Alley, but the styles are grooviest in the Gerry Building and Cooper Design Space.

Melrose Avenue
FASHION

(Map p74; Melrose Ave) A popular shopping strip as famous for its epic people-watching as it is for its consumer fruits. You'll see hair (and people) of all shades and styles, and everything from gothic jewels to custom sneakers to medical marijuana to stuffed porcupines available for a price. The strip is located between Fairfax and La Brea Aves.

Fred Segal
FASHION

(Map p74; ☑ 323-651-4129; www.fredsegal.com; 8100 Melrose Ave; ☺ 10am-7pm Mon-Sat, noon-6pm Sun) Celebs and beautiful people circle for the very latest from Babakul, Aviator Nation and Robbi & Nikki at this warren of high-end boutiques under one impossibly chic but slightly snooty roof. The only time you'll see bargains (sort of) is during the two-week blowout sale in September.

It's a Wrap!
VINTAGE

(www.itsawraphollywood.com; 3315 W Magnolia Blvd, Burbank; ☺ 10am-8pm Mon-Fri, 11am-6pm Sat & Sun) Here are fashionable, postproduction wares worn by TV and film stars. What that means to you is great prices on mainstream designer labels, including racks of casual and formal gear worn on such shows as *Nurse Jackie* and *Scandal*. The suits are a steal, and so is the denim. New arrivals are racked by show affiliation.

Raggedy Threads
VINTAGE

(Map p68; ☑ 213-620-1188; www.raggedythreads.com; 330 E 2nd St; ☺ noon-8pm Mon-Sat, to 6pm Sun) A tremendous vintage Americana store just off the main Little Tokyo strip. There's plenty of beautifully raggedy denim and overalls, soft T-shirts, a few Victorian dresses, and a wonderful turquoise collection at great prices. She also collects sensational glasses frames and watches.

Rose Bowl Flea Market
MARKET

(www.rgcshows.com; 1001 Rose Bowl Dr, Pasadena; admission from $8; ☺ 9am-4:30pm 2nd Sun each month, last entry 3pm) California's Marketplace of Unusual Items descends upon the Rose Bowl football field bringing forth the rummaging hordes. There are over 2500 vendors and 15,000 buyers here every month, and it's always a great time.

ℹ Information

DANGERS & ANNOYANCES
Crime rates are lowest in West LA, Beverly Hills, beach towns (except Venice and Long Beach) and Pasadena. Avoid walking alone and after dark around Downtown's 'Skid Row,' roughly bounded by 3rd, Alameda, 7th and Main Sts.

MEDIA
KCRW 89.9 FM (www.kcrw.org) Santa Monica–based National Public Radio (NPR) station for eclectic and indie music and intelligent talk.

LA Weekly (www.laweekly.com) Free alternative news, live music and entertainment listings newspaper.

Los Angeles Magazine (www.lamag.com) Glossy lifestyle monthly with a useful restaurant and bar guide.

Los Angeles Times (www.latimes.com) California's leading daily newspaper, winner of dozens of Pulitzer Prizes.

MEDICAL SERVICES
Cedars-Sinai Medical Center (☑ 310-423-3277; http://cedars-sinai.edu; 8700 Beverly Blvd, West Hollywood; ☺ 24hr) 24-hour emergency room.

MONEY
Travelex (☑ 310-659-6093; www.travelex.com; US Bank, 8901 Santa Monica Blvd, West Hollywood; ☺ 9:30am-5pm Mon-Thu, 9am-6pm Fri, to 1pm Sat)

Travelex (☑ 310-260-9219; www.travelex.com; 201 Santa Monica Blvd, Suite 101, Santa Monica; ☺ 9am-5pm Mon-Thu, to 6pm Fri)

TELEPHONE
LA County is covered by multiple area codes. Dial ☑ 1+(area code) before all local seven-digit numbers.

TOURIST INFORMATION
Downtown LA Visitor Center (Map p68; www.discoverlosangeles.com; 800 N Alameda St, Downtown; ☺ 8:30am-5pm Mon-Fri)

Hollywood Visitor Information Center (Map p71; ☑ 323-467-6412; http://discoverlosangeles.com; Hollywood & Highland complex, 6801 Hollywood Blvd, Hollywood; ☺ 10am-10pm Mon-Sat, to 7pm Sun) In the Dolby Theatre walkway.

Santa Monica Visitor Information Center (Map p76; ☑ 800-544-5319; www.santamonica.com; 2427 Main St, Santa Monica) Roving information officers patrol the promenade on Segways.

USEFUL WEBSITES

Discover Los Angeles (http://discover-losangeles.com) Official tourism site.

Experience LA (www.experiencela.com) Comprehensive cultural events calendar.

LAist (http://laist.com) Arts, entertainment, food and pop-culture gossip.

❶ Getting There & Away

AIR

LA's gateway hub is Los Angeles International Airport (www.lawa.org/lax; 1 World Way), the USA's second-busiest airport. Its nine terminals are linked on the lower (arrivals) level by free shuttle bus A. Hotel and car-rental shuttles stop there as well.

Smaller **Long Beach Airport** (www.lgb.org; 4100 Donald Douglas Dr, Long Beach) and Burbank's **Bob Hope Airport** (www.burbankairport.com; 2627 N Hollywood Way, Burbank) handle mostly domestic flights.

BUS

Greyhound's main **bus terminal** (☑213-629-8401; www.greyhound.com; 1716 E 7th St) is in an unsavory part of Downtown LA, so avoid arriving after dark.

CAR

The usual international car-rental agencies have branches at LAX airport and throughout LA.

TRAIN

Long-distance Amtrak trains roll into Downtown LA's historic **Union Station** (☑800-872-7245; www.amtrak.com; 800 N Alameda St). Pacific Surfliner regional trains run south to San Diego ($37, 2¾ hours) and north to Santa Barbara ($31, 2¾ hours) and San Luis Obispo ($41, 5½ hours).

❶ Getting Around

TO/FROM THE AIRPORT

Door-to-door shuttles, such as those operated by **Prime Time** (☑800-733-8267; www.prime-timeshuttle.com) and **Super Shuttle** (☑800-258-3826; www.supershuttle.com), leave from the lower level of LAX terminals. Destinations include Santa Monica ($21), Hollywood ($27) and Downtown LA ($16).

Curbside dispatchers summon taxis at LAX. A flat fare applies to Downtown LA ($46.50). Otherwise, metered fares (including $4 airport surcharge) average $30 to $35 to Santa Monica or $50 to Hollywood, excluding tip.

LAX FlyAway Buses (☑866-435-9529; www.lawa.org/FlyAway; one-way $8) depart hourly for Santa Monica ($8, 40 minutes) or Hollywood

($8, 60 to 90 minutes) from early morning until late night, and every 30 minutes around the clock to Downtown LA's Union Station ($8, 35 minutes).

Other public transportation is slower and less convenient but cheaper. From the lower level outside any LAX terminal, catch free shuttle bus C to the Metro Bus Center, a hub for buses serving all of LA; or take free shuttle bus G to light-rail Aviation Station on the Metro Green Line.

CAR & MOTORCYCLE

Driving in LA doesn't need to be a hassle, but be prepared for some of the worst traffic in the country during weekday rush hours (roughly 7am to 10am and 3pm to 7pm).

Self-parking at motels is usually free; most hotels charge from $10 to $40. Valet parking at restaurants, hotels and nightspots is common, with average rates of $5 to $10.

PUBLIC TRANSPORTATION

If you're not in a hurry, public transportation suffices around – but not necessarily between – LA's most touristed neighborhoods.

Online trip-planning help is available from LA's **Metro** (☑323-466-3876; www.metro.net), which operates 200 bus lines and the following six subway and light-rail lines:

Blue Line Downtown (7th St/Metro Center) to Long Beach.

Expo Line Downtown (7th St/Metro Center) to Culver City (and Santa Monica from early 2016), via Exposition Park.

Gold Line East LA to Pasadena via Little Tokyo, Union Station and Chinatown.

Green Line Norwalk to Redondo Beach via Aviation Station.

Purple Line Downtown LA (Union Station) to Koreatown.

Red Line Downtown LA (Union Station) to North Hollywood, via Hollywood and Universal City.

Metro train or bus fares are $1.75 upon boarding; for buses, bring cash (exact change). Metro 'TAP card' unlimited-ride passes cost $7/25 per day/week. Purchase TAP cards at ticket-vending machines inside Metro Rail stations. Day passes are also sold on board buses.

Local **DASH minibuses** (☑213-808-2273, 323-808-2273; www.ladottransit.com; per ride 50¢; ⏱info line 6:30am-7pm) run around Downtown LA, Hollywood and other neighborhoods; schedules vary, with reduced weekend services.

Big Blue Bus (☑310-451-5444; www.bigbluebus.com; fares from $1) covers much of West LA, including Santa Monica, Venice, Westwood, Culver City and LAX; Rapid 10 Express connects Santa Monica with Downtown LA ($2, 45 minutes to 1¾ hours).

TAXI

Because of LA's size and heavy traffic, getting around by cab will cost you. Metered taxis charge $2.85 at flagfall, then $2.70 per mile. Except for taxis lined up outside airports, train stations and major hotels, it's best to phone for a cab.

SOUTHERN CALIFORNIA COAST

Disneyland & Anaheim

The mother of all West Coast theme parks, aka the 'Happiest Place on Earth,' Disneyland is a parallel world that's squeaky-clean, enchanting and wacky all at once. It's an 'imagineered' hyper-reality where the employees – called 'cast members' – are always upbeat and there are parades every day of the year. More than 16 million kids, grandparents, honeymooners and international tourists stream through the front gates annually.

Disneyland opened to great fanfare in 1955 and the workaday city of Anaheim grew up around it. Today the Disneyland Resort comprises the original Disneyland Park and newer Disney California Adventure theme park. Anaheim itself doesn't have much in the way of attractions outside the Disney juggernaut.

◉ Sights & Activities

Going on all the rides at both theme parks requires at least two days, as queues for top attractions can be an hour or more. To minimize wait times, arrive midweek (especially during summer) before the gates open, buy print-at-home tickets online and take advantage of the parks' Fastpass system, which preassigns boarding times at select rides and attractions. For seasonal park hours and schedules of parades, shows and fireworks, check the official website.

Disneyland Park   THEME PARK
(☎714-781-4565; http://disneyland.disney.go.com; 1313 Disneyland Dr; adult/child $99/93, 1-day pass to both parks $155/149; ⊞) Spotless, wholesome Disneyland is still laid out according to Walt's original plans. It's here you'll find plenty of rides and some of the attractions most asscociated with the Disney name: Main Street, U.S.A, Sleeping Beauty Castle, Tomorrowland.

Disney California Adventure   THEME PARK
(DCA; ☎714-781-4400, 714-781-4565; www.disneyland.com; 1313 Harbor Blvd, Anaheim; adult/child $99/93, 1-day pass to both parks $155/149; ⊞) Disneyland resort's larger but less crowded park, Disney California Adventure celebrates the natural and cultural glories of the Golden State but lacks the density of attractions and depth of imagination. The best rides are Soarin' Over California, a virtual hang glide, and the famous Twilight Zone Tower of Terror that drops you 183ft down an elevator chute.

🛏 Sleeping

Chain motels and hotels are a dime a dozen in Anaheim.

HI Fullerton   HOSTEL $
(☎714-738-3721; www.hihostels.com; 1700 N Harbor Blvd, Fullerton; dm $26-29, r per person $52-56; ☺mid-Jun–mid-Sep; P☺❄@🐾) On a former dairy farm in Brea Dam State Park, 6 miles north of Disneyland, this two-story hacienda houses 20 beds in three dorm types (male, female, mixed), and the usual youth-hostel amenities. Rates include continental breakfast and parking. By bus from Disneyland, walk to Harbor Blvd and Ball Rd to catch OCTA bus 43 ($2, 30 minutes).

★ Anabella   HOTEL $$
(☎714-905-1050; www.anabellahotel.com; 1030 W Katella Ave; r $89-199, ste $109-199; P@🛜🏊🐾) Formerly three separate motels, this 7-acre complex has the feel of a laid-back country club, complete with trams that carry guests effortlessly from the lobby to their buildings. Large rooms have wooden floors and a whisper of Spanish Colonial style, with extras like minifridges and TV entertainment systems. Bunk-bedded kids' suites have Disney-inspired decor.

Alpine Inn   MOTEL $$
(☎714-535-2186; www.alpineinnanaheim.com; 715 W Katella Ave; r $60-190; P❄@🛜🏊🐾) Connoisseurs of kitsch will hug their Hummels over this 42-room, snow-covered chalet sporting an A-frame exterior and icicle-covered roofs – framed by palm trees, of course. Right on the border of DCA, the inn also has Ferris-wheel views. It's circa 1958, and air-con rooms are aging but clean. Simple continental breakfast (included) served in the lobby.

Paradise Pier Hotel
HOTEL $$$

(☑ info 714-999-0990, reservations 714-956-6425; http://disneyland.disney.go.com/paradise-pier-hotel; 1717 S Disneyland Dr; d from $240; P ✱ @ 🌐 ≋ 🐾) Sunbursts, surfboards and a giant superslide are all on deck at the Paradise Pier Hotel, the smallest (472 rooms), cheapest and maybe the most fun of the Disney hotel trio. Kids will love the beachy decor and game arcade, not to mention the roof deck pool and the tiny-tot video room filled with mini Adirondack chairs.

✗ Eating & Drinking

There are dozens of dining options inside the theme parks. Hit the walk-up food stands for carnival treats like giant turkey legs and sugar-dusted churros. For table reservations and meals with Disney characters, call **Disney Dining** (☑ 714-781-3463; http://disneyland.disney.go.com/dining).

No alcohol is allowed inside Disneyland Park; it's sold at DCA and Downtown Disney. Budget-conscious visitors and families with kids can store their own food and drinks (no glass) in the lockers (per day $7 to $15) along Disneyland's Main Street, USA, DCA's Buena Vista Street and outside both parks' main entrance.

An open-air pedestrian mall adjacent to the parks, Downtown Disney has mostly generic, yet family-friendly chain restaurants. The same is true of Anaheim GardenWalk (www.anaheimgardenwalk.com; 400 W Disney Way; h11am-9pm), an outdoor mall just east of the parks. If you want to steer clear of Mickey Mouse food, drive to the Anaheim Packing District (3 miles northeast), Old Towne Orange (7 miles southeast), Little Arabia (3 miles west) or Little Saigon (8 miles southwest).

Earl of Sandwich
SANDWICHES $

(☑ 714-817-7476; Downtown Disney; mains $4-7; ⊙ 8am-11pm Sun-Thu, to midnight Fri & Sat) This counter-service spot near the Disneyland Hotel serves grilled sandwiches that are both kid- and adult-friendly. The 'original 1762' is roast beef, cheddar and horseradish, or look for chipotle chicken with avocado or holiday turkey. There are also pizza, salad and breakfast options.

Café Orleans
CAJUN, CREOLE $$

(New Orleans Sq; mains $16-20; ⊙ seasonal hours vary; 🐾) This Southern-flavored restaurant is famous for its Monte Cristo sandwiches at lunch. Breakfast is served seasonally.

WORTH A TRIP

KNOTT'S BERRY FARM

What, Disney's not enough for you? Find even more thrill rides and cotton candy at **Knott's Berry Farm** (☑ 714-220-5200; www.knotts.com; 8039 Beach Blvd, Buena Park; adult/child $67/37; ⊙ from 10am, closing time varies 6-11pm; 🐾). This Old West–themed amusement park teems with packs of speed-crazed adolescents testing their mettle on a line-up of rides. Gut-wrenchers include the Boomerang 'scream machine,' wooden GhostRider and 1950s-themed Xcelerator, while younger kids will enjoy tamer action at Camp Snoopy. From late September through October, the park transforms at night into Halloween-themed 'Knott's Scary Farm.'

When summer heat waves hit, jump next door to **Soak City Orange County** (☑ 714-220-5200; www.soakcityoc.com; 8039 Beach Blvd, Buena Park; adult/child 3-11yr $38/27; ⊙ 10am-5pm, 6pm or 7pm mid-May–mid-Sep) water park. Save time and money by buying print-at-home tickets for either park online. Parking is $15.

★ Carthay Circle
AMERICAN $$$

(Buena Vista St; mains lunch $24-32, dinner $34-47; ⊙ lunch & dinner) Decked out like a Hollywood country club, new Carthay Circle is the best dining in either park, with steaks, seafood, pasta, smart service and a good wine list. Your table needs at least one order of fried biscuits, stuffed with white cheddar, bacon and jalapeño and served with apricot honey butter. Inquire about special packages including dinner and the World of Color show.

Napa Rose
CALIFORNIAN $$$

(☑ 714-300-7170; Grand Californian Hotel & Spa; mains $39-45, 4-course prix-fixe dinner from $90; ⊙ 5:30-10pm; 🐾) Soaring windows, high-back Arts and Crafts–style chairs, leaded-glass windows and towering ceilings befit the Disneyland Resort's top-drawer restaurant. On the plate, seasonal 'California Wine Country' (read: NorCal) cuisine is as impeccably crafted as Sleeping Beauty Castle. Kids' menu available. Reservations essential. Enter the hotel from DCA or Downtown Disney.

ℹ Information

ATMs, foreign-currency exchange and medical services are available inside both parks.

Disneyland Resort (☑ live assistance 714-781-7290, recorded info 714-781-4565; www.disneyland.com)

MousePlanet (www.mouseplanet.com) A one-stop fan site for all things Disney, with weekly park updates and discussion boards.

MouseWait (www.mousewait.com) This free mobile app reports up-to-the-minute ride wait times and park news.

ℹ Getting There & Around

Disneyland Resort is just off I-5 (Santa Ana Fwy), about 30 miles southeast of Downtown LA.

Disneyland Resort Express (☑ 800-828-6699; www.graylineanaheim.com; ⊙ 8am-8pm) buses travel between LAX (one way/round-trip $30/48) and Disneyland-area hotels; one child rides free with each paying adult.

The Anaheim Regional Transportation Intermodal Center (ARTIC), next to Angel Stadium, is a quick bus or taxi ride east of Disneyland. **Amtrak** (☑ 800-872-7245; www.amtrak.com; 2626 E Katella Ave) trains between LA's Union Station ($15, 40 minutes) and San Diego ($28, 2¼ hours) arrive almost hourly. **Metrolink** (☑ 800-371-5465; www.metrolinktrains.com; 2626 E Katella Ave) commuter trains from LA's Union Station ($8.75, 50 minutes) stop at the same station.

Anaheim Resort Transit (ART; ☑ 888-364-2787; www.rideart.org; adult/child fare $3/1, day pass $5/2) provides frequent bus service between Disneyland Resort and many area hotels and motels. Shuttles start running an hour before Disneyland opens, operating from 7am to midnight daily in summer.

A free tram connects Disneyland Resort's main parking structures (per day from $17) and Downtown Disney, a short walk from the parks.

Orange County Beaches

If you've seen *The OC* or *Real Housewives*, you might imagine you already know what to expect from this giant quilt of suburbia connecting LA and San Diego, lolling beside 42 miles of glorious coastline. In reality, Hummer-driving hunks and Botoxed beauties mix it up with hang-loose surfers and beatnik artists to give each of Orange County's beach towns a distinct vibe.

Just across the LA–OC county line, old-fashioned **Seal Beach** is refreshingly noncommercial, with a quaint walkable downtown. Less than 10 miles further south along the Pacific Coast Hwy (Hwy 1), **Huntington Beach** – aka 'Surf City, USA' –

epitomizes SoCal's surfing lifestyle. Fish tacos and happy-hour specials abound at bars and cafes along downtown HB's Main St, not far from a shortboard-sized **surfing museum** (www.surfingmuseum.org; 411 Olive Ave; donations welcome; ⊙ noon-5pm Wed-Fri & Sun, to 8pm Tue, to 7pm Sat).

Next up is the ritziest of the OC's beach communities: yacht-filled **Newport Beach**. Families and teens steer toward Balboa Peninsula for its beaches, vintage wooden pier and quaint amusement center. From near the 1906 Balboa Pavilion, **Balboa Island Ferry** (www.balboaislandferry.com; 410 S Bay Front; adult/child $1/50¢, car incl driver $2; ⊙ 6:30am-midnight Sun-Thu, to 2am Fri & Sat) shuttles across the bay to Balboa Island for strolls past historic beach cottages and boutiques along Marine Ave.

Continuing south, Hwy 1 zooms past the wild beaches of **Crystal Cove State Park** (☑ 949-494-3539; www.parks.ca.gov; 8471 N Coast Hwy; per car $15, campsites $25-75; ⊙ 6am-sunset) before winding downhill into **Laguna Beach**, the OC's most cultured seaside community. Secluded beaches, glassy waves and eucalyptus-covered hillsides create a Riviera-like feel. Art galleries dot the narrow streets of the 'village' and the coastal highway, where the **Laguna Art Museum** (☑ 949-494-8971; www.lagunaartmuseum.org; 307 Cliff Dr; adult/child/student & senior $7/free/5, 5-9pm 1st Thu of month free; ⊙ 11am-5pm Fri-Tue, to 9pm Thu) exhibits modern and contemporary Californian works. Soak up the natural beauty right in the center of town at **Main Beach**.

Another 10 miles south, detour inland to **Mission San Juan Capistrano** (☑ 949-234-1300; www.missionsjc.com; 26801 Ortega Hwy, San Juan Capistrano; adult/child $9/6; ⊙ 9am-5pm), one of California's most beautifully restored Spanish Colonial missions, with flowering gardens, a fountain courtyard and the charming 1778 Serra Chapel.

🛏 Sleeping & Eating

Oceanside motels and hotels along Pacific Coast Hwy (Hwy 1) charge surprisingly steep rates, especially on summer weekends. Dive inland near the freeways for better bargains.

★ **Crystal Cove Beach Cottages** CABIN $$
(☑ reservations 800-444-7275; www.crystalcovebeachcottages.com; 35 Crystal Cove, Newport

Beach; r without bath $42-127, cottages $162-249; ⊗ check-in 4-9pm; 🐾) To snag these historic oceanfront cottages, book on the first day of the month six months before your intended stay – or pray for last-minute cancellations.

Shorebreak Hotel BOUTIQUE HOTEL **$$$**
(📞 714-861-4470; www.shorebreakhotel.com; 500 Pacific Coast Hwy, Huntington Beach; r $189-495; P 🌼 @ 🛜 🐾) Stow your surfboard (lockers provided) as you head inside HB's hippest hotel, a stone's throw from the pier. The Shorebreak has a surf concierge, a fitness center and yoga studio, bean-bag chairs in the lobby and rattan and hardwood furniture in geometric-patterned air-con rooms (some pet-friendly). Have sunset cocktails on the upstairs deck at Zimzala restaurant. Parking is $27.

Sugar Shack CAFE **$**
(www.hbsugarshack.com; 213½ Main St, Huntington Beach; mains $4-10; ⊗ 6am-2pm Mon-Tue & Thu-Fri, to 8pm Wed, to 3pm Sat & Sun; 🐾) Expect a wait at this HB institution, or get here early to see surfer dudes don their wet suits. Breakfast is served all day on the bustling Main St patio and inside, where you can grab a spot at the counter or a two-top. Photos of surf legends plastering the walls raise this place almost to shrine status.

⭐ **Bear Flag Fish Company** SEAFOOD **$$**
(📞 949-673-3434; www.bearflagfishco.com; 3421 Via Lido, Newport Beach; mains $8-15; ⊗ 11am-9pm Tue-Sat, to 8pm Sun & Mon; 🐾) This is *the* place for generously sized, grilled and panko-breaded fish tacos, ahi burritos, spankin' fresh ceviche and oysters. Pick out what you want from the ice-cold display cases, then grab a picnic-table seat. About the only way this seafood could be any fresher is if you caught and hauled it off the boat yourself!

242 Cafe Fusion Sushi JAPANESE **$$$**
(www.fusionart.us; 242 N Coast Hwy, Laguna Beach; mains $18-45; ⊗ 4:30-10pm Sun-Thu, to 10:30pm Fri & Sat) One of the only female sushi chefs in Orange County, Miki Izumisawa slices and rolls organic rice into Laguna's best sushi, artfully presented. The place seats maybe two dozen people at a time, so expect a wait or come early. The 'sexy' handroll – spicy ahi and scallops with mint, cilantro, avocado and crispy potato – is date-enhancing.

DON'T MISS

LAGUNA'S FESTIVAL OF ARTS

Hey, did that painting just move? Welcome to the **Pageant of the Masters** (📞 800-487-3378; www.foapom.com; 650 Laguna Canyon Rd; tickets from $15; ⊗ 8:30pm daily mid-Jul–Aug), in which elaborately costumed humans step into painstaking re-creations of famous paintings on an outdoor stage. The pageant began in 1933 as a sideshow to Laguna Beach's **Festival of Arts** (www.foapom.com; 650 Laguna Canyon Rd; admission $7-10; ⊗ usually 10am-11:30pm Jul & Aug) and has been a prime attraction ever since. Our favorite part: watching the paintings deconstruct.

San Diego

San Diegans shamelessly promote their hometown as 'America's Finest City.' It's easy to see where that breezy confidence comes from: the sunny weather is practically perfect, and beaches are rarely more than a quick drive away. San Diego's population (1.38 million) makes it the USA's eighth-largest city and California's second largest (after LA), yet we're hard-pressed to think of a more laid-back metropolis anywhere.

The city grew by leaps and bounds during WWII, when the Japanese attack on Pearl Harbor prompted the US Navy to relocate the US Pacific Fleet from Hawaii to San Diego's natural harbor. The military, tourism, education and scientific-research industries (especially medicine and oceanography), as well as high-tech ventures cropping up in inland valleys, have helped shape this city set against the Mexico borderlands.

⊙ Sights

San Diego's compact downtown hinges on the historic Gaslamp Quarter, a beehive after dark. Coronado is reached via a stunning bridge, while museum-rich Balboa Park (home of the San Diego Zoo) is north of downtown. Heading west is touristy Old Town and Mission Bay's aquatic playground. Cruising up the coast, Ocean Beach, Mission Beach and Pacific Beach live the laid-back SoCal dream, while La Jolla sits pretty and privileged. The I-5 Fwy cuts through the region north–south.

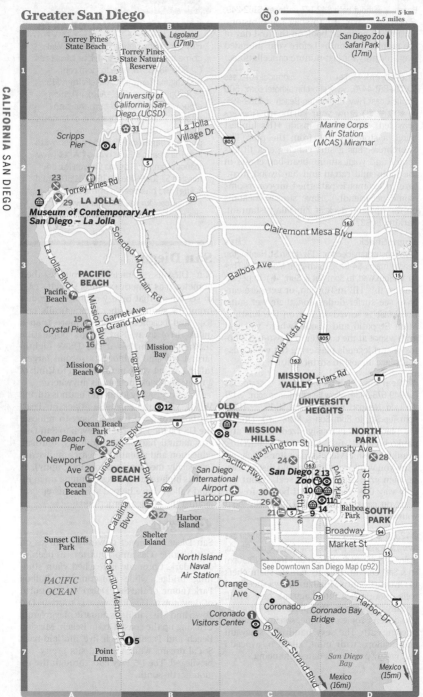

Greater San Diego

0 5 km
0 2.5 miles

Torrey Pines
State Beach

Legoland
(17mi)

San Diego Zoo
Safari Park
(17mi)

Torrey Pines
State Natural
Reserve

18

University of
California, San
Diego (UCSD)

Marine Corps
Air Station
(MCAS) Miramar

La Jolla
Village Dr

31

805

Scripps
Pier

4

Clairemont Mesa Blvd

163

17

23

Torrey Pines Rd

1

29 LA JOLLA

**Museum of Contemporary Art
San Diego – La Jolla**

52

Balboa Ave

15

Soledad Mountain Rd

PACIFIC
BEACH

Pacific
Beach

La Jolla Blvd

Mission Blvd

Garnet Ave

Grand Ave

19

Crystal Pier

16

Mission Bay

Ingraham St

Linda Vista Rd

805

163

Mission
Beach

7

3

5

12

MISSION
VALLEY

Friars Rd

8

UNIVERSITY
HEIGHTS

OLD
TOWN

7

8

MISSION
HILLS

Washington St

NORTH
PARK

University Ave

28

Ocean Beach
Park

Ocean Beach
Pier

25

Newport
Ave 20

Sunset Cliffs Blvd

Nimitz Blvd

OCEAN
BEACH

San Diego
International
Airport

Harbor Dr

Pacific Hwy

24

**San Diego
Zoo**

2 13

30

10

26

11

6th Ave

30th St

Park Blvd

Balboa
Park

SOUTH
PARK

Ocean
Beach

22

209

21

5

9

14

Catalina Blvd

27

Harbor
Island

Shelter
Island

5

Broadway

94

Market St

Sunset Cliffs
Park

Cabrillo Memorial Dr

209

North Island
Naval
Air Station

See Downtown San Diego Map (p92)

15

PACIFIC
OCEAN

Orange
Ave

15

Coronado

75

Coronado Bay
Bridge

Harbor Dr

5

Point
Loma

5

Coronado
Visitors Center

6

75

Silver Strand Blvd

San Diego
Bay

Mexico
(15mi)

Mexico
(16mi)

Greater San Diego

⊙ Downtown & Embarcadero

Downtown once harbored a notorious strip of saloons, gambling joints and bordellos known as Stingaree. These days, Stingaree has been beautifully restored and rechristened the **Gaslamp Quarter**, a heart-thumping playground of restaurants, bars, clubs, boutiques and galleries.

At downtown's northern edge, **Little Italy** has evolved into one of the city's hippest neighborhoods to live, eat and shop.

★**USS Midway Museum**   MUSEUM
(Map p92; ☑619-544-9600; www.midway.org; 910 N Harbor Dr; adult/child $20/10; ⊙10am-5pm, last entry 4pm; ⊛) The giant aircraft carrier USS *Midway* was one of the navy's flagships from 1945 to 1991, last playing a combat role in the first Gulf War. On the flight deck of the hulking vessel, walk right up to some 25 restored aircraft including an F-14 Tomcat and F-4 Phantom jet fighter. Admission includes an audio tour, along the narrow confines of the upper decks to the bridge, admiral's war room, brig and 'pri-fly' (primary flight control; the carrier's equivalent of a control tower).

Maritime Museum   MUSEUM
(Map p92; ☑619-234-9153; www.sdmaritime. org; 1492 N Harbor Dr; adult/child $16/8; ⊙9am-9pm late May-early Sep, to 8pm early Sep-late May; ⊛) This museum is easy to find: look for the 100ft-high masts of the iron-hulled square-rigger *Star of India*. Built on the Isle of Man and launched in 1863, the tall ship plied the England–India trade route, carried immigrants to New Zealand, became a trading ship based in Hawaii and, finally, ferried cargo in Alaska. It's a handsome vessel, but don't expect anything romantic or glamorous on board.

Museum of Contemporary Art   MUSEUM
(MCASD Downtown; Map p92; ☑858-454-3541; www.mcasd.org; 1001 Kettner Blvd; adult/child under 25yr/senior $10/free/$5, 5-7pm 3rd Thu each month free; ⊙11am-5pm Thu-Tue, to 7pm 3rd Thu each month) This Financial District museum has brought an ever-changing variety of innovative artwork to San Diegans since the 1960s here in the downtown location and **La Jolla branch** (MCASD; Map p90; ☑858-454-3541; www.mcasd.org; 700 Prospect St, La Jolla; adult/child $10/free, 5-7pm 3rd Thu each month free; ⊙11am-5pm Thu-Tue, to 7pm 3rd Thu each month); check the website for exhibits.

Downtown San Diego

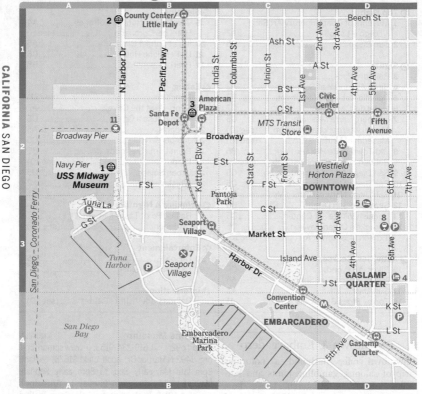

Across from the main building, a slickly renovated section of San Diego's train station houses permanent works by Jenny Holzer and Richard Serra. Tickets are valid for seven days in all locations.

⊙ Coronado

Technically a peninsula, Coronado Island is joined to the mainland by a 2.2-mile-long bridge. The peninsula's main draw is the Hotel del Coronado (p96), known for its seaside Victorian architecture and illustrious guest book, which includes Thomas Edison, Babe Ruth and Marilyn Monroe (its exterior stood in for a Miami hotel in the classic flick *Some Like it Hot*).

The hourly **Coronado Ferry** (Map p92; ☑ 619-234-4111; www.flagshipsd.com; tickets $4.75; ⊙ 9am-10pm) departs from the Embarcadero's Broadway Pier (990 N Harbor Dr) and from downtown's convention center. All

ferries arrive on Coronado at the foot of 1st St, where **Bikes & Beyond** (Map p90; ☑ 619-435-7180; www.bikes-and-beyond.com; 1201 1st St, Coronado; per hr/day from $8/30; ⊙ 9am-sunset) rents cruisers and tandems, perfect for pedaling past Coronado's white-sand beaches sprawling south along the **Silver Strand**.

⊙ Balboa Park

Balboa Park is an urban oasis brimming with more than a dozen museums, gorgeous gardens and architecture, performance spaces and a zoo. Early 20th-century beaux-arts and Spanish Colonial Revival–style buildings (the legacy of world's fairs) are grouped around plazas along east–west El Prado promenade.

A free tram shuttles visitors around the park, but it's more enjoyable to stroll around the botanical gardens, past the 1915 **Spreckels Organ Pavilion** (Map p90; http://

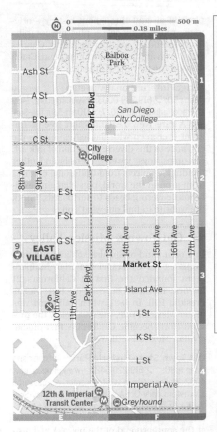

Downtown San Diego

◎ Top Sights
1 USS Midway Museum A2

◎ Sights
2 Maritime Museum A1
3 Museum of Contemporary Art...........B2

✦ Activities, Courses & Tours
Flagship Cruises.........................(see 11)

🛏 Sleeping
4 Hotel Solamar D3
5 USA Hostels San Diego.......................D3

✸ Eating
6 Basic...E3
7 Puesto at the Headquarters...............B3

🍸 Drinking & Nightlife
8 Bang Bang D3
9 Noble Experiment...............................E3

✪ Entertainment
10 Arts Tix D2

ⓘ Transport
11 Coronado Ferry...................................A2

spreckelsorgan.org), the shops and galleries of the **Spanish Village Art Center** (Map p90; ⏱11am-4pm) **FREE** and the international-themed exhibition cottages by the **United Nations Building**.

Stop by the Balboa Park Visitors Center (p99) for maps, events information and discount attraction passes. Free parking lots off Park Blvd fill quickly on weekends. From downtown, take MTS bus 7 ($2.25, 20 minutes).

★**San Diego Zoo**   ZOO
(Map p90; ☎619-231-1515; http://zoo.sandiego.org; 2920 Zoo Dr; 1-day pass adult/child from $48/38, 2-visit pass to zoo and/or safari park adult/child $86/66; ⏱9am-9pm mid-Jun–early Sep, to 5pm or 6pm early Sep–mid-Jun; 🅿🚻) 🏆 This justifiably famous zoo is one of SoCal's biggest attractions, showing more than 3000 animals representing over 800 species in a beautifully landscaped setting, typically in enclosures

that replicate their natural habitats. Its sister park is San Diego Zoo Safari Park (p99) in northern San Diego County.

Arrive early, as many of the animals are most active in the morning – though many perk up again in the afternoon. Pick up a map at the entrance to the zoo to find your own favorite exhibits.

Reuben H Fleet Science Center   MUSEUM
(Map p90; ☎619-238-1233; www.rhfleet.org; 1875 El Prado; adult/child incl IMAX $20/17; ⏱10am-5pm Mon-Thu, to 6pm Fri-Sun; 🚻) One of Balboa Park's most popular venues, this hands-on science museum features interactive displays and a toddler room. Look out for opportunities to build gigantic structures with Keva planks and visit the **Gallery of Illusions and Perceptions**. The biggest drawcard is the **Giant Dome Theater**, which screens several different films each day. The hemispherical, wraparound screen and 152-speaker state-of-the-art sound system create sensations ranging from pretty cool to mind-blowing.

San Diego Natural History Museum MUSEUM
(Map p90; ☎619-232-3821; www.sdnhm.org; 1788 El Prado; adult/child $19/11; ⏱10am-5pm; 🚻) The 'Nat' houses 7.5 million specimens,

including rocks, fossils and taxidermied animals, as well as an impressive dinosaur skeleton and a California fault-line exhibit, all in beautiful spaces. Kids love the movies about the natural world in the giant-screen cinema; the selections change frequently. Children's programs are held most weekends. Special exhibits (some with an extra charge) span pirates to King Tut. The museum also arranges field trips and nature walks in Balboa Park and further afield.

Museum of Man MUSEUM
(Map p90; ☑ 619-239-2001; www.museumofman. org; Plaza de California, 1350 El Prado; adult/child/student/child $12.50/5/8; ⊙10am-5pm Sun-Wed, to 8:30pm Thu-Sat) This is the county's only anthropological museum, with exhibits spanning ancient Egypt, the Mayans and local native Kumeyaay people, human evolution and the human life cycle. Recent temporary exhibits have covered everything from women's empowerment to beer. The basket and pottery collections are especially fine. The museum shop sells handicrafts from Central America and elsewhere.

Timken Museum of Art MUSEUM
(Map p90; ☑ 619-239-5548; www.timkenmuseum. org; 1500 El Prado; ⊙10am-4:30pm Tue-Sat, from noon Sun) FREE Don't skip the Timken, home of the Putnam collection, a small but impressive group of paintings, including works by Rembrandt, Rubens, El Greco, Cézanne and Pissarro, plus a wonderful selection of Russian icons. Built in 1965, the building stands out for *not* being in imitation Spanish style.

San Diego Museum of Art MUSEUM
(SDMA; Map p90; ☑ 619-232-7931; www.sdmart. org; 1450 El Prado; adult/child $12/4.50; ⊙10am-5pm Mon-Tue & Thu-Sat, from noon Sun, also 5-8pm Fri mid-Jul–mid-Sep) The SDMA is the city's largest art museum. The permanent collection has works by a number of European masters from the renaissance to the modernist eras (though no renowned pieces), American landscape paintings, and several fantastic pieces in the Asian galleries, and there are often important traveling exhibits. The **Sculpture Garden** has works by Alexander Calder and Henry Moore.

San Diego Air & Space Museum MUSEUM
(Map p90; ☑ 619-234-8291; www.sandiegoairandspace.org; 2001 Pan American Plaza; adult/child $18/9; ⊙10am-4:30pm; ☖) The round building at the southern end of the plaza houses an excellent museum with extensive displays of aircraft throughout history – originals, replicas, models – plus memorabilia from legendary aviators including Charles Lindbergh and astronaut John Glenn. Catch films in the new 3D/4D theater.

Mingei International Museum MUSEUM
(Map p90; ☑ 619-239-0003; www.mingei.org; 1439 El Prado; adult/child $10/7; ⊙10am-5pm Tue-Sun; ☖) A rare New Zealand kauri tree (a fragrant evergreen with flat leaves) marks the entrance to this diverse collection of folk art, costumes, toys, jewelry, utensils and other handmade objects from traditional cultures from around the world, plus changing exhibitions covering beads to surfboards. Check the website to find out what's on.

⊙ Old Town & Mission Valley

In 1769 a band of Spanish soldiers and missionaries led by Franciscan friar Junípero Serra founded the first of California's 21 historic mission churches on San Diego's Presidio Hill. In 1821, when California was under Mexican rule, the area below the presidio (fort) became California's first official civilian Mexican settlement.

Old Town State Historic Park HISTORIC SITE
(Map p90; ☑ 619-220-5422; www.parks.ca.gov; 4002 Wallace St; ⊙visitor center & museums 10am-4pm daily Oct-Apr, to 5pm Fri-Sun May-Sep; ☖☖) FREE This park has an excellent history museum in the **Robinson-Rose House** at the southern end of the plaza. You'll also find a diorama depicting the original pueblo and the park's **visitors center**, where you can pick up a copy of the *Old Town San Diego State Historic Park Tour Guide & Brief History* ($3), or take a guided tour (free) at 11am and 2pm daily.

**Mission Basilica
San Diego de Alcalá** CHURCH
(☑ 619-281-8449; www.missionsandiego.com; 10818 San Diego Mission Rd; adult/child $3/1; ⊙9am-4:30pm; ☖) Although the site of the first California mission (1769) was on Presidio Hill by present-day Old Town, in 1774 Padre Junípero Serra moved it about 7 miles upriver, closer to water and more arable land, now the Mission Basilica San Diego de Alcalá. In 1784 missionaries built a solid adobe-and-timber church, which was destroyed by an earthquake in 1803. The church was promptly rebuilt, and at least some of it still stands on a slope overlooking Mission Valley.

Junípero Serra Museum MUSEUM
(Map p90; 619-232-6203; www.sandiegohistory.org; 2727 Presidio Dr; adult/child $6/3; 10am-5pm Sat & Sun year-round, also 10am-5pm Fri early Jun-early Sep; P) Located in one of the most important historical buildings in the city, this small but interesting collection of artifacts and pictures is from the Mission and rancho periods, and it gives a good sense of the earliest days of European settlement up to 1929 when the museum was founded.

Point Loma

Cabrillo National Monument MONUMENT
(Map p90; 619-557-5450; www.nps.gov/cabr; 1800 Cabrillo Memorial Dr; per car $5; 9am-5pm; P) Atop a steep hill at the tip of the peninsula, this is San Diego's finest locale for history, views and nature walks. It's also the best place in town to see the gray-whale migration (January to March) from land. You may forget you're in a major metropolitan area.

The **visitor center** has a comprehensive, old-school presentation on Portuguese explorer Juan Rodríguez Cabrillo's 1542 voyage up the California coast, plus good exhibits on early Native Californian inhabitants and the area's natural history.

Mission Bay & Beaches

San Diego's big three beach towns all have ribbons of hedonism where armies of tanned, taut bodies frolic in the sand.

West of amoeba-shaped Mission Bay, surf-friendly **Mission Beach** and its northern neighbor, **Pacific Beach** (aka 'PB'), are connected by car-free **Ocean Front Walk**, which swarms with skaters, joggers and cyclists year-round. South of Mission Bay, bohemian **Ocean Beach** (OB) has a fishing pier, beach volleyball and good surf. Its main drag, **Newport Avenue**, is chockablock with scruffy bars, flip-flop eateries and shops selling surf gear, tattoos, vintage clothing and antiques.

Belmont Park AMUSEMENT PARK
(Map p90; 858-458-1549; www.belmontpark.com; 3146 Mission Blvd; per ride $3-6, all-day pass adult/child $29/18; from 11am daily, closing time varies; P) Pint-sized Belmont Park beckons with a historic wooden roller coaster, wave simulator and indoor pool.

SeaWorld San Diego THEME PARK
(Map p90; 800-257-4268; www.seaworldsandiego.com; 500 SeaWorld Dr; adult/child 3-9yr $89/83; daily; P) SeaWorld opened in San Diego in 1964 and for years has been one of California's most popular theme parks. Many visitors spend the whole day here, shuttling between aquatic-themed rides, animal encounters and exhibits. However, the park's best-known attraction is also its most controversial: live shows featuring trained dolphins, sea lions and killer whales. Since the release of the 2013 documentary *Blackfish,* SeaWorld's treatment of its captive orcas has come under intense scrutiny and the company has been hit by falling visitor numbers and a catalogue of negative PR.

La Jolla

Facing one of SoCal's loveliest sweeps of coastline, wealthy La Jolla (Spanish for 'the jewel,' pronounced la-*hoy*-ah) possesses shimmering beaches and an upscale downtown filled with boutiques and cafes. Oceanfront diversions include the **Children's Pool** (no longer for swimming, it's now home to barking sea lions), kayaking and exploring sea caves at **La Jolla Cove** and snorkeling at **San Diego-La Jolla Underwater Park**.

Torrey Pines State Natural Reserve PARK
(858-755-2063; www.torreypine.org; 12600 N Torrey Pines Park Rd; 7:15am-dusk, visitor center 10am-4pm Oct-Apr, 9am-6pm May-Sep; P) Between N Torrey Pines Rd and the ocean, and from the **Torrey Pines Gliderport** (Map p90; 858-452-9858; www.flytorrey.com; 2800 Torrey Pines Scenic Dr; 20min paragliding $175, hang gliding tandem flight per person $225) to Del Mar, this reserve preserves the last mainland stands of the Torrey pine *(Pinus torreyana),* a species adapted to sparse rainfall and sandy, stony soils. Steep sandstone gullies have eroded into wonderfully textured surfaces, and the views over the ocean and north, including whale-watching, are superb. Rangers lead nature walks on weekends and holidays. Several walking trails wind through the reserve and down to the beach. Parking fees per car vary from $4 per hour to $15 per day.

Birch Aquarium at Scripps AQUARIUM
(Map p90; 858-534-3474; www.aquarium.ucsd.edu; 2300 Expedition Way; adult/child $17/12.50; 9am-5pm; P) Marine scientists were working at the Birch Aquarium at Scripps Institution of Oceanography (SIO) as early as 1910 and, helped by donations from the ever-generous Scripps family, the institute has grown to be one of the world's largest

marine research institutions. It is now a part of University of California, San Diego (UCSD). Off N Torrey Pines Rd, the aquarium has brilliant displays. The **Hall of Fishes** has more than 30 fish tanks, simulating marine environments from the Pacific Northwest to tropical seas.

🏃 Activities

Surfing and windsurfing are both excellent, although beware of territorial locals in some places. Call ☑ 619-221-8824 for surf reports.

Pacific Beach Surf Shop   SURFING
(Map p90; ☑ 858-373-1138; www.pbsurfshop.com; 4150 Mission Blvd; ⊙ store 9am-7pm, lessons hourly until 4pm) This shop provides instruction through its Pacific Beach Surf School. It has friendly service, and also rents wetsuits and both soft (foam) and hard (fiberglass) boards. Call ahead for lessons.

Surf Diva   SURFING
(Map p90; ☑ 858-454-8273; www.surfdiva.com; 2160 Avenida de la Playa; ⊙ store 8:30am-6pm, varies seasonally) The wonderful women here offer surf classes from $75 and rent boards and wetsuits.

Flagship Cruises   BOAT TOUR
(Map p92; ☑ 619-234-4111; www.flagshipsd.com; 990 N Harbor Dr; tours adult/child from $23/11.50; ⊞) Harbor tours and seasonal whale-watching cruises from the Embarcadero, from one to several hours long.

🛏 Sleeping

Rates skyrocket in summer, especially by the beaches. Chain hotels and motels cluster inland off major freeways and in Mission Valley. Rates quoted here do not include lodging tax (10.5%).

🛏 Downtown & Around

★ USA Hostels San Diego   HOSTEL $
(Map p92; ☑ 619-232-3100; www.usahostels.com; 726 5th Ave; dm/r without bath from $33/79; @ ⓦ) Lots of charm and color at this convivial hostel in a former Victorian-era hotel. Look for cheerful rooms, a full kitchen, a communal lounge for chilling and in-house parties and beach barbecues. Rates include linens, lockers and pancakes for breakfast. It's smack-dab in the middle of Gaslamp nightlife. No air-con.

La Pensione Hotel   BOUTIQUE HOTEL $$
(Map p90; ☑ 619-236-8000; www.lapensione-hotel.com; 606 W Date St; r from $150; P ✳ ⓦ)

Despite the name, Little Italy's La Pensione isn't a pension but an intimate, friendly, recently renovated hotel of 68 rooms with queen-size beds and private bathrooms. It's set around a frescoed courtyard and it's just steps to the neighborhood's dining, cafes and galleries, and walking distance to most downtown attractions. There's an attractive cafe downstairs. Parking is $15.

Hotel Solamar   BOUTIQUE HOTEL $$
(Map p92; ☑ 877-230-0300, 619-819-9500; www. hotelsolamar.com; 435 6th Ave; r $169-299; P ✳ @ ⓦ ≋) A great compromise in the Gaslamp: hip style that needn't break the bank. Lounge beats animate your view of skyscrapers from the pool deck and bar, and rooms have sleek lines and nautical blue and neorococo accents for a touch of fun. There's a fitness center, in-room yoga kit, loaner bikes and a nightly complimentary wine hour. Parking costs $45.

🛏 Beaches

Pearl   MOTEL $$
(Map p90; ☑ 619-226-6100, 877-732-7574; www. thepearlsd.com; 1410 Rosecrans St; r $129-169; P ✳ ⓦ ≋) The midcentury modern Pearl feels more Palm Springs than San Diego. The 23 rooms in its 1959 shell have soothing blue hues, trippy surf motifs and bettas in fishbowls. There's a lively pool scene (including 'dive-in' movies on Wednesday nights), or play Jenga or Parcheesi in the groovy, shag-carpeted lobby. Light sleepers: request a room away from busy street traffic.

Inn at Sunset Cliffs   INN $$
(Map p90; ☑ 866-786-2453, 619-222-7901; www. innatsunsetcliffs.com; 1370 Sunset Cliffs Blvd; r/ ste from $175/289; P ✳ @ ⓦ ≋) At the south end of Ocean Beach, wake up to the sound of surf crashing onto the rocky shore. This low-key 1965 charmer wraps around a flower-bedecked courtyard with small heated pool. Its 24 breezy rooms are compact, but most have attractive stone-and-tile bathrooms, and some suites have full kitchens. Even if the ocean air occasionally takes its toll on exterior surfaces, it's hard not to love this place. Free parking.

★ Hotel del Coronado   LUXURY HOTEL $$$
(Hotel Del; Map p90; ☑ 619-435-6611; www.ho-teldel.com; 1500 Orange Ave; r from $289; P ⊖ ✳ @ ⓦ ⊞ ⓢ) San Diego's iconic hotel provides the essential Coronado experience: over a century of history, a pool, full-service

spa, shops, restaurants, manicured grounds, a white-sand beach and an ice-skating rink in winter. Even the basic rooms have luxurious marbled bathrooms. Note: half the accommodations are not in the main Victorian-era hotel (368 rooms) but in an adjacent seven-story building constructed in the 1970s. For a sense of place, book a room in the original hotel. Parking is $37.

★ **Crystal Pier**
Hotel & Cottages   COTTAGE $$$
(Map p90; ☑ 858-483-6983, 800-748-5894; www.crystalpier.com; 4500 Ocean Blvd; d $185-525; P 🖤 🌭) Charming, wonderful and unlike anyplace else in San Diego, Crystal Pier has cottages built right on the pier above the water. Almost all 29 cottages have full ocean views and kitchens; most date from 1936. Newer, larger cottages sleep up to six. Book eight to 11 months in advance for summer reservations. Minimum-stay requirements vary by season. No air-con. Rates include parking.

✖ Eating

Generally speaking, you'll find steakhouses and seafood institutions near downtown's waterfront, boisterous gastropubs in the Gaslamp Quarter, casual seafood and burgers by the beach, hip kitchens in neighborhoods around Balboa Park, and tacos and margaritas, well, everywhere.

✖ Downtown & Around

Basic   PIZZA $
(Map p92; ☑ 619-531-8869; www.barbasic.com; 410 10th Ave; small/large pizzas from $9/14; ⊙ 11:30am-2am) East Village hipsters feast on fragrant thin-crust, brick-oven-baked pizzas under Basic's high-ceilinged roof (it's in a former warehouse). Small pizzas have a large footprint but are pretty light. Toppings span the usual to the newfangled, like the mashed pie with mozzarella, mashed potatoes and bacon. Wash them down with beers (craft, naturally) or one of several mule cocktails.

★ **Puesto at the Headquarters** MEXICAN $$
(Map p92; ☑ 610-233-8800; www.eatpuesto.com; 789 W Harbor Dr, The Headquarters; mains $11-19; ⊙ 11am-10pm) This upscale eatery serves Mexican street food that knocked our *zapatos* off: innovative takes on traditional tacos such as chicken (with hibiscus, chipotle, pineapple and avocado) and some out-there

fillings such as potato-soy chorizo. Other highlights: crab guacamole, *barbacoa* short ribs (braised in chili sauce) and a Mexican street bowl (tropical fruits with chili, sea salt and lime).

Bencotto   ITALIAN $$
(Map p90; ☑ 619-450-4786; www.lovebencotto.com; 750 W Fir St; mains $14-26; ⊙ 11:30am-9:30pm Sun-Thu, to 10:30pm Fri & Sat; P) Bencotto melds the old with the new of Little Italy – contemporary, angular, multistory, architect-designed, arty and green – and the food is great too, from fresh-sliced prosciutto to pasta *a modo tuo* (your way), with more than 100 potential combos of fresh pasta and sauce.

Juniper & Ivy   MODERN AMERICAN $$$
(Map p90; ☑ 619-269-9036; www.juniperandivy.com; 2228 Kettner Blvd; small plates $9-17, mains $19-36; ⊙ 4-10pm Sun-Thu, to 11pm Fri & Sat) Chef Richard Blais has opened San Diego's restaurant of the moment. The menu changes daily, but if we mention molecular gastronomic takes on prawn and pork rigatoni; artisan-farmed strip steak with smoked potato, porcini onion rings and kimchi ketchup; and homemade Yodels snack cakes for dessert, do you get the idea? It's in a rockin' refurbished warehouse.

✖ Balboa Park & Around

Hash House a Go Go   AMERICAN $$
(Map p90; ☑ 619-298-4646; www.hashhouseagogo.com; 3628 5th Ave, Hillcrest; mains breakfast $9-18, dinner $15-29; ⊙ 7.30am-2pm Mon-Fri, to 2:30pm Sat & Sun, plus 5:30-9pm Tue-Thu, to 9:30pm Fri-Sun; 🌭) This buzzing bungalow makes biscuits and gravy straight outta Indiana, towering Benedicts, large-as-your-head pancakes and – wait for it – hash seven different ways. Eat your whole breakfast, and you won't need to eat the rest of the day. It's worth coming back for the equally massive burgers, sage fried chicken and award-winning meatloaf sandwich. No wonder it's called 'twisted farm food.'

Urban Solace   CALIFORNIAN $$
(Map p90; ☑ 619-295-6464; www.urbansolace.net; 3823 30th St, North Park; mains lunch $10-23, dinner $17-27; ⊙ 11am-10pm Mon-Thu, 11am-11pm Fri, 10:30am-11pm Sat, 9:30am-2:30pm & 4-9pm Sun) North Park's young hip gourmets revel in creative comfort food here: bluegrass burger; 'not your mama's' meatloaf of ground lamb, fig, pine nuts and feta;

'duckaroni' (mac 'n' cheese with duck confit); and chicken and dumplings. The setting's surprisingly chilled out for such great eats; maybe it's the creative cocktails.

Prado   CALIFORNIAN $$$

(Map p90; ☑ 619-557-9441; www.pradobalboa.com; House of Hospitality, 1549 El Prado; mains lunch $12-21, dinner $22-35; ⊙ 11:30am-3pm Mon-Fri, from 11am Sat & Sun, 5-9pm Sun & Tue-Thu, to 10pm Fri & Sat) In one of San Diego's most beautiful dining rooms, feast on Cal-eclectic cooking by one of San Diego's most renowned chefs: bakery sandwiches, chicken and orecchiette pasta, and pork prime rib. Go for a civilized lunch on the verandah or for afternoon cocktails and appetizers in the bar.

✗ Beaches

Hodad's   BURGERS $

(Map p90; ☑ 619-224-4623; www.hodadies.com; 5010 Newport Ave, Ocean Beach; dishes $4-13; ⊙ 11am-9pm Sun-Thu, to 10pm Fri & Sat) Since the flower-power days of 1969, OB's legendary burger joint has served great shakes, massive baskets of onion rings and succulent hamburgers wrapped in paper. The walls are covered in license plates, grunge/surf-rock plays (loud!) and your bearded, tattooed server might sidle in to your booth to take your order. No shirt, no shoes, no problem, dude.

Point Loma Seafoods   SEAFOOD $

(Map p90; www.pointlomaseafoods.com; 2805 Emerson St; mains $7-16; ⊙ 9am-7pm Mon-Sat, 10am-7pm Sun; ☑ ⚑) For off-the-boat-fresh seafood sandwiches, salads, fried dishes and icy-cold beer, order at the counter at this fish-market-cum-deli and grab a seat at a picnic table on the upstairs, harbor-view deck. In the Shelter Island Marina, it's a San Diego institution dating back to Portuguese fisherman days. It also does great sushi and takeout dishes from ceviche to clam chowder.

Whisknladle   CALIFORNIAN $$

(Map p90; ☑ 858-551-7575; www.wnlhosp.com; 1044 Wall St; mains lunch $14-21, dinner $15-36; ⊙ 11:30am-9pm Mon-Thu, to 10pm Fri, 10am-10pm Sat, 10am-9:30pm Sun) Gourmets and gourmands alike love Whisknladle's 'slow food' preparations of local, farm-fresh ingredients, served on a breezy covered patio and meant for sharing. Every minute preparation, from curing to pickling and macerating, is done in-house. The menu changes

daily, but it's always clever. So are the cocktails (the London's Burning mixes gin and jalapeño water).

★ George's at the Cove   CALIFORNIAN $$$

(Map p90; ☑ 858-454-4244; www.georgesatthecove.com; 1250 Prospect St, La Jolla; mains $13-50; ⊙ 11am-10pm Mon-Thu, to 11pm Fri-Sun) If you've got the urge to splurge, the Euro-Cal cooking is as dramatic as the oceanfront location thanks to the bottomless imagination of chef Trey Foshée. George's has graced just about every list of top restaurants in California, and indeed the USA. Three venues allow you to enjoy it at different price points: Ocean Terrace, George's Bar and George's California Modern.

🍷 Drinking & Nightlife

Downtown's Gaslamp Quarter has the rowdiest bars and hottest nightclubs. Lesbigay nightlife hits up Hillcrest and North Park.

Bang Bang   BAR

(Map p92; www.bangbangsd.com; 526 Market St; ⊙ closed Mon & Tue) Beneath lantern-light, the Gaslamp's hottest new spot has local and world-known DJs and serves sushi and Asian small plates like dumplings and panko-crusted shrimp to nurse the imaginative cocktails (some in giant goblets meant for sharing with your posse). Plus, the bathrooms are shrines to Ryan Gosling and Hello Kitty: in a word, awesome.

Noble Experiment   BAR

(Map p92; ☑ 619-888-4713; http://nobleexperimentsd.com; 777 G St; ⊙ 7pm-2am Tue-Sun) This place is literally a find. Open a secret door and enter a contemporary speakeasy with miniature gold skulls on the walls, classical paintings on the ceilings and some 400 cocktails on the list (from $12). The hard part: getting in. Text for a reservation, and staff will tell you if your requested time is available and how to find the place.

Ballast Point Tasting Room & Kitchen PUB

(Map p90; ☑ 619-255-7213; www.ballastpoint.com; 2215 India St; ⊙ 11am-11pm) Opened in 2013, this is the newest and funnest location from this San Diego–based brewery, and it does a lot of R&D for the rest of the company. Three 4oz tasters of beer for just $5 is the best deal in town. Enjoy them with a full menu including housemade pretzels, beer-steamed mussels, salads and grilled dishes.

☆ Entertainment

Arts Tix (Map p92; ☑ 858-381-5595; www.sdart-stix.com; 28 Horton Plaza) sells half-price and discounted tickets to plays, comedy shows and more.

Casbah   LIVE MUSIC
(Map p90; ☑ 619-232-4355; www.casbahmusic.com; 2501 Kettner Blvd; tickets $5-45) Bands from Smashing Pumpkins to Death Cab for Cutie all rocked the Casbah on their way up the charts and it's still a good place to catch tomorrow's headliners.

La Jolla Playhouse   THEATER
(Map p90; ☑ 858-550-1010; www.lajollaplayhouse.org; 2910 La Jolla Village Dr; tickets $20-75) Inside the Mandell Weiss Center for the Performing Arts, this theater has sent dozens of productions to Broadway including *Jersey Boys, Peter and the Starcatcher* and 2010 Tony winner *Memphis*.

❶ Information

MEDIA

San Diego Magazine (www.sandiegomagazine.com) Glossy monthly.

San Diego Reader (www.sandiegoreader.com) Free tabloid covers entertainment, food, beer and more.

U-T San Diego (www.utsandiego.com) The city's major daily newspaper.

MEDICAL SERVICES

Scripps Mercy Hospital (☑ 619-294-8111; www.scripps.org; 4077 5th Ave) Has a 24-hour emergency room.

MONEY

TravelEx (☑ 858-457-2412; www.travelex.com; Westfield UTC, 4417 La Jolla Village Dr; ◷10am-7pm Mon-Fri, to 6pm Sat, 11am-4pm Sun) For foreign-currency exchange.

TOURIST INFORMATION

Balboa Park Visitors Center (Map p90; ☑ 619-239-0512; www.balboapark.org; House of Hospitality, 1549 El Prado; ◷9:30am-4:30pm) In the House of Hospitality, the visitor center sells park maps and discount passports to museums and the zoo.

Coronado Visitors Center (Map p90; ☑866-599-7242, 619-437-8788; www.coronadovisitorcenter.com; 1100 Orange Ave; ◷9am-5pm Mon-Fri, 10am-5pm Sat & Sun)

USEFUL WEBSITES

Gaslamp Quarter Association (http://gaslamp.org) Everything you need to know about the bustling Gaslamp Quarter, including parking secrets.

San Diego Tourism (www.sandiego.org) Search sights, activities, neighborhoods and more, and make hotel reservations.

❶ Getting There & Away

Served mainly by domestic US and Mexico flights, **San Diego International Airport** (SAN; Map p90; www.san.org; 3325 N Harbor Dr; ☎) sits 3 miles northwest of downtown.

Greyhound (Map p92; ☑ 800-231-2222, 619-515-1100; www.greyhound.com; 1313 National Ave) has hourly direct buses to Los Angeles ($19, two hours).

Amtrak (☑ 800-872-7245; www.amtrak.com) runs the Pacific Surfliner several times daily to Los Angeles ($37, 2¾ hours) and Santa Barbara ($42, 5¾ hours) from downtown's historic **Union Station** (Santa Fe Depot; 1050 Kettner Blvd).

Major international car-rental companies have desks at the airport. Smaller, independent **West Coast Rent a Car** (☑ 619-544-0606; www.sandiegoautos.org; 834 W Grape St; ◷9am-6pm Mon-Sat) rents to under-25s, with free airport pickups.

❶ Getting Around

MTS bus 992 'The Flyer' ($2.25) runs every 15 to 30 minutes between the airport and Downtown from 5am until 11pm daily. Airport shuttles like **Super Shuttle** (☑ 800-258-3826; www.supershuttle.com) charge around $8 to $13 to downtown; book in advance. An airport taxi to downtown averages $10 to $16, plus tip.

City buses ($2.25 to $2.50) and trolleys ($2.50), including south to the Mexico border, are operated by **Metropolitan Transit System** (MTS; ☑ 619-233-3004; www.sdmts.com). MTS's **Transit Store** (Map p92; 102 Broadway; ◷9am-5pm Mon-Fri) sells regional passes (one/two/three/four days $5/9/12/15); purchase one-day passes on board buses (surcharge $2).

Metered taxis charge $2.80 at flag fall, then $3 per mile.

Around San Diego

San Diego Zoo Safari Park   ZOO
(☑ 760-747-8702; www.sdzsafaripark.org; 15500 San Pasqual Valley Rd, Escondido; admission adult/child $48/38, 2-visit pass to zoo and/or safari park $86/66; ◷9am-5pm late Aug–mid-Jun, to 7pm late Jun–mid-Aug; ▣). At this 1800-acre open-range zoo, giraffes graze, lions lounge and rhinos roam more or less freely on the valley floor.

For that instant safari feel, board the Africa Tram, which tours the second-largest continent in just 25 minutes.

The park is in Escondido, about 35 miles northeast of Downtown San Diego. Take the I-15 Fwy to the E Via Rancho Pkwy exit, then follow the signs. Parking is $12.

Legoland

Legoland THEME PARK
(☑ 760-918-5346; http://california.legoland.com; 1 Legoland Dr, Carlsbad; adult/child from $87/81; ⊗ open almost daily year-round, hours vary; P ⊛) This fun fantasy theme park of rides, shows and attractions is mostly suited to the elementary-school set. Tots can dig for dinosaur bones, pilot helicopters and earn their driver's license. Families with young children can overnight in the brand-new, colorful Lego-themed **hotel** (☑ 760-918-5346; 877-534-6526; http://california.legoland.com/legoland-hotel; 5885 The Crossings Dr; r incl breakfast from $369; P ⊖ ⊛ @ ⊚ ⊛ ⊛).

From Downtown San Diego (about 33 miles), take the I-5 Fwy north to Carlsbad's Cannon Rd exit. Parking is $15.

PALM SPRINGS & THE DESERTS

From swanky Palm Springs to desolate Death Valley, Southern California's desert region swallows up 25% of the entire state. At first what seems harrowingly barren may eventually be transformed in your mind's eye to perfect beauty: weathered volcanic peaks, booming sand dunes, purple-tinged mountains, cactus gardens, tiny wildflowers pushing up from hard-baked soil in spring, lizards scurrying beside colossal boulders, and in the night sky, uncountable stars. California's deserts are serenely spiritual, surprisingly chic and ultimately irresistible, whether you're a bohemian artist, movie star, rock climber or 4WD adventurer.

Palm Springs

The Rat Pack is back, baby – or, at least, its hangout is. In the 1950 and '60s, Palm Springs (population 45,000), some 100 miles east of LA, was the swinging getaway of Sinatra, Elvis and other stars. Once the Rat Pack packed it in, Palm Springs surrendered to retirees in golf clothing. Recently a new generation has rediscovered the city's retro-chic charms: kidney-shaped pools, 'starchitect' bungalows, Mid-Century Modern boutique hotels and bars serving perfect martinis. Today retirees mix comfortably with hipsters, hikers and an out-and-proud LGBTIQ community.

⊙ Sights & Activities

Palm Springs is the hub of the Coachella Valley, a string of desert towns along Hwy 111. In PS' compact downtown, one-way southbound Palm Canyon Dr is paralleled by northbound Indian Canyon Dr.

★**Palm Springs Aerial Tramway** CABLE CAR
(☑ 888-515-8726; www.pstramway.com; 1 Tram Way; adult/child $24/17; ⊗ from 10am Mon-Fri, 8am Sat & Sun, last tram up 8pm Sun-Thu, 9pm Fri & Sat, last tram down 9:45pm Sun-Thu, 10:30pm Fri & Sat) North of downtown, this rotating cable car is a highlight of any Palm Springs trip. It climbs nearly 6000 vertical feet through five different vegetation zones, from the Sonoran desert floor to the San Jacinto Mountains, in less than 15 minutes. The 2.5-mile ascent is said to be the temperature equivalent of driving from Mexico to Canada. It's 30°F to 40°F (up to 22°C) cooler as you step out into pine forests at the top, so bring warm clothing.

Sunnylands NOTABLE BUILDING
(☑ 760-202-2222; www.sunnylands.org; 37977 Bob Hope Dr, Rancho Mirage; admission free, tours $20-40; ⊗ 9am-4pm Thu-Sun, closed Jul & Aug) Sunnylands is the Mid-Century Modern estate of Walter and Leonore Annenberg, one of America's 'first families.' At their winter estate in Rancho Mirage, the Annenbergs entertained seven US presidents, royalty, Hollywood celebrities and international heads of state.

A new visitor center and museum screen a film and show changing exhibits about the estate. Just beyond is a magnificent desert garden. Reserve as early as possible for tours of the stunning house with its art collection, architecture and furniture.

Palm Springs Art Museum MUSEUM
(☑ 760-322-4800; www.psmuseum.org; 101 Museum Dr; adult/child $12.50/free, 4-8pm Thu free; ⊗ 10am-5pm Tue-Wed & Fri-Sun, noon-8pm Thu) See the evolution of American painting, sculpture, photography and glass art over the past century. Alongside well-curated

temporary exhibitions, the permanent collection is especially strong in modern painting and sculpture, with works by Henry Moore, Ed Ruscha, Mark di Suvero and other heavy hitters. There's also stunning glass art by Dale Chihuly and William Morris and a collection of pre-Columbian figurines.

Living Desert Zoo & Gardens
ZOO

(☑760-346-5694; www.livingdesert.org; 47900 Portola Ave, Palm Desert, off Hwy 111; adult/child $20/10; ☺9am-5pm Oct-May, 8am-1:30pm Jun-Sep; 🚼) 🐾 This amazing zoo exhibits a variety of desert plants and animals, alongside exhibits on desert geology and Native American culture. Highlights include a walk-through wildlife hospital and an African-themed village with a fair-trade market and storytelling grove. Camel rides, a spin on the endangered-species carousel, and a hop-on, hop-off shuttle cost extra. It's educational fun and worth the 30-minute (15-mile) drive down-valley.

Indian Canyons
HIKING

(☑760-323-6018; www.indian-canyons.com; 38520 S Palm Canyon Dr; adult/child $9/5, 90min guided hike $3/2; ☺8am-5pm Oct-Jun, Fri-Sun only Jul-Sep) Streams flowing from the San Jacinto Mountains sustain a rich variety of plants in oases around Palm Springs. Home to Native American communities for hundreds of years and now part of the Agua Caliente Indian Reservation, these canyons, shaded by fan palms and surrounded by towering cliffs, are a delight for hikers.

Smoke Tree Stables
HORSEBACK RIDING

(☑760-327-1372; www.smoketreestables.com; 2500 S Toledo Ave; 1/2hr guided ride $50/100) Near the Indian Canyons, this outfit arranges trail rides ranging from one-hour outings to all-day treks, for both novice and experienced riders. Reservations required.

🛏 Sleeping

High-season winter rates are quoted below; rates drop midweek and during summer. Motels hug Hwy 111 southeast of downtown. Book ahead, especially for weekends.

Caliente Tropics
MOTEL $

(☑760-327-1391; www.calientetropics.com; 411 E Palm Canyon Dr; r weekday/weekend from $54/109; P❄🐾☎📶🚼) Elvis once frolicked poolside at this premier budget pick, a nicely kept 1964 tiki-style motor lodge. Drift off to dreamland on quality mattresses

in rooms that are spacious and dressed in warm colors.

★ Orbit In
BOUTIQUE HOTEL $$

(☑877-966-7248, 760-323-3585; www.orbitin.com; 562 W Arenas Rd; r from $149; P❄📶🚼) Swing back to the '50s – pinkie raised and all – during the 'Orbitini' happy hour at this fabulously retro property, with high-end Mid-Century Modern furniture (Eames, Noguchi et al) in rooms set around a quiet saline pool with a Jacuzzi and fire pit. The long list of freebies includes bike rentals and daytime sodas and snacks.

Ace Hotel & Swim Club
HOTEL $$

(☑760-325-9900; www.acehotel.com/palmsprings; 701 E Palm Canyon Dr; r from $200; P❄@📶🚼🐾) Palm Springs goes Hollywood – with all the sass, but sans the attitude – at this former Howard Johnson motel turned hipster hangout. Rooms (many with patio) sport a glorified tent-cabin look and are crammed with lifestyle essentials (big flat-screen TVs, MP3 plugs). Happening pool scene and there's the **Feel Good Spa** (☑760-866-6188; www.acehotel.com/palmsprings/spa; 701 E Palm Canyon Dr), on-site restaurant and a bar to boot.

Del Marcos Hotel
BOUTIQUE HOTEL $$

(☑760-325-6902; www.delmarcoshotel.com; 225 W Baristo Rd; r incl breakfast $139-269; ❄📶🚼🐾) At this 1947 gem, designed by William F Cody, groovy lobby tunes usher you to a salt-water pool and ineffably chic rooms. And it's steps from the shops and eats of downtown Palm Springs' village.

WORLD'S BIGGEST DINOSAURS

World's Biggest Dinosaurs (☑951-922-0076; www.cabazondinosaurs.com; 50770 Seminole Dr, Cabazon; adult/child $9/8; ☺10am-8pm, off-season hours vary). You may do a double-take when you see this place, west of Palm Springs, near Cabazon's outlet malls. Claude K Bell, a sculptor for Knott's Berry Farm (p87), spent over a decade crafting these concrete behemoths, now owned by Christian creationists. In the gift shop, alongside the sort of dino-swag you might find at science museums, you can read about the alleged hoaxes and fallacies of evolution and Darwinism. To get here, exit the I-10 Fwy W at Main St in Cabazon.

El Morocco Inn & Spa　　BOUTIQUE HOTEL **$$**
(☑760-288-2527, 888-288-9905; www.elmoroc-coinn.com; 66810 4th St, Desert Hot Springs; $179-219; ✴🕸🛜🐕) Heed the call of the casbah at this drop-dead-gorgeous hideaway where the scene is set for romance. Twelve exotically furnished rooms wrap around a pool deck where your enthusiastic host serves free 'Moroccotinis' during happy hour. Other perks: on-site spa, huge DVD library and delicious homemade mint iced tea.

✗ Eating

Some restaurants keep shorter hours or even close for a few weeks during the hot, hot summer.

Tyler's Burgers　　BURGERS **$**
(www.tylersburgers.com; 149 S Indian Canyon Dr; dishes $3-9; ☺11am-4pm Mon-Sat; 🚲) This tiny shack in the center of downtown Palm Springs serves the best burgers in town, bar none. Waits are practically inevitable, which is presumably why there's an amazingly well-stocked magazine rack. Cash only.

★ Cheeky's　　CALIFORNIAN **$$**
(☑760-327-7595; www.cheekysps.com; 622 N Palm Canyon Dr; mains $8-13; ☺8am-2pm Wed-Mon, last seating 1:30pm) 🖉 Waits can be long and service only so-so, but the farm-to-table menu dazzles with witty inventiveness. Dishes change weekly, but custardy scrambled eggs, arugula pesto frittata and bacon bar 'flights' keep making appearances.

Sherman's　　DELI, BAKERY **$$**
(☑760-325-1199; www.shermansdeli.com; 401 E Tahquitz Canyon Way; mains $9-19; ☺7am-9pm; 🚲) Every community with a sizable retired contingent needs a good Jewish deli. Sherman's is it. With a breezy sidewalk patio, it pulls in an all-ages crowd with its 40 sandwich varieties (great hot pastrami!), finger-lickin' rotisserie chicken, lox and bagels and to-die-for pies. Walls are festooned with head shots of celebrity regulars, including Don Rickles.

Trio　　CALIFORNIAN **$$$**
(☑760-864-8746; www.triopalmsprings.com; 707 N Palm Canyon Dr; mains lunch $11-26, dinner $14-29; ☺11am-10pm Sun-Thu, to 11pm Fri & Sat) The winning formula in this '60s modernist space: updated American comfort food (awesome Yankee pot roast!), eye-catching artwork and picture windows. The $19 prix-fixe three-course dinner (served until 6pm) is a steal.

🍷 Drinking & Nightlife

Arenas Rd, east of Indian Canyon Dr, is gay and lesbian nightlife central.

Birba　　BAR
(www.birbaps.com; 622 N Palm Canyon Dr; ☺5-11pm Sun & Wed-Thu, to midnight Fri & Sat) It's cocktails and pizza at this fabulous indoor-outdoor space where floor-to-ceiling sliding glass doors separate the long marble bar from a hedge-fringed patio with sunken fire pits.

Koffi　　COFFEE
(www.kofficoffee.com; 515 N Palm Canyon Dr; snacks & drinks $3-6; ☺5:30am-7pm; 🛜) Tucked among the art galleries on N Palm Canyon Dr, this coolly minimalist, indie java bar serves strong organic coffee. There's a second Palm Springs location at 1700 S Camino Real, near the Ace Hotel.

🔒 Shopping

For art galleries, modern design stores and fashion boutiques, including fabulous **Trina Turk** (☑760-416-2856; www.trinaturk.com; 891 N Palm Canyon Dr; ☺10am-5pm Mon-Fri, to 6pm Sat, 11am-5pm Sun), head 'Uptown' to North Palm Canyon Dr. If you're riding the retro wave, uncover treasures in thrift, vintage and consignment shops scattered around downtown and along Hwy 111. For a local version of Rodeo Dr, drive down-valley to Palm Desert's El Paseo.

ℹ Information

Palm Springs Library (www.palmspringsca. gov; 300 S Sunrise Way; ☺10am-6pm Mon & Thu, to 8pm Tue & Wed, to 5pm Fri & Sat; @🛜) Free wi-fi and internet terminals.

Palm Springs Official Visitors Center (☑760-778-8418; www.visitpalmsprings.com; 2901 N Palm Canyon Dr; ☺9am-5pm) Well-stocked and well-staffed visitors center 3 miles north of downtown, in a 1965 Albert Frey–designed gas station at the tramway turnoff.

ℹ Getting There & Around

About 3 miles east of downtown, **Palm Springs International Airport** (PSP; ☑760-318-3800; www.palmspringsairport.com; 3400 E Tahquitz Canyon Way) is served by US and Canadian airlines; major car-rental agencies are on-site.

Thrice-weekly **Amtrak** trains to/from LA ($41, 2¾ hours) stop at the unstaffed, kinda-creepy North Palm Springs station, 5 miles north of downtown, as do a few daily **Greyhound** buses to/from LA ($27, 2½ to 3½ hours).

SunLine (☏ 800-347-8628; www.sunline.org; one way/day pass $1/3) runs slow-moving local buses throughout the valley.

Joshua Tree National Park

Like figments from a Dr Seuss book, whimsical-looking Joshua trees (actually tree-sized yuccas) welcome visitors to this wilderness park where the Sonora and Mojave Deserts converge. You'll find most of the main attractions, including all of the Joshua trees, in the park's northern half. 'J-Tree' is perennially popular with rock climbers and day hikers, especially in spring when the trees bloom with cream-colored flowers. The mystical quality of this stark, boulder-strewn landscape has inspired countless artists, most famously the rock band U2.

◉ Sights & Activities

Dominating the north side of the **park** (☏ 760-367-5500; www.nps.gov/jotr; 7-day entry per car $20), the epic **Wonderland of Rocks** calls to climbers, as does **Hidden Valley**. Sunset-worthy **Keys View** overlooks the San Andreas Fault and on clear days, you can see as far as Mexico. For pioneer history, tour **Keys Ranch** (☏ reservations 760-367-5522; tour adult/child $10/5; ⊘ tour schedules vary, reservations required). Hikers seek out native desert fan-palm oases like **49 Palms Oasis** (3-mile round-trip) and **Lost Palms Oasis** (7.2-mile round-trip). Kid-friendly nature trails include **Barker Dam** (1.1-mile loop), which passes Native American petroglyphs; **Skull Rock** (1.7-mile loop); and **Cholla Cactus Garden** (0.25-mile loop). For a scenic 4WD route, tackle bumpy 18-mile **Geology Tour Road**, also open to mountain bikers.

🛏 Sleeping

The park itself only has camping. Budget and midrange motels line Hwy 62.

Joshua Tree National Park Campgrounds   CAMPGROUND $
(www.nps.gov/jotr; tent & RV sites $10-15; ⊞❄) Of the park's eight campgrounds, only Cottonwood and Black Rock have potable water, flush toilets and dump stations. Indian Cove and Black Rock accept reservations; the others are first-come, first-served. None have showers. Backcountry camping (no campfires) is allowed 1 mile from any trailhead or road and 100ft from water sources; free self-registration is required at the park's

PIONEERTOWN
....

Less than 5 miles northwest of Hwy 62 in Yucca Valley, **Pioneertown** was built as a Hollywood movie set in 1946, and it hasn't changed much since. Witness mock gunfights at 2:30pm on Sundays from April to October. Enjoy BBQ, cheap beer and live music at honky-tonk **Pappy & Harriet's Pioneertown Palace** (☏ 760-365-5956; www.pappyandharriets. com; 53688 Pioneertown Rd; mains $8-29; ⊘ 11am-2am Thu-Sun, from 5pm Mon). Snooze at the **Pioneertown Motel** (☏ 760-365-7001; www.pioneertown-motel. com; 5040 Curtis Rd; r $70-120; ❄🛜❄), where old-timey movie stars once slept and simple rooms are crammed with Western-themed memorabilia.

12 backcountry boards at trailheads. **Joshua Tree Outfitters** (☏ 760-366-1848; www.joshuatreeoutfitters.com; 61707 Hwy 62) rents quality camping gear.

Harmony Motel   MOTEL $
(☏ 760-367-3351; www.harmonymotel.com; 71161 Twentynine Palms Hwy, Twentynine Palms; r $75-85; ℗❄🛜❄) This 1950s motel, where U2 stayed while working on the *Joshua Tree* album, has a small pool and large, cheerfully painted rooms; some have kitchenettes.

★**Spin & Margie's Desert Hide-a-Way**   INN $$
(☏ 760-366-9124; www.deserthideaway.com; 64491 Hwy 62; ste $145-175; ❄🛜) This handsome hacienda-style inn is perfect for restoring calm after a long day on the road. The five boldly colored suites are an eccentric symphony of corrugated tin, old license plates and cartoon art. Each has its own kitchen and flat-screen TV with DVD and CD player. Knowledgeable, gregarious owners ensure a relaxed visit. It's down the dirt Sunkist Rd, about 3 miles east of downtown Joshua Tree.

Joshua Tree Inn   MOTEL $$
(☏ 760-366-1188; www.joshuatreeinn.com; 61259 Twentynine Palms Hwy, Joshua Tree; r/ste incl breakfast from $89/159; ⊘ reception 3pm to 8pm; ❄🛜❄) This funky-cool, rock-and-roll–infused, wisteria-strewn motel has 11 spacious rooms behind turquoise doors leading off from a desert-garden courtyard with great views. It gained notoriety in 1973

when rock legend Gram Parsons overdosed in room 8, now decorated in tribute. Other famous guests have included John Wayne, Donovan and Emmylou Harris.

✖ Eating

Crossroads Cafe
AMERICAN $

(☑760-366-5414; 61715 Twentynine Palms Hwy, Joshua Tree; mains $5-12; ⊙7am-9pm Mon-Sat, to 8pm Sun; ☑) The much-loved Crossroads is the go-to place for carbo-loaded breakfasts, fresh sandwiches and dragged-through-the-garden salads that make both omnivores (burgers, Reuben sandwich) and vegans (spinach salad) happy.

Pie for the People
PIZZA $$

(☑760-366-0400; www.pieforthepeople.com; 61740 Hwy 62, Joshua Tree; pizzas $11-25; ⊙11am-9pm Mon-Thu, to 10pm Fri & Sat, to 8pm Sun; ☑) Thin-crust pizzas for takeout and delivery. Flavors span standards to the David Bowie: white pizza with mozzarella, Guinness caramelized onions, jalapenos, pineapple, bacon, and sweet plum sauce. Enjoy yours under the exposed rafters in the wood-and-corrugated-metal dining room, or under the tree on the back patio.

ℹ Information

Pick up park information at NPS visitor centers at **Joshua Tree** (6554 Park Blvd, Joshua Tree; ⊙8am-5pm), **Oasis** (74485 National Park Dr, Twentynine Palms; ⊙8:30am-5pm) and **Cottonwood** (Cottonwood Springs, 8 miles north of I-10 Fwy; ⊙8:30am-4pm), and at **Black Rock Nature Center** (9800 Black Rock Canyon Rd; ⊙8am-4pm Sat-Thu, noon-8pm Fri Oct-May; ☑). There are no park facilities aside from restrooms, so bring all the drinking water and food you'll need. Get gas and stock up in the three towns linked by the Twentynine Palms Hwy (Hwy 62) along the park's northern boundary: Yucca Valley, with the most services (banks, supermarkets etc); beatnik Joshua Tree, where outdoor outfitters and shops offering internet access cluster; and Twentynine Palms, home of the USA's largest marine base.

Anza-Borrego Desert State Park

Shaped by an ancient sea and tectonic forces, Anza-Borrego is the USA's largest state park outside Alaska. Cradling the park's only commercial hub – tiny Borrego Springs (pop 3429) – are more than 600,000 acres of mountains, canyons and badlands; a fab-

ulous variety of plants and wildlife; and intriguing historical relics of Native American tribes, Spanish explorers and gold-rush pioneers. Early spring wildflower blooms bring the biggest crowds. In summer Hades-like heat makes daytime exploring dangerous.

◉ Sights & Activities

Two miles west of Borrego Springs, the park **visitor center** (☑760-767-4205; www.parks.ca.gov; 200 Palm Canyon Dr, Borrego Springs; ⊙9am-5pm daily Oct 15-May 15, Sat & Sun only May 16-Sep 14) has natural-history exhibits, information handouts and updates on road conditions. Driving through the park is free, but if you camp, hike or picnic, a day-use parking fee ($5 per car) applies. You'll need a 4WD to tackle the 500 miles of backcountry dirt roads. If you're hiking, always bring extra water.

Park highlights include **Fonts Point** desert lookout, **Clark Dry Lake** for birding, the **Elephant Tree Discovery Trail** near Split Mountain's wind caves, and **Blair Valley**, with its Native American pictographs and pioneer traces. Further south, soak in concrete hot-springs pools at **Agua Caliente Regional Park** (☑760-765-1188; www.sdcounty.ca.gov/parks/; 39555 Rte S2; entry per car $5; ⊙9:30am-5pm Sep-May).

🛏 Sleeping & Eating

Free backcountry camping without a permit is permitted anywhere in the park at least 100ft from water or roads (no campfires).

For country-style B&Bs and famous apple pie, the gold-mining town of **Julian** (www.julianca.com) is a 30-mile drive southwest of Borrego Springs.

Borrego Palm Canyon Campground
CAMPGROUND $

(☑800-444-7275; www.reserveamerica.com; tent/RV sites $25/35; ☑☑☑) Near the visitor center, this campground has award-winning toilets, close-together campsites and an amphitheater with ranger programs.

Palm Canyon Hotel & RV Resort
MOTEL $$

(☑760-767-5341; www.palmcanyonrvresort.com; 221 Palm Canyon Dr, Borrego Springs; d $65-310; ☑☑☑☑) For that Old West flair, check into this welcoming motel, but don't be fooled: the place was only built in the '80s! It's about a mile from the park's visitor center and has two pools for unwinding, and a restaurant and saloon for sustenance.

★ **Borrego Valley Inn**   INN $$$
(☑760-767-0311;   www.borregovalleyinn.com;
405 Palm Canyon Dr; r $180-320; ⓟ🅿❄🛜🏊)
This petite, immaculately kept inn, filled
with Southwestern knickknacks and Native
American weavings, is an intimate spa-re-
sort, perfect for adults. There are 15 rooms
on 10 acres. One pool is clothing-optional.
Most rooms have kitchenettes. The grounds
are entirely nonsmoking.

Carlee's Place   AMERICAN $$
(☑760-767-3262; 660 Palm Canyon Dr; mains
lunch $8-14, dinner $12-27; ⊘11am-9pm) Even
though the decor feels like it hasn't been
updated since the 1970s, locals pick Carlee's
for its burgers, pastas and steak dinners.
The pool table, live music and karaoke are
big draws, too.

ℹ Information

Borrego Springs has banks with ATMs, gas stations, a supermarket, a post office and a public
library with free wi-fi and internet terminals, all
on Palm Canyon Dr.

Mojave National Preserve

If you're on a quest for the 'middle of nowhere,' you may find it in **Mojave National
Preserve** (☑760-252-6100; www.nps.gov/moja)
FREE, a 1.6-million-acre jumble of sand
dunes, Joshua trees, volcanic cinder cones
and habitat for endangered desert tortoises.
Warning: no gas is available here.

Southeast of Baker and the I-15 Fwy, Kel-
baker Rd crosses a ghostly landscape of cinder cones before arriving at **Kelso Depot**,
a 1920s Mission Revival–style railroad station. It now houses the park's main **visitor
center** (☑760-252-6108; ⊘9am-5pm), which
has excellent natural-and-cultural history
exhibits, and an old-fashioned lunch counter. It's another 11 miles southwest to 'singing' **Kelso Dunes**. When wind conditions
are right, they emanate low-pitched vibra-
tions caused by shifting sands – running
downhill can jump-start the effect.

From Kelso Depot, Kelso–Cima Rd takes
off northeast. After 19 miles, Cima Rd sling-
shots northwest toward I-15 around **Cima
Dome**, a 1500ft-high hunk of granite with
lava outcroppings, the slopes of which are
home to the world's largest **Joshua tree
forest**. For close-ups, summit **Teutonia
Peak** (3 miles round-trip); the trailhead is 6
miles northwest of Cima.

SALTON SEA & SALVATION MOUNTAIN

East of Anza-Borrego and south of Joshua Tree awaits a most unexpected sight:
the **Salton Sea** (☑760-393-3810; www.
parks.ca.gov; per car $5; ⊘visitor center
10am-4pm Oct-May, Fri-Sun only Jun-Sep),
California's largest lake in the middle of
its biggest desert. After the Colorado
River flooded in 1905, it took 1500 workers and half a million tons of rock to put
it back on course. With no natural outlet,
the artificial lake's surface is 220ft below sea level and its waters 50% saltier
than the Pacific – an environmental
nightmare that's yet to be cleaned up.

An even stranger sight near the lake's
eastern shore is **Salvation Mountain**
(www.salvationmountain.us), a 100ft-high
hill of hand-mixed clay slathered in colorful acrylic paint and found objects, and
inscribed with Christian messages. It was
the vision of folk artist Leonard Knight
(1931–2014). It's in Niland, about 3 miles
east of Hwy 111, via Main St/Beal Rd.

Further east, partly paved Mojave Rd
is a scenic backdoor route to first-come,
first-served campgrounds (campsites $12)
with potable water at Mid Hills (no RVs)
and Hole-in-the-Wall. The campgrounds
bookend a rugged 12-mile scenic drive along
dirt **Wild Horse Canyon Road**, ending near
Hole-in-the-Wall's **visitor center** (☑760-252-
6104; ⊘9am-4pm Wed-Sun Oct-Apr, 10am-4pm
Sat May-Sep) and the slot-canyon **Rings Loop
Trail**. Both roads usually don't require 4WD.

🛏 Sleeping & Eating

Free backcountry and roadside camping is
permitted in already impacted areas; ask at
the visitor center for details or consult the
free park newspaper.

For historical ambience, **Hotel Nipton**
(☑760-856-2335; http://nipton.com; 107355 Nipton
Rd; cabins/r without bath from $65/80; ⊘reception
8am-6pm; 🛜) encompasses a century-old adobe villa with rustic rooms and tent cabins in a
remote railway outpost, northeast of the preserve. Check in at the trading post next to a
simple Mexican-American cafe.

Off I-15, Baker (35 miles northwest of
Kelso) is the nearest town with bare-bones
motels and fast food.

CALIFORNIA MOJAVE NATIONAL PRESERVE

Death Valley National Park

The name itself evokes all that is harsh and hellish – a punishing, barren and lifeless place of Old Testament severity. Yet closer inspection reveals nature puts on a spectacular show of water-sculpted canyons, windswept sand dunes, palm-shaded oases, jagged mountains and wildlife aplenty here. It's also a land of superlatives, holding the US records for hottest temperature (134°F, or 57°C), lowest point (Badwater, 282ft below sea level) and largest national park outside Alaska (more than 5000 sq miles). Peak tourist season is when spring wildflowers bloom.

◉ Sights & Activities

In summer, stick to paved roads, limit your exertions outdoors to early morning hours and at night, and visit higher-elevation areas of the park.

From **Furnace Creek**, the central hub of the **park** (☏760-786-3200; www.nps.gov/deva; 7-day entry per car $20), drive southeast up to **Zabriskie Point** for spectacular sunset views across the valley and golden badlands eroded into waves, pleats and gullies. Twenty miles southeast at **Dante's View**, you can simultaneously spot the highest (Mt Whitney, 14,505ft) and lowest (Badwater) points in the contiguous USA.

Badwater itself, a timeless landscape of crinkly salt flats, is 17 miles south of Furnace Creek. Along the way, **Golden Canyon** and **Natural Bridge** are easily explored on short hikes. A 9-mile detour along **Artists Drive** through a narrow canyon is best in late afternoon when the eroded hillsides erupt in fireworks of color.

Northwest of Furnace Creek, near Stovepipe Wells Village, trek across Saharanesque **Mesquite Flat sand dunes** – magical under a full moon – and scramble along the smooth marble walls of **Mosaic Canyon**.

About 55 miles northwest of Furnace Creek at whimsical **Scotty's Castle** (☏877-444-6777; www.recreation.gov; tours adult/child from $15/7.50; ⊙grounds 8:30am-4:15pm, tour schedules vary, closed Tue-Thu mid-May–mid-Aug), tour guides in historical character dress bring to life the Old West tales of con man 'Death Valley Scotty' (reservations advised). Five miles west of Grapevine junction, circumambulate volcanic **Ubehebe Crater** and its younger sibling.

A scenic drive up **Emigrant Canyon**, starting 8 miles west of Stovepipe Wells, passes turnoffs to ghost towns and ends with a 3-mile unpaved stretch up to the historic beehive-shaped **Charcoal Kilns**. Nearby is the trailhead for the 8.4-mile round-trip hike up **Wildrose Peak** (9064ft). At the park's western edge, utterly remote **Panamint Springs** offers panoramic vistas and a 2-mile round-trip hike to tiny Darwin Falls.

Activities offered at the Ranch at Furnace Creek Ranch resort include horseback riding, golf, mountain biking and hot-springs pool swimming. For 4WD adventures, talk to **Farabee's Jeep Rentals** (☏760-786-9872; http://farabeesjeeprentals.com; 2-/4-door Jeep incl 200 miles $195/235; ⊙mid-Sep–late May) near the Inn at Furnace Creek.

🛏 Sleeping & Eating

In-park lodging is often booked solid, especially on weekends and during the spring wildflower bloom.

The closest town with a few roadside motels is Beatty, NV (40 miles northeast of Furnace Creek); many more accommodations are found in Las Vegas, NV (125 miles southeast) and Ridgecrest, CA (125 miles southwest).

Ranch at Furnace Creek RESORT **$$**
(☏760-786-2345; www.furnacecreekresort.com; Hwy 190, Furnace Creek; cabins $130-162, r $162-213; P ⊝ ❄ 🖥 ♨ 👪) Tailor-made for families, this rambling resort with multiple motel-style buildings has received a vigorous face-lift, resulting in spiffy rooms swathed in desert colors, updated bathrooms and French doors leading to porches with comfortable patio furniture. The grounds encompass a playground, spring-fed swimming pool, tennis courts, restaurants, shops and the **Borax Museum** (☏760-786-2345; ⊙9am-9pm Oct-May, variable in summer) **FREE**.

Stovepipe Wells Village MOTEL **$$**
(☏760-786-2387; www.escapetodeathvalley.com; Hwy 190, Stovepipe Wells; RV sites $33, r $117-176; P ❄ @ 🖥 ♨ 👪 🐾) The 83 rooms at this sea-level tourist village are newly spruced-up and have quality linens beneath Death Valley–themed artwork, cheerful Native American–patterned bedspreads, coffee-makers and TVs. The small pool is cool and the cowboy-style **Toll Road Restaurant** (dinner mains $13-26; ⊙7-10am & 6-10pm; 🖥 👪) serves breakfast and lunch daily.

Cynthia's HOSTEL, INN **$$**
([✆]760-852-4580; www.discovercynthias.com;
2001 Old Spanish Trail Hwy, Tecopa; dm $22-25, r
$75-118, tipis $165-225; [⊘]check-in 3-8pm; [P][🛜])
Match your budget to the bed at this congenial inn helmed by the friendly Cynthia, about 3 miles from central Tecopa. Your choices: a colorful and eclectically decorated private room in a vintage trailer, a bed in a dorm, or a Native American–style tipi (a short drive away) with thick rugs, fire pits and comfy king-size beds.

Inn at Furnace Creek HOTEL **$$$**
([✆]760-786-2345; www.furnacecreekresort.com;
Hwy 190; r/ste from $345/450; [⊘]mid-Oct–mid-
May; [P][⊘][✳][@][🛜][🏊]) Roll out of bed and count the colors of the desert as you pull back the curtains in your room at this elegant 1927 Mission-style hotel. After a day of sweaty touring, enjoy languid valley views while lounging by the spring-fed swimming pool, cocktail in hand. The lobby has a 1930s retro look.

ℹ Information

Purchase a seven-day entry pass (per car $20) at self-service pay stations throughout the park. For a free map and newspaper, show your receipt at the **visitor center** ([✆]760-786-3200; www.nps.gov/deva; [⊘]8am-5pm mid-Oct–mid-Jun, 9am-6pm mid-Jun–mid-Oct) in Furnace Creek, where you'll also find a general store, expensive gas station, post office, ATM, coin-op laundromat and pay showers. Stovepipe Wells Village, a 30-minute drive northwest, has a general store, expensive gas station, ATM and pay showers. Cell-phone reception is spotty to nonexistent in the park.

CENTRAL COAST

No trip to California would be worth its salt without a jaunt along the surreally scenic Central Coast. Among California's most iconic roads, Hwy 1 skirts past posh Santa Barbara, retro Pismo Beach, collegiate San Luis Obispo, fantastical Hearst Castle, soul-stirring Big Sur, cutesy Carmel, down-to-earth Monterey and hippie Santa Cruz, often within view of the Pacific. Slow down – this idyllic coast deserves to be savored, not gulped. (That same advice goes for the award-winning locally grown wines too.)

WORTH A TRIP

RHYOLITE

Four miles west of Beatty, NV, look for the turnoff to the ghost town of **Rhyolite** (www.rhyolitesite.com; off Hwy 374; [⊘]sunrise-sunset) **FREE**, which epitomizes the hurly-burly, boom-and-bust story of so many Western gold-rush mining towns. Don't miss the 1906 'bottle house' or the skeletal remains of a three-story bank. Next door is the bizarre **Goldwell Open Air Museum** (www.goldwellmuseum. org; off Hwy 374; [⊘]24hr) **FREE** of trippy art installations begun by Belgian artist Albert Szukalski in 1984.

Santa Barbara

Life is sweet in Santa Barbara, a coastal Shangri-La where the air is redolent of citrus and jasmine, flowery bougainvillea drapes whitewashed buildings with Spanish red-tiled roofs, and it's all cradled by pearly beaches – just ignore those pesky oil derricks out to sea. Downtown's main drag, State St, and the Funk Zone, south of the railroad tracks, abound with restaurants, bars, art galleries and boutiques.

◉ Sights

★**Mission Santa Barbara** CHURCH
(www.santabarbaramission.org; 2201 Laguna St; adult/child 5-15yr $7/2; [⊘]10am-5pm, last entry 4:15pm; [P]) California's 'Queen of the Missions' reigns above the city on a hilltop perch over a mile northwest of downtown. Its imposing Doric facade, an architectural homage to an ancient Roman chapel, is topped by an unusual twin bell tower. Inside the mission's 1820 stone church, notice the striking Chumash artwork. Outside is an eerie cemetery – skull carvings hang over the door leading outside – with 4000 Chumash graves and the elaborate mausoleums of early California settlers.

Santa Barbara
County Courthouse HISTORIC SITE
([✆]805-962-6464; www.santabarbaracourthouse. org; 1100 Anacapa St; [⊘]8am-4:45pm Mon-Fri, 10am-4:15pm Sat & Sun) **FREE** Built in Spanish-Moorish Revival style in 1929, the courthouse features hand-painted ceilings, wrought-iron chandeliers, and tiles from Tunisia and Spain. Step inside the hushed mural room depicting

Spanish-colonial history on the 2nd floor, then climb El Mirador, the 85ft clock tower, for arch-framed panoramas of the city, ocean and mountains. You're free to explore on your own, but you'll get a lot more out of a free docent-guided tour, usually at 2pm daily and 10:30am on weekdays.

Santa Barbara Museum of Art　　MUSEUM
(☑805-963-4364; www.sbmuseart.org; 1130 State St; adult/child 6-17yr $10/6, 5-8pm Thu free; ⏱11am-5pm Tue-Wed & Fri-Sun, to 8pm Thu) This thoughtfully curated, bite-sized art museum displays European and American masters – think Matisse and Diego Rivera – along with contemporary photography, classical antiquities and thought-provoking temporary exhibits. Traipse up to the 2nd floor, where impressive Asian art collections include an intricate, colorful Tibetan sand mandala and the iron-and-leather armor of a Japanese warrior. Guided tours usually start at 1pm daily. There's also an interactive children's space, a museum shop and a cafe.

Santa Barbara Maritime Museum　MUSEUM
(☑805-962-8404; www.sbmm.org; 113 Harbor Way; adult/child 6-17yr $7/4, 3rd Thu of month free; ⏱10am-5pm, to 6pm late May-early Sep; P☗) On the harborfront, this jam-packed, two-story exhibition hall celebrates the town's briny history with nautical artifacts, memorabilia and hands-on exhibits, including a big-game fishing chair from which you can 'reel in' a trophy marlin. Take a virtual trip through the Santa Barbara Channel, stand on a surfboard or watch deep-sea diving documentaries in the theater. There's 90 minutes of free parking in the public lot or take the Lil' Toot water taxi from Stearns Wharf.

🏃 Activities

Overlooking busy municipal beaches, 1872 **Stearns Wharf** is the West's oldest continuously operating wooden pier, strung with touristy shops and restaurants. Outside town off Hwy 101, bigger palm-fringed **state beaches** await at Carpinteria, 12 miles east, and El Capitan and Refugio, more than 20 miles west.

Wheel Fun Rentals　　　　CYCLING
(www.wheelfunrentals.com; 23 E Cabrillo Blvd; ⏱8am-8pm Mar-Oct, to 6pm Nov-Feb; ☗) Hourly rentals of beach cruisers ($10), mountain bikes ($11) and two-/four-person surreys ($29/39), with discounted half-day and full-day rates.

Santa Barbara Sailing Center　KAYAKING
(☑805-962-2826; www.sbsail.com; off Harbor Way; single/double kayak rental per hr $10/15, 2hr kayak tour $50; ☗) Just about the cheapest kayak rental and guided tours around, with paddling instruction available by prior arrangement. Call for seasonal hours.

Condor Express　　　　　CRUISE
(☑805-882-0088, 888-779-4253; www.condor-cruises.com; 301 W Cabrillo Blvd; adult/child 5-12yr 2½hr cruise $50/30, 4½hr cruise from $99/50; ☗) Take a whale-watching excursion aboard the high-speed catamaran *Condor Express*. Whale sightings are guaranteed, so if you miss out the first time, you'll get a free voucher for another cruise.

🛏 Sleeping

Hello, sticker shock: even basic motel rooms can command over $200 in summer. Less expensive motels line upper State St, north of downtown, and Hwy 101.

Santa Barbara Auto Camp　CAMPGROUND **$$**
(☑888-405-7553; http://autocamp.com/sb; 2717 De La Vina St; d $175-215; P☀☍☗☗) 🅿 Bed down with vintage style in one of five shiny metal Airstream trailers parked near upper State St, north of downtown. All five architect-designed trailers have unique perks, such as a clawfoot tub or extra twin-size beds for kiddos, as well as a full kitchen and complimentary cruiser bikes to borrow. Book ahead; two-night minimum may apply. Pet fee $25.

Agave Inn　　　　　　MOTEL **$$**
(☑805-687-6009; http://agaveinnsb.com; 3222 State St; r incl breakfast from $119; P☀☗) While it's still just a motel at heart, this boutique-on-a-budget property's 'Mexican pop meets modern' motif livens things up with a color palette from a Frieda Kahlo painting. Flat-screen TVs, microwaves, minifridges and air-con make it a standout option. Family-sized rooms have kitchenettes and pull-out sofa beds. Continental breakfast included.

Harbor House Inn　　　　MOTEL **$$**
(☑888-474-6789, 805-962-9745; www.harbor-houseinn.com; 104 Bath St; r from $180; P☗☗) Down by the harbor, this converted motel offers brightly lit studios with hardwood floors and a beachy design scheme. A few have full kitchens and fireplaces, but there's no air-con. Rates include a welcome basket of breakfast goodies (with a two-night minimum stay), and beach towels, chairs and

OFF THE BEATEN TRACK

CHANNEL ISLANDS NATIONAL PARK

Remote, rugged **Channel Islands National Park** (www.nps.gov/chis) earns the nickname 'California's Galápagos' for its unique wildlife. These islands offer superb snorkeling, scuba diving and sea kayaking. Spring, when wildflowers bloom, is a gorgeous time to visit; summer and fall are bone-dry, but the latter brings the calmest water and winds; winter can be stormy.

Anacapa, an hour's boat ride from the mainland, is the best island for day-tripping, with easy hikes and unforgettable views. Santa Cruz, the biggest island, is for overnight camping excursions, kayaking and hiking. Other islands require longer channel crossings and multiday trips. San Miguel is often shrouded in fog. Tiny Santa Barbara supports seabird and seal colonies. So does Santa Rosa, which also protects Torrey pine trees.

Boats leave from Ventura Harbor, off Hwy 101, where the park's **visitor center** (☑805-658-5730; www.nps.gov/chis; 1901 Spinnaker Dr, Ventura; ⊙8:30am-5pm; ♠) has info and maps. The main tour-boat operator is **Island Packers** (☑805-642-1393; www. islandpackers.com; 1691 Spinnaker Dr, Ventura; 3hr cruise adult/child 3-12yr from $36/26); book ahead. Primitive island campgrounds require reservations; book through Recreation.gov (p440) and bring food and water.

umbrellas and three-speed bicycles to borrow. Pet fee $20.

★**Inn of the**
Spanish Garden   BOUTIQUE HOTEL $$$
(☑866-564-4700, 805-564-4700; www.spanishgardeninn.com; 915 Garden St; d incl breakfast from $309; P❋@☞☜) At this Spanish Colonial-style inn, casual elegance, top-notch service and an impossibly romantic central courtyard will have you lording about like the don of your own private villa. Beds have luxurious linens, bathrooms have oversized bathtubs and concierge service is top-notch. Palms surround a small outdoor pool, or unwind with a massage in your room.

✗ Eating

Lilly's Taquería   MEXICAN $
(http://lillystacos.com; 310 Chapala St; items from $1.60; ⊙10:30am-9pm Sun-Mon & Wed-Thu, to 10pm Fri & Sat) There's almost always a line roping around this downtown taco shack at lunchtime. But it goes fast, so you'd best be snappy with your order – the *adobada* (marinated pork) and *lengua* (beef tongue) are standout choices. Second location in Goleta west of the airport, off Hwy 101.

Santa Barbara
Shellfish Company   SEAFOOD $$
(www.sbfishhouse.com; 230 Stearns Wharf; dishes $4-19; ⊙11am-9pm; P♠) 'From sea to skillet to plate' sums up this end-of-the-wharf seafood shack that's more of a buzzing counter joint than a sit-down restaurant. Chase away the seagulls as you chow down on garlic-baked

clams, crab cakes and coconut-fried shrimp at wooden picnic tables outside. Awesome lobster bisque, ocean views and the same location for over 25 years.

★**Lark**   CALIFORNIAN $$$
(☑805-284-0370; www.thelarksb.com; 131 Anacapa St; shared plates $5-32, mains $24-38; ⊙5-10pm Tue-Sun, bar till midnight) ✔ There's no better place in Santa Barbara County to taste the bountiful farm and fishing goodness of this stretch of SoCal coast. Named after an antique Pullman railway car, this chef-run restaurant in the Funk Zone morphs its menu with the seasons, presenting unique flavor combinations like fried olives with chorizo aioli and chili-spiced mussels in lemongrass-lime broth. Make reservations.

☐ Drinking & Nightlife

Nightlife orbits lower State St and the Funk Zone. You can ramble between a dozen wine-tasting rooms along the city's **Urban Wine Trail** (www.urbanwinetrailsb.com). Check the free alt-weekly *Santa Barbara Independent* (www.independent.com) for an entertainment calendar.

Figueroa Mountain Brewing Co   BAR
(www.figmtnbrew.com; 137 Anacapa St; ⊙11am-11pm) Father and son brewers have brought their gold-medal-winning hoppy IPA, Danish red lager and double IPA from Santa Barbara's Wine Country to the Funk Zone. Clink pint glasses on the taproom's open-air patio while acoustic acts play. Enter on Yanonali St.

ⓘ Information

Santa Barbara Car Free (www.santabarbara-carfree.org) is a helpful website for ecotravel tips and discounts.

Santa Barbara Visitors Center (☑ 805-965-3021, 805-568-1811; www.santabarbaraca.com; 1 Garden St; ☺ 9am-5pm Mon-Sat, 10am-5pm Sun, closing 1hr earlier Nov-Jan) Pick up maps and brochures while consulting with the helpful, but busy staff. The website offers free downloadable DIY touring maps and itineraries, from famous movie locations to wine trails, art galleries and outdoors fun. Self-pay metered parking lot nearby.

ⓘ Getting There & Around

From a downtown **bus station** (☑ 805-965-7551; www.greyhound.com; 224 Chapala St), Greyhound has a few daily buses to LA ($17, two to three hours) and via San Luis Obispo ($31, two hours) to Santa Cruz ($59, six hours) and San Francisco ($63, nine hours).

From the **train station** (☑ 800-872-7245; www.amtrak.com; 209 State St) south of downtown, Amtrak trains roll toward LA ($31, 2¾ hours) and San Luis Obispo ($35, 2¾ hours).

Metropolitan Transit District (MTD; ☑ 805-963-3366; www.sbmtd.gov) runs citywide buses ($1.75). Its electric shuttles (50¢) loop between downtown's State St and Stearns Wharf and along beachfront Cabrillo Blvd.

Santa Barbara to San Luis Obispo

You can speed up to San Luis Obispo in less than two hours along Hwy 101, or take all day detouring to wineries, historical missions and hidden beaches.

A scenic backcountry drive north of Santa Barbara follows Hwy 154, where you can go for the grape in the **wine country** (www.sbcountywines.com) of the Santa Ynez and Santa Maria Valleys. Ride along with **Sustainable Vine** (☑ 805-698-3911; www.sustainablevine.com) ☀ for ecoconscious winery tours ($150), or just follow the pastoral **Foxen Canyon Wine Trail** (www.foxencanyonwinetrail.com) north to discover cult winemakers' vineyards. In the town of **Los Olivos**, where two dozen more wine-tasting rooms await, **Los Olivos Wine Merchant & Café** (☑ 805-688-7265; www.losolivoscafe.com; 2879 Grand Ave; mains breakfast $9-12, lunch & dinner $12-29; ☺ 11:30am-8:30pm daily, also 8-10:30am Sat & Sun) is a charming Cal-Mediterranean bistro with a wine bar.

Further south, the Danish-immigrant village of **Solvang** (www.solvangusa.com) abounds with windmills and fairy-tale-esque bakeries. Fuel up on breakfast biscuits, buttermilk fried-chicken sandwiches and farm-fresh salads at **Succulent Café** (☑ 805-691-9444; www.succulentcafe.com; 1555 Mission Dr; mains breakfast & lunch $9-13, dinner $19-29; ☺ breakfast 8:30am-noon Sat & Sun, lunch 11am-3pm Mon & Wed-Fri, noon-3pm Sat & Sun, dinner 5-9pm Wed-Mon) ☀. For a picnic lunch or BBQ takeout, swing into **El Rancho Market** (http://elranchomarket.com; 2886 Mission Dr; ☺ 6am-11pm), east of Solvang's 19th-century Spanish colonial **mission** (☑ 805-688-4815; www.missionsantaines.org; 1760 Mission Dr; adult/child under 12yr $5/free; ☺ 9am-4:30pm).

Follow Hwy 246 about 15 miles west of Hwy 101 to **La Purísima Mission State Historic Park** (☑ 805-733-3713; www.lapurisimamission.org; 2295 Purísima Rd, Lompoc; per car $6; ☺ 9am-5pm; ♿) ☀. Exquisitely restored, it's one of California's most evocative Spanish Colonial missions, with flowering gardens, livestock pens and adobe buildings. South of Lompoc off Hwy 1, Jalama Rd travels 14 twisting miles to windswept **Jalama Beach County Park** (☑ recorded info 805-736-3616; http://cosb.countyofsb.org/parks/; 9999 Jalama Rd, Lompoc; per car $10). Book ahead for its crazy-popular **campground** (www.sbparks.org/reservations; tent/RV sites from $23/38, cabins $110-210), where simple cabins have kitchenettes.

Where Hwy 1 rejoins Hwy 101, **Pismo Beach** has a long, lazy stretch of sand and a **butterfly grove** (www.monarchbutterfly.org; ☺ sunrise-sunset; ♿) 🆓, where migratory monarchs perch in eucalyptus trees from late October until February. Adjacent **North Beach Campground** (☑ reservations 800-444-7275; www.reserveamerica.com; 399 S Dolliver St; tent & RV sites $35; ♿♿) offers beach access and hot showers. Dozens of motels and hotels stand by the ocean and along Hwy 101, but rooms fill quickly, especially on weekends. **Pismo Lighthouse Suites** (☑ 805-773-2411; www.pismolighthousesuites.com; 2411 Price St; ste incl breakfast from $275; @ ☎ ♨ ♿ ♿) has everything vacationing families need, even a life-sized outdoor chessboard; ask about off-season discounts. Near Pismo's seaside pier, **Old West Cinnamon Rolls** (861 Dolliver St; snacks $2-5; ☺ 6:30am-5:30pm) offers gooey goodness. Uphill at the **Cracked Crab** (☑ 805-773-2722; www.crackedcrab.com; 751 Price St; mains $12-45; ☺ 11am-9pm Sun-Thu, to 10pm Fri & Sat; ♿), make sure you don a plastic bib before a fresh bucket o' seafood gets dumped on your butcher-paper-covered table.

The nearby town of **Avila Beach** has a sunny waterfront promenade, an atmospherically creaky wooden fishing pier and a historical **lighthouse** (🅙 guided hike reservations 805-541-8735, trolley tour reservations 855-533-7843; www.sanluislighthouse.org; lighthouse admission adult/child under 12yr $5/free, trolley tour incl admission per adult/child 3-12yr $20/15; 🕐 guided hikes usually 8:45am-1pm Wed & Sat, trolley tours usually noon, 1pm & 2pm Wed & Sat). Back toward Hwy 101, pick juicy fruit and feed the goats at **Avila Valley Barn farmstand** (www.avilavalleybarn.com; 560 Avila Beach Dr; 🕐 usually 9am-6pm mid-Mar–late-Dec; 🚸), then do some stargazing from a private redwood hot tub at **Sycamore Mineral Springs** (🅙 805-595-7302; www.sycamoresprings.com; 1215 Avila Beach Dr; 1hr per person $13.50-17.50; 🕐 8am-midnight, last reservation 10:45pm).

San Luis Obispo

Halfway between LA and San Francisco, San Luis Obispo is a low-key place. But CalPoly university students inject a healthy dose of hubbub into the streets, bars and cafes, especially during the weekly **farmers market** (www.downtownslo.com; 🕐 6-9pm Thu; 🅙 🚸) 🐾, which turns downtown's Higuera St into a party with live music and sidewalk BBQs.

Like several other California towns, SLO grew up around a Spanish Catholic **mission** (🅙 805-543-6850; www.missionsanluisobispo.org; 751 Palm St; donation $2; 🕐 9am-5pm late Mar-Oct, to 4pm Nov–mid-Mar), founded in 1772 by Junípero Serra. These days, SLO is just a grape's throw from thriving **Edna Valley wineries** (www.slowine.com), known for crisp Chardonnay and subtle Pinot Noir.

🛏 Sleeping

SLO's motel row is north of downtown along Monterey St. Budget and midrange motels and hotels line Hwy 101.

HI Hostel Obispo　　　　　　HOSTEL $
(🅙 805-544-4678; www.hostelobispo.com; 1617 Santa Rosa St; dm $27-31, r from $60, all without bath; 🕐 check-in 4:30-10pm; @🛜) 🐾 On a tree-lined street near the train station, this solar-powered, avocado-colored hostel inhabits a converted Victorian, which gives it a bit of a B&B feel. Amenities include a kitchen, bike rentals (from $10 per day) and complimentary sourdough pancakes and coffee for breakfast. BYOT (bring your own towel).

Madonna Inn　　　　　　　　HOTEL $$
(🅙 805-543-3000; www.madonnainn.com; 100 Madonna Rd; r $189-309; ✱@🛜🏊🚸) The fantastically campy Madonna Inn is a garish confection visible from Hwy 101. Japanese tourists, vacationing Midwesterners and irony-loving hipsters adore the 110 themed rooms – including Yosemite Rock, Caveman and hot-pink Floral Fantasy (check out photos online). The urinal in the men's room is a bizarre waterfall. But the best reason to stop here? Old-fashioned cookies from the storybook bakery.

🍴 Eating & Drinking

Downtown abounds with cafes, restaurants, wine bars, brewpubs and the solar-powered **Palm Theatre** (🅙 805-541-5161; www.thepalmtheatre.com; 817 Palm St; tickets $5-8) 🐾, screening indie films.

Firestone Grill　　　　　　BARBECUE $
(www.firestonegrill.com; 1001 Higuera St; dishes $4-10; 🕐 11am-10pm Sun-Wed, to 11pm Thu-Sat; 🚸) If you can stomach huge lines, long waits for a table, and sports-bar-style service, you'll get to sink your teeth into an authentic Santa Maria–style tri-tip steak sandwich on a toasted garlic roll and a basket of super-crispy fries.

Big Sky Café　　　　　　CALIFORNIAN $$
(www.bigskycafe.com; 1121 Broad St; dinner mains $11-22; 🕐 7am-9pm Mon-Thu, to 10pm Fri, 8am-10pm Sat, to 9pm Sun; 🚸) 🐾 Big Sky is a big room, and still the wait can be long – its tagline is 'analog food for a digital world.' Vegetarians have almost as many options as carnivores, and many of the ingredients are sourced locally. Big-plate dinners can be a bit bland, but breakfast (served until 1pm daily) gets top marks.

Luna Red　　　　　　　　　FUSION $$$
(🅙 805-540-5243; www.lunaredslo.com; 1023 Chorro St; shared plates $6-20, mains $20-39; 🕐 11am-9pm Mon-Wed, to 11:30pm Thu & Fri, 9am-11:30pm Sat, 9am-9pm Sun; 🚸) 🐾 Local bounty from the land and sea, artisan cheeses and farmers-market produce pervade the chef's Californian, Asian and Mediterranean small-plates menu. Cocktails and glowing lanterns enhance a sophisticated ambience indoors, or linger over brunch on the mission-view garden patio. Reservations recommended.

ℹ Information

San Luis Obispo Car Free (http://slocarfree.org) A helpful website for ecotravel tips and discounts.

San Luis Obispo Visitor Center (☑ 805-781-2777; www.visitslo.com; 895 Monterey St; ☺ 10am-5pm Sun-Wed, to 7pm Thu-Sat) Free maps and tourist brochures.

ℹ Getting There & Around

Amtrak trains from Santa Barbara ($28 to $35, 2¾ hours) and LA ($41, 5½ hours) arrive at SLO's **train station** (☑ 800-872-7245; www.amtrak.com; 1011 Railroad Ave), a 10-minute walk from downtown. Inconveniently stopping 3.5 miles southwest of downtown off Hwy 101, **Greyhound** (☑ 800-231-2222; www.greyhound.com; 1460 Calle Joaquin) has a few daily buses to Santa Barbara ($31, two hours), LA ($33, 5¼ hours), Santa Cruz ($46, 3¾ hours) and San Francisco ($59, 6¾ hours). You'll have to call for a taxi to connect to downtown.

Operated by **SLO RTA** (RTA; ☑ 805-541-2228; www.slorta.org; single-ride fares $1.50-3, day pass $5), countywide buses with limited weekend services converge on downtown's **transit center** (cnr Palm & Osos Sts).

Morro Bay to Hearst Castle

A dozen miles northwest of San Luis Obispo via Hwy 1, Morro Bay is a sea-sprayed fishing town where **Morro Rock**, a volcanic peak jutting up from the ocean floor, is your first hint of the coast's upcoming drama. (Never mind those powerplant smokestacks obscuring the views.) Hop aboard boat cruises or rent kayaks along the **Embarcadero**, which is packed with touristy shops. A classic seafood shack, **Giovanni's** (www.giovannisfishmarket.com; 1001 Front St; mains $6-15; ☺ 9am-6pm; ⊞) cooks killer garlic fries and fish-and-chips. Midrange motels cluster uphill off Harbor and Main Sts and along Hwy 1.

Nearby are fantastic state parks for coastal hikes and **camping** (☑ reservations 800-444-7275; www.reserveamerica.com; tent & RV sites $20-50; ⊞ 雹). South of the Embarcadero, **Morro Bay State Park** (☑ 805-772-2694; www.parks.ca.gov; park entry free, museum admission adult/child under 17yr $3/free; ☺ museum 10am-5pm) has a natural-history museum for kids. Further south in Los Osos, west of Hwy 1, wilder **Montaña de Oro State Park** (☑ 805-772-7434; www.parks.ca.gov; 3550 Pecho Valley Rd, Los Osos; ☺ 6am-10pm) **FREE** features

coastal bluffs, tide pools, sand dunes, peak hiking and mountain-biking trails. Its Spanish name (which means 'mountain of gold') comes from native California poppies that blanket the hillsides in spring.

Heading north of downtown Morro Bay along Hwy 1, surfers love the Cal-Mexican **Taco Temple** (2680 Main St; mains $8-20; ☺ 11am-9pm Wed-Mon; ⊞), a cash-only joint, and **Ruddell's Smokehouse** (www.smokerjim.com; 101 D St; dishes $4-13; ☺ 11am-6pm; ⊞ 雹), serving smoked-fish tacos by the beach in Cayucos. Vintage motels on Cayucos' Ocean Ave include the cute, family-run **Seaside Motel** (☑ 805-995-3809; www.seasidemotel.com; 42 S Ocean Ave; d $80-160; 雹). You can fall asleep to the sound of the surf at the ocean-view **Shoreline Inn on the Beach** (☑ 805-995-3681; www.cayucosshorelineinn.com; 1 N Ocean Ave; r $139-199; ⊞ 雹).

North of Harmony (population: just 18 souls), Hwy 46 leads east into the vineyards of **Paso Robles wine country** (www.pasowine.com). Tired of wine? Off Hwy 101 in Paso Robles, **Firestone Walker Brewing Company** (☑ 805-225-5911; www.firestonebeer.com; 1400 Ramada Dr; ☺ tasting room 10am-5pm Mon-Thu, to 6pm Fri-Sun, tours 10:30am-3:30pm) offers brewery tours ($3; reservations recommended), or just stop by the taproom for samples.

Further north along Hwy 1, quaint **Cambria** has lodgings along unearthly pretty Moonstone Beach, where the **Blue Dolphin Inn** (☑ 805-927-3300; www.cambriainns.com; 6470 Moonstone Beach Dr; r from $199; 雹 雹) embraces modern rooms with romantic fireplaces. Inland, **HI Cambria Bridge Street Inn** (☑ 805-927-7653; www.bridgestreetinncambria.com; 4314 Bridge St; dm from $32, r $57-95, all without bath; ☺ check-in 5-9pm; 雹) sleeps like a hostel but feels like a grandmotherly B&B, while the retro **Cambria Palms Motel** (☑ 805-927-4485; www.cambriapalmsmotel.com; 2662 Main St; r $109-149; ☺ check-in 3-9pm; 雹) has clean-lined rooms and cruiser bicycles to borrow. An artisan cheese and wine shop, **Indigo Moon** (☑ 805-927-2911; www.indigomooncafe.com; 1980 Main St; lunch $9-14, dinner $14-33; ☺ 10am-9pm) has breezy bistro tables and market-fresh salads and sandwiches at lunch. With a sunny patio and takeout counter, **Linn's Easy as Pie Cafe** (www.linnsfruitbin.com; 4251 Bridge St; dishes $6-11; ☺ 10am-6pm Oct-Apr, to 7pm May-Sep; ⊞) is famous for its olallieberry pie.

About 10 miles north of Cambria, hilltop **Hearst Castle** (☑ info 805-927-2020, reservations 800-444-4445; www.hearstcastle.org; 750 Hearst Castle Rd, San Simeon; tours adult/ child 5-12yr from $25/12; ☺ from 9am daily except Thanksgiving, Christmas & New Year's Day, closing time varies) is California's most famous monument to wealth and ambition. William Randolph Hearst, the newspaper magnate, entertained Hollywood stars and royalty at this fantasy estate dripping with European antiques, accented by shimmering pools and surrounded by flowering gardens. Try to make tour reservations in advance or show up early in the day.

Across Hwy 1, overlooking a historic whaling pier, **Sebastian's Store** (442 SLO-San Simeon Rd; mains $7-12; ☺ 11am-5pm, kitchen closes at 4pm) sells Hearst Ranch beef burgers and giant sandwiches for impromptu beach picnics. Five miles back south along Hwy 1, past a forgettable row of budget and mid-range motels in San Simeon, **Hearst San Simeon State Park** (☑ reservations 800-444-7275; www.reserveamerica.com; Hwy 1; tent & RV sites $20-25) offers primitive and developed creekside campsites.

Heading north, Point Piedras Blancas is home to an enormous **elephant seal colony** that breeds, molts, sleeps, frolics and, occasionally, goes aggro on the beach. Keep your distance from these wild animals who move faster on the sand than you can. The signposted vista point, about 4.5 miles north of Hearst Castle, has interpretive panels. Seals haul out year-round, but the frenzied birthing and mating season runs from January through March. Nearby, the 1875 **Piedras Blancas Light Station** (☑ 805-927-7361; www.piedrasblancas.gov; tours adult/child 6-17yr $10/5; ☺ tours usually 9:45am Mon-Sat mid-Jun–Aug, 9:45am Tue, Thu & Sat Sep–mid-Jun) is an outstandingly scenic spot; call ahead to confirm tour schedules (no reservations) and directions to the meet-up point.

Big Sur

Much ink has been spilled extolling the raw beauty and energy of this 100-mile stretch of craggy coastline sprawling south of Monterey Bay. More a state of mind than a place you can pinpoint on a map, Big Sur has no traffic lights, banks or strip malls. When the sun goes down, the moon and stars are the only illumination – if summer fog hasn't extinguished them, that is.

Lodging, food and gas are all scarce and pricey in Big Sur. Demand for rooms is high

PINNACLES NATIONAL PARK

Named for the towering spires that rise abruptly out of the chapparal-covered hills, **Pinnacles National Park** (☑ 831-389-4486; www.nps.gov/pinn; per car $10) is a study in geologic drama, with craggy monoliths, sheer-walled canyons and ancient volcanic remnants. Besides hiking and rock climbing, the park's biggest attractions are talus caves and endangered California condors. Visit during spring or fall – summer heat and humidity are extreme. A **campground** (☑ 877-444-6777; www.recreation.gov; tent/ RV sites $23/36; ☀ ⊞ ☂) with a seasonal swimming pool lies near the park's east entrance, off Hwy 25 about 30 miles northwest of King City on Hwy 101.

year-round, especially on weekends, so book ahead. The free *Big Sur Guide* (www.bigsur-california.org), an info-packed newspaper, is available at roadside businesses. The day-use parking fee (per car $10) charged at Big Sur's state parks is valid for same-day entry to all except Limekiln.

It's about 25 miles from Hearst Castle to blink-and-you-miss-it Gorda, home of **Treebones Resort** (☑ 877-424-4787, 805-927-2390; www.treebonesresort.com; 71895 Hwy 1; d without bath from $265; ☎ ☂), which offers back-to-nature clifftop yurts. Basic United States Forest Service (USFS) campgrounds are just off Hwy 1 at shady **Plaskett Creek** (☑ reservations 877-477-6777; www.recreation.gov; Hwy 1; tent & RV sites $25) and oceanside **Kirk Creek** (☑ reservations 877-444-6777; www.recreation.gov; Hwy 1; tent & RV sites $25).

Ten miles north of Lucia is new-agey **Esalen Institute** (☑ 888-837-2536; www.esalen.org; 55000 Hwy 1), famous for its esoteric workshops and ocean-view hot springs. By reservation only (call ☑ 831-667-3047 between 9am and noon daily), you can frolic nekkid in the baths from 1am to 3am nightly ($30, credit cards only). It's surreal.

Another 3 miles north, **Julia Pfeiffer Burns State Park** (☑ 831-667-2315; www.parks.ca.gov; Hwy 1; per car $10; ☺ 30min before sunrise-30min after sunset; ♿) hides 80ft-high McWay Falls, one of California's only coastal waterfalls. From the viewpoint, you can photograph it tumbling over granite cliffs into the ocean – or onto the beach, depending on the tide.

> **ⓘ DRIVING HIGHWAY 1**
>
> Navigating the narrow two-lane highway through Big Sur can be slow going. Allow at least 2½ hours to drive nonstop between Hearst Castle and Monterey Bay, much more if you stop to explore. Driving after dark can be risky and, more to the point, it's futile because you'll miss all the scenery. Watch out for cyclists and please use signposted roadside pullouts to let faster-moving traffic pass. For current road conditions and temporary closures, call ☑ 800-427-7623.

Over 7 miles further north, the beatnik **Henry Miller Memorial Library** (☑ 831-667-2574; www.henrymiller.org; 48603 Hwy 1; ☉ 11am-6pm) is the art and soul of Big Sur bohemia, with a jam-packed bookstore, live-music concerts, open-mic nights and outdoor film screenings. Opposite, food takes a backseat to dramatic panoramic views at clifftop **Nepenthe** (☑ 831-667-2345; www.nepenthebigsur.com; 48510 Hwy 1; mains $15-42; ☉ 11:30am-4:30pm & 5-10pm), meaning 'island of no sorrow.'

Heading north, rangers at **Big Sur Station** (☑ 831-667-2315; www.fs.usda.gov/lpnf; 47555 Hwy 1; ☉ 8am-4pm, closed Mon & Tue Nov-Mar) have information on area camping and hiking, including the popular 10-mile one-way hike to **Sykes Hot Springs**. On the opposite side of Hwy 1 just south, turn onto Sycamore Canyon Rd, which drops two narrow, twisting miles to crescent-shaped **Pfeiffer Beach** (www.fs.usda.gov/lpnf; end of Sycamore Canyon Rd; per car $10; ☉ 9am-8pm; 🅿), with a towering offshore sea arch. Strong currents make it too dangerous for swimming. Dig down into the sand – it's purple!

Next up, **Pfeiffer Big Sur State Park** (☑ 831-667-2315; www.parks.ca.gov; 47225 Hwy 1; per car $10; ☉ 30min before sunrise-30min after sunset; 🅿) is crisscrossed by sun-dappled trails through redwood forests. Make **campground** (☑ reservations 800-444-7275; www.reserveamerica.com; 47225 Hwy 1; tent & RV sites $35-50; 🅿🅿) reservations or stay at the rambling, old-fashioned **Big Sur Lodge** (☑ 831-667-3100; www.bigsurlodge.com; 47225 Hwy 1; d $205-395; 🅿🅿), which has rustic duplex cottages (some with kitchenettes and wood-burning fireplaces), a simple restaurant and a well-stocked general store.

Most of Big Sur's commercial activity is concentrated just north along Hwy 1, including private campgrounds with rustic cabins, motels, restaurants, gas stations and shops. **Glen Oaks Motel** (☑ 831-667-2105; www.glenoaksbigsur.com; 47080 Hwy 1; d $225-390; 🅿) 🅿 is a redesigned 1950s redwood-and-adobe motor lodge with romantic, woodsy cabins and cottages. Nearby, the Big Sur River Inn's **general store** (www.bigsurriverinn.com; 46840 Hwy 1; mains $8-10; ☉ 11am-7pm; 🅿) hides a burrito and fruit-smoothie bar at the back, while **Maiden Publick House** (☑ 831-667-2355; Village Center Shops, Hwy 1; ☉ noon-2am) pulls off an encyclopedic beer menu and live-music jams. Back south by the post office, put together a picnic at **Big Sur Deli** (www.bigsurdeli.com; 47520 Hwy 1; dishes $2-7; ☉ 7am-8pm), attached to the laid-back **Big Sur Taphouse** (www.bigsurtaphouse.com; 47520 Hwy 1; ☉ noon-10pm Mon-Thu, to midnight Fri & Sat, 10am-10pm Sun; 🅿), a beer-centric bar with board games and pub grub.

Heading north again, don't skip **Andrew Molera State Park** (☑ 831-667-2315; www.parks.ca.gov; Hwy 1; per car $10; ☉ 30min before sunrise-30min after sunset; 🅿), a gorgeous trail-laced pastiche of grassy meadows, waterfalls, ocean bluffs and rugged beaches. Learn all about endangered California condors at the park's **Discovery Center** (☑ 831-624-1202; www.ventanaws.org/discovery_center/; ☉ 10am-4pm Sat & Sun late May-early Sep; 🅿) 🅿 **FREE**. From the dirt parking lot, a 0.3-mile trail leads to a primitive, no-reservations **campground** (www.parks.ca.gov; Hwy 1; tent sites $25).

Six miles before the landmark **Bixby Creek Bridge**, you can tour 1889 **Point Sur Lightstation** (☑ 831-625-4419; www.pointsur.org; off Hwy 1; adult/child 6-17yr from $12/5; ☉ tours usually at 1pm Wed, 10am Sat & Sun Nov-Mar, 10am & 2pm Wed & Sat, 10am Sun Apr-Oct, also 10am Thu Jul & Aug). Check online or call for tour schedules, including seasonal moonlight walks, and directions to the meeting point. Arrive early since space is limited (no reservations).

Carmel

Once a bohemian artists' seaside resort, quaint Carmel-by-the-Sea now has the well-manicured feel of a country club. Simply plop down in any cafe and watch the parade of behatted ladies toting fancy-label shopping bags and dapper gents driving top-down convertibles along Ocean Ave, the village's slow-mo main drag.

◉ Sights & Activities

Often foggy, municipal **Carmel Beach** is a gorgeous white-sand crescent, where pampered pups excitedly run off-leash.

San Carlos Borroméo de Carmelo Mission CHURCH

(www.carmelmission.org; 3080 Rio Rd; adult/child 7-17yr $6.50/2; ⊙9:30am-7pm) Monterey's original mission was established by Franciscan friar Junípero Serra in 1770, but poor soil and the corrupting influence of Spanish soldiers forced the move to Carmel two years later. Today this is one of California's most strikingly beautiful missions, an oasis of solemnity bathed in flowering gardens. The mission's adobe chapel was later replaced with an arched basilica made of stone quarried in the Santa Lucia Mountains. Museum exhibits are scattered throughout the meditative complex.

Point Lobos State Natural Reserve PARK

(⊉831-624-4909; www.pointlobos.org; Hwy 1; per car $10; ⊙8am-7pm, closes 30min after sunset early Nov-mid-Mar; 🖈) They bark, they bathe and they're fun to watch – sea lions are the stars here at Punta de los Lobos Marinos (Point of the Sea Wolves), almost 4 miles south of Carmel, where a dramatically rocky coastline offers excellent tide-pooling. The full perimeter hike is 6 miles, but shorter walks take in wild scenery too, including Bird Island, shady cypress groves, the historical Whaler's Cabin and Devil's Cauldron, a whirlpool that gets splashy at high tide.

✗ Eating & Drinking

Bruno's Market & Deli DELI, MARKET $

(www.brunosmarket.com; cnr 6th & Junípero Aves; sandwiches $6-9; ⊙7am-8pm) This small supermarket deli counter makes a saucy sandwich of oakwood-grilled tri-tip beef and stocks all the accoutrements for a beach picnic, including Sparkys root beer from Pacific Grove.

Mundaka SPANISH, TAPAS $$

(⊉831-624-7400; www.mundakacarmel.com; San Carlos St, btwn Ocean & 7th Aves; small plates $6-25; ⊙5:30-10pm Sun-Wed, to 11pm Thu-Sat) This stone courtyard hideaway is a svelte escape from Carmel's stuffy 'newly wed and nearly dead' crowd. Taste Spanish tapas and housemade sangria while world beats spin.

Monterey

Working-class Monterey is all about the sea. It lures visitors with a top-notch aquarium that's a veritable temple to Monterey Bay's underwater universe. A National Marine Sanctuary since 1992, the bay begs for exploration by kayak, boat, scuba or snorkel. Meanwhile, downtown's historic quarter preserves California's Spanish and Mexican roots. Don't waste too much time on touristy Fisherman's Wharf or Cannery Row, the latter immortalized by novelist John Steinbeck back when it was the hectic, smelly epicenter of the sardine-canning industry, Monterey's lifeblood until the 1950s.

◉ Sights

★ Monterey Bay Aquarium AQUARIUM

(ⓘinfo 831-648-4800, tickets 866-963-9645; www.montereybayaquarium.org; 886 Cannery Row; adult/child 3-12yr/youth 13-17yr $40/25/30; ⊙9:30am-6pm daily Jun, 9:30am-6pm Mon-Fri, to 8pm Sat & Sun Jul-Aug, 10am-5pm or 6pm daily Sep-May; 🖈) ✎ Monterey's most mesmerizing experience is its enormous aquarium, built on the former site of the city's largest sardine cannery. All kinds of aquatic creatures are featured, from kid-tolerant sea stars and slimy sea slugs to animated sea otters and surprisingly nimble 800lb tuna. The aquarium is much more than an impressive collection of glass tanks – thoughtful placards underscore the bay's cultural and historical contexts.

Monterey State Historic Park HISTORIC SITE

(ⓐaudio tour 831-998-9458, info 831-649-7118; www.parks.ca.gov) ✎ FREE Old Monterey is home to an extraordinary assemblage of 19th-century brick and adobe buildings, administered as Monterey State Historic Park, all found along a 2-mile self-guided walking tour portentously called the 'Path of History.' You can inspect dozens of buildings, many with charming gardens; expect some to be open while others aren't, according to a capricious schedule dictated by unfortunate state-park budget cutbacks.

Point Pinos Lighthouse LIGHTHOUSE

(⊉831-648-3176; www.pointpinoslighthouse.org; 90 Asilomar Ave; suggested donation adult/child 6-17yr $2/1; ⊙1-4pm Thu-Mon) The West Coast's oldest continuously operating lighthouse has been warning ships off the hazardous tip of the Monterey Peninsula since 1855. Inside are modest exhibits on the lighthouse's history and alas, its failures – local shipwrecks.

Monarch Grove Sanctuary PARK
(www.ci.pg.ca.us; off Ridge Rd, btwn Lighthouse Ave & Short St; ☉dawn-dusk; 🖪) 🅿 FREE Between October and February, over 25,000 migratory monarch butterflies cluster in this thicket of tall eucalyptus trees, secreted inland. During peak season, volunteer guides answer all of your questions.

🏃 Activities

Year-round, whale-watching boats depart from Fisherman's Wharf. Cycle or walk the paved **Monterey Peninsula Recreation Trail**, which edges the coast past Cannery Row, ending at Lovers Point in Pacific Grove. The overhyped **17-Mile Drive** (www.pebblebeach.com; per car/bicycle $10/free) toll road connects Monterey and Pacific Grove with Carmel-by-the-Sea.

Adventures by the Sea CYCLING, KAYAKING
(☑831-372-1807; www.adventuresbythesea.com; 299 Cannery Row; rental per day kayak or bicycle $30, SUP set $50, tours from $60; 🖪) Beach cruisers, electric bikes and water-sports gear rentals and tours available at multiple locations on Cannery Row and **downtown** (☑831-372-1807; www.adventuresbythesea.com; 210 Alvarado St; 🖪).

Aquarius Dive Shop DIVING
(☑831-375-1933; www.aquariusdivers.com; 2040 Del Monte Ave; snorkel/scuba-gear rental $35/65, dive tours from $65) Talk to this five-star PADI operation for gear rentals, classes and guided dives into Monterey Bay.

Sanctuary Cruises WHALE-WATCHING
(☑831-917-1042; www.sanctuarycruises.com; 7881 Sandholdt Rd; adult/child 12yr & under $50/40; 🖪) 🅿 Departing from Moss Landing, 20 miles north of Monterey, this biodiesel boat runs recommended whale-watching and dolphin-spotting tours (reservations essential).

🛏 Sleeping

No-frills motels (which are exorbitantly priced in summer) are found on Munras Ave south of downtown and N Fremont St east of Hwy 1.

HI Monterey Hostel HOSTEL $
(☑831-649-0375; www.montereyhostel.org; 778 Hawthorne St; dm $27-37, d $79-199, all without bath; ☉check-in 4-10pm; @🛜) Four blocks from Cannery Row and the aquarium, this simple, clean hostel houses single-sex and mixed dorms, as well as private rooms (call for rates). Budget backpackers stuff themselves silly with make-your-own pancake breakfasts. Reservations strongly recommended. Take MST bus 1 from downtown's Transit Plaza.

Monterey Hotel HISTORIC HOTEL $$
(☑831-375-3184; www.montereyhotel.com; 406 Alvarado St; r $80-220; 🛜) In the heart of downtown and a short walk from Fisherman's Wharf, this 1904 edifice harbors five-dozen small, somewhat noisy, but freshly renovated rooms with Victorian-styled furniture and plantation shutters. No elevator. Parking is $17.

★**InterContinental–Clement** HOTEL $$$
(☑831-375-4500, 866-781-2406; www.ictheclementmonterey.com; 750 Cannery Row; r from $250; ❄@🛜🐾🖪) Like an upscale version of a New England millionaire's seaside mansion, this all-encompassing resort presides over Cannery Row. For the utmost luxury and romance, book an ocean-view suite with a balcony and private fireplace, then breakfast in bayfront C Restaurant downstairs. Parking is $23.

🍴 Eating

Restaurants, bars and live-music venues line Cannery Row and downtown's Alvarado St.

LouLou's Griddle in the Middle AMERICAN $$
(www.loulousgriddle.com; Municipal Wharf 2; mains $8-16; ☉usually 7:30am-3pm & 5-8:30pm Wed-Mon; 🖪🐾) Stroll down the municipal wharf to this zany diner, best for breakfasts of ginormous pancakes and omelets with Mexican *pico de gallo* salsa or fresh seafood for lunch. Breezy outdoor tables are dog friendly.

Red House Cafe CAFE $$
(☑831-643-1060; www.redhousecafe.com; 662 Lighthouse Ave; mains breakfast & lunch $8-14, dinner $12-23; ☉8am-2:30pm daily, 5-9pm Tue-Sun; 🖪) Crowded with locals, this shingled late-19th-century house dishes up comfort food with haute touches, like cinnamon-brioche French toast, grilled eggplant-fontina sandwiches or spinach-cheese ravioli in lemon beurre blanc sauce. Oatmeal-apricot-pecan cookies are what's for dessert. Reservations helpful.

★**Passionfish** SEAFOOD $$$
(☑831-655-3311; www.passionfish.net; 701 Lighthouse Ave, Pacific Grove; mains $16-32; ☉5-9pm Sun-Thu, to 10pm Fri & Sat) 🅿 Fresh, sustainable

seafood is artfully presented in any number of inventive ways, and a seasonally inspired menu also carries slow-cooked meats and vegetarian dishes spotlighting local farms. The earth-tone decor is spare, with tables squeezed conversationally close together. An ambitious world-ranging wine list is priced near retail, and there are twice as many Chinese teas as wines by the glass.

Reservations strongly recommended.

ⓘ Information

Monterey Visitors Center (☑ 831-657-6400, 888-221-1010; www.seemonterey.com; 401 Camino El Estero; ⊙ 9am-6pm Mon-Sat, to 5pm Sun, closing 1hr earlier Nov-Mar) Free tourist brochures; ask for a *Monterey County Literary & Film Map*.

ⓘ Getting There & Around

Regional and local **Monterey-Salinas Transit** (MST; ☑ 888-678-2871; www.mst.org; single-ride fares $1.50-3.50, day pass $10) buses converge on downtown's **Transit Plaza** (cnr Pearl & Alvarado Sts), including routes to Pacific Grove, Carmel, Big Sur (daily in summer, otherwise weekends only) and Salinas (for Greyhound bus and Amtrak train connections). During summer, free trolleys shuttle between downtown Monterey and Cannery Row.

Santa Cruz

SoCal beach culture meets NorCal counter-culture here. The university student population makes this old-school radical town youthful, hip and lefty-liberal. Some worry that Santa Cruz' weirdness quotient is dropping, but you'll disagree when you witness the freak show (and we say that with love, man) along Pacific Ave downtown.

⊙ Sights & Activities

You'll find the most action at **Main Beach**, about a mile south of downtown. Locals favor less-trampled beaches off E Cliff Dr.

★**Santa Cruz**
Beach Boardwalk   AMUSEMENT PARK
(☑ 831-423-5590; www.beachboardwalk.com; 400 Beach St; per ride $3-6, all-day pass $32-40; ⊙ daily Apr-early Sep, seasonal hours vary; 🖐) The West Coast's oldest beachfront amusement park, this 1907 boardwalk has a glorious old-school Americana vibe. The smell of cotton candy mixes with the salt air, punctuated by the squeals of kids hanging upside down on

carnival rides. Famous thrills include the Giant Dipper, a 1924 wooden roller coaster, and the 1911 Looff carousel, both National Historic Landmarks. During summer, catch free midweek movies and Friday-night concerts by rock veterans you may have thought were already dead.

Santa Cruz Surfing Museum   MUSEUM
(www.santacruzsurfingmuseum.org; 701 W Cliff Dr; admission by donation; ⊙ 10am-5pm Wed-Mon Jul 4-early Sep, noon-4pm Thu-Mon early Sep-Jul 3) A mile southwest of the wharf along the coast, this tiny museum inside an old lighthouse is packed with memorabilia, including vintage redwood surfboards. Fittingly, Lighthouse Point overlooks two popular surf breaks.

Natural Bridges State Beach   BEACH
(www.parks.ca.gov; 2531 W Cliff Dr; per car $10; ⊙ 8am-sunset; 🖐) Best for sunsets, this family favorite has lots of sand, tide pools and monarch butterflies from mid-October through mid-February. It's at the far end of W Cliff Dr.

Seymour Marine Discovery Center MUSEUM
(☑ 831-459-3800; http://seymourcenter.ucsc.edu; 100 Shaffer Rd; adult/child 3-16yr $8/6; ⊙ 10am-5pm Tue-Sun year-round, also 10am-5pm Mon Jul & Aug; 🖐) 🖉 By Natural Bridges State Beach, this kids' educational center is part of UCSC's Long Marine Laboratory. Interactive natural-science exhibits include tidal touch pools and aquariums, while outside you can gawk at the world's largest blue-whale skeleton. Guided one-hour tours happen at 1pm, 2pm and 3pm daily, with a special half-hour tour for families with younger children at 11am; sign up for tours in person an hour in advance (no reservations).

Venture Quest   KAYAKING
(☑ 831-425-8445, 831-427-2267; www.kayaksantacruz.com; Municipal Wharf; kayak rental/tour from $30/55; ⊙ 10am-7pm Mon-Fri, from 9am Sat & Sun late May-late Sep, hours vary late Sep–mid-May) Convenient rentals on the wharf, plus whale-watching and coastal sea-cave tours, moonlight paddles and kayak-sailing trips. Book ahead for kayak-surfing lessons.

O'Neill Surf Shop   SURFING
(☑ 831-475-4151; www.oneill.com; 1115 41st Ave; wetsuit/surfboard rental from $10/20; ⊙ 9am-8pm Mon-Fri, from 8am Sat & Sun) Head east toward Pleasure Point to worship at this internationally renowned surfboard maker's flagship store, with branches on the beach boardwalk and downtown.

Richard Schmidt Surf School SURFING
(831-423-0928; www.richardschmidt.com; 849 Almar Ave; 2hr group/1hr private lesson $90/120) Award-winning, time-tested surf school can get you out there, all equipment included. Summer surf camps hook adults and kids alike.

Sleeping

Motels border Ocean St near downtown, Mission St by the university campus and Hwy 1 heading south. Make reservations for state-park **campgrounds** (reservations 800-444-7275; www.reserveamerica.com; tent & RV sites $35-65;) by beaches off Hwy 1 and in redwood forests off Hwy 9.

HI Santa Cruz Hostel HOSTEL $
(831-423-8304; www.hi-santacruz.org; 321 Main St; dm $26-29, r $60-110, all without bath; check-in 5-10pm; @) Budget overnighters dig this cute hostel at the century-old Carmelita Cottages surrounded by flowering gardens, just two blocks from the beach. Cons: midnight curfew, daytime lockout (11am to 5pm) and three-night maximum stay. Reservations are essential. Street parking costs $2.

★ **Adobe on Green B&B** B&B $$
(831-469-9866; www.adobeongreen.com; 103 Green St; r incl breakfast $169-219;) Peace and quiet are the mantras at this place, a short walk from Pacific Ave. The hosts are practically invisible, but their thoughtful touches are everywhere, from boutique-hotel amenities in spacious, stylish and solar-powered rooms to breakfast spreads from their organic gardens.

Pelican Point Inn INN $$
(831-475-3381; www.pelicanpointinn-santacruz.com; 21345 E Cliff Dr; ste $139-219;) Ideal for families, these roomy apartments near a kid-friendly beach come with everything you'll need for a lazy vacation, including kitchenettes. Weekly rates available. Pet fee $20.

Dream Inn HOTEL $$$
(866-774-7735, 831-426-4330; www.dreaminnsantacruz.com; 175 W Cliff Dr; r $249-479; @) Overlooking the wharf from a spectacular hillside perch, this chic boutique hotel is as stylish as Santa Cruz gets. Rooms have all mod cons, while the beach is just steps away. Don't miss happy hour at Aquarius restaurant's ocean-view bar. Parking is $25.

Eating

Downtown is chockablock with so-so cafes. Mission St near the university campus and 41st Ave in neighboring Capitola offer cheaper takeout and international flavors.

Picnic Basket DELI $
(http://thepicnicbasketsc.com; 125 Beach St; dishes $3-10; 7am-9pm, shorter off-season hours;) Across the street from the beach boardwalk, this locavarian kitchen puts together creative sandwiches such as beet with lemony couscous or 'fancy pants' grilled cheese with fruit chutney, plus homemade soups, breakfast burritos and baked goods. Staff can be sour, but ice-cream treats are sweet.

Pono Hawaiian Grill FUSION $$
(www.ponohawaiiangrill.com; 120 Union St; mains $7-15; 11am-10pm Sun-Wed, to 11pm Thu-Sat) Inside the Reef bar, this kitchen runs on 'island time' as it mixes up your fresh ahi tuna, salmon, shellfish or veggie *poke* (cubed raw salad) in a bowl or ladled on a plate with two-scoop rice and creamy macaroni or tossed green salad. The loco moco burrito with spicy gravy is a huge hit.

Soif BISTRO $$$
(831-423-2020; www.soifwine.com; 105 Walnut Ave; small plates $5-17, mains $19-25; 5-9pm Sun-Thu, to 10pm Fri & Sat) Bon vivants swoon over a heady selection of three dozen international wines by the glass, paired with a sophisticated, seasonally driven Euro-Cal menu. Expect tastebud-ticklers like roasted beet salad with fava beans and maple vinaigrette or squid-ink linguini with spicy chorizo.

Drinking & Nightlife

Downtown is jam-packed with bars, live-music lounges, low-key nightclubs and coffeehouses. Check the free *Good Times Santa Cruz* (www.gtweekly.com) tabloid for more venues and current events.

★ **Verve Coffee Roasters** CAFE
(www.vervecoffeeroasters.com; 1540 Pacific Ave; 6:30am-9pm;) To sip finely roasted artisan espresso or a cup of rich pour-over coffee, join the surfers and hipsters at this industrial-zen cafe. Single-origin brews and house blends rule.

Caffe Pergolesi CAFE
(www.theperg.com; 418 Cedar St; 7am-11pm;) Discuss conspiracy theories over stalwart coffee, tea or beer at this landmark Victori-

an house with a big ol' tree-shaded veranda. There's live music some evenings.

Discretion Brewing BREWERY
(www.discretionbrewing.com; 2703 41st Ave, Soquel; ⊙11:30am-9pm) Rye IPA, English ales and traditional Belgian and German brews are always on tap, off Hwy 1.

❶ Information

KPIG 107.5 FM (www.kpig.com) Streams the classic Santa Cruz soundtrack – think Bob Marley, Janis Joplin and Willie Nelson.
Santa Cruz Visitor Center (☑831-425-1234; www.santacruzca.org; 303 Water St; ⊙9am-noon & 1-4pm Mon-Fri, 11am-3pm Sat & Sun; @) Free public internet terminal, maps and brochures.

❶ Getting There & Around

Local and regional **Santa Cruz Metro** (☑831-425-8600; www.scmtd.com; single ride/day pass $2/6) buses converge on downtown's **Metro Center** (920 Pacific Ave). From there, Greyhound operates a few daily buses to San Francisco ($20, three hours), San Luis Obispo ($46, 3¾ hours), Santa Barbara ($59, six hours) and LA ($65, 8¾ hours). During summer, a trolley (25¢) shuttles between downtown and Main Beach and the wharf.

Santa Cruz to San Francisco

Far more scenic than any freeway, this curvaceous, 70-mile stretch of coastal Hwy 1 is bordered by wild beaches, organic farms and sea-salted villages, all scattered like loose diamonds in the rough.

About 20 miles northwest of Santa Cruz, **Año Nuevo State Reserve** (☑information 650-879-0227, tour reservations 800-444-4445; www.parks.ca.gov; off Hwy 1; entry per car $10, 2½hr tour per person $7; ⊙8:30am-5pm, last entry 3:30pm Apr-Nov, tours only mid-Dec–Mar) is the seasonal home of a gigantic colony of elephant seals. Book well in advance for a guided walking tour, given during the cacophonous winter birthing and mating season.

On a windswept coastal perch further north, **HI Pigeon Point Lighthouse Hostel** (☑650-879-0633; www.norcalhostels.org/pigeon; 210 Pigeon Point Rd; dm $26-31, d/tr from $76/104, all without bath; @🛜📶) ⊘ inhabits historic lightkeepers' quarters; it's popular, so reserve ahead. For more creature comforts, backtrack 4 miles south to bed down in a tent bungalow or a fireplace cabin at

Costanoa (☑877-262-7848, 650-879-1100; www.costanoa.com; 2001 Rossi Rd; tents/cabins without bath from $89/179, lodge r $203-291; 🛜📶).

Five miles north of Pigeon Point, turn off at **Pescadero State Beach** (www.parks.ca.gov; off Hwy 1; per car $8; ⊙8am-sunset) and drive a few miles inland to Pescadero village. Pick up picnic supplies at the bakery-deli inside **Arcangeli Grocery Co** (Norm's Market; www.normsmarket.com; 287 Stage Rd; ⊙10am-6pm). Nearby, family-owned **Harley Farms Cheese Shop** (☑650-879-0480; http://harleyfarms.com; 250 North St; 2hr tour adult/child $20/10; ⊙10am-5pm; 📶) offers goat-dairy farm tours by reservation.

Another 15 miles north, busy Half Moon Bay is bordered by 4-mile-long **Half Moon Bay State Beach** (www.parks.ca.gov; off Hwy 1; per car $10; ⊙8am-sunset; 📶), which has scenic campgrounds. Get out on the water with **Half Moon Bay Kayak** (☑650-773-6101; www.hmbkayak.com; 2 Johnson Pier; kayak/SUP rental per hour from $25; ⊙9am-5pm Wed-Mon, last rental 3:30pm). Offshore from Pillar Point Harbor, which has a decent brewpub with a sunset-view patio, dangerous **Mavericks** surf break attracts the world's top big-wave riders in winter. In Half Moon Bay's quaint downtown, eclectic shops, cafes and restaurants line Main St, just inland from Hwy 1.

North of Moss Beach off Hwy 1, **Fitzgerald Marine Reserve** (☑650-728-3584; www.fitzgeraldreserve.org; 200 Nevada Ave; ⊙8am-sunset; 📶) ⊘ **FREE** protects tide pools teeming with colorful sea life; time your visit for low tide. Another mile north, **HI Point Montara Lighthouse Hostel** (☑650-728-7177; www.norcalhostels.org/montara; cnr Hwy 1 & 16th St; dm $27-30, r $78-107, all without bath; @🛜) ⊘ perches on an ocean bluff (reservations essential). From there, it's less than 20 miles to San Francisco via beachy Pacifica and the Devil's Slide Tunnels.

SAN FRANCISCO & THE BAY AREA

San Francisco

If you've ever wondered where the envelope goes when it's pushed, here's your answer. Good times and social revolutions have often started here, from manic gold rushes to blissful hippie be-ins. Psychedelic drugs, newfangled technology, gay liberation, green ventures, free speech and culinary experimentation all became mainstream long ago in San Francisco.

Consider permission permanently granted to be outlandish: other towns may surprise you, but in San Francisco you may surprise yourself. Grab your coat and a handful of glitter, and enter the land of fog and fabulousness. So long, inhibitions; hello, San Francisco.

History

Before gold changed everything, San Francisco was a Spanish colonial mission built by conscripts from the indigenous Ohlone and Miwok communities. In 1849 the gold rush turned an 800-person village into a port city of 100,000 prospectors, con artists, prostitutes and honest folk.

Frustrated miners rioted against San Francisco's Chinese community, who from 1877 to 1943 were restricted to living and working in Chinatown by anti-Chinese laws. In the late 19th century, Chinese laborers had few options besides dangerous work building railroads for the city's robber barons, who dynamited, mined and clear-cut across the West, and built grand Nob Hill mansions. When the 1906 earthquake and fire reduced the city to rubble, San Franciscans rebuilt an astounding 15 buildings per day. By 1915, the rebuilt city hosted the Panama-Pacific International Exposition in grand style.

During WWII, soldiers accused of homosexuality and insubordination were dismissed in San Francisco, cementing the city's counterculture reputation. The 1967 'Summer of Love' brought free food, sex and music to the hippie Haight, while enterprising gay activists founded an out-and-proud community in the Castro. San Francisco's unconventional thinking is behind today's boom in social media, mobile apps and biotech.

◉ Sights

Let San Francisco's 43 hills stretch your legs and your imagination as they deliver breathtaking views.

◎ Embarcadero

★ Ferry Building   LANDMARK
(Map p128; ☑415-983-8030; www.ferrybuilding-marketplace.com; Market St & the Embarcadero; ☉10am-6pm Mon-Fri, 9am-6pm Sat, 11am-5pm Sun; P⛑; 🚃2, 6, 9, 14, 21, 31, Ⓜ Embarcadero,

Ⓑ Embarcadero) Hedonism is alive and well at this transit hub turned gourmet emporium, where foodies happily miss their ferries slurping local oysters and bubbly. Star chefs are frequently spotted at the farmers market (p136) that wraps around the building year-round.

★ Exploratorium   MUSEUM
(Map p128; ☑415-528-4444; www.exploratorium.edu; Pier 15; adult/child $29/19, 6-10pm Thu $15; ☉10am-5pm Tue-Sun, over 18yr only Thu 6-10pm; P⛑; ⓂF) ✐ Is there a science to skateboarding? Do toilets really flush counterclockwise in Australia? Find answers to questions you wished you'd learned in school, at San Francisco's thrilling hands-on science museum. Combining science with art, and investigating human perception, the Exploratorium nudges you to question how you perceive the world around you. The setting is thrilling – a 9-acre, glass-walled pier jutting straight into San Francisco Bay, with large outdoor portions you can explore free of charge, 24 hours a day.

◉ Union Square & Civic Center

Bordered by high-end department stores, **Union Square** (Map p128; intersection of Geary, Powell, Post & Stockton Sts; 🚃 Powell-Mason, Powell-Hyde, Ⓜ Powell, Ⓑ Powell) was named for pro-Union Civil War rallies held here 150 years ago. People-watch with espresso from **Emporio Rulli** (Map p128; ☑415-433-1122; www.rulli.com; Union Sq; ☉7am-7pm; Ⓜ Powell, Ⓑ Powell) cafe.

★ Asian Art Museum   MUSEUM
(Map p128; ☑415-581-3500; www.asianart.org; 200 Larkin St; adult/child/student $15/free/10, 1st Sun of month free; ☉10am-5pm Tue-Sun, to 9pm Thu; ⛑; Ⓜ Civic Center, Ⓑ Civic Center) Imaginations race from ancient Persian miniatures to cutting-edge Japanese fashion through three floors spanning 6000 years of Asian arts. Besides the largest collection outside Asia – 18,000 works – the museum offers excellent programs for all ages, from shadow-puppet shows and yoga for kids to mixers with cross-cultural DJ mash-ups.

Powell St Cable Car Turnaround   LANDMARK
(Map p128; cnr Powell & Market Sts; 🚃 Powell-Mason, Mason-Hyde, Ⓜ Powell, Ⓑ Powell) Stand awhile at Powell and Market Sts and spot arriving cable-car operators leaping out, gripping the trolley's chassis and slooowly turning the car atop a revolving wooden

platform. Cable cars can't go in reverse, so they need to be turned around by hand here at the terminus of Powell St lines. Riders queue up midmorning to early evening here to secure a seat, with raucous street performers and doomsday preachers on the sidelines as entertainment.

Chinatown

Since 1848, this community has survived riots, bootlegging gangsters and earthquakes.

Chinese Historical Society of America   MUSEUM
(CHSA; Map p128; ☑415-391-1188; www.chsa. org; 965 Clay St; ☺noon-5pm Tue-Fri, 11am-4pm Sat; ☑1, 8, 30, 45, ☑California St, Powell-Mason, Mason-Hyde) **FREE** Picture what it was like to be Chinese in America during the Gold Rush, transcontinental railroad construction or Beat heyday in this 1932 landmark, built as Chinatown's YWCA by Julia Morgan (chief architect of Hearst Castle). CHSA historians unearth fascinating artifacts, such as 1920s silk *qipao* dresses worn by socialites from Shanghai to San Francisco. Exhibits reveal once-popular views of Chinatown, including the sensationalist opium-den exhibit at San Francisco's 1915 Panama-Pacific International Expo, inviting fairgoers to 'Go Slumming' in Chinatown.

North Beach

City Lights   CULTURAL CENTER, LANDMARK
(Map p128; ☑415-362-8193; www.citylights.com; 261 Columbus Ave; ☺10am-midnight; ☑; ☑8, 10, 12, 30, 41, 45, ☑Powell-Mason, Powell-Hyde) Free speech and free spirits have flourished at City Lights since 1957, when founder and poet Lawrence Ferlinghetti and manager Shigeyoshi Murao won a landmark ruling defending their right to publish Allen Ginsberg's magnificent epic poem 'Howl.' Celebrate your right to read freely in the sunny upstairs Poetry Room, with its piles of freshly published verse and designated Poet's Chair.

Beat Museum   MUSEUM
(Map p128; ☑800-537-6822; www.kerouac.com; 540 Broadway; adult/student $8/5, walking tours $25; ☺museum 10am-7pm, walking tours 2-4pm Mon, Wed & Sat; ☑8, 10, 12, 30, 41, 45, ☑Powell-Mason) The closest you can get to the complete Beat experience without breaking a law. The 1000-plus artifacts in this museum's literary ephemera collection include the sublime (the banned edition of Ginsberg's *Howl*) and the ridiculous (those Kerouac bobble-head dolls are definite head-shakers). Downstairs, watch Beat-era films in ramshackle theater seats redolent with the odors of literary giants, pets and pot. Upstairs, pay respects at shrines to individual Beat writers. Guided two-hour walking tours cover the museum, Beat history and literary alleys.

San Francisco & the Bay Area

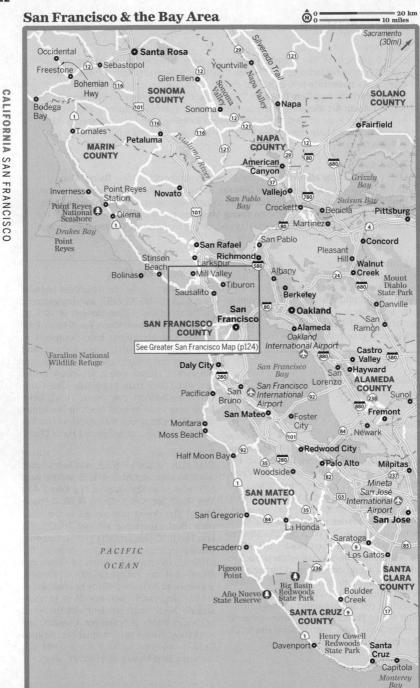

Russian Hill & Nob Hill

Lombard Street AREA

(Map p128; 900 block of Lombard St; 🚠 Powell-Hyde) You've seen its eight switchbacks in a thousand photographs. The tourist board has dubbed this 'the world's crookedest street,' which is factually incorrect. Vermont St in Potrero Hill deserves that award, but Lombard is much more scenic, with its red-brick pavement and lovingly tended flowerbeds. It wasn't always so bent; before the arrival of the automobile it lunged straight down the hill.

Cable Car Museum HISTORIC SITE

(Map p128; 📞 415-474-1887; www.cablecarmuseum.org; 1201 Mason St; donations appreciated; ⊙ 10am-6pm Apr-Sep, to 5pm Oct-Mar; 🚼; 🚠 Powell-Mason, Powell-Hyde) **FREE** Hear that whirring beneath the cable-car tracks? That's the sound of the cables that pull the cars, and they all connect inside the city's long-functioning cable-car barn. Grips, engines, braking mechanisms...if these warm your gearhead heart, you'll be besotted by the Cable Car Museum. See three original 1870s cable cars and watch cables whir over massive bull wheels – as awesome a feat of physics now as when Andrew Hallidie invented it in 1873.

Fisherman's Wharf

Maritime National Historical Park HISTORIC SITE

(Map p128; www.nps.gov/safr; 499 Jefferson St, Hyde St Pier; 7-day ticket adult/child $5/free; ⊙ 9:30am-5pm Oct-May, to 5:30pm Jun-Sep; 🚼; 🚌 19, 30, 47, 🚠 Powell-Hyde, 🚇 F) Four historic ships are floating museums at this national park, Fisherman's Wharf's most authentic attraction. Moored along Hyde St Pier, standouts include the 1891 schooner *Alma*, 1890 steamboat *Eureka*, paddle-wheel tugboat *Eppleton Hall* and iron-hulled *Balclutha*, which brought coal to San Francisco. It's free to walk the pier; pay only to board ships.

Maritime Museum MUSEUM

(Aquatic Park Bathhouse; Map p128; www.maritime.org; 900 Beach St; ⊙ 10am-4pm; 🚼; 🚌 19, 30, 47, 🚠 Powell-Hyde) **FREE** A monumental hint to sailors in need of a scrub, this restored, shipshape 1939 streamline-moderne landmark is decked out with Works Progress Administration (WPA) art treasures: playful seal and frog sculptures by Beniamino Bufano,

DON'T MISS

ALCATRAZ

Alcatraz (Map p124; 📞 Alcatraz Cruises 415-981-7625; www.alcatrazcruises.com; day tours adult/child/family $30/18/90, night tours adult/child $37/22; ⊙ call center 8am-7pm, ferries depart Pier 33 half-hourly 8:45am-3:50pm, night tours 5:55pm & 6:30pm) For more than 150 years, Alcatraz has given the innocent chills and the guilty cold sweats. It served as the nation's first military prison, a maximum-security penitentiary housing A-list criminals including Al Capone, and disputed territory between Native American activists and the FBI. No prisoners ever escaped Alcatraz alive, but since importing guards and supplies cost more than putting up prisoners at the Ritz, the prison was shuttered in 1963.

Day visits include the cruise to and from the island and captivating audio tours, with past prisoners and guards recalling life on 'the Rock.' Eerie night tours are led by a park ranger. Reserve tickets at least a month ahead.

Hilaire Hiler's surreal underwater dreamscape murals and recently uncovered wood reliefs by Richard Ayer. Acclaimed African American artist Sargent Johnson created the stunning carved green slate marquee doorway and the verandah's mesmerizing aquatic mosaics.

The Marina & Presidio

Crissy Field PARK

(Map p124; www.crissyfield.org; 1199 East Beach; 🅿; 🚌 30, PresidiGo Shuttle) War is for the birds at Crissy Field, a military airstrip turned waterfront nature preserve with knockout Golden Gate views. Where military aircraft once zoomed in for landings, bird-watchers now huddle in the silent rushes of a reclaimed tidal marsh. Joggers pound beachside trails and the only security alerts are raised by puppies suspiciously sniffing surfers. On foggy days, stop by the certified-green Warming Hut to browse regional-nature books and warm up with fair-trade coffee.

Presidio Officers' Club HISTORIC BUILDING

(Map p124; 📞 415-561-4165; www.presidioofficersclub.com; 50 Moraga Ave; ⊙ 10am-6pm Tue-Sun;

Greater San Francisco

See Downtown San Francisco Map (p128)

PresidiGo Shuttle) **FREE** The Presidio's oldest building dates to the late 1700s, and got a total renovation in 2015, revealing gorgeous Spanish-Moorish adobe architecture. The free Heritage Gallery shows the history of the Presidio, from Native American days to present. Moraga Hall – the former officers' club lounge – is a lovely spot to sit fireside and also has free wi-fi. Thursday and Friday evenings, the Club hosts a dynamic lineup of events and lectures; check the website.

Baker Beach BEACH
(Map p124; ☉ sunrise-sunset; **P**; ☐ 29, PresidiGo Shuttle) Picnic amid wind-sculpted pines, fish from craggy rocks or frolic nude at mile-long Baker Beach, with spectacular views of the bridge. Crowds come weekends, especially on fog-free days; arrive early. For nude sunbathing (mostly straight girls and gay boys), head to the north end. Families in clothing stick to the south end, nearer the parking lot. Mind the currents and the c-c-cold water.

The Mission & the Castro

⭐**Balmy Alley** PUBLIC ART
(Map p124; ☑ 415-285-2287; www.precitaeyes.org; btwn 24th & 25th Sts; ☐ 10, 12, 14, 27, 48, **B** 24th St Mission) Inspired by Diego Rivera's 1930s San Francisco murals and outraged by US foreign policy in Central America, 1970s Mission *muralistas* (muralists) set out to transform the political landscape, one mural-covered garage door at a time. Today, Balmy Alley murals span three decades, from an early memorial for El Salvador activist Archbishop Óscar Romero to a homage to Frida Kahlo, Georgia O'Keefe and other trailblazing modern women artists.

Mission Dolores CHURCH
(Misión San Francisco de Asís; ☑ 415-621-8203; www.missiondolores.org; 3321 16th St; adult/child

Greater San Francisco

$5/3; ⊘ 9am-4pm Nov-Apr, to 4:30pm May-Oct; 🚌 22, 33, Ⓑ 16th St Mission, Ⓜ J) The city's oldest building and its namesake, whitewashed adobe Misión San Francisco de Asís was founded in 1776 and rebuilt in 1782 with conscripted Ohlone and Miwok labor – a graveyard memorial hut commemorates 5000 Ohlone and Miwok laborers who died in mission measles epidemics in 1814 and 1826. Today the modest adobe mission is overshadowed by the ornate adjoining 1913 basilica, featuring stained-glass windows of California's 21 missions.

GLBT History Museum　　　　MUSEUM
(📞 415-621-1107; www.glbthistory.org/museum; 4127 18th St; admission $5, 1st Wed of month free; ⊘ 11am-7pm Mon-Sat, noon-5pm Sun; closed Tue fall-spring; Ⓜ Castro) America's first gay-history museum cobbles ephemera from the community – Harvey Milk's campaign literature, matchbooks from long-gone bathhouses, photographs of early activists – together with harder-hitting installations that focus on various aspects of queer history, incorporating electronic media to tell personal stories that illuminate the evolution of the struggle to gain rights and acceptance into the larger culture.

Dolores Park　　　　　　　　PARK
(http://sfrecpark.org/destination/mission-dolores-park/; Dolores St, btwn 18th & 20th Sts; 🚼 🐕; 🚌 14, 33, 49, Ⓑ 16th St Mission, Ⓜ J) Semiprofessional tanning, taco picnics and a Hunky Jesus Contest at Easter: welcome to San Francisco's sunny side. Dolores Park has something

for everyone, from street ball and tennis to the Mayan-pyramid playground (sorry kids: no blood sacrifice allowed). Political protests and other favorite local sports happen year-round, and there are free movie nights and Mime Troupe performances in summer. Climb to the upper southwest corner for the best views of downtown, framed by palm trees.

◉ The Haight & Around

Haight & Ashbury　　　　　LANDMARK
(🚌 6, 7, 33, 37, 43) This legendary intersection was the epicenter of the psychedelic '60s and remains a counterculture magnet. On average Saturdays here you can sign Green Party petitions, commission a poem, hear Hare Krishna on keyboards and Bob Dylan on banjo. The clock overhead always reads 4:20 – better known in herbal circles as International Bong-Hit Time. A local clockmaker recently fixed it; within a week it was stuck at 4:20.

Alamo Square Park　　　　　PARK
(www.sfparksalliance.org/our-parks/parks/alamo-square; Hayes & Scott Sts; ⊘ sunrise-sunset; 🐕; 🚌 5, 21, 22, 24) The pastel Painted Ladies of famed Postcard Row along the east side pale in comparison with the colorful characters along the northwest end of this 1857 Victorian hilltop park. Alamo Square's north side features Barbary Coast baroque mansions at their most bombastic, bedecked with fish-scale shingles and gingerbread trim dripping from peaked roofs.

Alcatraz

Book a ferry from Pier 33 and ride 1.5 miles across the bay to explore America's most notorious former prison. The trip itself is worth the money, providing stunning views of the city skyline. Once you've landed at the **Ferry Dock & Pier 1**, you begin the 580-yard walk to the top of the island and prison; if you're out of shape, there's a twice-hourly tram.

As you climb toward the **Guardhouse 2**, notice the island's steep slope; before it was a prison, Alcatraz was a fort. In the 1850s, the military quarried the rocky shores into near-vertical cliffs. Ships could then only dock at a single port, separated from the main buildings by a sally port (a drawbridge and moat in what became the guardhouse). Inside, peer through floor grates to see Alcatraz' original prison.

Volunteers tend the brilliant **Officer's Row Gardens 3** – an orderly counterpoint to the overgrown rose bushes surrounding the burned-out shell of the **Warden's House 4**. At the top of the hill, by the front door of the **Main Cellhouse 5**, beautiful shots unfurl all around, including a **view of the Golden Gate Bridge 6**. Above the main door of the administration building, notice the **historic signs & graffiti 7**, before you step inside the dank, cold prison to find the **Frank Morris cell 8**, former home to Alcatraz' most notorious jail-breaker.

TOP TIPS

➜ Book at least one month prior for self-guided daytime visits, longer for ranger-led night tours. For info on garden tours, see www.alcatraz gardens.org.

➜ Be prepared to hike; a steep path ascends from the ferry landing to the cell block. Most people spend two to three hours on the island. You need only reserve for the outbound ferry; take any ferry back.

➜ There's no food (just water) but you can bring your own; picnicking is allowed at the ferry dock only. Dress in layers as weather changes fast and it's usually windy.

EMMA DURNFORD / GETTY IMAGES ©

Historic Signs & Graffiti
During their 1969–71 occupation, Native Americans graffitied the water tower: 'Home of the Free Indian Land.' Above the cellhouse door, examine the eagle-and-flag crest to see how the red-and-white stripes were changed to spell 'Free.'

Warden's House
Fires destroyed the warden's house and other structures during the Indian Occupation. The government blamed the Native Americans; the Native Americans blamed agents provocateurs acting on behalf of the Nixon Administration to undermine public sympathy.

Parade Grounds

DAVID CLAPP / GETTY IMAGES ©

Ferry Dock & Pier
A giant wall map helps you get your bearings. Inside nearby Bldg 64, short films and exhibits provide historical perspective on the prison and details about the Indian Occupation.

View of Golden Gate Bridge
The Golden Gate Bridge stretches wide on the horizon. Best views are from atop the island at Eagle Plaza, near the cellhouse entrance, and at water level along the Agave Trail (September to January only).

Main Cellhouse
During the mid-20th century, the maximum-security prison housed the day's most notorious troublemakers, including Al Capone and Robert Stroud, the 'Birdman of Alcatraz' (who actually conducted his ornithology studies at Leavenworth).

Power House

Recreation Yard

Water Tower

Officers' Club

5

8

6

7

3

4

2

Lighthouse

Guard Tower

1

Frank Morris Cell
Peer into cell 138 on B-Block to see a re-creation of the dummy's head that Frank Morris left in his bed as a decoy to aid his notorious – and successful – 1962 escape from Alcatraz.

Guardhouse
Alcatraz' oldest building dates to 1857 and retains remnants of the original drawbridge and moat. During the Civil War the basement was transformed into a military dungeon – the genesis of Alcatraz as prison.

Officer's Row Gardens
In the 19th century soldiers imported topsoil to beautify the island with gardens. Well-trusted prisoners later gardened – Elliott Michener said it kept him sane. Historians, ornithologists and archaeologists choose today's plants.

Downtown San Francisco

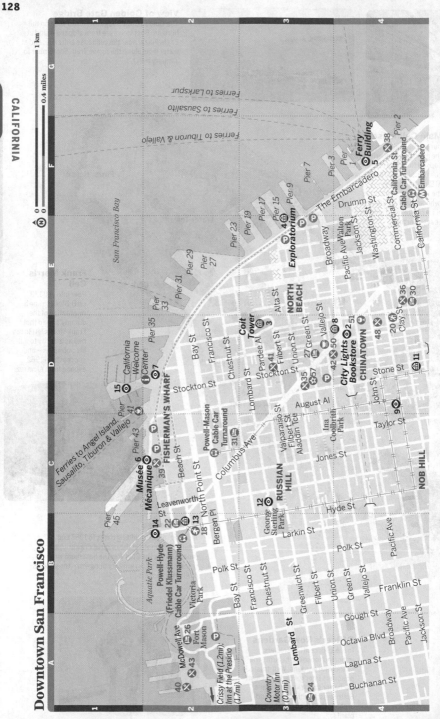

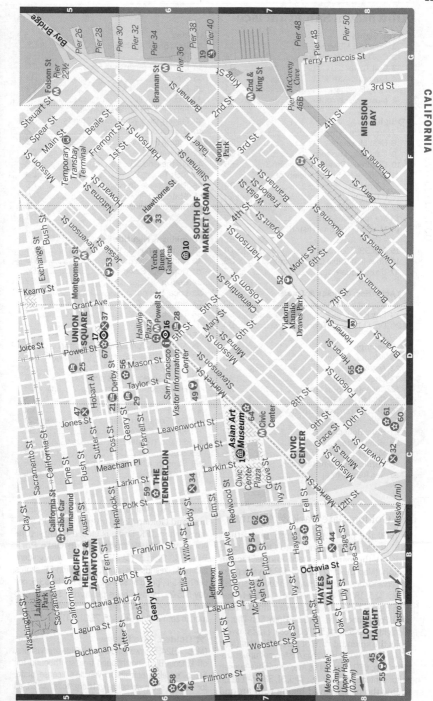

Downtown San Francisco

⊙ Golden Gate Park & Around

In 1865 the city voted to turn more than 1000 acres of sand dunes into Golden Gate Park. At the park's western end is **Ocean Beach** (Map p124; ☎ 415-561-4323; www.parks conservancy.org; Great Hwy; ☺ sunrise-sunset; P⊞; ☐ 5, 18, 31, Ⓜ N), where **Cliff House** (Map p124; ☎ 415-386-3330; www.cliffhouse.com; 1090 Point Lobos Ave; ☺ 9am-11pm Sun-Thu, to midnight Fri & Sat; ☐ 5, 18, 31, 38) FREE overlooks the splendid ruin of **Sutro Baths** (Map p124; www.nps.gov/goga/historyculture/sutrobaths.htm; 680 Point Lobos Ave; ☺ sunrise-sunset; visitor center 9am-5pm; P; ☐ 5, 31, 38) ✐ FREE. Follow the partly paved hiking trail around

Lands End (Map p124) for shipwreck sightings and Golden Gate Bridge views. On Sundays, when JFK Drive is closed to cars, rent your own wheels from **Golden Gate Park Bike & Skate** (☎ 415-668-1117; www.goldengateparkbikeandskate.com; 3038 Fulton St; skates per hr $5-6, per day $20-24, bikes per hr $3-5, per day $15-25, tandem bikes per hr/day $15/75, disc golf bags for 2 people $6/25; ☺ 10am-6pm summer, to 7pm winter; ⊞; ☐ 5, 21, 31, 44).

★ **Golden Gate Bridge**   BRIDGE
(Map p124; www.goldengatebridge.org/visitors; off Lincoln Blvd; northbound free, southbound toll $6, billed electronically to vehicle's license plate, for details, see www.goldengate.org/tolls; ☐ 28, all

Golden Gate Transit buses) San Franciscans have passionate perspectives on every subject, especially their signature landmark, though everyone agrees that it's a good thing that the navy didn't get its way over the bridge's design – naval officials preferred a hulking concrete span, painted with caution-yellow stripes, over the soaring art-deco design of architects Gertrude and Irving Murrow and engineer Joseph B Strauss, which, luckily, won the day.

★ **California Academy of Sciences** MUSEUM
(Map p124; ☑ 415-379-8000; www.calacademy.org; 55 Music Concourse Dr; adult/child $34.95/24.95; ☺9:30am-5pm Mon-Sat, 11am-5pm Sun; P 🚼; 🚍5, 6, 7, 21, 31, 33, 44, M N) 🐾 Architect Renzo Piano's 2008 landmark LEED-certified green building houses 40,000 weird and wonderful animals in a four-story rainforest and split-level aquarium under a 'living roof' of California wildflowers. After the penguins nod off to sleep, the wild rumpus starts at kids-only Academy Sleepovers ($109; ages five to 17, plus adult chaperones; 6pm to 8am including snack and breakfast) and over-21 NightLife Thursdays ($12), when rainforest-themed cocktails encourage strange mating rituals among shy internet daters.

de Young Museum MUSEUM
(☑ 415-750-3600; http://deyoung.famsf.org/; 50 Hagiwara Tea Garden Dr; adult/child $10/6, discount with Muni ticket $2, 1st Tue of month free, online booking fee per ticket $1; ☺9:30am-5:15pm Tue-Sun, to 8:45pm Fri Apr-Nov; 🚍5, 7, 44, M N) Follow sculptor Andy Goldsworthy's artificial fault line in the sidewalk into Herzog & de Meuron's sleek, copper-clad building that's oxidizing green to blend into the park. Don't be fooled by the de Young's camouflaged exterior: shows here boldly broaden artistic horizons, from Oceanic ceremonial masks and Oscar de la Renta gowns to James Turrell's domed 'Skyspace' installation, built into a hill in the sculpture garden.

Legion of Honor MUSEUM
(Map p124; ☑ 415-750-3600; http://legionofhonor. famsf.org; 100 34th Ave; adult/child $10/6, discount with Muni ticket $2, 1st Tue of month free; ☺9:30am-5:15pm Tue-Sun; 🚼; 🚍1, 2, 18, 38) A museum as eccentric and illuminating as San Francisco itself, the Legion showcases a wildly eclectic collection ranging from Monet water lilies to John Cage soundscapes, ancient Iraqi ivories to R Crumb comics. Upstairs are blockbust-

er shows of Old Masters and Impressionists, but don't miss selections from the Legion's Achenbach Foundation of Graphic Arts collection of 90,0000 works on paper, ranging from Rembrandt to Ed Ruscha.

Japanese Tea Garden GARDENS
(☑ tea ceremony reservations 415-752-1171; www. japaneseteagardensf.com; 75 Hagiwara Tea Garden Dr; adult/child $8/2, before 10am Mon, Wed & Fri free; ☺9am-6pm Mar-Oct, to 4:45pm Nov-Feb; P 🚼; 🚍5, 7, 44, M N) Since 1894, this picturesque 5-acre garden and bonsai grove has blushed with cherry blossoms in spring, turned flaming red with maple leaves in fall, and lost all track of time in the meditative Zen Garden.

🏃 Activities

Blazing Saddles CYCLING
(Map p128; ☑ 415-202-8888; www.blazingsaddles. com/san-francisco; 2715 Hyde St; bicycle rental per hour $8-15, per day $32-88, electric bikes per day $48-88; ☺8am-8pm; 🚼; 🚋Powell-Hyde) Blazing Saddles is tailored to visitors, with a main shop on Hyde St and six rental stands around Fisherman's Wharf, convenient for biking the Embarcadero or to the Golden Gate Bridge. It also rents electric bikes and offers 24-hour return service – a big plus. Reserve online for a 10% discount; rental includes all extras (bungee cords, packs etc).

DON'T MISS

COIT TOWER

Adding an exclamation mark to San Francisco's skyline, **Coit Tower** (Map p128; ☑ 415-249-0995; http://sfrecpark. org/destination/telegraph-hill-pioneer-park/ coit-tower; Telegraph Hill Blvd; elevator entry (nonresident) adult/child $8/5; ☺10am-6pm May-Oct, 9am-5pm Nov-Apr; 🚍39) offers views worth shouting about – especially after you climb the steep wooden **Filbert Street steps** up Telegraph Hill to get here. Check out 360-degree panoramas from the open-air viewing platform, and the wraparound 1930s lobby murals glorifying workers – once denounced as communist but now a landmark. To glimpse more murals hidden inside a stairwell, join a free docent-led tour at 11am on Wednesday or Saturday.

City Kayak KAYAKING
(Map p128; ☑ 415-294-1050; www.citykayak.com;
Pier 40, South Beach Harbor; kayak rentals per
hour $35-65, 3hr lesson & rental $59, tours $58-98;
⊘ rentals 11am-3pm, return by 5pm Thu-Mon; ☐ 30,
45, Ⓜ N,T) You haven't seen San Francisco until you've seen it from the water. Newbies to
kayaking can take lessons and paddle calm
waters near the Bay Bridge, alone or escort-
ed; experienced paddlers can brave choppy
Bay currents near the Golden Gate (conditions permitting; get advice first). Sporty
romantics take note: calm-water moonlight
tours are ideal for proposals. Check website
for details.

Tours

★ Precita Eyes Mission Mural Tours
WALKING TOUR
(☑ 415-285-2287; www.precitaeyes.org; adult $15-
20, child $3; ⊘ see website calendar for tour dates;
⧐; ☐ 12, 14, 48, 49, Ⓑ 24th St Mission) Muralists
lead weekend walking tours covering 60 to
70 Mission murals in a six- to 10-block radius of mural-bedecked Balmy Alley. Tours last
from 90 minutes and up to 2½ hours for the
more in-depth Classic Mural Walk. Proceeds
fund mural upkeep at this community arts
nonprofit.

Drag Me Along Tours
WALKING TOUR
(Map p128; http://www.dragmealongtours.com; tour
begins in Portsmouth Square; tours $20; ⊘ tours
usually 11am-1pm Sun; ☐ 1, 8, 10, 12, 30, 41, 45,
⧐ California, Powell-Mason, Powell-Hyde) Explore
San Francisco's bawdy Barbary Coast with a
bona-fide legend: Gold Rush burlesque star
Countess Lola Montez, reincarnated in drag
by San Francisco historian Rick Shelton.
Her Highness leads you through Chinatown
alleyways where Victorian ladies made and
lost reputations to Jackson Square saloons
where sailors were shanghaied, introducing
Barbary Coast characters who gambled big,
loved hard and lived large.
Adult content; reservations required;
cash only.

Haight-Ashbury Flower Power Walking Tour
WALKING TOUR
(☑ 415-863-1621; www.haightashburytour.com;
adult/under 10yr $20/free; ⊘ 10:30am Tue & Sat,
2pm Fri; ☐ 6, 71, Ⓜ N) Take a long, strange trip
through 12 blocks of hippie history, following in the steps of Jimi, Jerry and Janis – if
you have to ask for last names, you really
need this tour, man. Tours meet at the cor-

ner of Stanyan and Waller Sts and last about
two hours; reservations required.

Public Library City Guides
TOUR
(☑ 415-557-4266; www.sfcityguides.org; dona-
tions/tips welcome) FREE Volunteer local historians lead nonprofit tours organized by
neighborhood and theme: Art Deco Marina,
Gold Rush Downtown, Secrets of Fisherman's Wharf, Telegraph Hill Stairway Hike
and more.

★ Festivals & Events

Lunar New Year
CULTURAL
(www.chineseparade.com; ⊘ Feb) Chase the
200ft dragon, lion dancers and frozen-smile
runners-up for the Miss Chinatown title
during Lunar New Year celebrations. Fire-
crackers and fierce legions of tiny-tot mar-
tial artists make this parade at the end of
February the highlight of San Francisco
winters.

Bay to Breakers
SPORTS
(www.baytobreakers.com; race registration from
$64; ⊘ May) Run in costume or wearing not
much at all from Embarcadero to Ocean
Beach the third Sunday in May, while joggers dressed as salmon run upstream.

SF Pride Celebration
CULTURAL
(⊘ Jun) A day isn't enough to do SF proud:
June begins with the **International LGBT
Film Festival** (www.frameline.org; ⊘ mid-Jun),
and goes out in style the last weekend with
Saturday's **Dyke March** (www.dykemarch.org)
to the Castro's Pink Party and the joyous,
million-strong Pride Parade.

Hardly Strictly Bluegrass
MUSIC
(http://www.hardlystrictlybluegrass.com; ⊘ Oct)
The West goes wild for free bluegrass at
Golden Gate Park, with three days of concerts and three stages of headliners; held
early October.

Sleeping

Boutique and luxury hotels abound around
Union Square, Nob Hill and SoMa, while
Fisherman's Wharf and the Marina accommodations are mostly motels and chain hotels. Offbeat inns, small hotels and cozy B&Bs
await in less-touristed neighbourhoods.
Expect to pay $35 to $55 for overnight
parking.
Quoted rates do not include hotel tax
(15.5%), from which hostels are exempt.

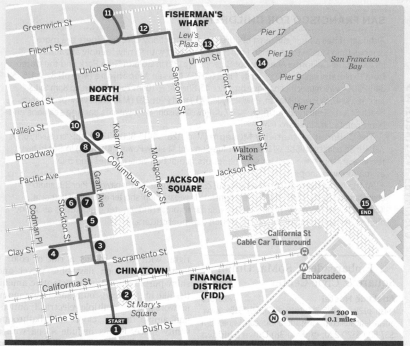

🏃 City Walk
Chinatown to the Waterfront

START CHINATOWN'S DRAGON GATE
END FERRY BUILDING
LENGTH 2.5 MILES; FIVE HOURS

Starting at Chinatown's ❶ **Dragon Gate**, head past Grant St's gilded dragon lamps to ❷ **Old St Mary's Square**, site of a brothel leveled in the 1906 fire. Today, renegade skateboarders turn different kinds of tricks under the watchful eye of Beniamino Bufano's 1929 statue of Chinese revolutionary Sun Yat-Sen. Pass flag-festooned temple balconies along ❸ **Waverly Place**, then head to the ❹ **Chinese Historical Society of America** (p121) museum, in the majestic Chinatown YWCA designed by Julia Morgan.

Enter ❺ **Spofford Alley**, where mahjongg tiles click, Chinese orchestras play and beauticians gossip over blow-dryers – hard to believe this is where Prohibition bootleggers fought turf wars, and Sun Yat-Sen plotted the 1911 overthrow of China's last dynasty at No 36. Once packed with brothels, ❻ **Ross Alley** turned movie star as a location for *Karate*

Kid II and *Indiana Jones and the Temple of Doom*. At No 56, make a fortune and watch it get folded into a warm cookie at the ❼ **Golden Gate Fortune Cookie Factory**.

Back on Grant Ave, take a shortcut through Jack Kerouac Alley, where the binge-prone author often wound up 'on the road'. Stop by ❽ **City Lights Bookstore** (p121) on Columbus Ave, champion of Beat poetry and free speech, then hop down Broadway into the ❾ **Beat Museum** (p121). Savor espresso at ❿ **Caffe Trieste**, under the Sardinian fishing mural where Francis Ford Coppola wrote *The Godfather* script.

Climb waaaay up to ⓫ **Coit Tower** (p131) for glorious bay-view panoramas and historic murals. Take the head-spinning ⓬ **Filbert Street Steps** downhill past wild parrots and hidden cottages to ⓭ **Levi's Plaza**, named for the coinventor of denim pants with rivets – aka American blue jeans. Head right on Embarcadero to the fun-for-all-ages ⓮ **Exploratorium** (p120) before having lunch bayside at the landmark ⓯ **Ferry Building** (p120), with its thrice-weekly outdoor farmers market.

SAN FRANCISCO FOR CHILDREN

Although it has almost the least children per capita of any US city – there are more canines than kids in town – San Francisco is packed with family-friendly attractions, including the California Academy of Sciences (p131) in Golden Gate Park and the waterfront Exploratorium (p120), Crissy Field (p123), **Musée Mécanique** (Map p128; ☑415-346-2000; www.museemechanique.org; Pier 45, Shed A; ⊙10am-7pm Mon-Fri, to 8pm Sat & Sun; ♿; ▢47, ▣Powell-Mason, Powell-Hyde, Ⓜ F) and **Pier 39** (Map p128; www.pier39.com; Beach St & the Embarcadero; Ⓟ♿; ▢47, ▣Powell-Mason, Ⓜ F), with its barking sea lions and hand-painted Italian carousel.

The **Children's Creativity Museum** (Map p128; ☑415-820-3320; http://creativity.org/; 221 4th St; admission $12; ⊙10am-4pm Tue-Sun; ♿; ▢14, Ⓜ Powell, Ⓑ Powell) in SoMa has technology that's too cool for school: robots, live-action video games and 3-D animation workshops.

At the **Aquarium of the Bay** (Map p128; www.aquariumofthebay.org; Pier 39; adult/child/family $21.95/12.95/64; ⊙9am-8pm late May-early Sep, shorter off-season hours; ♿; ▢49, ▣Powell-Mason, Ⓜ F) on Pier 39, wander through underwater glass tubes as sharks circle overhead, then let tots gently touch tide-pool critters.

🛏 Embarcadero, SoMa, Union Square & Civic Center

Adelaide Hostel
HOSTEL **$**

(Map p128; ☑415-359-1915, 877-359-1915; www.adelaidehostel.com; 5 Isadora Duncan Lane; dm $37-50, r $120-220; @🛜; ▢38) Down a hidden alley, the 22-room Adelaide has up-to-date furnishings and marble-tiled baths – also the occasional rust stain and dust bunny. Extras include breakfast, group activities and two common areas (one quiet). Good service; friendly crowd. Note: your private room may wind up being in the nearby Dakota or Fitzgerald Hotels; of the two, Fitzgerald is the better.

Golden Gate Hotel
HOTEL **$$**

(Map p128; ☑415-392-3702; www.goldengatehotel.com; 775 Bush St; r $215, without bathroom $145; @🛜; ▢2, 3, ▣Powell-Hyde, Powell-Mason) Like an old-fashioned pension, the Golden Gate has kindly owners and simple rooms with mismatched furniture, inside a 1913 Edwardian hotel safely up the hill from the Tenderloin. Rooms are small, clean and comfortable and most have private bathrooms (some with antique claw-foot bathtubs). Enormous croissants, homemade cookies and a resident cat provide TLC after long days of sightseeing.

★ Marker
BOUTIQUE HOTEL **$$**

(Map p128; ☑844-736-2753, 415-292-0100; http://themarkersanfrancisco.com; 501 Geary St; r from $209; ✴@🛜♿; ▢38, ▣Powell-Hyde, Powell-Mason) 🍃 Snazzy Marker gets details right, with guest rooms a riot of color – lipstick-red lacquer, navy-blue velvet and shiny-purple silk – plus substantive amenities like high-thread-count sheets, ergonomic workspaces, multiple electrical outlets, and ample drawer, closet and bathroom-vanity space. Extras include a spa with a Jacuzzi, small gym, evening wine reception and bragging rights to a stylin' address.

Hotel Zetta
HOTEL **$$$**

(Map p128; ☑415-543-8555, 855-212-4187; www.hotelzetta.com; 55 5th St; r from $324; ✴@🛜♿🛜; Ⓑ Powell St, Ⓜ Powell St) 🍃 Opened 2013, this snappy eco-conscious downtowner by the Viceroy group plays to techies who work too much, with a mezzanine-level 'play room' with billiards, shuffleboard and two-story-high Plinko wall rising above the art-filled lobby. Upstairs, bigger-than-average rooms look sharp with padded black-leather headboards and low-slung platform beds; web-enabled flat-screen TVs link with your devices.

🛏 North Beach

Pacific Tradewinds Hostel
HOSTEL **$**

(Map p128; ☑415-433-7970, 888-734-6783; http://san-francisco-hostel.com; 680 Sacramento St; dm $38; ⊙front desk 8am to midnight; @🛜; ▢1, ▣California St, Ⓑ Montgomery) San Francisco's smartest-looking all-dorm hostel has a blue-and-white nautical theme, fully equipped kitchen, spotless glass-brick showers and no lockout time. Bunks are bolted to the wall so there's no bed-shaking when your bunkmate shifts. Alas, no elevator means hauling bags up three flights but it's worth it. Great service, fun staff.

San Remo Hotel
HOTEL $

(Map p128; ☎ 415-776-8688; www.sanremohotel. com; 2237 Mason St; r without bathroom $119-159; @ ☎ ☎; ☐ 30, 47, ☐ Powell-Mason) One of the city's best-value stays, the San Remo dates to 1906 and is long on old-fashioned charm. Rooms are simply done with mismatched turn-of-the-century furnishings and all rooms share bathrooms. Think reputable, vintage boarding house. Note: least expensive rooms have windows onto the corridor, not the outdoors. Family suites accommodate up to five. No elevator.

Hotel Bohème
BOUTIQUE HOTEL $$

(Map p128; ☎ 415-433-9111; www.hotelboheme. com; 444 Columbus Ave; r $225-295; @ ☎; ☐ 10, 12, 30, 41, 45) Our favorite boutique hotel is a love letter to the Beat era, with moody color schemes, Chinese umbrellas as light fixtures and photos from the Beat years on the walls. Rooms are smallish, some front on noisy Columbus Ave (quieter rooms are in back) and bathrooms are teensy, but it's smack in North Beach's vibrant scene. No elevator.

🛏 Fisherman's Wharf, the Marina & Presidio

★ HI San Francisco Fisherman's Wharf
HOSTEL $

(Map p128; ☎ 415-771-7277; www.sfhostels.com; Bldg 240, Fort Mason; dm incl breakfast $30-42, r $75-109; P @ ☎; ☐ 28, 30, 47, 49) Trading downtown convenience for a glorious park-like setting with million-dollar waterfront views, this hostel occupies a former army hospital building, with bargain-priced private rooms and dorms (some coed) with four to 22 beds (avoid bunks one and two – they're by doorways). Huge kitchen. No curfew but no heat during daytime: bring warm clothes. Limited free parking.

Coventry Motor Inn
MOTEL $$

(Map p128; ☎ 415-567-1200; www.coventrymotorinn.com; 1901 Lombard St; r $160-225; P ☎ ☎ ♿; ☐ 22, 28, 30, 43) Of the many motels lining Lombard St (Hwy 101), the generic Coventry has the highest quality-to-value ratio with spacious, well-maintained (if plain) rooms and extras like air-con (good for quiet sleeps) and covered parking. Parents: there's plenty of floor space to unpack kids' toys, but no pool.

★ Inn at the Presidio
HOTEL $$$

(☎ 415-800-7356; www.innatthepresidio.com; 42 Moraga Ave; r $270-360; P @ ☎ ☎; ☐ 43, PresidiGo Shuttle) 🍃 Built in 1903 as bachelor quarters for army officers, this three-story red-brick building in the Presidio was transformed in 2012 into a spiffy national-park lodge, styled with leather, linen and wood. Oversized rooms are plush, including feather beds with Egyptian-cotton sheets. Suites have fireplaces. Nature surrounds you, with hiking trailheads out back, but taxis downtown cost $25.

Argonaut Hotel
BOUTIQUE HOTEL $$$

(Map p128; ☎ 415-563-0800; www.argonauthotel. com; 495 Jefferson St; r from $439, with view from $489; ❄ ☎ ♿ ☎; ☐ 19, 47, 49, ☐ Powell-Hyde) 🍃 Fisherman's Wharf's top hotel was built as a cannery in 1908 and has century-old wooden beams and exposed-brick walls. Rooms sport an over-the-top nautical theme, with porthole-shaped mirrors and plush, deep-blue carpets. Though all have the amenities of an upper-end hotel – ultracomfy beds, iPod docks – some rooms are tiny with limited sunlight.

🛏 The Mission & the Castro

Inn San Francisco
B&B $$

(☎ 415-641-0188; www.innsf.com; 943 S Van Ness Ave; r $215-255, without bathroom $165-225, cottages $385-475; P @ ☎ ☎; ☐ 14, 49) 🍃 This stately Mission-district inn occupies an elegant 1872 Italianate-Victorian mansion, impeccably maintained, packed with antiques. All rooms have fresh-cut flowers and sumptuous mattresses with featherbeds; some have a Jacuzzi. There's also a freestanding garden cottage that sleeps up to six. Outside there's an English garden and redwood hot tub open 24 hours (a rarity). Limited parking: reserve ahead. No elevator.

Inn on Castro
B&B $$

(☎ 415-861-0321; www.innoncastro.com; 321 Castro St; r incl breakfast $235-275, without bathroom $165-185, self-catering apt $235-290; ☎; Ⓜ Castro) A portal to the Castro's disco heyday, this Edwardian townhouse is decked out with top-end '70s-mod furnishings. Rooms are retro-cool and spotlessly kept. Exceptional breakfasts – the owner is a chef. Several nearby, great-value apartments are also available for rental. No elevator. LGBT friendly.

CALIFORNIA SAN FRANCISCO

The Haight

Metro Hotel HOTEL $
(☑415-861-5364; www.metrohotelsf.com; 319 Divisadero St; r $88-100; @☎; ☐6, 24, 71) On a thoroughfare bisecting the Upper and Lower Haight districts, this straightforward, zero-frills hotel provides cheap, clean rooms with private bathroom, an outdoor garden patio and 24-hour reception. Some rooms have two double beds; one room sleeps six ($150). The location is largely residential but you can walk to the Haight's bars and restaurants. No elevator.

Chateau Tivoli B&B $$
(Map p128; ☑415-776-5462; www.chateautivoli. com; 1057 Steiner St; r $175-300, without bathroom $130-200; ☎⊛; ☐5, 22) This imposing, glorious chateau on a secondary thoroughfare near Alamo Square once hosted Isadora Duncan and Mark Twain, and though its two-toned gabled roofs have faded, its grand domed turrets, cornices and gorgeous carved woodwork retain their luster. Guest rooms are full of soul, character and, rumor has it, the ghost of a Victorian opera diva. No elevator, no TVs.

✕ Eating

Hope you're hungry – there are more restaurants per capita in San Francisco than in any other US city. Most of the top-ranked restaurants are quite small, so reserve ahead. For bargain eats, hit Mission taquerias, Chinatown dim sum joints, North Beach delis and food trucks all around town.

✕ Embarcadero & SoMa

Ferry Plaza Farmers Market MARKET $
(Map p128; ☑415-291-3276; www.cuesa.org; Market St & the Embarcadero; ☺10am-2pm Tue & Thu, 8am-2pm Sat; ⓜEmbarcadero) The Ferry Building market showcases California-grown, organic produce, artisan meats and gourmet-prepared foods at moderate-to-premium prices – plus an excellent selection of food trucks on weekends.

1601 Bar & Kitchen CALIFORNIAN, FUSION $$
(Map p128; ☑415-552-1601; http://1601sf.com/; 1601 Howard St; mains $12-22; ☺6-10pm Tue-Thu, to 11pm Fri & Sat; ☐9, 12, 47, ⓜVan Ness) ⋒ Rising star-chef alert: Brian Fernando is turning Sri Lankan inspirations into Californian cravings. Velvety halibut ceviche in coconut milk is an instant obsession, Marin Sun Farms goat stew with red basmati rice for two is date worthy, and you'll want the pork belly and fenugreek-vinegar home fries again for breakfast. Ingenuity without pretension, at half the cost of most downtown tasting menus ($76 here).

★Benu CALIFORNIAN, FUSION $$$
(Map p128; ☑415-685-4860; www.benusf.com; 22 Hawthorne St; tasting menu $228; ☺5:30-8:30pm seatings Tue-Sat; ☐10, 12, 14, 30, 45) SF has set fusion-cuisine standards for 150 years, but chef-owner Corey Lee remixes California ingredients and Pacific Rim inspiration with a superstar DJ's finesse. Dungeness crab and truffle custard bring such outsize flavor to Lee's faux-shark's fin soup, you'll swear there's Jaws in there. The prix-fixe menu is pricey (plus 20% service), but don't miss star-sommelier Yoon Ha's ingenious pairings ($160).

✕ Union Square, Civic Center & Hayes Valley

Sweet Woodruff CALIFORNIAN $
(Map p128; ☑415-292-9090; www.sweetwood-ruffsf.com; 798 Sutter St; mains $8-14; ☺8am-9:30pm Mon-Fri, 9:30am-9:30pm Sat & Sun; ⋒; ☐2, 3, ⋒California) ⋒ Little sister to ground-breaking, Michelin-starred Sons & Daughters, this storefront gourmet hot spot uses ingredients grown on the restaurant's own farm in its abbreviated, affordable small-plates menu. There's limited service and a tiny kitchen, yet somehow it turns out sourdough pancakes, homemade soups, impeccable bone-marrow deviled eggs and inspired vegetarian options like beet burgers.

Brenda's French Soul Food CREOLE, SOUTHERN $$
(Map p128; ☑415-345-8100; www.frenchsoulfood. com; 652 Polk St; mains lunch $9-13, dinner $12-17; ☺8am-3pm Mon & Tue, to 10pm Wed-Sat, to 8pm Sun; ☐19, 31, 38, 47, 49) Chef-owner Brenda Buenviaje blends New Orleans–style Creole cooking with French technique into 'French soul food.' Expect updated classics like beignets, serious biscuits and grits, impeccable Hangtown Fry (eggs with bacon and fried oysters), and fried chicken with collard greens and hot-pepper jelly. Long waits on sketchy sidewalks are unavoidable – but Brenda serves takeout sandwiches two doors down.

Rich Table
CALIFORNIAN $$$

(Map p128; ☎415-355-9085; http://richtablesf.com; 199 Gough St; mains $12-30; ⊙5:30-10pm Sun-Thu, to 10:30pm Fri & Sat; ⊠5, 6, 7, 21, 47, 49, ⓂVan Ness) 🍴 Satisfy cravings for taste adventures at Rich Table, home of dried porcini doughnuts, octopus confit and totally trippy beet marshmallows. Married co-chefs/owners Sarah and Evan Rich riff on seasonal California fare like jazz masters, hitting their groove with exquisitely playful amuse-bouches like the Dirty Hippie: silky goat-buttermilk *panna cotta* with hemp – a dish as offbeat and entrancing as Hippie Hill drum circles.

🍴 Chinatown & North Beach

Liguria Bakery
BAKERY $

(Map p128; ☎415-421-3786; 1700 Stockton St; focaccia $4-5; ⊙8am-1pm Tue-Fri, from 7am Sat; 🍴📶; ⊠8, 30, 39, 41, 45, ⓆPowell-Mason) Bleary-eyed art students and Italian grandmothers are in line by 8am for cinnamon-raisin focaccia hot out of the 100-year-old oven, leaving 9am dawdlers a choice of tomato or classic rosemary/garlic and 11am stragglers out of luck. Take yours in wax paper or boxed for picnics – but don't kid yourself that you're going to save some for later. Cash only.

Molinari
DELI $

(Map p128; ☎415-421-2337; www.molinarisalame.com; 373 Columbus Ave; sandwiches $10-12.50; ⊙9am-6pm Mon-Fri, to 5:30pm Sat, 10am-4pm Sun; ⊠8, 10, 12, 30, 39, 41, 45, ⓆPowell-Mason) Grab a number and a crusty roll, and when your number rolls around, wise-cracking deli staff in paper hats will stuff it with translucent sheets of *prosciutto di Parma*, milky buffalo mozzarella, tender marinated artichokes or slabs of the legendary house-cured salami. Enjoy yours hot from the panini press at sidewalk tables or in Washington Sq.

City View
CHINESE $

(Map p128; ☎415-398-2838; http://cityviewdimsum.com; 662 Commercial St; dishes $3-8; ⊙11am-2:30pm Mon-Fri, from 10am Sat & Sun; 📶; ⊠1, 8, 10, 12, 30, 45, ⓆCalifornia St) Take your seat in the sunny dining room and your pick from carts loaded with delicate shrimp and leek dumplings, garlicky Chinese broccoli, tangy spare ribs, coconut-dusted custard tarts and other tantalizing dim sum. Arrive before the midday lunch rush, so you can nab seats in the sunny upstairs room and get first dibs from passing carts.

Cinecittà
PIZZA $$

(Map p128; ☎415-291-8830; www.cinecittarestaurant.com; 663 Union St; pizzas $12-15; ⊙noon-10pm Sun-Thu, to 11pm Fri & Sat; 🍴📶; ⊠8X, 30, 39, 41, 45, ⓆPowell-Mason) Follow tantalizing aromas into this tiny hot spot for thin-crust Roman pizza, made from scratch and served with sass by Roman owner Romina. Local loyalties are divided between the Roman Travestere (fresh mozzarella, arugula and prosciutto) and Neapolitan O Sole Mio (capers, olives, mozzarella and anchovies). Local brews are on tap, house wine is $5 from 4pm to 7pm, and Romina's tiramisu is San Francisco's best.

Z & Y
CHINESE $$

(Map p128; ☎415-981-8988; www.zandyrestaurant.com; 655 Jackson St; mains $9-20; ⊙11am-10pm Mon-Thu, to 11pm Fri-Sun; ⊠8, 10, 12, 30, 45, ⓆPowell-Mason, Powell-Hyde) Graduate from ho-hum sweet-and-sour and middling *mushu* to sensational Szechuan dishes that go down in a blaze of glory. Warm up with spicy pork dumplings and heat-blistered string beans, take on the housemade *tantan* noodles with peanut-chili sauce, and leave lips buzzing with fish poached in flaming chili oil and buried under red Szechuan chili peppers. Go early; it's worth the wait.

🍴 Fisherman's Wharf, the Marina & Presidio

Off the Grid
FOOD TRUCK $

(Map p128; www.offthegridsf.com; items $5-12; ⊙Fort Mason Center 5-10pm Fri Apr-Oct, Presidio 5-9pm Thu Apr-Oct, 11am-4pm Sun Apr-Nov; 📶; ⊠22, 28) Some 30 food trucks circle their wagons at SF's largest mobile-gourmet hootenannys on Friday night at Fort Mason Center (2 Marina Blvd), and Sunday midday for Picnic at the Presidio and Thursday evenings for Twilight at the Presidio (both on the Main Post Lawn). Arrive early for best selection and to minimize waits. Cash only.

Fisherman's Wharf Crab Stands
SEAFOOD $

(Map p128; Taylor St; mains $5-15; ⓂF) Brawny-armed men stir steaming cauldrons of Dungeness crab at several side-by-side takeout stands at the foot of Taylor St, the epicenter of Fisherman's Wharf. Crab season typically runs winter through spring, but you'll find shrimp and other seafood year-round.

⭐ Greens
VEGETARIAN, CALIFORNIAN $$

(Map p128; ☎415-771-6222; www.greensrestaurant.com; Bldg A, Fort Mason Center, cnr Marina

Blvd & Laguna St; lunch $15-18, dinner $18-25; ⏲11:45am-2:30pm & 5:30-9pm Tue-Fri, from 11am Sat, 10:30am-2pm & 5:30-9pm Sun, 5:30-9pm Mon; ⚲🚻; 📵28) 🖊 Career carnivores won't realize there's zero meat in the hearty black-bean chili, or in the other flavor-packed vegetarian dishes, made using ingredients from a Zen farm in Marin. And oh!, what views – the Golden Gate rises just outside the window-lined dining room. The on-site cafe serves to-go lunches. For sit-down meals, including Sunday brunch, reservations are essential.

✖ The Mission & the Castro

★**La Taqueria** MEXICAN $
(🖉415-285-7117; 2889 Mission St; burritos $6-8; ⏲11am-9pm Mon-Sat, to 8pm Sun; 🚻; 📵12, 14, 48, 49, 🅱24th St Mission) SF's definitive burrito has no debatable saffron rice, spinach tortilla or mango salsa – just perfectly grilled meats, slow-cooked beans and classic tomatillo or mesquite salsa wrapped in a flour tortilla. You'll pay extra without beans, because they pack in more meat. Spicy pickles and *crema* (Mexican sour cream) bring complete burrito bliss.

Craftsman & Wolves BAKERY, CALIFORNIAN $
(🖉415-913-7713; http://craftsman-wolves.com; 746 Valencia St; pastries $3-7; ⏲7am-7pm Mon-Thu, to 8pm Fri, 8am-8pm Sat, to 7pm Sun; 📵14, 22, 33, 49, 🅱16th St Mission, Ⓜ J) Conventional breakfasts can't compare to the Rebel Within: savory sausage-spiked Asiago cheese muffin with a silken soft-boiled egg baked inside. SF's surest pick-me-up is Highwire macchiato and *matcha* (green tea) snickerdoodle cookies; Thai coconut curry scone, chilled pea soup and Provence rosé make a sublime lunch. Exquisite hazelnut and *horchata* (cinnamon-rice) cube cakes are ideal for celebrating SF half-birthdays, foggy days and imaginary holidays.

Mission Chinese FUSION $$
(Lung Shan; 🖉415-863-2800; www.missionchinesefood.com; 2234 Mission St; mains $12-20; ⏲11:30am-3pm & 5-10:30pm Thu-Mon, 5-10:30pm Tue & Wed; 📵14, 33, 49, 🅱16th St Mission) Extreme gourmets and Chinese takeout fans converge on Danny Bowien's cult-food dive. Tiki pork belly with pickled pineapple and spicy lamb-face (sheep's cheek) noodles are big enough for two – though not for the salt-shy – and satisfy your conscience: 75¢ from each main is donated to San Francisco Food

Bank. Wine corkage is $10; parties of eight or less.

★**Frances** CALIFORNIAN $$$
(🖉415-621-3870; www.frances-sf.com; 3870 17th St; mains $22-30; ⏲5-10pm Sun-Thu, to 10:30pm Fri & Sat; Ⓜ Castro) Chef/owner Melissa Perello earned a Michelin star for fine dining, then ditched downtown to start this market-inspired neighborhood bistro. Daily menus showcase bright, seasonal flavors and luxurious textures: cloudlike sheep's-milk ricotta gnocchi with crunchy breadcrumbs and broccolini, grilled calamari with preserved Meyer lemon, and artisan wine served by the ounce, directly from Wine Country.

Commonwealth CALIFORNIAN $$$
(🖉415-355-1500; www.commonwealthsf.com; 2224 Mission St; small plates $13-18; ⏲5:30-10pm Sun-Thu, to 11pm Fri & Sat; 🖊; 📵14, 22, 33, 49, 🅱16th St Mission) Wildly imaginative farm-to-table dining where you'd least expect it: in a converted cinderblock Mission dive. Chef Jason Fox serves adventurous, exquisitely Instagrammable compositions like *uni* (sea urchin) and popcorn atop cauliflower pudding, and foie gras in an oatmeal crust with tangy rhubarb. Dishes are dainty but pack wallops of earthy flavors. Savor the $75 prix fixe, knowing $10 is donated to charity.

✖ The Haight & Fillmore

Rosamunde Sausage Grill FAST FOOD $
(Map p128; 🖉415-437-6851; http://rosamundesausagegrill.com; 545 Haight St; sausages $7-7.50; ⏲11:30am-10pm Sun-Wed, to 11pm Thu-Sat; 📵6, 7, 22, Ⓜ N) Impress a dinner date on the cheap: load up classic Brats or duck-fig links with complimentary roasted peppers, grilled onions, whole-grain mustard and mango chutney, and enjoy with your choice of 45 seasonal draft brews at Toronado (p139) next door. To impress a local lunch date, call ahead or line up by 11:30 Tuesdays for massive $6 burgers.

Magnolia Brewpub CALIFORNIAN, AMERICAN $$
(🖉415-864-7468; www.magnoliapub.com; 1398 Haight St; mains $14-26; ⏲11am-midnight Mon-Thu, to 1am Fri, 10am-1am Sat, 10am-midnight Sun; 📵6, 7, 33, 43) 🖊 Organic pub grub and homebrew samplers keep conversation flowing at communal tables, while grass-fed Prather Ranch burgers satisfy stoner appetites in booths – it's like the Summer of Love all over again, only with better food. Morning-after brunches of quinoa hash with brewer's yeast

are plenty curative, but Cole Porter pints are powerful enough to revive the Grateful Dead.

★**State Bird Provisions**   CALIFORNIAN **$$$**
(Map p128; ☑415-795-1272; http://statebirdsf.com; 1529 Fillmore St; dishes $9-26; ☺5:30-10pm Sun-Thu, to 11pm Fri & Sat; ☐22, 38) Even before winning back-to-back James Beard Awards, State Bird attracted lines for 5:30pm seatings not seen since the Dead played neighbouring Fillmore Auditorium. The draw is a thrilling play on dim sum, wildly inventive with seasonal-regional ingredients and esoteric flavors, like fennel pollen or garum. Plan to order multiple dishes. Book exactly 60 days ahead.

Golden Gate Park & Around

Outerlands   CALIFORNIAN **$$**
(Map p124; ☑415-661-6140; www.outerlandssf.com; 4001 Judah St; sandwiches & small plates $7-14, mains $18-22; ☺10am-3pm Tue-Fri, from 9am Sat & Sun, 5:30-10pm Tue-Sun; ☑♻; Ⓜ N) ◢ When windy Ocean Beach leaves you feeling shipwrecked, drift into this beach-shack bistro for organic, California-coastal comfort food. Brunch demands Dutch pancakes in iron skillets with housemade ricotta, lunch brings $12 grilled artisan cheese combos with surfer-warming soup, and dinner means light, creative coastal fare like clam stew with mezcal broth (hungry surfers: order house-baked levain bread). Reserve ahead.

Burma Superstar   BURMESE **$$**
(Map p124; ☑415-387-2147; www.burmasuperstar.com; 309 Clement St; mains $11-28; ☺11:30am-3:30pm & 5-9:30pm Sun-Thu, to 10pm Fri & Sat; ☐1, 2, 33, 38, 44) Yes, there's a wait, but do you see anyone walking away? Blame it on fragrant *moh hinga* (catfish curry) and traditional Burmese green-tea salads tarted up with lime and dried shrimp. Reservations aren't accepted; ask the host to call you so you can browse Burmese cookbooks at Green Apple Books while you wait.

🍷 Drinking & Nightlife

For a pub crawl, start with North Beach saloons or Mission bars around Valencia and 16th Sts. The Castro has historic gay bars; SoMa adds dance clubs. Downtown and around Union Square mix dives with speakeasies. Haight bars draw mixed alterna-crowds.

★**Smuggler's Cove**   BAR
(Map p128; ☑415-869-1900; www.smugglers covesf.com; 650 Gough St; ☺5pm-1:15am; ☐5, 21, 47, 49, Ⓜ Civic Center) Yo-ho-ho and a bottle of rum...or maybe a Dead Reckoning with Angostura bitters, Nicaraguan rum, tawny port and vanilla liqueur, unless someone will share the flaming Scorpion Bowl? Pirates are bedeviled by choice at this Barbary Coast shipwreck tiki bar, hidden behind a tinted-glass door. With 400-plus rums and 70 cocktails gleaned from rum-running around the world, you won't be dry-docked long.

Comstock Saloon   BAR
(Map p128; ☑415-617-0071; www.comstocksaloon.com; 155 Columbus Ave; ☺noon-2am Mon-Fri, 4pm-2am Sat, 4pm-midnight Sun; ☐8, 10, 12, 30, 45, ☐Powell-Mason) Relieving yourself in the marble trough below the bar is no longer advisable, but otherwise this 1907 Victorian saloon revives the Barbary Coast's glory days. Get the authentic Pisco Punch or martini-precursor Martinez (gin, vermouth, bitters, maraschino liqueur). Reserve booths or back-parlor seating, so you can hear dates when ragtime-jazz bands play. Call it dinner with pot pie and buckets of shrimp.

Ritual Coffee Roasters   CAFE
(☑415-641-1011; www.ritualroasters.com; 1026 Valencia St; ☺6am-8pm Mon-Thu, to 10pm Fri, 7am-10pm Sat, to 8pm Sun; ☐14, 49, Ⓑ24th St Mission) Cults wish they inspired the same devotion as Ritual, where regulars solemnly queue for house-roasted cappuccino with ferns drawn in foam and specialty drip coffees with highly distinctive flavor profiles – descriptions comparing roasts to grapefruit peel or hazelnut aren't exaggerating. Electrical outlets are limited to encourage conversation, so you can eavesdrop on dates, art debates and political-protest plans.

Local Edition   BAR
(Map p128; ☑415-795-1375; www.localeditionsf.com; 691 Market St; ☺5pm-2am Mon-Fri, from 7pm Sat; Ⓜ Montgomery, Ⓑ Montgomery) Get the scoop on the SF cocktail scene at this new speakeasy in the basement of the historic Hearst newspaper building. Lighting is so dim you might bump into typewriters, but all is forgiven when you get The Pulitzer – a scotch-sherry cocktail that goes straight to your head.

Toronado   PUB
(Map p128; ☑415-863-2276; www.toronado.com; 547 Haight St; ☺11:30am-2am; ☐6, 7, 22, Ⓜ N)

Glory hallelujah, beer lovers: your prayers have been answered. Be humbled before the chalkboard altar that lists 45-plus beers on tap and hundreds more bottled, including spectacular seasonal microbrews. Bring cash and order sausages from Rosamunde (p138) next door to accompany ale made by Trappist monks. It may get too loud to hear your date talk, but you'll hear angels sing.

Elixir
BAR

(☑ 415-522-1633; www.elixirsf.com; 3200 16th St; ☺ 3pm-2am Mon-Fri, from noon Sat, from 10am Sun; ☐ 14, 22, 33, 49, Ⓑ 16th St Mission, Ⓜ J) ✐ Do the planet a favor and have another drink at SF's first certified-green bar, in an actual 1858 Wild West saloon. Elixir expertly blends farm-fresh seasonal mixers with small-batch, organic, even biodynamic spirits – dastardly tasty organic basil Negronis and kumquat caipirinhas will get you air-guitar-rocking to the killer jukebox. Drink-for-a-cause Wednesdays encourage imbibing, with proceeds supporting local charities.

Trick Dog
BAR

(☑ 415-471-2999; www.trickdogbar.com; 3010 20th St; ☺ 3pm-2am; ☐ 12, 14, 49) Drink adventurously with ingenious cocktails inspired by local obsessions: SF landmarks, Chinese diners, '70s hits, horoscope signs. Every six months, Trick Dog adopts a new theme, and the entire menu changes – proof that you can teach an old dog new tricks, and improve on classics like the Manhattan. Arrive early for bar stools or hit the mood-lit loft for high-concept bar bites.

El Rio
CLUB

(☑ 415-282-3325; www.elriosf.com; 3158 Mission St; cover free-$8; ☺ 1pm-2am; ☐ 12, 14, 27, 49, Ⓑ 24th St Mission) Work it all out on the dance floor with SF's most down and funky crowd – SF's full rainbow spectrum of colorful characters is here to party. Calendar highlights include Wednesday's aptly named Mayhem Karaoke, Thursday ping-pong marathons, free oysters Fridays at 5:30pm, and monthly drag-star Daytime Realness. Expect knockout margaritas and shameless flirting in the back garden. Cash only.

☆ Entertainment

At Union Square, **TIX Bay Area** (Map p128; www.tixbayarea.org; 350 Powell St) sells last-minute theater tickets for half-price.

★ SFJAZZ Center
JAZZ

(Map p128; ☑ 866-920-5299; www.sfjazz.org; 201 Franklin St; tickets $25-120; ☺ showtimes vary; ☐ 5, 6, 7, 21, 47, 49, Ⓜ Van Ness) Jazz greats coast-to-coast and legends from Argentina to Yemen are showcased at America's newest, largest jazz center. Hear fresh takes on classic jazz albums like *Ah Um* and *Getz/Gilberto* downstairs in the Lab, or book ahead for extraordinary main-stage collaborations like Laurie Anderson with David Coulter playing the saw, or pianist Jason Moran's performance with skateboarders improvising moves on indoor ramps.

★ American Conservatory Theater
THEATER

(ACT; Map p128; ☑ 415-749-2228; www.act-sf.org; 415 Geary St; ☺ box office noon-6pm Mon, to curtain Tue-Sun; ☐ 8, 30, 38, 45, ☐ Powell-Mason, Powell-Hyde, Ⓑ Powell, Ⓜ Powell) Breakthrough shows launch at this turn-of-the-century landmark, which has hosted ACT's landmark productions of Tony Kushner's *Angels in America* and Robert Wilson's *Black Rider*, with William S Burroughs' libretto and music by Tom Waits. Major playwrights like Tom Stoppard, David Mamet and Sam Shepard premiere work here, while experimental works are staged at ACT's new **Strand Theater** (Map p128; 1127 Market St).

San Francisco Opera
OPERA

(Map p128; ☑ 415-864-3330; www.sfopera.com; War Memorial Opera House, 301 Van Ness Ave; tickets $10-350; ☐ 21, 45, 47, Ⓑ Civic Center, Ⓜ Van Ness) Opera was SF's Gold Rush soundtrack – and today, SF rivals NYC's the Met with world premieres of original works covering WWII Italy *(Two Women,* or *La Ciociara)*, Stephen King thrillers *(Dolores Claiborne)*, and Qing-dynasty Chinese courtesans *(Dream of the Red Chamber)*. Don't miss Tuscany-born musical director Nicola Liusotti's signature Verdi operas. Score $10 same-day standing-room tickets at 10am and two hours before curtain.

San Francisco Ballet
DANCE

(Map p128; ☑ tickets 415-865-2000; www.sfballet.org; War Memorial Opera House, 301 Van Ness Ave; tickets $15-160; ☺ ticket sales 10am-4pm Mon-Fri; ☐ 5, 21, 47, 49, Ⓜ Van Ness, Ⓑ Civic Center) America's oldest ballet company is looking sharp in more than 100 shows annually, from the *Nutcracker* (the US premiere was here) to modern Mark Morris originals. It performs mostly at War Memorial Opera House January to May, with occasional performances at Yerba Buena Center for the Arts. Score $15 to $20 same-day standing-room tickets at the box office (noon Tuesday to Friday, 10am weekends).

Fillmore Auditorium   LIVE MUSIC
(Map p128; ☑415-346-6000; http://thefillmore. com; 1805 Geary Blvd; admission $20-50; ⊙box office 10am-3pm Sun, plus 30min before doors open on show nights until 10pm; ☐22, 38) Jimi Hendrix, Janis Joplin, the Doors – they all played the Fillmore. Now you might catch the Indigo Girls, Duran Duran or Tracy Chapman in the historic 1250-capacity, standing-room theater (if you're polite and lead with the hip, you might squeeze up to

the stage). Don't miss the priceless collection of psychedelic posters in the upstairs gallery.

Great American Music Hall   LIVE MUSIC
(Map p128; ☑415-885-0750; www.gamh.com; 859 O'Farrell St; shows $16-26; ⊙box office 10:30am-6pm Mon-Fri & on show nights; ☐19, 38, 47, 49) Everyone busts out their best sets at this opulent 1907 former bordello – the Dead occasionally show up, Tuvan throat-singing supergroup Huun Huur Tu throws down and John Waters throws Christmas extravaganzas here. Pay $25 extra for dinner with priority admission and prime balcony seating where you can watch shows comfortably, or enter the standing-room scrum downstairs and rock out on the floor.

LGBTIQ SAN FRANCISCO

Doesn't matter where you're from, who you love or who your daddy is: if you're here, and queer, welcome home. The Castro is the heart of the gay cruising scene, but South of Market (SoMa) has leather bars and thump-thump clubs. The Mission is the preferred 'hood for many women and a diverse transgender community.

Bay Area Reporter (aka BAR; www.ebar.com) covers community news and listings. *San Francisco Bay Times* (www.sfbaytimes.com) focuses on LGBTIQ perspectives and events. Free *Gloss Magazine* (www.glossmagazine.net) locks down nightlife.

Over 1.5 million people come out for SF Pride (p132) parades and parties in late June. For weekly roving dance parties, check **Honey Soundsystem** (Map p128; http:// hnysndsystm.tumblr.com/).

Blackbird (☑415-503-0630; www.blackbirdbar.com; 2124 Market St; ⊙3pm-2am Mon-Fri, from 2pm Sat & Sun; Ⓜ Church) Castro's first-choice lounge offers craft cocktails, billiards and everyone's favorite: a photo booth.

Hi Tops (http://hitopssf.com; 2247 Market St; ⊙4pm-midnight Mon-Wed, 4pm-2am Thu & Fri, 11am-2am Sat, noon-2am Sun; Ⓜ Castro) Castro's prime-time sports bar for friendly guys, big-screen TVs, shuffleboard and pub grub.

Cafe Flore (☑415-621-8579; www.cafeflore.com; 2298 Market St; ⊙7am-1am Sun-Thu, to 2am Fri & Sat; ☎; Ⓜ Castro) You haven't done the Castro till you've lollygagged on the sun-drenched patio here.

Stud (Map p128; www.studsf.com; 399 9th St; admission $5-8; ⊙noon-2am Tue, 5pm-3am Thu-Sat, 5pm-midnight Sun; ☐12, 19, 27, 47) Rocking SoMa's gay scene since 1966. Anything goes here, especially on 'Club Some Thing' Fridays.

Oasis (Map p128; ☑415-795-3180; www.sfoasis.com/; 298 11th St; tickets $10-30; ☐9, 12, 14, 47, Ⓜ Van Ness) SoMa drag shows so fearless and funny, you'll laugh till it hurts. Afterwards, shake it on the dance floor.

EndUp (Map p128; ☑415-646-0999; www.theendup.com; 401 6th St; admission $5-20; ⊙10pm Thu-4am Fri, 11pm Fri-11am Sat, 10pm Sat-4am Mon, 10pm Mon-4am Tue; ☐12, 19, 27, 47) A mixed gay/straight crowd and marathon dance parties that don't end with sunrise over the 101 freeway ramp.

Aunt Charlie's Lounge (Map p128; ☑415-441-2922; www.auntcharlieslounge.com; 133 Turk St; admission free-$5; ⊙noon-2am Mon-Fri, from 10am Sat, 10am-midnight Sun; ☐27, 31, Ⓜ Powell, Ⓑ Powell) Tenderloin drag dive bar for fabulously seedy glamour and a vintage pulp fiction vibe.

Beach Blanket Babylon CABARET
(BBB; Map p128; ☑ 415-421-4222; www.beachblan-ketbabylon.com; 678 Green St; admission $25-100; ☑ shows 8pm Wed, Thu & Fri, 6:30pm & 9:30pm Sat, 2pm & 5pm Sun; ☑ 8, 30, 39, 41, 45, ☑ Powell-Mason) Snow White searches for Prince Charming in San Francisco: what could possibly go wrong? The Disney-spoof musical-comedy cabaret has been running since 1974, but topical jokes keep it outrageous and wigs big as parade floats are gasp-worthy. Spectators must be over 21 to handle racy humor, except at cleverly sanitized Sunday matinees. Reservations essential; arrive one hour early for best seats.

Independent LIVE MUSIC
(☑ 415-771-1421; www.theindependentsf.com; 628 Divisadero St; tickets $12-45; ☑ box office 11am-6pm Mon-Fri, to 9:30pm show nights; ☑ 5, 6, 7, 21, 24) Shows earn street cred at the intimate Independent, featuring indie dreamers (Magnetic Fields, Death Cab for Cutie), rock legends (Meat Puppets, Luscious Jackson), alterna-pop (The Killers, Imagine Dragons) and comedians (Dave Chapelle, Comedians of Comedy). Ventilation is poor, but drinks are cheap – and movie nights offer free shows with a two-drink minimum.

SAN FRANCISCO'S BEST SHOPPING AREAS

All those rustic-chic dens, well-stocked cupboards and fabulous outfits don't just pull themselves together – San Franciscans scoured their city for it all. Here's where to find what:

Ferry Building Local food, wine and kitchenware.

Hayes Valley Independent fashion designers, housewares, gifts.

Valencia Street Bookstores, local design collectives, art galleries, vintage whatever.

Haight Street Head shops, music, vintage, skate and surf gear.

Union Square Department stores, megabrands, discount retail, Apple store.

Russian Hill and the Marina Date outfits, urban accessories, housewares, gifts.

Grant Avenue From Chinatown souvenirs to funky North Beach boutiques.

Castro Theatre CINEMA
(☑ 415-621-6120; www.castrotheatre.com; 429 Castro St; adult/child $11/8.50; ☑ showtimes vary; Ⓜ Castro) The Mighty Wurlitzer organ rises from the orchestra pit before evening performances and the audience cheer for the Great American Songbook, ending with: 'San Francisco open your Golden Gate/You let no stranger wait outside your door..' If there's a cult classic on the bill, say, *Whatever Happened to Baby Jane?*, expect participation. Otherwise, crowds are well behaved and rapt.

Roxie Cinema CINEMA
(☑ 415-863-1087; www.roxie.com; 3117 16th St; regular screening/matinee $10/7.50; ☑ showtimes vary; ☑ 14, 22, 33, 49, Ⓑ 16th St Mission) This little neighborhood nonprofit cinema earns international clout for distributing documentaries and showing controversial films banned elsewhere. Tickets to film-festival premieres, rare revivals and raucous annual Oscars telecasts sell out – reserve tickets online – but if the main show is packed, check out documentaries in teensy next-door Little Roxy instead. No ads, plus personal introductions to every film.

Sundance Kabuki Cinema CINEMA
(Map p128; ☑ 415-346-3243; www.sundancecinemas.com; 1881 Post St; adult $10.50-15, child $9.75-13; ☑ 2, 3, 22, 38) ☞ Cinema-going at its best. Reserve a stadium seat, belly up to the bar, and order wine and surprisingly good food to enjoy during the film. A multiplex initiative by Robert Redford's Sundance Institute, Kabuki features big-name flicks and festivals – and it's green, with recycled-fiber seating, reclaimed-wood decor and local chocolates and booze. Validated parking available.

🛍 Shopping

Aggregate Supply CLOTHING, GIFTS
(☑ 415-474-3190; www.aggregatesupplysf.com; 806 Valencia St; ☑ 11am-7pm Mon-Sat, noon-6pm Sun; ☑ 14, 33, 49, Ⓑ 16th St Mission) Wild West modern is the look at Aggregate Supply, purveyors of West Coast cool fashion and home decor. Local designers and indie makers get pride of place, including vintage Heath stoneware mugs, Turk+Taylor's ombre plaid shirt-jackets, and ingeniously repurposed rodeo-saddle tassel necklaces. Souvenirs don't get more authentically local than Aggregate Supply's own op-art California graphic tee and NorCal-forest-scented organic soaps.

Betabrand CLOTHING
(☑ 800-694-9491; www.betabrand.com; 780 Valencia St; ⊙ 11am-7pm Mon-Fri, to 8pm Sat, noon-6pm Sun; 🚌 14, 22, 33, 49, Ⓑ 16th St Mission) Crowdsource your fashion choices at Betabrand, where experimental designs are put to an online vote and winners are produced in limited editions. Recent approved designs include office-ready dress yoga pants, discoball windbreakers and sundresses with a smiling-poo-emoji print. Some styles are clunkers – including the 'suitsy', a business-suit onesie – but at these prices you can afford to take fashion risks.

Local Take GIFTS
(www.localtakesf.com; 3979 B 17th St; ⊙ 11am-7pm; Ⓜ Castro) 🔖 This marvelous little shop, next to the F-Market terminus, carries the perfect gifts to take home: SF-specific merchandise, all made locally. Our favorite items include a miniature scale model of Sutro Tower; T-shirts emblazoned with iconic SF locales; cable-car and Golden Gate Bridge jewelry; woodcut city maps; knit caps; and snappy one-of-a-kind belt buckles.

ℹ Information

DANGERS & ANNOYANCES
Keep your city smarts and wits about you in the Tenderloin and SoMa.

MEDIA
KPFA 94.1 FM (www.kpfa.org) Alternative news, music and culture.

KPOO 89.5 FM (www.kpoo.com) Community radio plays jazz, blues, soul and world beats.

KQED 88.5 FM (www.kqed.org) NPR affiliate for news, talk, arts and educational programming.

San Francisco Chronicle (www.sfgate.com) The city's main daily newspaper.

SF Weekly (www.sfweekly.com) Free weekly tabloid covering food, arts, entertainment and events.

MEDICAL SERVICES
San Francisco General Hospital (☑ emergency 415-206-8111, main hospital 415-206-8000; www.sfdph.org; 1001 Potrero Ave; ⊙ 24hr; 🚌 9, 10, 33, 48) Best for serious trauma. Provides care to uninsured patients, including psychiatric care; no documentation required beyond ID.

MONEY
Currency Exchange International (☑ 415-974-6600; www.sanfranciscocurrencyexchange.com; Westfield Center, 865 Market St, Level 1; ⊙ 10am-8:30pm Mon-Sat, 11am-7pm Sun; Ⓜ Powell St, Ⓑ Powell St) Good rates on exchange; centrally located near Union Square.

TOURIST INFORMATION
San Francisco Visitor Information Center (Map p128; ☑ 415-391-2000; www.sanfrancisco.travel; Hallidie Plaza, Market & Powell Sts, lower level; ⊙ 9am-5pm Mon-Fri, to 3pm Sat & Sun; 🚃 Powell-Mason, Powell-Hyde, Ⓜ Powell St, Ⓑ Powell St) Provides practical multilingual information, sells transportation passes, publishes glossy maps and booklets, and provides interactive touch screens.

USEFUL WEBSITES
7x7 (www.7x7.com) Trend spotting SF restaurants, bars, style and tech.

SFGate (www.sfgate.com) News and arts, entertainment and events listings.

ℹ Getting There & Away

AIR
San Francisco International Airport (SFO; www.flysfo.com; S McDonnell Rd) is 14 miles south of downtown, off Hwy 101 and accessible by Bay Area Rapid Transit (BART). Serving primarily domestic destinations, **Oakland International Airport** (OAK; www.oaklandairport.com; 1 Airport Dr; ☎) is a 40-minute BART ride across the Bay, while **Mineta San José International Airport** (www.flysanjose.com; 1701 Airport Blvd, San Jose) is 45 miles south via Hwy 101.

BUS
Until 2017, San Francisco's intercity hub remains the **Temporary Transbay Terminal** (Map p128; Howard & Main Sts), where you can catch buses on **AC Transit** (☑ 511; www.actransit.org) to the East Bay, **Golden Gate Transit** (☑ 415-455-2000, 511; www.goldengatetransit.org) north to Marin and Sonoma Counties, and **SamTrans** (☑ 800-660-4287; www.samtrans.com) south to Palo Alto and along coastal Hwy 1. **Greyhound** (☑ 800-231-2222; www.greyhound.com) buses leave several times daily for Los Angeles ($59, eight to 12 hours) and many other destinations.

TRAIN
Two long-distance **Amtrak** (☑ 800-872-7245; www.amtrakcalifornia.com) trains, the Coast Starlight (Los Angeles–Seattle) and California Zephyr from Chicago, stop at Oakland's Jack London Sq. So do the Capitol Corridor and San Joaquin intra-California trains to/from Sacramento; the latter has connecting bus services to Yosemite Valley from Merced. Amtrak runs free shuttle buses for its passengers to San Francisco's Ferry Building and CalTrain station.

CalTrain (www.caltrain.com; cnr 4th & King Sts) connects San Francisco with Silicon Valley hubs and San Jose.

ⓘ Getting Around

For Bay Area transit options, call ☎ 511 or check http://511.org.

TO/FROM SAN FRANCISCO INTERNATIONAL AIRPORT

From SFO's **BART** (Bay Area Rapid Transit; www. bart.gov; one way $8.65) station, connected to the International Terminal, it's a 30-minute ride to downtown SF. A taxi to downtown SF from SFO costs $40 to $55, plus tip.

SuperShuttle (☎ 800-258-3826; www.supershuttle.com) offers shared van rides for $17 per person.

BOAT

Blue & Gold Fleet (☎ 415-705-8200; www. blueandgoldfleet.com) operates ferries to Sausalito ($11.50), Angel Island ($9) and Oakland's Jack London Sq ($6.40) from SF's Ferry Building and/or Pier 41.

Golden Gate Ferry (☎ 415-455-2000, 511; http://goldengateferry.org) runs from SF's Ferry Building to Sausalito ($11.25) in Marin County.

CAR & MOTORCYCLE

Street parking can be harder to find than true love, and meter readers are ruthless. Municipal parking garages charge $1 to $5.50 per hour, or around $16 to $36 per day; for more info, check www.sfmta.com.

PUBLIC TRANSPORTATION

Muni (Municipal Transit Agency; ☎ 511; www. sfmta.com) operates bus, streetcar and cable-car lines. Standard fare for buses or streetcars is $2.25; cable-car rides are $7. Ask for a free transfer (not valid on cable cars) when boarding.

A **Visitor Passport** (one/three/seven days $17/26/35) allows unlimited travel on all Muni transport, including cable cars; it's sold at the Powell St cable car turnaround (p120), San Francisco Visitor Information Center (p143) and Union Square's TIX Bay Area (p140) kiosk.

A nine-day **City Pass** (www.citypass.com; adult/child $94/69) covers Muni, a bay cruise and admission to three attractions.

BART links San Francisco with the East Bay and runs beneath Market St, down Mission St and south to SFO and Millbrae, where it connects with CalTrain.

TAXI

Fares run about $2.75 per mile; meters start at $3.50. Hailing a cab in the street can be difficult. Download the mobile app **Flywheel** (http://flywheel.com) for prompt service.

Marin County

Majestic redwoods cling to tawny coastal headlands just across the Golden Gate Bridge in laid-back Marin. The southernmost town, **Sausalito** (www.sausalito.org), is a tiny bayfront destination for cycling trips over the bridge (take the ferry back to San Francisco). Near the harbor, where picturesque bohemian houseboats are docked, the **Bay Model Visitors Center** (Map p124; ☎ 415-332-3871; www.spn.usace.army.mil/Missions/Recreation/BayModelVisitorCenter.aspx; 2100 Bridgeway Blvd; ☉ 9am-4pm Tue-Sat, plus 10am-5pm Sat & Sun in summer; ♿) **FREE** houses a giant hydraulic re-creation of the entire bay and delta.

Marin Headlands

These windswept, rugged headlands are laced with hiking trails, providing panoramic bay and city views. To find the **visitor center** (Map p124; ☎ 415-331-1540; www. nps.gov/goga/marin-headlands.htm; Fort Barry; ☉ 9:30am-4:30pm), take the Alexander Ave exit after crossing north over the Golden Gate Bridge, turn left under the freeway and follow the signs.

Attractions west of Hwy 101 include **Point Bonita Lighthouse** (Map p124; www.nps.gov/goga/pobo.htm; off Field Rd; ☉ 12:30-3:30pm Sat-Mon) **FREE**, Cold War-era **Nike Missile Site SF-88** (Map p124; ☎ 415-331-1453; www. nps.gov/goga/nike-missile-site.htm; off Field Rd; ☉ 12:30pm-3:30pm Thu-Sat) **FREE** and the educational **Marine Mammal Center** (Map p124; ☎ 415-289-7325; www.marinemammalcenter.org; 2000 Bunker Rd; ☉ 10am-5pm; ♿) ✔ **FREE** uphill from **Rodeo Beach** (Map p124). East of Hwy 101 at Fort Baker, the interactive **Bay Area Discovery Museum** (Map p124; ☎ 415-339-3900; www.baykidsmuseum.org; 557 McReynolds Rd; admission $14, 1st Wed each month free; ☉ 9am-5pm Tue-Sun; ♿) is awesome for kids.

Near the visitor center, **HI Marin Headlands Hostel** (Map p124; ☎ 415-331-2777; www. norcalhostels.org/marin; Fort Barry, Bldg 941; dm $26-30, r $72-92, all without bath; @) ✔ occupies two 1907 military buildings on a forested hill. For historical luxury, book a fireplace room with bay views at Fort Baker's LEED-certified **Cavallo Point** (Map p124; ☎ 888-651-2003, 415-339-4700; www.cavallopoint.com; 601 Murray Circle; r from $359; ❉@🛜🏊♿) ✔ lodge.

Muir Woods National Monument

Wander among an ancient stand of the world's tallest trees at 550-acre **Muir Woods National Monument** (Map p124; ☑415-388-2595; www.nps.gov/muwo; 1 Muir Woods Rd, Mill Valley; adult/child $10/free; ⊙8am-sunset), 10 miles northwest of the Golden Gate Bridge. Easy hiking trails loop past thousand-year-old coast redwoods at Cathedral Grove. By the entrance, **Muir Woods Trading Company** (Map p124; ☑415-388-7059; www.muirwoodstradingcompany.com; 1 Muir Woods Rd, Mill Valley; items $3-11; ⊙from 9am daily, closing varies 4pm to 7pm; ☻) ♠ serves light lunches, snacks and drinks in the cafe. Come midweek to avoid crowds, or arrive early morning or before sunset. Take Hwy 101 to the Hwy 1 exit, then follow the signs.

The **Muir Woods Shuttle** (Route 66F; www.marintransit.org; round-trip adult/child $5/free; ⊙weekends & holidays Apr-Oct) operates weekends and holidays from April through October (daily in peak summer season), connecting with Hwy 101 and Sausalito's ferry terminal.

Mt Tamalpais State Park

Majestic Mt Tam (2572ft) is a woodsy playground for hikers and mountain bikers. **Mt Tamalpais State Park** (Map p124; ☑415-388-2070; www.parks.ca.gov/mttamalpais; parking $8) encompasses 6300 acres of parklands and over 200 miles of trails. Don't miss driving up to East Peak Summit lookout. Panoramic Hwy passes through the park, connecting Muir Woods with **Stinson Beach**, a coastal town with a sandy crescent-shaped beach on Hwy 1.

Park headquarters are **Pantoll Station** (☑415-388-2070; www.parks.ca.gov/?page_id=471; 801 Panoramic Hwy; ⊙variable hours; ☎), the nexus of many trails, with a first-come, first-served **campground** (Map p124; Panoramic Hwy; tent sites $25). Book far ahead for a rustic cabin (no electricity or running water) or walk-in campsite at **Steep Ravine** (☑800-444-7275; www.reserveamerica.com; Nov-Sep; tent sites $25, cabins $100), off Hwy 1 south of Stinson Beach. Or hike in with a sleeping bag, towel and food to off-the-grid **West Point Inn** (Map p124; ☑info 415-388-9955, reservations 415-646-0702; www.westpointinn.com; 100 Old Railroad Grade Fire Rd, Mill Valley; r per adult/child $50/25); reservations required.

Point Reyes National Seashore

The windswept peninsula of **Point Reyes National Seashore** (www.nps.gov/pore) FREE juts 10 miles out to sea on an entirely different tectonic plate, protecting over 100 sq miles of beaches, lagoons and forested hills. A mile west of Olema, **Bear Valley Visitor Center** (☑415-464-5100; www.nps.gov/pore; ⊙10am-5pm Mon-Fri, from 9am Sat & Sun) has maps, information and natural-history displays. The 0.6-mile **Earthquake Trail**, which crosses the San Andreas Fault zone, starts nearby.

Crowning the peninsula's westernmost tip, **Point Reyes Lighthouse** (☑415-669-1534; ⊙lighthouse 10am-4:30pm Fri-Mon, lens room 2:30-4pm Fri-Mon) FREE is ideal for winter whale-watching. Off Pierce Point Rd, the 10-mile round-trip **Tomales Point Trail** rolls atop blustery bluffs past herds of tule elk to the peninsula's northern tip. To paddle out into Tomales Bay, **Blue Waters Kayaking** (☑415-669-2600; www.bluewaterskayaking.com; rentals/tours from $50/68; ☻) launches from Inverness and Marshall.

Nature-lovers bunk at the only in-park lodging, **HI Point Reyes Hostel** (☑415-663-8811; www.norcalhostels.org/reyes; 1390 Limantour Spit Rd; dm $26-29, r $87-130, all without bath; @☻) ♠, 8 miles inland from the visitor center. In the coastal town of Inverness, the **Cottages at Point Reyes Seashore** (☑415-669-7250; www.cottagespointreyes.com; 13275 Sir Francis Drake Blvd; r $129-239; ☎✲☻☻) is a family-friendly place tucked away in the woods. The **West Marin Chamber of Commerce** (☑415-663-9232; www.pointreyes.org) checks availability at more cozy inns, cottages and B&Bs.

Two miles north of Olema, the tiny town of **Point Reyes Station** has heart-warming bakeries, cafes and restaurants. Gather a picnic lunch at **Tomales Bay Foods & Cowgirl Creamery** (www.cowgirlcreamery.com; 80 4th St; sandwiches $6-12; ⊙10am-6pm Wed-Sun; ☻) ♠ or 2 miles west of town at **Perry's Deli** (http://perrysinvernesssparkgrocery.com; 12301 Sir Francis Drake Blvd, Inverness Park; sandwiches $5-11; ⊙7am-8pm Mon-Thu, to 9pm Fri & Sat, 8am-8pm Sun).

Berkeley

As the birthplace of the 1960s Free Speech Movement, and the home of the hallowed halls of the University of California,

Berkeley is no bashful wallflower. You can't legally walk around nude anymore, but 'Berserkeley' remains the Bay Area's radical hub, crawling with university students, punk skaters and aging Birckenstock-shod hippies. 'Nuclear Free Zone' signs mark the city limits.

◉ Sights & Activities

Leading to the campus's south gate, **Telegraph Avenue** is a youthful street carnival, packed with cheap cafes, music stores, street hawkers and buskers.

University of California, Berkeley   UNIVERSITY (www.berkeley.edu) 'Cal' is one of the country's top universities and home to 35,000 diverse, politically conscious students. The **Visitor Services Center** (☑510-642-5215; http://visitors.berkeley.edu; 101 Sproul Hall; ☺tours usually 10am Mon-Sat & 1pm Sun) has info and leads free campus tours (reservations required). Cal's landmark is the 1914 **Campanile** (Sather Tower; http://visitors.berkeley.edu/camp/; adult/child $3/2; ☺10am-3:45pm Mon-Fri, to 4:45pm Sat, 10am-1:30pm & 3-4:45pm Sun; ⏃), with elevator rides ($3) to the top. The **Bancroft Library** (☑510-642-3781; www.bancroft.berkeley.edu; ☺10am-5pm Mon-Fri) displays the small gold nugget that started the California gold rush in 1848.

🛏 Sleeping

Midrange motels line University Ave west of downtown.

Downtown Berkeley Inn   MOTEL **$$** (☑510-843-4043; www.downtownberkeleyinn.com; 2001 Bancroft Way; r $79-129; ❈ 🛜) A 27-room budget boutique-style motel with good-sized rooms and correspondingly ample flat-screen TVs.

Hotel Shattuck Plaza   HOTEL **$$$** (☑510-845-7300; www.hotelshattuckplaza.com; 2086 Allston Way; r from $195; ❈ @ 🛜) Peace is quite posh following a $15-million renovation and greening of this 100-year-old downtown jewel. A foyer of red Italian glass lighting, flocked Victorian-style wallpaper – and yes, a peace sign tiled into the floor – leads to comfortable rooms with down comforters, and an airy, columned restaurant serving all meals. Accommodations off Shattuck are quietest; cityscape rooms boast bay views.

✖ Eating & Drinking

Ippuku   JAPANESE **$$** (☑510-665-1969; www.ippukuberkeley.com; 2130 Center St; shared plates $5-20; ☺5-10pm Sun-Thu, to 11pm Fri & Sat) Specializing in *shōchū*, a distilled alcohol often made from rice or barley, Ippuku is similar to a Tokyo *izakaya* (Japanese pubs serving food) and beloved by its Japanese expat patrons. Choose from a menu of skewered meats and vegetables and handmade noodles as you settle in at one of the traditional tatami tables (no shoes, please) or cozy booth perches. Reservations essential.

★ Chez Panisse   CALIFORNIAN **$$$** (☑cafe 510-548-5049, restaurant 510-548-5525; www.chezpanisse.com; 1517 Shattuck Ave; cafe dinner mains $19-32, restaurant prix-fixe dinner $75-125; ☺cafe 11:30am-2:45pm & 5-10:30pm Mon-Thu, 11:30am-3pm & 5-11:30pm Fri & Sat, restaurant seatings 5:30pm & 8pm Mon-Sat) ✆ Foodies come to worship here at the church of Alice Waters, the inventor of California cuisine. It's in a lovely arts-and-crafts house in the Gourmet Ghetto, and you can choose to pull all the stops with a prix-fixe meal downstairs, or go less expensive and a tad less formal in the cafe upstairs. Reservations accepted one month ahead.

Jupiter   PUB (www.jupiterbeer.com; 2181 Shattuck Ave; ☺11:30am-1am Mon-Thu, to 1:30am Fri, noon-1:30am Sat, to midnight Sun) This downtown pub has loads of regional microbrews, a beer garden, good pizza and live bands most nights. Sit upstairs for a bird's-eye view of bustling Shattuck Ave.

☆ Entertainment

Freight & Salvage Coffeehouse   LIVE MUSIC (☑510-644-2020; www.thefreight.org; 2020 Addison St; ⏃) This legendary club has almost 50 years of history and is conveniently located in the downtown arts district. It features great traditional folk and world music and welcomes all ages, with half-price tickets for patrons under 21.

Berkeley Repertory Theatre   THEATER (☑510-647-2949; www.berkeleyrep.org; 2025 Addison St; tickets $40-100) This highly respected company has produced bold versions of classical and modern plays since 1968. Most shows have half-price tickets for patrons under 30.

ℹ️ Getting There & Around

BART (✆ 511, 510-465-2278; www.bart.gov) trains connect downtown Berkeley, a short walk from campus, with San Francisco ($3.90, 25 minutes). AC Transit (p143) runs local buses around Berkeley ($2.10) and to San Francisco ($4.20, 40 minutes).

NORTHERN CALIFORNIA

The Golden State goes wild in Northern California, with coast redwoods swirled in fog, Wine Country vineyards and hidden hot springs. Befitting this dramatic meeting of land and water is an unlikely mélange of local residents: timber barons and hippie tree huggers, dreadlocked Rastafarians and biodynamic ranchers, pot farmers and political radicals of every stripe. Come for the scenery, but stay for the top-notch wine and farm-to-fork restaurants, misty hikes among the world's tallest trees and rambling conversations that begin with 'Hey, dude!' and end hours later.

Wine Country

America's premier viticulture region has earned its reputation among the world's best. Century-old oaks and swaths of vineyards carpet rolling hillsides as far as the eye can see. Where they end, lush redwood forests follow serpentine rivers to the sea. Napa has art-filled tasting rooms by big-name architects, with prices to match. In down-to-earth Sonoma, you may drink in a tin-roofed shed and meet the vintner's dog.

ℹ️ Getting There & Around

Either Napa or Sonoma is at least an hour's drive north of San Francisco via Hwy 101 or I-80.

Getting to and around the valleys by public transportation (mainly buses, perhaps in combination with BART trains or ferries) is slow and complicated, but just possible; consult http://511.org for trip planning and schedules.

Rent bicycles from **Wine Country Cyclery** (✆ 707-966-6800; www.winecountrycyclery. com; 262 W Napa St, Sonoma; bicycle rental per day $30-65; ⏰ 10am-6pm), **Napa Valley Bike Tours** (✆ 707-251-8687; www.napavalleybike-tours.com; 6500 Washington St, Yountville; bicycle rental per day $45-90, tours from $109; ⏰ 8:30am-5pm), **Calistoga Bike Shop** (✆ 707-942-9687; www.calistogabikeshop.com; 1318 Lincoln Ave, Calistoga; bicycle rental from $12/39 per hour/day; ⏰ 10am-6pm) or **Spoke**

Folk Cyclery (✆ 707-433-7171; www.spokefolk. com; 201 Center St, Healdsburg; bicycle rental per hour/day from $15/40; ⏰ 10am-6pm Mon-Fri, to 5pm Sat & Sun).

Napa Valley

More than 200 wineries crowd 30-mile-long Napa Valley along three main routes. Traffic-jammed on weekends, **Highway 29** is lined with blockbuster wineries. Running parallel, **Silverado Trail** moves faster, passing boutique winemakers, bizarre architecture and cult-hit Cabernet Sauvignon. Heading west toward Sonoma, **Carneros Highway** (Hwy 121) winds by landmark vineyards specializing in sparkling wines and Pinot Noir.

At the southern end of the valley, **Napa** – the valley's workaday hub – lacks rusticity, but has trendy restaurants and tasting rooms downtown. Stop by the **Napa Valley Welcome Center** (✆ 855-847-6272, 707-251-5895; www.visitnapavalley.com; 600 Main St; ⏰ 9am-5pm; 📶) for wine-tasting passes and winery maps.

Heading north on Hwy 29, the former stagecoach stop of tiny **Yountville** has more Michelin-starred eateries per capita than San Francisco. Another 10 miles north, traffic snarls in charming **St Helena**, where there's genteel strolling and shopping – if you can find parking. At the valley's northern end, folksy **Calistoga** is home to hot-springs spas and mud-bath emporiums using volcanic ash from nearby Mt St Helena.

👁 Sights & Activities

Many Napa wineries require reservations. Plan to visit no more than a few tasting rooms each day.

⭐ **Hess Collection**   WINERY, GALLERY
(✆ 707-255-1144; www.hesscollection.com; 4411 Redwood Rd, Napa; museum entry free, tasting $20, tours free-$65; ⏰ 10am-5:30pm, last tasting 5pm, tours 10:30am-3pm) 🍷 Art-lovers: don't miss Hess Collection, the galleries of which display mixed-media and large-canvas works, including pieces by Francis Bacon and Robert Motherwell. In the cave-like tasting room, find well-known Cabernet Sauvignon and Chardonnay, but also try the Viognier. Hess overlooks the valley: be prepared to drive a winding road. Reservations recommended. Bottles: $20 to $100. (NB: don't confuse Hess Collection with Hess Select, the grocery-store brand.)

★ **Frog's Leap**   WINERY
(☑ 707-963-4704; www.frogsleap.com; 8815 Conn Creek Rd, Rutherford; tasting $20, incl tour $25; ⊙ 10am-4pm by appointment only; ☒ ☺) ✐ Meandering paths wind through magical gardens and fruit-bearing orchards surrounding an 1884 barn and farmstead with cats and chickens. The vibe is casual and down-to-earth, with a major emphasis on *fun*. Sauvignon Blanc is its best-known wine, but the Merlot merits attention. There's also a dry, restrained Cabernet, atypical of Napa.

All wines are organic. Appointments required. Bottles cost $22 to $42.

Castello di Amorosa   WINERY, CASTLE
(☑ 707-967-6272; www.castellodiamorosa.com; 4045 Hwy 29, Calistoga; admission & tasting $20-45, incl guided tour $35-75; ⊙ 9:30am-6pm Mar-Oct, to 5pm Nov-Feb) It took 14 years to build this perfectly replicated, 13th-century Italian castle, complete with moat, hand-cut stone walls, ceiling frescoes by Italian artisans, Roman-style cross-vault brick catacombs, and a torture chamber with period equipment. You can taste without an appointment, but this is one tour worth taking. Oh, the wine? Some respectable Italian varietals, including a velvety Tuscan blend, and a Merlot blend that goes great with pizza. Bottles are $29 to $95.

Casa Nuestra   WINERY
(☑ 707-963-5783,   866-844-9463;   www.casanuestra.com; 3451 Silverado Trail N, St Helena; tasting $10; ⊙ 10am-4:30pm by appointment only; ☒) ✐ A peace flag and portrait of Elvis greet you at this old-school, mom-and-pop winery, which produces unusual blends and interesting varietals (including good Chenin Blanc). Vineyards are all-organic; the sun provides power. Picnic free (call ahead and buy a bottle) beneath weeping willows shading happy goats. Bottles are $20 to $60.

di Rosa Art +
Nature Preserve   GALLERY, GARDENS
(☑ 707-226-5991; www.dirosaart.org; 5200 Hwy 121, Napa; admission $5, tours $12-15; ⊙ 10am-4pm Wed-Sun) West of downtown, scrap-metal sheep graze Carneros vineyards at 217-acre di Rosa Preserve, a stunning collection of Northern California art, displayed indoors in galleries and outdoors in sculpture gardens. Reservations recommended for tours.

Indian Springs Spa   SPA
(☑ 707-942-4913;   www.indianspringscalistoga.com; 1712 Lincoln Ave; ⊙ by appointment 9am-

8pm) California's longest continually operating spa, and original Calistoga resort, has concrete mud tubs and mines its own ash. Treatments include use of the huge, hot-spring-fed pool. Great cucumber body lotion.

Culinary Institute
of America at Greystone   COOKING COURSE
(☑ 707-967-2320;   www.ciachef.edu/california; 2555 Main St; mains $25-29, cooking demonstration $20; ⊙ cooking demonstrations 1:30pm Sat & Sun) Inside an 1889 stone chateau, now a cooking school, there's a gadget- and cookbook-filled culinary shop; fine restaurant; weekend cooking demonstrations; and wine-tasting classes by luminaries including Karen MacNeil, author of *The Wine Bible*.

🛏 Sleeping

The valley's best-value deals are midweek at Napa's less-than-exciting motels.

Maison Fleurie   INN $$
(☑ 707-944-2056; www.maisonfleurienapa.com; 6529 Yount St, Yountville; r $170-395; ☒ @ ☁ ☒) Rooms at this ivy-covered country inn are in a century-old home and carriage house, decorated in French-provincial style. Big breakfasts (included), afternoon wine and *hors d'oeuvres*, hot tub.

El Bonita   MOTEL $$
(☑ 707-963-3216; www.elbonita.com; 195 Main St, St Helena; r $169-239; ☒ @ ☁ ☒ ☒) Book in advance to secure this sought-after motel, with up-to-date rooms (quietest are in back), attractive grounds, hot tub and sauna.

Indian Springs Resort   RESORT $$
(☑ 707-942-4913;   www.indianspringscalistoga.com; 1712 Lincoln Ave, Calistoga; r/cottages from $239/359; ☒ ☁ ☒ ☒) The definitive old-school Calistoga resort, Indian Springs has cottages facing a central lawn with palm trees, shuffleboard, bocce, hammocks and Weber grills – not unlike a vintage Florida resort. Some sleep six. There are also top-end, motel-style lodge rooms (adults only). Huge hot-springs-fed swimming pool.

🍴 Eating

Many wine-country restaurants keep shorter hours in winter; book ahead for lunch and dinner.

★ **Oxbow Public Market**   MARKET $
(☑ 707-226-6529; http://oxbowpublicmarket.com; 610 & 644 1st St, Napa; items from $3; ⊙ 9am-7pm

Wed-Mon, to 8pm Tue, some restaurants open later) 🍽 Graze this gourmet market and plug into the Northern California food scene. Standouts: Hog Island Oyster Co; comfort cooking at celeb-chef Todd Humphries' Kitchen Door; Venezuelan arepa (corn-cake sandwiches) at Pica Pica; great Cal-Mexican tacos at C Casa; Italian pastries at Ca' Momi; espresso from Ritual Coffee; and Three Twins certified-organic ice cream.

Bouchon Bakery
BAKERY $

(☑707-944-2253; www.thomaskeller.com; 6528 Washington St, Yountville; items from $3; ☺7am-7pm) Bouchon makes as-good-as-in-Paris French pastries and strong coffee. There's always a line and rarely a seat: get it to go.

Gott's Roadside
AMERICAN $$

(☑707-963-3486; http://gotts.com; 933 Main St, St Helena; mains $8-16; ☺10am-10pm May-Sep, 8am-9pm Oct-Apr; 👪) 🍽 Wiggle your toes in the grass and feast on quality burgers – of beef or ahi tuna – plus Cobb salads and fish tacos at this classic roadside drive-in, whose original name, 'Taylor's Auto Refresher,' remains on the sign. Avoid weekend waits by phoning ahead or ordering online. There's another at Oxbow Public Market.

★French Laundry
CALIFORNIAN $$$

(☑707-944-2380; www.frenchlaundry.com; 6640 Washington St, Yountville; prix-fixe dinner $295; ☺seatings 11am-1pm Fri-Sun, 5:30-9:15pm daily) The pinnacle of California dining, Thomas Keller's French Laundry is epic, a high-wattage culinary experience on par with the world's best. Book two months ahead at 10am sharp, or log onto OpenTable.com precisely at midnight. Avoid tables before 7pm; first-service seating moves a touch quickly. This is the meal you can brag about the rest of your life.

Sonoma Valley

More laid-back and less commercial than Napa, Sonoma Valley shelters more than 40 wineries off Hwy 12 – and unlike in Napa, most don't require tasting appointments. Note there are actually three Sonomas: the town, the valley and the county.

◉ Sights & Activities

Downtown Sonoma was once the capital of the short-lived Bear Flag Republic. Today Sonoma Plaza – the state's largest town square – is bordered by historic hotels, busy restaurants, chic shops and a **visitor center** (☑866-966-1090, 707-996-1090; www.sonomavalley.com; 453 1st St E; ☺9am-5pm Mon-Sat, 10am-5pm Sun).

Bartholomew Park Winery
WINERY

(☑707-939-3026; www.bartpark.com; 1000 Vineyard Lane, Sonoma; tasting $10-30; ☺11am-4:30pm) 🍽 A great bike-to winery, Bartholomew Park occupies a 400-acre nature preserve, with oak-shaded picnicking and valley-view hiking. The vineyards were originally cultivated in 1857 and now yield certified-organic, citrusy Sauvignon Blanc, Cabernet Sauvignon softer in style than Napa and lush Zinfandel. Bottles are $21 to $48.

Gundlach-Bundschu Winery
WINERY

(☑707-939-3015; www.gunbun.com; 2000 Denmark St, Sonoma; tasting $10-25, incl tour $30-50; ☺11am-4:30pm, to 5:30pm Jun–mid-Oct) 🍽 California's oldest family-run winery looks like a castle, but has a down-to-earth vibe. Founded in 1858 by a Bavarian immigrant, its signatures are Gewürztraminer and Pinot Noir, but 'Gun-Bun' was the first American winery to produce 100% Merlot. Down a winding lane, it's a terrific bike-to winery, with picnicking, hiking and a lake. Tour the 1800-barrel cave by reservation only. Bottles are $21 to $90.

Benziger
WINERY

(☑707-935-3000, 888-490-2739; www.benziger.com; 1883 London Ranch Rd, Glen Ellen; tasting $15-40, tours $25-50; ☺10am-5pm, tram tours 11am-3:30pm; 👪🍷) 🍽 If you're new to wine, make Benziger your first stop for Sonoma's best crash course in winemaking. The worthwhile, nonreservable tour includes an open-air tram ride (weather permitting) through biodynamic vineyards, and a five-wine tasting. Great picnicking, plus a playground, make it tops for families. The large-production wine is OK (head for the reserves); the tour's the thing. Bottles are $15 to $80.

Jack London State Historic Park
STATE PARK

(☑707-938-5216; www.jacklondonpark.com; 2400 London Ranch Rd, Glen Ellen; per car $10, cottage entry adult/child $4/2; ☺park 9:30am-5pm, museum 10am-5pm, cottage noon-4pm) Napa has Robert Louis Stevenson, but Sonoma's got Jack London. This 1400-acre park frames that author's last years; don't miss the excellent on-site museum. Miles of hiking trails (some open to mountain bikes) weave through oak-dotted woodlands, between

600ft and 2300ft elevations; an easy 2-mile loop meanders to a lake, great for picnicking. Watch for poison oak.

Cline Cellars WINERY
(☑707-940-4030; www.clinecellars.com; 24737 Arnold Dr, Sonoma; tasting free-$20; ⊘ tasting room 10am-6pm, museum 10am-4pm) ✎ Balmy days are for pond-side picnics, and rainy ones for fireside tastings of old-vine Zinfandel and Mouvedre inside an 1850s farmhouse. Stroll out back to the California Mission Museum, housing 1930s miniature replicas of California's original 21 Spanish Colonial missions.

Kunde WINERY
(☑707-833-5501; www.kunde.com; 9825 Hwy 12, Kenwood; tasting $10-25, incl tour $30-40; ⊘10:30am-5pm) ✎ It's worth making reservations in advance for sustainable vineyard tours, mountain-top tastings and monthly guided hikes.

🛏 Sleeping

At the valley's north end, Santa Rosa has budget-saving motels and hotels.

Sonoma Hotel HISTORIC HOTEL **$$**
(☑707-996-2996; www.sonomahotel.com; 110 W Spain St; r from $160; ❋ 🐾) Long on charm, this good-value, vintage-1880s hotel, decorated with country-style willow-wood furnishings, sits right on the plaza. Double-pane glass blocks the noise, but there's no elevator or parking lot.

★ Beltane Ranch B&B **$$**
(☑707-833-4233; www.beltaneranch.com; 11775 Hwy 12, Glen Ellen; d $205-295; 🐾) ✎ Surrounded by horse pastures and vineyards, Beltane is a throwback to 19th-century Sonoma. The cheerful, lemon-yellow, 1890s ranch house has double porches, lined with swinging chairs and white wicker. Though it's technically a B&B, each country-Americana-style room has a private entrance – nobody will make you pet the cat. No phones or TVs mean zero distraction from pastoral bliss.

✗ Eating & Drinking

Fremont Diner AMERICAN, SOUTHERN **$$**
(☑707-938-7370; www.thefremontdiner.com; 2698 Fremont Dr, Sonoma; mains $9-22; ⊘8am-3pm Mon-Wed, to 9pm Thu-Sun; 🖈) ✎ Lines snake out the door peak times at this farm-to-table roadside diner. We prefer the indoor tables, but will happily accept a picnic table in the

big outdoor tent to feast on ricotta pancakes with real maple syrup, chicken and waffles, oyster po'boys, finger-licking barbecue and skillet-baked cornbread. Arrive early, or late, to beat queues.

fig cafe & winebar FRENCH, CALIFORNIAN **$$**
(☑707-938-2130; www.thefigcafe.com; 13690 Arnold Dr, Glen Ellen; mains $14-26, 3-course prix-fixe dinner $36; ⊘brunch 10am-2:30pm Sat & Sun, dinner 5-9pm Sun-Thu, to 9:30pm Fri & Sat) The fig's earthy California-Provençal comfort food includes flash-fried calamari with spicy-lemon aioli, duck confit and *moules-frites* (mussels and french fries). Good wine prices and weekend brunch give reason to return.

Hopmonk Tavern PUB FOOD **$$**
(☑707-935-9100; www.hopmonk.com; 691 Broadway, Sonoma; mains $11-23; ⊘11:30am-9pm Sun-Thu, to 9:30pm Fri & Sat) This happening gastropub and beer garden takes its brews seriously, with more than a dozen of its own and guest beers on tap, served in type-appropriate glassware. Live music Friday through Sunday.

★ Cafe La Haye CALIFORNIAN **$$$**
(☑707-935-5994; www.cafelahaye.com; 140 E Napa St, Sonoma; mains $18-30; ⊘5:30-9pm Tue-Sat; 🍽) ✎ One of Sonoma's top tables for earthy New American cooking, La Haye only uses produce sourced from within 60 miles. Its dining room gets packed cheek-by-jowl and service can border on perfunctory, but the clean simplicity and flavor-packed cooking make it many foodies' first choice. Reserve well ahead.

Russian River Valley

Redwoods tower over small wineries in the Russian River Valley, about 75 miles northwest of San Francisco (via Hwys 101 and 116), in western Sonoma County.

Famous for its apple orchards and farm-tour trails, **Sebastopol** has a new-age spiritual aura, with downtown bookshops, art galleries and boutiques, and antiques stores further south. Wander around the **Barlow** (☑707-824-5600; thebarlow.net; 6770 McKinley St; ⊘8:30am-9:30pm; 🖈), an indoor market of food producers, winemakers, coffee roasters, spirit distillers and indie chefs. Or go straight to the source by driving or cycling local farm trails (www.farmtrails.org).

Guerneville is the main river beach town, buzzing with Harleys and gay-friendly honky-tonks. Explore old-growth redwoods at **Armstrong Redwoods State Reserve** (☑ info 707-869-2015, visitor center 707-869-2958; www.parks.ca.gov; 17000 Armstrong Woods Rd; per car $8; ⊙ 8am-sunset; ⛿), next to no-reservations **Bullfrog Pond Campground** (☑ 707-869-2015; www.stewardscr.org; sites reserved/nonreserved $35/25; ⛿⛺). Paddle downriver with **Burke's Canoe Trips** (☑ 707-887-1222; www.burkescanoetrips.com; 8600 River Rd, Forestville; canoe/kayak rental incl shuttle $65/45, cash only; ⊙ 10am-6pm Mon-Fri, 9am-6pm Sat & Sun). Head southeast to sip sparkling wines at hilltop **Iron Horse Vineyards** (☑ 707-887-1507; www.ironhorsevineyards.com; 9786 Ross Station Rd, Sebastopol; tasting $20, incl tour $25-50; ⊙ 10am-4:30pm); reserve tours in advance. Other excellent wineries, many known for award-winning Pinot Noir, scatter along rural **Westside Road**, which follows the river toward Healdsburg. Guerneville's **visitor center** (☑ 877-644-9001, 707-869-9000; www.russianriver.com; 16209 1st St, Guerneville; ⊙ 10am-4:45pm Mon-Sat, plus 10am-3pm Sun May-Oct) offers winery maps and lodging info. It's worth the wait for a table at California-smart **Boon Eat + Drink** (☑ 707-869-0780; http://eatatboon.com; 16248 Main St; lunch mains $14-18, dinner $15-26; ⊙ lunch 11am-3pm Mon, Tue, Thu & Fri, brunch 10am-3pm Sat & Sun, dinner 5-9pm Sun-Thu, to 10pm Fri & Sat), which also manages boutique **Boon Hotel + Spa** (☑ 707-869-2721; www.boonhotels.com; 14711 Armstrong Woods Rd; r $165-275; 🛜⛿⛺) 🍴, a minimalist oasis with a saline pool.

The aptly named Bohemian Hwy winds 10 miles south of the river to tiny **Occidental**, where **Howard Station Cafe** (☑ 707-874-2838; www.howardstationcafe.com; 3611 Bohemian Hwy; mains $6-13; ⊙ 7am-2:30pm Mon-Fri, to 3pm Sat & Sun; ⛿⛺) serves hearty breakfasts like blueberry cornmeal pancakes (cash only), and **Barley & Hops Tavern** (☑ 707-874-9037; www.barleynhops.com; 3688 Bohemian Hwy; mains $10-15; ⊙ 4-9:30pm Mon-Thu, 11am-10pm Fri & Sat, 11am-9:30pm Sun) pours craft beers. It's another few miles south to **Freestone**, home of the phenomenal bakery **Wild Flour Bread** (www.wildflourbread.com; 140 Bohemian Hwy, Freestone; items from $3; ⊙ 8:30am-6:30pm Fri-Mon) and invigorating cedar-enzyme baths at **Osmosis** (☑ 707-823-8231; www.osmosis.com; 209 Bohemian Hwy, Freestone; ⊙ by appointment) spa.

Healdsburg & Around

More than 100 wineries dot the valleys within a 20-mile radius of Healdsburg, where upscale eateries, wine-tasting rooms and stylish hotels surround a leafy plaza. For tasting passes and maps, drop by the **visitor center** (☑ 07-433-6935; www.healdsburg.com; 217 Healdsburg Ave, Healdsburg; ⊙ 10am-4pm Mon-Fri, to 3pm Sat & Sun). Dine with California-chic locavores at the **Shed** (☑ 707-431-7433; healdsburgshed.com; 25 North St; dishes $3-15; ⊙ 8am-7pm Wed-Mon; 🍴 gourmet marketplace and culinary center, or grab lunch near the vineyards at country-style **Dry Creek General Store** (☑ 707-433-4171; www.drycreekgeneralstore1881.com; 3495 Dry Creek Rd; sandwiches $8-10; ⊙ 6:30am-6pm Mon-Thu, to 6:30pm Fri & Sat, 7am-6pm Sun). Afterward bed down at old-fashioned **L&M Motel** (☑ 707-433-6528; www.landmmotel.com; 70 Healdsburg Ave; r $150-180; ❄🛜⛿⛺) or romantic **Healdsburg Modern Cottages** (☑ 707-395-4684; www.healdsburgcottages.com; 425 Foss St; d $250-500; ❄🛜⛺).

Picture-perfect farmstead wineries await discovery in Dry Creek Valley, west of Hwy 101 and Healdsburg. Pedal a bicycle out to taste citrusy Sauvignon Blanc and peppery Zinfandel at biodynamic **Preston Vineyards** (www.prestonvineyards.com; 9282 W Dry Creek Rd; tasting $10; ⊙ 11am-4:30pm; ⛿ 🍴 and **Quivira Vineyards** (☑ 707-431-8333; www.quivirawine.com; 4900 W Dry Creek Rd; tasting $15, incl tour $25; ⊙ 11am-5pm; ⛿⛺) 🍴. Motor toward the Russian River and **Porter Creek Vineyards** (☑ 707-433-6321; www.portercreekvineyards.com; 8735 Westside Rd, Healdsburg; tasting $10; ⊙ 10:30am-4:30pm; ⛺) 🍴 for forest-floor Pinot Noir and fruity Viognier poured at a bar made from a bowling-alley lane.

Northwest of Healdsburg off Hwy 101, follow Hwy 128 through the **Anderson Valley**, known for its fruit orchards and family-owned wineries like **Navarro** (☑ 707-895-3686; www.navarrowine.com; 5601 Hwy 128, Philo; ⊙ 9am-6pm, to 5pm Nov-Mar) **FREE** and **Husch** (www.huschvineyards.com; 4400 Hwy 128, Philo; ⊙ 10am-6pm, to 5pm Nov-Mar) **FREE**. Outside **Boonville**, which has roadside cafes, bakeries and delis, brake for disc-golf and beer at solar-powered **Anderson Valley Brewing Company** (☑ 707-895-2337; www.avbc.com; 17700 Hwy 253, Boonville; tasting from $2, tours & disc-golf course free; ⊙ tasting room 11am-6pm Sat-Thu, to 7pm Fri, tours 1:30pm & 3pm daily) 🍴.

North Coast

Metropolitan San Francisco, only a few hours behind in the rearview mirror, feels eons away from the frothing, frigid crash of Pacific tide and two-stoplight towns on this jagged edge of the continent. Forested valleys brush up against moody ocean waves and rural farms here on California's weirdest coast, home to hippies, hoppy microbrews, marijuana farms and, most famously, the tallest trees on earth. The winding coastal drive gets more rewarding with every gorgeous, white-knuckled mile of narrow highway.

Coastal Highway 1 to Mendocino

Often winding precariously atop ocean cliffs, this serpentine slice of Hwy 1 passes salty fishing harbors and hidden beaches. Use roadside pullouts to scan the Pacific horizon for migrating whales or to amble coves bounded by startling rock formations and relentlessly pounded by the surf. The 110-mile stretch from Bodega Bay to Fort Bragg takes at least three hours of nonstop driving; at night or in the fog, it takes steely nerves and much, much longer.

Bodega Bay, the first pearl in a string of sleepy fishing villages, was the setting for Hitchcock's terrifying 1963 psycho-horror flick *The Birds*. Today the skies are free from bloodthirsty gulls, but you'd best keep an eye on that picnic basket as you explore the arched rocks, blustery coves and wildflower-covered bluffs of **Sonoma Coast State Park** (www.parks.ca.gov; per car $8), with beaches rolling beyond Jenner, 10 miles north. **Bodega Bay Sportfishing Center** (☑707-875-3495; www.bodegacharters.com; 1410 Bay Flat Rd) runs winter whale-watching trips (adult/child $50/35). Landlubbers hike Bodega Head or saddle up at **Chanslor Riding Stables** (☑707-875-2721, 707-875-3333; www.horsenaroundtrailrides.com; 2660 N Hwy 1; rides from $40).

Where the wide, lazy Russian River meets the Pacific, there isn't much to **Jenner**, a cluster of shops and restaurants dotting coastal hills. Informative volunteers protect the resident colony of harbor seals at the river's mouth during pupping season, between March and August. **Water Treks Ecotours** (☑707-865-2249; http://watertreks.com; kayak rental from $30; ⊘10am-3pm Mon-Thu, 9am-5pm Fri-Sun) rents kayaks on Hwy 1; reservations recommended.

Twelve miles north of Jenner, the salt-weathered structures of **Fort Ross State Historic Park** (☑707-847-3437; www.fortross.org; 19005 Hwy 1; per car $8; ⊘10am-4:30pm Fri-Mon) preserve an 1812 trading post and Russian Orthodox church. It's a quiet place, but the history is riveting: this was once the southernmost reach of Tsarist Russia's North American trading expeditions. The small, wood-scented museum offers historical exhibits and respite from the windswept cliffs.

Several miles further north, **Salt Point State Park** (☑707-847-3221; www.parks.ca.gov; per car $8; ⊘park sunrise-sunset, visitor center 10am-3pm Sat & Sun Apr-Oct) abounds with hiking trails and tide pools and has two **campgrounds** (☑800-444-7275; www.reserveamerica.com; tent & RV sites $25-35; ⊞). At neighboring **Kruse Rhododendron State Natural Reserve**, pink blooms spot the misty green woods between April and June. Cows graze the fields on the bluffs heading north to **Sea Ranch** (www.tsra.org), where public-access hiking trails lead downhill from roadside parking lots (per car $7) to pocket beaches.

Two miles north of Point Arena town, detour to wind-battered **Point Arena Lighthouse** (☑877-725-4448, 707-882-2809; www.pointarenalighthouse.com; 45500 Lighthouse Rd; adult/child $7.50/1; ⊘10am-3:30pm, to 4:30pm late May-early Sep), built in 1908. Ascend 145 steps to inspect the flashing Fresnel lens and get jaw-dropping coastal views. Eight miles north of the Little River crossing at Hwy 128 is **Van Damme State Park** (☑707-937-5804; www.parks.ca.gov; 8001 N Hwy 1, Little River; per car $8; ⊘8am-9pm), where the popular 5-mile round-trip **Fern Canyon Trail** passes through a lush river canyon with young redwoods, continuing another mile each way to a pygmy forest. The park's **campground** (☑800-444-7275; www.reserveamerica.com; tent & RV sites $25-35; ⊞⊞) has coin-op hot showers.

In **Mendocino**, a historical village perched on a gorgeous headland, baby boomers stroll around New England saltbox and water-tower B&Bs, quaint shops and art galleries. Wilder paths pass berry brambles, wildflowers and cypress trees standing guard over rocky cliffs and raging surf at **Mendocino Headlands State Park** (www.parks.ca.gov) FREE. The **Ford House Museum & Visitor Center** (☑707-537-5397;

http://mendoparks.org; 45035 Main St; ⊘11am-4pm) is nearby. Just south of town, paddle your way up the Big River with **Catch a Canoe & Bicycles, Too!** (✆707-937-0273; www.catchacanoe.com; Stanford Inn by the Sea, 44850 Comptche-Ukiah Rd; kayak & canoe rental adult/child from $28/14; ⊘9am-5pm). North of town, 1909 **Point Cabrillo Light Station** (✆707-937-6123; www.pointcabrillo.org; 45300 Lighthouse Rd; ⊘park sunrise-sunset, lighthouse 11am-4pm) **FREE** is a perfect winter whale-watching perch.

🛏 Sleeping

Every other building in Mendocino seems to be a pricey B&B; book ahead. Fort Bragg, just 10 miles north, has cheaper motels.

Gualala Point Regional Park CAMPGROUND $
(✆707-567-2267; http://parks.sonomacounty.ca.gov; 42401 Hwy 1, Gualala; tent & RV sites $35; ⊞) Shaded by a stand of redwoods and fragrant California bay laurel trees, a short trail connects this creekside campground to the windswept beach. The quality of sites, including several secluded hike-in spots, makes it the best drive-in camping on this part of the coast.

Andiron CABIN $$
(✆707-937-1543; http://theandiron.com; 6051 N Hwy 1, Little River; most r $109-199; 🕾⊞☎) ✈ Styled with hip vintage decor, this cluster of 1950s roadside cottages is a refreshingly playful option amid the cabbage-rose and lace aesthetic of Mendocino. Each cabin houses two rooms with complementing themes: 'Read' has old books, comfy vintage chairs and hip retro eyeglasses, while the adjoining 'Write' features a huge chalkboard and a ribbon typewriter.

Alegria B&B $$$
(✆707-937-5150; www.oceanfrontmagic.com; 44781 Main St, Mendocino; r $239-299; 🕾) A perfect romantic hideaway, beds have views over the coast, decks have ocean view and all rooms have wood-burning fireplaces; outside a gorgeous path leads to a big, amber-grey beach. Ever-so-friendly innkeepers whip up amazing breakfasts served in the sea-view dining area. Less expensive rooms are available across the street at bright and simple **Raku House** (www.rakuhouse.com; r $159-189).

Mar Vista Cottages CABIN $$$
(✆707-884-3522, 877-855-3522; www.marvista-mendocino.com; 35101 S Hwy 1, Gualala; cottages $185-305; 🕾⊞☎) ✈ The elegantly renovated 1930s fishing cabins offer a simple, stylish seaside escape with a vanguard commitment to sustainability. The harmonious environment is the result of pitch-perfect details: linens are line-dried over lavender, guests browse the organic vegetable garden to harvest their own dinner and chickens cluck around the grounds laying the next morning's breakfast. It often requires two-night stays.

🍴 Eating & Drinking

Even tiny coastal towns usually have a bakery, deli, natural-foods market and a couple of roadside cafes and restaurants.

★Franny's Cup & Saucer BAKERY $
(www.frannyscupandsaucer.com; 213 Main St, Point Arena; items from $2; ⊘8am-4pm Wed-Sat) The cutest patisserie on this stretch of coast is run by Franny and her mother, Barbara (a veteran of Chez Panisse). The fresh berry tarts and creative housemade chocolates seem too beautiful to eat, until you take the first bite and immediately want to order another. Several times a year they pull out all the stops for a Sunday garden brunch ($25).

Spud Point Crab Company SEAFOOD $
(www.spudpointcrab.com; 1910 Westshore Rd, Bodega Bay; dishes $4-12; ⊘9am-5pm; ⊞) In the classic tradition of dockside crab shacks, Spud Point serves salty-sweet crab cocktails and *real* clam chowder. Eat at picnic tables overlooking the marina. Take Bay Flat Rd to get here.

Café Aquatica CAFE $
(✆707-865-2251; 10439 Hwy 1, Jenner; items $3-10; ⊘8am-5pm; 🕾) This is the kind of North Coast coffee shop you've been dreaming of: fresh pastries, fog-lifting organic coffee and chatty locals. The expansive view of the Russian River from the patio and gypsy sea-hut decor make it hard to leave.

Piaci Pub & Pizzeria ITALIAN $$
(www.piacipizza.com; 120 W Redwood Ave, Fort Bragg; mains $8-18; ⊘11am-9:30pm Mon-Thu, to 10pm Fri & Sat, 4-9:30pm Sun) Fort Bragg's must-visit pizzeria is known for its sophisticated wood-fired, brick-oven pies as much as for its long list of microbrews. Try the 'Gusto-so' – with chèvre, pesto and seasonal pears – all carefully orchestrated on a thin crust. It's tiny, loud and fun, with much more of a bar atmosphere than a restaurant. Expect to wait at peak times.

North Coast Brewing Company BREWERY $$
(📞707-964-2739; www.northcoastbrewing.com; 455 N Main St, Fort Bragg; mains $16-25; ☺restaurant 4-10pm Sun-Thu, to 11pm Fri & Sat, bar from 2pm daily) Though thick, rare slabs of steak and a list of specials demonstrate that this brewery takes the food as seriously as the bevvies, it's burgers and garlic fries that soak up the fantastic selection of handcrafted brews. A great stop for serious beer-lovers.

Café Beaujolais CALIFORNIAN $$$
(📞707-937-5614; www.cafebeaujolais.com; 961 Ukiah St, Mendocino; mains lunch $10-18, dinner $23-38; ☺11:30am-2:30pm Wed-Sun, dinner from 5:30pm daily) 🍴 Mendocino's iconic, beloved country-Cal–French restaurant occupies an 1893 house restyled into a monochromatic urban-chic dining room, perfect for holding hands by candlelight. The refined, inspired cooking draws diners from San Francisco, who make this the centerpiece of their trip. The locally sourced menu changes with the seasons, but the Petaluma duck breast served with crispy skin is a gourmand's delight.

ℹ️ Getting There & Around

Mendocino Transit Authority (MTA; 📞707-462-1422; http://mendocinotransit.org; most one-way fares $1.50-6) bus 95 travels daily between Fort Bragg and Santa Rosa ($23, 2½ hours), while MTA bus 65 travels once or twice daily between Santa Rosa and Point Arena ($8.25, three hours) via Hwy 1. From Santa Rosa, catch Golden Gate Transit (p143) bus 101 to San Francisco ($12.50, 2½ hours, every 30 to 60 minutes). On weekdays, MTA bus 60 shuttles four times between Fort Bragg and Mendocino ($1.50, one hour), with two onward connections daily except Sunday to Point Arena ($4.50, 2¼ hours).

Along Highway 101 to Avenue of the Giants

To get into the most remote and wild parts of the North Coast behind the 'Redwood Curtain' on the quick, eschew winding Hwy 1 for inland Hwy 101, which occasionally pauses under the traffic lights of small towns. Diversions along the way include bountiful redwood forests past Leggett and the abandoned wilds of the Lost Coast.

Although **Ukiah** is mostly a place to gas up or grab a bite downtown, it's worth a 30-minute meandering mountain drive west to soak at clothing-optional **Orr Hot Springs** (📞707-462-6277; www.orrhotsprings.

org; 13201 Orr Springs Rd; day-use fee adult/child $30/20; ☺10am-10pm by appointment only).

Just north of tiny **Leggett** on Hwy 101, take a dip in the Eel River at **Standish-Hickey State Recreation Area** (📞707-925-6482; www.parks.ca.gov; 69350 Hwy 101; per car $8; 🐾), where hiking trails traipse through virgin and second-growth redwoods. South of **Garberville** on Hwy 101, **Richardson Grove State Park** (📞707-247-3318; www.parks. ca.gov; 1600 Hwy 101, Garberville; per car $8) also protects old-growth redwood forest beside the river. Both parks have developed **campgrounds** (📞800-444-7275; www.reserveamerica. com; tent & RV sites $35-45; 🐾).

The **Lost Coast** tempts hikers with the most rugged coastal backpacking in California. It became 'lost' when the state's highway bypassed the mountains of the King Range, which rises over 4000ft within a few miles of the ocean. From Garberville, it's 23 steep, twisting miles along a paved road to **Shelter Cove**, the main supply point but little more than a seaside subdivision with a general store, cafes and none-too-cheap ocean-view lodgings.

Along Hwy 101, 82-sq-mile **Humboldt Redwoods State Park** (📞707-946-2409; www.parks.ca.gov) FREE protects some of California's oldest redwoods, including more than half of the world's tallest 100 trees. Magnificent groves rival those in Redwood National Park, a long drive further north. If you don't have time to hike, at least drive the awe-inspiring **Avenue of the Giants**, a 31-mile, two-lane road parallel to Hwy 101. Book ahead for **campsites** (📞800-444-7275; www.reserveamerica.com; tent & RV sites $20-35; 🐾). Get hiking info and maps at the **visitor center** (📞707-946-2263; www.humboldt redwoods.org; ☺9am-5pm Apr-Oct, 10am-4pm Nov-Mar).

🛏️ Sleeping & Eating

Campgrounds and RV parks are plentiful along Hwy 101, where every one-horse town guarantees at least a natural-foods store with a deli, a drive-thru espresso stand, a hippie-owned cafe and a handful of motels. Woodsy cabin resorts and aging motels along Avenue of the Giants are mediocre.

Inn of the Lost Coast INN $$
(📞707-986-7521, 888-570-9676; www.innofthelost-coast.com; 205 Wave Dr, Shelter Cove; r $180-300; 🌐🐾🌐) Shelter Cove's most family-friendly hotel has clean rooms, some with basic cooking facilities, breathtaking ocean views

and fireplaces. Downstairs there's a serviceable takeout pizza place and coffee shop as well as ping-pong and a hot tub.

Benbow Inn
HISTORIC HOTEL $$$

(☑707-923-2124; www.benbowinn.com; 445 Lake Benbow Dr, Garberville; d $150-395; ✳ 🛜 🏊 🐾) This inn is a monument to 1920s rustic elegance; the Redwood Empire's first luxury resort is a National Historic Landmark. Hollywood's elite once frolicked in the Tudor-style resort's lobby, where you can play chess by the crackling fire, and enjoy complimentary afternoon tea and scones.

Saucy
PIZZA $$

(☑707-462-7007; http://saucyukiah.com; 108 W Standley St, Ukiah; mains $11-19; ⊘11:30am-9pm Mon-Thu, to 10pm Fri, noon-10pm Sat) Yes there are arty pizzas with toppings like Calabrian love sausage (really), fennel pollen and almond basil pesto but there are also amazing soups, salads, pastas and starters – Nana's meatballs are to die for and the 'kicking' minestrone lives up to its name. The small-town ambience is slightly chic but boisrous at the same time.

Woodrose Café
BREAKFAST, AMERICAN $$

(www.woodrosecafe.com; 911 Redwood Dr, Garberville; meals $10-18; ⊘8am-2pm; 🖊 🐾) Garberville's beloved cafe serves organic omelets, veggie scrambles and buckwheat pancakes with *real* maple syrup in a cozy room. Lunch brings crunchy salads, sandwiches with all-natural meats and good burritos. Plenty of gluten-free options.

❶ Getting There & Around

Daily Greyhound buses connect San Francisco with Ukiah ($39, three hours) and Garberville ($53, 5½ hours). **Redwood Transit System** (☑707-443-0826; www.redwoodtransit.org) operates infrequent weekday buses between Garberville and Eureka ($5.50, 1¾ hours), making a few stops along the Avenue of the Giants.

Highwayy 101 from Eureka to Crescent City

Past the strip malls sprawling around its edges, the heart of Eureka is Old Town, abounding with fine Victorians buildings, antique shops and restaurants. Cruise the harbor aboard the blue-and-white 1910 **Madaket** (☑707-445-1910; www.humboldtbaymaritimemuseum.com; narrated cruise adult/child $18/10), departing from the foot of C St; sunset cocktail cruises serve from the state's smallest licensed bar. The **visitor center** (☑707-442-3738; www.eurekachamber.com; 2112 Broadway; ⊘8:30am-5pm Mon-Fri; @🛜) is on Hwy 101, south of downtown.

On the north side of Humboldt Bay, **Arcata** is a patchouli-dipped hippie haven of radical politics. Biodiesel-fueled trucks drive in for the weekly **farmers market** (www.humfarm.org; ⊘9am-2pm Sat Apr-Nov) on the central plaza, surrounded by art galleries, shops, cafes and bars. Make reservations to soak at **Finnish Country Sauna & Tubs** (☑707-822-2228; http://cafemokkaarcata.com; 495 J St; 30min per adult/child $9.75/2; ⊘noon-11pm Sun-Thu, to 1am Fri & Sat). Northeast of downtown stands eco-conscious, socially responsible **Humboldt State University** (HSU; www.humboldt.edu; 1 Harpst St).

Sixteen miles north of Arcata, **Trinidad** sits on a bluff overlooking a breathtakingly beautiful fishing harbor. Stroll sandy beaches or take short hikes around Trinidad Head after meeting tide-pool critters at the **HSU Telonicher Marine Laboratory** (☑707-826-3671; www.humboldt.edu/marinelab; 570 Ewing St; self-guided tour $1; ⊘9am-4:30pm Mon-Fri, 10am-5pm Sat & Sun mid-Sep–mid-May; 🐾). Heading north of town, Patrick's Point Dr is dotted with forested campgrounds, cabins and lodges. **Patrick's Point State Park** (☑707-677-3570; www.parks.ca.gov; 4150 Patrick's Point Dr; per car $8) has stunning rocky headlands, beachcombing, an authentic reproduction of a Yurok village and a **campground** (☑reservations 800-444-7275; www.reserveamerica.com; tent & RV sites $35-45) with coin-op hot showers.

Heading north, Hwy 101 passes Redwood National Park's **Thomas H Kuchel Visitor Center** (☑707-464-6101; www.nps.gov/redw; Hwy 101; ⊘9am-6pm Jun-Aug, to 5pm Sep-Oct & Mar-May, to 4pm Nov-Feb). Together, the national park and three state parks – Prairie Creek, Del Norte and Jedediah Smith – are a World Heritage site containing more than 40% of the world's remaining old-growth redwood forests. The national park is free, while state parks have an $8 day-use parking fee and developed **campgrounds** (☑reservations 800-444-7275; www.reserveamerica.com; tent & RV sites $35).

This patchwork of state and federally managed land stretches all the way north to the Oregon border, interspersed with several towns. Furthest south, you'll encounter **Redwood National Park** (www.nps.gov/redw; 🐾) **FREE**, where a 1-mile nature trail winds through Lady Bird Johnson Grove.

Six miles north of Orick, the 10-mile Newton B Drury Scenic Parkway runs parallel to Hwy 101 through **Prairie Creek Redwoods State Park**. Roosevelt elk graze in the meadow outside the **visitor center** (707-488-2039; www.parks.ca.gov; 9am-5pm May-Sep, off-season hours vary;), where sunlight-dappled hiking trails begin. Three miles back south, mostly unpaved Davison Rd heads northwest to Gold Bluffs Beach, dead-ending at the trailhead for unbelievably lush **Fern Canyon**.

North of tiny Klamath, Hwy 101 passes the **Trees of Mystery** (707-482-2251; www.treesofmystery.net; 15500 Hwy 101, Klamath; adult/child $15/8; 8:30am-6:30pm Jun-Aug, 9:30am-4:30pm Sep-May;), a kitschy roadside attraction. Next up, **Del Norte Coast Redwoods State Park** preserves virgin redwood groves and unspoiled coastline. The 4.5-mile round-trip **Damnation Creek Trail** careens over 1000ft downhill past redwoods to a hidden rocky beach, best visited at low tide. Find the trailhead at a parking turn-out near mile-marker 16 on Hwy 101.

Backed by a fishing harbor and bay, Crescent City is drab because, after more than half the town was destroyed by a tidal wave in 1964, it was rebuilt with utilitarian architecture. When the tide's out, you can walk across to the 1856 **Battery Point Lighthouse** (707-467-3089; www.delnortehistory.org; adult/child $3/1; 10am-4pm daily Apr-Sep, Sat & Sun only Oct-Mar) from the south end of A St.

Beyond Crescent City, **Jedediah Smith Redwoods State Park** is the northernmost park in the system. The redwood stands here are so dense that there are few trails, but a couple of easy hikes start near riverside swimming holes along Hwy 199 and rough, unpaved Howland Hill Rd, a 10-mile scenic drive. The Redwood National & State Parks' **Crescent City Information Center** (707-465-7335; www.nps.gov/redw; 1111 2nd St; 9am-5pm Apr-Oct, to 4pm Nov-Mar) has maps and info.

🛏 Sleeping

A mixed bag of budget and midrange motels are scattered along Hwy 101, including in Eureka, Arcata and Crescent City.

Curly Redwood Lodge   MOTEL $
(707-464-2137; www.curlyredwoodlodge.com; 701 Hwy 101 S, Crescent City; r $69-100;) The Redwood Lodge is a marvel: it's entirely built and paneled from a single curly redwood tree which measured over 18ft thick in diameter. Progressively restored and pol-

ished into a gem of mid-20th-century kitsch, the inn is a delight for retro junkies. Rooms are clean, large and comfortable (request one away from the road). For truly modern accommodations, look elsewhere.

★ **Historic Requa Inn**   HISTORIC HOTEL $$
(707-482-1425; www.requainn.com; 451 Requa Rd, Klamath; r $119-199;) A woodsy country lodge on bluffs overlooking the mouth of the Klamath, the creaky and bright 1914 Requa Inn is a North Coast favorite and – even better – it's a carbon-neutral facility. Many of the charming old-timey Americana rooms have mesmerizing views over the misty river, as does the dining room, which serves locally sourced, organic New American cuisine.

Carter House Inns   B&B $$$
(707-444-8062; http://carterhouse.com; 301 L St, Eureka; r $179-385;) Recently constructed in period style, this hotel is a Victorian lookalike, holding rooms with top-quality linens and modern amenities; suites have in-room Jacuzzis and marble fireplaces. The same owners operate four other sumptuously decorated lodgings: a single-level house, two honeymoon hideaway cottages and a replica of an 1880s San Francisco mansion, which the owner built himself, entirely by hand.

✖ Eating & Drinking

Arcata has the biggest variety of dining options, from organic juice bars and vegan cafes to Californian and world-fusion bistros.

Wildberries Marketplace   MARKET, DELI $
(www.wildberries.com; 747 13th St, Arcata; sandwiches $4-10; 7am-midnight;) Wildberries Marketplace is Arcata's best grocery, with natural foods, a good deli, bakery and juice bar.

★ **Brick & Fire**   CALIFORNIAN $$
(707-268-8959; www.brickandfirebistro.com; 1630 F St, Eureka; dinner mains $14-23; 11:30am-9pm Mon & Wed-Fri, 5-9pm Sat & Sun) Eureka's best restaurant is in an intimate, warm-hued, bohemian-tinged setting that is almost always busy. Choose from thin-crust pizzas, delicious salads (try the pear and blue cheese) and an ever-changing selection of appetizers and mains that highlight local produce and wild mushrooms. There's a weighty wine list and servers are well-versed in pairings.

Lost Coast Brewery   BREWERY
(📞707-445-4480; www.lostcoast.com; 617 4th
St, Eureka; ⊙11am-10pm Sun-Thu, to 11pm Fri &
Sat; 🕿) The roster of the regular brews at
Eureka's colorful brewery might not knock
the socks off a serious beer snob (and can't
hold a candle to some of the others on the
coast), but highlights include the Downtown
Brown Ale, Great White and Lost Coast Pale
Ale. After downing a few pints, the fried pub
grub starts to look pretty tasty.

**Redwood Curtain Brewing
Company**   BREWERY
(www.redwoodcurtainbrewing.com; 550 S G St, Arcata; ⊙noon-11pm Sun-Tue, to midnight Wed-Sat)
A newer brewery (started in 2010), this tiny
gem has a varied collection of rave-worthy
craft ales and live music most Thursdays
and Saturdays. Plus it offers free wheat thins
and goldfish crackers to munch on.

❶ Getting There & Around

Arcata's **Greyhound depot** (📞707-825-8934;
925 E St at 9th St) has daily buses to San Fran-
cisco ($57, seven hours) via Eureka, Garberville,
Ukiah and Santa Rosa. Several daily Redwood
Transit System (p155) buses stop in Eureka and
Arcata on the Hwy 101 (Trinidad–Scotia) route
($3, 2½ hours).

Sacramento

In California's capital city, politicians in
SUVs go bumper-to-bumper with farmers
driving muddy, half-ton pickups at rush
hour. 'Sac' got its start when eccentric Swiss
immigrant John Sutter built a fort here
in 1839. Once gold was discovered in the
nearby Sierra foothills in 1848, the town's
population boomed. After much legislative
waffling, it became California's state capital
in 1854.

Old Sacramento remains a visitor's magnet – a riverside area with raised wooden
sidewalks that can feel like a ye olde tourist
trap. More interesting food and culture are
hidden on the grid of streets downtown and
in Midtown, where an arts scene quietly de-
fies the city's reputation as a cow town.

◉ Sights

California State Railroad Museum MUSEUM
(📞916-323-9280; www.csrmf.org; 125 I St; adult/
child $10/5; ⊙10am-5pm Fri-Wed, to 8pm Thu;
🚼) At Old Sac's north end is this impressive collection of railcars and locomotives

from miniature to true scale. While the
candy-coated recounting of the struggles of
those who laid the track is unsettling, the
fully outfitted Pullman sleeper and vintage
diner cars will thrill rail fans. Board a restored passenger train (adult/child $12/6)
from the Sacramento Southern Railroad
ticket office, across the plaza on Front St, for
a 40-minute jaunt along the river.

Weather permitting, train rides run hourly from 11am to 4pm on weekends from
April to September.

California State Capitol   HISTORIC BUILDING
(📞916-324-0333; http://capitolmuseum.ca.gov;
1315 10th St; ⊙8am-5pm Mon-Fri, from 9am Sat &
Sun) 𝗙𝗥𝗘𝗘 The gleaming dome of the California State Capitol is Sacramento's most
recognizable structure. A painting of Arnold
Schwarzenegger in a suit hangs in the West
Wing with the other governors' portraits.
Some will find **Capitol Park**, the 40 acres
of gardens and memorials surrounding the
building, more interesting than what's inside. Tours run hourly until 4pm.

California Museum   MUSEUM
(📞916-653-0650; www.californiamuseum.org;
1020 O St; adult/child $9/6.50; ⊙10am-5pm Tue-
Sat, from noon Sun; 🚼) This modern museum
is home to the California Hall of Fame and so
the only place to simultaneously encounter
César Chávez, Mark Zuckerberg and Amelia
Earhart. The *California Indians* exhibit is a
highlight, with artifacts and oral histories of
more than 100 distinct tribes.

Crocker Art Museum   MUSEUM
(📞916-808-7000; https://crockerartmuseum.
org; 216 O St; adult/child $10/5; ⊙10am-5pm
Tue, Wed & Fri-Sun, to 9pm Thu) Housed in the
Crocker family's ornate Victorian mansion
(and sprawling additions), this museum is
stunning as much for its striking architecture (old and new) as its collections. There
are some very fine works by both California
painters and European masters. The contemporary collection is most enthusiastically
presented.

🛏 Sleeping

Hotels cater to business travelers, so look for
weekend bargains. The freeways and suburbs around the city are glutted with budget
and midrange chain lodgings.

HI Sacramento Hostel   HOSTEL $
(📞916-443-1691; http://norcalhostels.org/sac; 925
H St; dm $30-33, r with/without bath from $86/58;

⊙check-in 2-10:30pm; 🖥 @ 📶) In a grand Victorian mansion, this hostel offers impressive trimmings at rock-bottom prices. It's within walking distance of the capitol, Old Sac and the train station and has a piano in the parlor and large dining room. It attracts an international crowd often open to sharing a ride to San Francisco or Lake Tahoe. Limited parking $5.

★**Citizen Hotel**   BOUTIQUE HOTEL **$$**
(🖉info 916-447-2700, reservations 916-492-4460; www.jdvhotels.com; 926 J St; r from $159; 🖥 @ 📶 🖥) With an elegant, ultrahip upgrade by the Joie de Vivre group, the long-vacant Citizen has suddenly become one of the coolest stays in these parts. Rooms are sleek, with luxe linen and bold-patterned decor. There's an upscale farm-to-fork restaurant, **Grange Sacramento** (🖉916-492-4450; www.grangesacramento.com; 926 J St; dinner mains $19-39; ⊙6:30-10:30am & 11:30am-2pm Mon-Fri, 8am-2pm Sat & Sun, 5:30pm-10pm Mon-Thu, to 11pm Fri & Sat, to 10pm Sun; 📶), on the ground floor.

Delta King   B&B **$$**
(🖉916-444-5464; www.deltaking.com; 1000 Front St; d incl breakfast from $145; 🖥📶) It's a treat to sleep aboard the *Delta King*, a 1927 paddle wheeler docked in Old Sac that lights up like a Christmas tree at night.

🍴 Eating & Drinking

For more restaurants and bars, make for Midtown, especially J St east of 16th St.

La Bonne Soupe Cafe   DELI **$**
(🖉916-492-9506; 920 8th St; items $5-8; ⊙11am-3pm Mon-Sat) Divine soup and sandwiches assembled with such care that the line of downtown lunchers snakes out the door. If you're in a hurry, skip it. This humble lunch counter is focused on quality that predates drive-through haste.

Mulvaney's B&L   MODERN AMERICAN **$$$**
(🖉916-441-6022; www.mulvaneysbl.com; 1215 19th St; mains $32-40; ⊙11:30am-2:30pm Tue-Fri, 5-10pm Tue-Sat) 🍴 With an obsessive commitment to seasonality, the menu at this swank converted firehouse includes delicate pastas and grilled meats that change every day.

Rubicon Brewing Company   BREWERY
(www.rubiconbrewing.com; 2004 Capitol Ave; ⊙11am-11:30pm Mon-Thu, to 12:30am Fri & Sat, to 10pm Sun) These people take their hops *seriously*. Their heady selection is brewed on-site. Monkey Knife Fight Pale Ale is ideal for washing back platters of hot wings.

❶ Getting There & Around

About 11 miles northwest of downtown off I-5, **Sacramento International Airport** (SMF; www.sacramento.aero/smf; 6900 Airport Blvd) is served mainly by domestic flights.

Inconveniently stopping 2 miles northwest of downtown, **Greyhound** (🖉800-231-2222; www.greyhound.com; 420 Richards Blvd) has several daily buses to San Francisco ($20, two to 2½ hours).

From downtown's **train station** (🖉877-974-3322; www.capitolcorridor.org; 401 I St), Amtrak runs frequent Capitol Corridor trains to/from the San Francisco Bay Area ($29, two hours); thrice-daily San Joaquin trains, with onward bus connections to Yosemite Valley ($38, five hours); and daily long-distance Coast Starlight and California Zephyr trains.

Sacramento Regional Transit (RT; 🖉916-321-2877; www.sacrt.com; fare/day pass $2.50/6) runs a bus and light-rail system around town.

Gold Country

Hard to believe, but this is where it all began – these quaint hill towns and drowsy oak-lined byways belie the wild, chaotic, often violent founding of California. After a glint caught James Marshall's eye in Sutter's Creek in 1848, the gold rush brought a 300,000-stong stampede of forty-niners to these Sierra foothills. The frenzy paid little heed to the starched moral decorum of Victorian society, populating lawless boom towns and wreaking environmental havoc.

Traveling here might be a thrill for history buffs – the fading historical markers tell tales of bloodlust and banditry – but more tactile pleasures await anyone willing to plunge into a swimming hole, rattle down a mountain-biking trail or go white-water rafting in the icy currents of local rivers.

Hwy 50 divides the Northern and Southern Mines. Winding Hwy 49, which connects everything, provides plenty of vistas of the famous hills. The **Gold Country Visitors Association** (www.calgold.org) has many more touring ideas.

❶ Getting There & Around

A patchwork of public buses sporadically serves some towns.

For the Northern Mines, several daily **Gold Country Stage** (🖉888-660-7433, 530-477-

0103; www.goldcountrystage.com; fares $1.50-3) buses link Nevada City via Grass Valley with Auburn, an **Amtrak** (☑800-872-7245; www.amtrak.com; 277 Nevada St) train stop. **Placer County Transit** (☑530-885-2877; www.placer.ca.gov/transit; fare $1.25) buses connect Auburn with Sacramento hourly.

Among the Southern Mines, weekday-only **Amador Transit** (☑209-267-9395; http://amadortransit.com; fares $1-3; ⊙Mon-Fri) runs twice-daily buses between Sutter Creek and Sacramento, Amador City, Plymouth and Jackson. A few buses **Calaveras Transit** (☑209-754-4450; http://transit.calaverasgov.us; fare $2) buses serve Jackson, Mokelumne Hill, Angels Camp and Murphys. Weekday-only **Tuolumne County Transit** (☑209-532-0404; www.tuolumnecountytransit.com; fare $1.50; ⊙Mon-Fri) buses and trolleys loop between Sonora, Columbia and Jamestown.

Northern Mines

Known as the 'Queen of the Northern Mines,' the narrow streets of Nevada City gleam with lovingly restored buildings, tiny theaters, art galleries, cafes and shops. The **visitor center** (☑530-265-2692; www.nevadacitychamber.com; 132 Main St; ⊙9am-5pm Mon-Fri, 11am-4pm Sat, 11am-3pm Sun) dispenses information and self-guided walking-tour maps. On Hwy 49, the **Tahoe National Forest Headquarters** (☑530-265-4531; www.fs.usda.gov/tahoe; 631 Coyote St; ⊙8am-4:30pm Mon-Fri) provides camping and hiking information and wilderness permits.

Just over a mile east of utilitarian **Grass Valley** and Hwy 49, **Empire Mine State Historic Park** (☑530-273-8522; www.empiremine.org; 10791 E Empire St; adult/child $7/3; ⊙10am-5pm) marks the site of one of the richest mines in California. From 1850 to 1956 it produced almost 6 million ounces of gold – over $6 billion in today's market.

When it's sweltering hot outside during summer, if you see a line of cars parked roadside along Hwy 49, that's your signal to discover a swimming hole. One of the best is where the North and Middle Forks of the American River join up at **Auburn State Recreation Area** (☑530-885-4527; www.parks.ca.gov; per car $10; ⊙7am-sunset). It's just east of **Auburn**, an I-80 pit stop about 25 miles south of Grass Valley.

Coloma is where California's gold rush started. Riverside **Marshall Gold Discovery State Historic Park** (☑530-622-3470; http://marshallgold.org; per car $8; ⊙8am-5pm, to 7pm late May-early Sep, museum 10am-5pm, to 4pm Nov-Mar; ♿) pays tribute to James Marshall's riot-inducing discovery, with restored buildings and gold-panning opportunities. There's a hilltop monument to Marshall himself, who ironically died a penniless ward of the state.

🛏 Sleeping & Eating

Nevada City has the biggest spread of restaurants and historical B&Bs. Motels speckle Hwy 49 in Grass Valley and I-80 in Auburn.

★**Outside Inn**   MOTEL, CABIN $$
(☑530-265-2233; www.outsideinn.com; 575 E Broad St, Nevada City; d $79-210; ❄🤖🏊♿🐕) The best option for active explorers, this is an unusually friendly and fun motel, with 12 rooms and three cottages maintained by staff that loves the outdoors and has excellent information about area hiking. Some rooms have a patio overlooking a small creek; all have nice quilts and access to BBQ grills. It's a 10-minute walk from downtown.

Broad Street Inn   INN $$
(☑530-265-2239; www.broadstreetinn.com; 517 W Broad St, Nevada City; r $115-125; ❄🤖🐕) 🐾 This six-room inn is a favorite because it keeps things simple. (No weird old dolls, no yellowing lace doilies.) The good-value rooms are modern, brightly furnished and elegant.

Ikedas   MARKET $
(www.ikedas.com; 13500 Lincoln Way; sandwiches $6-9; ⊙11am-7pm Mon-Thu, 10am-8pm Fri-Sun; 🐾) If you're cruising this part of the state without time to explore, the best pit stop is this expanded farm stand off I-80 a few miles north of downtown. Thick, grass-fed beef or tofu burgers, homemade pies and the seasonal fresh peach shake are deliriously good.

★**New Moon Café**   CALIFORNIAN $$$
(☑530-265-6399; www.thenewmooncafe.com; 203 York St; dinner mains $23-38; ⊙11:30am-2pm Tue-Fri, 5-8:30pm Tue-Sun) 🐾 Pure elegance, Peter Selaya's organic and local-ingredient menu changes with the seasons. If you visit during spring or summer, go for the line-caught fish or the housemade, moon-shaped fresh ravioli.

Southern Mines

The towns of the Southern Mines – from Placerville to Sonora – receive less traffic and their dusty streets have a whiff of Wild West, today evident in the motley crew of

Harley riders and gold prospectors (still!) who populate them. Some, like **Plymouth** (ol' Pokerville), **Volcano** and **Mokelumne Hill**, are virtual ghost towns, slowly crumbling into photogenic oblivion. Others, like **Sutter Creek**, **Murphys** and **Angels Camp**, are gussied-up showpieces of Victorian Americana. Get off the beaten path at family-run vineyards and subterranean caverns, where geological wonders reward those who first navigate the touristy gift shops above ground.

A short detour off Hwy 49, **Columbia State Historic Park** (209-588-9128; www.parks.ca.gov; 11255 Jackson St, Columbia; museum 10am-5pm Apr-Sep, to 4pm Oct-Mar;) **FREE** preserves blocks of authentic 1850s buildings complete with shopkeepers and street musicians in period costumes. Also near Sonora, **Railtown 1897 State Historic Park** (209-984-3953; www.railtown1897.org; 18115 5th Ave, Jamestown; adult/child $5/3, incl train ride $15/10; 9:30am-4:30pm Apr-Oct, 10am-3pm Nov-Mar, train rides 10:30am-3pm Sat & Sun Apr-Oct;) offers excursion trains through the surrounding hills where Hollywood Westerns including *High Noon* have been filmed.

🛏 Sleeping & Eating

Lacy B&Bs, cafes and ice-cream parlors are found in nearly every town. Sonora, about an hour's drive from Yosemite National Park, and Placerville have the most motels.

Indian Grinding Rock
State Historic Park   CAMPGROUND $
(reservations 800-444-7275; www.reserveamerica.com; 14881 Pine Grove-Volcano Rd, Pine Grove; tent & RV sites $30) The beautiful campground at Indian Grinding Rock State Historic Park has fresh water, plumbing and 22 nonreservable sites set among the trees, with tent sites and hookups for RVs.

City Hotel   HOTEL $$
(info 209-532-1479, reservations 800-444-7275; www.reserveamerica.com; 22768 Main St, Columbia; r $85-115;) Among the handful of restored Victorian hotels in the area, the City Hotel is the most elegant, with rooms that overlook a shady stretch of Main St and that open on lovely sitting rooms. The acclaimed restaurant (mains $15 to $30) is frequented by a Twain impersonator and the adjoining **What Cheer Saloon** is an atmospheric Gold Country joint with oil paintings of lusty ladies and striped wallpaper.

Imperial Hotel   B&B $$
(209-267-9172; www.imperialamador.com; 14202 Hwy 49, Amador City; r $105-155, ste $125-195;) Built in 1879, it's one of the area's most inventive updates to the typical antique-cluttered hotels, with sleek deco touches accenting the usual gingerbread flourish, a genteel bar and a very good, seasonally minded restaurant (dinner mains $14 to $30). On weekends and holidays, expect a two-night minimum.

Volcano Union Inn   HISTORIC HOTEL $$
(209-296-7711; www.volcanounion.com; 21375 Consolation St, Volcano; r incl breakfast $119-139;) The preferred of two historic hotels in Volcano, this one has four lovingly updated rooms with crooked floors: two have street-facing balconies. Flat-screen TVs and modern touches are a bit incongruous with the old building, but it's a comfortable place to stay. The on-site **Union Pub** (dinner mains $12 to $28) has a superb menu and will host the occasional fiddler.

Cozmic Café & Pub   HEALTH FOOD $
(www.ourcoz.com; 594 Main St; items $4-10; 7am-8pm;) In the historic Placerville Soda Works building, the menu is organic and boasts vegetarian and healthy fare backed by fresh smoothies. There's a good selection of microbrews and live music on weekends, when it stays open late.

Northern Mountains

Remote, empty and eerily beautiful, these are some of California's least visited wild lands, an endless show of geological wonders, clear lakes, rushing rivers and high desert. The major peaks – Lassen, Shasta and the Trinity Alps – have few geological features in common, but all offer backcountry camping under starry skies. Small towns dotting the region aren't attractions themselves, but are handy resupply points for further wilderness adventures.

Redding to Mt Shasta

Much of the drive north of Redding is dominated by **Mt Shasta**, a 14,180ft snowcapped goliath at the southern end of the volcanic Cascades Range. It arises dramatically, fueling the anticipation felt by mountaineers who seek to climb its slopes.

Don't believe the tourist brochures: Redding, the region's largest city, is a snooze. The best reason to detour off I-5 is the **Sundial Bridge**, a glass-bottomed pedestrian marvel designed by Spanish neofuturist architect Santiago Calatrava. It spans the Sacramento River at **Turtle Bay Exploration Park** (☏800-887-8532; www.turtlebay.org; 844 Sundial Bridge Dr; adult/child $16/12, after 3:30pm $11/7; ⊙9am-5pm Mon-Sat, 10am-5pm Sun, closing 1hr earlier Nov–mid-Mar; ♿), a kid-friendly science and nature center with botanical gardens.

Six miles west of Redding along Hwy 299, explore a genuine gold-rush town at **Shasta State Historic Park** (☏520-243-8194; www.parks.ca.gov; museum entry adult/child $3/2; ⊙10am-5pm Thu-Sun). Two miles further west, **Whiskeytown National Recreation Area** (☏530-246-1225; Hwy 299 at JFK Memorial Dr, Whiskeytown; ⊙10am-4pm) harbors **Whiskeytown Lake**, with sandy beaches, waterfall hikes and water-sports and camping opportunities. In sleepy **Weaverville**, another 35 miles further west, **Joss House State Historic Park** (☏530-623-5284; www.parks.ca.gov; 630 Main St; tour adult/child $4/2; ⊙tours hourly 10am-4pm Thu-Sun) preserves an ornate 1874 Chinese immigrant temple.

North of Redding, I-5 crosses deep-blue **Shasta Lake**, California's biggest reservoir, formed by colossal **Shasta Dam** (☏530-275-4463; www.usbr.gov/mp/ncao/shasta/; 16349 Shasta Dam Blvd; ⊙visitor center 8am-5pm, tours 9am-3:30pm) **FREE** and ringed by houseboat marinas and RV campgrounds. High in the limestone megaliths on the lake's northern side are prehistoric **Lake Shasta Caverns** (☏530-238-2341; http://lakeshastacaverns.com; 20359 Shasta Caverns Rd, Lakehead; 2hr tour adult/child $24/14; ⊙tours every 30min 9am-4pm late May-early Sep, hourly 9am-3pm Apr-late May & early-late Sep, 10am, noon & 2pm Oct-Mar; ♿), where tours include a catamaran ride.

Another 35 miles north on I-5, **Dunsmuir** is a teeny historic railroad town with vibrant art galleries inhabiting a quaint downtown district. Six miles south off I-5, **Castle Crags State Park** (☏530-235-2684; www.parks.ca.gov; per car $8; ⊙sunrise-sunset) shelters forested **campsites** (☏reservations 800-444-7275; www.reserveamerica.com; tent & RV sites $15-30). Be awed by stunning views of Mt Shasta from the top of the park's hardy 5.6-mile round-trip **Crags Trail**.

Nine miles north of Dunsmuir, **Mt Shasta city** lures climbers, new-age hippies and

back-to-nature types, all of whom revere the majestic mountain looming overhead. Usually open and snow free beyond Bunny Flat from June until October, **Everitt Memorial Hwy** ascends the mountain to a perfect sunset-watching perch at almost 8000ft – simply head east from town on Lake St and keep going. For experienced mountaineers, climbing the peak above 10,000ft requires a Summit Pass ($20), available from **Mt Shasta Ranger Station** (☏530-926-4511; www.fs.usda.gov/stnf; 204 W Alma St; ⊙8am-4:30pm Mon-Fri), which has weather reports and sells topographic maps. Stop by downtown's **Fifth Season** (☏530-926-3606; http://thefifthseason.com; 300 N Mt Shasta Blvd; ⊙9am-6pm Mon-Fri, from 8am Sat, 10am-5pm Sun) outdoor-gear shop for equipment rentals. **Shasta Mountain Guides** (☏530-926-3117; http://shastaguides.com) offers mountaineering trips (from $550).

🛏 Sleeping

Roadside motels are abundant, including in Mt Shasta city. Redding has the most chain lodgings, clustered near major highways. Campgrounds are abundant, especially on public lands.

★ **McCloud River Mercantile Hotel** INN $$
(☏530-964-2330; www.mccloudmercantile.com; 241 Main St, McCloud; r $129-250; 🕸) Stroll upstairs to the 2nd floor of McCloud's central Mercantile and try not to fall in love; it's all high ceilings, exposed brick and a perfect marriage of preservationist class and modern panache. The rooms with antique furnishings are situated within open floor plans.

Shasta MountInn B&B $$
(☏530-926-1810; www.shastamountinn.com; 203 Birch St, Mt Shasta city; r $150-175; 🕸) Only antique on the outside, this bright Victorian 1904 farmhouse is all relaxed minimalism, bold colors and graceful decor on the inside. Each airy room has a great bed and exquisite views of the luminous mountain. Enjoy the expansive garden, wraparound deck, outdoor hot tub and sauna. Not relaxed enough yet? Chill on the perfectly placed porch swings.

Railroad Park Resort INN, CAMPGROUND $$
(☏530-235-4440; www.rrpark.com; 100 Railroad Park Rd, Dunsmuir; tent/RV sites from $29/37, d $135-165; ❋🕸🌊♿🐾) About 2 miles south

of town, off I-5, visitors can spend the night inside refitted vintage railroad cars and cabooses. The grounds are fun for kids, who can run around the engines and plunge in a centrally situated pool. The deluxe boxcars are furnished with antiques and claw-foot tubs, although the cabooses are simpler and a bit less expensive.

Eating & Drinking

Dunsmuir Brewery Works PUB FOOD $
(530-235-1900; www.dunsmuirbreweryworks.com; 5701 Dunsmuir Ave, Dunsmuir; mains $10-15; 11am-9pm Tue-Sun;) It's hard to describe this little microbrew pub without veering into hyperbole. Start with the beer: the crisp ales and porter are perfectly balanced and the IPA is apparently pretty good too, because patrons are always drinking it dry. Soak it up with awesome bar food; a warm potato salad, bratwurst or a thick Angus burger.

Yaks AMERICAN $
(www.yaks.com; 4917 Dunsmuir Ave, Dunsmuir; mains $8-18; 11am-9pm Mon-Sat, to 8pm Sun;) Hiding under the Hitching Post sign just off I-5, this is where you come to blow your diet. Breakfast means Cuban peppersteak hash or perhaps home-baked cinnamon roll French toast with choice of house syrups like Baileys-and-bourbon. Lunch offers a huge range of burgers (try the one with the house-roasted coffee rub). There's also a takeout counter.

Berryvale Grocery MARKET, DELI $
(www.berryvale.com; 305 S Mt Shasta Blvd, Mt Shasta city; items $4-11; store 8am-8pm, cafe to 7pm;) This market sells groceries and organic produce to health-conscious eaters. The excellent cafe serves good coffee and an array of tasty – mostly veggie – salads, sandwiches and wraps.

★ **Café Maddalena** EUROPEAN, NORTH AFRICAN $$$
(530-235-2725; www.cafemaddalena.com; 5801 Sacramento Ave, Dunsmuir; mains $15-26; 5-9pm Thu-Sun Feb-Dec) Simple and elegant, this cafe put Dunsmuir on the foodie map. The menu was designed by chef Bret LaMott (of Trinity Cafe fame) and changes weekly to feature dishes from southern Europe and northern Africa. Some highlights include pan-roasted king salmon with basil cream, or sauteed rabbit with carrots and morel sauce.

Getting There & Around

Amtrak's Coast Starlight trains inconveniently stop in Redding and Dunsmuir in the dead of night. Thrice-daily **Greyhound** (800-231-2222; www.greyhound.com) buses connect Weed, 10 miles north of Mt Shasta via I-5, with Redding ($27, 80 minutes) and Sacramento ($63, 4½ to 5½ hours). **STAGE** (530-842-8295; www.co.siskiyou.ca.us; fares $1.75-6) buses travel the I-5 corridor a few times daily, linking Weed, Mt Shasta city, McCloud and Dunsmuir.

Northeast Corner

Site of California's last major Native American conflict and a half-million years of volcanic destruction, **Lava Beds National Monument** (530-667-8113; www.nps.gov/labe; 7-day entry per car $15) is a peaceful monument to centuries of turmoil. This park's got it all: lava flows, cinder and spatter cones, volcanic craters and amazing lava tubes. It was the site of the Modoc War, and ancient Native American petroglyphs are etched into rocks and pictographs painted on cave walls. Pick up info and maps at the **visitor center** (530-667-8113; www.nps.gov/labe; Tulelake; 8am-6pm late May-early Sep, to 5pm mid-Sep–mid-May), which sells basic spelunking gear (borrow flashlights for free). Nearby is the park's basic **campground** (tent & RV sites $10;), where drinking water is available. Over 20 miles northeast of the park, the dusty town of Tulelake off Hwy 139 has basic motels, roadside diners and gas.

Comprising six separate refuges in California and Oregon, **Klamath Basin National Wildlife Refuge Complex** is a prime stopover on the Pacific Flyway and an important wintering site for bald eagles. When the spring and fall migrations peak, more than a million birds can fill the sky. The **visitor center** (530-667-2231; http://klamathbasinrefuges.fws.gov; 4009 Hill Rd, Tulelake; 8am-4:30pm Mon-Fri, 9am-4pm Sat & Sun) FREE is off Hwy 161, about 4 miles south of the Oregon border. Self-guided 10-mile auto tours of the Lower Klamath and Tule Lake refuges provide excellent birding opportunities. Paddle the Upper Klamath refuge's 9.5-mile canoe trail by launching from **Rocky Point Resort** (541-356-2287; www.rockypointoregon.com; 28121 Rocky Point Rd, Klamath Falls, OR; canoe & kayak rental per hr/half-day/day $20/45/60). For gas, food and lodging, drive into Klamath Falls, OR, off Hwy 97.

Quietly impressive **Lassen Volcanic National Park** (☑530-595-4480; www.nps.gov/lavo; 7-day entry per car $20) has hydrothermal sulfur pools, boiling mud pots and steaming pools, as glimpsed from the **Bumpass Hell** boardwalk. Tackle **Lassen Peak** (10,457ft), the world's largest plug-dome volcano, on a strenuous, but nontechnical 5-mile round-trip trail. The park has two entrances: an hour's drive east of Redding off Hwy 44, near popular **Manzanita Lake Campground** (☑reservations 877-444-6777; www.recreation.gov; tent & RV sites $15-24, cabins $69-95; 🐾🚻); and a 40-minute drive northwest of Lake Almanor off Hwy 89, by the **Kohm Yah-ma-nee Visitor Center** (☑530-595-4480; www.nps.gov/lavo; ☺9am-5pm, closed Mon & Tue Nov-Mar; 🚻) 🐾. Hwy 89 through the park is typically snow free and open to cars from June though October.

SIERRA NEVADA

The mighty Sierra Nevada – baptized the 'Range of Light' by poet-naturalist John Muir – is California's backbone. This 400-mile phalanx of craggy peaks, chiseled and gouged by glaciers and erosion, both welcomes and challenges outdoor-sports enthusiasts. Cradling three national parks (Yosemite, Sequoia and Kings Canyon), the Sierra is a spellbinding wonderland of superlative wilderness, boasting the contiguous USA's highest peak (Mt Whitney), North America's tallest waterfall (Yosemite Falls) and the world's oldest and biggest trees (ancient bristlecone pines and giant sequoias, respectively).

Yosemite National Park

There's a reason why everybody's heard of it: the granite-peak heights are dizzying, the mist from thunderous waterfalls drenching, the Technicolor wildflower meadows amazing and the majestic silhouettes of El Capitan and Half Dome almost shocking against a crisp blue sky. It's a landscape of dreams, surrounding oh-so-small people on all sides.

Then, alas, the hiss and belch of another tour bus, disgorging dozens, rudely breaks the spell. While staggering crowds can't be ignored, these rules will shake most of 'em:

➡ Avoid summer in the valley. Spring's best, especially when waterfalls gush in May. Autumn is blissfully peaceful, and snowy winter days can be magical too.

➡ Park your car and leave it – by hiking a short distance up almost any trail, you'll lose car-dependent hordes.

➡ Forget jet lag. Get up for sunrise, or go for moonlit hikes with stargazing.

◉ Sights

The main entrances to the **park** (☑209-372-0200; www.nps.gov/yose; 7-day entry per car $30) are at Arch Rock (Hwy 140), Wawona (Hwy 41) and Big Oak Flat (Hwy 120 west). Tioga Pass (Hwy 120 east) is open only seasonally.

◉ Yosemite Valley

From the ground up, this dramatic valley cut by the meandering Merced River is song-inspiring: rippling green meadow-grass; stately pines; cool, impassive pools reflecting looming granite monoliths; and cascading ribbons of glacially cold white water. Often overrun and traffic-choked, **Yosemite Village** is home to the park's main visitor center (p166), **museum** (☺9am-5pm summer, 10am-4pm winter, often closed noon-1pm) **FREE**, photography gallery, movie theater, general store and many more services. **Curry Village** is another valley hub, offering public showers and outdoor-equipment rental and sales, including camping gear.

Spring snowmelt turns the valley's famous waterfalls into thunderous cataracts; most are reduced to a mere trickle by late summer. **Yosemite Falls** is North America's tallest, dropping 2425ft in three tiers. A wheelchair-accessible trail leads to the bottom of this cascade or, for solitude and different perspectives, you can trek the grueling trail to the top (6.8 miles round-trip). No less impressive are other waterfalls around the valley. A strenuous granite staircase beside **Vernal Fall** leads you, gasping, right to the waterfall's edge for a vertical view – look for rainbows in the clouds of mist.

You can't ignore the valley's monumental **El Capitan** (7569ft), an El Dorado for rock climbers. Toothed **Half Dome** (8842ft) soars above the valley as Yosemite's spiritual centerpiece. The classic panoramic photo op is at **Tunnel View** on Hwy 41 as you drive into the valley.

Glacier Point

Rising over 3000ft above the valley floor, dramatic Glacier Point (7214ft) practically puts you at eye level with Half Dome. It's at least an hour's drive from Yosemite Valley up Glacier Point Rd (usually open from May into November) off Hwy 41, or a strenuous hike along the **Four Mile Trail** (actually, 4.6 miles one way) or the less-crowded, waterfall-strewn **Panorama Trail** (8.5 miles one way). To hike one way downhill from Glacier Point, reserve a seat on the hikers' shuttle bus (adult/child $25/15).

Wawona

At Wawona, an hour's drive south of Yosemite Valley, drop by the **Pioneer Yosemite History Center** (rides adult/child $5/4; ⊙24hr, rides Wed-Sun Jun-Sep; 🚻) **FREE**, with its covered bridge, historic buildings and horse-drawn stagecoach rides. Further south stands towering **Mariposa Grove**, home of the Grizzly Giant and other giant sequoia trees. Free shuttle buses usually run to the grove from spring through fall. Note that the grove is closed to visitors for restoration until spring 2017.

Tuolumne Meadows

A 90-minute drive from Yosemite Valley, high-altitude Tuolumne Meadows (pronounced *twol*-uh-mee) draws hikers, backpackers and climbers to the park's northern wilderness. The Sierra Nevada's largest subalpine meadow (8600ft), it's a vivid contrast to the valley, with wildflower fields, azure lakes, ragged granite peaks, polished domes and cooler temperatures. Hikers and climbers have a paradise of options; lake swimming and picnicking are also popular. Access is via scenic Tioga Rd (Hwy 120), which is only open seasonally. West of Tuolumne Meadows and **Tenaya Lake**, stop at **Olmsted Point** for epic vistas of Half Dome.

Hetch Hetchy

A 40-mile drive northwest of Yosemite Valley, it's the site of perhaps the most controversial dam in US history. Despite not existing in its natural state, Hetch Hetchy Valley remains pretty and mostly crowd free. A 5.4-mile round-trip hike across the dam and through a tunnel to the base of **Wapama Falls** lets you get thrillingly close to an avalanche of water crashing down into the sparkling reservoir.

🏃 Activities

With more than 800 miles of varied hiking trails, you're spoiled for choice. Easy valley-floor routes can get jammed; escape the teeming masses by heading up. The ultimate hike summits **Half Dome** (14 to 16 miles round-trip), but be warned: it's very strenuous, and advance lottery permits (from $12.50) are required even for day hikes. Without a permit, it's rewarding to hike as far as the top of Vernal Fall (2.4 miles round-trip) or Nevada Fall (5.4 miles round-trip) via the **Mist Trail**.

CAMPING IN YOSEMITE

From mid-March through mid-October or November, many park campgrounds accept or require **reservations** (☎518-885-3639, 877-444-6777; www.recreation.gov), which are available starting five months in advance. Campsites routinely sell out online within *minutes*. All campgrounds have bear-proof lockers and campfire rings; most have potable water.

In summer most campgrounds are noisy and booked to bulging, especially **North Pines** (tent & RV sites $26; ⊙Apr-Oct; 🐻), **Lower Pines** (tent & RV sites $26; ⊙Apr-Oct; 🐻) and **Upper Pines** (tent & RV sites $26; ⊙year-round; 🐻) in Yosemite Valley; **Tuolumne Meadows** (tent & RV sites $26; ⊙Jul-Sep; 🚻🐻) off Tioga Rd; and riverside **Wawona** (tent & RV sites $18-26; ⊙year-round; 🐻).

Year-round the following are all first-come, first served: **Camp 4** (shared tent sites per person $6; ⊙year-round), a rock climber's hangout in the valley; **Bridalveil Creek** (tent & RV sites $18; ⊙Jul-early Sep; 🐻), off Glacier Point Rd; and **White Wolf** (tent & RV sites $18; ⊙Jul-early Sep; 🐻), off Tioga Rd. They often fill before noon, especially on weekends.

Looking for a quieter, more rugged experience? Try the primitive campgrounds (no potable water) off Tioga Rd at **Tamarack Flat** (tent sites $12; ⊙late Jun-Sep; 🐻), **Yosemite Creek** (tent sites $12; ⊙Jul-early Sep; 🐻) and **Porcupine Flat** (tent & RV sites $12; ⊙Jul–mid-Oct; 🐻), all first-come, first-served.

For overnight backpacking trips, wilderness permits (from $10) are required year-round. A quota system limits the number of hikers leaving daily from each trailhead. Make reservations up to 26 weeks in advance, or try your luck at the **Yosemite Valley Wilderness Center** (☑ 209-372-0745; Yosemite Village; ⊙ 8am-5pm May-Sep) or another permit-issuing station, starting at 11am on the day before you aim to hike.

Yosemite
Mountaineering School   ROCK CLIMBING
(☑ 209-372-8344; Curry Village; ⊙ Apr-Oct) Offers topflight instruction for novice to advanced climbers, plus guided climbs and equipment rental.

🛏 Sleeping & Eating

Concessionaire **DNC** (☑ 801-559-4884; www.yosemitepark.com) has a monopoly on park lodging and eating establishments, including fast-food courts and snack bars. Lodging reservations (up to 366 days in advance) are essential for peak season (May to September). During summer, DNC sets up simple canvas-tent cabins at riverside **Housekeeping Camp** (q $106; ⊙ Apr-Oct) in Yosemite Valley and at busy **Tuolumne Meadows Lodge** (tent cabins $123; ⊙ mid-Jun–mid-Sep) and quieter **White Wolf Lodge** (tent cabins $126, cabins with bath $158; ⊙ Jul–mid-Sep) off Tioga Rd.

Curry Village   CABIN $$
(tent cabins $121-126, cabins $193, without bath $146; 🗺🖼) Founded in 1899 as a summer camp, Curry has hundreds of units squished tightly together beneath towering evergreens. The canvas cabins are basically glorified tents, so for more comfort, quiet and privacy get one of the cozy wood cabins, which have bedspreads, drapes and vintage posters. There are also 18 attractive motel-style rooms in the **Stoneman House** (r $202), including a loft suite sleeping up to six.

Wawona Hotel   HISTORIC HOTEL $$
(r $226, without bath $155; ⊙ mid-Mar–Dec; 🗺🖼) This National Historic Landmark, dating from 1879, is a collection of six graceful, whitewashed New England–style buildings flanked by wide porches. The 104 rooms – with no phone or TV – come with Victorian-style furniture and other period items, and about half the rooms share bathrooms, with nice robes provided for the walk there.

ⓘ IMPASSABLE TIOGA PASS

Hwy 120 is the only road connecting Yosemite National Park with the Eastern Sierra, climbing through Tioga Pass (9945ft). Most maps mark this road 'closed in winter,' which, while literally true, is also misleading. Tioga Rd is usually closed from the first heavy snowfall in October or November, not reopening until May or June. Call ☑ 209-372-0200 or check www.nps.gov/yose/planyourvisit/conditions.htm for current road conditions.

★**Ahwahnee Hotel**   HISTORIC HOTEL $$$
(r from $458; @🗺🖼) The crème de la crème of Yosemite's lodging, this sumptuous historic property dazzles with soaring ceilings, Turkish kilims lining the hallways and atmospheric lounges with mammoth stone fireplaces. It's the gold standard for upscale lodges, though if you're not blessed with bullion, you can still soak up the ambience during afternoon tea, a drink in the bar or a gourmet meal.

Yosemite Lodge at the Falls   MOTEL $$$
(r from $235; @🗺🖼) 🖊 Situated a short walk from Yosemite Falls, this multibuilding complex contains a wide range of eateries, a lively bar, big pool and other handy amenities. Delightful rooms, thanks to a recent eco-conscious renovation, now feel properly lodge-like, with rustic wooden furniture and striking nature photography. All have cable TV, telephone, fridge and coffeemaker, and great patio or balcony panoramas.

Degnan's Loft   PIZZA $
(Yosemite Village; mains $8-12.50; ⊙ 11am-9pm late May-Sep; 🖊🖼) Head upstairs to this convivial place with high-beamed ceilings and a many-sided fireplace, and kick back under the dangling lift chair for decent salads, lasagna and pizza.

★**Mountain Room Restaurant** AMERICAN $$$
(☑ 209-372-1403; Yosemite Lodge; mains $17-36; ⊙ 5:30-9:30pm; 🖊🖼) 🖊 With killer views of Yosemite Falls, the window tables at this casual and elegant contemporary steakhouse are a hot commodity. The chefs whip up the best meals in the park, with flat-iron steak and locally caught mountain trout wooing diners under a rotating display of nature photographs. Reservations are

DON'T MISS

SUPERSIZED FORESTS

In California you can stand under the world's oldest trees (ancient bristlecone pines) and its tallest (coast redwoods), but the record for biggest in terms of volume belongs to giant sequoias (*Sequoiadendron giganteum*). They grow only on the western slope of the Sierra Nevada range and are most abundant in Sequoia, Kings Canyon and Yosemite National Parks. John Muir called them 'Nature's forest masterpiece,' and anyone who's ever craned their neck to take in their soaring vastness has probably done so with the same awe. These trees can grow to almost 275ft tall and 100ft in circumference, protected by bark up to 2ft thick. The Giant Forest Museum in Sequoia National Park has exhibits about the trees' unusual ecology.

accepted only for groups larger than eight; casual dress OK.

Outside Yosemite National Park

Gateway towns that have a mixed bag of motels, hotels, lodges and B&Bs include Fish Camp, Oakhurst, El Portal, Midpines, Mariposa, Groveland and, in the Eastern Sierra, Lee Vining.

★ Yosemite Bug
Rustic Mountain Resort   HOSTEL, CABIN **$**
(☎ 209-966-6666, 866-826-7108; www.yosemitebug.com; 6979 Hwy 140, Midpines; dm $30, tent cabins $45-75, r with/without bath from $150/75; @🔧🏠) ✈ The highlight of the almost nonexistent town of Midpines is this folksy oasis, tucked away on a forested hillside about 25 miles from Yosemite. It's more like a convivial mountain retreat than a hostel: at night, friendly folks of all ages and backgrounds share stories, music and delicious freshly prepared meals and beer and wine in the woodsy cafe before retreating to their beds.

★ Evergreen Lodge   CABIN, CAMPGROUND **$$$**
(☎ 209-379-2606; www.evergreenlodge.com; 33160 Evergreen Rd; tents $90-125, cabins $180-415; @🔧🏠) ✈ Outside the park near the entrance to Hetch Hetchy, this classic 90-year-old resort consists of a series of lovingly decorated and comfy cabins (each with its own cache of board games) spread out among the trees. Accommodations run from rustic to deluxe, and all cabins have private porches without distracting phone or TV. Roughing-it guests can cheat with comfy, prefurnished tents.

The place has just about everything you could ask for, including a tavern (complete with pool table), a general store, a fantastic restaurant serving all meals, live music, horseshoes, ping-pong, a giant outdoor chess set, a kids' zip line and all sorts of guided hikes and outdoor activities – many of them family-oriented. Seasonal equipment rentals are also available.

🛈 Information

Yosemite Village, Curry Village and Wawona stores all have ATMs. Drivers should fill up before entering the park. High-priced gas is sold at Wawona and Crane Flat year-round and at Tuolumne Meadows in summer. Cell-phone service is spotty throughout the park. Check the free park newspaper for wi-fi hot spots and pay-as-you-go internet terminals.

Yosemite Medical Clinic (☎ 209-372-4637; 9000 Ahwahnee Dr, Yosemite Village; ⊙ 9am-7pm daily late May-late Sep, 9am-5pm Mon-Fri late Sep-late May) Twenty-four-hour emergency service available.

Yosemite Valley Visitor Center (☎ 209-372-0200; Yosemite Village; ⊙ 9am-5pm) The main office, with exhibits and free film screenings in the theater.

🛈 Getting There & Around

From the Greyhound and Amtrak stations in Merced, **Yosemite Area Regional Transportation System** (YARTS; ☎ 877-989-2787; www.yarts.com) buses travel year-round to Yosemite Valley via Hwy 140, stopping at towns along the way. In summer YARTS buses run from Yosemite Valley to Mammoth Lakes via Tuolumne Meadows along Hwys 120 and 395. One-way fares (including park entry fee) are $13 from Merced, $18 from Mammoth Lakes.

Free shuttle buses loop around Yosemite Valley year-round and, in summer, the Tuolumne Meadows/Tioga Rd area. Bicycle rentals (per hour/day $12/34) are available seasonally at Curry Village and Yosemite Lodge at the Falls, both in the valley.

In winter highways to the park are kept open (except Tioga Rd/Hwy 120), although snow chains may be required at any time; Glacier Point Rd remains open only as far as Badger Pass ski area, with free shuttle service from the valley.

Sequoia & Kings Canyon National Parks

In these neighboring parks, giant sequoia trees are bigger – up to 27 stories high! – and more numerous than anywhere else in the Sierra Nevada. Tough and fire-charred, they'd easily swallow two freeway lanes each. Giant, too, are the mountains – including Mt Whitney (14,505ft), the tallest peak in the lower 48 states. Finally, there is the deep Kings Canyon, carved out of granite by ancient glaciers and a powerful river. For quiet, solitude and close-up sightings of wildlife, including black bears, hit the trails and lose yourself in wilderness.

🅞 Sights

Sequoia was designated a national park in 1890; Kings Canyon, in 1940. Though distinct, these **parks** (☑ 559-565-3341; www.nps. gov/seki; 7-day entry per car $20) operate as one unit with a single admission fee. From the south, Hwy 198 enters Sequoia National Park beyond the town of Three Rivers at Ash Mountain, then ascends the zigzagging Generals Hwy to Giant Forest. From the west, Hwy 180 enters Kings Canyon National Park near Grant Grove, then plunges down into the canyon all the way to Cedar Grove.

🅞 Sequoia National Park

We dare you to try hugging the trees in **Giant Forest**, a 3-sq-mile grove protecting gargantuan specimens – the world's largest is the **General Sherman Tree**. With sore arms and sticky sap fingers, lose the crowds on a network of forested hiking trails (bring a map).

Worth a detour is **Mineral King Valley**, a late-19th-century mining and logging camp ringed by craggy peaks and alpine lakes. The 25-mile one-way scenic drive – navigating almost 700 hair-raising hairpin turns – is usually open from late May until late October.

Giant Forest Museum   MUSEUM
(☑ 559-565-4480; Generals Hwy, at Crescent Meadow Rd; ☺ 9am-4:30pm; 🖈) `FREE` For a primer on the intriguing ecology and history of giant sequoias, this pint-sized modern museum will entertain both kids and adults. Hands-on exhibits teach about the life stages of these big trees, which can live for over 3000 years, and the fire cycle that releases

their seeds and allows them to sprout on bare soil. The museum itself is housed in a 1920s historic building designed by Gilbert Stanley Underwood, famed architect of Yosemite's Ahwahnee Hotel.

Crystal Cave   CAVE
(☑ 559-565-3759; www.explorecrystalcave.com; Crystal Cave Rd, off Generals Hwy; tours adult/child/ youth from $16/5/8; ☺ May-Nov; 🖈) Discovered in 1918, the cave has marble formations estimated to be 10,000 years old. First-come, first-served tickets for the 50-minute introductory tour are only available in person at the Lodgepole and Foothills visitor centers, *not* at the cave. Bring a jacket.

🅞 Kings Canyon National Park & Scenic Byway

Just north of Grant Grove Village, **General Grant Grove** brims with majestic giants. Beyond, Hwy 180 begins its 30-mile descent into **Kings Canyon**, serpentining past chiseled rock walls laced with waterfalls. The road meets the Kings River, its roar ricocheting off granite cliffs soaring over 8000ft high, making this one of North America's deepest canyons.

At the bottom of the canyon, **Cedar Grove** is the last outpost before the rugged grandeur of the Sierra Nevada backcountry begins. A popular day hike climbs 4.6 miles one way to gushing **Mist Falls** from Roads End. A favorite of birders, an easy 1.5-mile nature trail loops around **Zumwalt Meadow**, just west of Roads End. Watch for lumbering black bears and springy mule deer.

The scenic byway past Hume Lake to Cedar Grove Village is usually closed from mid-November to late April.

Boyden Cavern   CAVE
(☑ 888-956-8243;   www.caverntours.com/ BoydenRt.htm; Hwy 180; tours adult/child from $14.50/8.75; ☺ late Apr-Sep; 🖈) While the rooms are smaller and the interiors less eye-popping than Crystal Cave in Sequoia National Park, touring the beautiful and fantastical formations here requires no advance tickets. Just show up for the basic 45-minute tour, which departs hourly from 10am to 5pm during peak summer season. Reaching the cave entrance requires a short walk up a steep, paved grade.

🏃 Activities

Hiking is why people come here – with over 800 miles of marked trails to prove it. Cedar Grove and Mineral King offer the best backcountry access. Trails at higher elevations usually start opening by early summer. Overnight backcountry trips require wilderness permits (per trip $15), subject to a quota system from late May to late September; reserve well in advance for popular routes.

In summer cool off by swimming in **Hume Lake**, on national forest land off Hwy 180, and at riverside swimming holes in both parks. In winter you can cross-country ski or snowshoe among giant sequoias; equipment rental is available at Grant Grove Village and Wuksachi Lodge.

🛏 Sleeping & Eating

Camping reservations (p440) are accepted only from late spring through early fall at Lodgepole, Potwisha and Buckeye Flat Campgrounds (tent and RV sites $22) in Sequoia National Park. The parks' 10 other developed campgrounds (tent and RV sites $10 to $20) are first-come, first-served. Potwisha, Azalea and remote South Fork are open year-round. Overflow camping is available on surrounding national-forest land.

The markets at Lodgepole, Grant Grove and Cedar Grove have limited groceries. Lodgepole and Cedar Grove snack bars serve basic, budget-friendly meals. Grant Grove has a simple restaurant and espresso cart.

Outside Sequoia's southern entrance, mostly well-worn cabins and chain motels, as well as down-home eateries, line Hwy 198 through Three Rivers town.

Wuksachi Lodge   LODGE $$
(📞 559-565-4070, 866-807-3598; www.visitsequoia.com; 64740 Wuksachi Way, off Generals Hwy; r $185-290; 🛜📶) Built in 1999, Wuksachi Lodge is the park's most upscale lodging and dining option. But don't get too excited – the wood-paneled atrium lobby has an inviting stone fireplace and forest views, but charmless motel-style rooms with coffee makers, minifridges, oak furniture and thin walls have an institutional feel. The lodge's location near Lodgepole Village, however, can't be beat.

John Muir Lodge   LODGE $$
(📞 559-335-5500, 866-807-3598; www.visitsequoia.com; off Hwy 180, Grant Grove Village; r from $170; 🛜📶) An atmospheric wooden building hung with historical black-and-white photographs, this year-round hotel is a place to lay your head and still feel like you're in the forest. Wide porches have wooden rocking chairs, and homespun rooms contain rough-hewn wood furniture and patchwork bedspreads. Cozy up to the big stone fireplace on chilly nights with a board game.

Cedar Grove Lodge   LODGE $$
(📞 559-565-3096, 866-807-3598; www.visitsequoia.com; Hwy 180, Cedar Grove Village; r from $130; ⊙ early May–mid-Oct; ✳🛜📶) The only indoor sleeping option in the canyon, the riverside lodge offers 21 unexciting motel-style rooms. A recent remodel has dispelled some of the frumpy decor. Three ground-floor rooms with shady furnished patios have spiffy river views and kitchenettes. All rooms have phones and TVs.

ℹ Information

Lodgepole Village and Grant Grove Village are the parks' main commerical hubs. Both have visitor centers, post offices, markets, ATMs, a coin-op laundry and public showers (summer only).

The following visitor centres are open year-round:

Foothills Visitor Center (📞 559-565-4212; 47050 Generals Hwy; ⊙ 8am-4:30pm) At Ash Mountain.

Lodgepole Visitor Center (📞 559-565-4436; off Generals Hwy, Lodgepole Village; ⊙ 8am-5pm early May-early Oct, 7am-7pm peak season) Near Giant Forest.

Kings Canyon Visitor Center (📞 559-565-4307; Hwy 180, Grant Grove Village; ⊙ 8am-noon & 1-5pm late May-early Sep, shorter off-season hours) In Grant Grove.

The following open seasonally:

Cedar Grove Visitor Center (📞 559-565-3793; Hwy 180, Cedar Grove Village; ⊙ 9am-5pm late May-late Sep) In Kings Canyon.

Mineral King Ranger Station (📞 559-565-3768; Mineral King Rd; ⊙ 8am-4pm late May-late Sep)

Check the free park newspaper for other visitor services, including wi-fi hot spots.

Expensive gas is available at Hume Lake (year-round) and Stony Creek (closed in winter) outside the parks on national-forest land.

ℹ Getting There & Around

From late May to early September, free shuttle buses loop around the Giant Forest, Lodgepole/Wuksachi and Foothills areas of Sequoia and also Grant Grove in Kings Canyon. **Sequoia**

Shuttle (☑ 877-287-4453; www.sequoiashuttle.com; round-trip incl park entry $15; ☺ late May-late Sep) links the Giant Forest to Three Rivers and Visalia (for onward connections to Amtrak), while **Big Trees Transit** (☑ 800-325-7433; www.bigtreestransit.com; round-trip incl park entry fee $15; ☺ late May-early Sep) connects Grant Grove with Fresno's airport and Amtrak and Greyhound stations; round-trip fares include the park entry fee (reservations required).

Eastern Sierra

Vast, empty and majestic, here jagged peaks plummet down into the desert, a dramatic juxtaposition that creates a potent scenery cocktail. Hwy 395 runs the entire length of the eastern side of the Sierra Nevada, with turnoffs leading to pine forests, wildflower-strewn meadows, placid lakes, hot springs and glacier-gouged canyons. Hikers, backpackers, mountain bikers, fishers and skiers all find escapes here.

At **Bodie State Historic Park** (☑ 760-647-6445; www.parks.ca.gov/bodie; Rte 270; adult/child $5/3; ☺ 9am-6pm mid-May–Oct, to 4pm Nov–mid-May), the weathered buildings of a gold-rush boomtown sit frozen in time on a dusty, windswept plain. To get there, head east for 13 miles (the last three unpaved) on Hwy 270, about 7 miles south of Bridgeport. Snow usually closes the access road in winter and early spring.

Further south at **Mono Lake** (www.monolake.org), unearthly tufa towers rise from the alkaline water like drip sand castles. Off Hwy 395, **Mono Basin Scenic Area Visitor Center** (☑ 760-647-3044; www.fs.usda.gov/inyo; ☺ 8am-5pm, shorter spring & fall hours, closed Dec-Mar) has excellent views and educational exhibits, but the best photo ops are from the mile-long nature trail at the **South Tufa Area** (adult/child $3/free). From the nearby town of Lee Vining, Hwy 120 heads west into Yosemite National Park via seasonal Tioga Pass.

Continuing south on Hwy 395, detour along the scenic 16-mile **June Lake Loop** or push on to **Mammoth Lakes**, a popular four-seasons resort guarded by 11,053ft **Mammoth Mountain** (☑ 760-934-2571, 24hr snow report 888-766-9778; www.mammothmountain.com; lift tickets adult/child 7-12yr/youth/senior 13-18yr/$105/35/82/89), a top-notch skiing area. The slopes morph into a mountain-bike park in summer, when scenic gon-

dola rides run. There's also camping and day hiking around Mammoth Lakes Basin and Reds Meadow, the latter near the 60ft-high basalt columns of **Devils Postpile National Monument** (☑ 760-934-2289; www.nps.gov/depo; shuttle day pass adult/child $7/4; ☺ late May-Oct), formed by volcanic activity. Hot-springs fans can soak in primitive pools off Benton Crossing Rd or view the geysering water at **Hot Creek Geological Site**, both off Hwy 395 southeast of town. The in-town **Mammoth Lakes Welcome Center & Ranger Station** (☑ 760-924-5500, 888-466-2666; www.visitmammoth.com; ☺ 8am-5pm) has helpful maps and information.

Further south, Hwy 395 descends into the Owens Valley. In frontier-flavored **Bishop**, **Mountain Light Gallery** (☑ 760-873-7700; www.mountainlight.com; 106 S Main St; ☺ 10am-5pm Mon-Sat, 11am-4pm Sun) FREE and the historical **Laws Railroad Museum** (☑ 760-873-5950; www.lawsmuseum.org; Silver Canyon Rd, off Hwy 6; donation $5; ☺ 10am-4pm early Sep-late May, 9:30am-4pm late May-early Sep; ♠) are minor attractions. A gateway for packhorse trips, Bishop accesses the Eastern Sierra's best fishing and rock climbing.

Budget a half-day for the thrilling drive up to the **Ancient Bristlecone Pine Forest**. These gnarled, otherworldly looking trees – the world's oldest – are found above 10,000ft on the slopes of the White Mountains. The road (closed by snow in winter and early spring) is paved to the **visitor center** (☑ 760-873-2500; www.fs.usda.gov/inyo; per person/car $3/6; ☺ 10am-4pm Fri-Mon late May-early Nov) at Schulman Grove, where hiking trails await. From Hwy 395 in Big Pine, take Hwy 168 east for 12 miles, then follow White Mountain Rd uphill for 10 miles.

Hwy 395 barrels south to **Manzanar National Historic Site** (☑ 760-878-2194; www.nps.gov/manz; 5001 Hwy 395, Independence; ☺ dawn-dusk, visitor center 9am-4:30pm, to 5:30pm Apr-Oct; ♠) FREE, which memorializes the camp where some 10,000 Japanese Americans were unjustly interned during WWII following the attack on Pearl Harbor. Interpretive exhibits and a short film vividly chronicle life at the camp, which today is marked by a short self-guided auto-tour route.

Further south in Lone Pine, you'll finally glimpse **Mt Whitney** (14,505ft), the highest mountain in the lower 48 states. The heart-stopping, 12-mile scenic drive up **Whitney Portal Road** (closed in winter and early spring) is spectacular. Climbing the peak is hugely popular, but requires a permit (per person $15) awarded via annual lottery. Just south of town, the **Eastern Sierra Interagency Visitor Center** (✆760-876-6222; www.fs.fed.us/r5/inyo; cnr Hwys 395 & 136; ⊙8am-5pm) issues wilderness permits, dispenses outdoor-recreation info and sells books and maps.

West of Lone Pine, the bizarrely shaped boulders of the **Alabama Hills** have enchanted filmmakers of Hollywood Westerns. Peruse vintage memorabilia and movie posters back in town at the **Museum of Western Film History** (✆760-876-9909; www.museumofwesternfilmhistory.org; 701 S Main St; adult/child $5/free; ⊙10am-5pm Mon-Sat, to 4pm Sun, longer summer hours).

🛌 Sleeping

The Eastern Sierra is freckled with campgrounds; backcountry camping requires a wilderness permit, available at ranger stations. Bishop, Lone Pine and Bridgeport have the most motels. Mammoth Lakes has a few motels and hotels and dozens of inns, B&Bs, condos and vacation rentals. Reservations are essential everywhere in summer.

El Mono Motel MOTEL $
(✆760-647-6310; www.elmonomotel.com; 51 Hwy 395, Lee Vining; r $69-99; ⊙mid-May–Oct; ☎) Grab a board game or soak up some mountain sunshine in this friendly flower-ringed place attached to an excellent cafe. In operation since 1927, and often booked solid, each of its 11 simple rooms (a few share bathrooms) is unique, decorated with vibrant and colorful art and fabrics.

**Whitney Portal
Hostel & Hotel** HOSTEL, MOTEL $
(✆760-876-0030; www.whitneyportalstore.com; 238 S Main St; dm/d $25/85; ✴☎☎) A popular launching pad for Whitney trips and for posthike wash-ups (public showers available), its hostel rooms are the cheapest beds in town – reserve them months ahead for July and August. There's no common space for the carpeted single-sex bunk-bed rooms, though amenities include towels, TVs, in-room kitchenettes and stocked coffeemakers. The majority of the establishment consists of plush and modern motel rooms, and many look out towards Whitney and its neighbors.

Dow Hotel & Dow Villa Motel HOTEL, MOTEL $$
(✆760-876-5521; www.dowvillamotel.com; 310 S Main St; hotel r with/without bath $87/69, motel r $115-173; ✴@☎☎☎) John Wayne and Errol Flynn are among the stars who have stayed at this venerable hotel. Built in 1922, the place has been restored but retains much of its rustic charm. The rooms in the newer motel section have air-con and are more comfortable and bright, but also more generic.

Tamarack Lodge LODGE, CABIN $$$
(✆760-934-2442; www.tamaracklodge.com; 163 Twin Lakes Rd; r with/without bath $219/169, cabins from $299; @☎☎) ✏ In business since 1924, this charming year-round resort on Lower Twin Lake has a cozy fireplace lodge, a bar and excellent restaurant, 11 rustic-style rooms and 35 cabins. The cabins range from very simple to simply deluxe, and come with full kitchen, private bathroom, porch and wood-burning stove. Some can sleep up to 10 people. Daily resort fee $20.

🍴 Eating & Drinking

Alabama Hills Cafe DINER $
(111 W Post St; mains $8-14; ⊙7am-2pm; ✏) Everyone's favorite breakfast joint, the portions here are big, the bread fresh-baked, and the hearty soups and scratch-made fruit pies make lunch an attractive option too.

Mammoth Tavern PUB FOOD $$
(www.mammothtavern.com; 587 Old Mammoth Rd; mains $12-35; ⊙3:30-11pm Tue-Sun) Warm lighting, wood-paneled walls rising to a circular ceiling and drop-dead gorgeous views of the snowcapped Sherwin Range mean the big screen TVs here are an unnecessary distraction. A newcomer to the local dining scene, Mammoth Tavern hits the spot with comfort food like shepherd's pie, oysters, gorgeous salads and fondue garlic turkey meatballs. Worthy libations include tasty house cocktails, local drafts, interesting whiskeys and over two-dozen wines by the glass.

Whoa Nellie Deli CALIFORNIAN $$
(✆760-647-1088; www.whoanelliedeli.com; Tioga Gas Mart, Hwys 120 & 395, Lee Vining; mains $10-22; ⊙6:30am-9pm late Apr-Oct; ☎) After putting this unexpected gas-station restaurant on the map, its famed chef has moved on to Mammoth, but locals think the food is still damn good. Stop in for delicious fish tacos, wild-buffalo meatloaf and other tasty morsels, and live bands two nights a week.

Mammoth Brewing Company Tasting Room   BREWERY
(www.mammothbrewingco.com; 18 Lake Mary Rd; ⊙10am-9:30pm Sun-Thu, to 10:30pm Fri & Sat) In a large and central location, this place has a dozen brews on tap (flights $5 to $7) – including special seasonal varieties not found elsewhere. Pick up some IPA 395 or Double Nut Brown to go. Tasty bar food available.

June Lake Brewing   MICROBREWERY
(www.junelakebrewing.com; 131 S Crawford Ave, June Lake; ⊙11am-8pm Wed-Mon, to 9pm Fri & Sat; 🕭) A top new regional draw, June Lake Brewing's open tasting room serves 10 drafts, including a 'SmoKin' Porter, Deer Beer Brown Ale and some awesome IPAs. Brewers swear the June Lake water makes all the difference. Flights $4 to $6.

Lake Tahoe

Shimmering in myriad blues and greens, Lake Tahoe is the USA's second-deepest lake. Driving around its spellbinding 72-mile scenic shoreline gives you quite a workout behind the wheel. The north shore is quiet and upscale; the west shore, rugged and old-timey; the east shore, largely undeveloped; and the south shore, busy with families and flashy casinos. Horned peaks surrounding the lake (elevation 6255ft), which straddles the California–Nevada state line, are four-seasons outdoor playgrounds.

Tahoe gets packed in summer, on winter weekends and during holidays, when camping and lodging reservations are essential.

ℹ Information

Lake Tahoe Visitors Authority (☎530-541-5255; www.tahoesouth.com; 3066 Lake Tahoe Blvd, South Lake Tahoe; ⊙9am-5pm) and **North Lake Tahoe Visitors' Bureaus** (☎800-468-2463; www.gotahoenorth.com) run multiple visitor information centers.

ℹ Getting There & Around

South Tahoe Airporter (☎775-325-8944, 866-898-2463; www.southtahoeexpress.com; adult/child 4-12yr $30/17) runs several daily shuttles from Nevada's Reno-Tahoe International Airport to Stateline. **North Lake Tahoe Express** (☎866-216-5222; www.northlaketahoeexpress.com; per person $49) connects Reno's airport with Truckee, Northstar, Squaw Valley and north-shore towns.

Truckee's **Amtrak depot** (☎800-872-7245; www.amtrak.com; 10065 Donner Pass Rd) has daily trains to Reno ($13, 1¼ hours) and Sacramento ($41, 4½ hours), and twice-daily **Greyhound** (☎800-231-2222; www.greyhound.com) buses to Reno ($16, one hour), Sacramento ($40, 2½ hours) and San Francisco ($41, 5¾ hours). Daily Amtrak buses connect South Lake Tahoe with Sacramento ($34, 2¾ hours).

Tahoe Area Rapid Transit (TART; ☎530-550-1212; www.laketahoetransit.com; single/day pass $1.75/3.50) operates local buses from Truckee around the north and west shores. South Lake Tahoe is served by **BlueGO** (☎530-541-7149; www.tahoetransportation.org/transit; fare/day pass $2/5) buses. Making limited runs during summer, **Emerald Bay Trolley** (fare $2) connects BlueGo with TART.

If you're driving, tire chains are often required in winter on I-80, US 50 and other mountain highways, which may close temporarily due to heavy snow. Call ☎800-427-7623 to check current road condtions and closures.

South Lake Tahoe & West Shore

With retro motels and eateries lining busy Hwy 50, South Lake Tahoe gets crowded. Gambling at Stateline's casino hotels, just across the Nevada border, attracts thousands, as does the world-class ski resort of **Heavenly** (☎775-586-7000; www.skiheavenly.com; 4080 Lake Tahoe Blvd, South Lake Tahoe; adult/child 5-12yr/youth 13-18yr $99/59/89; ⊙9am-4pm Mon-Fri, 8:30am-4pm Sat, Sun & holidays; 🕭). In summer a trip up Heavenly's **gondola** (adult/child $42/20) guarantees fabulous views of the lake and the **Desolation Wilderness**, with its raw granite peaks, glacier-carved valleys and alpine lakes favored by hikers. Get maps, information and wilderness permits (per adult $5 to $10) from the **USFS Taylor Creek Visitor Center** (☎530-543-2674; www.fs.usda.gov/ltbmu; Visitor Center Rd, off Hwy 89; ⊙8am-5pm late May-Sep, to 4pm Oct). It's 3 miles north of the 'Y' intersection of Hwys 50/89, at **Tallac Historic Site** (www.tahoeheritage.org; Tallac Rd; optional tour adult/child $10/5; ⊙10am-4pm daily mid-Jun–Sep, Fri & Sat late May–mid-Jun; 🕭) **FREE**, preserving swish early-20th-century vacation estates.

From sandy, swimmable **Zephyr Cove** (www.zephyrcove.com; 760 Hwy 50; per car $10; 🕭) across the Nevada border or the in-town Ski Run Marina, **Lake Tahoe Cruises** (☎800-238-2463; www.zephyrcove.com; adult/child from $51/15) plies the 'Big Blue' year-round. Paddle under your own power with

Kayak Tahoe (☏530-544-2011; www.kayak-tahoe.com; 3411 Lake Tahoe Blvd; kayak single/double 1hr $25/35, 1 day $65/85, lessons & tours from $40; ⏰9am-5pm Jun-Sep). Back on shore, boutique-chic motels include the Alder Inn (☏530-544-4485; www.thealderinn.com; 1072 Ski Run Blvd; r $99-150; 🛜🖥) and the hip Basecamp Hotel (☏530-208-0180; www.basecamp hotels.com; 4143 Cedar Ave; d $109-229, 8-person bunkroom $209-299; 🛜🖥) 🅿, which has a rooftop hot tub, or pitch a tent at lakeside Fallen Leaf Campground (☏info 530-544-0426, reservations 877-444-6777; www.recreation. gov; 2165 Fallen Leaf Lake Rd; tent & RV sites $33-35, yurts $84; ⏰mid-May–mid-Oct; 🐾). Fuel up at vegetarian-friendly Sprouts (www.sprouts-cafetahoe.com; 3123 Harrison Ave; mains $7-10; ⏰8am-9pm; 🖊🍴) natural-foods cafe, or with a peanut-butter-topped burger and garlic fries at the Burger Lounge (☏530-542-2010; www.burgerloungeintahoe.com; 717 Emerald Bay Rd; dishes $4-10; ⏰10am-8pm daily Jun-Sep, 11am-7pm Wed-Sun Oct-May; 🍴).

Hwy 89 threads northwest along the thickly forested west shore to Emerald Bay State Park (☏530-541-6498; www.parks. ca.gov; per car $10; ⏰late May-Sep), where granite cliffs and pine trees frame a sparkling fjordlike inlet. A 1-mile trail leads steeply downhill to Vikingsholm Castle (tour adult/child $10/8; ⏰11am-4pm late May-Sep), a 1920s Scandinavian-style mansion. From there, the Rubicon Trail ribbons 4.5 miles north along the lakeshore past petite coves to DL Bliss State Park (☏530-525-7277; www.parks. ca.gov; per car $10; ⏰late May-Sep; 🍴), offering sandy beaches. Further north, Tahoma Meadows B&B Cottages (☏866-525-1553, 530-525-1553; www.tahomameadows.com; 6821 W Lake Blvd, Tahoma; cottages $99-389; 🛜🍴🐾) rents darling country cabins.

North & East Shores

A busy commercial hub, Tahoe City is great for grabbing food and supplies and renting outdoor-sports gear. It's not far from Squaw Valley USA (☏530-452-4331; www.squaw.com; 1960 Squaw Valley Rd, off Hwy 89, Olympic Valley; adult/child under 13yr/youth 13-22yr $114/66/94; 🍴), a megasized ski resort that hosted the 1960 Winter Olympics. Après-ski crowds gather at woodsy Bridgetender Tavern & Grill (www.tahoebridgetender.com; 65 W Lake Blvd; ⏰11am-11pm, to midnight Fri & Sat) back in

town. In the morning, gobble eggs Benedict with house-smoked salmon at down-home Fire Sign Cafe (www.firesigncafe.com; 1785 W Lake Blvd; mains $7-13; ⏰7am-3pm; 🖊🍴), 2 miles further south.

In summer, swim or kayak at Tahoe Vista or Kings Beach. Overnight at Cedar Glen Lodge (☏530-546-4281; www.tahoecedar glen.com; 6589 N Lake Blvd; r/ste/cottages $139-350; @🛜🖥🍴🐾), where rustic-themed cottages and rooms have kitchenettes, or well-kept, compact Hostel Tahoe (☏530-546-3266; www.hosteltahoe.com; 8931 N Lake Blvd; dm $35, d/q $70/85, all incl tax; @🛜) 🅿. East of Kings Beach's casual lakeside eateries, Hwy 28 barrels into Nevada. Catch a live-music show at Crystal Bay Club Casino (☏775-833-6333; www.crystalbaycasino.com; 14 Hwy 28), but for more happening bars and bistros, drive further to Incline Village.

With pristine beaches, lakes and miles of multiuse trails, Lake Tahoe-Nevada State Park (www.parks.nv.gov; per car $7-12) is the east shore's biggest draw. Summer crowds splash in the turquoise waters of Sand Harbor. The 13-mile Flume Trail, a mountain biker's holy grail, ends further south at Spooner Lake. Back in Incline Village, Flume Trail Bikes (☏775-298-2501; http://flumetrailtahoe.com; 1115 Tunnel Creek Rd, Incline Village; mountain-bike rental per day $35-85, shuttle $15) offers bicycle rentals and shuttles.

Truckee & Around

North of Lake Tahoe off I-80, Truckee is not in fact a truck stop but a thriving mountain town, with coffee shops, trendy boutiques and dining in downtown's historical district. Ski bums have several resorts to pick from, including glam Northstar California (☏530-562-1010; www.northstarcalifornia.com; 5001 Northstar Dr, off Hwy 267, Truckee; adult/child 5-12yr/youth 13-22yr $116/69/96; ⏰8:30am-4pm; 🍴); kid-friendly Sugar Bowl (☏530-426-9000; www.sugarbowl.com; 629 Sugar Bowl Rd, off Donner Pass Rd, Norden; adult/child 6-12yr/youth 13-22yr $82/30/70; ⏰9am-4pm; 🍴), cofounded by Walt Disney; and Royal Gorge (☏530-426-3871; www.royalgorge.com; 9411 Pahatsi Rd, off I-80 exit Soda Springs/Norden, Soda Springs; adult/youth 13-22yr $29/22; ⏰9am-5pm during snow season; 🍴🐾), paradise for cross-country skiers.

West of Hwy 89, Donner Summit is where the infamous Donner Party became trapped during the fierce winter of 1846–47. Fewer than half survived – some by cannibalizing their dead friends. The grisly tale is chronicled at the museum inside **Donner Memorial State Park** (☑530-582-7892; www.parks.ca.gov; Donner Pass Rd; per car $8; ☺museum 10am-5pm, closed Tue & Wed Sep-May; ⊞), which offers **camping** (☑530-582-7894, reservations 800-444-7275; www.reserveamerica.com; tent & RV sites $35; ☺late May-late Sep; ⊞). Nearby **Donner Lake** is popular with swimmers and paddlers.

On the outskirts of Truckee, green-certified **Cedar House Sport Hotel** (☑866-582-5655, 530-582-5655; www.cedarhousesporthotel.com; 10918 Brockway Rd; r $180-295; @🛜🐾) 🍃 offers stylish boutique rooms and an outstanding restaurant. Down pints of Donner Party Porter at **Fifty Fifty Brewing Co** (www.fiftyfiftybrewing.com; 11197 Brockway Rd; ☺11:30am-9am Sun-Thu, to 9:30pm Fri & Sat).

Pacific Northwest

Best Places to Eat

➡ Sitka & Spruce (p187)

➡ Toulouse Petit (p187)

➡ Saffron Mediterranean Kitchen (p204)

➡ Andina (p212)

➡ Chow (p223)

Best Places to Stay

➡ Ace Hotel (p185)

➡ Davenport Hotel (p201)

➡ Kennedy School (p210)

➡ Timberline Lodge (p220)

➡ Moore Hotel (p185)

Why Go?

As much a state of mind as a geographical region, the northwest corner of the US is a land of subcultures and new trends, where evergreen trees frame snow-dusted volcanoes, and inspired ideas scribbled on the back of napkins become tomorrow's start-ups. You can't peel off the history in layers here, but you *can* gaze wistfully into the future in fast-moving, innovative cities such as Seattle and Portland, which are sprinkled with food carts, streetcars, microbreweries, green belts, coffee connoisseurs and weird urban sculpture.

Ever since the days of the Oregon Trail, the Northwest has had a hypnotic lure for risk takers and dreamers, and the metaphoric carrot still dangles. There's the air, so clean they ought to bottle it; the trees, older than many of Rome's Renaissance palaces; and the end-of-the-continent coastline, holding back the force of the world's largest ocean. Cowboys take note: it doesn't get much more 'wild' or 'west' than this.

When to Go

Seattle

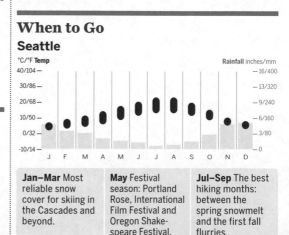

Jan–Mar Most reliable snow cover for skiing in the Cascades and beyond.

May Festival season: Portland Rose, International Film Festival and Oregon Shakespeare Festival.

Jul–Sep The best hiking months: between the spring snowmelt and the first fall flurries.

History

Native American societies, including the Chinook and the Salish, had long-established coastal communities by the time Europeans arrived in the Pacific Northwest in the 18th century. Inland, on the arid plateaus between the Cascades and the Rocky Mountains, the Spokane, Nez Percé and other tribes thrived on seasonal migration between river valleys and temperate uplands.

Three hundred years after Columbus landed in the New World, Spanish and British explorers began probing the northern Pacific coast, seeking the fabled Northwest Passage. In 1792 Captain George Vancouver was the first explorer to sail the waters of Puget Sound, claiming British sovereignty over the entire region. At the same time, an American, Captain Robert Gray, found the mouth of the Columbia River. In 1805 the explorers Lewis and Clark crossed the Rockies and made their way down the Columbia to the Pacific Ocean, extending the US claim on the territory.

In 1824 the British Hudson's Bay Company established Fort Vancouver in Washington as headquarters for the Columbia region. This opened the door to waves of settlers, but had a devastating impact on the indigenous cultures, which were assailed by European diseases and alcohol.

In 1843 settlers at Champoeg, on the Willamette River south of Portland, voted to organize a provisional government independent of the Hudson's Bay Company, thereby casting their lot with the US, which formally acquired the territory from the British by treaty in 1846. Over the next decade, some 53,000 settlers came to the Northwest via the 2000-mile Oregon Trail.

Arrival of the railroads set the region's future. Agriculture and lumber became the pillars of the economy until 1914, when WWI and the opening of the Panama Canal brought increased trade to Pacific ports. Shipyards opened along Puget Sound, and the Boeing aircraft company set up shop near Seattle.

Big dam projects in the 1930s and '40s provided cheap hydroelectricity and irrigation. WWII offered another boost for aircraft manufacturing and shipbuilding, and agriculture continued to thrive. In the postwar period, Washington's population, especially around Puget Sound, grew to twice that of Oregon.

In the 1980s and '90s, the economic emphasis shifted with the rise of the high-tech industry, embodied by Microsoft in Seattle and Intel in Portland.

Hydroelectricity production and massive irrigation projects along the Columbia have threatened the river's ecosystem in the past few decades, and logging has also left its scars. But the region has reinvigorated its eco-credentials by attracting some of the country's most environmentally conscious companies, and its major cities are among the greenest in the US. It stands at the forefront of US efforts to tackle climate issues.

Local Culture

The stereotypical image of a Pacific Northwesterner is a casually dressed latte-sipping urbanite who drives a Prius, votes Democrat and walks around with an unwavering diet of Nirvana-derived indie rock programmed into their iPod. But, as with most fleeting

PACIFIC NORTHWEST HISTORY

THE PACIFIC NORTHWEST IN...

Four Days

Hit the ground running in **Seattle** to see the main sights, including Pike Place Market and the Seattle Center. On day three, head down to **Portland**, where you can do like the locals do and cycle to bars, cafes, food carts and shops.

One Week

Add a couple highlights such as **Mt Rainier, Olympic National Park**, the **Columbia River Gorge** or **Mt Hood**. Or explore the spectacular Oregon Coast (try the **Cannon Beach** area) or the historic seaport of **Port Townsend** on the Olympic Peninsula.

Two Weeks

Crater Lake is unforgettable, and can be combined with a trip to **Ashland** and its Shakespeare Festival. Don't miss the ethereal **San Juan Islands** up near the watery border with Canada, or **Bend**, the region's biggest outdoor draw. If you like wine, Washington's **Walla Walla** is your mecca, while the **Willamette Valley** is Oregon's Pinot Noir paradise.

Pacific Northwest Highlights

1 Cycling and kayaking around the quieter corners of the **San Juan Islands** (p196).

2 Exploring the gorgeous **Oregon Coast** (p224), from scenic Astoria to balmy Port Orford.

3 Admiring trees older than Europe's Renaissance castles in Washington's **Olympic National Park** (p192).

4 Watching the greatest outdoor show in the Pacific Northwest in Seattle's theatrical **Pike Place Market** (p179).

5 Walking the green and serene neighborhoods of **Portland** (p205), energized by beer, coffee and food-cart treats.

6 Witnessing the impossibly deep-blue waters and scenic panoramas of **Crater Lake National Park** (p223).

7 Going mountain biking, rock climbing or skiing in the outdoor mecca of **Bend** (p221).

8 Tasting sumptuous reds and whites in the wine regions around **Walla Walla** (p204).

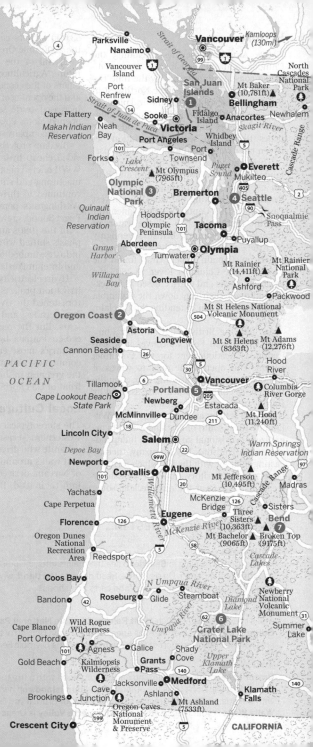

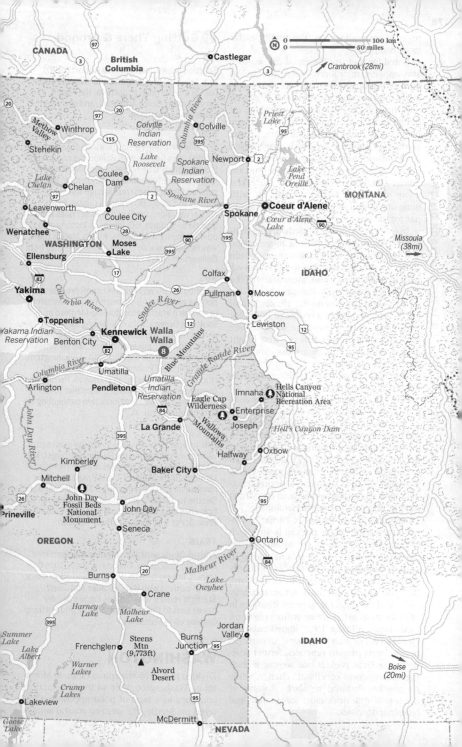

regional generalizations, the reality is far more complex.

Noted for their sophisticated cafe culture and copious microbrew pubs, the urban hubs of Seattle and Portland are the Northwest's most emblematic cities. But head east into the region's drier and less verdant interior, and the cultural affiliations become increasingly more traditional. Here, strung along the Columbia River Valley or nestled amid the arid steppes of southeastern Washington, small towns host raucous rodeos, tourist centers promote cowboy culture, and a cup of coffee is served 'straight up' with none of the chai lattes and frappés that are par for the course in the bigger cities.

In contrast to the USA's hardworking eastern seaboard, life out west is more casual and less frenetic. Ideally, Westerners would rather work to live than live to work. Indeed, with so much winter rain, the citizens of the Pacific Northwest will dredge up any excuse to shun the nine-to-five treadmill and hit the great outdoors a couple of hours (or even days) early. Witness the scene in late May and early June, when the first bright days of summer prompt a mass exodus of hikers and cyclists making enthusiastically for the national parks and wilderness areas for which the region is justly famous.

Creativity is another strong Northwestern trait, be it in redefining the course of modern rock music or reconfiguring the latest Microsoft computer program. The Pacific Northwest has redefined itself internationally in recent decades through celebrated TV shows (*Frasier* and *Portlandia*, for example), iconic global personalities (Bill Gates) and a groundbreaking music scene that has spawned everything from grunge rock to riot grrrl feminism.

Tolerance is widespread in Pacific Northwestern society, from gay rights to physician-assisted suicide to recreational drugs (recreational marijuana use is now legal in both Washington and Oregon). Commonly voting Democrat in presidential elections, the population has also enthusiastically embraced the push for 'greener' lifestyles in such forms as extensive recycling programs, restaurants utilizing 'local' ingredients and biodiesel whale-watching tours. An early exponent of ecofriendly practices, former Seattle mayor Greg Nickels has become a leading spokesperson on climate change, while progressive Portland regularly features at the top of America's most sustainable and bike-friendly cities.

ⓘ Getting There & Around

AIR
Seattle-Tacoma International Airport (p190), aka 'Sea-Tac,' and Portland International Airport (p215) are the main airports for the region, serving many North American, and several international, destinations.

BOAT
Washington State Ferries (www.wsdot.wa.gov/ferries) links Seattle with Bainbridge and Vashon Islands. Other WSF routes cross from Whidbey Island to Port Townsend on the Olympic Peninsula, and from Anacortes through the San Juan Islands to Sidney, BC. Victoria Clipper (www.clippervacations.com) operates services from Seattle to Victoria, BC; ferries to Victoria also operate from Port Angeles. Alaska Marine Highway ferries (www.dot.state.ak.us/amhs) go from Bellingham, WA, to Alaska.

BUS
Greyhound (www.greyhound.com) provides service along the I-5 corridor from Bellingham in northern Washington down to Medford in southern Oregon, with connecting services across the US and Canada. East–west routes fan out toward Spokane, Yakima, the Tri-Cities (Kennewick, Pasco and Richland in Washington), Walla Walla and Pullman in Washington, and Hood River and Pendleton in Oregon. Private bus companies service most of the smaller towns and cities across the region, often connecting to Greyhound or Amtrak.

CAR
Driving your own vehicle is by far the most convenient way of touring the Pacific Northwest. Major and minor rental agencies are commonplace throughout the region. I-5 is the major north–south artery. In Washington I-90 heads east from Seattle to Spokane and into Idaho. In Oregon I-84 branches east from Portland along the Columbia River Gorge to link up with Boise in Idaho.

TRAIN
Amtrak (www.amtrak.com) runs train services north (to Vancouver, Canada) and south (to California), linking Seattle, Portland and other major urban centers with the *Cascades* and *Coast Starlight* routes. The famous *Empire Builder* heads east to Chicago from Seattle and Portland (joining up in Spokane).

WASHINGTON

Divided in two by the spinal Cascade Mountains, Washington isn't so much a land of contrasts as a land of polar opposites. Centered on Seattle, the western coastal zone is wet, urban, liberal and famous for its fecund evergreen forests; splayed to the east between the less celebrated cities of Spokane and Yakima, the inland plains are arid, rural, conservative and covered by mile after mile of scrublike steppe.

Of the two halves it's the west that harbors most of the quintessential Washington sights, while the more remote, less heralded east is understated and full of surprises.

Seattle

Combine the brains of Portland, OR, with the beauty of Vancouver, BC, and you'll get something approximating Seattle. It's hard to believe that the Pacific Northwest's largest metropolis was considered a 'secondary' US city until the 1980s, when a combination of bold innovation and unabashed individualism turned it into one of the dot-com era's biggest trendsetters, spearheaded by an unlikely alliance of coffee-sipping computer geeks and navel-gazing musicians.

Reinvention is the buzzword these days in a city where grunge belongs to the history books and Starbucks is just one in a cavalcade of precocious indie coffee providers eking out their market position.

Surprisingly elegant in places and coolly edgy in others, Seattle is notable for its strong neighborhoods, top-rated university, monstrous traffic jams and proactive city mayors who harbor green credentials. Although it has fermented its own pop culture in recent times, it has yet to create an urban mythology befitting Paris or New York, but it does have 'the Mountain.' Better known as Rainier to its friends, Seattle's unifying symbol is a 14,411ft mass of rock and ice, which acts as a perennial reminder to the city's huddled masses that raw wilderness, and potential volcanic catastrophe, are never far away.

◉ Sights

◎ Downtown

★ **Pike Place Market**   MARKET
(www.pikeplacemarket.org; 85 Pike St; ☺9am-6pm Mon-Sat, to 5pm Sun; ◙Westlake) 🍃 Take a bunch of small-time businesses and sprinkle them liberally around a waterside strip amid crowds of old-school bohemians, new-wave restaurateurs, tree-huggers, students, artists, buskers and tourists, and the result: Pike Place Market, a cavalcade of noise,

smells, personalities, banter and urban theater. You'll find produce stalls, vintage shops, handmade crafts, souvenir kitsch and funky eateries. In operation since 1907, Pike Place is a wonderfully 'local' experience that highlights the city for what it really is: all-embracing, eclectic and proudly singular.

Seattle Art Museum   MUSEUM
(SAM; ☑206-654-3210; www.seattleartmuseum.org; 1300 1st Ave; adult/student $19.50/12.50; ☺10am-5pm Wed & Fri-Sun, to 9pm Thu; ◙University St) Over the last decade, SAM has added over 100,000 sq ft to its gallery space and acquired about $1 billion worth of new art, including works by Zurbarán and Murillo. The museum is known for its extensive Native American artifacts and work from the local Northwest School, in particular by

PACIFIC NORTHWEST

Seattle

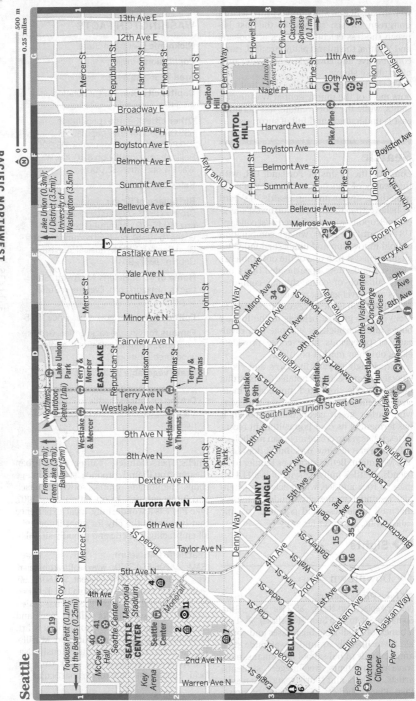

500 m
0.25 miles

Lake Union (0.3m);
U District (3.5mi);
University of
Washington (3.5mi)

13th Ave E
12th Ave E
E Mercer St
E Republican St
E Harrison St
E Thomas St
E John St
E Denny Way
E Howell St
E Olive St
Cascina
Spinasse (0.1mi)
31
11th Ave
10th Ave E
44
42
E Union St
E Madison St

Lincoln
Reservoir
Nagle Pl
Capitol Hill
CAPITOL HILL
Broadway E
Harvard Ave E
Harvard Ave
Boylston Ave E
Boylston Ave
Belmont Ave E
Belmont Ave
Summit Ave E
Summit Ave
Bellevue Ave E
Bellevue Ave
Melrose Ave E
Melrose Ave
29
36
Pike/Pine
E Pine St
E Pike St
Union St
University St
Boylston Ave
Boren Ave
Terry Ave

E Olive Way
E Howell St

Eastlake Ave E
Yale Ave N
Pontius Ave N
Minor Ave N
Fairview Ave N
Mercer St
John St

Denny Way
Yale Ave
Minor Ave
34
Boren Ave
Terry Ave
9th Ave
8th Ave
Seattle Visitor Center
& Concierge Services

Northwest
Outdoor
Center (1mi)
Lake Union
Park
Terry &
Mercer
EASTLAKE
Republican St
Harrison St
Thomas St
Terry &
Thomas
Terry Ave N
Westlake Ave N
Westlake
& Mercer
Westlake
& Thomas
9th Ave N
8th Ave N
Dexter Ave N

Fremont (2mi);
Green Lake (3mi);
Ballard (5mi)

John St
Denny
Park
Aurora Ave N

Westlake & 9th
Howell St
Virginia St
9th Ave
Terry Ave
Stewart St
Olive Way
Westlake
Westlake
& 7th
Westlake
Hub
Westlake
Center
South Lake Union Street Car
Lenora St
8th Ave
7th Ave

Mercer St
Broad St
6th Ave N
Taylor Ave N
5th Ave N
4th Ave N
Roy St

Denny Way
6th Ave
5th Ave
DENNY
TRIANGLE
17
Bell St
3rd Ave
35
39
15
Battery St
16
Blanchard St
Virginia St
28
20

19
40
41
McCaw Hall
Seattle Center
SEATTLE
CENTER
Seattle
Memorial
Stadium
4
Memorial
11
2
Seattle
Center
7

Toulouse Petit (0.1mi);
On the Boards (0.25mi)

Key
Arena
2nd Ave N
Warren Ave N

Eagle St
Clay St
Cedar St
Vine St
Wall St
4th Ave
BELLTOWN
1st Ave
Western Ave
Elliott Ave
Alaskan Way
14

Pier 69
Victoria Clipper
Pier 67
6

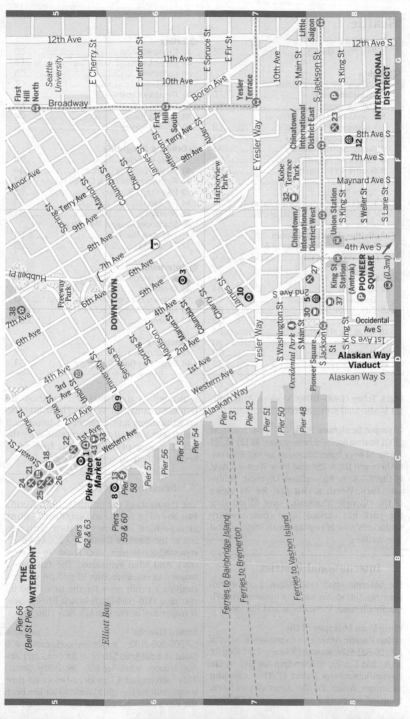

Seattle

Mark Tobey (1890–1976). Modern American art is also well represented.

Olympic Sculpture Park PARK, SCULPTURE
(2901 Western Ave; ☺ sunrise-sunset; ☒ 13) FREE
Terraced over train tracks, in an unlikely oasis between the water and busy Western Ave, is the 8.5-acre, $85-million Olympic Sculpture Park. Worth a visit just for its views of the Olympic Mountains over Elliott Bay, the park has various large contemporary sculptures and is popular with joggers and dog-walkers.

◎ International District

For 'international', read Asian. East of Pioneer Sq, the shops and businesses are primarily Chinese, Vietnamese and Filipino.

**Wing Luke Museum of the
Asian Pacific American Experience** MUSEUM
(☎ 206-623-5124; www.wingluke.org; 719 S King St; adult/child $15/10; ☺ 10am-5pm Tue-Sun; ☒ Chinatown/International District E) This museum examines Asian Pacific American culture, focusing on prickly issues such as Chinese

settlement in the 1880s and Japanese internment camps in WWII. There are also art exhibitions and a preserved immigrant apartment. Guided tours are available; the first Thursday of the month is free, when hours are 10am to 8pm.

◎ Seattle Center

The remnants of the futuristic 1962 World's Fair hosted by Seattle and subtitled 'Century 21 Exposition' are now into their sixth decade at the **Seattle Center** (☎ 206-684-8582; www.seattlecenter.com; 400 Broad St; ☒ monorail). And what remnants! The fair was a major success, attracting 10 million visitors, running a profit (rare for the time) and inspiring a skin-crawlingly kitsch Elvis movie, *It Happened at the World's Fair* (1963).

Space Needle LANDMARK
(☎ 206-905-2100; www.spaceneedle.com; 400 Broad St; adult/child $21/13; ☺ 8am-midnight Jun-Aug, reduced hours Sep-May; ☒ Seattle Center) This streamlined, modern-before-its-time tower built for the 1962 World's Fair has been the city's defining symbol for more than 50

years. The needle anchors the complex now called Seattle Center and draws over one million annual visitors to its flying-saucer-like observation deck and pricey rotating restaurant. Purchase a combination ticket with Chihuly Garden and Glass for $36.

EMP Museum　　　　　　　　　MUSEUM
(☎206-770-2700; www.empmuseum.org; 325 5th Ave N; adult/child $25/16; ☉10am-7pm Jun-Aug, to 5pm Sep-May; Ⓜ Seattle Center) This museum, a marriage of super modern architecture and rock-and-roll history, was founded by Microsoft co-creator Paul Allen. It was inspired by the music of Seattle-born guitar icon, Jimi Hendrix, though today its collection has morphed to include pop-culture and science-fiction history. Buy discounted tickets online.

Chihuly Garden and Glass　　　MUSEUM
(☎206-753-4940; www.chihulygardenandglass.com; 305 Harrison St; adult/child $25/16; ☉8am-9pm Sun-Thu, to 10pm Fri & Sat; Ⓜ Seattle Center) Opened in 2012 and reinforcing Seattle's position as the Venice of North America, this exquisite exposition of the life and work of dynamic local glass sculptor Dale Chihuly might just take your breath away. It shows off Chihuly's colorfully creative designs within an airy glass atrium and landscaped gardens. Hours vary throughout the year; check the website.

◉ Capitol Hill

Millionaires mingle with goth musicians in Capitol Hill, a well-heeled but liberal neighborhood rightly renowned for its fringe theater, alternative music scene, indie coffee bars, and vital gay and lesbian culture. You can take your dog for a herbal bath here, go shopping for ethnic crafts on Broadway, or blend in (or not) with the young punks and old hippies on the eclectic Pike–Pine corridor. The junction of Broadway and E John St is the nexus from which to navigate the quarter's various restaurants, brewpubs, boutiques and dingy, but not dirty, dive bars.

◉ Fremont

Fremont pitches young hipsters among old hippies in an unlikely urban alliance, and vies with Capitol Hill as Seattle's most irreverent neighborhood. It's full of junk shops, urban sculpture, and a healthy sense of its own ludicrousness.

HIGHER THAN THE SPACE NEEDLE

Columbia Center (☎206-386-5564; www.skyviewobservatory.com; 701 5th Ave; adult/student $15/9; ☉9am-10pm) Everyone makes a rush for the iconic Space Needle, but it's not the tallest of Seattle's glittering viewpoints. That honor goes to the sleek, tinted-windowed Columbia Center (1985); at 943ft high, it's the loftiest building in the Pacific Northwest. From the plush observation deck on the 73rd floor you can look down on ferries, cars, islands – even the Space Needle!

Waiting for the Interurban　　MONUMENT
(cnr N 34th St & Fremont Ave N) Seattle's most popular piece of public art, *Waiting for the Interurban,* is cast in recycled aluminum and depicts six people waiting for a train that never comes. Occasionally locals will lovingly decorate the people in outfits corresponding to a special event, the weather, someone's birthday, a Mariners win – whatever. Check out the human face on the dog; it's Armen Stepanian, once Fremont's honorary mayor, who made the mistake of objecting to the sculpture.

Fremont Troll　　　　　　　SCULPTURE
(cnr N 36th St & Troll Ave) The Fremont Troll lurks beneath the north end of the Aurora Bridge at N 36th St. The troll's creators – artists Steve Badanes, Will Martin, Donna Walter and Ross Whitehead – won a competition sponsored by the Fremont Arts Council in 1990. The 18ft-high cement figure snacking on a Volkswagen Beetle is now a favorite place for late-night beer drinking.

◉ The U District

U-dub, a neighborhood of young, studious out-of-towners, places the beautiful, leafy University of Washington campus next to the shabbier 'Ave,' an eclectic strip of cheap boutiques, dive bars and ethnic restaurants.

Burke Museum　　　　　　　MUSEUM
(☎206-543-5590; www.burkemuseum.org; cnr 17th Ave NE & NE 45th St; admission $10; ☉10am-5pm; 🚌70) One of the Northwest's best natural history museums, the Burke boasts an impressive stash of fossils, including a 20,000-year-old sabre-toothed cat. Equally compelling is the focus on over a dozen different Native

DON'T MISS

PIONEER SQUARE

Pioneer Sq is Seattle's oldest quarter, which isn't saying much if you're visiting from Rome or London. Most of the buildings here date from just after the 1889 fire (a devastating inferno that destroyed 25 city blocks, including the entire central business district), and are referred to architecturally as Richardsonian Romanesque, a redbrick revivalist style in vogue at the time. In the early years, the neighborhood's boom-bust fortunes turned its arterial road, Yesler Way, into the original 'skid row' – an allusion to the skidding logs that were pulled downhill to Henry Yesler's pier-side mill. When the timber industry fell on hard times, the road became a haven for the homeless, and its name subsequently became a byword for poverty-stricken urban enclaves countrywide.

Thanks to a concerted public effort, the neighborhood avoided being laid to waste by the demolition squads in the 1960s and is now protected in the Pioneer Sq–Skid Rd Historic District.

The quarter today mixes the historic with the seedy while harboring art galleries, cafes and nightlife. Its most iconic building is the 42-story **Smith Tower** (206-622-4004; www.smithtower.com; 506 2nd Ave), completed in 1914 and, until 1931, the tallest building west of the Mississippi. Other highlights include the 1909 **Pergola** (cnr Yesler Way & James St), a decorative iron shelter reminiscent of a Parisian Metro station, and **Occidental Park** (btwn S Washington & S Main Sts; Pioneer Sq), containing totem poles carved by Chinook artist Duane Pasco.

The **Klondike Gold Rush National Historical Park** (206-553-3000; www.nps. gov/klse; 319 2nd Ave S; 9am-5pm; International District/Chinatown) FREE is a city-based visitor-center outpost. It shows off exhibits, photos and news clippings from the 1897 Klondike gold rush, when a Seattle-on-steroids acted as a fueling depot for prospectors bound for the Yukon in Canada

American cultures. There's free admission on the first Thursday of the month, when the museum stays open until 8pm.

Ballard

A former seafaring community with a strong Scandinavian heritage, Ballard still feels like a small town engulfed by a bigger city. Traditionally gritty, no-nonsense and uncommercial, it's slowly being condo-ized, but remains a good place to down a microbrew or see a live band.

Hiram M Chittenden Locks   CANAL
(3015 NW 54th St; locks 24hr, ladder & gardens 7am-9pm, visitor center 10am-6pm May-Sep; 62) Seattle shimmers like an impressionist painting on sunny days at the Hiram M Chittenden Locks. Here, the fresh waters of Lake Washington and Lake Union drop 22ft into salt-water Puget Sound. Construction of the canal and locks began in 1911; today 100,000 boats pass through them annually. You can view fish-ladder activity through underwater glass panels, stroll through botanical gardens and visit a small museum.

Activities

Cycling

A cycling favorite, the 16.5-mile **Burke-Gilman Trail** winds from Ballard to Log Boom Park in Kenmore on Seattle's Eastside. There, it connects with the 11-mile **Sammamish River Trail**, which winds past the Chateau Ste Michelle winery in Woodinville before terminating at Redmond's Marymoor Park.

More cyclists pedal the popular loop around **Green Lake**, situated just north of Fremont and 5 miles north of the downtown core. From Belltown, the 2.5-mile **Elliott Bay Trail** runs along the Waterfront to Smith Cove.

Get a copy of the *Seattle Bicycling Guide Map*, published by the City of Seattle's Transportation Bicycle & Pedestrian Program online (www.seattle.gov/transportation/bike-maps.htm) or at bike shops.

For bicycle rentals and tours, try **Recycled Cycles** (206-547-4491; www.recycledcycles.com; 1007 NE Boat St; rental per day $40-50; 10am-8pm Mon-Fri, to 6pm Sat & Sun; 66), a friendly U District shop that also rents out chariots and trail-a-bike attachments for kids, or **SBR Seattle Bicycle Rental & Tours** (800-349-0343; www.seattlebicyclerentals.com; Pier 58; rental per hour $10-15, per day $45-65; 11am-7pm Wed-

Mon; ⓇUniversity St), which offers reasonable rates and daily tours (book online).

Water Sports

Seattle is not just on a network of cycling trails. With Venice-like proportions of downtown water, it is also strafed with kayak-friendly marine trails. The **Lakes to Locks Water Trail** links Lake Sammamish with Lake Washington, Lake Union and – via the Hiram M Chittenden Locks – Puget Sound. For launching sites and maps, check the website of the Washington Water Trails Association (www.wwta.org).

Northwest Outdoor Center   KAYAKING
(📌206-281-9694; www.nwoc.com; 2100 Westlake Ave N; rental per hour from $15; 🚌62) On Lake Union, rents kayaks and offers tours and instruction in sea and white-water kayaking.

👉 Tours

Seattle Free Walking Tours   WALKING TOUR
(www.seattlefreewalkingtours.org) A nonprofit set up in 2012 by two world travelers. Choose from a general downtown tour or a Pike Place Market option. Suggested $15 donation.

Seattle by Foot   WALKING TOUR
(📌206-508-7017; www.seattlebyfoot.com; tours $25-35) Offers different tours focusing on the city's coffeehouses, pubs, downtown areas or the Fremont neighborhood. Book online for a $5 discount.

⚜ Festivals & Events

Seattle International Film Festival   FILM
(SIFF; www.siff.net) Held in mid-May, the city's biggest film festival uses a half dozen cinemas, but also has its own dedicated cinema, in McCaw Hall's **Nesholm Family Lecture Hall** (321 Mercer St).

Seafair   FAIR
(www.seafair.com) Huge crowds attend this festival held on the water in late July/August, with hydroplane races, a torchlight parade, an air show, music and even a Milk Carton Derby (look it up!).

Bumbershoot   MUSIC, PERFORMING ARTS
(www.bumbershoot.com) A major arts and cultural event at Seattle Center on the Labor Day weekend in September, with live music, comedy, theater, visual arts and dance.

🛏 Sleeping

Reserve ahead in summer, when hotels book up and prices tend to skyrocket.

ⓘ SEATTLE CITY PASS

If you're planning on visiting the Space Needle, Seattle Aquarium, Woodland Park Zoo and Chihuly Garden and Glass (among other sights), consider buying the Seattle City Pass (www.citypass.com/seattle), which will save you nearly 50% on admission costs.

Moore Hotel   HOTEL $
(📌206-448-4851; www.moorehotel.com; 1926 2nd Ave; r with private/shared bath from $112/87; 🛜; ⓇWestlake) Old-world and allegedly haunted, the central, hip and whimsical Moore offers 119 good-size budget rooms at bargain rates. Two rooms sleep up to eight, and the suites have kitchenettes. The cute cafe serves up great coffee. Reserve in summer.

Hotel Hotel   HOSTEL $
(📌206-257-4543; www.hotelhotel.co; 3515 Fremont Ave N; dm $29-35, r $79-99; @🛜; 🚌26) This slick hostel almost feels like a boutique hotel – walls are painted dark earth colors and there are cool retro touches. Dorms are wonderful and spacious, while private rooms have trendy sliding bathroom doors. All boast hardwood floors. A kitchen is available, or eat downstairs in the wood-fired-pizza restaurant-bar.

City Hostel Seattle   HOSTEL $
(📌206-706-3255; www.hostelseattle.com; 2327 2nd Ave; dm/d from $29/79; @🛜; ⓇWestlake) Every awesome room in this well-located, boutique 'art hostel' has colorful murals on its walls painted by local artists. There's also a common room, hot tub, in-house movie theater and all-you-can-eat breakfast.

★ Ace Hotel   HOTEL $$
(📌206-448-4721; www.acehotel.com; 2423 1st Ave; r with private/shared bath from $219/119; 🅿✳🛜📺; 🚌13) The original locale of the trendy Ace Hotel chain, sports minimal decor, sliding barn-door bathrooms and Pendleton wool blankets. Some rooms even come with record players. Continental breakfast is free, but parking costs $26.

Pensione Nichols   GUESTHOUSE $$
(📌206-441-7125; www.pensionenichols.com; 1923 1st Ave; r from $180; 🛜✳) For a homey stay right near Pike Place, this cozy guesthouse is hard to beat. Interior rooms are quiet, but still bright with skylights, while deluxe rooms offer street views. Apartment suites

PACIFIC NORTHWEST SEATTLE

DON'T MISS

DISCOVERY PARK

A former military installation that has been transformed into a wild coastal park, **Discovery Park** (www.seattle.gov/parks/environment/discovery.htm; 🖳33) is a relatively recent addition to the city landscape – it wasn't officially inaugurated until 1973, and the American military finally left in 2012. Comprising the largest green space in the city, the park's 534 acres are laced with cliffs, meadows, sand dunes, forest and beaches, all of which provide a welcome breathing space for hemmed-in Seattleites and a vital corridor for wildlife.

For a map of the park's trail and road system, stop by the **Discovery Park Environmental Learning Center** (📞206-386-4236; 3801 W Government Way; ⊘8:30am-5pm) near the Government Way entrance. The park is five miles northwest of downtown Seattle in the neighborhood of Magnolia. To get there, catch bus 33 from 3rd Ave & Union St downtown.

sleep four to six and boast full kitchens. There are great water views from the common room, where continental breakfast is served.

Maxwell Hotel BOUTIQUE HOTEL **$$**
(📞206-286-0629; www.themaxwellhotel.com; 300 Roy St; r from $240; P❋@🛜🏊; 🚌Rapid Ride D-Line) Located in Lower Queen Anne, the Maxwell's huge designer-chic lobby welcomes you, while the 139 gorgeously modern rooms offer up hardwood floors and Scandinavian bedding. There's a small pool, a gym and free bike rentals.

★**Inn at the Market** BOUTIQUE HOTEL **$$$**
(📞206-443-3600; www.innatthemarket.com; 86 Pine St; r with/without water view from $385/325; P❋@🛜🏊; 🚌Westlake) Just a block from Pike Place Market, this 71-room boutique hotel has elegant, good-size rooms, many with large windows or small balconies. There's an awesome communal terrace offering views of market activity and Puget Sound. A swimming pool is available at a nearby gym; parking costs $32.

Hotel Five BOUTIQUE HOTEL **$$$**
(📞206-448-0924; www.hotelfiveseattle.com; 2200 5th Ave; r from $285; P❋🛜; 🖳13) This

trendy hotel mixes retro-'70s furniture with sharp color accents to produce something dazzlingly modern. The ultra comfortable beds are a valid cure for insomnia, while the large reception area invites lingering, especially when they lay out the complimentary cupcakes and coffee in the late afternoon. Day-of or online rates can be a good deal.

Belltown Inn HOTEL **$$$**
(📞206-529-3700; www.belltown-inn.com; 2301 3rd Ave; r from $239; P❋@🛜; 🚌Westlake) Rooms at this modern, centrally located hotel are modestly sized but very comfortable, and offer good amenities (some have kitchenettes). There's a roof terrace and free bike rentals. It's popular with cruises, so reserve in summer.

🍴 Eating

The best budget meals are to be found in Pike Place Market. Take your pick from fresh produce, baked goods, deli items and takeout ethnic foods.

★**Salumi** SANDWICHES **$**
(📞206-621-8772; www.salumicuredmeats.com; 309 3rd Ave S; sandwiches $8.50-11; ⊘11am-1:30pm Mon, to 3:30pm Tue-Fri; 🚇International District/Chinatown) Be ready for a queue outside Salumi, well known and loved for its delicious salami and cured-meat sandwiches (grilled lamb, pork shoulder, meatball...). Vegetarians can go for the seasonal veggie offering or eggplant balsamico. Meats and cheeses are also sold by the pound.

Green Leaf VIETNAMESE **$**
(📞206-340-1388; www.greenleaftaste.com; 418 8th Ave S; pho $9, specials $10-12; ⊘11am-10pm; 🚇Chinatown/International District E) Popular Green Leaf, located in Chinatown, shoots out rapid-fire dishes from its tiny kitchen to its small, crowded dining room. Choose the traditional *pho* (beef noodle soup) or go for the excellent rice- or vermicelli-noodle dishes. Also located in Belltown at 2800 1st Ave.

Piroshky Piroshky BAKERY **$**
(www.piroshkybakery.com; 1908 Pike Pl; snacks $3-6; ⊘8am-6pm; 🚌Westlake) Piroshky knocks out its delectable sweet and savory Russian pies and pastries in a space about the size of a walk-in closet. Get the savory smoked-salmon pâté or the sauerkraut with cabbage and onion, and follow it with the chocolate-cream hazelnut roll or a fresh rhubarb piroshki.

Crumpet Shop
BAKERY $

(☑206-682-1598; www.thecrumpetshop.com; 1503 1st Ave; crumpets $3-6; ⊙7am-3pm Mon-Thu, to 4pm Fri-Sun; ⋒Westlake) The treasured British crumpet has been given a distinct American twist with lavish toppings such as pesto, wild salmon or lemon curd at this casual Pike Place Market eatery, family-owned and operated for almost 40 years. Organic ingredients make it very Pacific Northwest, though there's marmite for homesick Brits.

★ Toulouse Petit
CAJUN, CREOLE $$

(☑206-432-9069; www.toulousepetit.com; 601 Queen Anne Ave N; mains $13-17; ⊙8am-2am; ⋒13) Hailed for its generous happy hours, cheap brunches and rollicking atmosphere, this perennially busy Queen Anne eatery has something for everyone. The menu is large and varied, offering choices such as blackened ribeye steak, freshwater gulf prawns and housemade gnocchi with artichoke hearts.

Revel
ASIAN $$

(☑206-547-2040; www.revelseattle.com; 403 N 36th St; small plates $12-16; ⊙11am-2pm & 5-10pm Mon-Fri, 10am-2pm & 5-10pm Sat & Sun) Walk into this slick, modern restaurant and you'll notice this isn't your typical Asian eatery. The menu is small but delicious, from the short-rib dumplings to the lemongrass beef with cilantro noodles. Dishes are small-ish and meant to be shared; down them with a creative cocktail or two.

Serious Pie
PIZZA $$

(☑206-838-7388; www.tomdouglas.com; 316 Virginia St; pizzas $16-18; ⊙11am-11pm; ⋒Westlake) In the crowded confines of Serious Pie you can enjoy beautifully blistered pizza bases topped with such unconventional ingredi-ents as clams, potatoes, nettles, soft eggs, truffle cheese and more. Other locations around town.

Jack's BBQ
BARBECUE $$

(☑206-467-4038; www.jacksbbq.com; 3924 Airport Way S; mains $12-23; ⊙11am-9pm Tue-Sat) Some of Seattle's best BBQ can be had at this casual, family-friendly joint, located south towards the airport. Meats are smoked slowly over hardwoods and come out tender and delicious – the ribs are a mainstay, and on Tuesdays they serve up a giant beef rib (reserve ahead).

Pink Door
ITALIAN $$

(☑206-443-3241; www.thepinkdoor.net; 1919 Post Alley; mains $18-27; ⊙11:30am-4pm & 5-11pm Mon-Thu, 11.30am-midnight Fri & Sat, 4-10pm Sun) Finding this upscale Italian restaurant is an adventure in itself – look for the unsigned pink door down a busy alleyway near Pike Place Market. Pastas are the specialty here, with a few seafood and meat options, and there's an emphasis on organic, seasonal ingredients.

Le Pichet
FRENCH $$

(☑206-256-1499; www.lepichetseattle.com; 1933 1st Ave; mains $11-25; ⊙8am-midnight; ⋒Westlake) Say *bonjour* to Le Pichet, just up from Pike Place Market, a cute and very French bistro with pâtés, cheeses, wine, *chocolat* and a refined Parisian feel. Dinner means delicacies such as wild boar shoulder or grilled rabbit sausage.

Sitka & Spruce
MODERN AMERICAN $$$

(☑206-324-0662; www.sitkaandspruce.com; 1531 Melrose Ave; small plates $8-33; ⊙11:30am-2pm & 5-10pm Mon-Fri, 10am-2pm & 5-11pm Sat, 10am-2pm & 5-9pm Sun; ⋒10) Located in a

---

SEATTLE FOR CHILDREN

Make a beeline for the Seattle Center, preferably on the monorail, where food carts, street entertainers, fountains and green spaces will make the day fly by. One essential stop is the **Pacific Science Center** (☑206-443-2001; www.pacificsciencecenter.org; 200 2nd Ave N; adult/child exhibits only $19.50/14.50, with Imax $23.50/18.50; ⊙10am-5pm Mon-Fri, to 6pm Sat & Sun; ⋒; Ⓜ Seattle Center), which entertains and educates with virtual-reality exhibits, laser shows, holograms, an Imax theater and a planetarium. Parents won't be bored either.

Downtown on Pier 59, **Seattle Aquarium** (☑206-386-4300; www.seattleaquarium.org; 1483 Alaskan Way, at Pier 59; adult/child 4-12yr $23/16; ⊙9:30am-5pm; ⋒; ⋒University St) is a fun way to learn about the natural world of the Pacific Northwest. Even better is **Woodland Park Zoo** (☑206-548-2500; www.zoo.org; 5500 Phinney Ave N; adult/child 3-12yr May-Sep $20/12.25, Oct-Apr $13.75/9.25; ⊙9:30am-6pm May-Sep, to 4pm Oct-Apr; ⋒; ⋒5) in the Green Lake neighborhood, one of Seattle's greatest tourist attractions and consistently rated as one of the top 10 zoos in the country.

marketplace-like building on trendy Capitol Hill, this small-plates fine diner has won acclaim for its casual vibe, constantly changing menu and good wine selection. Sample items such as the house-made charcuterie, conica morels or king-trumpet escabeche. All the ingredients are obtained from local producers. Reserve ahead.

Cascina Spinasse ITALIAN $$$
(☑206-251-7673; www.spinasse.com; 1531 14th Ave; mains $28-31; ⏱5-10pm Sun-Thu, to 11pm Fri & Sat; ☐11) Spinasse specializes in cuisine of the Piedmont region of northern Italy. This means seasonally inspired dishes such as roasted morels stuffed with pork, or milk-braised chicken with roasted baby artichokes. The finely curated wine list includes a number of impressive Piedmontese reds.

♟ Drinking & Nightlife

Starbucks is the tip of the iceberg when it comes to coffee culture in Seattle; the city has spawned plenty of smaller indie chains, many with their own roasting rooms. Look out for Uptown Espresso, Caffe Ladro and Espresso Vivace.

You'll find cocktail bars, dance clubs and live music on Capitol Hill. The main drag in Ballard has brick taverns both old and new, filled with the hard-drinking older set in daylight hours and indie rockers at night. Belltown has gone from grungy to shabby chic, and has the advantage of many drinking holes neatly lined up in rows.

★Starbucks Reserve Roastery & Tasting Room COFFEE
(www.starbucks.com/roastery; 1124 Pike St; coffees $3-12; ⏱7am-11pm) Often likened to Willy Wonka's Chocolate Factory, this roastery – Starbucks' largest venue to date – is a multi-leveled mecca of over-caffeinated proportions. Up front a greeter welcomes you with a map, while in back gigantic roasters spin beans. It's a Scandinavian-inspired arena of glass, wood, copper and concrete – a perfect place to sip your cup of siphoned West Java Preanger ($12). Coffee flights available.

★Fremont Brewing BREWERY
(☑206-420-2407; www.fremontbrewing.com; 3409 Woodland Park Ave N; ⏱11am-9pm; ☐26) ⌇ Hipsters and cyclists frequent this trendy brewery for its award-winning beers and sustainable practices. On sunny days, sitting at the communal tables out back in the beer garden is mandatory. Free pretzels and apples to snack on, but no real food.

Noble Fir BAR
(☑206-420-7425; www.thenoblefir.com; 5316 Ballard Ave NW; ⏱4pm-midnight Tue-Thu, to 1am Fri & Sat, 1-9pm Sun; ☐17) Possibly the first bar devoted to the theme of wilderness-hiking, the upscale Noble Fir is a bright, shiny spot in the Ballard neighborhood with an epic beer list that might just make you want to abandon all your plans for outdoor adventure. Fine wine and hard ciders, too, along with meat and cheese plates.

Zeitgeist CAFE
(☑206-583-0497; www.zeitgeistcoffee.com; 171 S Jackson St; ⏱6am-7pm Mon-Fri, 7am-7pm Sat, 8am-6pm Sun; 🛜; ☐Pioneer Sq) Possibly Seattle's best indie coffee bar, Zeitgeist brews up smooth *doppio macchiatos* to go along with the sweet almond croissants (and other luscious baked goods). The atmosphere is airy industrial, with brick walls and large windows for people-watching. Soups, salads and sandwiches on offer.

Pike Pub & Brewery BREWERY
(☑206-622-6044; www.pikebrewing.com; 1415 1st Ave; ⏱11am-midnight; ☐University St) Leading the way in the microbrewery revolution, this brewpub was an early starter, opening in 1989 underneath Pike Place Market. Today it continues to serve good pub food (mains $11 to $20) and hop-heavy beers in a busily decorated but fun multilevel space. Free tours available.

Elysian Brewing Company BREWERY
(☑206-860-1920; www.elysianbrewing.com; 1221 E Pike St; ⏱11:30am-2am Mon-Fri, noon-2am Sat & Sun; ☐Pike-Pine) Located on hip Capitol Hill, the Elysian's huge windows are great for people-watching. This is one of Seattle's best brewpubs, loved in particular for its spicy pumpkin beers on draft, available in the fall. The Elysian has other locations around town.

Panama Hotel Tea & Coffee House CAFE
(☑206-515-4000; www.panamahotel.net; 607 S Main St; ⏱8am-9pm; ☐Chinatown/International District W) The Panama, a historic 1910 building containing the only remaining Japanese bathhouse in the US, doubles as a memorial to the neighborhood's Japanese residents forced into internment camps during WWII. The beautifully relaxed cafe has a wide selection of teas, serves Lavazza Italian coffee, and boasts a National Treasure designation.

Caffè Umbria CAFE
(📞206-624-5847; www.caffeumbria.com; 320 Occidental Ave S; ⊗6am-7pm Mon-Fri, 7am-6pm Sat, 8am-5pm Sun; 🚇Pioneer Sq) Umbria has a European flavor with its 8oz cappuccinos, chatty clientele, pretty Italianate tiles and baguettes so fresh they must have been teleported over from Milan. Beautiful pastry and gelato case, too. Ideal for Italophiles and Starbucks-phobes.

Shorty's DIVE BAR
(📞206-441-5449; www.shortydog.com; 2222 2nd Ave; ⊗noon-2am; 🚇13) Shorty's is all about beer, arcade games and music, which is mostly punk and metal. A remnant of Belltown's grungier days that refuses to become an anachronism, it keeps the lights low and the music loud. Pinball machines are built into every table, and basic snacks (hot dogs, nachos) soak up the booze.

Blue Moon DIVE BAR
(📞206-675-9116; www.bluemoonseattle.wordpress.com; 712 NE 45th St; ⊗2pm-late Mon-Fri, noon-late Sat, 1pm-late Sun; 🚇66) A legendary counterculture dive near the university that first opened in 1934 to celebrate the repeal of the prohibition laws, the Blue Moon makes much of its former literary patrons – doyens Dylan Thomas, Allen Ginsberg and Tom Robbins get mentioned a lot. These days you're more likely to run into its comedy, open-mic and vinyl-revival nights.

Re-Bar GAY
(📞206-233-9873; www.rebarseattle.com; 1114 Howell St; 🚇70) This storied indie dance club, where many of Seattle's defining cultural events happened (such as Nirvana album releases), welcomes gay, straight, bi or undecided revelers to its lively dance floor. Also come

for its offbeat theater, burlesque shows and poetry slams – among other wacky offerings.

☆ Entertainment

Consult *The Stranger, Seattle Weekly* or the daily papers for listings. Tickets for big events are available at TicketMaster (www.ticketmaster.com).

Live Music

Crocodile LIVE MUSIC
(📞206-441-4618; www.thecrocodile.com; 2200 2nd Ave; 🚇13) Nearly old enough to be called a Seattle institution, the Crocodile is a clamorous 560-capacity music venue that first opened in 1991, just in time to grab the coattails of the grunge explosion. Everyone who's anyone in Seattle's alt-music scene has since played here, including a famous occasion in 1992 when Nirvana appeared unannounced supporting Mudhoney.

Tractor Tavern LIVE MUSIC
(📞206-789-3599; www.tractortavern.com; 5213 Ballard Ave NW; 🚇17) The premier venue for folk and acoustic music, Tractor Tavern books local songwriters and regional bands, plus quality touring acts. Music runs towards country, rockabilly, folk, blues and old-time. It's an intimate place with a small stage and great sound; occasional square dancing is frosting on the cake.

Neumo's LIVE MUSIC
(📞206-709-9442; www.neumos.com; 925 E Pike St; 🚇Pike-Pine) This punk, hip-hop and alternative-music Capitol Hill venue counts Radiohead and Bill Clinton (not together) among its former guests. It can get hot and sweaty, and even smelly, but that's rock and roll.

GRUNGE & OTHER MUSICAL SUBCULTURES

Synthesizing Gen X angst with a questionable approach to personal hygiene, grunge first dive-bombed onto Seattle's music scene in the early 1990s like a clap of thunder on an otherwise dry and sunny afternoon. The anger had been fermenting for years. Hardcore punk originated in Portland in the late 1970s, led by resident contrarians the Wipers, whose antifashion followers congregated in legendary dive bars such as Satyricon. Another musical blossoming occurred in Olympia, where DIY–merchants Beat Happening invented 'lo-fi' and coyly mocked the corporate establishment. Scooping up the fallout of a disparate youth culture, Seattle quickly became grunge's pulpit, spawning bands such as Pearl Jam, Soundgarden and Alice in Chains. The genre went global in 1991 when Nirvana's *Nevermind* album knocked Michael Jackson off the number-one spot, but the movement was never meant to be successful, and the kudos quickly killed it. Since the mid-1990s the Pacific Northwest has kept its subcultures largely to itself, though the music's no less potent or relevant.

PACIFIC NORTHWEST SEATTLE

Performing Arts

A Contemporary Theatre   THEATER

(ACT; ☑ 206-292-7676; www.acttheatre.org; 700 Union St; ☒ University St) One of the three big companies in the city, this theater fills its $30-million home at Kreielsheimer Place with performances by Seattle's best thespians and occasional big-name actors. Terraced seating surrounds a central stage, and the interior has gorgeous architectural embellishments.

Intiman Theater Company   THEATER

(☑ 206-441-7178; www.intiman.org; 201 Mercer St; Ⓜ Seattle Center) Artistic director Andrew Russell curates magnificent stagings of Shakespeare and Ibsen, among others.

On the Boards   DANCE, THEATER

(☑ 206-217-9888; www.ontheboards.org; 100 W Roy St; 🖥13) *The* place for avant-garde performance art, the nonprofit On the Boards makes its home at the intimate Behnke Center for Contemporary Performance, and showcases some innovative and occasionally weird dance and music.

🛍 Shopping

The main big-name shopping area is downtown between 3rd and 6th Aves and University and Stewart Sts. Pike Place Market is a maze of arts-and-crafts stalls, galleries and small shops. Pioneer Sq and Capitol Hill have locally owned gift and thrift shops. There are many only-in-Seattle shops worth seeking out.

DeLaurenti's   FOOD

(☑ 206-622-0141; 1435 1st Ave; ◷9am-6pm Mon-Sat, 10am-5pm Sun; ☒ University St) Offers a stunning selection of wine, cheese, sausages, hams and pasta, along with a large range of capers, olive oils and anchovies. The sandwich counter is a great place to order panini, salads and pizza slices.

Elliott Bay Book Company   BOOKS

(☑ 206-624-6600; www.elliottbaybook.com; 1521 10th Ave; ◷10am-10pm Mon-Fri, to 11pm Sat, 11am-9pm Sun; ☒ Pike-Pine) This beloved local bookstore offers over 150,000 titles in a large, airy, wood-beamed space with cozy nooks that can inspire hours of serendipitous browsing.

ℹ Information

EMERGENCY

Seattle Police (☑ 206-625-5011; www.seattle.gov/police)

MEDICAL SERVICES

Harborview Medical Center (☑ 206-744-3000; www.uwmedicine.org/harborview; 325 9th Ave) Full medical care, with emergency room.

MEDIA

KEXP 90.3 FM (www.kexp.org) Legendary independent music and community station.

Seattle Times (www.seattletimes.com) The state's largest daily paper.

Stranger (www.thestranger.com) Irreverent and intelligent free weekly, edited by Dan Savage of 'Savage Love' fame.

POST

Post Office (☑ 206-748-5417; www.usps.com; 301 Union St; ◷8:30am-5:30pm Mon-Fri)

TOURIST INFORMATION

Seattle Visitor Center & Concierge Services (☑ 206-461-5840; www.visitseattle.org; cnr Pike St & 7th Ave, Washington State Convention Center; ◷9am-5pm daily Jun-Sep, Mon-Fri Oct-May) Also look for an information kiosk at the entrance to Pike Place Market.

ℹ Getting There & Away

AIR

Seattle-Tacoma International Airport (SEA; ☑ 206-787-5388; www.portseattle.org/Sea-Tac; 17801 International Blvd; 🛜), 13 miles south of Seattle on I-5, has daily services to Europe, Asia, Mexico and points throughout the USA and Canada, with frequent flights to and from Portland, OR, and Vancouver, BC.

BOAT

Victoria Clipper (☑ 206-448-5000; www.clippervacations.com; 2701 Alaskan Way, Pier 69) Operates several high-speed passenger ferries to the San Juan Islands and Victoria, BC, as well as offering package tours.

Washington State Ferries (WSF; ☑ 888-808-7977; www.wsdot.wa.gov/ferries) Routes, prices and schedules available on the website; fares depend on the destination, vehicle size and trip duration, and are collected either for round-trip or one-way travel depending on the departure terminal. Reserve ahead, as bookings are becoming almost mandatory to some destinations (ie San Juan Islands).

BUS

Various intercity coaches serve Seattle at different drop-off points.

Bellair Airporter Shuttle (☑ 866-235-5247; www.airporter.com) Buses connect downtown Seattle and Sea-Tac airport with Anacortes (for the San Juan Island ferries) and Bellingham.

Greyhound (206-628-5526; www.greyhound.com; 503 S Royal Brougham Way) Greyhound connects Seattle with cities all over the country, including Chicago, Spokane, San Francisco and Vancouver, BC.

Quick Shuttle (800-665-2122; www.quickcoach.com;) Fast and efficient Quick Shuttle has several daily buses to Vancouver, BC.

TRAIN

King Street Station (206-296-0100; www.amtrak.com; 303 S Jackson St) Amtrak serves Seattle's King Street Station. Three main routes run through town: the *Amtrak Cascades* (connecting Vancouver, Seattle, Portland and Eugene); the very scenic *Coast Starlight* (connecting Seattle, Oakland and Los Angeles) and the *Empire Builder* (a cross-continental to Chicago).

❶ Getting Around

TO/FROM THE AIRPORT

There are a number of options for making the 13-mile trek from the airport to downtown Seattle. The most efficient is via the new light-rail service run by Sound Transit (www.soundtransit.org).

Seattle's Link Light Rail operates between Sea-Tac Airport and downtown (Westlake Center). It runs every 10 to 15 minutes between 5am and midnight; the ride takes 36 minutes. There are additional stops in Pioneer Sq and the International District.

Shuttle Express (425-981-7000; www.shuttleexpress.com) has a pickup and drop-off point on the 3rd floor of the airport garage; it charges approximately $18 and is handy if you have a lot of luggage.

Taxis are available at the parking garage on the 3rd floor. The average fare to downtown is $46 (not including tip).

CAR & MOTORCYCLE

Trapped in a narrow corridor between mountains and sea, Seattle is a horrendous traffic bottleneck and its nightmarish jams are famous. I-5 has a high-occupancy vehicle lane for vehicles carrying two or more people. Otherwise, try to work around the elongated 'rush hours.'

PUBLIC TRANSPORTATION

Buses are operated by Metro Transit (www.metro.kingcounty.gov), part of the King County Department of Transportation.

Seattle has a bike share system (www.prontocycleshare.com) with 50 stations around the city.

Monorail (206-905-2620; www.seattlemonorail.com; adult/child 5-12yr $2.25/1) Travels only between two stops: Seattle Center and Westlake Center.

Seattle Streetcar (www.seattlestreetcar.org) Runs about every 15 minutes from downtown Seattle (Westlake) to South Lake Union; stops allow connections with numerous bus routes. Expansion lines are planned.

TAXI

All Seattle taxi cabs operate at the same rate, set by King County; $2.60 at meter drop, then $2.70 per mile.

Seattle Orange Cab (206-522-8800; www.orangecab.net)

Seattle Yellow Cab (206-622-6500; www.seattleyellowcab.com)

Around Seattle

Olympia

Small in size, but big in clout, state capital Olympia is a musical, political and outdoor powerhouse. Look no further than the street-side buskers on 4th Ave belting out acoustic grunge, the smartly attired bureaucrats marching across the lawns of the state legislature, or the Goretex-clad outdoor fiends overnighting before sorties into the Olympic Mountains. Progressive Evergreen State College has long lent the place an artsy turn (Matt Groening, creator of the *Simpsons,* studied here), while the dive bars and secondhand guitar shops of downtown provided an original pulpit for riot grrrl music and grunge.

◎ Sights & Activities

Washington State Capitol LANDMARK
(360-902-8880; 416 Sid Snyder Ave SW; 7am-5:30pm Mon-Fri, 11am-4pm Sat & Sun) FREE Olympia's capitol complex is set in a 30-acre park overlooking Capitol Lake with the Olympic Mountains glistening in the background. The campus' crowning glory is the magnificent **Legislative Building**. Completed in 1927, it's a dazzling display of craning columns and polished marble, topped by a 287ft dome that is only slightly smaller than its namesake in Washington, DC. Tours available.

Olympia Farmers Market MARKET
(360-352-9096; www.olympiafarmersmarket.com; 700 N Capitol Way; 10am-3pm Thu-Sun Apr-Oct, Sat & Sun Nov & Dec) Second only to Seattle's Pike Place in size and character, Olympia's local market is a great place to shop for organic herbs, vegetables, flowers, baked goods and the famous specialty oysters.

🛏 Sleeping & Eating

Fertile Ground Guesthouse GUESTHOUSE $$
(☑360-352-2428; www.fertileground.org; 311 9th
Ave SE; s/d from $110/120; 🐾) Surrounded by
a lush and leafy organic garden, this comfortable and homey guesthouse offers three
lovely rooms, one en suite and two with
shared bath. Breakfast is made mostly from
organic and locally sourced ingredients.
Sauna on premises. More rooms (including
a dorm) are available at other locations;
check the website for details.

Traditions Cafe & World Folk Art AMERICAN $
(☑360-705-2819; www.traditionsfairtrade.com;
300 5th Ave SW; sandwiches $9-10; ⊙9am-6pm
Mon-Fri, 10am-6pm Sat, 11am-5pm Sun; 🍴) 🍃
Fair Trade hippy enclave of fresh salads
(lemon-tahini, smoked salmon etc), sandwiches (meat, veggie and vegan), a few Mexican and Italian plates, coffee drinks, herbal teas and local ice cream. Attached is an
eclectic folk-art store. Check the website for
music, poetry nights and more.

ℹ Information

State Capitol Visitor Center (☑360-704-
7544; www.visitolympia.com; 103 Sid Snyder
Ave SW; ⊙10am-3pm Mon-Fri, 11am-3pm Sat &
Sun) Offers information on the capitol campus,
the Olympia area and Washington state. Note
the limited opening hours.

Olympic Peninsula

Surrounded on three sides by sea and exhibiting many of the characteristics of a full-blown island, the remote Olympic Peninsula
is about as 'wild' and 'west' as America gets.
What it lacks in cowboys it makes up for in
rare, endangered wildlife and dense primeval forest. The peninsula's roadless interior
is largely given over to the notoriously wet
Olympic National Park, while the margins
are the preserve of loggers, Native American
reservations and a smattering of small but
interesting settlements, most notably Port
Townsend. Equally untamed is the western
coastline, America's isolated end point, where
tempestuous ocean and misty old-growth Pacific rainforest meet in aqueous harmony.

Olympic National Park

Declared a national monument in 1909 and
a national park in 1938, the 1406-sq-mile
Olympic National Park (www.nps.gov/olym)

shelters one of the world's only temperate
rainforests and a 57-mile strip of Pacific
coastal wilderness that was added in 1953.
Opportunities for independent exploration
abound, with activities from hiking and fishing to kayaking and skiing.

EASTERN ENTRANCES

The graveled Dosewallips River Rd follows
the river from US 101 (turnoff approximately 1km north of Dosewallips State Park) for
15 miles to **Dosewallips Ranger Station**,
where hiking trails begin; call ☑360-565-
3130 for road conditions. Even hiking smaller portions of the two long-distance paths,
including the 14.9 mile Dosewallips River
Trail, with views of glaciated **Mt Anderson**,
is reason enough to visit the valley. Another eastern entry for hikers is the **Staircase
Ranger Station** (☑360-877-5569), just inside
the national-park boundary, 15 miles from
Hoodsport on US 101. Two state parks along
the eastern edge of the national park are
popular with campers: **Dosewallips State
Park** (☑888-226-7688; www.parks.wa.gov/499/
Dosewallips; 306996 Hwy 101; tent sites $12-35, RV
sites $30-45) and **Lake Cushman State Park**
(☑888-226-7688; campsites $15-66). Both have
running water, flush toilets and some RV
hookups. Reservations are accepted.

NORTHERN ENTRANCES

The park's easiest – and hence most popular
– entry point is at **Hurricane Ridge**, 18 miles
south of Port Angeles. At the road's end, an
interpretive center gives a stupendous view
of Mt Olympus (7965ft) and dozens of other
peaks. The 5200ft altitude can mean you'll
hit inclement weather, and the winds here
(as the name suggests) can be ferocious.
Aside from various summer trekking opportunities, the area maintains the small, family-friendly **Hurricane Ridge Ski & Snowboard Area** (www.hurricaneridge.com; 🎿).

Popular for boating and fishing is **Lake
Crescent**, the site of the park's oldest and
most reasonably priced **lodge** (☑888-896-
3818; www.olympicnationalparks.com; 416 Lake
Crescent Rd; lodge r from $120, cabins from $260;
P✳🐾). Delicious sustainable food is served
in the lodge's ecofriendly restaurant. From
Storm King Information Station (☑360-
928-3380; 343 Barnes Point Rd; ⊙May-Sep) on
the lake's south shore, a 1-mile hike climbs
through old-growth forest to Marymere
Falls.

Along the Sol Duc River, the **Sol Duc Hot Springs Resort** (☏360-327-3583; www.olym-picnationalparks.com; 12076 Sol Duc Hot Springs Rd, Port Angeles; day use $12.25, RV sites $43, cabins from $196; ☺Apr-Oct; ✸✸) ✐ has lodging, dining, massage and, of course, hot-spring pools, as well as great day hikes.

WESTERN ENTRANCES

Isolated by distance and home of one of the country's rainiest microclimates, the Pacific side of the Olympics remains the wildest. Only US 101 offers access to its noted temperate rainforests and untamed coastline. The **Hoh River Rainforest**, at the end of the 19-mile Hoh River Rd, is a Tolkienesque maze of dripping ferns and moss-draped trees. The **Hoh Visitor Center and Campground** (☏360-374-6925; ☺9am-5pm) has information on guided walks and longer backcountry hikes. There are no hookups or showers, and it's first-come, first-served.

A little to the south lies **Lake Quinault**, a beautiful glacial lake surrounded by forested peaks. It's popular for fishing, boating and swimming, and is surrounded by some of the nation's oldest trees. **Lake Quinault Lodge** (☏360-288-2900; www.olympicnational-parks.com; 345 S Shore Rd; r from $269; ✸☎✸), a luxury classic of 1920s 'parkitecture,' has a heated pool and sauna, a crackling fireplace and a memorable dining room. For a cheaper sleep nearby, try the ultrafriendly **Quinault River Inn** (☏360-288-2237; www.quinaultriverinn.com; 8 River Dr; r from $139; ✸☎) in Amanda Park, a favorite with anglers.

A number of short hikes begin just outside the Lake Quinault Lodge, or you can try the longer **Enchanted Valley Trail**, a medium-grade 13-miler that begins from the Graves Creek Ranger station at the end of South Shore Rd and climbs up to a large meadow resplendent with wildflowers and copses of alder trees.

❶ Information

The park entry fee is $5/15 per person/vehicle, valid for one week and payable at park entrances. Many park visitor centers double as United States Forestry Service (USFS) ranger stations, where you can pick up permits for wilderness camping (per group $5, valid up to 14 days, plus $2 per person per night).

Forks Visitor Information Center (☏360-374-2531; www.forkswa.com; 1411 S Forks Ave; ☺10am-5pm Mon-Sat, 11am-4pm Sun)

Olympic National Park Visitor Center (☏360-565-3130; www.nps.gov/olym; 3002

Mt Angeles Rd, Port Angeles; ☺9am-5pm) The best overall center is situated at the Hurricane Ridge gateway, a mile off Hwy 101 in Port Angeles. Hours vary according to the season.

Wilderness Information Center (☏360-565-3100; www.nps.gov/olym; 3002 Mt Angeles Rd, Port Angeles; ☺8am-6pm Jul & Aug, to 4pm Sep-Jun) Provides backcountry permits and backpacking information.

Port Townsend

Historic relics are rare in the Pacific Northwest, which makes time-warped Port Townsend all the more fascinating. Small, nostalgic and culturally vibrant, this showcase of 1890s Victorian architecture is the 'New York of the West that never was,' a one-time boomtown that went bust at the turn of the 20th century, only to be rescued 70 years later by a group of far-sighted locals. Port Townsend today is a buoyant blend of inventive eateries, historic hotels and quirky annual festivals.

⊙ Sights

Jefferson Art & History Museum MUSEUM
(www.jchsmuseum.org; 540 Water St; adult/child $6/1; ☺11am-4pm daily Mar-Dec, Sat & Sun Jan & Feb) The local historic society runs this well-maintained exhibition area that includes mock-ups of an 1892 jail, maritime artifacts and an art-gallery room. You can also learn about the history of prostitution in innocent-seeming Port Townsend.

Fort Worden State Park PARK
(☏360-344-4431; www.parks.wa.gov/511/Fort-Worden; 200 Battery Way; ☺6:30am-dusk Apr-Oct, 8am-dusk Nov-Mar) This attractive park located within Port Townsend's city limits is the remains of a large fortification system constructed in the 1890s to protect the strategically important Puget Sound area from outside attack – supposedly from the Spanish during the 1898 war. Sharp-eyed film buffs might recognize the area as the backdrop for the movie *An Officer and a Gentleman*.

The Commanding Officer's Quarters, a 12-bedroom mansion, is open for tours, and part of one of the barracks is now the Puget Sound Coast Artillery Museum, which tells the story of early Pacific coastal fortifications.

Hikes lead along the headland to **Point Wilson Lighthouse Station** and some wonderful windswept beaches. On the park's fishing pier is the **Port Townsend**

Marine Science Center (www.ptmsc.org; 532 Battery Way; adult/child $5/3; ⊙11am-5pm Wed-Mon Jun-Aug, reduced hours Sep-May) featuring four touch tanks and daily interpretive programs. There are also several camping and lodging possibilities.

🛏 Sleeping & Eating

Waterstreet Hotel   HOTEL $
(☑360-385-5467; www.watersthotel.com; 635 Water St; r $60-175; ✳🐾) Homey and friendly, the Waterstreet offers great-value rooms, some with shared bathrooms. If you're a family or group go for suite 5 – it's essentially an apartment with a loft, full kitchen and charming back porch with views of Puget Sound. Reception is in the gift shop next door to the hotel.

Palace Hotel   HISTORIC HOTEL $$
(☑360-385-0773; www.palacehotelpt.com; 1004 Water St; r $109-229; 🐾✳) Built in 1889, this beautiful Victorian building is a former brothel that was once run by the locally notorious Madame Marie, who did business out of the 2nd-floor corner suite. It's been reincarnated as an attractive period hotel with antique furnishings. Pleasant common spaces; kitchenettes available.

Doc's Marina Grill   AMERICAN $$
(☑360-344-3627; www.docsgrill.com; 141 Hudson St; mains $13-24; ⊙11am-11pm) With a great location by Port Townsend's marina, Doc's offers up something for everyone. There are burgers, sandwiches, fish and chips, various salads, pastas, steaks, seafood and a few vegetarian selections. It is housed in a historic building that was a nurses' barracks back in the 1940s.

Waterfront Pizza   PIZZA $$
(☑360-379-9110; 951 Water St; large pizzas $16-28; ⊙11am-8pm Sun-Thu, to 9pm Fri & Sat) If you're craving a quick snack, grab a slice downstairs – just be prepared for lines in the closet-size dining room. For more relaxed, sit-down service, climb the stairs and sample the pies topped with treats such as Cajun sausage, feta cheese, artichoke hearts and pesto.

ℹ Information

Visitor Center (☑360-385-2722; www.ptchamber.org; 2409 Jefferson; ⊙9am-5pm)

ℹ Getting There & Away

Washington State Ferries (☑206-464-6400; www.wsdot.wa.gov/ferries) Goes to/from Coupeville on Whidbey Island (35 minutes); reserve ahead.

Port Angeles

Despite the name, there's nothing Spanish or particularly angelic about Port Angeles, propped up by the lumber industry and backed by the steep-sided Olympic Mountains. Rather than visiting to see the town per se, people come here to catch a ferry for Victoria, BC, or to plot an outdoor excursion into the nearby Olympic National Park.

🏃 Activities

The **Olympic Discovery Trail** (www.olympicdiscoverytrail.com) is a 30-mile off-road hiking and cycling trail between Port Angeles and Sequim, starting at the end of **Ediz Hook**, the sand spit that loops around the bay. Bikes can be rented at **Sound Bikes & Kayaks** (www.soundbikekayaks.com; 120 Front St; bike rental per hour/day $10/45).

🛏 Sleeping & Eating

Toadlily House   HOSTEL $
(☑360-797-3797; www.toadlilyhouse.com; 105 E 5th St; dm $25-30; 🐾) This bright and clean hostel in a lime-green heritage home has several bunk rooms and one private room ($40) off the back garden. The bathroom and kitchen are shared, the layout is perfect for socializing, and the owner is hip and friendly.

Olympic Lodge   HOTEL $$
(☑360-452-2993; www.olympiclodge.com; 140 Del Guzzi Dr; r from $190; ✳@🐾✳) This is the most comfortable place in town, offering gorgeous rooms, on-site bistro, swimming pool with hot tub, and complimentary cookies and soup in the afternoon. Prices vary widely depending on the day and month.

Bella Italia   ITALIAN $$
(☑360-457-5442; www.bellaitaliapa.com; 118 E 1st St; mains $14-24; ⊙4pm-late) Bella Italia has been around a lot longer than Bella, the heroine of the *Twilight* saga, but its mention in the book as the place where Bella and Edward Cullen go for their first date has turned what was already a popular restaurant into an icon. Try the clam linguine, chicken marsala or smoked duck breast, washed down with an outstanding wine from a list featuring 500 selections.

ℹ Information

Port Angeles Visitor Center (☑360-452-2363; www.portangeles.org; 121 E Railroad Ave; ⊙8am-5pm Mon-Sat, noon-3pm Sun) Adjacent to the ferry terminal. Open later in summer if volunteers are available.

ℹ Getting There & Away

Clallam Transit (☎ 360-452-4511; www.clallamtransit.com) Buses go to Forks and Sequim, where they link up with other transit buses that circumnavigate the Olympic Peninsula.

Coho Vehicle Ferry (☎ 888-993-3779; www.cohoferry.com) Runs to/from Victoria, BC (1½ hours).

Dungeness Line (www.olympicbuslines.com; 123 East Front St, Gateway Transit Center) Runs twice daily to Seattle.

Northwest Peninsula

Several Native American reservations cling to the extreme northwest corner of the continent, and are welcoming to visitors. The small weather-beaten settlement of **Neah Bay** on Hwy 112 is home to the Makah Indian Reservation, whose **Makah Museum** (☎ 360-645-2711; www.makahmuseum.com; 1880 Bayview Ave; admission $5; ⊙ 10am-5pm) displays artifacts from one of North America's most significant archaeological finds, the 500-year-old Makah village of Ozette. Several miles beyond the museum, a short boardwalk trail leads to stunning **Cape Flattery**, a 300ft promontory that marks the most northwesterly point in the lower 48 states.

Convenient to the Hoh River Rainforest and the Olympic coastline is **Forks**, a one-horse lumber town that's now more famous for its *Twilight* paraphernalia. It's a central town for exploring Olympic National Park; a good accommodation choice is the **Miller Tree Inn** (☎ 360-374-6806; www.millertreeinn.com; 654 E Division St; r $135-235; 🛜🐾).

Northwest Washington

Wedged between Seattle, the Cascades and Canada, northwest Washington draws influences from three sides. Its urban hub is collegiate Bellingham, while its outdoor highlight is the pastoral San Juan Islands, an extensive archipelago that glimmers like a sepia-toned snapshot from another era. Anacortes is the main hub for ferries to the San Juan Islands and Victoria, BC.

Whidbey Island

While not as detached (there's a bridge connecting it to adjacent Fidalgo Island at its

northernmost point) or nonconformist as the San Juans, life is almost as slow, quiet and pastoral on Whidbey Island. Having six state parks is a bonus, along with a plethora of B&Bs, two historic fishing villages (Langley and Coupeville), famously good clams and a thriving artist's community.

Deception Pass State Park (☎ 360-675-2417; 41229 N State Hwy 20) straddles the eponymous steep-sided water chasm that flows between Whidbey and Fidalgo Islands, and incorporates lakes, islands, campsites and 38 miles of hiking trails.

Ebey's Landing National Historical Reserve (☎ 360-678-6084; www.nps.gov/ebla; 162 Cemetery Rd) comprises 17,400 acres encompassing working farms, sheltered beaches, two state parks and the town of **Coupeville**. This small settlement is one of Washington's oldest towns and has an attractive seafront, antique stores and a number of old inns, including the **Coupeville Inn** (☎ 800-247-6162; www.thecoupevilleinn.com; 200 NW Coveland St; r $110-170, condos $175-300; ✳@📶🐾), which bills itself as a French-style motel (if that's not an oxymoron), with fancy furnishings and a substantial breakfast. For the famous fresh local clams, head to **Christopher's** (☎ 360-678-5480; www.christopherson-whidbey.com; 103 NW Coveland St; mains $18-23; ⊙ 11:30am-2pm & 5pm-close).

ℹ Getting There & Around

Washington State Ferries (www.wsdot.wa.gov/ferries) link Clinton to Mukilteo (20 minutes, every 30 minutes). They also ply the waters between Coupeville and Port Townsend (35 minutes, every 45 minutes). Free **Island Transit** (☎ 360-678-7771; www.islandtransit.org) buses run the length of Whidbey every hour daily, except Sundays, from the Clinton ferry dock.

Bellingham

Welcome to a green, liberal and famously livable settlement that has taken the libertine, nothing-is-too-weird ethos of Oregon's 'City of Roses' and given it a peculiarly Washingtonian twist. Mild in both manners and weather, the 'city of subdued excitement,' as a local mayor once dubbed it, is an unlikely alliance of espresso-sipping students, venerable retirees, all-weather triathletes and placard-waving peaceniks. Publications such as *Outside Magazine* have consistently lauded it for its abundant outdoor opportunities.

◉ Sights & Activities

Bellingham offers outdoor sights and activities by the truckload. **Whatcom Falls Park** is a natural wild region that bisects Bellingham's eastern suburbs. The change in elevation is marked by four sets of waterfalls, including **Whirlpool Falls**, a popular summer swimming hole.

Fairhaven Bike & Mountain Sports   CYCLING
(✪ 360-733-4433; www.fairhavenbike.com; 1103 11th St; rental per 4hr $25-37.50) Bellingham is one of the most bike-friendly cities in the Northwest, with a well-maintained intra-urban trail going as far south as Larrabee State Park. This outfit rents bikes and has maps on local routes.

San Juan Cruises   CRUISE
(✪ 360-738-8099; www.whales.com; 355 Harris Ave; cruises $35-99) Runs cruises around Bellingham Bay with beer- or wine-tasting, plus whale-watching around the San Juan Islands and more.

🛏 Sleeping & Eating

GuestHouse Inn   MOTEL $
(✪ 360-671-9600; www.guesthouseintl.com; 805 Lakeway Dr; r from $90; ❋@☎☎) This clean, comfortable and friendly motel is just off I-5 and about a 20-minute walk from downtown Bellingham. Rooms come with modern amenities such as flat-screen TV, fridge and microwave. Continental breakfast and hot-tub use included.

★ Hotel Bellwether   BOUTIQUE HOTEL $$$
(✪ 360-392-3100; www.hotelbellwether.com; 1 Bellwether Way; r from $250; ❋@☎☎) Bellingham's finest and most charismatic hotel lies on the waterfront and offers views of Lummi Island. Standard rooms come with Italian furnishings and Hungarian-down duvets, but the finest stay is the 900-sq-ft lighthouse suite (from $500), an old converted three-story lighthouse with a wonderful private lookout. Spa and restaurant on premises.

Old Town Cafe   CAFE $
(✪ 360-671-4431; www.theoldtowncafe.com; 316 W Holly St; mains $7-10; ⊙6:30am-3pm Mon-Sat, 8am-2pm Sun) Very popular for its casual, artsy atmosphere, this bohemian breakfast joint cooks up tasty dishes such as custom omelets, egg tortillas and whole wheat French toast. There's also homemade granola, gluten-free hot cakes, organic tofu scrambles, garden salads and 10 different kinds of sandwiches.

★ Pepper Sisters   MODERN AMERICAN $$
(✪ 360-671-3414; www.peppersisters.com; 1055 N State St; mains $10-18; ⊙4:30-9pm Tue-Sun; ❋) This cheerful, colorful restaurant serves innovative food that is hard to categorize – let's call it Mexican cuisine with a Northwestern twist. Try the grilled eggplant tostada, chipotle-and-pink-peppercorn enchilada or Southwest pizza; there's even a chicken-strip-free kids' menu.

❶ Information

Downtown Info Center (✪ 360-671-3990; www.bellingham.org; 1306 Commercial St; ⊙9am-5pm)

❶ Getting There & Away

Alaska Marine Highway (AMHS; ✪ 800-642-0066; www.dot.state.ak.us/amhs; 355 Harris Ave) ferries go to Juneau (60 hours) and other southeast Alaskan ports (from $326 without car). The Bellair Airporter Shuttle (www.airporter.com) runs to Sea-Tac Airport, with connections en route to Anacortes and Whidbey Island.

San Juan Islands

Take the ferry west out of Anacortes and you'll feel like you've dropped off the edge of the continent. A thousand metaphoric miles from the urban inquietude of Puget Sound, the nebulous San Juan archipelago conjures up Proustian flashbacks from another era and often feels about as American as – er – Canada (which surrounds it on two sides).

There are 172 landfalls in this expansive archipelago, but unless you're rich enough to charter your own yacht or seaplane, you'll be restricted to seeing the big four – San Juan, Orcas, Shaw and Lopez Islands – all served daily by Washington State Ferries. Communally, the islands are famous for their tranquillity, whale-watching opportunities, sea kayaking and seditious nonconformity.

A great way to explore the San Juans is by sea kayak or bicycle. Expect a guided half-day trip to cost from $45 to $65. Cycling-wise, Lopez is flat and pastoral and San Juan is worthy of an easy day loop, while Orcas offers the challenge of undulating terrain and a steep 5-mile ride to the top of Mt Constitution.

❶ Getting There & Around

Airlines serving the San Juan Islands include **San Juan Airlines** (✪ 800-874-4434; www.

sanjuanairlines.com) and **Kenmore Air** (☏ 866-435-9524; www.kenmoreair.com).

Washington State Ferries (www.wsdot.wa.gov/ferries) leave Anacortes for the San Juans; some continue to Sidney, BC, near Victoria. Ferries run to Lopez Island (45 minutes), Orcas Landing (60 minutes) and Friday Harbor on San Juan Island (75 minutes). Fares vary by season; the cost of the entire round-trip is collected on westbound journeys only (except those returning from Sidney, BC). To visit all the islands, it's cheapest to go to Friday Harbor first and work your way back through the other islands.

Shuttle buses ply Orcas and San Juan Island in the summer months.

San Juan Island

San Juan Island is the archipelago's unofficial capital, a harmonious mix of low forested hills and small rural farms that resonate with a dramatic and unusual 19th-century history. The only real settlement is Friday Harbor, home to the **visitor center** and **Chamber of Commerce** (www.sanjuanisland.org; 135 Spring St, Friday Harbor; ⊙10am-5pm) located inside a small mall off the main street.

⦿ Sights

San Juan Island
National Historical Park   HISTORIC SITE
(☏360-378-2240; www.nps.gov/sajh; ⊙visitor center 8:30am-5pm Jun-Aug, to 4:30pm Sep-May) ✐ **FREE** More known for their scenery than their history, the San Juans nonetheless hide one of the 19th century's oddest political confrontations, the so-called 'Pig War' between the USA and Britain. This curious stand-off is showcased in two separate historical parks on either end of the island that once housed opposing American and English military encampments.

Lime Kiln Point State Park   PARK
(☏360-902-8844;   www.parks.wa.gov/540/Lime-Kiln-Point; 1567 Westside Rd, Friday Harbor; ⊙8am-dusk) ✐ Clinging to the island's rocky west coast, this beautiful park overlooks the deep Haro Strait and is, reputedly, one of the best places in the world to view whales from the shoreline. Word is out, however, so the view areas are often packed with hopeful picnickers. There is a small **interpretive center** (☏360-378-2044; ⊙Jun-Aug) in the park, along with trails, a restored lime kiln and the landmark Lime Kiln Lighthouse, built in 1919.

🛏 Sleeping & Eating

There are hotels, B&Bs and resorts scattered around the island, but Friday Harbor has the highest concentration.

Wayfarer's Rest   HOSTEL $
(☏360-378-6428; www.hostelssanjuan.com; 35 Malcolm St, Friday Harbor; dm $40, r from $85; 🛜) A short walk from the ferry terminal, this pleasant hostel is located in a homey house with comfortable dorms and affordable private rooms. The main kitchen overlooks the grassy backyard, and there's also a suite that sleeps six ($245). Reserve two months ahead in summer.

Juniper Lane Guest House   INN $$
(☏360-378-7761;   www.juniperlaneguesthouse.com; 1312 Beaverton Valley Rd, Friday Harbor; r $85-135, cabins $219; 🛜) ✐ The five great rooms at this cozy, hip inn are decorated with an eclectic assortment of furnishings, much of it refurbished. In summer, there are hammocks in the backyard and views over the surrounding countryside. Communal kitchen and two-bedroom cabin available. It's 1.3 miles from the ferry dock.

Market Chef   DELI $
(☏360-378-4546; 225 A St, Friday Harbor; sandwiches $9; ⊙10am-4pm Mon-Fri) ✐ Super popular and famous for its delicious sandwiches, such as roast beef and rocket or (their signature) curried egg salad with roasted peanuts and chutney. Salads are also available; local ingredients used. If you're in town on a Saturday in summer, visit Market Chef at the San Juan Island Farmer's Market (10am to 1pm).

Backdoor Kitchen   FUSION $$$
(☏360-378-9540; www.backdoorkitchen.com; 400 A St, Friday Harbor; mains $30-37; ⊙11:30am-2:30pm Mon, 5-9pm Wed-Sun) One of San Juan Island's finest restaurants, Backdoor Kitchen uses fresh local ingredients to serve up creative multi-ethnic dishes such as Spanish-style pork with wild prawn stew and east Indian spiced lentils with spinach cake. Dine in the pretty garden in summer. Reserve ahead.

Orcas Island

Precipitous, unspoiled and ruggedly beautiful, Orcas Island is the San Juans' emerald icon, excellent for hiking and, more recently, gourmet food. The ferry terminal is at Orcas Landing, 8 miles south of the main village, Eastsound.

On the island's eastern lobe is **Moran State Park** (☏360-376-6173; 3572 Olga Rd; Discover Pass required at some parking lots, $10; ⊙6:30am-dusk Apr-Sep, 8am-dusk Oct-Mar), dominated by Mt Constitution (2409ft), with 40 miles of trails and an amazing 360-degree mountaintop view.

🛏 Sleeping

Doe Bay Village Resort & Retreat   HOSTEL $
(☏360-376-2291; www.doebay.com; campsites from $60, cabins from $100, yurts from $125; 🕾🐾) 🐾 By far the least expensive resort in the San Juans, Doe Bay has the atmosphere of an artists' commune combined with a hippie retreat. Accommodations include sea-view campsites and various cabins and yurts, some with views of the water.

Golden Tree Hostel   HOSTEL $$
(☏360-317-8693; www.goldentreehostel.com; 1159 North Beach Rd, Eastsound; dm/d with shared bath $45/115; @🕾) Located in an 1890s-era heritage house, this hip hostel offers cozy rooms and pleasant common spaces, along with a hot tub and sauna in the grassy garden. There's even a separate recreation building with pool, foosball, shuffleboard and darts. Friday pizza nights. Reserve in summer.

Outlook Inn   HOTEL $$
(☏360-376-2200; www.outlookinn.com; 171 Main St, Eastsound; r with shared/private bath from $79/99; @🕾🐾) Eastsound's oldest and most eye-catching building, the Outlook Inn (1888) is an island institution. Budget rooms are cozy and neat (try for room 30), while the luxurious suites have fireplaces, Jacuzzi tubs and stunning water views from their balconies. Excellent attached cafe.

🍴 Eating & Drinking

Kitchen   ASIAN $
(☏360-376-6958; www.thekitchenorcas.com; 249 Prune Alley, Eastsound; mains $10-15; ⊙11am-8pm Mon-Fri, to 4pm Sat) 🐾 By using mostly local, organic and sustainably produced ingredients, Kitchen serves up some of the island's freshest and tastiest 'fast' food. Choose from various wraps, all made with sprouted-wheat tortillas, or go for a noodle or fried rice bowl with creative sauces.

Mijita's   MEXICAN $$
(☏360-376-6722; 310 A St, Eastsound; mains $14-22; ⊙4-9pm Mon-Sat) It's difficult to go wrong in this creative, indoor-outdoor restaurant with its rustic Mexican furnishings

and fairy-lit garden. The Mexican native chef's family recipes include delicacies such as slow-braised short ribs with blackberry mole or vegetarian quinoa cakes with mushrooms, chèvre, almonds and *pipian* – but there are also the basics such as fish tacos and enchiladas. Reserve ahead.

Island Hoppin' Brewery   BREWERY
(www.islandhoppinbrewery.com; 33 Hope Lane, Eastsound; ⊙noon-9pm Tue-Sun) The location, just off Mt Baker Rd near the airport, makes this tiny brewery hard to find, but the locals sure know it's there – this is *the* place to go to enjoy seven changeable brews on tap. Don't come hungry – only snacks are served. Happy hour runs from 7pm to 9pm Sunday to Thursday, while a ping-pong table adds some action.

Lopez Island

If you're going to Lopez – or 'Slow-pez,' as locals prefer to call it – take a bike. With its undulating terrain and salutation-offering residents (who are famous for their three-fingered 'Lopezian wave'), this is the ideal cycling isle. A leisurely pastoral spin can be tackled in a day, with good overnight digs available next to the marina in the **Lopez Islander Resort** (☏360-468-2233; www.lopezfun.com; 2864 Fisherman Bay Rd; r from $119; 🕾🐾), which has a restaurant, gym and pool and offers free parking in Anacortes (another incentive to dump the car). If you arrive cycleless, call up **Village Cycles** (☏360-468-4013; www.villagecycles.net; 214 Lopez Rd; rental per hour $7-16), which can deliver a bicycle to the ferry terminal for you.

North Cascades

Geologically different from their southern counterparts, the North Cascade Mountains are peppered with sharp, jagged peaks, copious glaciers and a preponderance of complex metamorphic rock. Thanks to their virtual impregnability, the North Cascades were an unsolved mystery to humans until relatively recently. The first road was built across the region in 1972 and, even today, it remains one of the Northwest's most isolated outposts.

Mt Baker

Rising like a ghostly sentinel above the sparkling waters of upper Puget Sound, Mt Baker has been mesmerizing visitors to the

Northwest for centuries. A dormant volcano that last belched smoke in the 1850s, this haunting 10,781ft peak shelters 12 glaciers, and in 1999 registered a record-breaking 95ft of snow in one season.

Well-paved Hwy 542, known as the Mt Baker Scenic Byway, climbs 5100ft to **Artist Point**, 56 miles from Bellingham. Near here you'll find the **Heather Meadows Visitor Center** (Mt Baker Hwy, Mile 56; ⊘8am-4:30pm May-Sep) and a plethora of varied hikes, including the 7.5-mile **Chain Lakes Loop** that leads you around a half-dozen lakes surrounded by huckleberry meadows.

Receiving more annual snow than any ski area in North America, the **Mt Baker Ski Area** (⊉360-734-6771; www.mtbakerskiarea. com) has 38 runs, eight lifts and a vertical rise of 1500ft. The resort has gained something of a cult status among snowboarders, who have been coming here for the Legendary Baker Banked Slalom every January since 1985.

On your way up the mountain, stop for a bite at authentic honky-tonk bar and restaurant **Graham's** (⊉360-599-9883; 9989 Mt Baker Hwy; mains $6-14; ⊘noon-9pm Mon-Fri, 8-11am & noon-9pm Sat & Sun) and grab trail munchies at **Wake & Bakery** (⊉360-599-1658; www. getsconed.com; 6903 Bourne St, Glacier; snacks from $4; ⊘7:30am-5pm), both in the town of **Glacier**.

Leavenworth

Blink hard and rub your eyes. This isn't some strange Germanic hallucination. This is Leavenworth, a former lumber town that underwent a Bavarian makeover back in the 1960s after the rerouting of the cross-continental railway threatened to put it permanently out of business. Swapping wood for tourists, Leavenworth today has successfully reinvented itself as a traditional Romantische Strasse village, right down to the beer, sausages and lederhosen-loving locals (25% of whom are German). The classic *Sound of Music* mountain setting helps, as does the fact that Leavenworth serves as the main activity center for sorties into the nearby Alpine Lakes Wilderness.

The **Leavenworth Ranger Station** (⊉509-548-2550; 600 Sherbourne St; ⊘8am-4:30pm Mon-Sat) can advise on the local outdoor activities. Highlights include the best climbing in the state at **Castle Rock** in Tumwater Canyon, about 3 miles northwest of town off US 2.

The **Devil's Gulch** is a popu' mountain bike trail (25 miles hours). Local outfitters **Der** (⊉509-548-5623; www.dersportsn. Front St; ⊘9am-6pm) rents mountain bik

🛏 Sleeping & Eating

Hotel Pension Anna　　　　　HOTEL **$$**
(⊉509-548-6273; www.pensionanna.com; 926 Commercial St; r from $155) The most authentic Bavarian hotel in town is also spotless and incredibly friendly. Each room is decorated in imported Austrian decor, and the European-inspired breakfasts (included) may induce joyful yodels. Our favorite room is the double with hand-painted furniture, but the spacious suite in the adjacent St Joseph's chapel is perfect for families.

Enzian Inn　　　　　　　　HOTEL **$$**
(⊉509-548-5269; www.enzianinn.com; 590 Hwy 2; d from $125; 🐾🖳) At this Leavenworth classic, long-term owner Bob Johnson starts the day with a blast on his famous alpenhorn before breakfast. If this doesn't send you running for your lederhosen, cast an eye over the free putting green (with resident grass-trimming goats), the indoor and outdoor swimming pools, or the nightly pianist pounding out requests in the Bavarian lobby.

München Haus　　　　　　　GERMAN **$**
(⊉509-548-1158; www.munchenhaus.com; 709 Front St; snacks from $6; ⊘11am-9pm Mon-Wed, to 10pm Thu & Sun, to 11pm Fri & Sat; ⊋) The Haus is 100% alfresco, meaning that the hot German sausages and pretzels are essential stomach-warmers in winter, while the Bavarian brews will cool you down in summer. The casual beer-garden atmosphere is complemented by vibrant flower baskets, laid-back staff and a stash of top-quality relishes, including cider kraut and mustard. Hours vary outside summer.

Lake Chelan

Long, slender Lake Chelan is central Washington's water playground. The town of **Chelan**, at the lake's southeastern tip, is the primary base for accommodations and services, and has a **USFS ranger station** (⊉509-682-4900; 428 W Woodin Ave).

Lake Chelan State Park (⊉509-687-3710; 7544 S Lakeshore Rd; primitive/standard tent sites from $12/25) has 144 campsites; a number of lakeshore campgrounds are accessible only by boat. If you'd rather sleep in a real bed, try he great-value **Midtowner Motel** (📞800-572-0943; www.midtowner.com; 721 E Woodin Ave; r $92-129; 🅿️@🛜🏊) in town.

Several wineries have also opened in the area and many have excellent restaurants. Try **Tsillan Cellars** (📞509-682-9463; www.tsillancellars.com; 3875 Hwy 97A; ⊗noon-5pm).

Link Transit (📞509-662-1155; www.linktransit.com) buses connect Chelan with Wenatchee and Leavenworth ($1).

Beautiful **Stehekin**, on the northern tip of Lake Chelan, is accessible only by **boat** (📞509-682-4584; www.ladyofthelake.com), **seaplane** (📞509-682-5555; www.chelanairways.com) or a long hike across Cascade Pass, 28 miles from the lake. You'll find lots of information about hiking, campgrounds and cabin rentals at www.stehekin.com. Most facilities are open from mid-June to mid-September.

Methow Valley

The Methow's combination of powdery winter snow and abundant summer sunshine has transformed this valley into one of Washington's primary recreation areas. You can bike, hike and fish in summer, and cross-country ski on the second-biggest snow trail network in the US in winter.

The 200km of trails are maintained by the nonprofit **Methow Valley Sport Trails Association** (MVSTA; 📞509-996-3287; www.mvsta.com; 309 Riverside Ave, Winthrop) 🚲, which in winter provides the most comprehensive network of hut-to-hut (and hotel-to-hotel) skiing in North America. An extra blessing is that few people seem to know about it. For classic accommodations and easy access to the skiing, hiking and cycling trails, decamp at the exquisite **Sun Mountain Lodge** (📞509-996-2211; www.sunmountainlodge.com; 604 Patterson Lake Rd, Winthrop; r from $300, cabins from $405; ⊗Dec-late Oct; 🅿️🛜🏊), 10 miles west of the town of Winthrop. While the rooms and facilities are cosy cabin-style (including a lot of taxidermy), it's the views from up here, and the endless choice of hiking and cross-country skiing trails surrounding the resort, that make it so special.

North Cascades National Park

Even the names of the lightly trodden dramatic mountains in **North Cascades National Park** (www.nps.gov/noca) sound wild and untamed: Desolation Peak, Jagged Ridge, Mt Despair and Mt Terror. Not sur-prisingly, the region offers some of the best backcountry adventures outside of Alaska.

The **North Cascades Visitor Center** (📞206-386-4495, ext 11; 502 Newhalem St, Newhalem; ⊗9am-6pm Jun-Sep, reduced hours Oct-May) 🚲, in the small settlement of Newhalem on Hwy 20, is the best orientation point for visitors and is staffed by expert rangers who can enlighten you on the park's highlights.

Built in the 1930s for loggers working in the valley which was soon to be flooded by Ross Dam, the floating cabins at the **Ross Lake Resort** (📞206-386-4437; www.rosslakeresort.com; 503 Diablo St, Rockport; cabins $175-350; ⊗mid-Jun–late Oct) on the eponymous lake's west side are the state's most unique accommodations. There's no road in – guests can either hike the 2-mile trail from Hwy 20 or take the resort's tugboat-taxi-and-truck shuttle from the parking area near Diablo Dam.

Northeastern Washington

Spokane

Washington's second-biggest population center is one of the state's latent surprises and a welcome break after the treeless monotony of the eastern scablands. Situated at the nexus of the Pacific Northwest's so-called 'Inland Empire,' this understated yet confident city sits on the banks of the Spokane River, close to where British fur traders founded a short-lived trading post in 1810. Though rarely touted in national tourist blurbs, Spokane hosts one of the world's largest mass-participation running events (May's annual Bloomsday).

⊙ Sights

Riverfront Park PARK
(www.spokaneriverfrontpark.com; 🅿️) The former site of the 1974 World's Fair and Exposition, this park's highlights include a 17-point **sculpture walk** and **Spokane Falls**, a gushing combination of scenic waterfalls and foaming rapids. A short **gondola ride** (adult/child under 12yr $7.50/5; ⊗10am-8pm Sun-Thu, to 9pm Fri & Sat Jul & Aug, reduced hours Sep-Jun) takes you directly above the falls, as does the cheaper and equally spectacular **Monroe St Bridge**, built in 1911 and one of the largest concrete arches in the USA.

Northwest Museum of Arts & Culture

MUSEUM

(MAC; ☎509-456-3931; www.northwestmuseum.org; 2316 W 1st Ave; adult/child $10/5; ⊙10am-5pm Wed-Sun) In a striking state-of-the-art building in the historic Browne's Addition neighborhood, this museum has – arguably – one of the finest collections of indigenous artifacts in the Northwest. Leading off a plush glass foyer overlooking the Spokane River are four galleries showcasing Spokane's history, as well as a number of rotating exhibitions that change every three to four months. Your ticket also earns you the right to visit the adjacent English Tudor–revival **Campbell House**.

🛏 Sleeping & Eating

Hotel Ruby

MOTEL $

(☎509-747-1041; www.hotelrubyspokane.com; 901 W 1st Ave; r from $90; ❇🐾🛜❇) This basic motel, retrofitted in hip, artistic decor, retains its '70s feel. Diagonally opposite the Davenport Hotel, it's walking distance to dining and drinking establishments.

★ Davenport Hotel

HISTORIC HOTEL $$

(☎509-455-8888; www.thedavenporthotel.com; 10 S Post St; r from $220; ❇🛜❇) This historical landmark (opened in 1914) is considered one of the best hotels in the country. Even if you're not staying here, linger in the gorgeous lobby or have a drink in the Peacock Lounge. The adjacent modern Davenport Tower sports a safari-themed lobby and bar.

Mizuna

FUSION $$$

(☎509-747-2004; www.mizuna.com; 214 N Howard St; mains lunch $12-14, dinner $27-32; ⊙11am-10pm Mon-Sat, 4-10pm Sun; 🍴) This fine restaurant is located in an antique brick building with simple furnishings, and is well-known for its specialties such as seed-crushed quinoa croquettes and pan-seared pork tenderloin. Wash dinner down with an exquisite wine for a memorable experience.

🍷 Drinking & Entertainment

With a vibrant student population based at Gonzaga University, Spokane has a happening nighttime scene.

NoLi Brewhouse

BREWERY

(☎509-242-2739; www.nolibrewhouse.com; 1003 E Trent Ave; ⊙11am-9pm Sun & Mon, to 10pm Tue-Sat) A student hangout situated near Gonzaga University, Spokane's best microbrewery serves some weird and wonderful flavors, including a tart cherry ale and an imperial stout with coffee, chocolate and brown-sugar tones. Food-wise, check out the cod and chips cooked in batter made with the brewery's own pale ale.

Mootsy's

BAR

(☎509-838-1570; 406 W Sprague Ave) This popular bar is the hub for the nightlife and alternative-music scene that hops all along this block between Stevens and Washington Sts. Its cheap Pabst Blue Ribbon (PBR) during happy hour keeps its customer base loyal.

Bing Crosby Theater

THEATER

(☎509-227-7638; www.bingcrosbytheater.com; 901 W Sprague Ave) Yes, Bing Crosby hailed from Spokane, and now the 'Bing' presents concerts, plays and festivals in a fairly intimate setting.

WORTH A TRIP

GRAND COULEE DAM

While the more famous Hoover Dam (conveniently located between Las Vegas and the Grand Canyon) gets over a million visitors per year, the much larger (four times) and arguably more significant **Grand Coulee Dam** (inconveniently located far from everything) gets only a trickle of tourism. It's the largest concrete structure in the US and also the largest producer of electricity in the US.

The **Grand Coulee Visitor Arrival Center** (☎509-633-9265; www.usbr.gov/pn/grandcoulee/visit; ⊙8:30am-10:30pm Jun-Aug, to 9:30pm Sep, 9am-5pm Oct-May) details the history of the dam and surrounding area with movies, photos and interactive exhibits, while free guided tours of the facility run on the hour from 10am to 5pm (from May to September); there are fewer tours outside summer.

Similarly spectacular is the nightly **laser show** (www.usbr.gov/pn/grandcoulee/visit; ⊙10pm Jun & Jul, 9:30pm Aug, 8:30pm Sep) – purportedly the world's largest – which illustrates the history of the Columbia River and its various dams against a gloriously vivid backdrop.

ℹ Information

Spokane Area Visitor Information Center
(☑ 888-776-5263; www.visitspokane.com; 808 W Main Ave; ⊘ 8am-5pm Mon-Sat, 11am-6pm Sun)

ℹ Getting There & Away

Spokane Intermodal Transportation Station
(221 W 1st Ave) Buses and trains depart from this station.

South Cascades

The South Cascades are taller but less clustered than their northern counterparts, extending from Snoqualmie Pass east of Seattle down to the mighty Columbia River on the border with Oregon. The highpoint in more ways than one is 14,411ft Mt Rainier. Equally compelling for different reasons is Mt St Helens (8363ft), still recovering from a devastating 1980 volcanic eruption. Lesser-known Mt Adams (12,276ft) is notable for the huckleberries and wildflowers that fill its grassy alpine meadows during the short but intense summer season.

Mt Rainier National Park

The USA's fourth-highest peak (outside Alaska), majestic Mt Rainier is also one of its most beguiling. Encased in a 368-sq-mile national park (the world's fifth national park when it was inaugurated in 1899), the mountain's snowcapped summit and forest-covered foothills boast numerous hiking trails, huge swaths of flower-carpeted meadows, and an alluring conical peak that presents a formidable challenge for aspiring climbers.

Mt Rainier National Park (www.nps.gov/mora; entry per car $25) has four entrances. Call ☑ 800-695-7623 for road conditions. The National Park Service (NPS) website includes downloadable maps and descriptions of dozens of park trails. The most famous trail is the hardcore, 93-mile-long Wonderland Trail that completely circumnavigates Mt Rainier and takes around 10 to 12 days to tackle.

Campgrounds in the park have running water and toilets, but no showers or RV hookups. Reservations at **park campsites** (☑ 800-365-2267; www.nps.gov/mora; campsites $20) are strongly advised during summer months and can be made up to two months in advance by phone or online. For overnight backcountry trips, you'll need a wilderness permit; check the NPS website for details.

NISQUALLY ENTRANCE

The busiest and most convenient gate to Mt Rainier National Park, Nisqually lies on Hwy 706 via Ashford, near the park's southwest corner. It's open year-round. **Longmire**, 7 miles inside the Nisqually entrance, has a **museum and information center** (☑ 360-569-6575; ⊘ 9am-4:30pm), a number of important trailheads, and the rustic **National Park Inn** (☑ 360-569-2275; www.mtrainierguestservices. com; r with shared/private bath from $119/169, units $252; P ❋), complete with an excellent restaurant. More hikes and interpretive walks can be found 12 miles further east at loftier **Paradise**, which is served by the informative **Henry M Jackson Visitor Center** (☑ 360-569-6571; Paradise; ⊘ 10am-7pm daily Jun-Sep, 10am-5pm Sat & Sun Oct-May), and the vintage **Paradise Inn** (☑ 360-569-2275; www.mtrainier-guestservices.com; r with shared/private bath from $117/174; ⊘ May-Oct), a historical 'parkitecture' inn constructed in 1916 and long part of the national park's fabric. Climbs to the top of Rainier leave from the inn; excellent four-day guided ascents are led by **Rainier Mountaineering Inc** (☑ 888-892-5462; www.rmiguides. com; 30027 SR 706 E, Ashford).

OTHER ENTRANCES

The three other entrances to Mt Rainier National Park are **Ohanapecosh**, via Hwy 123 and accessed via the town of **Packwood**, where lodging is available; **White River**, off Hwy 410, which literally takes the high road (6400ft) to the beautiful viewpoint at the **Sunrise Lodge Cafeteria** (snacks $6-9; ⊘ 10am-7pm Jul & Aug); and remote **Carbon River** in the northwest corner, which gives access to the park's inland rainforest.

Mt St Helens National Volcanic Monument

What it lacks in height, Mt St Helens makes up for in fiery infamy – 57 people perished on the mountain when it erupted with a force of 1500 atomic bombs on May 18, 1980. The cataclysm began with an earthquake measuring 5.1 on the Richter scale, which sparked the biggest landslide in human history and buried 230 sq miles of forest under millions of tons of volcanic rock and ash. Today it's a fascinating landscape of recovering forests, new river valleys and ash-covered slopes. There's an $8 per person fee to use the services at Coldwater Lake Recreation Area and Johnston Ridge Observatory.

NORTHEASTERN ENTRANCE

From the main northeast entrance on Hwy 504, your first stop should be the **Silver Lake Visitor Center** (www.parks.wa.gov/245/ Mount-St-Helens; 3029 Spirit Lake Hwy; adult/child $5/2.50; ☺9am-5pm mid-May–mid-Sep, reduced hours mid-Sep–mid-May; 🖭) 🖋, which has films, exhibits and free information about the mountain (including trail maps). For a closer view of the destructive power of nature, venture to the **Johnston Ridge Observatory** (🗷360-274-2140; 24000 Spirit Lake Hwy; admission $8; ☺10am-6pm mid-May–Oct), situated at the end of Hwy 504, which looks directly into the mouth of the crater.

A welcome stop in an accommodations-light area, the **Eco Park Resort** (🗷360-274-7007; www.ecoparkresort.com; 14000 Spirit Lake Hwy, Toutle; campsites $22, yurts $75-150, cabins $125-130) offers seven rooms in a large house opposite the Silver Lake Visitor Center.

SOUTHEASTERN & EASTSIDE ENTRANCES

The southeastern entrance via the town of **Cougar** on Hwy 503 holds some serious lava terrain, including the 2-mile-long **Ape Cave** lava tube, which you can explore year-round; be prepared for the chill as it remains a constant 41°F (5°C). Bring two light sources per adult or rent lanterns at **Apes' Headquarters** (🗷360-449-7800; ☺10am-5pm Jun-Sep) for $5 each.

The eastside entrance is the most remote, but the harder-to-reach **Windy Ridge** viewpoint on this side gives you a palpable, if eerie, sense of the destruction from the blast. It's often closed until June. A few miles down the road you can descend 600ft on the 1-mile-long **Harmony Trail** (hike 224) to Spirit Lake.

Central & Southeastern Washington

The sunny, dry near-California-looking central and southeastern parts of Washington harbor one not-so-secret weapon: wine. The fertile land that borders the Nile-like Yakima and Columbia River Valleys is awash with enterprising new wineries producing quality grapes that now vie with the Napa and Sonoma Valleys for national recognition. Yakima and its more attractive cousin Ellensburg

once held the edge, but nowadays the real star is Walla Walla, where talented restaurateurs and a proactive local council are crafting a wine destination par excellence.

Yakima & Ellensburg

Situated in its eponymous river valley, the city of Yakima is a rather bleak trading center that doesn't really live up to its 'Palm Springs of Washington' tourist label. The main reason to stop here is to visit one of the numerous wineries that lie between Yakima and Benton City; pick up a map at the **Yakima Valley Visitors & Convention Bureau** (🗷800-221-0751; www.visityakima.com; 101 N Fair Ave; ☺9am-5pm Mon-Sat, 10am-4pm Sun Jun-Aug, reduced hours Sep-May).

A better layover is Ellensburg, a diminutive settlement 36 miles to the northwest that juxtaposes the state's largest rodeo (each Labor Day) with a town center that has more coffee bars per head than anywhere else in the world (allegedly). Grab your latte at local roaster **D&M Coffee** (🗷509-962-9333; www. dmcoffee.com; 301 N Pine St; ☺7am-5pm) 🖋 and overnight at centrally located and charming Victorian **Guesthouse Ellensburg** (🗷509-962-3706; www.guesthouseellensburg.com; 606 Main St; r from $145), which also runs the excellent **Yellow Church Cafe** (🗷509-933-2233; www.theyellowchurchcafe.com; 111 S Pearl St; mains brunch $9-13, dinner $13-20; ☺11am-9pm Tue-Thu, 8am-9pm Fri-Mon).

Greyhound services both cities, with buses to Seattle, Spokane and points in between.

Walla Walla

Over the last decade, Walla Walla has converted itself from an obscure agricultural backwater, famous for its sweet onions and large state penitentiary, into the hottest wine-growing region outside of California. While venerable Marcus Whitman College is the town's most obvious cultural attribute, you'll also find zany coffee bars, cool wine-tasting rooms, fine Queen Anne architecture, and one of the state's freshest and most vibrant farmers markets.

◉ Sights & Activities

You don't need to be sloshed on wine to appreciate Walla Walla's historical and cultural heritage. Its Main St has won countless historical awards, and to bring the settlement to life, the local **chamber of commerce** (🗷509-525-0850; www.wallawalla.org; 29 E Sumach St;

DON'T MISS

YAKIMA VALLEY WINE TOUR

If you find yourself driving between Ellensburg and Walla Walla, why not go wine-tasting? The Yakima Valley AVA (American Viticultural Area) is the oldest, largest and most diverse in the state. You'll find www.wineyakimavalley.org is a good resource for finding wineries.

Bonair Winery (☑509-829-6027; www.bonairwine.com; 500 S Bonair Rd, Zillah; ⊙10am-5pm) In the Rattlesnake Hills near Zillah, this winery has lovely gardens and is a laid-back place to sample luscious reds.

Terra Blanca (☑509-588-6082; www.terrablanca.com; 34715 N DeMoss Rd, Benton City; ⊙10am-6pm Apr-Oct, 11am-6pm Nov-Mar) Majestically located up on Red Mountain with views over the valley, this is one of the fanciest vineyards in the region, and perfect for sipping sweet dessert wines on the patio. There is a restaurant on-site.

Maison Bleue (☑509-525-9084; www.mbwinery.com; 20 N 2nd Ave, Walla Walla; ⊙11am-5pm Thu-Sun Apr-Dec) Family-owned winery producing lauded Rhône-style wines.

⊙8:30am-5pm Mon-Fri) has concocted some interesting walking tours, complete with leaflets and maps.

Fort Walla Walla Museum　　　MUSEUM
(☑509-525-7703; www.fwwm.org; 755 Myra Rd; adult/child 6-12yr $8/3; ⊙10am-5pm Mar-Oct, to 4pm Nov-Feb; ⊕) This is a pioneer village of 17 historical buildings, with the museum housed in the old cavalry stables. There are collections of farm implements, ranching tools and what could be the world's largest plastic replica of a mule team.

Waterbrook Wine　　　WINERY
(☑509-522-1262; www.waterbrook.com; 10518 W US 12; ⊙11am-6pm Sun-Thu, to 7pm Fri & Sat) About 10 miles west of town, the pond-side patio of this large winery is a great place to imbibe a long selection of wines on a sunny day. Food served Thursday to Sunday; hours vary outside summer.

Amavi Cellars　　　WINERY
(☑509-525-3541; www.amavicellars.com; 3796 Peppers Bridge Rd; ⊙10am-4pm) South of Walla Walla, amid a scenic spread of grape and apple orchards, you can sample some of the most talked-about wines in the valley (try the Syrah and Cabernet Sauvignon). The classy yet comfortable outdoor patio has views of the Blue Mountains.

🛏 Sleeping & Eating

Colonial Motel　　　MOTEL $
(☑509-529-1220; www.colonial-motel.com; 2279 Isaacs Ave; r $68-129; ❄️🐾) A simple family-run motel halfway to the airport, the Colonial is welcoming and bike-friendly with safe bike storage and plenty of local maps.

Marcus Whitman Hotel　　　HOTEL $$
(☑509-525-2200; www.marcuswhitmanhotel.com; 6 W Rose St; r from $144; ❄️🐾🐾) Walla Walla's best-known landmark is also the town's only tall building, impossible to miss with its distinctive rooftop turret. In keeping with the settlement's well-preserved image, the red-brick 1928 beauty has been elegantly renovated and decorated, with ample rooms in rusts and browns, embellished with Italian-crafted furniture, huge beds and great views over the nearby Blue Mountains.

Graze　　　CAFE $
(☑509-522-9991; 5 S Colville St; sandwiches from $8; ⊙10am-7:30pm Mon-Sat, to 3:30pm Sun; 🐾) Amazing sandwiches are packed for your picnic, or (if you can get a table) eaten in at this simple cafe. Try the turkey pear panini with provolone and blue cheese, or the flank-steak torta with pickled jalapeños, avocado, tomato, cilantro and chipotle dressing. Plenty of vegetarian and non-vegetarian options.

Saffron Mediterranean Kitchen　　　MEDITERRANEAN $$$
(☑509-525-2112; www.saffronmediterraneankitchen.com; 125 W Alder St; mains $17-30; ⊙2-10pm Tue-Sat, to 9pm Sun May-Oct, 2-9pm Tue-Sun Nov-Apr) This place isn't about cooking, it's about alchemy: Saffron takes seasonal, local ingredients and turns them into pure gold. The Med-inspired menu lists dishes such as bison rib eye, nettle pappardelle with duck ragù, and wild Burgundy snail flatbread. Then there are the intelligently paired wines – and beers. Reserve ahead.

❶ Getting There & Away

Greyhound buses run once daily to Seattle via Yakima and Ellensburg; change buses in Pasco for buses east to Spokane and beyond.

Walla Walla Regional Airport (www.wallawallaairport.com) Alaska Airlines services Walla Walla Regional Airport with several daily flights to Seattle.

OREGON

It's hard to slap a single characterization onto Oregon's geography and people. Its landscape ranges from rugged coastline and thick evergreen forests to barren, fossil-strewn deserts, volcanoes and glaciers. As for its denizens, you name it – Oregonians run the gamut from pro-logging conservatives to tree-hugging liberals to beer-making, sideburn-wearing hipsters. What they all have in common is an independent spirit, a love of the outdoors and a fierce devotion to where they live.

Portland

Call it what you want – PDX, Stumptown, City of Roses, Bridge City, Beervana or Portlandia – Portland positively rocks. It's a city with a vibrant downtown, pretty residential neighborhoods, ultragreen ambitions and zany characters. Here, liberal idealists outnumber conservative stogies, Gortex jackets are acceptable in fine restaurants and everyone supports countless brewpubs, coffeehouses, knitting circles, lesbian potlucks and eclectic book clubs. Portland is an up-and-coming destination that has finally arrived, and makes for an appealing, can't-miss stop on your adventures in the Pacific Northwest.

◉ Sights

◎ Downtown

★**Tom McCall Waterfront Park**   PARK
This popular riverside park, which lines the west bank of the Willamette River, was finished in 1978 after four years of construction. It replaced an old freeway with 1.5 miles of paved sidewalks and grassy spaces, and attracts heaps of joggers, in-line skaters, strollers and cyclists. During summer the park is perfect for hosting large outdoor events such as the Oregon Brewers Festival. Walk over the Steel and Hawthorne bridges to the **Eastbank Esplanade**, making a 2.6-mile loop.

★**Pioneer Courthouse Square**   LANDMARK
(www.thesquarepdx.org) The heart of downtown Portland, this brick plaza is nicknamed 'Portland's living room' and is the most-visited public space in the city. When it isn't full of Hacky Sack players, sunbathers or office workers lunching, the square hosts concerts, festivals, rallies, farmers markets, and even summer Friday-night movies (aka 'Flicks on the Bricks').

Portland Building   LANDMARK
(cnr SW 5th Ave & SW Main St) This controversial 15-story building (1982) was designed by Michael Graves and catapulted the postmodern architect to celebrity status. The people working inside the blocky, pastel-colored edifice, however, have had to deal with tiny windows, cramped spaces and general user-unfriendliness. The building suffered from major design flaws that later proved very costly to fix – not a great start for what was considered to be the world's first major postmodern structure. At least it's been made somewhat green: an ecofriendly roof was installed in 2006.

Oregon Historical Society   MUSEUM
(🖉503-222-1741; www.ohs.org; 1200 SW Park Ave; adult/child $11/5; ⊙10am-5pm Mon-Sat, noon-5pm Sun) Along the tree-shaded South Park Blocks sits the state's primary history museum, which dedicates most of its space to the story of Oregon and the pioneers who made it. There are interesting sections on Native American tribes and the travails of the Oregon Trail. Temporary exhibitions furnish the downstairs space. Check their website for free admission days.

Portland Art Museum   MUSEUM
(🖉503-226-2811; www.portlandartmuseum.org; 1219 SW Park Ave; adult/child $15/free; ⊙10am-5pm Tue, Wed, Sat & Sun, to 8pm Thu & Fri) Just across the South Park Blocks, the art museum's excellent exhibits include Native American carvings, Asian and American art, and English silver. The museum also houses the Whitsell Auditorium, a first-rate theater that frequently screens rare or international films.

Aerial Tram   CABLE CAR
(www.gobytram.com; 3303 SW Bond Ave; round trip $4.50; ⊙5:30am-9:30pm Mon-Fri, 9am-5pm Sat, 1-5pm Sun Oct–mid-May, 1-5pm Sun mid-May–Sep) Portland's aerial tram runs from the

OREGON FACTS

Nickname Beaver State

Population 4 million

Area 98,466 sq miles

Capital city Salem (population 160,000)

Other cities Portland (population 610,000), Eugene (population 160,000), Bend (population 82,000)

Sales tax Oregon has no sales tax

Birthplace of Former US president Herbert Hoover (1874–1964), actor and dancer Ginger Rogers (1911–95), writer and merry prankster Ken Kesey (1935–2001), filmmaker Gus Van Sant (b 1952), *The Simpsons* creator Matt Groening (b 1954)

Home of Oregon Shakespeare Festival, Nike, Crater Lake

Politics Democrat governors since 1987

Famous for Forests, rain, microbrews, coffee, Death with Dignity Act

State beverage Milk (dairy's big here)

Driving You can't pump your own gas in Oregon; Portland to Eugene, 110 miles; Portland to Astoria, 96 miles

south Waterfront (there's a streetcar stop) to Marquam Hill. The tram runs along a 3300ft line up a vertical ascent of 500ft and the ride takes four minutes. The tram opened in 2007, far exceeding its budget predictions and causing much public controversy.

Old Town & Chinatown

The core of rambunctious 1890s Portland, the once-notorious Old Town used to be the lurking grounds of unsavory characters, but today disco queens outnumber drug dealers. It's one of the livelier places in town after dark, when nightclubs and bars open their doors and hipsters start showing up.

Saturday Market MARKET
(☑503-222-6072; www.portlandsaturdaymarket. com; 2 SW Naito Pkwy; ☺10am-5pm Sat, 11am-4:30pm Sun Mar-Dec) The best time to hit the river walk is on a weekend to catch this famous market, which showcases handicrafts, street entertainers and food booths.

Lan Su Chinese Garden GARDENS
(☑503-228-8131; www.lansugarden.org; 239 NW Everett St; adult/child $9.50/7; ☺10am-6pm mid-Apr–mid-Oct, to 5pm mid-Oct–mid-Apr) This classical Chinese garden is a one-block haven of tranquillity, reflecting ponds and manicured greenery. Guided tours are available.

Shanghai Tunnels HISTORIC SITE
(☑503-622-4798; www.shanghaitunnels.info; 120 NW 3rd Ave; adult/child under 12yr $13/8) Downtown Portland's basements were once connected by tunnels running beneath the streets and down to riverside docks. While built for shipping and flood control, rumors persist they were also used to transport unconscious men to be sold to unscrupulous ship's captains. Though long sealed, remnants can be visited on tour; book at www. portlandwalkingtours.com.

Chinatown Gates GATE
(cnr W Burnside St & NW 4th Ave) Don't expect flashbacks of Shanghai in Portland's lackluster Chinese quarter, which begins (and largely ends) at the deceptively impressive pagoda-style Chinatown Gates.

The Pearl District & Northwest

Pearl District NEIGHBORHOOD
(www.explorethepearl.com) Slightly to the northwest of downtown, the Pearl District is an old industrial quarter that has transformed its once grotty warehouses into expensive lofts, upscale boutiques and creative restaurants. On the first Thursday of every month, the zone's abundant art galleries extend their evening hours and the area turns into a fancy street party of sorts. The **Jamison Square Fountain** (810 NW 11th Ave) is one of its prettier urban spaces.

Northwest 23rd Avenue NEIGHBORHOOD
Nob Hill – or 'Snob Hill' to its detractors – has its hub on NW 23rd Ave, a trendy thoroughfare that brims with clothing boutiques, home-decor shops and cafes. The restaurants – including some of Portland's finest – lie mostly along NW 21st Ave. This is a perfect neighborhood for strolling, window-shopping and looking at houses that most of us will never be able to afford.

West Hills

Behind downtown Portland is the West Hills area, known for its exclusive homes, huge parks and – if you're lucky – peek-a-boo views of up to five Cascade volcanoes.

Forest Park   PARK
(☑503-223-5449; www.forestparkconservancy.org) Abutting the more manicured Washington Park to the south (to which it is linked by various trails) is the far wilder 5100-acre Forest Park, a temperate rainforest that harbors plants, animals and an avid hiking fraternity. The **Portland Audubon Society** (☑503-292-6855; www.audubonportland.org; 5151 NW Cornell Rd; ⊙9am-5pm, nature store 10am-6pm Mon-Sat, to 5pm Sun) maintains a bookstore, wildlife rehabilitation center and 4.5 miles of trails within its Forest Park sanctuary.

Washington Park   PARK
(www.washingtonparkpdx.org) Tame and well-tended Washington Park contains several key attractions within its 400 acres of greenery. The **International Rose Test Garden** (www.rosegardenstore.org; 400 SW Kingston Ave; ⊙7:30am-9pm) FREE is the centerpiece of Portland's famous rose blooms; there are 400 types on show here, plus great city views. Further uphill is the **Japanese Garden** (☑503-223-1321; www.japanesegarden.com; 611 SW Kingston Ave; adult/child $9.50/6.75; ⊙noon-7pm Mon, 10am-7pm Tue-Sun mid-Mar–Sep, noon-4pm Mon, 10am-4pm Tue-Sun Oct–mid-Mar), another oasis of tranquillity. If you have kids, the Oregon Zoo and Portland Children's Museum should be on your docket.

Northeast & Southeast

Across the Willamette River from downtown is the **Lloyd Center** (www.lloydcenter.com; 2201 Lloyd Center), Oregon's largest shopping mall and where notorious ice-queen Tonya Harding first learned to skate in the rink here. A few blocks to the southwest are the unmissable glass towers of the **Oregon Convention Center** (www.oregoncc.org; 777 NE Martin Luther King Jr Blvd), and nearby is the **Moda Center** (☑503-235-8771; www.center-or.com; 1 N Center Court St) (previously called the Rose Quarter), home of professional basketball team the Trailblazers.

Further up the Willamette, **N Mississippi Ave** used to be full of run-down buildings, but is now a hot spot of trendy shops and eateries. Northeast is artsy **NE Alberta St**, a long ribbon of art galleries, boutiques and cafes (don't miss the Last Thursday street-art event here, taking place the last Thursday of each month). **SE Hawthorne Blvd** (near SE 39th Ave) is affluent hippy territory, with gift stores, cafes, coffeeshops and two branches of Powell's bookstores. One leafy mile to the south, **SE Division St** has become a foodie destination, with plenty of excellent restaurants, bars and pubs. The same is true of **E Burnside at NE 28th Ave**, though it has a more concentrated and upscale feel.

🏃 Activities

Hiking

The best hiking is found in Forest Park (p207), which harbors an unbelievable 80 miles of trails and often feels more like Mt Hood's foothills than Portland's city limits.

PACIFIC NORTHWEST PORTLAND

PORTLAND FOR CHILDREN

Washington Park has the most to offer families with young kids. Here you'll find the world-class **Oregon Zoo** (☑503-226-1561; www.oregonzoo.org; 4001 SW Canyon Rd; adult/child 3-11yr $11.50/8.50; ⊙9am-6pm Jun-Aug, reduced hours Sep-May; ⊞), which is set in a beautiful natural environment even parents will enjoy. Next door is the **Portland Children's Museum** (☑503-233-6500; www.portlandcm.org; 4015 SW Canyon Rd; admission $10.75; ⊙9am-5pm; ⊞) and **World Forestry Center** (☑503-228-1367; www.worldforestry.org; 4033 SW Canyon Rd; adult/child $9/6; ⊙10am-5pm; ⊞), both offering fun learning activities and exhibits.

On the other side of the Willamette River, the **Oregon Museum of Science and Industry** (OMSI; ☑503-797-4000; www.omsi.edu; 1945 SE Water Ave; adult/child 3-13yr $13.50/9.75; ⊙9.30am-7pm Jun-Aug, reduced hours Sep-May; ⊞) is a top-notch destination with a theater, planetarium and even a submarine to explore. And finally, further south is **Oaks Amusement Park** (☑503-233-5777; www.oakspark.com; 7805 SE Oaks Park Way; ride bracelets $13-26, individual rides $2.75; ⊙hours vary; ⊞), home to pint-size roller coasters, miniature golf and carnival games.

Portland

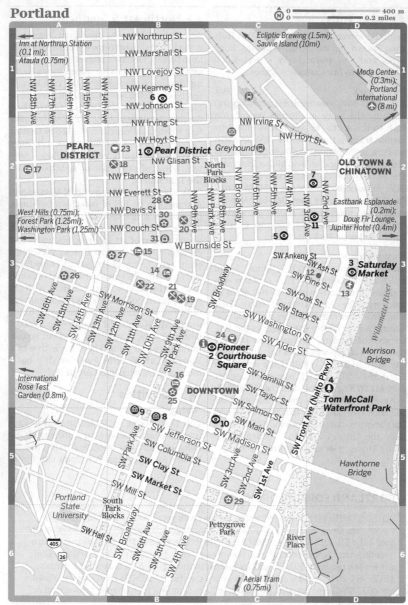

The park's **Wildwood Trail** starts at the Hoyt Arboretum and winds through 30 miles of forest, with many spur trails that allow for loop hikes. Other trailheads into Forest Park are located at the western ends of NW Thurman and NW Upshur Sts.

Cycling

Portland has been voted the 'most bike-friendly city in the US' several times in the media by the likes of CNN Travel, NBC News and *Bicycling Magazine*. There are many streets that cater to bicycles, and

Portland

drivers are used to watching out for cyclists. Riding along downtown riverside paths is a great way to see the city.

To the east of downtown the **Springwater Corridor** starts near the Oregon Museum of Science & Industry (as an extension of the Eastbank Esplanade) and goes all the way to the suburb of Boring – 21 miles away. In the northwest, **Leif Erikson Dr** is an old logging road leading 11 miles into Forest Park and offering occasional peeks over the city.

For scenic farm country, head to **Sauvie Island**, 10 miles northwest of downtown Portland. This island is prime cycling land – it's flat, has relatively little traffic and much of it is wildlife refuge.

Good cycling maps can be found at the tourist office and any bike store.

Waterfront Bicycle Rentals   BICYCLE RENTAL
(☑503-227-1719; www.waterfrontbikes.com; 10 SW Ash St; rental per hour from $9; ☺10am-6pm Mon-Fri, to 4pm Sat & Sun) Bike rentals near the waterfront bike trails.

Kayaking

Situated close to the confluence of the Columbia and Willamette Rivers, Portland has miles of navigable waterways.

Portland Kayak Company   KAYAKING
(☑503-459-4050; www.portlandkayak.com; 6600 SW Macadam Ave; rental per hour from $12) Kay-

aking rentals (minimum two hours), instruction and tours, including a three-hour circumnavigation of Ross Island on the Willamette River ($45).

🖝 Tours

Pedal Bike Tours   BICYCLE TOUR
(☑503-243-2453; www.pedalbiketours.com; 133 SW 2nd Ave; tours $49-199; ☺10am-6pm) Bike tours with all sorts of themes – history, food carts, beer – plus trip to the coast or gorge.

Portland Walking Tours   WALKING TOUR
(☑503-774-4522; www.portlandwalkingtours.com; tours $20-59) Food, chocolate, underground and even ghost-oriented tours.

🎎 Festivals & Events

Portland Rose Festival   CULTURAL
(www.rosefestival.org; ☺late May–mid-Jun) Rose-covered floats, dragon-boat races, a riverfront carnival, fireworks, roaming packs of sailors and the crowning of a Rose Queen all make this Portland's biggest celebration.

Oregon Brewers Festival   BEER
(www.oregonbrewfest.com) In the last full weekend in July you can quaff microbrews from near and far in Waterfront Park – everyone's happy and even nondrinkers have fun. Plenty of food stalls.

Bite of Oregon FOOD

(www.biteoforegon.com; ⊘early Aug) All the food (and beer) you could think of consuming, much of it from great local restaurants – and some of it from Portland's famous food carts. Good microbrews too. The festival benefits Special Olympics Oregon.

🛏 Sleeping

Reserve ahead in summer, when many Portland hotels book up solid. Prices noted here don't include lodging taxes, which can range up to 14.5%.

Northwest Portland Hostel HOSTEL $

(✆503-241-2783; www.nwportlandhostel.com; 425 NW 18th Ave; dm $29-34, d with shared bath $63-114; ✳@🛜) Perfectly located between the Pearl District and NW 21st and 23rd Aves, this friendly and clean hostel takes up four old buildings and features plenty of common areas (including a small deck) and discounted bike rentals. Dorms are spacious and private rooms can be as nice as in hotels, though all share outside bathrooms. Non-HI members pay $3 extra.

Hawthorne Portland Hostel HOSTEL $

(✆503-236-3380; www.portlandhostel.org; 3031 SE Hawthorne Blvd; dm $29-34, d with shared bath $80; ✳@🛜) ⚐ This ecofriendly hostel has a great Hawthorne location. The two private rooms are good and the dorms are spacious; all share outside bathrooms. There are summertime open-mic nights in the grassy backyard, and bike rentals (and a fix-it station) are available. The hostel composts and recycles, uses rainwater to flush toilets, and has a nice eco-roof. Discounts offered to those bike-touring.

★Kennedy School HOTEL $$

(✆503-249-3983; www.mcmenamins.com/KennedySchool; 5736 NE 33rd Ave; d from $145; 🛜) Portland's most unusual institution, this former elementary school is now home to a hotel (sleep in old classrooms!), a restaurant with a great garden courtyard, several bars, a microbrewery and a movie theater. Guests can use the soaking pool for free, and the whole school is decorated in funky art style – mosaics, fantasy paintings and historical photographs. It's a unique stay and very Portland.

★Ace Hotel BOUTIQUE HOTEL $$

(✆503-228-2277; www.acehotel.com; 1022 SW Stark St; d with shared/private bath from $185/285; P✳@🛜🛁) One of Portland's trendiest places to sleep is this hipster hotel fusing industrial, minimalist and retro styles. From the photo booth and sofa lounge in its lobby to the recycled fabrics and furniture in its rooms, the Ace makes the warehouse feel work. A Stumptown coffee shop and underground bar are on the premises, and the fancy Clyde Common restaurant is next door. Parking costs $25.

McMenamins Edgefield HOTEL $$

(✆503-669-8610; www.mcmenamins.com/54-edgefield-home; 2126 SW Halsey St, Troutdale; dm $30, d with shared/private bath from $130/165; 🛜) This former county poor farm, restored by the McMenamin brothers, is now a one-of-a-kind, 38-acre hotel complex with a dizzying variety of services. Taste wine and homemade beer, play golf, watch movies, shop at the gift store, listen to live music, walk the extensive gardens and eat at one of its restaurants. It's about a 20-minute drive east from downtown.

Jupiter Hotel BOUTIQUE MOTEL $$

(✆503-230-9200; www.jupiterhotel.com; 800 E Burnside St; d from $179; ✳🛜🛁) This slick, remodeled motel is within walking distance of downtown and right next to Doug Fir, a top-notch live-music venue. Standard rooms are tiny – go for the Metro rooms instead – and ask for a pad away from the bar patio if you're more into sleeping than staying up late. Bike rentals are available; walk-ins after midnight get a discount if there are vacancies.

Caravan BOUTIQUE HOTEL $$

(✆503-288-5225; www.tinyhousehotel.com; 5009 NE 11th Ave; r from $145; ✳🛜) Only in Portland: stay in a tiny-house (84 to 170 sq ft – smaller than most hotel rooms!), complete with kitchen and bathroom, in the artsy Alberta neighborhood. It's the first and, currently, only tiny house hotel in the country. Free s'mores nightly and Wednesday night live music from 7pm to 10pm. Book way ahead in summer.

Crystal Hotel HOTEL $$

(✆503-972-2670; www.mcmenamins.com/CrystalHotel; 303 SW 12th Ave; r with shared/private bath from $145/175; ✳🛜🛁) Each room here is dedicated to a different artist, musician or poet at this funky McMenamins hotel. It's located smack-dab in the middle of town, and on the premises are Zeus Café (a good restaurant) and Al's Den (a speakeasy bar). An original, creaky wood elevator and basement saltwater soaking pool complete the picture.

Clinton Street Guesthouse   GUESTHOUSE **$$**
(☑503-234-8752; www.clintonstreetguesthouse.
com; 4220 SE Clinton St; d $150; ❖❁) Just two
simple but beautiful rooms are on offer in
this lovely Craftsman house in a residential
neighborhood near trendy Division St. Fur-
nishings are elegant, the linens luxurious,
and your hosts hands-off. Simple continen-
tal breakfast included. There are also two
small houses available to rent less than a
mile away.

Inn at Northrup Station   BOUTIQUE HOTEL **$$$**
(☑503-224-0543; www.northrupstation.com; 2025
NW Northrup St; d from $225; ❐❖@❁) Almost
over the top with its bright color scheme and
funky decor, this super-trendy hotel boasts
huge artsy suites, many with patio or balcony, and all with kitchenettes or full kitchens.
There's a cool rooftop patio with plants, and
complimentary streetcar tickets are included
(the streetcar runs just outside).

Heathman Hotel   LUXURY HOTEL **$$$**
(☑503-241-4100; www.heathmanhotel.com; 1001
SW Broadway; d from $300; ❐❖@❁❖) A
Portland institution, the Heathman has top-
notch services and one of the best restau-
rants in the city. Rooms are elegant, stylish
and luxurious, and the location is very cen-
tral. It also hosts high tea in the afternoons,
jazz from Wednesday to Saturday evenings
and has a library stocked with 1700 signed
books by authors who have stayed here.
Parking costs $39.

🍴 Eating

Portland's rapidly evolving food scene tore
up the rule book years ago and has branched
out into countless genres and subgenres.
Vegetarianism is well represented, as is
brunch, Asian fusion and the rather loose
concept known as 'Pacific Northwest.' Then
there are the city's famous food carts, repre-
senting dozens of cuisines and quirky food
niches.

Little Big Burger   BURGERS **$**
(☑503-274-9008; www.littlebigburger.com; 122
NW 10th Ave; burgers $4; ⊙11am-10pm) A sim-
ple six-item menu takes fast food to the next
level with mini burgers made from prime
ingredients. Try a beef burger topped with
cheddar, Swiss, chèvre or blue cheese, with
a side of truffled fries – then wash it down
with a gourmet root-beer float. Several loca-
tions; check the website.

Paadee   THAI **$$**
(☑503-360-1453; www.paadeepdx.com; 6 SE 28th
Ave; mains $11-17; ⊙11:30am-3pm & 5-10pm) Lo-
cated on a strip of 28th Ave dubbed 'Restaurant Row' is this beautiful dining room
with bird cages as lampshades. Bright, fresh
flavors come alive in plates such as the steak
salad or *gra prao muu grob* (crispy pork
belly with basil and chili). Tasty cocktails
are available, too, and the lauded restaurant
Langbaan is secreted away behind a wall –
though it's booked out months in advance.

Tasty n Sons   AMERICAN **$$**
(☑503-621-1400; www.tastynsons.com; 3808 N Wil-
liams Ave; ⊙9am-2:30pm & 5:30-10pm Sun-Thu, to
11pm Fri & Sat) Superb small plates in a trendy,
high-ceilinged, industrial-feel dining room.
Share delicacies such as bacon-wrapped
dates, grilled quail with couscous, and lamb
souvlaki. Especially popular for brunch,
when a wait is guaranteed. There is a more
extensive menu at their other location, **Tasty
n Alder** (☑503-621-9251; www.tastynalder.com;
580 SW 12th Ave; mains $15-20; ⊙9am-2pm & 5:30-
10pm Sun-Thu, to 11pm Fri & Sat).

Olympia Provisions   FRENCH **$$**
(☑503-894-8136; www.olympiaprovisions.com;
1632 NW Thurman St; mains lunch $9-15, dinner $19-
28; ⊙11am-10pm Mon-Fri, 10am-10pm Sat, to 9pm
Sun) This French-inspired rotisserie bistro
serves up charcuterie and cheese boards,
gourmet sandwiches, salads and deli items,
and main plates such as rotisserie chicken
and confit duck leg. Delicious Benedicts for
brunch. Also at 107 SE Washington St.

Ken's Artisan Pizza   PIZZA **$$**
(☑503-517-9951; www.kensartisan.com; 304 SE
28th Ave; pizza for one $11-13; ⊙5-10pm Mon-Sat,
4-9pm Sun) Glorious wood-fired, thin-crust
pizzas with toppings such as prosciutto, fen-
nel sausage and green garlic. Super-trendy
atmosphere, with huge sliding windows that
open to the street on warm nights. Expect a
long wait – no reservations taken.

Pambiche   CUBAN **$$**
(☑503-233-0511; www.pambiche.com; 2811 NE
Glisan St; mains $12-20; ⊙11am-10pm Mon-Thu, to
midnight Fri, 9am-midnight Sat, to 10pm Sun) Portland's best Cuban food, with a trendy and
riotously colorful atmosphere. All your regular favorites are available, but leave room
for dessert. Lunch is a good deal, but happy
hour is even better (2pm to 6pm Monday to
Friday, 10pm to midnight Friday and Saturday). Be prepared to wait for dinner.

PORTLAND'S FOOD CARTS

One of the most fun ways to explore Portland's cuisine is to eat at a food cart. These semipermanent kitchens-on-wheels inhabit parking lots around town and are usually clustered together in 'pods', often with their own communal tables, ATMs and portaloos. As many of the owners are immigrants (who can't afford a hefty restaurant start-up), the carts are akin to an international potluck.

Food-cart locations vary, but the most significant cluster is at SW Alder St and SW 9th Ave. For a current list and some background information, see www.foodcartsportland. com. Highlights in a highly competitive field:

Nong's Khao Man Gai (✆971-255-3480; www.khaomangai.com; cnr SW 10th Ave & SW Alder St; mains $8; ⊙10am-4pm Mon-Fri) Tender poached chicken with rice. That's it – and enough. Also at 411 SW College St (another food cart) and 609 SE Ankeny St (a brick-and-mortar restaurant), both of which have a more extensive menu.

Holy Mole (✆503-347-4270; www.facebook.com/holymoleportlandor; 1419 SE 33rd Ave; mains $7-11) Not your typical taco cart (though Fernando Otero does have one taco choice on his menu). Try the *pozole* (a hearty corn soup) or his trademark mole dishes. Hours change daily; check the website.

Viking Soul Food (✆971-506-5579; www.vikingsoulfood.com; 4262 SE Belmont St; mains $7-9; ⊙noon-8pm Tue-Thu & Sun, to 9pm Fri & Sat) Delicious Norwegian wraps. Savory stuffings include meatballs, chicken sausage, house-smoked salmon and mushroom-hazelnut patties. Sweet stuffings include rhubarb chèvre, lemon curd and lingonberry preserves. Several pickled sides available, too.

Bing Mi! (www.bingmiportland.com; cnr SW 9th Ave & SW Alder St; savory crepes $6; ⊙7:30am-3pm Mon-Fri, 11am-4pm Sat) Savory grilled crepes in Northern Chinese style, stuffed with scrambled egg, pickled vegetables, fried crackers, black-bean paste and chili sauce. That's all you get, and that's all you'll need.

Bollywood Theater INDIAN $$
(✆971-200-4711; www.bollywoodtheaterpdx.com; 2039 NE Alberta St; small plates $9-12, thalis $15-17; ⊙11am-10pm; ☑) This popular Indian restaurant serves up 'street food' such as lamb samosas and *kati* rolls (meat and chutney rolled up in flatbread), along with small plates (chicken curry, pork vindaloo) and *thalis* (platters with several dishes). Plenty of vegetable and side dishes as well; wash it all down with a chai, yogurt *lassi*.

Podnah's Pit BARBECUE $$
(✆503-281-3700; www.podnahspit.com; 1625 NE Killingsworth St; mains $12-30; ⊙11am-10pm Mon-Fri, 9am-10pm Sat & Sun) Possibly Portland's best barbecue joint, serving amazingly tender and tasty pork ribs that have been smoked for four hours. There's also brisket, chicken and pulled-pork sandwiches, along with typical sides such as coleslaw, potato salad and collard greens.

★**Andina** PERUVIAN $$$
(✆503-228-9535; www.andinarestaurant.com; 1314 NW Glisan St; mains $23-35; ⊙11:30am-2:30pm & 5-9:30pm Sun-Thu, to 10:30pm Fri & Sat) A modern take on traditional Peruvian food produces delicious mains such as slow-cooked lamb shank in cilantro-and-black-beer sauce or wok-fried wild mushrooms served with garlic rice. For lighter fare, hit the bar for tapas, great cocktails and Latin-inspired live music.

★**Ned Ludd** AMERICAN $$$
(✆503-288-6900; www.nedluddpdx.com; 3925 NE Martin Luther King Jr Blvd; small plates $9-25; ⊙5pm-late Wed-Sat, 9am-2pm & 5pm-close Sun) ✔ Too quintessentially Portland, this offbeat, upscale joint exudes artisan vibes, from its rustic-peasant decor to the prominent brick wood-fired oven where all dishes are cooked. The beautifully presented small plates are rotated daily. Not a place to simply fill your tummy, but rather to sample eclectic 'American craft' delicacies. Also does a good brunch.

★**Ox** STEAK $$$
(✆503-284-3366; www.oxpdx.com; 2225 Martin Luther King Jr Blvd; mains $23-42; ⊙5-10pm Tue-Thu & Sun, to 11pm Fri & Sat) One of Portland's most popular restaurants is this upscale, Ar-

gentine-inspired steakhouse. Start with the smoked bone-marrow clam chowder, then go for the gusto: the grass-fed beef rib eye. Or, if there's two of you, the *asado* ($60) is a good choice for trying several different cuts. Reserve ahead.

Ataula
SPANISH $$$

(☑503-894-8904; www.ataulapdx.com; 1818 NW 23rd Pl; tapas $7-12, paella dishes $32-37; ⊘4:30-10pm Tue-Sat) This critically acclaimed Spanish tapas restaurant offers outstanding cuisine. If they're on the menu, try the *nuestras bravas* (sliced, fried potatoes in milk alioli), *croquetas* (salt-cod fritters), *xupa-xup* (chorizo lollipop) or *ataula montadito* (salmon with marscapone yogurt and black-truffle honey). Great cocktails, too. Reserve ahead.

Ava Gene's
ITALIAN $$$

(☑971-229-0571; www.avagenes.com; 3377 SE Division St; mains $20-32; ⊘5-11pm) Renowned trattoria-inspired eatery owned by Duane Sorenson, who founded Stumptown Coffee. Rustic Italian cuisine rules the menu, with exquisite pasta and vegetable dishes as highlights. Exceptional ingredients, great wine list and cocktails, and outstanding service. Reserve ahead.

🍸 Drinking & Nightlife

Portland is world famous for its coffee, and boasts more than 70 breweries within its metro area – more than any other city on earth. It also offers a wide range of excellent bars, from dive bars to hipster joints to pubs and ultra-modern lounges. You'll never get thirsty in these parts.

★ Barista
COFFEE

(☑503-274-1211; www.baristapdx.com; 539 NW 13th Ave; ⊘6am-6pm Mon-Fri, 7am-6pm Sat & Sun) One of Portland's best coffeeshops, owned by award-winning barista Billy Wilson and known for its lattes. Beans are sourced from specialty roasters. Three other locations in town.

Breakside Brewery
BREWERY

(☑503-719-6475; www.breakside.com; 820 NE Dekum St; ⊘3-10pm Mon-Thu, noon-11pm Fri & Sat, to 10pm Sun) Over 20 taps of some of the most experimental, tastiest beer you'll ever drink, laced through with fruits, vegetables and spices (try the hoppy Breakside IPA). Past beers have included a Meyer lemon kolsch, a mango IPA and a beet beer with ginger. For dessert,

pray they have the salted-caramel stout. Good food and nice outdoor seating, too.

Departure Lounge
BAR

(☑503-802-5370; www.departureportland.com; 525 SW Morrison St; ⊘4pm-midnight Sun-Thu, to 1am Fri & Sat) This rooftop restaurant-bar, atop the 15th floor of the Nines Hotel, fills a deep downtown void: a cool bar with unforgettable views of Portland. The vibe is distinctly spaceship-LA, with mod couches and sleek lighting. Hit happy hour from 4pm to 6pm Tuesday to Thursday (or late night) for select drinks and appetizers.

Stumptown Coffee Roasters
COFFEE

(☑503-230-7702; www.stumptowncoffee.com; 4525 SE Division St; ⊘6am-7pm Mon-Fri, 7am-7pm Sat & Sun) The microroaster who put Portland on the coffee map, and still its most famous coffeeshop – though some bemoan the fact that it has 'gone corporate.' See the website for other Portland (and US) locations.

Coava Coffee
COFFEE

(☑503-894-8134; www.coavacoffee.com; 1300 SE Grand Ave; ⊘6am-6pm Mon-Fri, 7am-6pm Sat, 8am-6pm Sun) The decor takes the concept of 'neo-industrial' to extremes, but most people love that – and Coava delivers where it matters. The pour-over makes for a fantastic cup of java, and the espressos are exceptional, too. Also at 2631 SE Hawthorne Blvd.

Heart
COFFEE

(☑503-206-6602; www.heartroasters.com; 2211 E Burnside St; ⊘7am-6pm) Artsy-industrial atmosphere on busy E Burnside; check out its large visible roaster. A bit too hipster-y for some, but most of the beans are well (and lightly) roasted. Also at 537 SW 12th Ave.

Ecliptic Brewing
BREWERY

(☑503-265-8002; www.eclipticbrewing.com; 825 N Cook St; ⊘11am-10pm Sun-Thu, to 11pm Fri & Sat) Founded by John Harris, who previously brewed for the McMenamins, Deschutes and Full Sail before starting Ecliptic, his own brewery-restaurant. Instantly popular, it now puts out interesting creations such as Spica Pilsner (an unfiltered ale) and Mintaka Stout (a dry beer with caramel and coffee notes).

Migration
BREWERY

(☑503-206-5221; www.migrationbrewing.com; 2828 NE Glisan St; ⊘11am-midnight Mon-Sat, to 10pm Sun) Popular neighborhood brewpub with great casual-industrial atmosphere. Wood picnic tables outside make it easy to see and be seen, and are especially wonderful

A BRIEF HISTORY OF MICROBREWING IN THE PACIFIC NORTHWEST

Beer connoisseurship is a nationwide phenomenon these days, but the campaign to put a dash of flavor into commercially brewed beer was first ignited in the Pacific Northwest in the 1980s.

One of America's first microbreweries was the mercurial Cartwright Brewing Company, set up in Portland in 1980. The nation's first official brewpub was the now defunct Grant's, which opened in the Washington city of Yakima in 1982. The trend went viral in 1984 with the inauguration of Bridgeport Brewing Company in Portland, followed a year later by Beervana's old-school brewing brothers Mike and Brian McMenamin, whose quirky beer empire still acts as a kind of personification of the craft-brewing business in the region.

Today, Washington and Oregon operate over 450 microbreweries (the Portland metro area alone has over 70). These take classic, natural ingredients – malt, hops and yeast – to produce high-quality beer in small batches.

on a warm day. There's great food, too – the gringo bowl and steak salad are favorites – while sports fans will appreciate a Blazers or Timbers game on the screens inside.

Hair of the Dog Brewing   BREWERY
(☑ 503-232-6585; www.hairofthedog.com; 61 SE Yamhill St; ⊙ 11:30am-10pm Tue-Sat, to 8pm Sun) HOTD brews unusual beer styles, some of which are 'bottle-conditioned,' whereby the brewing cycle is finished inside the bottle. This results in complex flavors and high alcohol content, and the beer ages like a fine wine. Food is served to complement the beer's flavors.

Rontoms   BAR
(☑ 503-236-4536; 600 E Burnside St; ⊙ 11am-2:30am Mon-Fri, 2pm-2:30am Sat & Sun) First the downside – the food's just OK, the service is mediocre and if you're not a hipster you'll feel out of place. But if it's a nice day, the large patio in back is *the* place to be. It's at the corner of E Burnside and 6th (too cool for a sign).

☆ Entertainment

The best guide to local entertainment is the free *Willamette Week* (www.wweek.com), which comes out on Wednesday and lists theater, music, clubs, cinema and events in the metro area. Also, try the *Portland Mercury* (www.portlandmercury.com).

For summer outdoor concerts, check what's happening at the Oregon Zoo (www.oregonzoo.org) or at McMenamins Edgefield (p210).

Live Music

Doug Fir Lounge   LIVE MUSIC
(☑ 503-231-9663; www.dougfirlounge.com; 830 E Burnside St) Combining futuristic elements with a rustic log-cabin aesthetic, this ultra-trendy venue has helped transform the LoBu (lower Burnside) neighborhood from seedy to slick. Doug Fir books edgy, hard-to-get talent, drawing crowds from tattooed youth to suburban yuppies. Its decent restaurant has long hours. Find it next door to the rock-star-quality Jupiter Hotel.

Crystal Ballroom   LIVE MUSIC
(☑ 503-225-0047; www.mcmenamins.com; 1332 W Burnside St) This large, historic ballroom has hosted some major acts, including the Grateful Dead, James Brown and Jimi Hendrix. The 'floating' dance floor makes dancing a balancing act. If you like '80s music, come on a Friday night.

Mississippi Studios   LIVE MUSIC
(☑ 503-288-3895; www.mississippistudios.com; 3939 N Mississippi Ave) Good for checking out budding acoustic talent, along with more established musical acts. Excellent sound system and good restaurant-bar with patio next door. Located right on trendy N Mississippi Ave.

Jimmy Mak's   LIVE MUSIC
(☑ 503-295-6542; www.jimmymaks.com; 221 NW 10th Ave) Stumptown's premier jazz venue, serving excellent Mediterranean food in its dining room.

Performing Arts

Portland Center Stage   THEATER
(☑ 503-445-3700; www.pcs.org; 128 NW 11th Ave) The city's main theater company now performs in the Portland Armory – a renovated Pearl District landmark with state-of-the-art features.

Arlene Schnitzer
Concert Hall CLASSICAL MUSIC
(☑503-248-4335; www.portland5.com; 1037 SW
Broadway) The Oregon Symphony performs
in this beautiful, if not acoustically brilliant,
downtown venue.

Artists Repertory Theatre THEATER
(☑503-241-1278; www.artistsrep.org; 1515 SW
Morrison St) Some of Portland's best plays,
including regional premieres, are performed
in two intimate theaters.

Keller Auditorium PERFORMING ARTS
(☑503-248-4335; www.portland5.com; 222 SW
Clay St) The Portland Opera and Oregon Ballet Theatre stage performances here, along
with some Broadway productions.

🏬 Shopping

Portland's downtown shopping district extends in a two-block radius from Pioneer
Courthouse Sq and hosts all of the usual
suspects. The Pearl District is dotted with
high-end galleries, boutiques and home-
decor shops. On weekends, you can visit the
quintessential Saturday Market (p206) by
the Skidmore Fountain. For a pleasant, upscale shopping street, head to NW 23rd Ave.

Eastside has lots of trendy shopping
streets that also host restaurants and cafes.
SE Hawthorne Blvd is the biggest, N Mississippi Ave is the newest and NE Alberta St
is the most artsy and funkiest. Down south,
Sellwood is known for its antique shops.

ℹ Information

EMERGENCY
Portland Police Bureau (☑503-823-0000;
www.portlandoregon.gov/police; 1111 SW 2nd
Ave)

INTERNET ACCESS
Central Library (☑503-988-5123; www.mult-
colib.org; 801 SW 10th Ave; ⊘10am-8pm Mon,
noon-8pm Tue & Wed, 10am-6pm Thu-Sat, to
5pm Sun) Downtown; for other branches check
the website.

MEDIA
KBOO 90.7 FM (www.kboo.fm) Progressive
local station run by volunteers; alternative
news and views.
Portland Mercury (www.portlandmercury.
com) Free local sibling of Seattle's *The
Stranger*.
Willamette Week (www.wweek.com) Free
weekly covering local news and culture.

DON'T MISS

POWELL'S CITY OF BOOKS

You remember bookstores, don't you?
Well they haven't all disappeared. **Powell's City of Books** (☑800-878-7323;
www.powells.com; 1005 W Burnside St;
⊘9am-11pm), an empire of reading that
takes up a whole city block on multiple
stories, once claimed to be 'the largest independent bookstore in the world.' Don't
miss it during your Portland tenure; it's a
local institution, tourist attraction and a
worthy place to hang out for a few hours
(it'll take you that long to get through it).
There are other branches around town
and at the airport, but none as large.

MEDICAL SERVICES
Legacy Good Samaritan Medical Center
(☑503-413-7711; www.legacyhealth.org; 1015
NW 22nd Ave) Convenient to downtown.

POST
Post Office (☑503-525-5398; www.usps.
com; 715 NW Hoyt St; ⊘8am-6:30pm Mon-Fri,
8:30am-5pm Sat)

TOURIST INFORMATION
Portland Oregon Visitors Association
(☑503-275-8355; www.travelportland.com;
701 SW 6th Ave; ⊘8:30am-5:30pm Mon-Fri,
10am-4pm Sat, to 2pm Sun May-Oct, 8:30am-
5:30pm Mon-Fri, 10am-4pm Sat Nov-Apr)
Super-friendly volunteers staff this office in
Pioneer Courthouse Sq. There's a small theater
with a 12-minute film about the city, and Tri-Met
bus and light-rail offices inside.

ℹ Getting There & Away

AIR
Portland International Airport (PDX; ☑503-
460-4234; www.flypdx.com; 7000 NE Airport
Way; 🛜) Award-winning Portland International
Airport has daily flights all over the US, as
well as to several international destinations.
It's situated just east of I-5 on the banks of
the Columbia River (20 minutes' drive from
downtown).

BUS
Greyhound (☑503-243-2361; www.greyhound.
com; 550 NW 6th Ave) Greyhound connects
Portland with cities along I-5 and I-84. Destina-
tions include Chicago, Denver, San Francisco,
Seattle and Vancouver, BC.

Bolt Bus (☑877-265-8287; www.boltbus.com)
Connects Portland with Seattle, Bellingham,
Eugene and San Francisco, among other cities.

TRAIN
Amtrak (☑800-872-7245; www.amtrak.com; 800 NW 6th Ave) Amtrak serves Chicago, Oakland, Seattle and Vancouver, BC.

❶ Getting Around

TO/FROM THE AIRPORT
Portland International Airport (PDX) is about 10 miles northeast of downtown, next to the Columbia River. Tri-Met's light-rail MAX line takes about 40 minutes to get from downtown to the airport. **Blue Star** (☑503-249-1837; www.bluestarbus.com) offers shuttle services between PDX and several downtown stops.

Taxis charge around $40 from the airport to downtown (not including tip).

BICYCLE
It's easy riding a bicycle around Portland, often voted 'the most bike-friendly city in America.'

Rental companies include **Clever Cycles** (☑503-334-1560; www.clevercycles.com/rentals; 900 SE Hawthorne Blvd; rentals per day from $30; ⊙11am-6pm Mon-Fri, to 5pm Sat & Sun) and Waterfront Bicycle Rentals (p209).

PUBLIC TRANSPORTATION
Portland has a good public-transportation system, which consists of local buses, streetcars and the MAX light-rail. All are run by **TriMet** (☑503-238-7433; www.trimet.org; 701 SW 6th Ave; ⊙8:30am-5:30pm Mon-Fri), which has an information center at Pioneer Courthouse Sq.

Tickets for the transportation systems are completely transferable within 2½ hours of the time of purchase. Buy tickets for local buses from the fare machines as you enter; for streetcars, you can buy tickets either at streetcar stations or on the streetcar itself. Tickets for the MAX must be bought from ticket machines at MAX stations (before you board); there is no conductor or ticket seller on board (but there are enforcers).

Be aware that there are fewer services at night, and only a few run past 1am; check the website for details on a specific line.

CAR
Most major car-rental agencies have outlets both downtown and at Portland International Airport. Many of these agencies have added hybrid vehicles to their fleets. **Zipcar** (www.zipcar.com) is a popular car-sharing option, but there are many. For cheap parking downtown, see www.portlandoregon.gov/transportation/35272.

CHARTER SERVICE
EcoShuttle (☑503-548-4480; www.ecoshuttle.net) For custom bus or van charters and tours, try EcoShuttle. Vehicles are run on 100% biodiesel.

PEDICAB
PDX Pedicab (☑503-828-9888; www.pdxpedicab.com) For an ecofriendly option, there are several pedicab operators in town, including PDX Pedicab. Bicycle pedicabs come with 'drivers' that pedal you around downtown.

TAXI
Cabs are available 24 hours by phone. Downtown, you can sometimes just flag them down.
Broadway Cab (☑503-333-3333; www.broadwaycab.com)
Radio Cab (☑503-227-1212; www.radiocab.net)

Willamette Valley

The Willamette Valley, a fertile 60-mile-wide agricultural basin, was the Holy Grail for Oregon Trail pioneers who headed west more than 170 years ago. Today it's the state's breadbasket, producing more than 100 kinds of crops – including renowned Pinot Noir grapes. Salem, Oregon's capital, is about an hour's drive from Portland at the northern end of the valley, and most of the other attractions in the area make easy day trips as well. Toward the south is Eugene, a dynamic college town worth a day or two of exploration.

Salem

Oregon's legislative center (not the Salem associated with witches, which is in Massachusetts) is renowned for its cherry trees, art-deco capitol building and Willamette University.

Willamette University's **Hallie Ford Museum of Art** (☑503-370-6855; www.willamette.edu/arts/hfma; 900 State St; adult/child $6/free; ⊙10am-5pm Tue-Sat, 1-5pm Sun) showcases the state's best collection of Pacific Northwest art, including an impressive Native American gallery.

The **Oregon State Capitol** (☑503-986-1388; www.oregonlegislature.gov; 900 Court St NE; ⊙8am-5pm Mon-Fri) FREE, built in 1938, looks like a background prop from a lavish Cecil B DeMille movie; free tours are offered. Rambling 19th-century **Bush House** (☑503-363-4714; www.salemart.org; 600 Mission St SE; adult/child $6/3; ⊙1-4pm Wed-Sun Mar-Dec) is an Italianate mansion now preserved as a museum with historical accents, including original wallpapers and marble fireplaces.

You can get oriented at the **Visitors Information Center** (☑503-581-4325; www.travelsalem.com; 181 High St NE; ⊙9am-5pm Mon-Fri, 10am-4pm Sat).

Salem is served daily by **Greyhound** (☎503-362-2428; www.greyhound.com; 500 13th St SE) buses and **Amtrak** (☎503-588-1551; www.amtrak.com; 500 13th St SE) trains.

Eugene

Eclectic Eugene – also known as 'Tracktown' – is full of youthful energy and liberal politics, and famous for its track-and-field champions (Nike was born here, after all). And while the city maintains a working-class base in timber and manufacturing, some unconventional citizens live here as well, from ex-hippie activists to eco-green anarchists to upscale entrepreneurs to high-tech heads.

Eugene offers a great arts scene, exceptionally fine restaurants, boisterous festivals, miles of riverside paths and several lovely parks. It's an awesome place to be, both for energetic visitors and those lucky enough to settle here.

◉ Sights

Alton Baker Park   PARK
(100 Day Island Rd) This popular, 400-acre riverside park, which provides access to the **Ruth Bascom Riverbank Trail System**, a 12-mile bikeway that flanks both sides of the Willamette, is heaven for cyclists and joggers. There's good downtown access via the DeFazio Bike Bridge.

University of Oregon   UNIVERSITY
(☎541-346-1000; www.uoregon.edu; 1585 E 13th Ave) Established in 1872, the University of Oregon is the state's foremost institution of higher learning, with a focus on the arts, sciences and law. The campus is filled with historical ivy-covered buildings and includes a **Pioneer Cemetery**, with tombstones that give vivid insight into life and death in the early settlement. Campus tours are held in the summer.

☰ Sleeping

Eugene has all the regular chain hotels and motels. Prices rise sharply during key football games and graduation.

Campus Inn   MOTEL **$**
(☎541-343-3376; www.campus-inn.com; 390 E Broadway; d $70-80; ❇@🐾🛜🏊) This very pleasant motel near the university offers spacious business-style rooms in simple, stylish decor. Go for the $10 upgrade: it's worth it for a bigger bed and more space. Small gym, communal Jacuzzi and upstairs outside patio available.

WORTH A TRIP

WILLAMETTE VALLEY WINE COUNTRY

Just a hour's drive from Portland is the Willamette Valley, home to hundreds of wineries producing world-class tipples, especially Pinot Noir. McMinnville, Newberg and Dundee provide many of this region's services, which include some very fine restaurants, shops, B&Bs and wine-tasting rooms. Check out www.willamettewines.com for more information on the region's wineries.

Meandering through plush green hills on winding country roads from one wine-tasting room to another is a delightful way to spend an afternoon (just make sure you designate a driver). If you'd rather go on a tour, **Grape Escape** (☎503-283-3380; www.grapeescapetours.com) offers some good ones. If you like to bicycle, Portland-based **Pedal Bike Tours** (p209) runs five-hour bike tours ($89).

For something more cerebral, head to McMinnville's **Evergreen Aviation & Space Museum** (☎503-434-4185; www.evergreenmuseum.org; 500 NE Captain Michael King Smith Way; adult/child incl 3-D movie $25/23; ⊙9am-5pm) and check out Howard Hughes' **Spruce Goose**, the world's largest wood-framed airplane. There's also a replica of the Wright brothers' *Flyer,* along with a 3-D theater and – oddly enough – an excellent water park.

For an interesting place to stay, head to **McMenamins Hotel Oregon** (☎503-472-8427; www.mcmenamins.com; 310 NE Evans St; d $83-138; ❇🛜🏊), an older building renovated into a charming hotel. It has a wonderful rooftop bar. And for a spectacular restaurant experience, consider **Joel Palmer House** (☎503-864-2995; www.joelpalmerhouse.com; 600 Ferry St, Dayton; prix fixe menus from $55; ⊙4:30-9:30pm Tue-Sat) 🍴 Its dishes are peppered with wild mushrooms collected locally by the chefs.

Eugene Whiteaker International Hostel HOSTEL $
(✆541-343-3335; www.eugenehostels.com; 970 W 3rd Ave; dm $30-35, r $40-75; ☺@⛾) This casual hostel in an old rambling house has an artsy vibe, nice front and back patios to hang out in, and a free simple breakfast. Campsites are available ($25 per person), and there's a second location (the Emerald Garden Hostel) nearby.

C'est La Vie Inn B&B $$
(✆541-302-3014; www.cestlavieinn.com; 1006 Taylor St; d $150-170, ste $260; ✳@⛾) This gorgeous Victorian house, run by a friendly French/American couple, is a neighborhood showstopper. Beautiful antique furniture fills the living and dining areas, while the three tastefully appointed rooms offer comfort and luxury. Also available is an amazing suite with kitchenette.

✗ Eating & Drinking

Papa's Soul Food Kitchen SOUTHERN $
(✆541-342-7500; www.papassoulfoodkitchen.com; 400 Blair Blvd; mains $8-12; ⊙noon-2pm & 5-10pm Tue-Fri, 2-10pm Sat) This popular Southern-food spot grills up awesome jerk chicken, pulled-pork sandwiches, crawfish jambalaya and fried okra. The best part is the live blues music that keeps the joint open late on Friday and Saturday nights. Nice back patio, too.

Sweet Life Patisserie BAKERY $
(✆541-683-5676; www.sweetlifedesserts.com; 755 Monroe St; pastries $2.50-5; ⊙7am-11pm Mon-Fri, 8am-11pm Sat & Sun) ∅ Eugene's best dessert shop: think pecan sticky buns, savory croissants and *pain au chocolat*. Even the day-old pastries are delicious (and half-price). Organic coffee, too.

★**Beppe & Gianni's Trattoria** ITALIAN $$
(✆541-683-6661; www.beppeandgiannis.net; 1646 E 19th Ave; mains $15-20; ⊙5-9pm Sun-Thu, to 10pm Fri & Sat) One of Eugene's most beloved restaurants and its favorite Italian food. Homemade pastas are the real deal here, and the desserts are excellent. Expect a wait, especially on weekends.

Pizza Research Institute PIZZA $$
(PRI; ✆541-343-1307; www.pizzaresearchinstitute. com; 325 Blair Blvd; pizzas $16-24; ⊙4-9:30pm; ∅) Located in a cute bungalow house, PRI bakes up some of Eugene's best (vegetarian, vegan, gluten-free) pies. Try the pear with vegan pesto, apple and smoked gouda, or chèvre with marinated eggplant. You can build your own pizza, too, adding toppings such as artichoke hearts, asparagus or roasted zucchini.

Ninkasi Brewing Company BREWERY
(✆541-344-2739; www.ninkasibrewing.com; 272 Van Buren St; ⊙noon-9pm Sun-Wed, to 10pm Thu-Sat) Head to this tasting room to sample some of Oregon's best microbrews. There's a sweet outdoor patio with snacks to purchase, and there's usually a food cart or two nearby. Brewery tours available.

ⓘ Information

Visitor Center (✆541-484-5307; www.eugenecascadescoast.org; 754 Olive St; ⊙8am-5pm Mon-Fri) On weekends, stop by the visitor center at 3312 Gateway St in Springfield for information.

WORTH A TRIP

HOT SPRINGS

Oregon has an abundance of hot springs and there are some not far from Salem:

Bagby Hot Springs (www.bagbyhotsprings.org; admission $5) A couple of hours' drive east of Salem is this rustic hot spring with various wood tubs in semiprivate bathhouses. It's accessible via a lovely 1.5-mile hiking trail.

Terwilliger Hot Springs (admission $6) About 40 miles east of Eugene, Terwilliger Hot Springs (aka Cougar Hot Springs) is a beautiful cluster of terraced outdoor pools framed by large rocks. They're rustic, but well-maintained, with the hottest on top. Clothing is optional, no alcohol is allowed and it's day-use only. From the parking lot, you'll have to walk a quarter-mile to the springs. To get here, turn south onto Aufderheide Scenic Byway from Hwy 126 and drive 7.5 miles.

Breitenbush Hot Springs (✆503-854-3320; www.breitenbush.com) Enjoy salubrious climes at Breitenbush Hot Springs, a fancy spa with massages, yoga and the like. Day-use prices are $16 to $30, but you can also stay in the dorm, cabins or lodge.

Getting There & Around

Eugene's **Amtrak station** (541-687-1383; www.amtrak.com; 433 Willamette St) runs daily trains to Vancouver, BC, and LA, and everywhere in between on its *Cascade* and *Coast Starlight* lines. **Greyhound** (541-344-6265; www.greyhound.com; 987 Pearl St) runs north to Salem and Portland, and south to Grants Pass and Medford. **Porter Stage Lines** (www.kokkola-bus.com) runs a daily bus from outside the train station to the coast.

Local bus service is provided by **Lane Transit District** (541-687-5555; www.ltd.org). For bike rentals, try **Paul's Bicycle Way of Life** (541-344-4105; www.bicycleway.com; 566 Charnelton St; rentals per day $24-48; 9am-7pm Mon-Fri, 10am-5pm Sat & Sun).

Columbia River Gorge

The fourth-largest river in the US by volume, the mighty Columbia runs 1243 miles from Alberta, Canada, into the Pacific Ocean just west of Astoria. For the final 309 miles of its course, the heavily dammed waterway delineates the border between Washington and Oregon and cuts though the Cascade Mountains via the spectacular Columbia River Gorge. Showcasing numerous ecosystems, waterfalls and magnificent vistas, the land bordering the river is protected as a National Scenic Area and is a popular sporting nexus for windsurfers, cyclists, anglers and hikers.

Not far from Portland, **Multnomah Falls** is a huge tourist draw, while **Vista House** offers stupendous gorge views. And if you want to stretch your legs, the **Eagle Creek Trail** is the area's premier tromping ground – provided you don't get vertigo!

Hood River & Around

Famous for its surrounding fruit orchards and wineries, the small town of Hood River – 63 miles east of Portland on I-84 – is also a huge mecca for windsurfing and kiteboarding. Strong river currents, prevailing westerly winds and the vast Columbia River provide the perfect conditions for these wind sports.

Sights & Activities

Mt Hood Railroad   HISTORIC SITE
(800-872-4661; www.mthoodrr.com; 110 Railroad Ave) Built in 1906, the railroad once transported fruit and lumber from the upper Hood River Valley to the main railhead

in Hood River. The vintage trains now transport tourists beneath Mt Hood's snowy peak and past fragrant orchards, on various excursions. See the website for schedules and fares. Reserve in advance.

Cathedral Ridge Winery   WINERY
(800-516-8710; www.cathedralridgewinery.com; 4200 Post Canyon Dr) Attractive winery with signature red blends and an award-winning Barbera.

Hood River Waterplay   WATER SPORTS
(541-386-9463; www.hoodriverwaterplay.com; Port of Hood River Marina) To partake in Hood River's wind sports, such as catamaran sailing and windsurfing, contact this outfitter for rentals and classes.

Discover Bicycles   CYCLING
(541-386-4820; www.discoverbicycles.com; 210 State St; rentals per day $30-80; 10am-6pm Mon-Sat, to 5pm Sun) Rents road, hybrid and mountain bikes and can give advice on area trails.

Sleeping & Eating

Inn of the White Salmon   INN $$
(509-493-2335; www.innofthewhitesalmon.com; 172 West Jewett Blvd; d $129-189;) Over in White Salmon, WA, is this very pleasant and contemporary 18-room inn with comfortable accommodations and a lovely patio-garden out back. There's also a very nice four-bed dorm (single bunk $25, queen bunk for two $40), along with a common-use kitchenette area.

Hood River Hotel   HISTORIC HOTEL $$
(541-386-1900; www.hoodriverhotel.com; 102 Oak St; d $109-209;) Located right in the heart of downtown, this fine 1913 hotel offers comfortable old-fashioned rooms with four-poster or sleigh beds, some with tiny baths. The suites have the best amenities and views. Kitchenettes are also available, and there's a restaurant and sauna on the premises.

Double Mountain Brewery   PUB $$
(541-387-0042; www.doublemountainbrewery.com; 8 4th St; sandwiches $7.50-10, pizzas $16-22; 11am-11pm Sun-Thu, to midnight Fri & Sat) For a casual bite, step into this popular brewpub-restaurant for a tasty sandwich or excellent brick-oven pizza. The menu is limited, but the food is great and the beer even better. Live music on weekends.

❶ Information

Chamber of Commerce (☎541-386-2000; www.hoodriver.org; 720 E Port Marina Dr; ⊙9am-5pm Mon-Fri, 10am-5pm Sat & Sun Apr-Oct, 9am-5pm Mon-Fri Nov-Mar)

❶ Getting There & Away

Hood River is connected to Portland by daily **Greyhound** (☎541-386-1212; www.greyhound.com; 110 Railroad Ave) buses. Amtrak runs on the Washington side.

Oregon Cascades

The Oregon Cascades offer plenty of dramatic volcanoes that dominate the skyline for miles around. Mt Hood, overlooking the Columbia River Gorge, is the state's highest peak, and has year-round skiing plus a relatively straightforward summit ascent. Tracking south you'll pass Mt Jefferson and the Three Sisters before reaching Crater Lake, the ghost of erstwhile Mt Mazama that collapsed in on itself after blowing its top approximately 7000 years ago.

Mt Hood

The state's highest peak, Mt Hood (11,240ft) pops into view over much of northern Oregon whenever there's a sunny day, exerting an almost magnetic tug on skiers, hikers and sightseers. In summer, wildflowers bloom on the mountainsides and hidden ponds shimmer blue, making for some unforgettable hikes; in winter, downhill and cross-country skiing dominates people's minds and bodies.

Mt Hood is accessible year-round from Portland on US 26 and from Hood River on Hwy 35. Together with the Columbia River Hwy, these routes comprise the **Mt Hood Loop**, a popular scenic drive. **Government Camp** is at the pass over Mt Hood and is the center of business on the mountain.

🏃 Activities

Skiing

Hood is rightly revered for its skiing. There are six ski areas on the mountain, including **Timberline** (☎503-272-3158; www.timberlinelodge.com), which lures snow-lovers with the only year-round skiing in the US. Closer to Portland, **Mt Hood SkiBowl** (☎503-272-3206; www.skibowl.com) is no slacker either. It's the nation's largest night-ski area and popular with city slickers who ride up for an evening of powder play from the metro zone. The largest ski area on the mountain is **Mt Hood Meadows** (☎503-337-2222; www.skihood.com), and the best conditions usually prevail here.

Hiking

The Mt Hood National Forest protects an astounding 1200 miles of trails. A Northwest Forest Pass ($5) is required at most trailheads.

One popular trail loops 7 miles from near the village of Zigzag to beautiful **Ramona Falls**, which tumbles down mossy columnar basalt. Another heads 1.5 miles up from US 26 to **Mirror Lake**, continues 0.5 miles around the lake, then tracks 2 miles beyond to a ridge.

The 41-mile **Timberline Trail** circumnavigates Mt Hood through scenic wilderness. Noteworthy portions include the hike to McNeil Point and the short climb to Bald Mountain. From Timberline Lodge, Zigzag Canyon Overlook is a 4.5-mile round-trip. At the time of writing, however, part of the trail was washed out, with no timetable for when it would be repaired.

Climbing Mt Hood should be taken seriously, as deaths do occur, though dogs have made it to the summit and the climb can be done in a long day. Contact **Timberline Mountain Guides** (☎541-312-9242; www.timberlinemtguides.com) for guided climbs.

🛏 Sleeping & Eating

Reserve **campsites** (☎877-444-6777; www.recreation.gov) in summer. On US 26 are streamside campgrounds **Tollgate** and **Camp Creek**. Large and popular **Trillium Lake** has great views of Mt Hood.

★Timberline Lodge　　　　　　　LODGE **$$**
(☎800-547-1406;　www.timberlinelodge.com; 27500 Timberline Rd; d from $135; ⚡🏊) More a community treasure than a hotel, this gorgeous historical lodge offers a variety of rooms, from bunk rooms that sleep up to 10 to deluxe fireplace rooms. Huge wooden beams tower over multiple fireplaces, there's a year-round heated outdoor pool, and the ski lifts are close by. Enjoy awesome views of Mt Hood, nearby hiking trails, two bars and a good dining room. Rates can vary widely, so check ahead.

Huckleberry Inn　　　　　　　　　INN **$$**
(☎503-272-3325;　www.huckleberry-inn.com; 88611 E Government Camp Loop; r $90-160; ⚡) Simple and comfortably rustic rooms are

available here, and there are bunk rooms that sleep up to 14. It's in a great central location in Government Camp, and has a casual restaurant (which doubles as the hotel's reception). Peak holiday rates go up 20%.

Mt Hood Brewing Co PUB $
(☑ 503-272-3172; www.mthoodbrewing.com; 87304 E Government Camp Loop, Government Camp; mains $12-18; ☺ 11am-10pm) Government Camp's only brewery-restaurant offers a friendly, family-style atmosphere and pub fare including hand-tossed pizzas, sandwiches and short ribs.

Rendezvous Grill & Tap Room AMERICAN $$
(☑ 503-622-6837; www.rendezvousgrill.net; 67149 E US 26, Welches; mains lunch $10-17, dinner $18-23; ☺ 11:30am-9pm) In a league of its own is this excellent restaurant with outstanding dishes such as wild salmon with caramelized shallots and artichoke hash or chargrilled pork chop in rhubarb chutney. Lunch means gourmet sandwiches, burgers and salads on the outdoor patio.

ⓘ Information

If you're approaching from Hood River, visit the **Hood River Ranger Station** (☑ 541-352-6002; 6780 Hwy 35, Parkdale; ☺ 8am-4:30pm Mon-Fri). The **Zigzag Ranger Station** (☑ 503-622-3191; 70220 E Hwy 26; ☺ 7:45am-4:30pm Mon-Sat) is more handy for Portland arrivals. **Mt Hood Information Center** (☑ 503-272-3301; 88900 E US 26; ☺ 9am-5pm) is in Government Camp. The weather changes quickly here; carry chains in winter.

ⓘ Getting There & Away

From Portland, Mt Hood is one hour (56 miles) by car along Hwy 26. Alternatively, you can take the prettier and longer approach via Hwy 84 to Hood River, then Hwy 35 south (1¾ hours, 95 miles). The **Central Oregon Breeze** (☑ 800-847-0157; www.cobreeze.com) shuttle between Bend and Portland stops briefly at Government Camp, 6 miles from the Timberline Lodge. There are regular **shuttles** (☑ 503-286-9333; www.seatosummit.net) from Portland to the ski areas during the winter.

Sisters

Straddling the Cascades and high desert, where mountain pine forests mingle with desert sage and juniper, is the darling town of Sisters. Once a stagecoach stop and a trade town for loggers and ranchers, today Sisters is a bustling tourist destination

whose main street is lined with boutiques, art galleries and eateries housed in Western-facade buildings. Visitors come for the mountain scenery, spectacular hiking, fine cultural events and awesome climate – there's plenty of sun and little precipitation here. And while the town's atmosphere is a bit upscale, people are still friendly and the back streets are still undeveloped enough that deer are often seen nibbling in neighborhood garden plots.

At the southern end of Sisters, the city park has **camp sites** ($15), but no showers. For ultracomfort, bag a room in the luxurious **Five Pine Lodge** (☑ 866-974-5900; www.fivepinelodge.com; 1021 Desperado Trail; d $170-293, cabins $179-329; ❈@☎❋❋). On the quieter and cheaper side is **Sisters Motor Lodge** (☑ 541-549-2551; www.sistersmotorlodge.com; 511 W Cascade St; r $129-229; ❈☎❋), offering 11 cozy rooms with homey decor (and some with kitchenettes).

For great gourmet treats head to **Porch** (☑ 541-549-3287; www.theporch-sisters.com; 243 N Elm St; small plates $8-17, mains $24-29; ☺ 5-9pm Fri-Tue), which offers morsels such as truffle fries and creamy butternut-squash risotto. **Three Creeks Brewing** (☑ 541-549-1963; www.threecreeksbrewing.com; 721 Desperado Ct; ☺ 11:30am-9pm Sun-Thu, till 10pm Fri & Sat) is the place to go for home brew and pub grub.

ⓘ Information

Chamber of Commerce (☑ 541-549-0251; www.sisterscountry.com; 291 Main St; ☺ 10am-4pm Mon-Sat)

ⓘ Getting There & Away

Valley Retriever (☑ 541-265-2253; www.kokkola-bus.com/VRBSchedule; cnr Cascade & Spruce Sts) Buses connect Sisters with Bend, Newport, Corvallis, Salem, McMinnville and Portland.

Bend

Bend is where all outdoor-lovers should live – it's an absolute paradise. You can ski fine powder in the morning, paddle a kayak in the afternoon and take in a game of golf into the evening. Or would you rather go mountain biking, hiking, mountaineering, stand-up paddleboarding, fly-fishing or rock climbing? It's all close by, and top-drawer. Plus, you'll probably be enjoying it all in great weather, as the area gets nearly 300 days of sunshine each year.

With the lovely Deschutes River carving its way through the heart of the city, Bend also offers a vibrant and attractive downtown area full of shops, galleries and upscale dining. South of downtown, the Old Mill District has been renovated into a large shopping area full of brand-name stores, fancy eateries and modern movie theaters. Bend has also become a beer-lover's dream; it has more than a dozen breweries per capita more than any other city in Oregon.

⊙ Sights

★ High Desert Museum
MUSEUM

(☑ 541-382-4754; www.highdesertmuseum.org; 59800 S US 97; adult/child 5-12yr $15/9; ⊙ 9am-5pm May-Oct, 10am-4pm Nov-Apr) Don't miss this excellent museum about 3 miles south of Bend on US 97. It charts the exploration and settlement of the West, using reenactments of a Native American camp, a hardrock mine and an old Western town. The region's natural history is also explored; kids love the live snake, tortoise and trout exhibits, and watching the birds of prey and otters is always fun.

⚡ Activities

Cycling

Bend is a mountain biking paradise, with hundreds of miles of awesome bike trails to explore. For a good bike-trails map, get the *Bend Oregon Adventure Map* ($12), available at the Visit Bend tourist office and elsewhere.

The king of Bend's mountain biking trails is **Phil's Trail** network, which offers a variety of excellent fast single-track forest trails just minutes from town. If you want to catch air, don't miss the **Whoops Trail**.

Cog Wild
BICYCLE TOUR

(☑ 541-385-7002; www.cogwild.com; 255 SW Century Dr, ste 201; half-day tours from $60) Offers organized tours and shuttles to the best trailheads. Separate rental shop downstairs.

Rock Climbing

Smith Rock State Park
ROCK CLIMBING

(☑ 800-551-6949; www.oregonstateparks.org; 9241 NE Crooked River Dr; day use $5) About 25 miles northeast of Bend lies Smith Rock State Park, where 800ft cliffs over the Crooked River offer gorgeous lead and trad climbing. The park's 1800-plus routes are among the best in the nation.

Smith Rock Climbing Guides Inc
ROCK CLIMBING

(☑ 541-788-6225; www.smithrockclimbingguides.com) Offers a variety of climbing instruction (basic, lead, trad, multi-pitch, aid and self-rescue), along with guided climbs to famous routes at Smith Rock State Park.

Skiing

Mount Bachelor Ski Resort
SKIING

(☑ 800-829-2442; www.mtbachelor.com) Bend hosts Oregon's best skiing, 22 miles southwest of town, at the glorious Mount Bachelor Ski Resort, famous for its 'dry' powdery snow, long season and ample terrain (it's the largest ski area in the Pacific Northwest). The mountain has long advocated cross-country skiing in tandem with downhill, and maintains 35 miles of groomed trails.

🛏 Sleeping & Eating

Mill Inn
INN $$

(☑ 541-389-9198; www.millinn.com; 642 NW Colorado Ave; d incl breakfast $95-165; ⊛ 🐾 🔊) A 10-room boutique hotel with small, classy rooms decked out with velvet drapes and comforters; four share outside bathrooms. Full breakfast and hot-tub use is included, and there are nice small patios on which to hang out.

★ McMenamins Old St Francis School
HOTEL $$

(☑ 541-382-5174; www.mcmenamins.com; 700 NW Bond St; d $135-185, 5-bedroom cottage from $350; ⊛ 🔊) One of McMenamins' best venues, this old schoolhouse has been remodeled into a classy 19-room hotel – two rooms even have side-by-side clawfoot tubs. The fabulous tiled saltwater Turkish bath is worth the stay alone, though nonguests can soak for $5. A restaurant-pub, three bars, a movie theater and creative artwork complete the picture.

★ Oxford Hotel
BOUTIQUE HOTEL $$$

(☑ 541-382-8436; www.oxfordhotelbend.com; 10 NW Minnesota Ave; d $389-599; ⊛ 🔊 🔊) 🦮 Bend's premier boutique hotel is deservedly popular. The smallest rooms are still huge (470 sq ft) and are decked out with eco-friendly features such as soy-foam mattresses and cork flooring. High-tech aficionados will love the smart-panel desks. Suites (with kitchen and steam-shower) are available, and the basement restaurant is slick.

★ **Chow** AMERICAN $

(541-728-0256; www.chowbend.com; 1110 NW
Newport Ave; mains $8-15; 7am-2pm) The
signature poached-egg dishes here are spectacular and beautifully presented, coming
with sides such as crab cakes, house-cured
ham and corn-meal-crusted tomatoes (don't
miss their housemade hot sauces). Gourmet
sandwiches and salads are served for lunch,
some with an Asian influence. Much of the
produce is grown in the garden, and there
are good cocktails, too.

Jackson's Corner AMERICAN $

(541-647-2198; www.jacksonscornerbend.com;
845 NW Delaware Ave; mains $10-16; 7am-9pm;
) This homey corner restaurant, very popular with families, has a market-like feel and
boasts seasonal ingredients. Homemade
pizzas and pastas are always good, as are
the organic salads (add on chicken, steak or
prawns). There's a kids' menu and outside
seating for sunny days; just remember to
order at the counter first. Also at 1500 NE
Cushing Dr.

10 Barrel Brewing Co AMERICAN $

(541-678-5228; www.10barrel.com; 1135 NW
Galveston; mains $10-14; 11am-11pm Mon-Thu, to
midnight Fri-Sun) Located in a charming house,
this popular brewery-restaurant has a great
patio for warm nights. The tasty pub-food
menu includes starters such as fried brussels
sprouts and steak and gorgonzola nachos,
while mains run the gamut from gourmet
burgers to fish tacos with chipotle slaw.
Sports-lovers should head to the bar in back.

Zydeco AMERICAN $$$

(541-312-2899; www.zydecokitchen.com; 919
NW Bond St; mains $16-30; 11:30am-2:30pm &
5-9pm Mon-Fri, 5-9pm Sat & Sun) One of Bend's
most acclaimed restaurants, and with good
reason. Start with the duck fries (french
fries fried in duck fat) or tri-colored beet sal-
ad with goat's cheese, then move onto your
main course: pan-roasted steelhead, craw-
fish jambalaya or roasted wild mushroom
pork tenderloin. Reserve ahead.

ℹ Information

Visit Bend (800-949-6086; www.visitbend.
com; 750 NW Lava Rd; 9am-5pm Mon-Fri,
10am-4pm Sat & Sun) Great information, plus
maps and recreation passes.

ℹ Getting There & Around

Central Oregon Breeze (www.cobreez…
offers transport to Portland two or m…
daily. Connect to Sisters, Willamette …
destinations and the coast with Valley Retriever
(www.kokkola-bus.com/VRBSchedule) and Por-
ter Stage Lines (www.pslporterstageline.com).

Cascades East Transit (541-385-8680;
www.cascadeseasttransit.com) The regional
bus company in Bend, covering La Pine, Mt
Bachelor, Sisters, Prineville and Madras. It also
provides bus transport within Bend.

High Desert Point (541-923-1732; www.
highdesert-point.com) Buses link Bend with
Chemult, where the nearest train station is
located (65 miles south). High Desert Point also
has bus services to Eugene, Ontario and Burns.

Newberry National Volcanic Monument

Newberry National Volcanic Monument (day
use $5) showcases 400,000 years of dramatic
seismic activity. Start your visit at the **Lava
Lands Visitor Center** (541-593-2421; 58201
S Hwy 97; 9am-5pm late May-Sep, reduced hours
Oct-late May), 13 miles south of Bend. Nearby
attractions include **Lava Butte**, a perfect
cone rising 500ft, and **Lava River Cave**, Or-
egon's longest lava tube. Four miles west of
the visitor center is **Benham Falls**, a good
picnic spot on the Deschutes River.

Newberry Crater was once one of the
most active volcanoes in North America, but
after a large eruption a caldera was born.
Close by are **Paulina Lake** and **East Lake**,
deep bodies of water rich with trout, while
looming above is 7985ft **Paulina Peak**.

Crater Lake National Park

It's no exaggeration: Crater Lake is so blue,
you'll catch your breath. And if you get to see
it on a calm day, the surrounding cliffs are
reflected in those deep waters like a mirror.
It's a stunningly beautiful sight. Crater Lake
is Oregon's only **national park** (541-594-
3000; www.nps.gov/crla; 7-day vehicle pass $15).

The secret lies in the water's purity. No
rivers or streams feed the lake, meaning
its content is made up entirely of rain and
melted snow. It is also exceptionally deep –
at 1949ft, it's the deepest lake in the US. The
classic tour is the 33-mile rim drive (open
from approximately June to mid-October),
but there are also exceptional hiking and

oss-country skiing opportunities. Note that because the area receives some of the highest snowfalls in North America, the rim drive and north entrance are sometimes closed up until early July.

You can stay from late May to mid-October at the Cabins at Mazama Village (📞888-774-2728; www.craterlakelodges.com; d $144; ☉late May–mid-Oct) or the majestic and historic Crater Lake Lodge (📞888-774-2728; www.craterlakelodges.com; d $169-295; ☉late May–mid-Oct; ♿🐾), opened in 1915. Campers head to Mazama Campground (📞888-774-2728; www.craterlakelodges.com; tent/RV sites from $22/31; 🐾🚿).

For more information, head to Steel Visitors Center (📞541-594-3000; ☉9am-5pm May-Oct, 10am-4pm Nov-Apr).

Oregon Coast

Thanks to a far-sighted government in the 1910s, Oregon's 363-mile Pacific Coast was set aside as public land. This magnificent littoral is paralleled by US 101, a scenic highway that winds its way through towns, resorts, state parks (more than 70 of them) and wilderness areas. Everyone from campers to gourmet-lovers will find a plethora of ways to enjoy this exceptional region, which is especially popular in summer (reserve accommodations in advance).

Astoria

Astoria sits at the 5-mile-wide mouth of the Columbia River and was the first US settlement west of the Mississippi. The city has a long seafaring history and has seen its old harbor, once home to poor artists and writers, attract fancy hotels and restaurants in recent years. Inland are many historical houses, including lovingly restored Victorians – a few converted into romantic B&Bs.

👁 Sights

Adding to the city's scenery is the 4.1-mile Astoria-Megler Bridge, the longest continuous truss bridge in North America, which crosses the Columbia River into Washington state. See it from the Astoria Riverwalk, which follows the trolley route. Pier 39 is an interesting covered wharf with informal cannery museum and a couple of places to eat.

Columbia River Maritime Museum MUSEUM
(📞503-325-2323; www.crmm.org; 1792 Marine Dr; adult/child $12/5; ☉9:30am-5pm) Astoria's

seafaring heritage is well interpreted at this wave-shaped museum. It's hard to miss the Coast Guard boat, frozen in action, through a huge outside window. Other exhibits highlight the salmon-packing industry, local lighthouses and the river's commercial history; also check out the Columbia River Bar exhibit and 3-D theater.

Flavel House HISTORIC BUILDING
(📞503-325-2203; www.cumtux.org; 441 8th St; adult/child $6/2; ☉10am-5pm) The extravagant Flavel House was built by Captain George Flavel, one of Astoria's leading citizens during the 1880s. This Queen Anne house has been repainted in its original colors and the grounds have been returned to Victorian-era landscaping; it has great views of the Columbia River, too.

Astoria Column LANDMARK
(📞503-325-2963; www.astoriacolumn.org; 1 Coxcomb Dr; parking $2; ☉9am-5:30pm Mon-Fri, to 5pm Sat & Sun) Rising high on Coxcomb Hill, the Astoria Column (built in 1926) is a 125ft tower painted with scenes from the westward sweep of US exploration and settlement. The top of the column (up 164 steps) offers excellent views over the area.

Fort Stevens State Park PARK
(📞503-861-3170 ext 21; www.oregonstateparks.org; 100 Peter Iredale Rd, Hammond; day use $5) Ten miles west of Astoria, this park holds the historical military installation that once guarded the mouth of the Columbia River. Near the Military Museum (📞503-861-2000; ☉10am-6pm May-Sep, to 4pm Oct-Apr) FREE are gun batteries dug into sand dunes – interesting remnants of the fort's mostly demolished military stations (truck and walking tours available). There's a popular beach at the small *Peter Iredale* 1906 shipwreck, and good ocean views from parking lot C. There's also camping and 12 miles of paved bike trails.

🛏 Sleeping & Eating

Norblad Hotel & Hostel HOSTEL $
(📞503-325-6989; www.norbladhotel.com; 443 14th St; dm $29, d $59-99; 🐾🚿) This central hostel-hotel offers six simple but elegant, private rooms, most with shared bathroom (just one is en suite). There are also several dorm rooms and a communal kitchen. Some rooms have flat-screen TVs and views of the river.

LEWIS & CLARK: JOURNEY'S END

In November 1805 William Clark and his fellow explorer Meriwether Lewis of the Corps of Discovery staggered, with three dozen others, into a sheltered cove on the Columbia River, 2 miles west of the present-day Astoria-Megler Bridge, completing what was indisputably the greatest overland trek in American history.

After the first truly democratic ballot in US history (in which a woman and a black slave both voted), the party elected to make their bivouac 5 miles south of Astoria at Fort Clatsop, where the Corps spent a miserable winter in 1805–06. Today this site is called the **Lewis and Clark National Historical Park** (☑503-861-2471; www.nps.gov/lewi; 92343 Fort Clatsop Rd; adult/child $3/free; ☺9am-6pm mid-Jun–Aug, to 5pm Sep–mid-Jun), where you'll find a reconstructed Fort Clatsop, along with a visitors center and historical reenactments in summer.

Commodore Hotel　　BOUTIQUE HOTEL **$$**
(☑503-325-4747;　　www.commodoreastoria.com; 258 14th St; d with shared/private bath from $89/199; ☻☎) Hip travelers should beeline to this slick and trendy hotel, which offers small, chic, minimalist rooms. Choose either private bathrooms or go Euro-style (sinks in rooms, but baths down the hall; 'deluxe' rooms have better views). There's a great living-room-style lobby with attached cafe. Room 309 has the best river view.

Blue Scorcher Bakery Café　　CAFE **$**
(☑503-338-7473; www.bluescorcher.com; 1493 Duane St; mains $7-13; ☺7am-4pm; ☑🍴) 🍴 This artsy, organic co-op coffeehouse and bakery with free wi-fi boasts tasty salads, sandwiches, pizza, and egg dishes for breakfast. Vegetarian/vegan friendly; doughnut-free.

Fort George Brewery　　PUB **$**
(☑503-325-7468;　　www.fortgeorgebrewery.com; 1483 Duane St; mains $9-14; ☺11am-11pm Mon-Thu, to midnight Fri & Sat, noon-11pm Sun) Atmospheric brewery-restaurant in a historical building – this was the original settlement site of Astoria. Today you can get gourmet burgers, house-made sausages, organic salads and a few eclectic dishes. Afternoon brewery tours on weekends.

❶ Information

Visitors Center (☑503-325-6311; www.oldoregon.com; 111 W Marine Dr; ☺9am-5pm Mon-Fri, 10am-4pm Sat) Sells permits such as the Oregon Pacific Coast Passport and State Park Recreation Pass.

❶ Getting There & Away

Northwest Point (☑503-484-4100; www.northwest-point.com) Daily buses head to Seaside, Cannon Beach and Portland; check the website for schedules.

Sunset Empire Transit (☑503-861-7433; www.ridethebus.org; 900 Marine Dr) Local transport; buses also head to Warrenton, Cannon Beach and Seaside.

Cannon Beach

Charming Cannon Beach is one of the most popular and upscale beach resorts on the Oregon coast. The streets are full of boutiques and art galleries, and lined with colorful flowers. Lodging is expensive, and the streets are jammed; on a warm sunny Saturday, you'll spend a good chunk of time just finding a parking spot.

◉ Sights & Activities

Photogenic **Haystack Rock**, a 295ft sea stack, is the most spectacular landmark on the Oregon coast and is accessible from the beach at low tide. Birds cling to its ballast cliffs and tide pools ring its base.

The coast to the north, protected inside **Ecola State Park** (☑503-436-2844; www.oregonstateparks.org; day use $5), is the Oregon you may have already visited in your dreams: sea stacks, crashing surf, hidden beaches and gorgeous pristine forest. The park is 1.5 miles from town and is crisscrossed by paths, including part of the **Oregon Coast Trail**, which leads over Tillamook Head to the town of Seaside.

The Cannon Beach area is good for surfing, though not the beach itself. The best spots are **Indian Beach** in Ecola State Park, 3 miles to the north, and **Oswald West State Park**, 10 miles south. **Cleanline Surf Shop** (☑503-738-2061; www.cleanlinesurf.com; 171 Sunset Blvd) is a friendly local shop that rents out boards and mandatory wetsuits.

WORTH A TRIP

SCENIC DRIVE: THREE CAPES

Cape Meares, Cape Lookout and Cape Kiwanda, about halfway between Cannon Beach and Newport, are some of the coast's most stunning headlands, strung together on a slow, winding and sometimes bumpy 40-mile alternative to US 101. It's a worthwhile drive, though in March 2013 a section of road north of Cape Meares began sinking and was closed. Repairs are ongoing, so you might have to drive to Cape Meares via Netarts and Oceanside, then backtrack.

The forested headland at **Cape Meares** offers good views from its 38ft-tall lighthouse (Oregon's shortest). Short trails lead to Oregon's largest Sitka spruce and the 'Octopus Tree,' another Sitka shaped like a candelabra.

A panoramic vista atop sheer cliffs that rise 800ft above the Pacific makes **Cape Lookout State Park** a highlight. In winter, the end of the cape, which juts out nearly a mile, is thronged with whale-watchers. There are wide sandy beaches, hiking trails and a popular campground near the water.

Finally there's **Cape Kiwanda**, a sandstone bluff that rises just north of the little town of Pacific City. You can hike up tall dunes, or drive your truck onto the beach. It's the most developed of the three capes, with plenty of services nearby (don't miss **Pelican Pub & Brewery** (📞503-965-7007; www.yourlittlebeachtown.com/pelican; 33180 Cape Kiwanda Dr, Pacific City; mains $12-32; ⊙8am-10pm Sun-Thu, to 11pm Fri & Sat) if you like beer). Watch the dory fleet launch their craft or, after a day's fishing, land as far up the beach as possible.

🛏 Sleeping & Eating

Cannon Beach Hotel   HISTORIC HOTEL **$$**
(📞503-436-1392; www.cannonbeachhotel.com; 1116 S Hemlock St; d from $139; 🛜) If you don't need much space, check out this classy, centrally located hotel with just 10 rooms. Standard rooms are lovely, but very small; even the regular suites are tight. A good breakfast at the cafe on the premises is included.

Blue Gull Inn Motel   MOTEL **$$**
(📞800-507-2714; www.haystacklodgings.com; 487 S Hemlock St; d $119-219; 🛜🐾) These are some of the more affordable rooms in town, with comfortable atmosphere and toned-down decor, except for the colorful Mexican headboards and serapes on the beds. Kitchenette and Jacuzzi units are available. It's run by Haystack Lodgings, which also manages six other properties in town and does vacation rentals.

Sleepy Monk Coffee   CAFE **$**
(📞503-436-2796; www.sleepymonkcoffee.com; 1235 S Hemlock St; ⊙8am-3pm Mon, Tue & Thu, to 4pm Fri-Sun) 🌿 For organic, certified-fair-trade coffee, try this little coffee shop on the main street. Sit on an Adirondack chair in the tiny front yard and enjoy the rich brews, all tasty and roasted on the premises. Good homemade pastries, too.

Newman's at 988   FRENCH, ITALIAN **$$$**
(📞503-436-1151; www.newmansat988.com; 988 Hemlock St; mains $21-35; ⊙5:30-9pm daily Jul–mid-Oct, Tue-Sun mid-Oct–Jun) Expect a fine dining experience at this small, quality restaurant on the main drag. Award-winning chef John Newman comes up with a fusion of French and Italian dishes such as marinated rack of lamb and char-grilled portabello mushrooms with spinach and Gorgonzola. Desserts are sublime; reserve ahead.

ℹ Information

Chamber of Commerce (📞503-436-2623; www.cannonbeach.org; 207 N Spruce St; ⊙10am-5pm) Has good local information, including tide tables.

ℹ Getting There & Away

Northwest Point (📞541-484-4100; www.northwest-point.com) buses head from Astoria to Portland (and vice versa) every morning, stopping at Cannon Beach; buy tickets at the Beach Store, next to Cannon Beach Surf.

The **Cannon Beach Shuttle** (📞503-861-7433; www.ridethebus.org), also known as 'the Bus', runs the length of Hemlock St to the end of Tolovana Beach; the schedule varies seasonally. Both buses go to Seaside and Astoria, too.

Wave (www.tillamookbus.com) buses go south towards Manzanita and Lincoln City several times daily.

Newport

Home to Oregon's largest commercial fishing fleet, Newport is a lively tourist city with several fine beaches and a world-class aquarium. In 2011 it became the host of NOAA, the National Oceanic and Atmospheric Administration. Good restaurants – along with some tacky attractions, gift shops and barking sea lions – abound in the historic bay-front area, while bohemian Nye Beach offers art galleries and a friendly village atmosphere. The area was first explored in the 1860s by fishing crews who found oyster beds at the upper end of Yaquina Bay.

◉ Sights

The world-class **Oregon Coast Aquarium** (☑ 541-867-3474; www.aquarium.org; 2820 SE Ferry Slip Rd; adult/child 3-12yr/child 13-17yr $19.95/12.95/17.95; ⊙ 9am-6pm May-Aug, to 5pm Sep-Apr; ⊕) is an unmissable attraction, featuring a sea-otter pool, surreal jellyfish tanks and Plexiglas tunnels through a shark tank. Nearby, the **Hatfield Marine Science Center** (☑ 541-867-0100; www.hmsc.oregonstate.edu; 2030 SE Marine Science Dr; ⊙ 10am-5pm daily Jun-Aug, 10am-4pm Thu-Mon Sep-May) **FREE** is much smaller, but still worthwhile. For awesome tide-pooling and views, don't miss the **Yaquina Head Outstanding Area** (☑ 541-574-3100; 750 NW Lighthouse Dr; vehicle fee $7; ⊙ 8am-sunset, interpretive center 10am-6pm), site of the coast's tallest lighthouse and an interesting interpretive center.

🛏 Sleeping & Eating

Campers can head to large and popular **South Beach State Park** (☑ 541-867-4715; www.oregonstateparks.org; tent sites/RV sites/yurts $21/29/44; ⊛), two miles south on US 101. Book-lovers can stay at the **Sylvia Beach Hotel** (☑ 541-265-5428; www.sylviabeachhotel.com; 267 NW Cliff St; d $165-230), which has simple but comfy rooms, each named after a famous author; reservations are mandatory.

For tasty seafood, head to **Local Ocean Seafoods** (☑ 541-574-7959; www.localocean.net; 213 SE Bay Blvd; mains $10-28; ⊙ 11am-9pm) 🍴 – it's especially great for lunch, when the glass walls open to the port area.

❶ Information

Visitors Center (☑ 541-265-8801; www.newportchamber.org; 555 SW Coast Hwy; ⊙ 8:30am-5pm Mon-Fri, 10am-2pm Sat)

Yachats & Around

One of the Oregon coast's best-kept secrets is the neat and friendly little town of Yachats (ya-hots). People come here and to the small remote inns and B&Bs just south of town to get away from it all, which isn't hard to do along this relatively undeveloped coast.

Three miles to the south, lofty **Cape Perpetua** was first sighted by Captain Cook in 1778. Volcanic intrusions have formed a beautifully rugged shoreline, with dramatic features such as the **Devil's Churn**, where powerful waves crash through a 30ft inlet. For an easy hike, take the paved **Captain Cook Trail** (a 1.2-mile round trip) down to tide pools near **Cooks Chasm**, where at high tide the geyser-like spouting horn blasts water out of a sea cave. For information head to the **Cape Perpetua Visitor Center** (☑ 541-547-3289; www.fs.usda.gov/siuslaw; 2400 US 101; vehicle fee $5; ⊙ 10am-5pm Jun-Aug, reduced hours Sep-May).

Fifteen miles to the south on US 101 is the almost-tourist-trap, but fun, **Sea Lion Caves** (☑ 541-547-3111; www.sealioncaves.com; 91560 US 101; adult/child 5-12yr $14/8; ⊙ 9am-5pm), a noisy grotto filled with groaning sea lions accessed via an elevator.

Camp at **Beachside State Park** (☑ 541-563-3220; www.oregonstateparks.org; tent sites/RV sites/yurts $21/29/44; ⊛), five miles north of Yachats on US 101. The **Ya'Tel Motel** (☑ 541-547-3225; www.yatelmotel.com; cnr US 101 & 6th St; d $64-84; ⊖ @ ⊛ ⊛) is a good, inexpensive place to sleep, and for snacks there's the **Green Salmon Coffee House** (☑ 541-547-3077; www.thegreensalmon.com; 220 US 101; mains $7-11; ⊙ 7:30am-2:30pm; ⊿) 🍴.

Oregon Dunes National Recreation Area

Stretching for 50 miles between Florence and Coos Bay, the Oregon Dunes form the largest expanse of coastal dunes in the USA. They tower up to 500ft and undulate inland as far as three miles to meet coastal forests, harboring curious ecosystems that sustain an abundance of wildlife. Hiking trails, bridle paths, and boating and swimming areas are available, but avoid the stretch south of Reedsport as noisy dune buggies dominate. Find out more at the Oregon Dunes National Recreation Area's **headquarters** (☑ 541-271-6000; www.fs.usda.gov/siuslaw; 855 Highway

Ave; ⊙8am-4:30pm Mon-Sat Jun-Aug, Mon-Fri Sep-May) in Reedsport.

State parks with camping include popular **Jessie M Honeyman** (☑541-997-3641, 800-452-5687; www.oregonstateparks.org; 84505 US 101 S; tent sites/RV sites/yurts $21/28/44; 🐾), 3 miles south of Florence, and pleasant **Umpqua Lighthouse** (☑541-271-4118; www.oregonstateparks.org; 460 Lighthouse Rd; tent sites/RV sites/yurts/deluxe yurts from $19/26/40/80; 🐾), 4 miles south of Reedsport. There's plenty of other camping in the area, too.

Port Orford

Occupying a rare natural harbor and guarding plenty of spectacular views, the scenic hamlet of Port Orford sits on a headland wedged between two magnificent state parks. **Cape Blanco State Park** (☑541-332-2973; www.oregonstateparks.org; US 101), nine miles to the north, is the second-most-westerly point in the continental US, and the promontory is often lashed by fierce 100mph winds. As well as hiking, visitors can tour the **Cape Blanco Lighthouse** (☑541-332-2207; www.oregonstateparks.org; US 101; tour $2; ⊙10am-3:30pm Wed-Mon Apr-Oct) built in 1870; it's the oldest and highest operational lighthouse in Oregon.

Six miles south of Port Orford, in **Humbug Mountain State Park** (☑541-332-6774), mountains and sea meet in aqueous disharmony with plenty of angry surf. You can climb the 1750ft peak on a 3-mile trail through old-growth cedar groves.

For an affordable stay try **Castaway-by-the-Sea Motel** (☑541-332-4502; www.castawaybythesea.com; 545 W 5th St; d $75-165; @🐾🏠🐾). Food in this fishing village means a visit to slick **Redfish** (☑541-336-2200; www.redfishportorford.com; 517 Jefferson St; mains lunch $12-14, dinner $22-25; ⊙11am-3pm & 5-9pm Mon-Fri, 9am-3pm & 5-9pm Sat & Sun) 🍴 for the freshest seafood in town.

Southern Oregon

With a warm and sunny climate that belongs in nearby California, southern Oregon is the state's banana belt. Rugged landscapes, scenic rivers and a couple of attractive towns top the highlights list.

Ashland

Oregon was unknown territory to the Elizabethan explorers of William Shakespeare's day, so it might seem a little strange to find that the pretty settlement of Ashland in southern Oregon has established itself as the English playwright's second home. The irony probably wouldn't have been lost on Shakespeare himself. 'All the world's a stage,' the great Bard once opined, and fittingly people come from all over to see Ashland's famous Shakespeare Festival, which has been held here under various guises since the 1930s. The 'festival' moniker is misleading; the shows here are a semipermanent fixture occupying nine months of the annual town calendar and attracting up to 400,000 theater-goers per season.

Even without the shows, Ashland is an attractive town, propped up by various wineries, upscale B&Bs and fine restaurants.

◉ Sights & Activities

Lithia Park PARK
(59 Winburn Way) Adjacent to Ashland's three splendid theaters (one of which is outdoors) lies what is arguably the loveliest city park in Oregon, and its 93 acres wind along Ashland Creek above the center of town. Unusually, the park is in the National Register of Historic Places. It is embellished with fountains, flowers, gazebos and an ice-skating rink (winter only).

Schneider Museum of Art MUSEUM
(☑541-552-6245; www.sou.edu/sma; 1250 Siskiyou Blvd; suggested donation $5; ⊙10am-4pm Mon-Sat) Ashland's culture extends beyond the OSF; if you like contemporary art, check out this Southern Oregon University museum. The university also puts on theater performances of its own, along with classical concerts and opera performances.

Jackson Wellsprings SPA
(☑541-482-3776; www.jacksonwellsprings.com; 2253 Hwy 99; ⊙8am-midnight mid-Apr–mid-Oct, noon-midnight mid-Oct–mid-Apr) For a good soak check out this casual, New Age–style place, which boasts a mineral-fed swimming pool, private soaking tubs, saunas and steam rooms. There's also yoga, massages and spa services, and you can camp or stay in tipis in summer. It's 1 mile north of town. Note that Monday night is women only.

DON'T MISS

OREGON SHAKESPEARE FESTIVAL

One of Southern Oregon's highlights is Ashland's wildly popular Oregon Shakespeare Festival (OSF). Despite being deeply rooted in Shakespearean and Elizabethan drama, the festival also features plenty of revivals and contemporary theater from around the world.

Productions run from February to October in three theaters near Main and Pioneer Sts: the outdoor **Elizabethan Theatre** (⊘Jun-Oct), the **Angus Bowmer Theatre** and the intimate **Thomas Theatre**. Children under six are not allowed. There are no performances on Mondays.

Performances sell out quickly; obtain tickets at www.osfashland.org. The **box office** (✍541-482-4331; 15 S Pioneer St; tickets $30-96) also has last-minute tickets. Be sure to book backstage **tours** well in advance.

Check the **OSF Welcome Center** (76 N Main St; ⊘10am-6pm Tue-Sun) for other events, which may include scholarly lectures, play readings, concerts and preshow talks.

Mt Ashland Ski Resort SKIING
(✍541-482-2897; www.mtashland.com) Powdery snow is abundant at this resort, 16 miles southwest of town on 7533ft Mt Ashland.

Siskiyou Cyclery CYCLING
(✍541-482-1997; www.siskiyoucyclery.com; 1729 Siskiyou Blvd; rental per hour $10-15; ⊘10am-6pm Mon-Sat) Rent a bike and explore the countryside on Bear Creek Greenway, a 21-mile bike path between Ashland and the town of Central Point.

🛏 Sleeping

Reserve ahead in summer when the thespians descend in droves. There are many B&Bs in town.

Ashland Hostel HOSTEL $
(✍541-482-9217; www.theashlandhostel.com; 150 N Main St; dm $28, d $45-64; ❀@⊛) Central and somewhat upscale hostel (shoes off inside!). Most private rooms share bathrooms; some are connected to dorms. Hangout spaces include the cozy basement living room and the shady front porch. No alcohol or smoking on the premises. Call ahead, as reception times are limited.

Ashland Commons HOSTEL $
(✍541-482-6753; www.ashlandcommons.com; 437 Williamson Way; dm from $26, s $45-65, d $60-80; ❀⊛) These unconventional dorm or private room accommodations are provided within three large apartments. All vary in atmosphere, and are either two- or four-bedroom, with kitchen and living areas. Great for large groups, as entire apartments can be rented. Located in a mixed industrial-residential area just outside the center.

Palm BOUTIQUE HOTEL $$
(✍541-482-2636; www.palmcottages.com; 1065 Siskiyou Blvd; d $98-239; ❀⊛⊛⊛) Fabulous small motel remodeled into 16 charming garden cottage rooms and suites (some with kitchens). It's an oasis of green on a busy avenue, complete with grassy lawns and a saltwater pool. A house nearby harbors three large suites ($299).

Columbia Hotel HOTEL $$
(✍541-482-3726; www.columbiahotel.com; 262 1/2 E Main St; d $89-179; ❀⊛) Awesomely located 'European-style' hotel – which means most rooms share outside bathrooms. It's the best deal in downtown Ashland, with 24 quaint vintage rooms (no TVs), a nice lobby and a historical feel. Park in back for fewer stairs to climb.

🍴 Eating & Drinking

There are plenty of great eating choices in Ashland, which levies a 5% restaurant tax. Dinner reservations in summer are a good idea at the fancier spots.

Morning Glory CAFE $
(✍541-488-8636; 1149 Siskiyou Blvd; mains $11-14; ⊘8am-1:30pm) This colorful, casual cafe is one of Ashland's best breakfast joints. Creative dishes include the Alaskan crab omelet, vegetarian hash with roasted chilis, and shrimp cakes with poached eggs. For lunch there's gourmet salad and sandwiches. Go early or late to avoid a long wait.

Agave MEXICAN $
(✍541-488-1770; www.agavetaco.net; 92 N Main St; tacos $3-4.25; ⊘11am-10pm Sun-Thu, to 11pm Fri & Sat) Tasty and creative tacos are cooked

up at this popular restaurant. There's the regular stuff such as *carnitas* and grilled chicken, but for something more exotic go for the shredded duck or sautéed main lobster ($8.25). A few salads and tamales, too.

Standing Stone Brewery　　　AMERICAN $
(☑541-482-2448; www.standingstonebrewing. com; 101 Oak St; mains $9-15; ⊙11am-midnight) Popular and hip brewery-restaurant with gourmet burgers, salads, sandwiches and wood-fired pizzas, along with a few seafood dishes. Wash it all down with some microbrews or a cocktail. Great back patio.

Caldera Tap House　　　　BREWERY
(☑541-482-4677; www.calderabrewing.com; 590 Clover Lane; ⊙11am-11pm) This bright and airy brewery-restaurant just off I-5 has pleasant outdoor seating and views of the countryside. It serves dishes such as pizza, housemade gnocchi, flat-iron steak and white truffle mac 'n' cheese (mains $10 to $21). Wash it all down with one of 40 beers on tap. Also located at 31 Water St in downtown Ashland, but the vibe is more local and the atmosphere darker.

❶ Information

Ashland Chamber of Commerce (☑541-482-3486; www.ashlandchamber.com; 110 E Main St; ⊙9am-5pm Mon-Fri) There is also an information booth at the Plaza (open summer weekends only).

Jacksonville

This small but endearing ex-gold-prospecting town is the oldest settlement in southern Oregon and a National Historic Landmark. The main drag is lined with well-preserved buildings dating from the 1880s, now converted into boutiques and galleries. Music-lovers shouldn't miss the September **Britt Festival** (www.brittfest.org; ⊙Jun-Sep), a world-class musical experience with top-name performers. Seek more enlightenment at the **Chamber of Commerce** (☑541-899-8118; www.jacksonvilleoregon.org; 185 N Oregon St; ⊙10am-3pm daily May-Oct, Mon-Sat Nov-Apr).

Jacksonville is full of fancy B&Bs; for budget motels head 6 miles east to Medford. The **Jacksonville Inn** (☑541-899-1900; www. jacksonvilleinn.com; 175 E California St; d from $159; ❇☞❇) is the most pleasant abode, shoehorned downtown in an 1863 building

with regal antique-stuffed rooms. There's a fine restaurant on-site.

Wild Rogue Wilderness

Situated between the town of Grants Pass on I-5 and Gold Beach on the Oregon coast, the aptly named Wild Rogue Wilderness is anchored by the turbulent Rogue River, which cuts through 40 miles of untamed, roadless canyon. The area is known for challenging white-water rafting (classes III and IV) and long-distance hikes.

The humble city of **Grants Pass** is the gateway to adventures along the Rogue. For information, the **Chamber of Commerce** (☑541-450-6180; www.visitgrantspass.org; 1995 NW Vine St; ⊙8am-5pm Mon-Fri) is right off I-5, exit 58. For raft permits and backpacking advice, contact the Bureau of Land Management's **Smullin Visitors Center** (☑541-479-3735; www.blm.gov/or/resources/recreation/rogue; 14335 Galice Rd, Galice; ⊙7am-3pm mid-May–mid-Oct) in Galice, 16 miles northwest of Grants Pass.

Rafting the Rogue is legendary, but not for the faint of heart. A typical trip takes three days and costs around $1000. A good outfitter is **Rogue Wilderness Adventures** (☑800-336-1647; www.wildrogue.com; 325 Galice Rd, Merlin). Kayaking the river is equally exhilarating; for instruction and guidance, contact **Sundance Kayak**. (☑541-708-3601; www.sundancekayak.com; day trips from $95).

Another highlight of the region is the 42-mile **Rogue River Trail**, once a supply route from Gold Beach. The full trek takes four to five days; day hikers might aim for Whiskey Creek Cabin, a 6-mile round-trip from the Grave Creek trailhead. The trail is dotted with rustic lodges ($130 to $165 per person including meals; reservations required) – try **Black Bar** (☑541-479-6507; www.blackbarlodge. com; Merlin; s/d from $230/260). There are also primitive campgrounds along the way.

North Umpqua River

This 'Wild and Scenic' river boasts world-class fly-fishing, fine hiking and serene camping. The 79-mile **North Umpqua Trail** begins near Idleyld Park, 3 miles east of Glide, and passes through Steamboat en route to the Pacific Crest Trail. A popular sideline is pretty **Umpqua Hot Springs**, east of Steamboat near Toketee Lake. Not far away, stunning, two-tiered **Toketee Falls**

(113ft) flows over columnar basalt, while **Watson Falls** (272ft) is one of the highest waterfalls in Oregon. For information, stop by Glide's **Colliding Rivers Information Center** (✑541-496-0157; 18782 N Umpqua Hwy, Glide; ⊙9am-5pm May-Sep). Adjacent is the **North Umpqua Ranger District** (✑541-496-3532; 18782 N Umpqua Hwy, Glide; ⊙8am-4:30pm Mon-Fri).

Between Idleyld Park and Diamond Lake are dozens of riverside campgrounds; these include lovely **Susan Creek** and primitive **Boulder Flat** (no water). Area accommodations fill up quickly in summer; try the log-cabin-like rooms at **Dogwood Motel** (✑541-496-3403; www.dogwoodmotel.com; 28866 N Umpqua Hwy; d $70-75; ❋ 🛜 🐾).

Oregon Caves National Monument & Preserve

This very popular cave (there's only one) lies 19 miles east of Cave Junction on Hwy 46. Three miles of passages are explored via 90-minute cave tours that include 520 rocky steps and dripping chambers running along the River Styx. Dress warmly, wear shoes with good traction and be prepared to get dripped on.

Cave Junction, 28 miles south of Grants Pass on US 199 (Redwood Hwy), provides the region's services – though the best area sleeps are at the **Holiday Motel** (✑541-592-3003; www.holidaymotelkerby.com; 24810 Redwood Hwy; d $75-85; ❋ 🛜), two miles north in Kerby. For fancy lodgings right at the cave there's the impressive **Oregon Caves Chateau** (✑541-592-3400; www.oregoncaveschateau.com; 20000 Caves Hwy; r $109-199; ⊙May-Oct); grab a milkshake at the old-fashioned soda fountain here. Campers should head to **Cave Creek Campground** (✑541-592-4000; campsites $10), 14 miles up Hwy 46, about 4 miles from the cave.

Eastern Oregon

Oregon east of the Cascades bears little resemblance to its wetter western cohort, either physically or culturally. Few people live here – the biggest town, Pendleton, numbers only 20,000 – and the region hoards high plateaus, painted hills, alkali lakebeds and the country's deepest river gorge.

John Day Fossil Beds National Monument

Within the soft rocks and crumbly soils of John Day country lies one of the world's greatest fossil collections, laid down between six and 50 million years ago. Roaming the forests at the time were saber-toothed nimravids, pint-sized horses, bear-dogs and other early mammals.

The national monument includes 22 sq miles at three different units: Sheep Rock Unit, Painted Hills Unit and Clarno Unit. Each has hiking trails and interpretive displays. To visit all of the units in one day requires quite a bit of driving, as more than 100 slow miles of curvy roads separate the fossil beds – it's best to take it easy and spend the night somewhere.

Visit the excellent **Thomas Condon Paleontology Center** (✑541-987-2333; www.nps.gov/joda; 32651 Hwy 19, Kimberly; ⊙10am-5pm), 2 miles north of US 26 at the **Sheep Rock Unit**. Displays include a three-toed horse and petrified dung-beetle balls, along with many other fossils and geologic history exhibits. If you feel like walking, take the short hike up the Blue Basin Trail.

The **Painted Hills Unit**, near the town of Mitchell, consists of low-slung, colorfully banded hills formed about 30 million years ago. Ten million years older is the **Clarno Unit**, which exposes mud flows that washed over an Eocene-era forest and eroded into distinctive, sheer white cliffs topped with spires and turrets of stone.

Rafting is popular on the John Day River, the longest free-flowing river in the state. **Oregon River Experiences** (✑800-827-1358; www.oregonriver.com) offers trips of up to five days. There's also good fishing for smallmouth bass and rainbow trout; find out more at the Oregon Department of Fish & Wildlife (www.dfw.state.or.us).

Most towns in the area have at least one hotel; these include the atmospheric **Historic Oregon Hotel** (✑541-462-3027; www.theoregonhotel.net; 104 E Main St; dm $20, d $49-69; 🛜) in Mitchell and the economical **Dreamers Lodge** (✑800-654-2849; www.dreamerslodge.com; 144 N Canyon Blvd; d from $70; ❋ 🛜 🐾) in the town of John Day (which has most of the area's services). There are several public campgrounds in the area (sites $5), including **Lone Pine** and **Big Bend** on Hwy 402.

Wallowa Mountains Area

The Wallowa Mountains, with their glacier-hewn peaks and crystalline lakes, are among the most beautiful natural areas in Oregon. The only drawback is the large number of visitors who flock here in summer, especially in the pretty Wallowa Lake area. Escape them all on one of several long hikes into the nearby Eagle Cap Wilderness, such as the 6-mile one-way jaunt to Aneroid Lake or the 8-mile trek on the Ice Lake Trail.

Just north of the mountains, in the Wallowa Valley, Enterprise is a homely backcountry town with several motels; try the Ponderosa (541-426-3186; 102 E Greenwood St; d from $82;). If you like beer and good food, don't miss the town's microbrewery, Terminal Gravity Brewing (541-426-0158; www.terminalgravitybrewing.com; 803 SE School St; mains $9-12; 11am-9pm Sun-Tue, to 10pm Wed-Sat). Just 6 miles south is Enterprise's fancy cousin, the upscale town of Joseph. Expensive bronze galleries and artsy boutiques line the main strip, along with some good eateries.

Hells Canyon

North America's deepest river gorge (yes, even deeper than the Grand Canyon when measured from the highest mountain peak) provides visitors with some wild and scenic vistas. The mighty Snake River has taken 13 million years to carve its path through the high plateaus of eastern Oregon to its present depth of 8000ft. The canyon itself is a true wilderness bereft of roads, but open to the curious and the brave.

For perspective, drive 30 miles northeast from Joseph to Imnaha, where a slow-going 24-mile gravel road leads up to the excellent lookout at Hat Point. From here you can see the Wallowa Mountains, Idaho's Seven Devils, the Imnaha River and the wilds of the canyon itself. This road is open from late May until snowfall; give yourself two hours each way for the drive.

For white-water action and spectacular scenery, head down to Hells Canyon Dam, 25 miles north of the small community of Oxbow. A few miles past the dam, the road ends at the Hells Canyon Visitor Center (8am-4pm May-Sep), which has good advice on the area's campgrounds and hiking trails. Beyond here, the Snake River drops 1300ft in elevation through wild rapids accessible only by jet boat or raft. Hells Canyon Adventures (800-422-3568; www.hellscanyon adventures.com; jet-boat tours from $60; May-

Sep) is the main operator running raft trips and jet-boat tours (reservations required).

The area has many campgrounds. Just outside Imnaha is the beautiful Imnaha River Inn (541-577-6002; www.imnahariver inn.com; 73946 Rimrock Rd; s/d from $70/130), a B&B replete with Hemingway-esque animal trophies, while Oxbow has the good-value Hells Canyon B&B (541-785-3373; www. hcbb.us; 49922 Homestead Rd; s/d $80/90;). For more services, head to the towns of Enterprise, Joseph and Halfway.

Steens Mountain & Alvord Desert

The highest peak in southeastern Oregon, Steens Mountain (9773ft) is part of a massive, 30-mile-long fault-block range that was formed about 15 million years ago. On the western slope of the range, Ice Age glaciers bulldozed trenches that formed massive U-shaped gorges and hanging valleys. To the east, 'the Steens' – as the range is usually referred to – drop off to the Alvord Desert, 5000ft below.

Beginning in Frenchglen, the gravel 59-mile Steens Mountain Loop Rd is Oregon's highest road and offers the range's best sights with its awesome overlooks, and also has access to camping and hiking trails. You'll see sagebrush, bands of junipers and aspen forests, and finally fragile rocky tundra at the top. Kiger Gorge Viewpoint is especially stunning; it's 25 miles up from Frenchglen. It takes about three hours all the way around if you're just driving through, but you'll want to see the sights, so give yourself much more time. You can also see the eastern side of the Steens via the Fields-Denio Rd, which goes through the Alvord Desert between Hwys 205 and 78. Take a full tank of gas and plenty of water, and be prepared for weather changes at any time of year.

Frenchglen (population 12) has the charming Frenchglen Hotel (541-493-2825; www. frenchglenhotel.com; 39184 Hwy 205; d from $75; mid-Mar–Oct;) with its small dining room (reserve for dinners), a small store with seasonal gas pump and not much else. There are camping options on the Steens Mountain Loop Rd, such as the BLM's pretty Page Springs, open year-round. A few other campgrounds (sites $6 to $8), further into the loop, are very pleasant, but accessible in summer only. Water is available at all of these campgrounds. Free backcountry camping is also allowed in the Steens. For more accommodation information in the region, check www. steensmountain.net/lodging.htm.

Rocky Mountains

Best Places to Eat

➜ Root Down (p241)

➜ Salt (p248)

➜ Rickshaw (p298)

➜ Sweet Melissa's (p273)

➜ Silk Road (p291)

Best Places to Sleep

➜ Curtis (p239)

➜ Boise Guest House (p296)

➜ Chautauqua Lodge (p246)

➜ Alpine House (p275)

➜ Old Faithful Inn (p282)

Why Go?

The high backbone of the lower 48, the Rockies are nature on steroids, with rows of snowcapped peaks, rugged canyons and wild rivers running buckshot over the western states. With its beauty and vitality, it's no wonder that 100 years ago, this region beckoned ailing patients with last-ditch hopes for cures.

The healing power of the Rocky Mountains persists. You can choose between tranquillity (try Wyoming, the USA's least-populated state) and adrenaline (measured in vertical drop). Locals love a good frozen, wet or mud-spattered adventure and, with plenty of climbing, skiing and white-water paddling, it's easy to join in. Afterwards, relax by soaking in hot springs under a roof of stars, sipping cold microbrews or feasting farm-to-table style.

Lastly, don't miss the super-sized charms of Yellowstone, Rocky Mountain, Grand Teton and Glacier National Parks, where the big five (grizzly bears, moose, bison, mountain lions and wolves) still roam wild.

When to Go
Denver

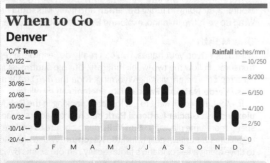

Jun-Aug Long days of sunshine for biking, hiking, farmers markets and summer festivals.

Sep & Oct Fall foliage coincides with terrific lodging deals.

Jan & Feb Snow-dusted peaks, powdery slopes and deluxe après-ski parties.

History

Before the late 18th century, when French trappers and Spaniards stepped in, the Rocky Mountain area was a land of many tribes, including the Nez Percé, the Shoshone, the Crow, the Lakota and the Ute.

Meriwether Lewis and William Clark claimed enduring fame after the USA bought almost all of present-day Montana, Wyoming and eastern Colorado in the 1803 Louisiana Purchase. Their epic survey covered 8000 miles in three years. Their success urged on other adventurers, setting migration in motion. Wagon trains voyaged to the Rockies right into the 20th century, only temporarily slowed by the completion of the Transcontinental Railroad across southern Wyoming in the late 1860s.

To accommodate settlers, the US purged the western frontier of the Spanish, the British and, in a truly shameful era, most of the Native American population. The government signed endless treaties to defuse Native American objections to increasing settlement but always reneged and shunted tribes onto smaller reservations. Gold-miners' incursions into Native American territory in Montana and the building of US Army forts along the Bozeman Trail ignited a series of wars with the Lakota, Cheyenne, Arapaho and others.

Gold and silver mania preceded Colorado's entry to statehood in 1876. Statehood soon followed for Montana (1889), Wyoming (1890) and Idaho (1890). Miners, white farmers and ranchers were the people with power in the late 19th century.

Mining, grazing and timber played major roles in regional economic development, sparking growth in financial and industrial support. They also subjected the region to boom-and-bust cycles by unsustainable resource management.

ROCKY MOUNTAINS IN...

Two Weeks

Start your Rocky Mountain odyssey in the **Denver** area. Go tubing, vintage-clothes shopping or biking in outdoor-mad, boho **Boulder**, then soak up the liberal rays eavesdropping at a sidewalk cafe. Enjoy the vistas of the **Rocky Mountain National Park** before heading west on I-70 to play in the mountains around **Breckenridge**, which also has some of the best beginner slopes in Colorado. Go to ski and mountain-bike mecca **Steamboat Springs** before crossing the border into Wyoming.

Get a taste of prairie-town life in **Laramie**, then stop in **Lander**, rock-climbing destination extraordinaire. Continue north to chic **Jackson** and the majestic **Grand Teton National Park** before hitting iconic **Yellowstone National Park**. Save at least three days for exploring this geyser-packed wonderland.

Cross the state line into 'big sky country' and slowly make your way northwest through Montana, stopping in funky **Bozeman** and lively **Missoula** before visiting **Flathead Lake**. Wrap up your trip in Idaho, exploring Basque culture in up-and-coming **Boise**.

One Month

With a month on your hands, you can really delve into the region's off-the-beaten-path treasures. Follow the two-week itinerary, but dip southwest in Colorado – a developing wine region – before visiting Wyoming. Ride the 4WD trails around **Ouray**. Be sure to visit **Mesa Verde National Park** and its ancient cliff dwellings.

In Montana, you'll want to get lost backpacking in the **Bob Marshall Wilderness Complex** and visit **Glacier National Park** before the glaciers disappear altogether. In Idaho, spend more time playing in **Sun Valley** and be sure to explore the shops, pubs and yummy organic restaurants in delightful little **Ketchum**. With a one-month trip, you also have time to drive along a few of Idaho's fantastically remote scenic byways. Make sure you cruise Hwy 75 from Sun Valley north to **Stanley**. Situated on the wide banks of the Salmon River, this stunning mountain hamlet is completely surrounded by national forestland and wilderness areas. Stanley is also blessed with world-class trout fishing and mild to wild rafting.

Take **Hwy 21** (the Ponderosa Pine Scenic Byway) from Stanley to Boise. This scenic drive takes you through miles of dense ponderosa forests and past some excellent, solitary riverside camping spots – some of which come with their own natural hot-springs pools.

After the economy boomed post-WWII, national parks started attracting vacationers. Tourism is now a leading industry in all four states, with the military trailing close behind, particularly in Colorado.

Land & Climate

Extending from Alaska's Brooks Range and Canada's Yukon Territory all the way to Mexico, the Rockies sprawl northwest to southeast, from the steep escarpment of Colorado's Front Range westward to Nevada's Great Basin. Their towering peaks and ridges form the Continental Divide: to the west, waters flow to the Pacific, and to the east, toward the Atlantic and the Gulf of Mexico.

For many travelers, the Rockies are a summer destination. It starts to feel summery around June, and the warm weather generally lasts until about mid-September (though warm outerwear is recommended). The winter, which brings in packs of powder hounds, doesn't usually hit until late November, though snowstorms can start in the mountains as early as September. Winter usually lasts until March or early April. In the mountains, the weather is constantly changing (snow in summer is not uncommon), so always be prepared. Fall, when the aspens flaunt their autumn gold, and early summer, when wildflowers bloom, are wonderful times to visit.

① Getting There & Around

Travel here takes time. The Rockies are sparsely developed, with attractions spread across long distances and linked by roads that meander between mountains and canyons. With limited public transportation, touring in a private vehicle is best. After all, road-tripping is one of the reasons to explore this scenic region.

In rural areas services are few and far between – the I-80 across Wyoming is a notorious offender. It's not unusual to go more than 100 miles between gas stations. When in doubt, fill up.

The main travel hub is Denver International Airport (p245), although if you are coming on a domestic flight, check out **Colorado Springs Airport** (☑719-550-1900; www.springsgov. com; 7770 Milton E Proby Pkwy; ☎) as well: fares are often lower, it's quicker to navigate than DIA and it's nearly as convenient. Both Denver and Colorado Springs offer flights on smaller planes to cities and resort towns around the region – Jackson, WY, Boise, ID, Bozeman, MT, and Aspen, CO, are just a few options. Salt Lake City, UT, also has connections with destinations in all four states.

Greyhound (☑800-231-2222; www.greyhound.com) has fixed routes throughout the Rockies, and offers the most comprehensive bus service. Two **Amtrak** (☑toll-free 800-872-7245; www.amtrak.com) routes serve the region:

California Zephyr Daily between Emeryville, CA (in the Bay Area), and Chicago, IL, with six stops in Colorado, including Denver, Fraser–Winter Park, Glenwood Springs and Grand Junction.

Empire Builder Daily from Seattle, WA, or Portland, OR, to Chicago, IL, with 12 stops in Montana (including Whitefish and East and West Glacier) and one in Idaho (Sandpoint).

COLORADO

From double-diamond runs to stiff espressos, Colorado is all about vigor. This is also the state graced with the greatest concentration of high peaks – dubbed 14ers for their height over 14,000ft.

But it isn't all about the great outdoors. Universities and high-tech hubs show the state's industrious side, though even workaholics might call in sick when snow starts falling.

① Information

Colorado Road Conditions (☑877-315-7623; www.state.co.us) Highway advisories.
Colorado State Parks (☑303-470-1144; www.parks.state.co.us) Tent sites cost from $10 to $20 per night, depending on facilities, while RV hook-ups are $24 per night. Advance reservations for specific campsites are taken, and are subject to an $10 nonrefundable booking fee.
Colorado Travel & Tourism Authority (☑800-265-6723; www.colorado.com) State-wide tourism information.

Denver

Denver's mile-high gravity is growing, pulling all objects in the Rocky Mountain West toward the glistening downtown towers, hopped-up brewpubs, hemped-out cannabis dispensaries, mountain trails, and growing western cosmopolitanism that's fostered a burgeoning arts scene and brought great restaurants and hip bars to a cow town gone worldwide crazy.

While most of the tourist action centers on the Downtown and Lower Downtown (LoDo) Districts, travelers in the know will also explore outlying neighborhoods like Highlands, Washington Park, Cherry Creek, Five Points, South Santa Fe and the River North (RiNo).

Rocky Mountains Highlights

1 Spotting bears, bison and geysers at **Yellowstone National Park** (p277).

2 Reveling in Hollywood-gone-cowboy in the party resort of **Aspen** (p257).

3 Hiking and climbing the craggy wilderness of **Grand Teton National Park** (p284).

4 Paddling top-notch white water at the **Middle Fork of the Salmon River** (p299).

5 Getting your groove on in the outdoor mecca of **Boulder** (p245).

6 Roaming the San Juan range's picturesque Wild West towns in **Southern Colorado** (p263).

300 km
180 miles

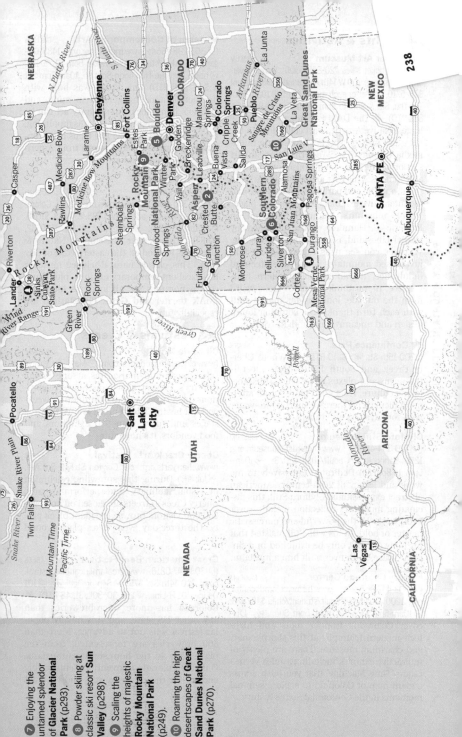

7 Enjoying the untamed splendor of **Glacier National Park** (p293).

8 Powder skiing at classic ski resort **Sun Valley** (p298).

9 Scaling the heights of majestic **Rocky Mountain National Park** (p249).

10 Roaming the high desertscapes of **Great Sand Dunes National Park** (p270).

238

Sights & Activities

★ Denver Art Museum   MUSEUM

(DAM; ✪ ticket sales 720-865-5000; www.denver-artmuseum.org; 100 W 14th Ave; adult/child/student $13/5/10, 1st Sat of each month free; ⊙10am-5pm Tue-Thu, Sat & Sun, to 8pm Fri; P⬥; ☐9, 16, 52, 83L RTD) ✦ The DAM is home to one of the largest Native American art collections in the USA and puts on special avant-garde multimedia exhibits. The Western American Art section of the permanent collection is justifiably famous. This isn't an old, stodgy art museum, and the best part of a visit is diving into the interactive exhibits – kids love this place.

The museum's landmark $110-million Frederic C Hamilton wing, designed by Daniel Libeskind, is quite simply awesome. Whether you see it as expanding crystals, juxtaposed mountains or just architectural indulgence, it's an angular modern masterpiece. If you think the place looks weird from the outside, look inside: shapes shift with each turn thanks to a combination of design and uncanny natural-light tricks.

★ Confluence Park   PARK

(2200 15th St; ⬥; ☐10 RTD) ✦ Where Cherry Creek and South Platte River meet is the nexus and plexus of Denver's sunshine-loving culture. It's a good place for an afternoon picnic, and there's a short white-water park for kayakers and tubers.

Clyfford Still Museum   MUSEUM

(✪720-354-4880; www.clyffordstillmuseum.org; 1250 Bannock St; adult/child $10/3; ⊙10am-5pm, to 8pm Fri) Dedicated exclusively to the work and legacy of 20th-century American abstract expressionist Clyfford Still, this fascinating museum's collection includes over 2400 works by the powerful and narcissistic master of bold. In his will, Still insisted that his body of work only be exhibited in a singular space, so Denver built him a museum.

History Colorado Center   MUSEUM

(✪303-447-8679; www.historycoloradocenter.org; 1200 Broadway; adult/student/child $10/8/8; ⊙10am-5pm Mon-Sat, noon-5pm Sun; P) Discover Colorado's frontier roots and high-tech modern triumphs at this sharp, smart and charming museum. There are plenty of interactive exhibits, including a Jules Verne-esque 'Time Machine' that you push across a giant map of Colorado to explore seminal moments in the Centennial State's history.

Museum of Contemporary Art   GALLERY

(✪303-298-7554; www.mcadenver.org; 1485 Delgany St; adult/student/child/after 5pm $8/5/1/5; ⊙noon-7pm Tue-Thu, noon-8pm Fri, 10am-7pm Sat & Sun; ☐6 RTD) This space was built with interaction and engagement in mind, and Denver's home for contemporary art can be provocative, delightful or a bit disappointing, depending on the show. The focus is on contemporary mixed-media works from American and international artists.

Denver Museum of Nature & Science   MUSEUM

(✪303-370-6000; www.dmns.org; 2001 Colorado Blvd; museum adult/child $13/8, IMAX $10/8, Planetarium $5/4; ⊙9am-5pm; P⬥; ☐20, 32, 40 RTD) The Denver Museum of Nature & Science is located on the eastern edge of City Park. This classic natural-science museum has excellent temporary exhibits, plus those cool panoramas we all loved as kids. The IMAX theater and Gates Planetarium are especially fun.

✪✪ Festivals & Events

Cinco de Mayo   CULTURAL

(www.cincodemayodenver.com; ⊙May; ⬥) Enjoy salsa music and margaritas at one of the country's biggest Cinco de Mayo celebrations, held over two days on the first weekend in May in Civic Center Park. With three stages and more than 350 exhibitors and food vendors, it's huge fun.

Cherry Creek Arts Festival   ARTS

(www.cherryarts.org; cnr Clayton St & E 3rd Ave; ⊙Jul; ⬥) During this sprawling celebraion of visual, culinary and performing arts, Cherry Creek's streets are closed off and over 250,000 visitors browse the giant block party. The three-day event takes place around July 4.

Great American Beer Festival   BEER

(✪303-447-0816; www.greatamericanbeerfestival.com; 700 14th St; $75; ⊙Sep or Oct; ⬥; ☐101 D-Line, 101 H-Line, ☐1, 8, 30, 30L, 31, 48 RTD) ✦ Colorado has more microbreweries than any other US state, and this hugely popular festival sells out in advance. More than 500 breweries are represented, from the big players to the home-brew enthusiasts. Only the Colorado Convention Center is big enough for these big brewers and their fat brews.

🛏 Sleeping

11th Avenue Hotel HOTEL **$**
(📞303-894-0529; www.11thavenuehotel.com; 1112 Broadway; dm $19-22, r with/without bath $45/39; 🌐❄🏠) This budget hotel has a good location for art lovers in the Golden Triangle district. The lobby looks vaguely like something from a Jim Jarmusch movie. The upstairs rooms, some with attached bathrooms, are bare but clean. It's safe, secure and a decent place for budget travelers.

Denver International Youth Hostel HOSTEL **$**
(📞303-832-9996; www.youthhostels.com/denver; 630 E 16th Ave; dm $19; ℗@🏠; 🚌15, 15L, 20 RTD) If cheap really matters, then the Denver International Youth Hostel might be the place for you. It's basic and vaguely chaotic, but it has a ramshackle charm and a great downtown location. All dorms have attached bathroom facilities and the common area in the basement has a large-screen TV, library and computers for guests to use.

★Curtis BOUTIQUE HOTEL **$$**
(📞303-571-0300; www.thecurtis.com; 1405 Curtis St; d $159-279; 🌐❄@🏠; 🚌15 RTD) It's like stepping into a doo-wop Warhol wonderworld at this temple to postmodern pop culture. Attention to detail – be it through the service or the decor in the rooms – is paramount at the Curtis, a one-of-a-kind hotel in Denver.
There are 13 themed floors and each is devoted to a different genre of American pop culture. Rooms are spacious and very mod without being too out there to sleep. The hotel's refreshingly different take on sleeping may seem too kitschy for some – you can get a wake-up call from Elvis – but if you're tired of the same old international brands, this joint in the heart of downtown might be your tonic.

★Queen Anne Bed & Breakfast Inn B&B **$$**
(📞303-296-6666; www.queenannebnb.com; 2147 Tremont Pl; r $135-215; ℗🌐❄🏠) 🌿 Soft chamber music wafting through public areas, fresh flowers, manicured gardens and evening wine tastings create a romantic ambience at this ecoconscious B&B in two late-1800s Victorian homes. Featuring period antiques, private hot tubs and exquisite hand-painted murals, each room has its own personality.

Patterson Historic Inn HISTORIC HOTEL **$$**
(📞303-955-5142; www.pattersoninn.com; 420 E 11th Ave; r from $169; ❄@🏠) This 1891 grande dame was once a senator's home. It's now

COLORADO FACTS

Nickname Centennial State

Population 5 million

Area 104,247 sq miles

Capital city Denver (population 649,495)

Other cities Boulder (population 103,000), Colorado Springs (population 439,800)

Sales tax 2.9% state tax, plus individual city taxes

Birthplace of Ute tribal leader Chief Ouray (1833–80); *South Park* creator Trey Parker (b 1969); actor Amy Adams (b 1974); climber Tommy Caldwell (b 1978)

Home of Naropa University (made famous by Beat poets), powder slopes, boutique beers

Politics Swing state

Famous for Sunny days (300 per year), the highest-altitude vineyards and longest ski run in the continental USA

Kitschiest souvenir Deer-hoof bottle opener

Driving distances Denver to Vail 100 miles, Boulder to Rocky Mountain National Park 38 miles

one of the best historic bed-and-breakfasts in town. The gardens are limited, but the Victorian charm, sumptuous breakfast and well-appointed chambers in the nine-room château will delight. Rooms come with modern touches such as silk robes, down comforters and flat-screen TVs.

Brown Palace Hotel HISTORIC HOTEL **$$$**
(📞303-297-3111; www.brownpalace.com; 321 17th St; r from $299; ℗🌐❄@🏠) Standing agape under the stained-glass crowned atrium, it's clear why this palace is shortlisted among the country's elite historic hotels. There's deco artwork, a four-star spa, imported marble and staff who discreetly float down the halls.

🍴 Eating

While the downtown restaurants offer the greatest depth and variety in Denver, it's also worth heading out to strollable neighborhoods like Highlands, Cherry Creek,

Denver

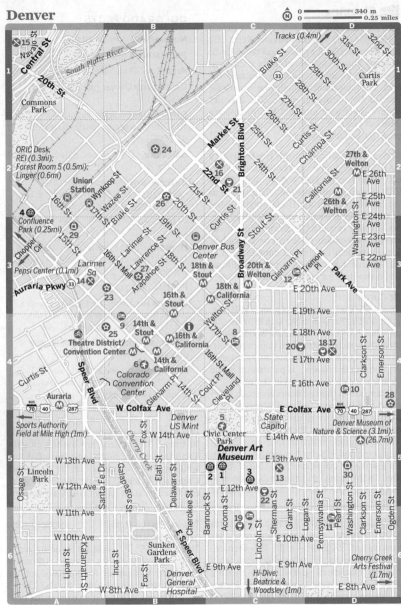

ROCKY MOUNTAINS DENVER

Uptown, Five Points and Washington Park, where little five-block commercial strips hold some of Denver's best eateries. Check out www.5280.com or www.diningout.com/denver for new eats.

Snooze BREAKFAST $

(☑303-297-0700; www.snoozeeatery.com; 2262 Larimer St; mains $6-12; ⊙6:30am-2:30pm Mon-Fri, 7am-2:30pm Sat & Sun; ⊛⊕) ⊘ This retro-styled cheery breakfast-and-brunch spot is one of the hottest post-party breakfast

Denver

joints in town. It dishes up spectacularly crafted breakfast burritos and a smokin' salmon benedict. The coffee's always good, but you have the option of an early-morning Bloody Mary. The wait can be up to an hour on weekends!

City O' City VEGETARIAN $
(✆303-831-6443; www.cityocitydenver.com; 206 E 13th Ave; mains $8-15; ☺7am-2am Mon-Fri, 8am-2am Sat, 8am-midnight Sun; ✍💺; 📵2, 9, 52 RTD) ✐ This popular vegan/vegetarian restaurant mixes stylish decor with an innovative spin on greens, grains, faux meat and granola. The menu offers tapas boards, big salads, some good transnational noodle dishes and the best vegan pizza pie in D-Town...the bar has drinks for accompaniment. The comfy dining room also features shifting artworks by local artists.

★**Beatrice & Woodsley** TAPAS $$
(✆303-777-3505; www.beatriceandwoodsley. com; 38 S Broadway; small plates $9-13; ☺5-11pm Mon-Fri, 10am-2pm & 5-10pm Sat & Sun; 📵0 RTD) Beatrice and Woodsley is the most artfully designed dining room in Denver. Chainsaws are buried into the wall to support shelves, there's an aspen growing through the back of the dining room and the feel is that of a mountain cabin being elegantly reclaimed by nature. The menu of small plates is whimsical and European inspired.

★**Steuben's Food Service** AMERICAN $$
(✆303-803-1001; www.steubens.com; 523 E 17th Ave; mains $8-21; ☺11am-11pm Sun-Thu, to midnight Fri & Sat; 💺) ✐ Although styled as a midcentury drive-in, the upscale treatment of comfort food (mac and cheese, fried chicken, lobster rolls) and the solar-powered kitchen demonstrate Steubens' contemporary smarts. In summer, open garage doors lining the street create a breezy atmosphere and after 10pm it has the most unbeatable deal around: a burger, hand-cut fries and beer for $7.

★**Root Down** MODERN AMERICAN $$$
(✆303-993-4200; www.rootdowndenver.com; 1600 W 33rd Ave; small plates $7-17, mains $18-28; ☺5-10pm Sun-Thu, 5-11pm Fri & Sat, 10am-2:30pm Sat & Sun; ✍) ✐ In a converted gas station, chef Justin Cucci has undertaken one of the city's most ambitious culinary concepts, marrying sustainable 'field-to-fork' practices, high-concept culinary fusions and a low-impact, energy-efficient ethos. The menu changes seasonally, but consider yourself lucky if it includes the sweet-potato falafel or hoisin-duck confit sliders.

★**Rioja** MODERN AMERICAN $$$
(✆303-820-2282; www.riojadenver.com; 1431 Larimer St; mains $18-29; ☺11:30am-2:30pm Wed-Fri, 10am-2:30pm Sat & Sun, 5-10pm daily; ✳✍; 📵2, 12, 15, 16th St Shuttle) This is one of Denver's

most innovative restaurants. Smart, busy and upscale, yet relaxed and casual – just like Colorado – Rioja features modern cuisine inspired by Italian and Spanish traditions and powered by modern culinary flavors.

🍷 Drinking & Nightlife

Top nightlife districts include Uptown for gay bars and a young professional crowd, LoDo for loud sports bars, heavy drinking and dancing, River North for hipsters, Lower Highlands for an eclectic mix and sweet decks, and Broadway and Colfax for old school wannabees.

★ Forest Room 5   BAR
(☑303-433-7001; www.forestroom5.com; 2532 15th St; ☺4pm-2am) One of the best damn bars in Denver, this LoHi (that's Lower Highlands) juggernaut has an outdoor patio with fire circles (where you can smoke!), streams and a funked-out Airstream. It plays kitsch movies nightly and has art openings in the upstairs area. It's an odd mix of Grizzly Adams meets Andy Warhol – and it works.

Linger   LOUNGE
(☑303-993-3120; www.lingerdenver.com; 2030 W 30th Ave; mains $8-14; ☺11:30am-2:30pm & 4pm-2am Tue-Sat, 10am-2:30pm Sun) This rambling LoHi complex sits in the former Olinger mortuary. Come nighttime, they black out the 'O' and it just becomes Linger. There's an interesting international menu, but most people come for the tony feel and light-up-the-night rooftop bar, which even has a replica of the RV made famous by the Bill Murray smash *Stripes*.

Bar Standard   CLUB
(☑303-534-0222; www.coclubs.com; 1037 Broadway; ☺8pm-2am Fri & Sat; ☐0 RTD) From the sleek deco interior to the DJ roster that spins *way* outside the typically mindless thump, Bar Standard is an inimitable gem in Denver's nightclub scene. It's ice cold without the attitude, and when the right DJ is on the tables it can be some of the best dancing in town.

Tracks   GAY
(☑303-863-7326; www.tracksdenver.com; 3500 Walnut St; ☺9pm-2am Fri & Sat, hours vary Sun-Thu) Denver's best gay dance club has an 18-and-up night on Thursdays, Friday drag shows and lesbian nights (just once a month). There's a definite pretty-boy focus, with good music and a scene to match. Saturday is the biggest dance night.

Denver Wrangler   GAY
(☑303-837-1075; www.denverwrangler.com; 1700 Logan St; ☺11am-2am; ☐101 RTD) Denver Wrangler attracts an amiable crowd of gay male professionals after work, and its central location endows Denver's premier bear bar with a flirty pick-up scene on the weekend. The sidewalk seating is a plus.

Great Divide Brewing Company   BREWERY
(www.greatdivide.com; 2201 Arapahoe St; ☺2-8pm Mon & Tue, to 10pm Wed-Sat) This excellent local brewery does well to skip the same old burger menu and the fancy digs to keep its focus on what it does best: crafting exquisite beer. Bellying up to the bar, looking onto the copper kettles and sipping Great Divide's spectrum of seasonal brews is an experience that will make a beer drinker's eyes light up.

Ace   BAR
(☑303-800-7705; www.acedenver.com; 501 E 17th Ave; ☺11am-midnight Mon-Fri, 2pm-midnight Sat & Sun) The best ping-pong bar in Denver. Come here for fun tournaments, hipster sightings, great food and a raucous indoor-outdoor party that takes you deep into the pong underground – street rules apply.

The Church   CLUB
(www.coclubs.com; 1160 Lincoln St; ☺9pm-2am Thu-Sun) There's nothing like ordering a stiff drink inside a cathedral built in 1865. Yes, this club, which draws a large and diverse crowd, is in a former house of the Lord. Lit by hundreds of altar candles and flashing blue strobe lights, the Church has three dance floors, acrobats, a couple of lounges and even a sushi bar!

☆ Entertainment

To find out what's happening with music, theater and other performing arts, pick up a free copy of **Westword** (www.westword.com).

★ Denver Performing Arts Complex   PERFORMING ARTS
(☑720-865-4220; www.artscomplex.com; cnr 14th & Champa Sts) This massive complex – one of the largest of its kind – occupies four city blocks and houses several major theaters, including the historic Ellie Caulkins Opera House and the Seawell Grand Ballroom. It's also home to the Colorado Ballet, Denver Center for the Performing Arts, Opera Colorado and the Colorado Symphony Orchestra.

WORTH A TRIP

BEST MILE-HIGH DAY HIKES

There are hundreds of day hikes within an hour of Denver. Here are a few we like:

Jefferson County Open Space Parks (www.jeffco.us/openspace; ♿) Top picks include Matthews Winters, Mount Falcon, Elk Meadow and Lair o' the Bear.

Golden Gate Canyon State Park (☎303-582-3707; www.parks.state.us/parks; 92 Crawford Gulch Rd, Golden; entrance/camping $7/24; ☺5am-10pm) Halfway between Denver and Nederland, this 12,000-acre state park can be reached in about 45 minutes.

Staunton State Park (☎303-816-0912; www.parks.state.co.us/parks) Colorado's newest state park sits on a historic ranch site 40 miles west of Denver, on Hwy 285 between Conifer and Bailey.

Waterton Canyon (☎303-634-3745; www.denverwater.org/recreation/watertoncanyon; Kassler Center) South of the city, just west of Chatfield Reservoir, this pretty canyon has an easy 6.5-mile trail to the Strontia Springs Dam. From there, the **Colorado Trail** (CTF; ☎303-384-3729; www.coloradotrail.org; PO Box 260876; ☺9am-5pm Mon-Fri) will take you all the way to Durango!

★**El Chapultepec**   JAZZ
(☎303-295-9126; www.thepeclodo.com; 1962 Market St; ☺11am-2am, music from 9pm) This smoky, old-school jazz joint attracts a diverse mix of people. Since it opened in 1951, Frank Sinatra, Tony Bennett and Ella Fitzgerald have played here, as have Jagger and Richards. Local jazz bands take the tiny stage nightly, but you never know who might drop by.

Hi-Dive   LIVE MUSIC
(☎303-733-0230; www.hi-dive.com; 7 S Broadway) Local rock heroes and touring indie bands light up the stage at the Hi-Dive, a venue at the heart of Denver's local music scene. During big shows it gets deafeningly loud, cheek-to-jowl with hipsters and humid as an armpit. In other words, it's perfect.

Grizzly Rose   LIVE MUSIC
(☎303-295-1330; www.grizzlyrose.com; 5450 N Valley Hwy; ☺from 6pm Tue-Sun; ♿) This is one kick-ass honky-tonk – 40,000 sq ft of hot live music – attracting real cowboys from as far as Cheyenne. The Country Music Association called it the best country bar in America. If you've never experienced line dancing, then put on the boots, grab the Stetson and let loose.

Ogden Theatre   LIVE MUSIC
(☎303-832-1874; www.ogdentheatre.net; 935 E Colfax Ave; ♿; 🚌15 RTD) One of Denver's best live-music venues, the Ogden Theatre has a checkered past. Built in 1917, it was derelict for many years and might have been dozed in the early 1990s, but it's now listed on the National Register of Historic Places. Bands such as Edward Sharpe & the Magnetic Zeros and Lady Gaga have played here.

Comedy Works   COMEDY
(☎303-595-3637; www.comedyworks.com; 1226 15th St; 🚌6, 9, 10, 15L, 20, 28, 32, 44, 44L RTD) Denver's best comedy club occupies a basement space in Larimer Sq (enter down a set of stairs at the corner of Larimer and 15th) and routinely brings in up-and-coming yucksters from around the country. It can be a bit cramped if you're claustrophobic, but the seats are comfortable and the quality of acts is excellent.

Lannie's Clocktower Cabaret   CABARET
(☎303-293-0075; www.lannies.com; 1601 Arapahoe St; tickets $25-40; ☺1-5pm Tue, to 11pm Wed & Thu, to 1:30am Fri & Sat; 🚌Arapahoe) Bawdy, naughty and strangely romantic, Lannie's Clocktower Cabaret is a wild-child standout among LoDo's rather straight-laced (or at least straight) night spots. A table right up near the front will get you in the sparkling heart of the action, and if you parse the schedule, you might get a glance at the sexiest drag queens in Denver.

Coors Field   BASEBALL
(☎800-388-7625; www.mlb.com/col/ballpark/; 2001 Blake St; ♿) Denver is a city known for manic sports fans, and it boasts five pro teams. The Colorado Rockies play baseball at the highly rated Coors Field. Tickets for the outfield – the Rockpile – cost $4. Not a bad deal.

LIVE AT RED ROCKS!

Red Rocks Amphitheatre (☑303-640-2637; www.redrocksonline.com; 18300 W Alameda Pkwy; ☺5am-11pm; ♿) is set between 400ft-high red sandstone rocks 15 miles southwest of Denver. Acoustics are so good many artists record live albums here. The 9000-seat theater offers stunning views and draws big-name bands all summer.

When the setting sun brings out a rich, orange glow from the rock formations and the band on stage launches into the right tune, Red Rocks Amphitheatre is a captivating experience, wholly befitting the park's 19th-century name, 'Garden of Angels.'

The natural amphitheater, once a Ute camping spot, has been used for performances for decades, but it wasn't until 1936 that members of the Civilian Conservation Corps built a formal outdoor venue with seats and a stage. Though it originally hosted classical performances and military bands, it debuted as a rock venue with style; the first rock quartet on this stage was John, Paul, George and Ringo.

You scored tickets? Great. Now for the nitty gritty. Eat beforehand, as the food vendors are predictably expensive. You can bring a small cooler into the show, as long as there's no booze and it'll fit under your seat. Climbing on the stunning formations is prohibited; however, 250-plus steps lead to the top of the theater, offering views of both the park and Denver, miles off to the east.

Amazingly, Red Rocks Park can be almost as entertaining when it's silent. The amphitheater is only a tiny part of the 600-acre space. There are miles of hiking trails, opportunities to lose the crowds and take in lovely rock formations. There's information about the entire area on the website.

Sports Authority Field at Mile High
STADIUM

(☑720-258-3000; www.sportsauthorityfieldatmile-high.com; 1701 S Bryant St; ♿) The much-lauded Denver Broncos football team and the Denver Outlaws lacrosse team play at Mile High Stadium, 1 mile west of downtown. This stadium also has an eclectic schedule of events, including major rock concerts for superstars such as U2. Stadium tours are organized through the **Colorado Sports Hall of Fame** (☑720-258-3888; www.coloradosports.org; 1701 Bryant St; ☺10am-3pm Thu-Sun Sep-May, 10am-3pm Tue-Sat Jun-Aug; ♿; ☐16, 16L, 28, 30, 30L, 31, 36L RTD) FREE.

Pepsi Center
STADIUM

(☑303-405-1111; www.pepsicenter.com; 1000 Chopper Circle) The mammoth Pepsi Center hosts the Denver Nuggets basketball team, the Colorado Mammoth of the National Lacrosse League and the Colorado Avalanche hockey team. Off season it's a mega concert venue.

🔒 Shopping

Head to the pedestrian mall on 16th St or LoDo for downtown shopping. Cherry Creek, Highlands Square and South Broadway are other top shopping districts.

★Tattered Cover Bookstore
BOOKS

(www.tatteredcover.com; 1628 16th St; ☺6:30am-9pm Mon-Fri, 9am-9pm Sat, 10am-6pm Sun) There are plenty of places to curl up with a book in Denver's beloved independent bookstore, which has two locations in the Denver area. Bursting with new and used books, it has a good stock of regional travel guides and nonfiction titles dedicated to the Western states and Western folklore.

★REI
OUTDOOR EQUIPMENT

(Recreational Equipment Incorporated; ☑303-756-3100; www.rei.com; 1416 Platte St; ♿) The flagship store of this outdoor-equipment super supplier is an essential stop if you are heading to the mountains or just cruising through Confluence Park. In addition to top gear for camping, cycling, climbing and skiing, it has a rental department, maps and the Pinnacle, a 47ft-high indoor structure of simulated red sandstone for climbing and rappelling.

Wax Trax Records
MUSIC

(☑303-831-7246; www.waxtraxrecords.com; 638 E 13th Ave; ☐2, 10, 15, 15L RTD) For more than 30 years, Wax Trax Records has been trading at this Denver location, stocking a huge quantity of CDs, DVDs, vinyl and music paraphernalia. Indie, alternative, punk, goth, folk, rock, hip-hop, jazz, reggae – anything that's a bit edgy you'll either find in store or it'll order for you.

ℹ Information

Visitors & Convention Bureau Information Center (☎ 303-892-1112; www.denver.org; 1600 California St; 🛜; 🖥 California) When you get to town, make for the largest and most centrally located information center, located on the 16th St Mall. You can load up on brochures and get information about local transportation. There's also a tourist info desk in the Colorado Convention Center.

ORIC Desk (Outdoor Recreation Information Center; ☑ REI main line 303-756-3100; www.oriconline.org; 1416 Platte St; 🛜) Inside REI, this information desk is a must for those looking to get out of town. It has maps and expert information on trip planning and safety information. The desk is staffed by volunteers, so hours vary wildly, but arriving on a weekend afternoon is a good bet.

ℹ Getting There & Away

Denver International Airport (DIA; ☑ 303-342-2000; www.flydenver.com; 8500 Peña Blvd; 🛜) is served by around 20 airlines and offers flights to nearly every major US city. Located 24 miles east of downtown, DIA is connected with I-70 exit 238 by 12-mile-long Peña Blvd. Tourist and airport information is available at a **booth** (☑ 303-342-2000) in the terminal's central hall.

Greyhound buses stop at **Denver Bus Center** (☎ 303-293-6555; 1055 19th St), which runs services to Boise (19 hours), Los Angeles (22 hours) and other destinations.

The **Colorado Mountain Express** (CME; ☑ 800-525-6363; www.coloradomountainexpress.com; DIA; 🛜) has shuttle service from DIA, downtown Denver or Morrison to Summit County, including Breckenridge and Keystone (2½ hours) and Vail (three hours).

Amtrak's *California Zephyr* runs daily between Chicago and San Francisco via Denver's **Union Station** (☑ Amtrak 800-872-7245; www.denverunionstation.org; cnr 17th & Wynkoop Sts; 🖥 31X, 40X, 80X, 86X, 120X RTD).

ℹ Getting Around

TO/FROM THE AIRPORT

Several transportation companies have booths near the baggage-claim area. Public **Regional Transit District** (RTD; ☑ 303-299-6000; www.rtd-denver.com) runs a SkyRide service to the airport from downtown Denver hourly ($9–13, about one hour) and Boulder (1½ hours). **Super-Shuttle** (☑ 303-370-1300; www.supershuttle.com) offers shared van services between the Denver area and the airport.

In early 2016 a transit center will open at DIA, linking the airport with downtown Denver via a 35-minute commuter rail trip.

BICYCLE

BikeDenver.org (www.bikedenver.org) or **City of Denver** (www.denvergov.org) have downloadable bike maps for the city.

Denver B-Cycle (http://denver.bcycle.com) is the first citywide bicycle-share program in the US, with more than 80 stations throughout the city. Helmets are not included, and are not required by law in Denver.

CAR & MOTORCYCLE

Street parking can be a pain, but there are slews of pay garages in downtown and LoDo. Nearly all the major car-rental agencies have counters at DIA; a few have offices in downtown Denver.

PUBLIC TRANSPORTATION

RTD provides public transportation throughout the Denver and Boulder area. Free shuttle buses operate along the 16th St Mall. RTD's light rail line currently has six lines servicing 46 stations. Fares are $2.25 for one to two stops, $4 for three fare zones and $5 for all zones.

TAXI

Companies offering 24-hour cab service:
Metro Taxi (☑ 303-333-3333; www.metrotaxidenver.com)
Yellow Cab (☑ 303-777-7777; www.denveryellowcab.com)

Boulder

Tucked against the Flatirons' cragged and near-vertical rock face, this idyllic town has a sweet location and a palpable idealism that's a magnet to entrepreneurs, athletes, hippies and hard-bodies. It's also home to the University of Colorado and the Buddhist-founded, Beat-inspired Naropa University.

Boulder's love of the outdoors was officially legislated in 1967, when it became the first US city to tax itself specifically to preserve open space. Thanks to such vision, packs of cyclists whip up and down the Boulder Creek corridor, which links city and county parks those taxpayer dollars have purchased. The pedestrian-only Pearl St Mall is lively and perfect for strolling, especially at night, when residents promenade until the wee hours.

In fact, for outdoorsy types, Boulder, not Denver, is the region's tourist hub. The city is about the same distance from Denver International Airport, and staying here puts you closer to trails, ski resorts and Rocky Mountain National Park.

◉ Sights & Activities

Boulder's two areas to see and be seen are the downtown Pearl St Mall and the University Hill district (next to campus), both off Broadway, though the Hill is rarely the haunt of anyone over 25. Overlooking the city from the west are the Flatirons, an eye-catching rock formation.

★**Chautauqua Park** PARK
(www.chautauqua.com; 900 Baseline Rd; 🖵HOP 2) This historic landmark park is not just the gateway to Boulder's most magnificent slab of open space adjoining the iconic Flatirons, the wide, lush lawn attracts picnicking families, sunbathers, Frisbee folk and students from nearby CU. It also gets copious hikers, climbers and trail runners.

Boulder Creek Bike Path CYCLING
(⊘24hr; 🖈) The most utilized commuter bike path in town, this smooth and mostly straight creekside concrete path follows Boulder Creek from Foothills Parkway all the way uphill to the split of Boulder Canyon and Four Mile Canyon Rd west of downtown – a total distance of over 5 miles one-way. It also feeds urban bike lanes that lead all over town.

Eldorado Canyon State Park OUTDOORS
(☑303-494-3943; ⊘visitor center 9am-5pm) Among the country's best rock-climbing areas, Eldorado has class 5.5 to 5.12 climbs. Suitable to all visitors, a dozen miles of hiking trails also link up to Chautauqua Park. A public pool (summer only) offers chilly swims in the canyon's famous spring water.

THE THOUSAND-YEAR FLOOD

It came after a drought that followed the worst wildfire in Colorado history. On September 12, 2013, the Front Range woke up to flooding canyons and inundations that isolated mountain communities. Eight people died and thousands lost their homes. A disaster of this magnitude is considered a thousand-year flood, with a 0.1% probability in any given year. The month's 17in of rainfall blasted September's usual 1.7in average. Now cited as the second-largest natural disaster in US history, after Hurricane Katrina, it will take years to recover. The affected area was roughly the size of Connecticut. Losses were estimated at $2 billion.

University Bicycles CYCLING
(www.ubikes.com; 839 Pearl St; 4hr rental $15; ⊘10am-6pm Mon-Sat, 10am-5pm Sun) There are plenty of rental shops, but this has the widest range of rides and the most helpful staff. For $18 you can get a townie bike for the day.

Boulder Rock Club ROCK CLIMBING
(☑303-447-2804; http://boulderrockclub.com; 2829 Mapleton Ave; day pass adult/child $17/10; ⊘8am-10pm Mon, 6am-11pm Tue-Thu, 8am-11pm Fri, 10am-8pm Sat & Sun; 🖈) An incredible indoor climbing gym popular with local rock rats. This massive warehouse is full of artificial rock faces cragged with ledges and routes, and the auto-belay system allows solo climbers an anchor. Lessons and courses available, with a special kids' program. Staff are a great resource for local climbing routes.

✸ Festivals & Events

Boulder Creek Festival MUSIC, FOOD
(☑303-449-3137; www.bceproductions.com; Canyon Blvd, Central Park; ⊘May; 🖈; 🖵206, JUMP) **FREE** Billed as the kick-off to summer and capped with the Bolder Boulder, this summer festival is massive. Over 10 event areas feature more than 30 live entertainers and 500 vendors. There will be food and drink, music and sunshine. What's not to love?

Bolder Boulder ATHLETICS
(☑303-444-7223; www.bolderboulder.com; adult from $59; ⊘May; 🖈) With 54,000 runners and pros mingling with costumed racers, live bands and sideline merrymakers, this may be the most fun 10k in America, ending at the CU Stadium.

🛏 Sleeping

Boulder has dozens of options – drive down Broadway or Hwy 36 to take your pick.

★**Chautauqua Lodge** HISTORIC HOTEL **$$**
(☑303-442-3282; www.chautauqua.com; 900 Baseline Rd; r from $73, cottages $125-183; 🅿⊘❄🛜🐾; 🖵HOP 2) Adjoining beautiful hiking trails to the Flatirons, these cottages, in a leafy neighborhood inside Chautauqua Park, are our top pick. It has contemporary rooms and one- to three-bedroom cottages with porches, and beds with patchwork quilts. It's perfect for families and pets. All cottages have full kitchens, though the wraparound porch of the Chautauqua Dining Hall is a local favorite for breakfast.

Hotel Boulderado
BOUTIQUE HOTEL **$$$**

(📞303-442-4344; www.boulderado.com; 2115 13th St; r from $264; 🅿❋🛜; 🚐HOP, SKIP) With a century of service, the charming Boulderado, full of Victorian elegance and wonderful public spaces, is a National Register landmark and a romantic getaway. Each antique-filled room is uniquely decorated. The stained-glass atrium and glacial water fountain accent the jazz-washed lobby. Guesthouse rooms across the street are slightly bigger and cheaper, but lack the historical gravitas.

St Julien Hotel & Spa
HOTEL **$$$**

(📞720-406-9696, reservations 877-303-0900; www.stjulien.com; 900 Walnut St; r from $309; 🅿❋@🛜🏊) In the heart of downtown, Boulder's finest four-star option is modern and refined, with photographs of local scenery and cork walls that warm the ambience. With fabulous Flatiron views, the back patio hosts live world music, jazz concerts and wild salsa parties. Rooms are plush, and so are the robes.

🍴 Eating

Boulder's dining scene has dozens of great options. Most are centered on the Pearl St Mall, while bargains are more likely to be found on the Hill. Between 3:30pm and 6:30pm nearly every restaurant in the city features a happy hour with some kind of amazing food and drink special. It's a great way to try fine dining on a budget – check websites for details.

Spruce Confections
BAKERY **$**

(📞303-449-6773; 767 Pearl St; cookies from $3.25; ⊙6:30am-6pm Mon-Fri, 7am-6pm Sat & Sun; 🖕; 🚐206) Boulder's go-to bakehouse, where the favorites are the Ol' B Cookie (chocolate, oats, cinnamon and coconut) and the Black Bottom Cupcake (chocolate with cheesecake filling). Pair either with the Spruce Juice, possibly the world's greatest iced vanilla latte. It has sinful scones, good homemade soups and salads too. There's another branch at 4684 Broadway.

Dish
SANDWICHES **$**

(📞720-565-9933; www.dishgourmet.com; 1918 Pearl St; mains $10; ⊙9am-6pm Mon-Fri, 11am-4pm Sat; 🖕; 🚐204, HOP) Bank-length lines flank this gourmet deli at lunchtime. At $10 the sandwiches are hardly cheap but they are satisfying. Think roasted turkey carved in chunks, pâté, natural beef, slow-cooked brisket and baguettes smothered with butter and top-tier cheeses. Side salads are alluring too.

Zoe Ma Ma
CHINESE **$**

(2010 10th St; mains $5-13; ⊙11am-10pm Sun-Thu, 11am-11pm Fri & Sat; 🚐206, SKIP, HOP) 🌱 At Boulder's hippest noodle bar you can find fresh street food at a long outdoor counter. Mama, the Taiwanese matriarch, is on hand, cooking and chatting up customers in her Crocs. Organic noodles are made from scratch, as are the garlicky melt-in-your-mouth pot stickers.

Sink
PUB FOOD **$**

(www.thesink.com; 1165 13th St; mains $5-12; ⊙11am-2am, kitchen to 10pm; 🍸; 🚐203, 204, 225, DASH, SKIP) A Hill landmark since 1923, the low-slung, graffiti-scrawled Sink even employed Robert Redford during his CU years. While he dropped out, it hasn't. The dimly lit, cavernous space still churns out legendary Sink burgers and slugs of local microbrews to the latest generation of students.

Alfalfa's
SUPERMARKET **$**

(www.alfalfas.com; 1651 Broadway St; ⊙7:30am-10pm; 🚐AB, B, JUMP, SKIP) A small, community-oriented natural market with a wonderful selection of prepared food and an inviting indoor-outdoor dining area to enjoy it in.

Cafe Aion
SPANISH **$$**

(📞303-993-8131; www.cafeaion.com; 1235 Pennsylvania Ave; tapas $5-13; ⊙11am-10pm Tue-Fri, 9am-3pm Sat & Sun; 🚐203, 204, 225, DASH, SKIP) Though fancy fare on the Hill sounds odd, don't skip this one. Original and unpretentious, this side-street cafe captures the relaxed rhythms of Spain with fresh tapas and delectable housemade sangria. Papas bravas wedges have the perfect crisp, and the grilled spring onions and dolmas are light and flavorful. Happy hour goes all night on Tuesdays.

Lucile's
CAJUN **$**

(📞303-442-4743; www.luciles.com; 2142 14th St; mains $8-14; ⊙7am-2pm Mon-Fri, from 8am Sat & Sun; 🖕; 🚐205, 206, HOP) 🌱 This New Orleans–style diner has perfected breakfast, and the Creole egg dishes (served over creamy spinach alongside cheesy grits or perfectly blackened trout) are the thing to order. Start with a steaming mug of chai or chicory coffee and an order of beignets drenched in powdered sugar which are the house specialty. Go early or be prepared to wait.

★ Salt
MODERN AMERICAN $$$

(☎303-444-7258; www.saltboulderbistro.com; 1047 Pearl St; mains $14-28; ⊙11am-10pm Mon-Wed, to 11pm Thu-Sat, 10am-10pm Sun; ◈; ☐208, HOP, SKIP) While farm-to-table is ubiquitous in Boulder, this is one spot that delivers and surpasses expectations. The sweet pea ravioli with lemon beurre blanc and shaved radishes is a feverish delight. But Salt also knows meat: local and grass-fed, basted, braised and slow roasted to utter perfection. When in doubt, ask – the servers really know their stuff.

Kitchen
MODERN AMERICAN $$$

(☎303-544-5973; http://thekitchen.com; 1039 Pearl St; mains $18-32; ☎; ☐206, HOP) ✔ The pioneer of farm-to-table cuisine in Boulder, Kitchen features clean lines, stacks of crusty bread and a daily menu. Super-fresh ingredients are crafted into rustic tapas: think roasted root vegetables, shaved prosciutto and steamed mussels in cream. The pulled-pork sandwich rocks, but save room for the sticky toffee pudding. Visitors shouldn't miss the community hour, with sips and nibbles at a communal table 3pm to 5pm weekdays.

Upstairs there's a more casual atmosphere and menu.

☻ Drinking & Entertainment

Playboy didn't vote CU the best party school for nothing – the blocks around the Pearl St Mall and the Hill churn out fun, with many restaurants doubling as bars or turning into all-out dance clubs come 10pm.

★ Mountain Sun Pub & Brewery
BREWERY

(www.mountainsunpub.com; 1535 Pearl St; ⊙11am-1am; ◈; ☐HOP, 205, 206) Boulder's favorite brewery cheerfully serves a rainbow of fine brews and packs in all from yuppies to hippies. But best of all is its community atmosphere. The pub grub, especially the burgers and chili, is delicious and its fully family-friendly, with board games and kids' meals. It often has live bluegrass, reggae and jam-bands on Sunday and Monday nights.

Bitter Bar
COCKTAIL BAR

(☎303-442-3050; www.thebitterbar.com; 835 Walnut St; cocktails $9-15; ⊙5pm-midnight Mon-Thu, 5pm-2am Fri & Sat; ☐HOP) A chic Boulder speakeasy where killer cocktails, such as the scrumptious lavender-infused Blue Velvet, make the evening slip happily out of focus. The patio is great for conversation and Thursdays at 9pm there's live music.

Boulder Dushanbe Teahouse
TEAHOUSE

(☎303-442-4993; 1770 13th St; mains $8-19; ⊙8am-10pm; ☐203, 204, 205, 206, 208, 225, DASH, JUMP, SKIP) It's impossible to find better ambience than this incredible Tajik teahouse, a gift from Dushanbe, Boulder's sister city. The elaborate carvings and paintings were reassembled over a decade on Central Park's edge. It's too bad the fusion fare is surprisingly dull, but it's very worth coming for a pot of tea.

Boulder Theater
CINEMA, LIVE MUSIC

(☎303-786-7030; www.bouldertheatre.com; 2032 14th St) This old movie-theater-turned-historic-venue brings in slightly under-the-radar acts like jazz great Charlie Hunter, the madmen rockers of Gogol Bordello and West Afro–French divas, Les Nubians. But it also screens classic films like *The Big Lebowski* and hosts short-film festivals that can and should be enjoyed with a glass of beer.

🛍 Shopping

★ Pearl Street Mall
MALL

The main feature of downtown Boulder is the Pearl St Mall, a vibrant pedestrian zone filled with kids' climbing boulders and splash fountains, bars, galleries and restaurants.

Momentum
HANDICRAFTS

(www.ourmomentum.com; 1625 Pearl St; ⊙10am-7pm Tue-Sat, 11am-6pm Sun) ✔ Committed to socially responsible and environmentally friendly business practices, Momentum makes you feel good about shopping. It sells the kitchen sink of unique global gifts – Zulu wire baskets, fabulous scarves from India, Nepal and Ecuador – all handcrafted and purchased at fair value from disadvantaged artisans. Every item purchased provides a direct economic lifeline to the artists.

Common Threads
CLOTHING

(www.commonthreadsboulder.com; 2707 Spruce St; ⊙10am-6pm Mon-Sat, noon-5pm Sun) Vintage shopping at its most haute couture, this fun place is where to go for secondhand Choos and Prada purses. Prices are higher than at your run-of-the-mill vintage shop, but clothes, shoes and bags are always in good condition, and the authenticity of the designer clothing is guaranteed. Offers fun classes on altering and innovating clothes.

Boulder Bookstore BOOKS
(www.boulderbookstore.indiebound.com; 1107 Pearl St; 🛜📶) Boulder's favorite indie bookstore has a huge travel section downstairs, along with all the hottest new fiction and nonfiction. Check the visiting-authors lineup posted at the entry.

ℹ Information

Boulder Visitor Center (📞303-442-2911; www.bouldercoloradousa.com; 2440 Pearl St; ⊙8:30am-5pm Mon-Thu, 8:30am-4pm Fri) Set in the Boulder Chamber of Commerce, this visitor center offers basic information, maps and tips on nearby hiking trails and other activities. There's a more accessible tourist info kiosk on the Pearl St Mall in front of the courthouse.

ℹ Getting There & Around

Boulder has fabulous public transportation, with services extending to Denver and its airport. Ecofriendly buses are run by **RTD** (📞303-299-6000; www.rtd-denver.com; per ride $2-4.50; 📶). Maps are available at **Boulder Station** (cnr 14th & Walnut Sts). RTD buses (route B) operate between Boulder Station and Denver's Market St Bus Station ($5, 55 minutes). RTD's SkyRide bus (route AB) heads to Denver International Airport ($9–13, one hour, hourly). **SuperShuttle** (📞303-444-0808; www.supershuttle.com) provides hotel ($27) and door-to-door ($33) shuttle service from the airport.

For two-wheel transportation, **Boulder B-Cycle** (http://boulder.bcycle.com; 24hr rental $7) is a new citywide program with townie bikes available at strategic locations, but riders must sign up online first.

Northern Mountains

With one foot on either side of the continental divide and behemoths of granite in every direction, Colorado's Northern Mountains offer out-of-this-world alpine adventures, laid-back skiing, kick-butt hiking and biking, and plenty of rivers to raft, fish and float.

Rocky Mountain National Park

Rocky Mountain National Park showcases classic alpine scenery, with wildflower meadows and serene mountain lakes set under snowcapped peaks. There are over four million visitors annually, but many stay on the beaten path. Hike an extra mile and enjoy the incredible solitude. Elk are the park's signature mammal – you will even see them grazing hotel lawns – but also keep an eye out for bighorn sheep, moose, marmots and black bears.

⊙ Sights & Activities

With over 300 miles of trail, traversing all aspects of its diverse terrain, the park is suited to every hiking ability.

Those with kids in tow might consider the easy hikes to **Calypso Falls** in the Wild Basin, **Gem Lakes** in the Lumpy Ridge area or the trail to **Twin Sisters Peak** south of Estes Park, while those with unlimited ambition, strong legs and enough trail mix will be lured by the challenge of **Longs Peak's** summit.

Regardless, it's best to spend at least one night at 7000ft to 8000ft prior to setting out to allow your body to adjust to the elevation. Before July, many trails are snowbound and high water runoff makes passage difficult. In the winter, avalanches are a hazard.

⭐**Moraine Park Museum** MUSEUM
(📞970-586-1206; Bear Lake Rd; ⊙9am-4:30pm Jun-Oct) Built by the Civilian Conservation Corps in 1923 and once the park's proud visitors lodge, this building has been renovated in recent years to host exhibits on geology, glaciers and wildlife.

🛏 Sleeping

The only overnight accommodations in the park are at campgrounds. Dining options and the majority of motel or hotel accommodations are around Estes Park or Grand Lake, located on the other side of the Trail Ridge Road Pass (open late May to October).

You will need a backcountry permit to stay outside developed park campgrounds. None of the campgrounds have showers, but they do have flush toilets in summer and outhouse facilities in winter. Sites include fire rings, picnic tables and one parking spot.

Olive Ridge Campground CAMPGROUND $
(📞303-541-2500; State Hwy 7; tent sites $19; ⊙mid-May–Nov) This well-kept USFS campground has access to four trailheads: St Vrain Mountain, Wild Basin, Longs Peak and Twin Sisters. In the summer it can get full, though sites are mostly first-come, first-served.

Longs Peak Campground CAMPGROUND $
(📞970-586-1206; Longs Peak Rd, off State Hwy 7; tent sites $20; 🅿) This is the base camp of choice for the early morning ascent of Longs Peak, one of Colorado's most easily accessible 14ers. The scenery is striking and its 26

spaces are for tents only, but don't expect much solitude in the peak of the summer.

Moraine Park Campground CAMPGROUND $
(☑ 877-444-6777; www.recreation.gov; off Bear Lake Rd; summer tent & RV sites $20) In the middle of a stand of ponderosa pine forest off Bear Lake Road, this is the biggest of the park's campgrounds, approximately 2.5 miles south of the Beaver Meadows Visitor Center, and with 245 sites. The walk-in, tent-only sites in the D Loop are recommended if you want quiet. Make reservations through the website.

Reservations are accepted and recommended from the end of May through to the end of September; other times of the year the campground is first-come, first-served. At night in the summer, there are numerous ranger-led programs in the amphitheater.

The campground is served by the shuttle buses on Bear Lake Rd through the summer.

Aspenglen Campground CAMPGROUND $
(☑ 877-444-6777; www.recreation.gov; State Hwy 34; summer tent & RV sites $20) With only 54 sites, this is the smallest of the park's reservable camping. There are many tent-only sites, including some walk-ins, and a limited number of trailers are allowed. This is the quietest campground in the park while still being highly accessible (5 miles west of Estes Park on US 34). Make reservations through the website.

Timber Creek Campground CAMPGROUND $
(Trail Ridge Rd, US Hwy 34; tent & RV sites $20) This campground has 100 sites and remains open through the winter. No reservations accepted. The only established campground on the west side of the park, it's 7 miles north of Grand Lake.

ⓘ Information

For private vehicles, the park entrance fee is $20, valid for seven days. Individuals entering the park on foot, bicycle, motorcycle or bus pay $10 each. All visitors receive a free copy of the park's information brochure, which contains a good orientation map and is available in English, German, French, Spanish and Japanese.

Backcountry permits ($26 for a group of up to 12 people for seven days) are required for overnight stays in the 260 designated backcountry camping sites in the park. They are free between November 1 and April 30. Phone reservations can be made only from March 1 to May 15. Reservations by snail mail or in person are accepted via the **Backcountry Office**. (☑ 970-586-1242;

www.nps.gov/romo; 1000 W Hwy 36 Estes Park CO 80517)

A bear box to store your food is required if you are staying overnight in the backcountry (established campsites already have them). These can be rented for around $3 to $5 per day from REI (p244) or the **Estes Park Mountain Shop** (☑ 970-586-6548; www.estesparkmountain-shop.com; 2050 Big Thompson Ave; 2-person tent $10, bear box per night $3; ⊘ 8am-9pm).

Alpine Visitor Center (www.nps.gov/romo; Fall River Pass; ⊘ 10:30am-4:30pm late May–mid-Jun, 9am-5pm late Jun-early Sep, 10:30am-4:30pm early Sep–mid-Oct; ♿) The views from this popular visitor center and souvenir store at 11,796ft, and right in the middle of the park, are extraordinary. You can see elk, deer and sometimes moose grazing on the hillside on the drive up Old Fall River Rd.

Much of the traffic that clogs Trail Ridge Road all summer pulls into Alpine Visitor Center, so the place is a zoo. Rangers here give programs and advice about trails. You can also shop for knick-knacks or eat in the cafeteria-style dining room.

Beaver Meadows Visitor Center (☑ 970-586-1206; www.nps.gov/romo; US Hwy 36; ⊘ 8am-9pm late Jun-late Aug, to 4:30pm or 5pm rest of yr; ♿) The primary visitor center and best stop for park information if you're approaching from Estes Park. You can see a film about the park, browse a small gift shop and reserve backcountry camping sites.

Kawuneeche Visitor Center (☑ 970-627-3471; 16018 US Hwy 34; ⊘ 8am-6pm last week May-Labor Day, 8am-4:30pm Oct-May; ♿) This visitor center is on the west side of the park, and offers a film about the park ranger-led walks and discussions, backcountry permits and family activities.

ⓘ Getting There & Away

Trail Ridge Rd (US 34) is the only east–west route through the park and is closed in winter. The most direct route from Boulder follows US 36 through Lyons to the east entrances.

There are two entrance stations on the east side, **Fall River** (US 34) and **Beaver Meadows** (US 36). The **Grand Lake Station** (also US 34) is the only entry on the west side. Year-round access is available through **Kawuneeche Valley** along the Colorado River headwaters to Timber Creek Campground.

The main centers of visitor activity on the park's east side are the Alpine Visitor Center, high on Trail Ridge Rd and Bear Lake Rd, which leads to campgrounds, trailheads and the Moraine Park Museum.

North of Estes Park, Devils Gulch Rd leads to several hiking trails. Further out on Devils Gulch Rd, you pass through the village of Glen Haven to reach the trailhead entry to the park along the North Fork of the Big Thompson River.

❶ Getting Around

In summer a free shuttle bus operates from the Estes Park Visitor Center multiple times daily, bringing hikers to a park-and-ride location where you can pick up other shuttles. The year-round option leaves the Glacier Basin parking area toward Bear Lake, in the park's lower elevations. During the summer peak, a second shuttle operates between Moraine Park Campground and the Glacier Basin parking area. Shuttles run on weekends only from mid-August through September.

Estes Park

It's no small irony that becoming a nature-lovers hub has turned the gateway of one of the most pristine outdoor escapes in the US into a kind of Great Outdoors Disney. And while there are plenty of t-shirt shops and mountain kitsch, a nice river runs through town, and there are cool parks, decent restaurants and a haunted hotel.

🏃 Activities

★Colorado Mountain School ROCK CLIMBING
(☑800-836-4008; www.totalclimbing.com; 341 Moraine Ave; half-day guided climbs per person from $125) Simply put, there's no better resource for climbers in Colorado – this outfit is the largest climbing operator in the region, has the most expert guides and is the only organization allowed to operate within Rocky Mountain National Park. It has a clutch of classes taught by world-class instructors.

🛏 Sleeping

Estes Park's dozens of hotels fill up fast in summer. There are some passable budget options but the many lovely area campgrounds are the best value.

Try the **Estes Park Visitor Center** (☑970-577-9900; www.estesparkresortcvb.com; 500 Big Thompson Ave; ⊙9am-8pm Jun-Aug, 8am-5pm Mon-Fri, 9am-5pm Sat, 10am-4pm Sun Sep-May), just east of the US 36 junction, for help with lodging; note that many places close in winter.

Estes Park Hostel HOSTEL $
(☑970-237-0152; www.estesparkhostel.com; 211 Cleave St; dm/s/d $26/38/52; 🛜) This hostel, with a handful of shared rooms and simple privates, isn't going into history books as the plushest digs ever, but there's a kitchen on site, and Terri, the owner, is helpful. The price is right too.

**★YMCA of the Rockies –
Estes Park Center** RESORT $$
(☑970-586-3341; www.ymcarockies.org; 2515 Tunnel Rd; r from $109, cabins from $129; P⊖❄🛜🐾) Estes Park Center is not your typical YMCA boarding house. Instead it's a favorite vacation spot with families, boasting upmarket motel-style accommodations and cabins set on hundreds of acres of high alpine terrain. Choose from roomy cabins that sleep up to 10 or motel-style rooms for singles or doubles. Both are simple and practical.

This very kid-friendly resort sits in a serene and ultrapristine location in the mountains just outside town. The 860-acre plot is home to cabins and motel rooms along with lots of wide open spaces dotted with forests and fields of wildflowers. Just a few minutes outside Estes Park (but definitely away from the hustle of town), it offers a range of activities for adults, kids or the whole family, throughout the year. It also runs special themed weekends and longer summer camps where environmental education is taught in a fun and engaging manner. This YMCA is unapologetically outdoorsy, and most guests come to participate in the activities.

Riversong BOUTIQUE HOTEL $$
(☑970 586 4666; www.romanticriversong.com; 1766 Lower Broadview Dr; d from $165; P⊖) Tucked down a dead-end dirt road overlooking the Big Thompson River, Riversong offers nine romantic rooms with private bath in a Craftsman-style mansion. The minimum stay is two nights, and prices vary by amenities. West of town take Moraine Ave, turn onto Mary's Lake Rd and take the first right.

Stanley Hotel HOTEL $$
(☑970-577-4000; www.stanleyhotel.com; 333 Wonderview Ave; r from $199; P🛜♿) The white Georgian Colonial Revival hotel stands in brilliant contrast to the towering peaks of Rocky Mountain National Park that frame the skyline. A favorite local retreat, this best-in-class hotel served as the inspiration for Stephen King's famous cult novel *The Shining*. Rooms are decorated to retain some of the Old West feel while still ensuring all the creature comforts.

✗ Eating

Ed's Cantina & Grill MEXICAN $
(☑970-586-2919; www.edscantina.com; 390 E
Elkhorn Ave; mains $9-13; ⊙11am-late Mon-Fri,
8am-10pm Sat & Sun; ♿) With an outdoor
patio right on the river, Ed's is a great place
to kick back with a margarita. Serving
Mexican and American staples, the restaurant is in a retro woodsy space with leather
booth seating and bold primary colors.

Estes Park Brewery PUB FOOD $$
(www.epbrewery.com; 470 Prospect Village Dr;
⊙11am-2am Mon-Sun) The town's brewpub
serves pizza, burgers and wings, and at least
eight different house beers, in a big, boxy
room resembling a cross between a class-
room and a country kitchen. Pool tables and
outdoor seating keep the place rocking late
into the night.

ⓘ Getting There & Away

From Denver International Airport, **Estes Park
Shuttle** (☑970-586-5151; www.estespark-
shuttle.com) runs four times daily to Estes Park
(one-way/return $45/85).

Steamboat Springs

With tree-skiing in luxuriant areas, top-
notch trails for mountain-biking and a laid-
back Western feel, Steamboat beats other ski
towns in both ambience and offerings. Its
historic center is cool for rambling, the hot
springs top off a hard day of play and locals
couldn't be friendlier.

🏃 Activities

Steamboat Mountain Resort SNOW SPORTS
(☑ticket office 970-871-5252; www.steamboat.
com; lift ticket adult/child $94/59; ⊙ticket office
8am-5pm) The stats of the Steamboat Ski
Area speak volumes for the town's claim as
'Ski Town, USA' – 165 trails, 3668ft vertical
and nearly 3000 acres. With excellent pow-
der and trails for all levels, this is the main
draw for winter visitors and some of the best
skiing in the US. In the ski area there are
(overpriced) food and equipment vendors
galore.

★ Strawberry Park Hot Springs HOT SPRING
(☑970-870-1517; www.strawberryhotsprings.
com; 44200 County Rd; per day adult/child $10/5;
⊙10am-10:30pm Sun-Thu, to midnight Fri & Sat;
♿) 🚭 Steamboat's favorite hot springs are
actually outside the city limits but offer

great back-to-basics relaxation. There are
very rustic cabins ($60 to $70) and camping
($55) here, too – though you are probably
better off back in Steamboat. It has no elec-
tricity (you get gas lanterns) and you'll need
your own linens. Be sure to reserve. Week-
end reservations require a two-night stay.

Note that the thermal pools are clothing
optional after dark. Check website for direc-
tions.

Orange Peel Bikes BICYCLE RENTAL
(☑970-879-2957; www.orangepeelbikes.com; 1136
Yampa St; bike rental per day $20-65; ⊙10am-6pm
Mon-Fri, to 5pm Sat; ♿) In a funky old build-
ing at the end of Yampa, this is perfectly
situated for renting a bike to ride the trails
criss-crossing Howelsen Hill. A staff of se-
rious riders and mechanics can offer tons
of information about local trails, including
maps. This is the coolest bike shop in town,
hands down.

**Bucking Rainbow
Outfitters** RAFTING, FLY-FISHING
(☑970-879-8747; www.buckingrainbow.com; 730
Lincoln Ave; inner tubes $17, rafting $43-100, fishing
$150-340; ⊙daily) This excellent outfitter has
fly-fishing, rafting, and outdoor apparel and
the area's best fly shop, but it's renowned for
its rafting trips on the Yampa and beyond.
Rafting half-days start at $71. Two-hour in-
town fly-fishing trips start at $155 per per-
son. It has a tube shack that runs shuttles
from Sunpies Bistro on Yampa St.

Old Town Hot Springs HOT SPRING
(☑970-879-1828; www.oldtownhotsprings.org;
136 Lincoln Ave; adult/child $16/9, waterslide $6;
⊙5:30am-10pm Mon-Fri, 7am-9pm Sat, 8am-9pm
Sun; ♿) Smack dab in the center of town,
the water here is warmer than most other
springs in the area. Known by the Utes as
the 'medicine springs,' the mineral waters
here are said to have special healing powers.

🛏 Sleeping & Eating

Hotel Bristol HOTEL $$
(☑970-879-3083; www.steamboathotelbristol.
com; 917 Lincoln Ave; d $129-149; ❀🐾🛜) The ele-
gant Hotel Bristol has small-but-sophisticat-
ed Western digs, with dark-wood and brass
furnishings and Pendleton wool blankets on
the beds. It has a ski shuttle, a six-person indoor Jacuzzi and a cozy restaurant.

The Boathouse MODERN AMERICAN $$
(☑970-879-4797; 609 Yampa; $12-20; ⊙restau-
rant 11am-10pm, bar to 1am) You can't beat the

view from the riverfront deck and the creative menu takes you on a cruise of the continents with innovative dishes like 'When Pigs Fly' (wasabi-kissed pork chops). Great for evening stargazing, it gets moving as a favorite pub after dinner.

Carl's Tavern   AMERICAN **$$**
(☑970-761-2060; www.carlstavern.com; 700 Yampa St; mains $14-31) This local's favorite has great pub grub, a happening patio, live music, hot wait staff, and a raucous spirit that will get your heart thumping.

ⓘ Information

Steamboat Springs Visitor Center (☑970-879-0880; www.steamboat-chamber.com; 125 Anglers Drive; ⊘8am-5pm Mon-Fri, 10am-3pm Sat) This visitor center, facing Sundance Plaza, has a wealth of local information, and its website is also excellent for planning.

ⓘ Getting There & Away

Buses between Denver and Salt Lake City stop at the **Greyhound Terminal** (☑800-231-2222; www.greyhound.com; 1505 Lincoln Ave), about half a mile west of town. **Steamboat Springs Transit** (☑970-879-3717, for pick-up in Mountain Area 970-846-1279; http://steamboat-springs.net) runs free buses between Old Town and the ski resort year-round. Steamboat is 166 miles northwest of Denver via US 40.

Central Colorado

Colorado's central mountains are well known for their plethora of world-class ski resorts, sky-high hikes and snow-melt rivers. To the southeast are Colorado Springs and Pikes Peak, which anchor the southern Front Range.

Winter Park

Less than two hours from Denver, unpretentious Winter Park is a favorite ski resort with Front Rangers, who flock here from as far away as Colorado Springs to ski fresh tracks each weekend. Beginners can frolic on miles of powdery groomers while experts test their skills on Mary Jane's world-class bumps. Most services are along US 40 (the main drag), including the **visitor center** (☑970-726-4118; www.winterpark-info.com; 78841 Hwy 40; ⊘9am-5pm daily).

South of town, **Winter Park Resort** (☑970-726-1564; www.winterparkresort.com; Hwy 40; lift ticket adult/child $104/62; ♿) covers five

mountains and has a vertical drop of more than 2600ft. Experts love it here because more than half of the runs are geared solely for highly skilled skiers. It also has 45 miles of lift-accessible **mountain-biking trails** (www.trestlebikepark.com; day pass adult/child $39/29; ⊘mid-Jun–mid-Sep) connecting to a 600-mile trail system running through the valley.

Devil's Thumb Ranch (☑800-933-4339; www.devilsthumbranch.com; 3530 County Rd 83; bunkhouse $100-180, lodge $240-425, cabins from $365; ❋ 🎱 🎱 🎱) ♪, with a cowboy-chic lodge and cabins alongside a 65-mile network of trails, makes an ultra-romantic getaway for the active-minded. Geothermal heat, reclaimed wood and low-emission fireplaces make it green. It's ideal for **cross-country skiing and horseback rides** (☑970-726-5632; trail passes adult/child $20/8, horseback riding $95-175; ♿) in the high country.

The best deal around is the friendly **Rocky Mountain Chalet** (☑970-726-8256; www.therockymountainchalet.com; 15 County Rd 72; dm $30, r summer/winter $89/149; Ⓟ❋🎱), with plush, comfortable doubles, dorm rooms and a sparkling kitchen.

For inspired dining, **Tabernash Tavern** (☑970-726-4430; www.tabernashtavern.com; 72287 US Hwy 40; mains $20-34; ⊘5-9pm Tue-Sat) ♪ whets the appetite with buffalo rib ragu or venison burgers. Reserve ahead. It's north of town.

Breckenridge & Around

Set at 9600ft, at the foot of a marvelous range of treeless peaks, Breck is a sweetly surviving gold-mining town with a lovely national historic district. With down-to-earth grace, the town boasts family-friendly ski runs that don't disappoint and always draw a giddy crowd. If you should happen to grow restless, there are five great ski resorts and outlet shopping less than an hour away.

◉ Sights & Activities

Peak 8 Fun Park   AMUSEMENT PARK
(☑800-789-7669; www.breckenridge.com; Peak 8; day pass 3-7yr/8yr & up $34/68; ⊘9:30am-5:30pm mid-Jun–mid-Sep; ♿) This park has a laundry list of made-for-thrills activities, including a big-air trampoline, climbing wall, mountain-bike park and the celebrated SuperSlide – a luge-like course taken on a sled at exhilarating speeds. Get the day pass, do activities à la carte ($10 to $18) or simply take a scenic ride up the chair lift (without/

with bike $10/17). This will eventually morph into the impressive eco-playground Epic Discovery (www.epicdiscovery.com), though not until 2016 at the earliest.

Breckenridge Ski Area
SNOW SPORTS

(☑ 800-789-7669; www.breckenridge.com; lift ticket adult/child $115/68; ☺ 8:30am-4pm Nov–mid-Apr; 🕭) Breckenridge spans five mountains (Peaks 6 to 10), covering 2900 acres and featuring some of the best beginner and intermediate terrain in the state, as well as plenty of exhilarating high-alpine runs and hike-to bowls. There are also five terrain parks and two half-pipes here.

Arapahoe Basin Ski Area
SNOW SPORTS

(☑ 970-468-0718; www.arapahoebasin.com; Hwy 6; lift adult/child 6-14yr $79/40; ☺ 9am-4pm Mon-Fri, from 8:30am Sat & Sun) Near the Continental Divide where US 6 crosses 11,992-foot Loveland Pass, 6 miles east of Keystone Resort and 90 miles west of Denver, Arapahoe Basin, aka A-Basin, is Colorado's second-oldest, and North America's highest ski area. Locals dig it because the lack of lodging and dining options (it's a day-use ski area only) keeps the package tourists away.

🎉 Festivals & Events

Ullr Fest
CULTURAL

(www.gobreck.com; ☺ early to mid Jan) The Ullr Fest celebrates the Norse god of winter, with a wild parade and four-day festival featuring a twisted version of the Dating Game, an ice-skating party and a bonfire.

International Snow Sculpture Championship
ARTS

(www.gobreck.com; ☺ mid-Jan; 🕭) The International Snow Sculpture Championship begins in mid-January and lasts for three weeks. It starts with 'Stomping Week,' when the snow blocks are made, proceeds with Sculpting Week, when the sculptures are created, and concludes with Viewing Week, when the sculptures decorate the River Walk and are enjoyed and judged by the public.

🛏 Sleeping

For upscale slope-side rentals, contact **Great Western Lodging** (☑ 888-453-1001; www.gw-lodging.com; 322 N Main St; condos summer/winter from $125/275; 🅿 ✳ 🛜). Campers can look for **USFS campgrounds** (☑ 877-444-6777; www.recreation.gov) outside of town.

Fireside Inn
B&B, HOSTEL $

(☑ 970-453-6456; www.firesideinn.com; 114 N French St; summer/winter dm $30/41, d $101/140; 🅿 ✳ @ 🛜) The best deal for budget travelers in Summit County, this chummy hostel and B&B is a find. All guests can enjoy the chlorine-free barrel hot tub, fridge and microwave, movie nights with fellow ski bums and the resident snuggly dog. The English hosts are a delight and all but dorm dwellers get breakfast in the morning. It's a 10-minute walk to the gondola in ski boots.

★ Abbett Placer Inn
B&B $$

(☑ 970-453-6489; www.abbettplacer.com; 205 S French St; r summer $99-179, winter $119-229; 🅿 ✳ @ 🛜) This violet house has five large rooms decked-out with wood furnishings, iPod docks and fluffy robes. It's very low key. The warm and welcoming hosts cook big breakfasts, and guests can enjoy a lovely outdoor Jacuzzi deck and use of a common kitchenette. The top-floor room has massive views of the peaks from a private terrace. Check-in is from 4pm to 7pm.

🍴 Eating & Drinking

Clint's Bakery & Coffee House
CAFE $

(131 S Main St; sandwiches $4.95-7.25; ☺ 7am-8pm; 🛜 🕭) The coolest coffee shop in town, where brainy baristas will steam up a chalkboard full of latte and mocha flavors and dozens of loose-leaf teas. If you're hungry, the downstairs bagelry stacks burly sandwiches and tasty breakfast bagels with egg and ham, lox, sausage and cheese. Good pastries too. The bagelry closes at 3pm.

Hearthstone
MODERN AMERICAN $$$

(☑ 970-453-1148; http://hearthstonerestaurant.biz; 130 S Ridge St; mains $26-44; ☺ 4pm-late; 🍴) 🌿 One of Breck's favorites, this restored 1886 Victorian churns out creative mountain fare such as blackberry elk and braised buffalo ribs with tomatillos, roasted chilies and polenta. Fresh and delicious, it's definitely worth a splurge, or hit happy hour (4pm to 6pm) for $5 plates paired with wine.

Downstairs at Eric's
BAR

(www.downstairsaterics.com; 111 S Main St; ☺ 11am-midnight; 🕭) Downstairs at Eric's is a Breckenridge institution. Locals flock to this game-room-style basement joint for the brews, burgers and delicious mashed potatoes. There are over 100 beers (20 on tap) to choose from and plenty of sports bar–arcade action.

CLIMBING YOUR FIRST FOURTEENER

Known as Colorado's easiest fourteener, **Quandary Peak** (www.14ers.com; County Rd 851), near Breckenridge, is the state's 15th-highest at 14,265ft. Though you will see plenty of dogs and children, 'easiest' may be misleading – the summit remains three grueling miles from the trailhead.

The trail ascends to the west; after about 10 minutes of moderate climbing, follow the right fork to a trail junction. Head left, avoiding the road, and almost immediately you will snatch some views of Mt Helen and Quandary (although the real summit is still hidden).

Just below the timberline you'll meet the trail from Monte Cristo Gulch – note it so you don't take the wrong fork on your way back down. From here it's a steep haul to the top.

Go between June and September. Start early and aim to turn around by noon, as afternoon lightning is typical during summer. It's a 6-mile round-trip, taking roughly seven to eight hours. To get here, take Colorado 9 to County Rd 850. Make a right and turn right again onto 851. Drive 1.1 miles to the unmarked trailhead. Park parallel on the fire road.

ℹ Information

Visitor Center (☎877-864-0868; www.go-breck.com; 203 S Main St; ☉9am-9pm; 🛜 ♿) Along with a host of maps and brochures, this center has a fantastic riverside museum that delves into Breck's gold-mining past.

ℹ Getting There & Around

Breckenridge is about 80 miles from Denver, 9 miles south of I-70 on Hwy 9.

Colorado Mountain Express (☎800-525-6363; www.coloradomountainexpress.com; adult/child $70/36; 🛜) runs shuttles between Breckenridge and Denver International Airport.

Free buses (www.townofbreckenridge.com; 150 Watson Ave; ☉8am-11:45pm) run along four routes throughout town.

To get between Breckenridge, Keystone and Frisco, hop on free **Summit Stages buses** (☎970-668-0999; www.summitstage.com; 150 Watson Ave). To get to Vail, take the **Fresh Tracks shuttle** (☎970-453-4052; www.freshtrackstransportation.com; $20 1-way).

Vail

Darling of the rich and sometime famous, Vail resembles an elaborate adult amusement park, with everything man-made from the golf greens down to the indoor waterfalls. It's compact and highly walkable, but the location (I-70 runs alongside) lacks the natural drama of other Rocky Mountain destinations. That said, no serious skier would dispute its status as the best ski resort in Colorado, with its powdery back bowls, chutes and wickedly fun terrain.

◉ Sights & Activities

Colorado Ski Museum   MUSEUM
(www.skimuseum.net; 3rd fl, Vail Village parking lot exit; ☉10am-5pm; ♿) FREE Humble but informative, this museum takes you from the invention of skiing to the trials of the Tenth Mountain Division, a decorated WWII alpine unit that trained in these mountains. There are also hilarious fashions from the past, as well as the fledgling Colorado Ski and Snowboard Hall of Fame.

★**Vail Mountain**   SNOW SPORTS
(☎970-754-8245; www.vail.com; lift ticket adult/child $129/89; ☉9am-4pm Dec–mid-Apr; ♿) Vail Mountain is our favorite in the state, with 5289 skiable acres, 193 trails, three terrain parks and (ahem) the highest lift-ticket prices on the continent. If you're a Colorado ski virgin, it's worth paying the extra bucks to pop your cherry here – especially on a blue-sky fresh-powder day. Multiday tickets are good at four other resorts (Beaver Creek, Breck, Keystone and Arapahoe Basin).

Vail to Breckenridge Bike Path   CYCLING
(www.fs.usda.gov) This paved car-free bike path stretches 8.7 miles from East Vail to the top of Vail Pass (elevation gain 1831ft), before descending 14 miles into Frisco (nine more if you go all the way to Breckenridge). If you're only interested in the downhill, hop on a shuttle from a **Bike Valet** (☎970-476-5385; www.bikevalet.net; 520 E Lionshead Cir; bike rental per day from $30; ☉10am-5pm; ♿) and enjoy the ride back to Vail.

THE ROCKIES FOR POWDER HOUNDS

Well worth the five-hour road trip from Denver, **Crested Butte** promises deep powder and lovely open terrain, next to a mining outpost re-tooled to be one of Colorado's coolest small towns. If you're short on travel time, go directly to Summit County. Use lively **Breckenridge** as your base and conquer five areas on one combo lift ticket, including the mastodon resort of **Vail**, our favorite for remote back bowl terrain, and the ultra-local and laid-back Arapahoe Basin Ski Area. A-Basin stays open into June, when spring skiing means tailgating with beer and barbecue in between slush runs.

From Crested Butte, you can head a little further south and ski the slopes at **Telluride**; from Summit County and Vail, **Aspen** is nearby. Both are true old gold towns. Be sure to devote at least a few hours to exploring Aspen's glitzy shops and Telluride's down-to-earth bars for a local vibe in a historic Wild West setting.

From Aspen, catch a local flight up to **Jackson Hole Mountain Resort** to do some vertical powder riding in the Grand Tetons.

🛏 Sleeping

Vail is as expensive as Colorado gets, and lodging – generally private condo rentals – is very hit or miss.

Gore Creek Campground   CAMPGROUND $
(📞877-444-6777; www.recreation.gov; Bighorn Rd; tent sites $18; ⊙mid-May–Sep; 🐾) This campground at the end of Bighorn Rd has 25 tent sites with picnic tables and fire grates nestled in the woods by Gore Creek. There is excellent fishing near here. Try the Slate Creek or Deluge Lake trails; the latter leads to a fish-packed lake. The campground is 6 miles east of Vail Village via exit 180 (East Vail) off I-70.

★**Minturn Inn**   B&B $$
(📞970-827-9647; www.minturninn.com; 442 Main St; r summer/winter from $100/150; 🅿🛜) If you don't need to be at the heart of the action in Vail, the rustic Minturn Inn should be your pick. Set in a 1915 log-hewn building in Minturn, this cozy B&B turns on the mountain charm with handcrafted log beds, river rock fireplaces and antlered decor. Reserve one of the newer River Lodge rooms for private Jacuzzi access.

★**The Sebastian**   HOTEL $$$
(📞800-354-6908; www.thesebastianvail.com; 16 Vail Rd; r summer/winter from $230/500; 🅿❄🛜🏊🐾) Deluxe and modern, this sophisticated hotel showcases tasteful contemporary art and an impressive list of amenities, including a mountainside ski valet, luxury spa and adventure concierge. Room rates dip to reasonable in the summer, the perfect time to enjoy the tapas bar and spectacular pool area with hot tubs frothing and spilling over like champagne.

🍴 Eating & Drinking

★**Yellowbelly**   SOUTHERN $
(www.yellowbellychicken.com; unit 14, 2161 N Frontage Rd; plates $10; ⊙11am-8:30pm; 🅿🛜🐾) It may be hidden in West Vail, but man is this fried chicken good. Although we could tout the healthy side of things (non-GMO, free-range, veggie-fed birds), it's the dynamite gluten-free batter that earns this place its stars. Spicy, tender pieces of chicken come with two sides (brussel slaw, citrus quinoa, mac and cheese) and a drink; alternatively, order an entire rotisserie bird for the whole gang.

★**bōl**   MODERN AMERICAN $$
(📞970-476-5300; www.bolvail.com; 141 E Meadow Dr; mains $14-28; ⊙5pm-1am, from 2pm in winter; 🛜🚲🐾) Half hip eatery, half space-age bowling alley, bōl is hands down the funkiest hangout in Vail. You can take the kids bowling in the back ($50 per hour), but it's the surprisingly eclectic menu that's the real draw: creations range from a filling chicken paillard salad with gnocchi to shrimp and grits with grapefruit. Prices are relatively affordable by Vail standards. Reserve.

Matsuhisa   JAPANESE $$$
(📞970-476-6628; www.matsuhisavail.com; 141 E Meadow Dr; mains $29-39, 2 pieces sushi $8-12; ⊙6-10pm) Legendary chef Nobu Matsuhisa has upped Vail's culinary standards with this modern, airy space, set at the heart of the Solaris complex. Expect traditional sushi and tempura alongside his signature 'new-style' sashimi – Matsuhisa opened his first restaurant in Peru, and continues to incorporate South American influences into his cuisine. Star dishes include black cod with miso and scallops with jalapeño salsa. Reserve.

Los Amigos
BAR

(400 Bridge St; ⊗11:30am-9pm) If you want views, tequila, and rock and roll with your après-ski ritual, come to Los Amigos. The Mexican food is decent at best, but the happy-hour prices and slope-side seating more than make up for any culinary shortcomings.

ℹ Information

Vail Visitor Center (☑970-479-1385; www.visitvailvalley.com; 241 S Frontage Rd; ⊗8:30am-5:30pm winter, to 8pm summer; 🛜)

ℹ Getting There & Around

Eagle County Airport (☑970-328-2680; www.flyvail.com; 219 Eldon Wilson Dr), 35 miles west of Vail, has services to destinations across the country (many of which fly through Denver) and rental-car counters.

Colorado Mountain Express (☑800-525-6363; www.coloradomountainexpress.com; 🛜) shuttles run between Denver International Airport and Eagle County Airport ($84–99). Greyhound buses stop at the **Vail Transportation Center** (☑970-476-5137; 241 S Frontage Rd) en route to Denver ($37, 2½ hours) or Grand Junction ($33, three hours).

Vail's **free buses** (www.vailgov.com; ⊗6:30am-1:50am) shuttle between West Vail, Lionshead and Vail Village; most have ski/bike racks. **ECO regional buses** (ECO) (www.eaglecounty.us; per ride $4, to Leadville $7) also run to Beaver Creek, Minturn and Leadville. To get to Breckenridge and other Summit County resorts, take the Fresh Tracks shuttle (p255).

Compact Vail Village, filled with upscale restaurants, bars and boutiques, is traffic free. Motorists must park in the public parking garage ($25 per day in winter, free in summer) before entering the pedestrian mall area near the chairlifts. Lionshead is a secondary base about half a mile to the west; it also has a parking garage (same rates). It has direct lift access and is usually less crowded.

Aspen

Immodestly posh Aspen is Colorado's glitziest high-octane resort, playing host to some of the wealthiest skiers in the world. The handsome, historic red-brick downtown is as alluring as the glistening slopes, but Aspen's greatest asset is its magnificent scenery. The stunning alpine environment – especially during late September and October, when the aspen trees put on a spectacular display – just adds extra sugar to an already sweet cake.

◉ Sights & Activities

★ Aspen Center for Environmental Studies
WILDLIFE SANCTUARY

(ACES; ☑970-925-5756; www.aspennature.org; 100 Puppy Smith St, Hallam Lake; ⊗9am-5pm Mon-Fri; 🅿 ♿) **FREE** The Aspen Center for Environmental Studies is a 22-acre wildlife sanctuary that hugs the Roaring Fork River. With a mission to advance 'the ethic that the earth must be respected and nurtured,' the center's naturalists provide summertime guided walks, raptor demonstrations and special programs for youngsters.

Aspen Art Museum
MUSEUM

(☑970-925-8050; www.aspenartmuseum.org; 637 East Hyman Ave; ⊗Tue- Sun, 10am-8pm) **FREE** No permanent collection here, just edgy, innovative contemporary exhibitions featuring paintings, mixed media, sculpture, video installations and photography by artists such as Mamma Andersson, Mark Manders and Susan Phiipsz. Art lovers will not leave disappointed. Visit in August and you can experience its annual artCRUSH event, an art auction and wine-tasting extravaganza.

★ Aspen Mountain
SNOW SPORTS

(☑800-525-6200; www.aspensnowmass.com; lift ticket adult/child $117/82; ⊗9am-4pm Dec–mid-Apr; ♿) The Aspen Skiing Company operates the area's four resorts – Snowmass (best all-around choice with the longest vertical drop in the US), Aspen (intermediate/expert), the Highlands (expert) and Buttermilk (beginner/terrain parks) – which are spread out through the valley and connected by free shuttles. Both Aspen and Snowmass are open in summer (lift ticket adult/child $28/11; mid-June to September) for hiking, mountain biking and kids' activities.

Maroon Bells
WILDERNESS AREA

If you have but one day to enjoy a slice of the pristine, you'd be wise to spend it in the shadow of Colorado's most iconic mountain peaks. Hikes range from a mile-long excursion (Crater Lake) to more serious challenges like Buckskin Pass (12,462ft). To get here, you'll need to catch a **shuttle** (Aspen Highlands; adult/child $6/4; ⊗9am-4:30pm daily Jun 15-Aug, Fri-Sun Sep-Oct 6) from the Highlands.

The access road is only open to vehicle traffic ($10) from 5pm to 9am in summer.

CYCLING TO MAROON BELLS

According to the Aspen cycling gurus, the most iconic road-bike ride in Aspen is the one to the stunning **Maroon Bells** (p257). The climb is 11 lung-wrenching miles to the foot of one of the most picturesque wilderness areas in the Rockies. If you crave sweet, beautiful pain, rent two-wheelers at **Aspen Bike Tours** (☑970-925-9169; www.aspenbikerentals.com; 430 S Spring St; half/full day adult from $33/40, child $22/29; ⊙9am-6pm; ⊛).

🛏 Sleeping

Aspen is popular year-round. Reserve well in advance.

The **Aspen Ranger District** (☑970-925-3445; www.fs.usda.gov/whiteriver; 806 W Hallam St; ⊙8am-4:30pm Mon-Fri) operates some 20 **campgrounds** (☑877-444-6777; www.recreation.gov; campsites $15-21) in the Maroon Bells, Independence Pass and Hunter–Fryingpan wilderness areas.

St Moritz Lodge   HOSTEL $
(☑970-925-3220; www.stmoritzlodge.com; 334 W Hyman Ave; dm summer/winter $60/66, d summer $130-269, d winter $155-299; 🅿❄@🛜🏊) St Moritz is the best no-frills deal in town. Perks include a heated outdoor pool and grill overlooking Aspen Mountain, and a lobby with games, books and a piano. The European-style ski lodge offers a wide variety of options, from quiet dorms to two-bedroom condos; the cheapest options share bathrooms. There's a kitchen downstairs.

Annabelle Inn   HOTEL $$
(☑877-266-2466; www.annabelleinn.com; 232 W Main St; r summer/winter from $169/199; 🅿❄@🛜) Personable and unpretentious, the cute and quirky Annabelle Inn resembles an old-school European-style ski lodge in a central location. Rooms are cozy without being too cute, and come with flat-screen TVs and warm duvets. We enjoyed the after-dark ski video screenings from the upper-deck hot tub (one of two on the property).

★Limelight Hotel   HOTEL $$$
(☑800-433-0832; www.limelighthotel.com; 355 S Monarch St; r summer/winter from $245/395; 🅿❄🛜🏊⚑) Sleek and trendy, the Limelight's brick-and-glass modernism reflects Aspen's vibe. Rooms are spacious and have

their perks: granite washbasins, leather headboards and mountain views from the balconies and rooftop terraces. In addition to the ski valet and transportation services, you can also catch live music most winter nights in the lobby's Italian restaurant. Breakfast is included.

🍴 Eating & Drinking

★Justice Snow's   MODERN AMERICAN $$
(☑970-429-8192; www.justicesnows.com; 328 E Hyman Ave; mains $10-22; ⊙11am-2am; 🛜🍴) 🌱 Located in the historic Wheeler Opera House, Justice Snow's is a retro-fitted old saloon that marries antique wooden furnishings with a deft modern touch. Although nominally a bar – the speakeasy cocktails are the soul of the place – the affordable and locally sourced menu ($10 gourmet burger! in Aspen!) is what keeps the locals coming back.

★Pine Creek Cookhouse   AMERICAN $$$
(☑970-925-1044; www.pinecreekcookhouse. com; 12700 Castle Creek Rd; lunch & summer dinner mains $13-41, winter dinner with ski tour/sleigh $90/110; ⊙11:30am-2:30pm daily, 2:30-8:30pm Wed-Sun Jun-Sep, seatings at noon & 1:30pm daily, plus 7pm Wed-Sun Dec-Mar; 🚗⊛) 🌱 This log-cabin restaurant, located 1.5 miles past the Ashcroft ghost town at the end of Castle Creek Rd (about 30min from Aspen), boasts the best setting around. In summer you can hike here; in winter it's cross-country skis or horse-drawn sleigh in the shadow of glorious white-capped peaks. Sample alpine delicacies like house-smoked trout, buffalo tenderloin and grilled elk brats.

Meatball Shack   ITALIAN $$$
(☑970-925-1349; www.themeatballshack.com; 312 S Mill St; lunch $13, dinner $21-28; ⊙11:30am-11:30pm; ⊛) 🌱 Helmed by Florentine chef Eddie Baida and NYC transplant Michael Gurtman, the shack specializes in – you guessed it – fettuccine and meatballs (nonna's, chicken or veal). It's quite the happening place come evening, but forget about the scene for a minute and concentrate on what's on your plate: those locally sourced ingredients definitely make a difference.

★Aspen Brewing Co   BREWERY
(www.aspenbrewingcompany.com; 304 E Hopkins Ave; ⊙noon-late; 🛜) With six signature flavors and a sun-soaked balcony facing the mountain, this is definitely the place to unwind after a hard day's play. Brews range from the flavorful This Year's Blonde and

high-altitude Independence Pass Ale (its IPA) to the mellower Conundrum Red Ale and the chocolaty Pyramid Peak Porter.

Woody Creek Tavern PUB
(☎970-923-4585; www.woodycreektavern.com; 2 Woody Creek Plaza, 2858 Upper River Rd; ⌚11am-10pm) Enjoying a 100% agave tequila and fresh-lime margarita at the late, great gonzo journalist Hunter S Thompson's favorite watering hole is well worth the 8-mile trek from Aspen. Here since 1980, this rustic funky tavern, a local haunt for decades now, has walls that are plastered with newspaper clippings and paraphernalia (mostly dedicated to Thompson).

Information

Aspen Visitor Center (☎970-925-1940; www.aspenchamber.org; 425 Rio Grande Pl; ⌚8:30am-5pm Mon-Fri) Located across from Rio Grande Park.

Getting There & Around

Four miles north of Aspen on Hwy 82, **Aspen-Pitkin County Airport** (☎970-920-5380; www.aspenairport.com; 233 E Airport Rd; 📶) has direct flights from Denver, Los Angeles, Dallas and Chicago. **Colorado Mountain Express** (☎800-525-6363; www.coloradomountainexpress.com; adult/child to DIA $118/61; 📶) runs frequent shuttles to/from Denver International Airport (three hours).

Roaring Fork Transit Agency (www.rfta.com) buses connect Aspen with all four ski areas (free) and runs free trips to and from Aspen-Pitkin County Airport.

If you're driving, it's easiest to park in the public garage ($15 per day) next to the Aspen Visitor Center on Rio Grande Pl.

Salida

Blessed with one of the state's largest historic downtowns, Salida is not only a charming spot to explore, it also has an unbeatable location, with the Arkansas River on one side and the intersection of two mighty mountain ranges on the other. The plan of attack here is to raft, bike or hike during the day, then come back to town to refuel with grilled buffalo ribs and a cold IPA at night.

Activities

Most rafting companies are based just south of Buena Vista (25 miles north of Salida), near where Hwys 24 and 285 diverge.

Buffalo Joe's Whitewater Rafting RAFTING
(☎866-283-3563; www.buffalojoe.com; 113 N Railroad St; half/full day adult $64/98, child $54/78; ⌚May-Sep; 👪) One of the top river outfitters in the Buena Vista–Salida swirl, offering a range of trips that run every bit of the 99 miles of the Arkansas River.

River Runners RAFTING
(☎800-723-8987; www.riverrunnersltd.com; 24070 County Rd 301; half/full day adult $60/98, child $50/88; ⌚May-Sep; 👪) Recommended river outfitter based in both Buena Vista and Cañon City, and in the business of guiding trips since 1972. It does everything from placid float trips to thrilling outings on class V rapids.

Absolute Bikes BICYCLE RENTAL
(☎719-539-9295; www.absolutebikes.com; 330 W Sackett Rd; bike rental $40-80, tours from $90; ⌚9am-7pm; 👪) The place to go for bike enthusiasts, offering maps, gear, advice and rentals. Check out the selection of guided rides, ranging from St Elmo ghost town to the Monarch Crest.

Sleeping

The Arkansas Headwaters Recreation Area operates six campgrounds (bring your own water) along the river. The nicest one is **Hecla Junction** (☎800-678-2267; http://coloradostateparks.reserveamerica.com; Hwy 285, Mile 135; tent/RV sites $16/24 ; 🐾), located north of Salida. Reserve in summer.

★**Simple Lodge & Hostel** HOSTEL $
(☎719-650-7381; www.simplelodge.com; 224 E 1st St; dm/d/q $24/55/76; P📶🐾) If only Colorado had more spots like this. Run by a super-friendly husband-wife team (Jon and Julia), this hostel is simple but stylish, with a fully stocked kitchen and a comfy communal area that feels just like home. It's a popular stopover for touring cyclists following the coast-to-coast Rte 50 – you're likely to meet some interesting folks here.

Eating

★**Amícas** PIZZA $
(www.amicassalida.com; 136 E 2nd St; pizzas & paninis $8-12; ⌚11:30am-9pm; 🍺👪) Thin-crust wood-fired pizzas and six microbrews on tap? Amícas can do no wrong. This laid-back, high-ceilinged hangout (formerly a funeral parlor) is the perfect spot to replenish all those calories you burned off during the day. Savor a Michelangelo (pesto, sausage and

WORTH A TRIP

RAFTING THE ARKANSAS RIVER

The headwaters of the Arkansas form Colorado's most popular stretch of river for rafters and kayakers, with everything from extreme rapids to mellow flat water. Although most rafting companies cover the river from Leadville to the Royal Gorge, the most popular trips descend **Brown's Canyon**, a 22-mile stretch that includes class III/IV rapids. If you're with young kids or just looking for something mellower, **Bighorn Sheep Canyon** is a good bet. Those after more of an adrenaline rush can head upstream to the **Numbers** or downstream to the **Royal Gorge**, both of which are class IV/V.

Water flow varies by season, so time your visit for early June for a wilder ride – by the time August rolls around, the water level is usually pretty low. If you're rafting with kids, note that they need to be six or older and weigh at least 50lb.

goat cheese) or Vesuvio (artichoke hearts, sun-dried tomatoes, roasted peppers) alongside a cool glass of Headwaters IPA.

Fritz TAPAS $
(☑719-539-0364; http://thefritzdowntown.com; 113 East Sackett St; tapas $4-8, mains $9-14; ☺11am-2am; 🐾) This fun and funky riverside watering hole serves up clever American-style tapas. Think three-cheese mac with bacon, fries and truffle aioli, shrimp curry, and even bone marrow with red-onion jam. It also does a mean grass-fed beef burger and other sandwiches at lunch. Good selection of local beers on tap.

ⓘ Information

USFS Ranger Office (☑719-539-3591; www.fs.usda.gov; 5575 Cleora Rd; ☺8am-4:30pm Mon-Fri) Located east of town off Hwy 50, with camping and trail info for the Sawatch and northern Sangre de Cristo Ranges.

ⓘ Getting There & Away

Salida is located at the intersection of Hwys 285 and 50, west of Cañon City and south of Leadville. You'll need your own car to get here.

Colorado Springs

The site of one of the country's first destination resorts, Colorado Springs sits at the foot of majestic Pikes Peak. Pinned down with four military bases and recently beset by a series of devastating summer wildfires, the city has evolved into a strange and sprawling quilt of neighborhoods – visitors can best come to grips with the layout by dividing it in three.

From east to west along Hwy 24 is the downtown district, an odd mix of fine art, Olympic dreams and downbeat desperation; Old Colorado City, whose Old West brothels and saloons now host restaurants and shops; and new-agey Manitou Springs, whose mountainside location makes it the most visitor-friendly part of town.

⦿ Sights & Activities

★**Pikes Peak** MOUNTAIN
(☑719-385-7325; www.springsgov.com; highway per adult/child $12/5; ☺7:30am-8pm Jun-Aug, 7:30am-5pm Sep, 9am-3pm Oct-May; 🅿) Pikes Peak (14,110ft) may not be the tallest of Colorado's 54 14ers, but it's certainly the most famous. The Ute originally called it the Mountain of the Sun, an apt description for this majestic peak, which crowns the southern Front Range. Rising 7400ft straight up from the plains, the mountain is climbed by over half a million visitors every year.

Its location as the easternmost 14er has contributed heavily to its place in American myth. Zebulon Pike first made note of it in 1806 (he called it 'Grand Peak' but never made it to the top) when exploring the Louisiana Purchase. Katherine Bates, a guest lecturer at Colorado College in 1893, wrote the original draft of *America the Beautiful* after reaching the summit.

Today there are three ways to ascend the peak: the Pikes Peak Hwy (about a five hour round-trip), which was built in 1915 by Spencer Penrose and winds 19 miles to the top from Hwy 24 west of town; the **cog railway** (☑719-685-5401; www.cograilway.com; 515 Ruxton Ave; round-trip adult/child $35/19; ☺8am-5:20pm May-Oct, reduced hours Nov-Apr; 🅿); and on foot via the Barr Trail.

Garden of the Gods PARK
(www.gardenofgods.com; 1805 N 30th St; ☺5am-11pm May-Oct, 5am-9pm Nov-Apr; 🅿🐾) **FREE**
This gorgeous vein of red sandstone (about

290 million years old) appears elsewhere along Colorado's Front Range, but the exquisitely thin cathedral spires and mountain backdrop of the Garden of the Gods are particularly striking. Explore the network of paved and unpaved trails, enjoy a picnic and watch climbers test their nerve on the sometimes flaky rock.

★ **Colorado Springs**

Fine Arts Center   MUSEUM
(FAC; ☑ 719-634-5583; www.csfineartscenter.org; 30 W Dale St; adult/student $10/8.50; ☉ 10am-5pm Tue-Sun; 𝗣) Fully renovated in 2007, this expansive museum and 400-seat theater originally opened in 1936. The museum's collection is surprisingly sophisticated, with some terrific Latin American art and photography, and great rotating exhibits that draw from the 23,000 pieces in its permanent collection.

US Air Force Academy   MILITARY ACADEMY
(☑ 719-333-2025; www.usafa.af.mil; I-25 exit 156B; ☉ visitor center 9am-5pm; 𝗣) FREE It is one of the highest-profile military academies in the country, and a visit to this campus offers a limited but nonetheless fascinating look into the lives of an elite group of cadets. The visitor center provides general background on the academy; from here you can walk over to the dramatic chapel (1963) or embark on a driving tour of the expansive grounds.

Barr Trail   HIKING
(www.barrcamp.com; Hydro St) The tough 12.5-mile Barr Trail ascends Pikes Peak with a substantial 7400ft of elevation gain. Most hikers split the trip into two days, stopping to overnight at Barr Camp, the halfway point at 10,200ft. The trailhead is near the Manitou Springs cog railway depot; parking is $5.

🛏 **Sleeping**

Barr Camp   CAMPGROUND $
(www.barrcamp.com; tent sites $12, lean-tos $17, cabin dm $28; 🐾) At the halfway point on the Barr Trail, about 6.5 miles from the Pikes Peak summit, you can pitch a tent, shelter in a lean-to or reserve a bare-bones cabin. It has drinking water and showers; dinner ($8) is available Wednesday to Sunday. Reservations are essential and must be made online in advance. It's open year-round.

Mining Exchange   HOTEL $$
(☑ 719-323-2000; www.wyndham.com; 8 S Nevada Ave; r $135-200; 𝗣✳🛜) Opened in 2012 and set in the former turn-of-the-century bank

where Cripple Creek prospectors traded in their gold for cash (check out the vault door in the lobby), the Mining Exchange takes the prize for Colorado Spring's most stylish hotel. Twelve-foot-high ceilings, exposed brick walls and leather furnishings make for an inviting, contemporary feel, though its downtown location is better suited to businesspeople than tourists. Excellent-value rates.

Two Sisters Inn   B&B $$
(☑ 719-685-9684; www.twosisinn.com; 10 Otoe Pl, Manitou Springs; r without bath $79-94, with bath $135-155; 𝗣✳🛜) A longtime favorite among B&B aficionados, this place has five rooms (including the honeymoon cottage out back) set in a rose-colored Victorian home, built in 1919 by two sisters. It was originally a boarding house for school teachers, and has been an inn since 1990. It has a magnificent stained-glass front door and an 1896 piano in the parlor. The inn has won awards for its breakfast recipes.

Broadmoor   RESORT $$$
(☑ 855-634-7711; www.broadmoor.com; 1 Lake Ave; r from $280-500; 𝗣✳🛜🏊🐾) One of the top five-star resorts in the US, the 744-room Broadmoor sits in a picture-perfect location against the blue-green slopes of Cheyenne Mountain. Everything here is exquisite: acres of lush grounds and a lake, a glimmering pool, world-class golf, myriad bars and restaurants, an incredible spa and ubercomfortable guest rooms (which, it must be said, are of the 'grandmother' school of design).

🍴 **Eating & Drinking**

Shuga's   CAFE $
(www.shugas.com; 702 S Cascade St; dishes $8-9; ☉ 11am-midnight; 🛜♿) If you thought Colorado Springs couldn't be hip, stroll to Shuga's, a Southern-style cafe with a knack for knockout espresso drinks and hot cocktails. Cuter than buttons, this little white house is decked out in paper cranes and red vinyl chairs. There's also patio seating. The food – brie BLT on rosemary toast, Brazilian coconut shrimp soup – comforts and delights. Don't miss vintage-movie Saturdays.

★ **Marigold**   FRENCH $$
(☑ 719-599-4776; www.marigoldcafeandbakery.com; 4605 Centennial Blvd; lunch $8.25-11, dinner $9-19; ☉ 11am-2:30pm & 5-9pm Mon-Sat, bakery 8am-9pm) Way out by the Garden of the Gods is this buzzy French bistro and bakery that's easy on both the palate and the wallet. Feast

WORTH A TRIP

CRIPPLE CREEK CASINOS

Just an hour from Colorado Springs yet worlds away, Cripple Creek hurls you back into the Wild West. This once lucky lady had produced a staggering $413 million in gold by 1952.

The booze still flows and gambling still thrives, but yesteryear's saloons and brothels are now modern casinos. If you're more interested in regional history or simply need a break from the slots, check out the **Heritage Center** (www.visitcripplecreek.com; 9283 Hwy 67; ⊗8am-7pm; ♿), the popular **gold mine tour** (www.goldminetours.com; 9388 Hwy 67; adult/child $18/10; ⊗8:45am-6pm mid-May–Oct; ♿) and the **narrow gauge railroad** (http://cripplecreekrailroad.com; Bennet Ave; adult/child $13/8; ⊗10am-5pm mid-May–mid-Oct; ♿🐾) to historic Victor.

Cripple Creek is 50 miles southwest of Colorado Springs on scenic Hwy 67. For an even more impressive drive, check out the old Gold Camp Rd (Hwy 336) out of Victor on the way home. It's unpaved and narrow, but provides spectacular views. It takes about 90 minutes down to the Springs. Alternatively, catch the **Ramblin' Express** (☎719-590-8687; www.ramblinexpress.com; round-trip tickets $25; ⊗departures 7am-midnight Wed-Sun) from Colorado Springs' 8th St Depot.

on delicacies such as snapper Marseillaise, garlic and rosemary rotisserie chicken, and gourmet salads and pizzas, and be sure to leave room for the double (and triple!) chocolate mousse cake and lemon tarts.

Adam's Mountain Cafe   MODERN AMERICAN $$

(☎719-685-1430; www.adamsmountain.com; 934 Manitou Ave; mains $9-19; ⊗8am-3pm daily, 5-9pm Tue-Sat; 🐾♿) In Manitou Springs, this slow-food cafe makes a lovely stop. Breakfast includes orange-almond French toast and huevos rancheros (eggs and beans on a tortilla). Lunch and dinner are more eclectic with offerings such as Moroccan chicken, pasta *gremolata* and grilled watermelon salad. The interior is airy and attractive with marble floors and exposed rafters, and it has patio dining and occasional live music too.

Jake & Telly's   GREEK $$

(☎719-633-0406; www.greekdining.com; 2616 W Colorado Ave; lunch $9-12, dinner $16-25; ⊗11:30am-9pm; 🐾♿) One of the best choices in Old Colorado City, this Greek eatery looks and sounds slightly touristy – lots of Greek monument murals on the walls and themed music on the stereo – but the food is absolutely delicious. It does a nice Greek-dip sandwich as well as traditional dishes such as souvlaki, dolmades and spanakopita. It's set on a 2nd-story terrace above a magic wand shop.

★ Swirl   WINE BAR

(www.swirlwineemporium.com; 717 Manitou Ave; ⊗noon-10pm Sun-Thu, to midnight Fri & Sat) Behind a stylish bottle shop in Manitou Springs, this nook bar is intimate and cool.

The garden patio has dangling lights and vines while inside are antique armchairs and a fireplace. If you're feeling peckish, sample the tapas and homemade pasta.

Bristol Brewing Co   BREWERY

(www.bristolbrewing.com; 1604 S Cascade Ave; ⊗11am-10pm; 🐾) Although a bit out of the way in south Colorado Springs, this brewery – which in 2013 spearheaded a community market center in the shuttered Ivywild Elementary School – is worth seeking out for its Laughing Lab ale and pub grub from the owner of the gourmet **Blue Star** (☎719-632-1086; www.thebluestar.net; 1645 S Tejon St; mains $21-35; ⊗from 3pm; 🅿🐾). Other back-to-school tenants include a bakery, deli, cafe, art gallery and movie theater in the old gym.

❶ Information

Colorado Springs Convention & Visitors Bureau (☎719-635-7506; www.visitcos.com; 515 S Cascade Ave; ⊗8:30am-5pm; 🐾) All the usual tourist pamphlets.

❶ Getting There & Around

Colorado Springs Municipal Airport (p235) is a smaller and much more easily navigable alternative to Denver. The **Yellow Cab** (☎719-777-7777) fare from the airport to the city center is around $30.

Buses between Cheyenne, WY, and Pueblo, CO, stop daily at **Greyhound** (☎719-635-1505; 120 S Weber St). **Mountain Metropolitan Transit** (www.springsgov.com; per trip $1.75, day pass $4) offers local bus information online.

Southern Colorado

Home to the dramatic San Juan and Sangre de Cristo mountain ranges, Colorado's bottom half is just as pretty as its top.

Crested Butte

Remote and ringed by three wilderness areas, this former mining village is counted among Colorado's best ski resorts (some say it's *the* best). The old town center features beautifully preserved Victorian-era buildings refitted with shops and businesses. Strolling two-wheel traffic matches its laidback, happy attitude.

Most everything in town is on Elk Ave, including the **visitor center** (✆970-349-6438; www.crestedbuttechamber.com; 601 Elk Ave; ⊙9am-5pm).

Two miles north of the town at the base of the impressive mountain of the same name, **Crested Butte Mountain Resort** (✆970-349-2222; www.skicb.com; 12 Snowmass Rd; lift ticket adult/child $98/54; ♿) is surrounded by forests, rugged mountain peaks and the West Elk, Raggeds and Maroon Bells-Snowmass Wilderness Areas. The scenery is breathtakingly beautiful. It caters mostly to intermediate and expert riders.

Crested Butte International Hostel (✆970-349-0588, toll-free 888-389-0588; www.crestedbuttehostel.com; 615 Teocalli Ave; dm/d shared bath $36/89, r $104-109; ☎) is one of Colorado's nicest hostels. The best private rooms have their own baths. Dorm bunks come with reading lamps and lockable drawers. The communal area is mountain rustic with a stone fireplace and comfortable couches. Rates vary dramatically by season, with fall being cheapest.

With phenomenal food, the funky-casual **Secret Stash** (✆970-349-6245; www.thesecretstash.com; 303 Elk Ave; mains $8-24; ⊙8am-late; ♿) is adored by locals, who also dig the original cocktails. The house specialty is pizza; its Notorious Fig (with prosciutto, fresh figs and truffle oil) won the World Pizza Championship.

Crested Butte's air link to the outside world is **Gunnison County Airport** (✆970-641-2304), 28 miles south of the town. Shuttle **Alpine Express** (✆970-641-5074; www.alpineexpressshuttle.com; per person $34) goes to Crested Butte; reserve ahead in summer. The free **Mountain Express** (✆970-349-7318; www.mtnexp.org) connects Crested Butte with Mt Crested Butte every 15 minutes in winter, less often in other seasons; check times at bus stops.

Ouray

With gorgeous ice falls draping the box canyon and soothing hot springs that dot the valley floor, Ouray is a privileged place for nature, even for Colorado. For ice-climbers it's a world-class destination, but hikers and 4WD fans can also appreciate its rugged charms. The town is a well-preserved quarter-mile mining village sandwiched between imposing peaks.

Between Silverton and Ouray, US 550 is one of the state's most memorable drives and is paved, but the road is scary in rain or snow, so take extra care.

🏃 Activities

The visitor center is at the hot-springs pool. Check out their leaflet on an excellent walking tour that takes in two-dozen houses and other buildings constructed between 1880 and 1904.

Ouray Ice Park   ICE CLIMBING
(✆970-325-4061; www.ourayicepark.com; Hwy 361; ⊙7am-5pm mid-Dec–Mar; ♿) **FREE** Enthusiasts from around the globe come to ice climb at the world's first public ice park, spanning a 2-mile stretch of the Uncompahgre Gorge. The sublime (if chilly) experience offers something for all skill levels. Get instruction through a local guide service.

Ouray Hot Springs   HOT SPRING
(✆970-325-7073; www.ourayhotsprings.com; 1200 Main St; adult/child $12/8; ⊙10am-10pm Jun-Aug, noon-9pm Mon-Fri & 11am-9pm Sat & Sun Sep-May; ♿) For a healing soak, try the historic Ouray Hot Springs. The natural springwater is crystal-clear and free of the sulphur smells plaguing other hot springs around here, and the giant pool features a variety of soaking areas at temperatures from 96°F to 106°F (36°C to 41°C). The complex also offers a gym and massage service.

San Juan Mountain Guides   CLIMBING, SKIING
(✆800-642-5389, 970-325-4925; www.ourayclimbing.com; 725 Main St; ♿) Ouray's own professional guiding and climbing group is certified with the International Federation of Mountain Guides Association (IFMGA). It specializes in ice and rock climbing and wilderness backcountry skiing.

✦ Festivals & Events

Ouray Ice Festival
ICE CLIMBING

(📞970-325-4288; www.ourayicefestival.com; donation for evening events; ⊘ Jan; ⊞) The Ouray Ice Festival features four days of climbing competitions, dinners, slide shows and clinics. There's even a climbing wall set up for kids. You can watch the competitions for free, but various evening events require a donation to the ice park. Once inside, you'll get free brews from popular Colorado brewer New Belgium.

🛏 Sleeping & Eating

Amphitheater Forest Service Campground
CAMPGROUND $

(📞877-444-6777; www.recreation.gov; US Hwy 550; tent sites $20; ⊘ Jun-Aug) With great tent sites under the trees, this high-altitude campground is a score. On holiday weekends a three-night minimum applies. South of town on Hwy 550, take a signposted left-hand turn.

★ Wiesbaden
HOTEL $$

(📞970-325-4347; www.wiesbadenhotsprings.com; 625 5th St; r $132-347; ⊘🛜♨) Quirky, quaint and new age, Wiesbaden even boasts a natural indoor vapor cave, which, in another era, was frequented by Chief Ouray. Rooms with quilted bedcovers are cozy and romantic, but the sunlit suite with a natural rock wall tops all. In the morning, guests roam in thick robes, drinking the free organic coffee or tea, post-soak or awaiting massages.

Box Canyon Lodge & Hot Springs
LODGE $$

(📞800-327-5080, 970-325-4981; www.boxcanyonouray.com; 45 3rd Ave; r $120-218; 🛜) 🅿 It's not every hotel that offers geothermal heated rooms, and pine-board rooms prove spacious and fresh. Spring-fed barrel hot tubs are perfect for a romantic stargazing soak. With good hospitality that includes free apples and bottled water, it's popular, so book ahead.

Buen Tiempo Mexican Restaurant & Cantina
MEXICAN $$

(📞970-325-4544; 515 Main St; mains $7-20; ⊘6-10pm; 🅿) This good-time spot bursts with bar-stool squatters and booths of families. From the chili-rubbed sirloin to the posole with warm tortillas, Buen Tiempo delivers. Start with a signature margarita with chips and spicy homemade salsa. End with a satisfying scoop of deep-fried ice cream. But to find out how the dollars got on the ceiling, it will cost you.

ℹ Information

Ouray Visitors Center (📞800-228-1876, 970-325-4746; www.ouraycolorado.com; 1230 Main St; ⊘10am-5pm Mon-Sat, 10am-3pm Sun; 🛜⊞) Staffed by volunteers, this useful visitor center has brochures and the usual information. It's near the Ouray hot-springs pool.

ℹ Getting There & Away

Ouray is 24 miles north of Silverton along US 550 and best reached by private vehicle.

DON'T MISS

SCENIC DRIVE: SAN JUAN MOUNTAIN PASSES

With rugged peaks and deep canyon drops, the scenery of the San Juan mountain range is hard to beat. Suitable for all vehicles, the **Million Dollar Highway** (US 550) takes its name from the valuable ore in the roadbed. But the scenery is also golden – the paved road clings to crumbly mountains, passing old mine-head frames and big alpine scenery.

A demanding but fantastic drive, the 65-mile **Alpine Loop Backcountry Byway** (www.alpineloop.com) begins in **Ouray** and travels east to **Lake City** – a wonderful mountain hamlet worth a visit – before looping back to its starting point. Along the way you'll cross two 12,000ft mountain passes and swap pavement and people for solitude, spectacular views and abandoned mining haunts. You'll need a high-clearance 4WD vehicle and some off-road driving skills to conquer this drive; allow six hours.

Spectacular during autumn for the splendor of its yellow aspens, **Ophir Pass** connects Ouray to Telluride via a former wagon road. The moderate 4WD route passes former mines, with a gradual ascent to 11,789ft. To get there, drive south of Ouray on Hwy 550 for 18.1 miles to the right-hand turnoff for National Forest Access, Ophir Pass.

As with all 4WD routes and mountain passes, check for road closures before going. The road can be dangerous in wet or frozen conditions, so drive carefully.

Telluride

Surrounded on three sides by mastodon peaks, exclusive Telluride feels cut off from the hubbub of the outside world, and it often is. Once a rough mining town, today it's dirt-bag-meets-diva – mixing the few who can afford the real estate with those scratching out a slope-side living for the sport of it. The town center still has palpable old-time charm and the surroundings are simply gorgeous.

Colorado Ave, also known as Main St, is where you'll find most businesses. From downtown you can reach the ski mountain via two lifts and the gondola. The latter also links Telluride with Mountain Village, the true base for the Telluride Ski Area. Located 7 miles from town along Hwy 145, Mountain Village is a 20-minute drive east, but is only 12 minutes away by gondola (free for foot passengers).

🏃 Activities

Telluride Ski Resort SNOW SPORTS
(☑970-728-7533, 888-288-7360; www.tellurideskiresort.com; 565 Mountain Village Blvd; adult/child full-day lift ticket $112/67) Covering three distinct areas, Telluride Ski Resort is served by 16 lifts. Much of the terrain is for advanced and intermediate skiers, but there's still ample choice for beginners.

✨ Festivals & Events

★ Mountainfilm FILM
(www.mountainfilm.org; ☉May) A four-day screening of outdoor adventure and environmental films.

Telluride Bluegrass Festival MUSIC
(☑800-624-2422; www.planetbluegrass.com; 4-day pass $205; ☉late Jun) This festival attracts thousands for a weekend of top-notch rollicking alfresco bluegrass. Stalls sell all sorts of food and local microbrews to keep you happy, and acts continue well into the night. Camping out for the four-day festival is very popular. Check the website for info on sites, shuttle services and combo ticket-and-camping packages – it's all very organized!

Telluride Film Festival FILM
(☑603-433-9202; www.telluridefilmfestival.com; ☉early Sep) National and international films are premiered throughout town, and the event attracts big-name stars. For more information on the relatively complicated pricing scheme, visit the film-festival website.

COLORADO HUT-TO-HUT

An exceptional way to enjoy hundreds of miles of single-track in summer or virgin powder slopes in winter, **San Juan Hut Systems** (☑970-626-3033; www.sanjuanhuts.com; per person $30) continues the European tradition of hut-to-hut adventures with five backcountry mountain huts. Bring just your food, flashlight and sleeping bag: amenities include padded bunks, propane stoves, wood stoves for heating and firewood.

The website has helpful tips and information on rental skis, bikes and (optional) guides based in Ridgway or Ouray.

🛏 Sleeping

Telluride's lodgings can fill quickly, and for the best rates it's best to book online. Unless you're planning to camp, however, don't expect budget deals.

Telluride Town Park Campground CAMPGROUND $
(☑970-728-2173; 500 E Colorado Ave; campsite with/without vehicle space $23/17; ☉mid-May–mid-Oct; 🖥🏊) Right in the center of town, it has 20 sites with shower access ($1.50 for a hot shower). It fills up quickly in the high season. There are many other campgrounds within 10 miles of town; check with the visitor center for more info.

Victorian Inn LODGE $$
(☑970-728-6601; www.victorianinntelluride.com; 401 W Pacific Ave; r from $124; ☉❄🖥) The smell of fresh cinnamon rolls greets visitors at one of Telluride's better deals, offering comfortable rooms (some with kitchenettes) and a hot tub and dry sauna. Best off all, there are fantastic lift-ticket deals for guests. Kids aged 12 years and under stay free, and you can't beat the downtown location.

Hotel Columbia HOTEL $$$
(☑970-728-0660, toll-free 800-201-9505; www.columbiatelluride.com; 300 W San Juan Ave; d/ste from $265/365; 🅿❄🖥🏊) Since pricey digs are a given, skiers might as well stay right across the street from the gondola. Locally owned and operated, this stylish and swank hotel pampers. Store your gear in the ski and boot storage and head directly to a room with espresso maker, fireplace and heated tile floors. With shampoo dispensers and recycling, it's also pretty eco-friendly.

DON'T MISS

TELLURIDE'S GREAT OUTDOORS

Sure, the festivals are great, but there's much more to a Telluride summer.

Mountain Biking

Follow the River Trail from Town Park to Hwy 145 for 2 miles. Join **Mill Creek Trail** west of the Texaco gas station, it climbs and follows the contour of the mountain and ends at the Jud Wiebe Trail (hikers only).

Hiking

Just over 2 miles, **Bear Creek Trail** ascends 1040ft to a beautiful cascading waterfall. From here you can access the strenuous **Wasatch Trail**, a 12-mile loop that heads west across the mountains to **Bridal Veil Falls** – Telluride's most impressive waterfalls. The Bear Creek trailhead is at the south end of Pine St, across the San Miguel River.

Cycling

A 31-mile (one-way) trip, **Lizard Head Pass** features amazing mountain panoramas.

Eating & Drinking

For the best deals, look for food carts serving Mediterranean food, hot dogs, tacos and coffee on Colorado Ave.

The Butcher & The Baker CAFE $
(970-728-3334; 217 E Colorado Ave; mains $10; 7am-7pm Mon-Sat, 8am-2pm Sun;) Two veterans of upscale local catering started this heartbreakingly cute cafe, and no one beats it for breakfast. Hearty sandwiches with local meats are the perfect takeout for the trail and there are heaps of baked goods and fresh sides.

There TAPAS, COCKTAIL BAR $$
(970-728-1213; http://therebars.com; 627 W Pacific Ave; mains $6-28; 5pm-midnight Mon-Fri, 10am-3pm Sat & Sun) A hip social alcove for cocktails and nibbling, plus weekend brunch. Bigger appetites can dine on shareable mains such as whole Colorado trout. On a comic-book-style menu, East meets West in yummy lettuce wraps, duck ramen and sashimi tostadas, paired with original hand-shaken drinks. We liked the jalapeño kiss.

La Cocina de Luz MEXICAN, ORGANIC $$
(www.lacocinatelluride.com; 123 E Colorado Ave; mains $9-19; 9am-9pm;) As they lovingly serve two Colorado favorites (organic and Mexican), it's no wonder that the lunch line runs deep at this healthy taqueria. Order the achiote pulled pork and you might be full until tomorrow. Delicious details include a salsa and chip bar, handmade tortillas and margaritas with organic lime and agave nectar. With vegan and gluten-free options too.

New Sheridan Bar BAR
(970-728-3911; www.newsheridan.com; 231 W Colorado Ave; 5pm-2am) Well worth a visit in low season for some real local flavor and opinions. At other times, it's a rush hour of beautiful people. But old bullet holes in the wall testify to the plucky survival of the bar itself, even as the adjoining hotel sold off chandeliers and antiques to pay the heating bills when mining fortunes waned.

Entertainment

Fly Me to the Moon Saloon LIVE MUSIC
(970-728-6666; 132 E Colorado Ave; 3pm-2am) Let your hair down and kick up your heels to the tunes of live bands at this saloon, the best place in Telluride to party hard.

Sheridan Opera House THEATER
(970-728-4539; www.sheridanoperahouse.com; 110 N Oak St;) This historic venue has a burlesque charm and is always the center of Telluride's cultural life. It hosts the Telluride Repertory Theater and frequently has special performances for children.

Information

Visitor Center (888-353-5473, 970-728-3041; www.telluride.com; 398 W Colorado Ave; 9am-5pm)

Getting There & Around

Commuter aircraft serve the mesa-top **Telluride Airport** (970-778-5051; www.tellurideairport.com; Last Dollar Rd), 5 miles east of town on Hwy 145. If the weather is poor, flights may be diverted to Montrose, 65 miles north. For car rental, National and Budget both have airport locations.

In ski season Montrose has direct flights to and from Denver (on United), Houston, Phoenix and limited cities on the East Coast.

Shared shuttles by **Telluride Express** (☑ 970-728-6000; www.tellurideexpress.com) go from the Telluride Airport to town or Mountain Village for $15. Shuttles between the Montrose Airport and Telluride cost $50.

Silverton

Ringed by snowy peaks and steeped in sooty tales of a tawdry mining town, Silverton seems like it would be more at home in Alaska than the lower 48. But here it is. Whether you're into snowmobiling, powder skiing, fly-fishing, beer on tap or just basking in some very high-altitude sunshine, Silverton delivers.

It's a two-street town, but only one is paved. The main drag, Greene St, is where you'll find most businesses. Notorious Blair St, still unpaved, runs parallel to Greene and is a blast from the past. During the silver rush, Blair St was home to thriving brothels and boozing establishments.

🏃 Activities

In summer, Silverton has some of the West's best 4WD trails. Traveling in modified Chevy Suburbans without the top, **San Juan Backcountry** (☑ 970-387-5565, toll-free 800-494-8687; www.sanjuanbackcountry.com; 1119 Greene St; 2hr tour adult/child $60/40; ☺ May-Oct; ⊕) ⌀ offers both tours and rental jeeps.

🛏 Sleeping & Eating

Red Mountain Motel & RV Park   MOTEL, CAMPGROUND $$
(☑ 970-382-5512, toll-free 800-970-5512; www.redmtmotelrvpk.com; 664 Greene St; motel r from $80, cabins from $70, RV/tent sites $38/22; ☺ year-round; P ⊕ ≋ ☻) The tiny log cabins stay warm and make good use of their limited space with a double bed, a bunk, a tiny TV and a fully outfitted kitchenette. The managers are friendly and keen to make sure guests and customers have a good time. It's a pet-friendly place that stays open year-round.

Inn of the Rockies at the Historic Alma House   B&B $$
(☑ 970-387-5336, toll-free 800-267-5336; www.innoftherockies.com; 220 E 10th St; r incl breakfast $109-173; P ⊕ ≋) Opened by a local named Alma in 1898, this inn has nine unique rooms furnished with Victorian antiques. The hospitality is first-rate and its New

Orleans–inspired breakfasts, served in a chandelier-lit dining room, merit special mention. Cheaper rates are available without breakfast. There's also a garden hot tub for soaking after a long day.

Stellar   ITALIAN $$
(☑ 970-387-9940; 1260 Blair St; mains $8-20; ☺ 4-9:30pm; ⊕) This friendly place is a good choice for dinner. Locals come here for the stellar pizzas, friendly service and easy atmosphere. There's a full bar with beers on tap, and the lasagna and freshly made salads are always good.

🍷 Drinking & Nightlife

★ **Montanya Distillers**   BAR
(www.montanyadistillers.com; 1309 Greene St; mains $6-14; ☺ noon-10pm) Under new management, this regional favorite still delivers, now in a spacious minimalist bar on Greene St. On a summer day, score a seat on the rooftop deck. Bartenders here can talk you into anything, crafting exotic cocktails with homemade syrups and their very own award-winning rum. It's worth it just for the fun atmosphere. Note: low season hours change.

ℹ Getting There & Away

Silverton is 50 miles north of Durango and 24 miles south of Ouray off US 550.

Mesa Verde National Park

Shrouded in mystery, **Mesa Verde**, with its cliff dwellings and verdant valley walls, is a fascinating, if slightly eerie, national park to explore. It is here that a civilization of Ancestral Puebloans appears to have vanished in AD 1300, leaving behind a complex civilization of cliff dwellings, some accessed by sheer climbs. Mesa Verde is unique among parks for its focus on preserving this civilization's cultural relics so that future generations may continue to interpret the puzzling settlement, and subsequent abandonment, of the area.

Mesa Verde rewards travelers who set aside a day or more to take the ranger-led tours of Cliff Palace and Balcony House, explore Wetherill Mesa or participate in one of the campfire programs. But if you only have time for a short visit, check out the Chapin Mesa Museum and walk through the Spruce Tree House, where you can climb down a wooden ladder into the cool chamber of a *kiva* (ceremonial structure, usually partly underground).

◉ Sights & Activities

Chapin Mesa Museum   MUSEUM
(☑970-529-4475; www.nps.gov/meve; Chapin Mesa Rd; admission incl with park entry; ⊙8am-6:30pm Apr–mid-Oct, 8am-5pm mid-Oct–Apr; ℗⚑) The Chapin Mesa Museum has exhibits pertaining to the Mesa Verde National Park. It's a good first stop. Staff at the museum provide information on weekends when the park headquarters is closed.

Chapin Mesa   ARCHAEOLOGICAL SITE
The largest concentration of Ancestral Puebloan sites is at Chapin Mesa, where you'll see the densely clustered **Far View Site** and the large **Spruce Tree House**, the most accessible of sites, with a paved half-mile round-trip path.

If you want to see **Cliff Palace** or **Balcony House**, the only way is through an hour-long ranger-led tour booked in advance at the visitor center ($4). These tours are extremely popular; go early in the morning or a day in advance to book. Balcony House requires climbing a 32ft and 60ft ladder.

Wetherill Mesa   ARCHAEOLOGICAL SITE
This is the second-largest concentration of Ancestral Puebloan sites. Visitors may enter stabilized surface sites and two cliff dwellings, including the **Long House**, open from late May through August. South from Park Headquarters, the 6-mile **Mesa Top Road** connects excavated mesa-top sites, accessible cliff dwellings and vantage points to view inaccessible dwellings from the mesa rim.

★ Aramark Mesa Verde   HIKING
(☑970-529-4421; www.visitmesaverde.com; adult $42-48) The park concessionaire, Aramark Mesa Verde, offers guided tours to excavated pit homes, cliff dwellings and the Spruce Tree House daily from May to mid-October.

⛺ Sleeping & Eating

The nearby towns of Cortez and Mancos have plenty of midrange places to stay; inside the park there's camping and a lodge.

Morefield Campground   CAMPGROUND $
(☑970-529-4465; www.visitmesaverde.com; North Rim Rd; tent/RV sites $30/40; ⊙May-early Oct; 🐾) 🍴 The park's camping option, located 4 miles from the entrance gate, also has 445 regular tent sites on grassy grounds conveniently located near Morefield Village. The village has a general store, gas station, restaurant, showers and laundry. It's managed by Aramark. Dry RV campsites (without hookup) cost the same as tent sites.

Far View Lodge   LODGE $$
(☑970-529-4421, toll-free 800-449-2288; www.visitmesaverde.com; North Rim Rd; r $117-177; ⊙mid-Apr–Oct; ℗🐾❄🛜🐾) Perched on a mesa top 15 miles inside the park entrance, this tasteful Pueblo-style lodge has 150 Southwestern-style rooms, some with *kiva* fireplaces. Don't miss sunset over the mesa from your private balcony. Standard rooms don't have air con (or TV) and summer daytimes can be hot. You can even bring your dog for an extra $10 per night.

Far View Terrace Café   CAFE $
(☑970-529-4421, toll-free 800-449-2288; www.visitmesaverde.com; North Rim Rd; dishes from $6; ⊙7-10am, 11am-3pm & 5-8pm May–mid-Oct; 🐾⚑) Housed in Far View Lodge immediately south of the visitor center, this self-service place offers reasonably priced meals and a convenient espresso bar. Don't miss the house special: the Navajo Taco.

Metate Room   MODERN AMERICAN $$$
(☑800-449-2288; www.visitmesaverde.com; North Rim Rd; mains $18-29; ⊙7-10am & 5-7:30pm Apr–mid-Oct, 5-7:30pm mid-Oct–Mar; 🐾⚑) 🍴 With an award in culinary excellence, this upscale restaurant in the Far View Lodge offers an innovative menu inspired by Native American food and flavors. Interesting dishes include stuffed poblano chilies, cinnamon chili pork tenderloin and grilled quail with prickly pear jam.

ℹ Information

The park entrance is off US 160, midway between Cortez and Mancos. The 2012 **Mesa Verde Visitor and Research Center** (☑800-305-6053, 970-529-5034; www.nps.gov/meve; North Rim Rd; ⊙8am-7pm Jun-early Sep, 8am-5pm early Sep–mid-Oct, closed mid-Oct–May; ⚑), located near the entrance, has information and news on park closures (many areas are closed in winter). It also sells tickets for **tours** ($3) of the magnificent Cliff Palace or Balcony House.

Durango

An archetypal old Colorado mining town, Durango is a regional darling that is nothing short of delightful. Its graceful hotels, Victorian-era saloons and tree-lined streets of sleepy bungalows invite you to pedal around soaking up all the good vibes. There is plenty to do outdoors. Style-wise, Durango is torn between its ragtime past and a cool, cutting-edge future where townie bikes, caffeine and farmers markets rule.

The town's historic central precinct is home to boutiques, bars, restaurants and theater halls. Foodies will revel in the innovative organic and locavore fare that is making it the best place to eat in the state. But the interesting galleries and live music, combined with a relaxed and congenial local populace, also make it a great place to visit.

🏃 Activities

Mountain Biking
CYCLING

From steep single-track to scenic road rides, Durango is a national hub for mountain biking. The easy **Old Railroad Grade Trail** is a 12.2-mile loop that uses both US Hwy 160 and a dirt road following the old railway tracks. From Durango take Hwy 160 west through the town of Hesperus. Turn right into the Cherry Creek Picnic Area, where the trail starts.

For something a bit more technical, try **Dry Fork Loop**, accessible from Lightner Creek just west of town. It has some great drops, blind corners and vegetation. Cycling shops on Main or Second Ave rent out mountain bikes.

★ Durango & Silverton Narrow Gauge Railroad
RAILWAY

(📞970-247-2733; www.durangotrain.com; 479 Main Ave; return adult/child 4-11yr from $85/51; ⊙May-Oct; 🚻) Riding the Durango & Silverton Narrow Gauge Railroad is a Durango must. These vintage steam locomotives have been making the scenic 45-mile trip north to Silverton (3½ hours each way) for more than 125 years. The dazzling journey allows two hours for exploring Silverton. This trip operates only from May through October. Check online for winter options.

Durango Mountain Resort
SNOW SPORTS

(📞970-247-9000; www.durangomountainresort. com; 1 Skier Pl; lift tickets adult/child from $77/45; ⊙mid-Nov–Mar; 🚻) Durango Mountain Resort, 25 miles north of Durango on US 550, is Durango's winter highlight. The resort, also known as Purgatory, offers 1200 skiable acres of varying difficulty and boasts 260in of snow per year. Two terrain parks offer plenty of opportunities for snowboarders to catch big air.

Check local grocery stores and newspapers for promotions and 2-for-1 lift tickets and other ski season specials before purchasing directly from the ticket window.

🛏 Sleeping

Adobe Inn
MOTEL $

(📞970-247-2743; www.durangohotels.com; 2178 Main Ave; d $84; ⊛❄@🛜) Locally voted the best lodging value, this friendly motel gets the job done with clean, decent rooms and friendly service. You might even be able to talk staff into giving their best rate if you arrive late at night. Check out the Durango tip sheet.

★ Rochester House
HOTEL $$

(📞970-385-1920, toll-free 800-664-1920; www. rochesterhotel.com; 721 E 2nd Ave; d $169-229; ⊛❄🛜🏊) Influenced by old Westerns (movie posters and marquee lights adorn the hallways), the Rochester is a little bit of old Hollywood in the new West. Rooms are spacious, with high ceilings. Two formal sitting rooms, where you're served cookies, and a breakfast room in an old train car are other perks at this pet-friendly establishment.

Strater Hotel
HOTEL $$$

(📞970-247-4431; www.strater.com; 699 Main Ave; d $197-257; ⊛❄@🛜) The past lives large in this historical Durango hotel with walnut antiques, hand-stenciled wallpapers and relics ranging from a Stradivarius violin to a gold-plated Winchester. Rooms lean toward the romantic, with comfortable beds amid antiques, crystal and lace. The boast-worthy staff goes out of its way to assist with inquiries.

🍴 Eating & Drinking

Durango Diner
DINER $$

(📞970-247-9889; www.durangodiner.com; 957 Main Ave; mains $7-18; ⊙6am-2pm Mon-Sat, 6am-1pm Sun; 📷🚻) To watch Gary work the grill in this lovable greasy spoon is to be in the presence of greatness. Backed by button-cute waitstaff, Gary's fluid, graceful wielding of a Samurai spatula turns out downright monstrous plates of eggs, smothered potatoes and French toast. The best diner in the state? No doubt.

Jean Pierre Bakery
FRENCH, BAKERY $$

(📞970-247-7700; www.jeanpierrebakery.com; 601 Main Ave; mains $9-22; ⊙8am-9pm; 📷🚻) A charming patisserie serving mouthwatering delicacies made from scratch. Breakfasts are all-out while dinner is a much more formal affair. Prices are dear, but the soup-and-sandwich lunch special with a sumptuous

French pastry (we recommend the sticky pecan roll) is a deal.

East by Southwest
FUSION, SUSHI $$

(☑ 970-247-5533; http://eastbysouthwest.com; 160 E College Dr; sushi $4-13, mains $12-24; ☺ 11:30am-3pm & 5-10pm Mon-Sat, 5-10pm Sun; ☑ ☺) 🍴 Low-lit but vibrant, it's packed with locals on date night. Skip the standards for goose-bump–good sashimi with jalapeño or rolls with mango and wasabi honey. Fish is fresh and endangered species are off the menu. Fusion plates include Thai, Vietnamese and Indonesian, well matched with creative martinis or sake cocktails. The best deals are the happy-hour food specials (5pm to 6:30pm).

Steamworks Brewing
BREWERY

(☑ 970-259-9200; www.steamworksbrewing.com; 801 E 2nd Ave; ☺ 11am-midnight Mon-Thu, 11am-2am Fri-Sun) Industrial meets ski lodge at this popular microbrewery, with high sloping rafters and metal pipes. It has a large bar area, as well as a separate dining room with a Cajun-influenced menu. At night there are DJs and live music.

ℹ Information

Visitor Center (☑ 800-525-8855; www.durango.org; 111 S Camino del Rio) South of town at the Santa Rita exit from US 550.

ℹ Getting There & Around

Durango-La Plata County Airport (DRO; ☑ 970-247-8143; www.flydurango.com; 1000 Airport Rd) is 18 miles southwest of Durango via US 160 and Hwy 172. Greyhound buses run daily from the **Durango Bus Center** (☑ 970 259 2755; 275 E 8th Ave), north to Grand Junction and south to Albuquerque, NM.

Check **Durango Transit** (☑ 970-259-5438; www.getarounddurango.com; 250 W 8th St) for local travel information. Durango buses are fitted with bicycle racks. It's free to ride the red T shuttle bus that circulates Main St.

Durango is at the junction of US 160 and US 550, 42 miles east of Cortez, 49 miles west of Pagosa Springs and 190 miles north of Albuquerque.

Great Sand Dunes National Park

Landscapes collide in a shifting sea of sand at **Great Sand Dunes National Park** (☑ 719-378-6399; www.nps.gov/grsa; 11999 Hwy 150; adult/child $3/free; ☺ visitor center 8:30am-6:30pm summer, shorter hr rest of yr), making you wonder whether a spaceship has whisked you to another planet. The 55-sq-mile dune park – the tallest sand peak rises 700ft above the valley floor – is squeezed between the jagged 14,000ft peaks of the Sangre de Cristo and San Juan Mountains and flat, arid scrub brush of the San Luis Valley.

Plan a visit to this excellent-value national park (at just $3, admission is a steal) around a full moon. Stock up on supplies, stop by the visitor center for your free backcountry camping permit and hike into the surreal landscape to set up camp in the middle of nowhere (bring plenty of water). You won't be disappointed.

There are numerous **hiking trails**, like the half-mile **Zapata Falls** (BLM Road 5415), reached through a fun slot canyon (wear grippy shoes, you may be in standing water). And there's always **sandboarding**, where you ride a snowboard down the dunes, though it's best left to those who already snowboard.

The most popular month to visit is June, when Medano Creek is flowing and kids get a natural refreshment from wading in. Be sure to bring lots of water. Walking in loose sand is difficult, and summer temperatures on the dunes can exceed 130°F (54°C).

🛏 Sleeping

Pinyon Flats Campground
CAMPGROUND $

(☑ 888-448-1474; www.recreation.gov; Great Sand Dunes National Park; tent & RV sites $20; 🐾) This is the official park campground, with a great location not far from the dune field. There are 88 sites here, but be warned: it is very popular and regularly fills up from mid-May through August. Half are available on a first-come, first-served basis (open year round); the other 44 (open May to November 15) can be reserved online.

Zapata Falls Campground
CAMPGROUND $

(www.fs.usda.gov; BLM Rd 5415; tent & RV sites $11; ☺ yr round; 🐾) Seven miles south of the national park, this campground offers glorious panoramas of the San Luis Valley from its 9000ft perch in the Sangre de Cristos. There are 23 first-come, first-served sites, but note that there is no water and that the 3.6-mile access road is steep and fairly washed out, making for slow going.

Zapata Ranch
RANCH $$$

(☑ 719-378-2356; www.zranch.org; 5303 Hwy 150; d $300) Ideal for horseback-riding enthusiasts, this exclusive preserve is a working cattle and bison ranch set amid groves of cottonwood trees. Owned and operated by the Nature Conservancy, the main inn is a refurbished 19th-century log structure, with distant views of the sand dunes.

ⓘ Getting There & Away

The national park is about 35 miles northeast of Alamosa and 250 miles south of Denver. From Denver, take I-25 south to Hwy 160 west and turn onto Hwy 150 north. There is no public transportation.

WYOMING

With wind, restless grasses and wide blue skies, the most sparsely populated state offers solitude to spare. Wyoming may be nuzzled in the bosom of America, but emptiness defines it.

Though steeped in ranching culture – just see the line of Stetsons at the local credit union – Wyoming is the number-one coal producer in the US and is also big in natural gas, crude oil and diamonds. Deeply conservative, its propensity toward industry has sometimes made it an uneasy steward of the land.

But wilderness may be Wyoming's greatest bounty. Its northwestern corner is home to the magnificent national parks of Yellowstone and Grand Teton. Chic Jackson and sporty Lander make great bases for epic hiking, climbing and skiing. For a truer taste of Western life, check out the plain prairie towns of Laramie and Cheyenne.

ⓘ Information

Even on highways, distances are long, with gas stations few and far between. Driving hazards include frequent high gusty winds and fast-moving snow squalls that can create whiteout blizzard conditions. If the weather gets too rough, the highway patrol will shut the entire interstate until it clears.

Wyoming Road Conditions (☑888-996-7623; www.wyoroad.info) Up-to-date info on road conditions and closures.

Wyoming State Parks & Historic Sites (☑307-777-6323; www.wyo-park.com; admission $6, historic site $4, campsite per person $17) Wyoming has 12 state parks. Camping reservations are taken online or over the phone.

Wyoming Travel & Tourism (☑800-225-5996; www.wyomingtourism.org; 5611 High Plains Rd, Cheyenne) At a rest area just south of Cheyenne on I-25, this info center has tons of information and kid-friendly displays about local wildlife, activities and the environment. Worth a stop!

Cheyenne

Many a country tune has been penned about Wyoming's state capital and largest city, though Cheyenne is more like the Hollywood Western *before* the shooting begins. That is, until Frontier Days festival, a raucous July celebration of cowboy fun. At the junction of I-25 and I-80, the city is a useful pit stop.

⊙ Sights

Frontier Days Old West Museum   MUSEUM
(☑307-778-7290; www.oldwestmuseum.org; 4610 N Carey Ave; adult/child $10/free; ⊙9am-5pm Mon-Fri, from 10am Sat & Sun) For a peek into the pioneer past, visit the lively Frontier Days Old West Museum at I-25 exit 12. It is chock-full of rodeo memorabilia – from saddles to trophies. For the audio tour, call ☑307-316-0079.

Big Boy Steam Engine   PARK
(Holliday Park; ⊙24hr) Inside pretty Holliday Park you'll find the world's largest steam engine – Old Number 4004, now retired. The locomotive made its name pulling 3600-ton trains across about a million miles of steep mountain terrain.

✪ Festivals & Events

★ **Cheyenne Frontier Days**   RODEO
(☑1-800-227-6336; www.cfdrodeo.com; 4501 N Carey Ave; free-$39; ⊙Jul; ⸭) If you've never seen a steer wrestler leap into action, this very Western event is bound to brand an impression. Beginning in late July, Wyoming's largest celebration features 10 days of rodeos, concerts, dances, air shows and chili cook-offs. Free events include morning 'slack' rodeos, pancake breakfasts and parades. There's also an art sale and 'Indian village.'

⫩ Sleeping & Eating

Reservations are a must during Frontier Days, when rates double and everything within 50 miles is booked; see www.cheyenne.org/availability for bookings. The cheapest motels line noisy Lincolnway (I-25 exit 9).

Nagle Warren Mansion Bed & Breakfast   B&B $$
(☑307-637-3333; www.naglewarrenmansion.com; 222 E 17th St; r from $163; ❈❢❀) This lavish spread is a fabulous find. The historic 1888 house is decked out with late-19th-century regional antiques. Spacious and elegant, it boasts a hot tub, a reading room tucked into

WYOMING FACTS

Nickname Equality State

Population 584,000

Area 97,100 sq miles

Capital city Cheyenne (population 62,400)

Other cities Laramie (population 31,800), Cody (population 9,800), Jackson (population 10,100)

Sales tax 4%

Birthplace of Artist Jackson Pollock (1912–56)

Home of Women's suffrage, coal mining, geysers, wolves

Politics Conservative to the core

Famous for Rodeo, ranches, former vice-president Dick Cheney

Kitschiest souvenir Fur bikini from a Jackson boutique

Driving distances Cheyenne to Jackson 432 miles

a turret and classic 1954 Schwinn bikes for cruising. There are six individually decorated rooms in the mansion and another six in the carriage house, all with private bath.

Tortilla Factory   MEXICAN $
(2706 S Greeley Hwy; mains $2-11; ⊙7am-8pm Mon-Sat, 8am-5pm Sun) A delicious Mexican fast-food joint serving homemade tamales for $2 and authentic classics such as *menudo* (Mexican soup) and green chili.

🍷 Drinking & Entertainment

Cheyenne Brewing Company   BREWERY
(Depot Station; ⊙11am-11pm) The name and ownership have changed, but the ambience is still cool at this brewpub inside the 1860s Union Pacific depot. There are good craft brews on tap, and three seating areas – a bar, an all-ages dining room and an outdoor terrace.

Cheyenne Gunslingers   WILD WEST SHOW
(☑800-426-5009; www.cheyennegunslingers.com; cnr Lincolnway & Carey Ave; ⊙noon Sat & 6pm Mon-Fri Jun-Jul; 🖱) FREE A nonprofit group of actors puts on a lively, if not exactly accurate, Old West show in Gunslinger Sq – from near hangings to slippery jailbreaks. Stars include corrupt judges, smiling good guys and, of course, the bad-ass villains.

❶ Information

Cheyenne Visitor Center (☑307-778-3133; www.cheyenne.org; 1 Depot Sq; ⊙8am-5pm Mon-Sat, 11am-5pm Sun, closed Sat & Sun winter)

❶ Getting There & Around

Cheyenne Airport (CYS; ☑307-634-7071; www.cheyenneairport.com; 200 E 8th Ave) Daily flights to Denver.

Black Hills Stage Lines (☑307-635-1327; www.blackhillsstagelines.com; 5401 Walker Rd) Greyhound buses depart from the Black Hills Stage Lines daily for Billings, MT ($96, 8½ hours), and Denver, CO ($34, 2¾ hours), among other destinations.

Cheyenne Street Railway Trolley (☑800-426-5009; 121 W 15th St; adult/child $10/5; ⊙10am, 11:30am, 1pm, 2:30pm and 4pm May-Sep) Takes visitors on tours through downtown, leaving from Depot Plaza.

Laramie

Home to the state's only four-year university, Laramie can be both hip and boisterous, a vibe which is missing from most Wyoming prairie towns. Well worth exploring is the small historic downtown, a lively five-block grid of attractive two-story brick buildings with hand-painted signs and murals pushed up against the railroad tracks.

◎ Sights

Wyoming Territorial Prison   MUSEUM
(www.wyomingterritorialprison.com; 975 Snowy Range Rd; adult/child $5/2.50; ⊙8am-7pm May-Oct; 🖱) The only prison ever to hold Butch Cassidy – he was in for grand larceny from 1894 to '96 and emerged to become one of history's greatest robbers – the Wyoming Territorial Prison operated until 1903, holding about a thousand 'malicious and desperate outlaws.' While inside, convicts produced over 700 brooms a day. The restored prison is surrounded by other historical buildings of the era; guided tours at 11am and 2pm are included in admission.

Geological Museum   MUSEUM
(☑307-766-2646; www.uwyo.edu/geomuseum; UW, Hwy 287 at I-80; ⊙10am-4pm Mon-Sat) FREE This University of Wyoming museum features an impressive collection of dinosaur remains, including a 75ft Apatosaurus skeleton.

🛏 Sleeping

Gas Lite Motel
MOTEL $

(📞 307-742-6616; www.facebook.com/GasLiteMotel; 960 N 3rd St; s/d $50/55; ❀❀🐾❀) The Gas Lite Motel stands out, even on a street lined with eye-catching, neon-signed retro motels. A plastic horse and rooster perch on the roof, and tattered plywood cowboys lean here and there. The swimming pool is in a greenhouse, surrounded by fake deer and grizzlies. Rooms are pet-friendly and dressed with playful Wild West touches.

Mad Carpenter Inn
B&B $$

(📞 307-742-0870; http://madcarpenter.com; 353 N 8th St; r $95-125; 🐾) With landscaped gardens, homemade granola and two comfy, snug rooms plus a backyard cottage, the homey Mad Carpenter Inn has warmth to spare. A serious game room features billiards and ping-pong.

🍴 Eating & Drinking

★ Sweet Melissa's
VEGETARIAN $

(213 S 1st St; mains $7-11, cocktails $5-7; ⊙ 11am-9pm Mon-Sat; 🐾) Doubtless the healthiest food for miles, Sweet Melissa's makes delicious vegetarian food, like portabella fajitas or black bean and sweet potato sliders. Tip: grab a seat at the adjoining Front Street Tavern and watch the trains roll by – it's usually less crowded, and the two places share a kitchen.

Coal Creek Coffee Co
CAFE $

(110 E Grand Ave; panini $9-10; ⊙ 6am-11pm; 🐾) With superlative brews, Coal Creek Coffee Co is modern and stylish, even borderline hipster – but not in a bad way. That just means you'll get a really good latte, made with fair-trade beans by people who know what they're doing. Sandwiches and quiches are tasty, too.

Old Buckhorn Bar
BAR

(📞 307-742-3554; 114 Ivinson St; ⊙ 9am-midnight Sun-Wed, to 2am Thu-Sat) For live country music and beers, you'll want to head to the Old Buckhorn Bar. Established in 1900, it's Laramie's oldest standing bar and a fantastic example of what a good Wild West saloon should look like in this century – check out the hand-scratched graffiti and half-century-old condom dispenser in the bathroom.

❶ Getting There & Away

Laramie Regional Airport (LAR; 📞 307-742-4164; www.laramieairport.com) Located 4 miles west of town via I-80 exit 311, Laramie Regional Airport has daily flights to Denver (40 minutes).

Lander

Lander is a cheerful example of the many cool little one-street towns across Wyoming. Just a stone's throw from the Wind River Reservation, it's a rock-climbing and mountaineering mecca in a friendly foothills setting.

◉ Sights & Activities

Sinks Canyon State Park
PARK

(📞 307-332-3077; 3079 Sinks Canyon Rd; admission $6; ⊙ visitor center 9am-6pm Jun-Sep) The beautiful Sinks Canyon State Park, 6 miles south of Lander, features a curious underground river. Flowing through a narrow

ROCKY MOUNTAINS LANDER

IF YOU HAVE A FEW MORE DAYS IN WYOMING

Wyoming is full of great places to get lost – here's a taster.

With vast grassy meadows, seas of wildflowers and peaceful conifer forests, the **Bighorn Mountains** in north-central Wyoming are truly awe-inspiring. Factor in gushing waterfalls and abundant wildlife and you've got a stupendous natural playground with hundreds of miles of marked trails.

Nestled in the shadow of the Bighorn Mountains, the town of **Sheridan** boasts century-old buildings once home to Wyoming cattle barons. It's popular with adventure fanatics who come to play in the Bighorns.

Rising a dramatic 1267ft above the Belle Fourche River, the nearly vertical monolith of **Devil's Tower National Monument** is an awesome sight. Known as Bears Lodge by some of the 20-plus Native American tribes who consider it sacred, it's a must-see if you are traveling between the Black Hills (on the Wyoming–South Dakota border) and the Tetons or Yellowstone.

West of Laramie, the lofty national forest stretching across **Medicine Bow Mountains** and **Snowy Range** is a wild and rugged place, perfect for multi-day hiking and camping trips.

canyon, the Middle Fork of the Popo Agie River disappears into the soluble Madison limestone called the Sinks and returns warmer a quarter-mile downstream in a pool called the Rise.

National Outdoor Leadership School
ADVENTURE TOUR

(NOLS; www.nols.edu; 284 Lincoln St) The renowned NOLS leads trips around the world and locally into the Wind River Range.

Gannett Peak Sports
MOUNTAIN BIKING

(351b Main St; ⊙10am-6pm Mon-Fri, 9am-5pm Sat, 10am-2pm Sun) If you want to check out the single-track trails outside town, head to Gannett Peak Sports for advice, gear and equipment rentals.

Wild Iris Mountain Sports
OUTDOOR EQUIPMENT

(☑307-332-4541; 166 Main St; ⊙9:30am-6:30pm Mon-Sat, 10am-5pm Sun) If you've come to hike, camp or climb, pop into this gear shop for good advice and climbing rental or snowshoes. Pick up their cheat sheet with local tips.

🛏 Sleeping

Sinks Canyon State Park Campgrounds
CAMPGROUND $

(☑877-444-6777; htttp://recreation.gov; campsites $15; ⊙May-Sep) This scenic campground, run by Shoshone National Forest, is highly recommended.

Holiday Lodge
MOTEL $

(☑307-332-2511; www.holidaylodgelander.com; 210 McFarlane Dr; tent sites per person $10, RV sites $38, s/d from $85/90; ❋🐾) It's under new ownership, but this funky motor lodge still offers a great alternative to the standard chains lining Main St. The look says 1961, but it's scrubbed shiny and friendly, with thoughtful extras like an iron, makeup remover and sewing kits. Riverside camping includes breakfast and showers.

✗ Eating & Drinking

Gannett Grill
AMERICAN $

(☑307-332-8227; 128 Main St; mains $8-11; ⊙11am-9pm) Decompress from long hours of travel or adventure at the backyard patio of Gannett Grill, an institution serving local beef burgers, crisp waffle fries and stone-oven pizzas. If you're feeling fancy, try the adjoining Cowfish, a more upscale dinner offering (mains $17–33) from the same folks.

Lander Bar
BAR

(☑307-332-8228; 126 Main St; ⊙11am-late) Adjoining the Gannett Grill, this big, wooden, barn-like place is the place to go for climbing and mountain-biking gossip. There's live music many nights.

ℹ Information

Lander Visitor Center
(☑307-332-3892; www.landerchamber.org; 160 N 1st St; ⊙9am-5pm Mon-Fri)

ℹ Getting There & Away

Wind River Transportation Authority
(☑307-856-7118; www.wrtabuslines.com; fare one-way $1, airport shuttle $30) Wind River Transportation Authority provides scheduled Monday-to-Friday services between Lander, Riverton, Dubois, Rock Springs and Riverton Regional Airport, plus bus service to Jackson ($160) and other destinations; check the website for schedules.

Jackson

Technically this is Wyoming, but you may have a hard time believing it. With a median age of 32, this Western town has evolved into a mecca for mountain lovers, hard-core climbers and skiers, easily recognizable as sunburned baristas.

The upside of being posh and popular? Jackson is abuzz with life: trails and outdoor opportunities abound. Fresh sushi is flown in daily and generous purse-strings support a vigorous cultural life. Skip the souvenirs and remember why you came to Jackson in the first place: to visit its glorious backyard, Grand Teton National Park.

⊙ Sights & Activities

★ National Museum of Wildlife Art
MUSEUM

(☑307-733-5771; www.wildlifeart.org; 2820 Rungius Rd; adult/child $14/6; ⊙9am-5pm, from 11am Sun spring & fall) If you visit one area museum, make it this one, with major works by Bierstadt, Rungius, Remington and Russell. It's worth driving up just for the outdoor sculptures and the building itself (inspired by a ruined Scottish castle). The discovery gallery has a kids' studio for drawing and print rubbing that adults plainly envy. Check the website for summer film-series and art-class schedules.

National Elk Refuge WILDLIFE RESERVE
(📞307-733-9212; www.fws.gov/refuge/national_elk_refuge; Hwy 89; ⊙8am-5pm Sep-May, to 7pm Jun-Aug) FREE This refuge protects Jackson's herd of several thousand elk, offering them a winter habitat from November to March. During summer, ask at the Jackson visitor center for the best places to see elk. An hour-long horse-drawn sleigh ride is the highlight of a winter visit; buy tickets at the visitor center.

★**Jackson Hole
Mountain Resort** SNOW SPORTS
(📞307-733-2292; www.jacksonhole.com; day pass adult/child $121/75; ⊙late Nov-early Apr) 'The Hole' is all about vertical, boasting a continuous vertical rise of 4139ft – beaten only by Big Sky, by 41ft (we're sure that some front loader is poised to adjust this injustice). Among the world's top ski destinations, the resort has 2500 acres of ski terrain blessed by an average of 380in of snow annually.

The runs (10% beginner, 40% intermediate and 50% advanced) are served by six lifts, an aerial tram, two high-speed quads and the Bridger gondola. Depending on snowfall, the ski season may start early or end late.

⭐ **Festivals & Events**

Town Square Shoot-out WILD WEST SHOW
(Jackson Town Sq; ⊙6:15pm Mon-Sat Memorial Day-Labor Day; 👪) FREE This hokey tourist draw takes place in summer.

🛏 **Sleeping**

Jackson has plenty of lodging, both in town and around the ski hill. There are also great camping options scattered outside of town. Reservations are essential in summer and winter.

Hostel HOSTEL $
(📞307-733-3415; www.thehostel.us; 3315 Village Dr, Teton Village; dm $34-40, r $79-119; ◉) The area's only budget option, this old ski lodge in Teton Village offers private doubles and bunk-bed rooms with renovated showers for up to four. The spacious lounge with fireplace is ideal for movies or Scrabble tournaments and there's a playroom for tots. There's a microwave and outdoor grill, coin laundry and ski-waxing area. Rates drop in fall and spring.

Antler Inn HOTEL $$
(📞307-733-2535; www.townsquareinns.com/ant-ler-inn; 43 W Pearl; s/d from $110/115) The 'cedar

log' rooms at this comfy motor inn give the place an appreciably Western feel, and it's right in the midst of the Jackson action. Rates drop sharply in winter.

★**Alpine House** B&B $$$
(📞307-739-1570; www.alpinehouse.com; 285 N Glenwood St; r $240-330, cottage $330-515; ◉) Two former Olympic skiers have infused this downtown home with sunny Scandinavian style and personal touches, like great service and a cozy mountaineering library. Amenities include plush robes, down comforters, a shared Finnish sauna and an outdoor Jacuzzi. Save your appetite for the creative breakfast options, like lemon-ricotta blueberry pancakes or eggs Benedict.

🍴 **Eating**

Jackson Whole Grocer HEALTH FOOD $
(📞307-733-0450; http://jacksonwholegrocer.com; 1155 S Hwy 89; ⊙7am-10pm; 🅿👪) A health-food market and deli, this is a good place to load up for a day's hiking or skiing adventure. There's even wine and beer by the glass, so you can sip while you shop.

Lotus Cafe VEGETARIAN $$
(📞307-734-0882; http://tetonlotuscafe.com; 145 N Glenwood; mains $7-24; ⊙8am-10pm; 🥗) You can hardly swing a cat in this town without hitting a primo steak, but good veggie fare is harder to find. The Lotus solves that with things like kale-avocado salad, veggie lasagna and giant grain-and-veg bowls. (There is some meat on the menu too, all organic.)

Bubba's Bar-B-Que BARBECUE $$
(📞307-733-2288; 100 Flat Creek Dr; mains $7-23; ⊙7am-10pm; 👪) Get the biggest, fluffiest breakfast biscuits for miles at this friendly and energetic diner. Later on, bring your own bottle (BYOB) and settle in for some BBQ ribs and racks.

Snake River Grill MODERN AMERICAN $$$
(📞307-733-0557; 84 E Broadway; mains $23-51; ⊙from 5:30pm) With a roaring stone fireplace, an extensive wine list and snappy white linens, this grill creates notable American haute cuisine. Try the wild game Korean hot bowl, with venison and spring veggies in spicy black-bean sauce. Or munch on a cast-iron bucket of truffle fries. Splurge-desserts like buttermilk *panna cotta* or homemade ice cream easily satisfy two.

🍷 Drinking & Nightlife

Stagecoach Bar BAR
(📞307-733-4407; http://stagecoachbar.net; 5800 W Hwy 22, Wilson; ⊙11am-late) Wyoming has no better place to shake your booty. Thursday is disco night plus Ladies' Night, and most Sundays the long-standing house band croons country-and-western favorites until 10pm. Worth the 6-mile drive to Wilson (just past the Teton Village turnoff).

The Rose COCKTAIL BAR
(http://therosejh.com; 50 W Broadway; cocktails $9-14; ⊙5:30pm-2am) A swank little lounge upstairs inside the Pink Garter theater, with red-leather booths, low lighting and chandeliers, the Rose is the place for craft cocktails in Jackson.

Snake River Brewing Co MICROBREWERY
(📞307-739-2337; www.snakeriverbrewing. com; 265 S Millward St; pints $4-5, mains $11-14; ⊙11:30am-midnight) With an arsenal of more than 20 microbrews crafted on the spot, some award-winning, it's no wonder this is a local favorite. Food includes wood-fired pizzas, bison burgers and wild-game stew.

Million Dollar Cowboy Bar BAR
(📞307-733-4790; 25 N Cache Dr; ⊙from 11am) Touristy to the gills, but you kind of have to give it a whirl. Plunk your hindquarters on a saddle stool and order a shot of Wyoming whiskey or a pint of the bar's namesake beer. Most nights there's Western swing dancing, and there's an upscale steakhouse downstairs (reservations recommended).

ℹ Information

Jackson Hole & Greater Yellowstone Visitor Center (📞307-733-3316; www.jacksonhole-chamber.com; 532 N Cache Dr; ⊙9am-5pm) Provides information, books, restrooms, an ATM and a courtesy phone for free local calls.

ℹ Getting There & Around

Jackson Hole Airport (JAC; 📞307-733-7682; www.jacksonholeairport.com) Jackson Hole Airport is 7 miles north of Jackson off US 26/89/189/191 within Grand Teton National Park. Daily flights serve Denver, Salt Lake City, LA, San Francisco, Chicago, Dallas and Houston.

START Bus (www.startbus.com; Teton Village one-way $3) This Teton County commuter bus system runs free shuttles within Jackson as well as approximately hourly trips to and from Teton Village; check current schedules online.

Alltrans' Jackson Hole Express (📞307-733-3135; www.jacksonholebus.com; ⊙park shuttle mid-May–Oct) Alltrans' Jackson Hole Express buses provide a shuttle to Grand Teton National Park ($14 per day) and the airport ($16). Buses also depart at 6:30am daily from Maverik County Store (on the corner of Hwy 89 S and S Park Loop Rd) for Salt Lake City ($75, 5½ hours).

Cody

Raucous Cody revels in its Wild West image (the town is named after legendary showman William 'Buffalo Bill' Cody, who founded it). Summer is high season, and Cody puts on quite an Old West show for the throngs of visitors making their way to Yellowstone National Park, 52 miles to the west.

From Cody, the approach to geyserland through the Wapiti Valley is dramatic to say the least. The **visitor center** (📞307-587-2777; www.codychamber.org; 836 Sheridan Ave; ⊙8am-7pm Jun-Aug, to 5pm Mon-Fri Sep-May) is the logical starting point.

◉ Sights

★**Buffalo Bill Center of the West** MUSEUM
(www.centerofthewest.org; 720 Sheridan Ave; adult/child $19/11; ⊙8am-6pm May–mid-Sep, 8am-5pm mid-Sep–Oct, 10am-5pm Nov, Mar & Apr, 10am-5pm Thu-Sun Dec-Feb) Cody's major tourist attraction is the superb Buffalo Bill Historical Center of the West. A sprawling complex of five museums, it showcases everything Western: from posters, grainy films and artifacts pertaining to Buffalo Bill's world-famous Wild West shows, to galleries showcasing frontier-oriented artwork, to museums dedicated to Native Americans. Its **Draper Museum of Natural History** explores the Yellowstone region's ecosystem with excellent results. The galleries are given regular overhauls to keep presentations fresh. There's also a daily (1pm) **raptor presentation**.

Entry is valid for two consecutive days. Save a couple of bucks by booking online.

🛏 Sleeping

Irma Hotel HISTORIC HOTEL $$
(📞800-745-4762; www.irmahotel.com; 1192 Sheridan Ave; r $132-152, ste $162-197) Built in 1902 by Buffalo Bill himself, and named for his daughter, this old-fashioned saloon has charming original historical suites named after past guests (Annie Oakley, Calamity Jane), plus

---

less-inspiring modern rooms in an annex. The creaky hallways, dining room and lobby drip with atmosphere – the ornate cherrywood bar was a gift from Queen Victoria.

It's well worth stopping in for dinner or drinks. Gunfights break out nightly at 6pm in front of the hotel from June through September.

Chamberlin Inn INN $$
(☑ 307-587-0202; http://chamberlininn.com; 1032 12th St; d/ste from $175/255) An elegant downtown retreat, this historic boutique hotel (built in 1903) has a library and a pretty inner courtyard. The registry claims Hemingway crashed in room 18 ($275) on a 1932 fishing trip.

Drinking & Entertainment

Silver Dollar Bar BAR
(1313 Sheridan Ave; mains $9-11; ⊙11am-late) The Silver Dollar Bar is a historic watering hole with lots of TV screens and live music or DJs nightly. The tap list is strong, with lots of great regional craft beers, and the burgers are tasty (the signature half-pounder goes for $15). In nice weather, an outdoor bar offers excellent views of street life.

Cody Nite Rodeo SPECTATOR SPORT
(www.codystampederodeo.com; 519 W Yellowstone Ave; adult/child $20/10; ⊙8pm Jun-Aug) If you're wondering why Cody is known as the 'rodeo capital of the world,' check out this nightly event, where you'll see future (and some current) pro-rodeo superstars putting in the hours all summer. It's rain or shine, with fireworks at dusk.

Getting There & Away

Yellowstone Regional Airport (COD; www.flyyra.com) Yellowstone Regional Airport is 1 mile east of Cody and runs daily flights to Salt Lake City and Denver.

Yellowstone National Park

They grow their critters and geysers big up in Yellowstone, America's first national park and Wyoming's flagship attraction. From shaggy grizzlies to oversized bison and magnificent packs of wolves, this park boasts the lower 48's most enigmatic concentration of wildlife. Throw in half the world's geysers, the country's largest high-altitude lake and a plethora of blue-ribbon rivers and waterfalls, all sitting pretty atop a giant supervolcano, and you'll quickly realize you've stumbled across one of Mother Nature's most fabulous creations.

When John Colter became the first white man to visit the area in 1807, the inhabitants were Tukadikas (aka Sheepeaters), a Shoshone Bannock people who hunted bighorn sheep. Colter's reports of exploding geysers and boiling mud holes (at first dismissed as tall tales) brought in expeditions and tourism interest eagerly funded by the railroads. The park was established in 1872 (as the world's first) to preserve Yellowstone's spectacular geography: the geothermal phenomena, the fossil forests and Yellowstone Lake.

Of the park's five entrance stations, only the North Entrance, near Gardiner, MT, is open year-round. The others, typically open mid-May to October, offer access from the

ROCKY MOUNTAINS YELLOWSTONE NATIONAL PARK

NATIONAL PARKS

The Rocky Mountains region is home to some of the USA's biggest national parks. The heavy-hitters include the following:

Rocky Mountain National Park (Colorado) Awesome hiking through alpine forests and tundra.

Great Sand Dunes National Park (Colorado) Sahara-like wonder.

Mesa Verde National Park (Colorado) An archaeological preserve with elaborate cliff-side dwellings.

Grand Teton National Park (Wyoming) Dramatic craggy peaks.

Yellowstone National Park (Wyoming) The country's first, a true wonderland of volcanic geysers, hot springs and forested mountains.

Glacier National Park (Montana) High sedimentary peaks, glaciers and lots of wildlife.

Hells Canyon National Recreation Area (Idaho) The Snake River carves the deepest canyon in North America. The **National Park Service** (NPS; www.nps.gov) also manages over two dozen other historic sites, monuments, nature preserves and recreational areas in Idaho.

northeast (Cooke City, MT), east (Cody, WY), south (Grand Teton National Park) and west (West Yellowstone, MT). The park's main road is the 142-mile Grand Loop Rd scenic drive.

◉ Sights

Just sitting on the porch of the Old Faithful Inn with a cocktail in hand waiting for Old Faithful geyser to erupt could be considered enough activity by itself but there's plenty else to keep you busy here, from hiking and backpacking to kayaking and fly-fishing. Most park trails are not groomed, but unplowed roads and trails are open for cross-country skiing.

Yellowstone is split into five distinct regions, each with unique attractions. Upon entering the national park you'll be given a basic map and a park newspaper detailing the excellent ranger-led talks and walks (well worth attending). All the visitor centers have information desks staffed by park rangers who can help you tailor a hike to your tastes, from great photo spots to best chance of spotting a bear.

◉ Geyser Country

With the densest collection of geothermal features in the park, **Upper Geyser Basin** contains 180 of the park's 250-odd geysers. For an easy walk, check out the predicted eruption times at the brand-new visitor center and then follow the easy boardwalk trail around the **Upper Geyser Loop**. The Firehole and Madison Rivers offer superb fly-fishing and wildlife viewing.

Old Faithful GEYSER
(Old Faithful Rd, Upper Geyser Basin) FREE You can feel the tension build as you wait for an eruption of Old Faithful – not the biggest, not the most frequent, but easily the most iconic geyser in the park. Erupting every 90 minutes, Old Faithful spouts some 30,000L (8000 gallons) of water up to 55m (180ft) in the air. Tip: the first thing to do when you arrive is to check the predicted geyser eruption times at the visitor center and then plan your explorations around these.

Old Faithful Visitor Center VISITOR CENTER
(☑307-545-2750; ☺8am-8pm mid-Apr–early Nov & mid-Dec–mid-Mar; ⬤) The new, improved and environmentally friendly center offers a bookstore and information booth and shows films 30 minutes before and 15 minutes after an eruption of Old Faithful. Kids will enjoy the Young Scientist displays, which include a working laboratory geyser and experiments involving elk jaw bones. The center closes at 5pm or 6pm outside of summer.

Grand Prismatic Spring SPRING
(Midway Geyser Basin) The park's most beautiful thermal feature is Grand Prismatic Spring.

◉ Mammoth Country

Known for the geothermal terraces and elk herds of historic **Mammoth** and the hot springs of **Norris Geyser Basin**, Mammoth Country is North America's most volatile and oldest-known continuously active thermal area. The peaks of the Gallatin Range rise to the northwest, towering above the area's lakes, creeks and numerous hiking trails.

Mammoth Hot Springs HOT SPRINGS
The imposing **Lower** and **Upper Terraces** of Mammoth Hot Springs are the product of dissolved subterranean limestone (itself originally deposited by ancient seas), which is continuously deposited as the spring waters cool on contact with air. The mountain is in effect turning itself inside out, depositing over a ton of travertine (limestone deposits) here every year. The colored runoff from the naturally white terraces is due to the bacteria and algae that flourish in the warm waters.

An hour's worth of boardwalks wend their way around the Lower Terraces and connect to the **Upper Terraces Loop**. The rutting Rocky Mountain elk that sometimes lounge on **Opal Terrace** in fall are a favorite photo opportunity.

Surreal **Palette Springs** (accessed from the bottom parking lot) and sulfur-yellow **Canary Springs** (accessed from the top loop) are the most beautiful sites, but thermal activity is constantly in flux, so check the current state of play at the visitor center.

◉ Roosevelt Country

Fossil forests, the commanding **Lamar River Valley** and its tributary trout streams, Tower Fall and the Absaroka Mountains' craggy peaks are the highlights of Roosevelt Country, the park's most remote, scenic and undeveloped region. Several good hikes begin near **Tower Junction**.

Tower Fall   WATERFALL

Two-and-a-half miles south of Tower-Roosevelt Junction, Tower Creek plunges over 132ft Tower Fall before joining the Yellowstone River. The fall gets its name from the volcanic breccia towers around it, which are like a demonic fortress and earn it the nickname the Devil's Den. Local storytellers claim that prominent Minaret Peak gets its name from one Minnie Rhett, the girlfriend of an early park visitor, but that sounds to us like one of Jim Bridger's tall tales. Iconic landscape painter Thomas Moran created one of his most famous paintings here.

◉ Canyon Country

A series of scenic overlooks linked by hiking trails highlight the colorful beauty and grandeur of the Grand Canyon of the Yellowstone and its impressive Lower Falls. South Rim Dr leads to the canyon's most spectacular overlook, at **Artist Point**. **Mud Volcano** is Canyon Country's primary geothermal area.

**★Grand Canyon
of the Yellowstone**   CANYON
(☑307 242 2550; ☉Canyon Visitor Education Center late May–mid-Oct) This is one of the park's true blockbuster sights. After its placid meanderings north from Yellowstone Lake, the Yellowstone River suddenly plummets over **Upper Falls** and then the much larger **Lower Falls**, before raging through the 300m-deep (1000ft) canyon.

◉ Lake Country

Yellowstone Lake, the centerpiece of Lake Country and one of the world's largest alpine lakes, is a watery wilderness lined with volcanic beaches and best explored by boat or sea kayak. Rising east and southeast of the lakes, the wild and snowcapped Absaroka Range hides the wildest lands in the lower 48, perfect for epic backpacking or horseback trips.

🏃 Activities

Hiking

Hikers can explore Yellowstone's backcountry from more than 92 trailheads that give access to 1100 miles of hiking trails. A free backcountry-use permit, which is available at visitor centers and ranger stations, is required for overnight trips. Backcountry camping is allowed in 300 designated sites, 60% of which can be reserved in advance by

---

ⓘ BEAT THE CROWDS

Yellowstone's wonderland attracts up to 30,000 visitors daily in July and August and over three million gatecrashers annually. Avoid the worst of the crowds with the following advice:

➡ Visit in May, September or October for decent weather and few people; or even in winter.

➡ Ditch 95% of the crowds by hiking a backcountry trail. Lose 99% by camping in a backcountry site (permit required).

➡ Mimic the wildlife and be most active in the golden hours after dawn and before dusk.

➡ Pack lunch for one of the park's many scenic picnic areas.

➡ Make reservations for park lodging months in advance and book concession campgrounds *at least* the day before.

---

mail; a $25 fee applies to all bookings that are more than three days in advance.

After much debate and a narrowly avoided fistfight, we have settled on the following as our five favorite day hikes in the park.

Lone Star Geyser Trail   HIKING
This paved and pine-lined hike is an easy stroll along a former service road to one of the park's largest backcountry geysers. It's popular with both day hikers and cyclists, yet is quite a contrast to the chaotic scene around Old Faithful. Isolated Lone Star erupts every three hours for between two and 30 minutes and reaches 30ft to 45ft in height, and it's definitely worth timing your visit with an eruption – check with Old Faithful Visitor Center for predicted times.

The hike begins at the Lone Star Trailhead, above **Kepler Cascades** (where the Firehole River speeds through a spectacular gorge). The 4.8-mile round-trip walk takes 2½ hours at most.

South Rim Trail & Ribbon Lake   HIKING
Southeast of the canyon's South Rim, a network of trails meanders through meadows and forests and past several small lakes. This loop links several trails and makes a nice antidote to seeing canyon views from your car. It's an incredibly varied hike, with awesome views of the Grand Canyon of the

Yellowstone & Grand Teton National Parks

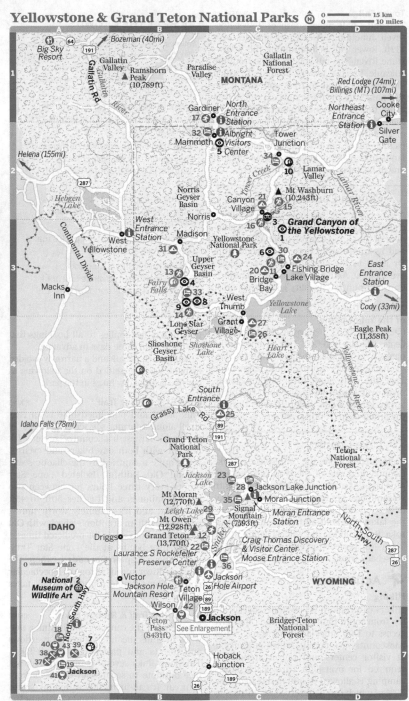

0   15 km
0   10 miles

Big Sky Resort

64
191
Bozeman (40mi)

Gallatin Valley
Ramshorn Peak (10,789ft)

Paradise Valley

Gallatin National Forest

MONTANA

Red Lodge (74mi); Billings (MT) (107mi)

Helena (155mi)

287

Hebgen Lake

Continental Divide

Gardiner
17
North Entrance Station

32
Mammoth
Albright Visitors Center
5

Tower Junction

34
10

Lamar Valley

Cooke City
Silver Gate

Northeast Entrance Station

Norris Geyser Basin

Mt Washburn (10,243ft)

West Entrance Station

West Yellowstone

Madison

Norris

Canyon Village

21
15

16

1 3 Grand Canyon of the Yellowstone

Macks Inn

31

Yellowstone National Park

Upper Geyser Basin

13 4

Fairy Falls

33

9 8
14

Lone Star Geyser

West Thumb

Grant Village

6
30
20 11
Bridge Bay

24
Fishing Bridge Lake Village

East Entrance Station

Cody (33mi)

Eagle Peak (11,358ft)

Yellowstone Lake

Shoshone Geyser Basin

Shoshone Lake

Heart Lake

27
26

Yellowstone River

Idaho Falls (78mi)

Grassy Lake Rd

South Entrance
25

89
191

Grand Teton National Park

Jackson Lake

23
28
35

Jackson Lake Junction
Moran Junction

Teton National Forest

287

Mt Moran (12,770ft)
Leigh Lake
29

Mt Owen (12,928ft)
Grand Teton (13,770ft)
12
22

Signal Mountain (7593ft)

Moran Entrance Station

North-South Hwy

287
26

IDAHO

Driggs

Laurance S Rockefeller Preserve Center

Craig Thomas Discovery & Visitor Center
Moose Entrance Station

36

WYOMING

Victor
Jackson Hole Mountain Resort
Wilson
Teton Pass (8431ft)

Teton Village
42

Jackson Hole Airport

26
89
189

Jackson

See Enlargement

Bridger-Teton National Forest

Hoback Junction

26
189

Enlargement

0   1 mile

National Museum of Wildlife Art
2

North-South Hwy

18
7
40 43 39
38
37 19
41
Jackson

Yellowstone & Grand Teton National Parks

ROCKY MOUNTAINS YELLOWSTONE NATIONAL PARK

Yellowstone (p279) and even a backcountry thermal area.

Park at Uncle Tom's parking area on the canyon's South Rim Dr and, after checking out the views of the Upper and Lower Falls from Uncle Tom's Trail, take the South Rim Trail east along the rim of the canyon to Artist Point for some of the finest canyon views available.

From Artist Point take the trail east toward Point Sublime, then branch right past Lily Pad Lake for 0.3 miles to another junction. Branch left here and descend to Ribbon Lake, actually two conjoined ponds, with a good chance of spotting moose. Allow about four hours.

Mt Washburn Trail   HIKING

Opt for this fairly strenuous uphill hike from Dunraven Pass trailhead to a mountaintop fire tower for 360-degree views over the park and likely sightings of bighorn sheep (6.4 miles).

Elephant Back Mountain Trail   HIKING

This popular ascent is a great short-but-sweet picnic option, suitable for families with teenagers. The stunning views from the panoramic overlook (8600ft) include Yellowstone Lake and Stevenson Island, Pelican Valley and the Absaroka Range.

The trailhead is 1 mile south of Fishing Bridge Junction and 0.5 miles north of the Lake Village turnoff on the Grand Loop Rd. From Lake Hotel it is 0.25 miles one way through the woods past Section J of the hotel's cabins. Allow about 2½ hours for the 3.5-mile loop.

Fairy Falls Trail & Twin Buttes   HIKING

Tucked away in the northwest corner of the Midway Geyser Basin, 197ft Fairy Falls is a popular hike, largely because it's only a short jaunt from Old Faithful. Beyond Fairy Falls the lollipop-loop trail continues to a hidden thermal area at the base of the Twin Buttes, two conspicuous bald hills severely charred in the 1988 fires.

The geysers are undeveloped, and you're likely to have them to yourself – in stark contrast to the throngs around Grand Prismatic Spring.

The Fairy Falls (Steel Bridge) Trailhead is just west of the Grand Loop Rd, 1 mile south of the Midway Geyser Basin turnoff and 4.5 miles north of the Old Faithful overpass.

Cycling

Cyclists can ride on public roads and a few designated service roads, but not on the backcountry trails. The best season is May to October, when the roads are usually snow-free. From mid-March to mid-April the Mammoth–West Yellowstone park road is closed to cars but open to cyclists, offering a long but stress-free ride.

White-Water Rafting

Yellowstone Raft Company   RAFTING
(☑ 800-858-7781; www.yellowstoneraft.com; half-day adult/child $42/32) There is exhilarating white water through Yankee Jim Canyon on the Yellowstone River just north of the park boundary in Montana. This company offers a range of guided adventures out of Gardiner starting in late May.

🛏 Sleeping

NPS and private campgrounds, along with cabins, lodges and hotels, are all available in the park. Reservations are essential in summer. Contact the park concessionaire **Xanterra** (☑ 866-439-7375, 307-344-7311; www.yellowstonenationalparklodges.com) to reserve a spot at its campsites, cabins or lodges, including all those reviewed here.

Plentiful accommodations can also be found in the gateway towns of Cody, Gardiner and West Yellowstone.

The best budget options are the seven NPS-run campgrounds (campsites from $15 to $20) in Mammoth, Tower Falls, Indian Creek, Pebble Creek, Slough Creek, Norris and Lewis Lake, which are first-come, first-served. Xanterra runs five more campgrounds (listed here; reservations accepted, $20 to $45 per night), all with cold-water bathrooms, flush toilets and drinking water. RV sites with hookups are available at Fishing Bridge.

Xanterra-run cabins, hotels and lodges are spread around the park and are open from May or June to October. Mammoth Hot Springs Hotel and Old Faithful Snow Lodge are the exceptions; these are also open mid-December through March. All places are nonsmoking and none have air-con or TV. Where wi-fi is available, it costs extra.

Bridge Bay Campground   CAMPGROUND $
(sites $22.50; ☺ late May–mid-Sep) Near the west shore of Yellowstone Lake, popular with boaters, and with 430-plus sites for tents and RVs.

Canyon Campground   CAMPGROUND $
(sites $27; ☺ late May-early Sep) Centrally located, with pay showers and coin laundry nearby. There are 273 sites for tents and RVs.

Fishing Bridge RV Park   CAMPGROUND $
(RV site $47.75; ☺ early May-late Sep) Full hookups for hard-shell RVs only ($37). Pay showers and coin laundry. There are 325 sites.

Grant Village Campground   CAMPGROUND $
(sites $27; ☺ mid-Jun–mid-Sep) On Yellowstone Lake's southwest shore, it has 430 sites for tents and RVs. Pay showers and coin laundry nearby.

Madison Campground   CAMPGROUND $
(☑ 307-344-7311; www.yellowstonenationalparklodges.com; sites $22.50; ☺ early May–mid-Oct) The closest campground to Old Faithful, with 278 sites for tents and RVs.

★ Old Faithful Inn   HOTEL $$
(☑ 866-439-7375; www.yellowstonenationalparklodges.com; old house d with shared/private bath from $108/162, standard $199-260; ☺ early May-early Oct) Next to the signature geyser, this grand inn is the most requested lodging in the park. A national historic landmark, it features an immense timber lobby, with its huge stone fireplaces and sky-high knotted-pine ceilings. Rooms come in all price ranges, and many of the most interesting historic rooms share baths. Public areas offer plenty of allure.

It's worth staying two nights to soak up the atmosphere.

Old Faithful Lodge Cabins   CABIN $$
(cabins with/without bath $140/83; ☺ mid-May-early Oct) Views of Old Faithful; simple, rustic cabins.

Roosevelt Lodge   CABIN $$
(☑ 866-439-7375; www.yellowstonenationalparklodges.com; cabins with/without bath $135/80; ☺ Jun-early Sep; 🐾) These cabins are good for families. With a cowboy vibe, the place offers nightly 'Old West dinner cookouts,' during which guests travel by horse or wagon to

a large meadow 3 miles from the lodge for open-air buffets (book ahead).

Lake Lodge CABIN $$
(cabins $83-194) The main lodge boasts a large porch with lakeside mountain views and a cozy room with two fireplaces. Choose from rustic 1920s wooden cabins or more modern motel-style modules.

Old Faithful Snow Lodge HOTEL $$
(cabins $109-155, r from $240-259; ☺ May–mid-Oct & late Dec-Feb; 🛜) A stylish modern option that combines timber lodge style with modern fittings and park motifs.

Lake Yellowstone Hotel HOTEL $$
(📿 866-439-7375; www.yellowstonenationalparklodges.com; cabins $149, annex r $160, hotel r $363-405; ☺ mid-May–early Oct; @🛜) Oozing grand 1920s Western ambience, this romantic, historic hotel is a classy option. It has Yellowstone's most divine lounge, which was made for daydreaming, with big picture windows overlooking the lake, ample natural light and a live string quartet playing in the background. Rooms are well appointed, cabins more rustic.

Canyon Lodge LODGE $$
(cabins $194, r $122-222; ☺ Jun-Sep) Centrally located, the Canyon area has the largest number of accommodations options in Yellowstone and is adding more: several new lodges were under construction at press time.

Mammoth Hot Springs Hotel HOTEL $$
(cabins $93-250, r with/without bath $140/90; ☺ May–mid-Oct) Wide variety of sleeping options, including cabins with hot tubs; elk are often seen grazing on the front lawn.

Grant Village HOTEL $$
(Grant Village; r $160-201; ☺ late May-Sep; 🛜) Near the southern edge of the park with comfortable but uninspiring motel-style rooms. Two nearby restaurants have fabulous lake views.

✖ Eating

Snack bars, delis, burger counters and grocery stores are scattered around the park. In addition, most of the lodges offer breakfast buffets, salad bars, and serves lunch and dinner in formal dining rooms. Food, while not always exceptional, is quite good, considering how many people the chef is cooking for, and not too overpriced for the exceptional views.

WORTH A TRIP

SCENIC DRIVE: THE ROOF OF THE ROCKIES

The most scenic route into Yellowstone Park, **Beartooth Highway** (www.beartoothhighway.com; US 212; ☺ Jun–mid-Oct) connects Red Lodge to Cooke City and Yellowstone's north entrance by an incredible 68-mile journey alongside 11,000ft peaks and wildflower-sprinkled alpine tundra. It's been called both America's most scenic drive and its premier motorcycle ride. There are a dozen USFS campgrounds (reservations for some accepted at www.recreation.gov) along the highway, four within 12 miles of Red Lodge. Open late May or early June through early October.

★**Lake Yellowstone Hotel Dining Room** AMERICAN $$$
(📿 307-344-7311; mains $14-40; ☺ 6:30-10am, 11:30am-2:30pm & 5-10pm mid-May–Oct; 🖋) Keep one unwrinkled outfit to dine in style at the dining room of the Lake Yellowstone Hotel, the best in the park. Lunch options include Montana lamb sliders, lovely salads and bison burgers. There's a focus on local and sustainable ingredients as well as gluten-free options. Dinner reservations are strongly suggested.

Old Faithful Inn Dining Room AMERICAN $$$
(📿 307-545-4999; dinner mains $13-29, breakfast/lunch/dinner buffet $13/16/30; ☺ 6:30-10:30am, 11:30am-2:30pm & 5-10pm early May-Oct; 🖋) The buffets here will maximize your time spent geyser gazing but the à la carte options are more innovative, with things like bison and pheasant sausages, red trout hash and the ever-popular pork osso bucco. With gluten-free options. Reservations strongly encouraged.

❶ Information

The park is open year-round, but most roads close in winter. Park entrance permits (hiker/vehicle $12/25) are valid for seven days for entry into both Yellowstone and Grand Teton National Parks. Summer-only visitor centers are evenly spaced every 20 to 30 miles along Grand Loop Rd.

Albright Visitor Center (📿 307-344-2263; www.nps.gov/yell; ☺ 8am-7pm Jun-Sep, 9am-5pm Oct-May) This newly renovated visitor center in Mammoth Hot Springs serves as park headquarters. The park website is a fantastic resource.

❶ Getting There & Away

The closest year-round airports are Yellowstone Regional Airport (p277) in Cody (52 miles); Jackson Hole Airport (p276) in Jackson (56 miles); Gallatin Field Airport (p287) in Bozeman, MT, (65 miles); and Idaho Falls Regional Airport (IDA) in Idaho Falls, ID, (107 miles). The airport (WYS) in West Yellowstone, MT, is usually open June to September. It's often more affordable to fly into Billings, MT, 170 miles away, Salt Lake City, UT, (390 miles) or Denver, CO, 563 miles away, and rent a car. There is no public transportation to or within Yellowstone National Park.

Grand Teton National Park

With its jagged, rocky peaks, cool alpine lakes and fragrant forests, the Tetons rank among the finest scenery in America. Directly south of Yellowstone, Grand Teton National Park has 12 glacier-carved summits, which frame the singular Grand Teton (13,770ft). For mountain enthusiasts, this sublime and crazy terrain is thrilling. Less crowded than Yellowstone, the Tetons also have plenty of tranquillity, along with wildlife such as bear, moose, grouse and marmot.

The park has two entrance stations: Moose (south), on Teton Park Rd west of Moose Junction; and Moran (east), on US 89/191/287 north of Moran Junction. The park is open year-round, although some roads and entrances close from around November to May 1, including part of Moose–Wilson Rd, restricting access to the park from Teton Village.

🏃 Activities

With 200 miles of **hiking trails** you can't really go wrong. Consult at the visitor center where you can grab a hiking map. A free backcountry-use permit, also available at the visitor center, is required for overnight trips. The Tetons are also known for excellent short-route **rock climbs** as well as classic longer routes to summits like Grant Teton, Mt Moran and Mt Owen; Jenny Lake Ranger Station has information.

Fishing is another draw, with several species of whitefish and cutthroat, lake and brown trout thriving in local rivers and lakes. Get a license at the Moose Village store, Signal Mountain Lodge or Colter Bay Marina.

Cross-country skiing and **snowshoeing** are the best ways to take advantage of

park winters. Pick up a brochure detailing routes at Craig Thomas Discovery & Visitor Center in Moose.

Exum Mountain Guides   ROCK CLIMBING
(☎307-733-2297; www.exumguides.com) For instruction and guided climbs.

🛏 Sleeping

Three different concessionaires run the park's six campgrounds. Demand is high from early July to Labor Day. Most campgrounds fill by 11am (Jenny Lake fills much earlier; Gros Ventre rarely fills up). Colter Bay and Jenny Lake have tent-only sites reserved for backpackers and cyclists.

Climbers' Ranch   CABIN $
(☎307-733-7271; www.americanalpineclub.org; Teton Park Rd; dm $25; ☉Jun-Sep) Started as a refuge for serious climbers, these rustic log cabins run by the American Alpine Club are now available to hikers who can take advantage of the spectacular in-park location. There is a bathhouse with showers and sheltered cook station with locking bins for coolers. Bring your own sleeping bag and pad (bunks are bare, but still a steal).

Flagg Ranch Campground   CAMPGROUND $
(www.flaggranch.com; 2-person campsites $35, RV sites $69) Flagg Ranch campground, which also has cabins, is run by Flagg Ranch Resorts.

Grand Teton Lodge Company   ACCOMMODATION SERVICES $
(☎307-543-2811; www.gtlc.com; campsites $24) This company runs most of the park's private lodges, cabins and the campgrounds of Colter Bay, Jenny Lake and Gros Ventre. It's best to reserve ahead, as nearly everything is completely booked by early June.

Colter Bay Village   CABIN $$
(☎307-543-2811; www.gtlc.com; tent cabins $66, cabins with bath $155-290, without bath $85; ☉Jun-Sep) Half a mile west of Colter Bay Junction, the village has two types of accommodations. Tent cabins (June to early September) are very basic structures with bare bunks and shared bathrooms in a separate building. At these prices, you're better off camping. The log cabins, some original, are much more comfortable and a better deal; they're available late May to late September.

Signal Mountain Lodge   LODGE $$
(☎307-543-2831; www.signalmtnlodge.com; r $221-326, cabins $173-233, ste $350, tent/RV sites

$22/45; ⊙May–mid-Oct) 🏊 This spectacularly located place at the edge of Jackson Lake offers cozy, well-appointed cabins and rather posh rooms with stunning lake and mountain views.

Spur Ranch Log Cabins CABIN **$$**
(✑307-733-2522; www.dornans.com; cabins $195-285; ⊙year-round) Gravel paths running through a broad wildflower meadow link these tranquil duplex cabins on the Snake River in Moose. Lodgepole pine furniture, Western styling and down bedding create a homey feel, but the views are what make it.

★**Jenny Lake Lodge** LODGE **$$$**
(✑307-733-4647; www.gtlc.com; Jenny Lake; cabins from $699; ⊙Jun-Sep) Worn timbers, down comforters and colorful quilts imbue this elegant lodging off Teton Park Rd with a cozy atmosphere. It doesn't come cheap, but includes breakfast, a five-course dinner, bicycle use and guided horseback riding. Rainy days are for hunkering down at the fireplace in the main lodge with a game or book from the stacks.

The log cabins sport a deck but no TVs or radios (phones on request).

Jackson Lake Lodge LODGE **$$$**
(✑307-543-2811; www.gtlc.com; r & cottages $289-385; ⊙mid-May–Sep; 🛜🐾🏊) Aim for the main lodge, with its enormous, breathtaking picture window in the lobby framing views of the peaks. The cottages are more modern than cozy; if you go this route, ask for one with a view of Moose Pond. There's a heated pool and pets are OK in designated cottages.

✗ Eating

Colter Bay Village, Jackson Lake Lodge, Signal Mountain and Moose Junction have several reasonably priced cafes for breakfast and fast meals.

Pioneer Grill DINER **$$**
(✑307-543-1911; Jackson Lake Lodge; mains $9-25; ⊙6am-10:30pm; 🚸) A casual classic lunch counter with leatherette stools lined up in a maze, the Pioneer serves solid diner fare – wraps, burgers and salads. Kids adore the hot-fudge sundaes. A takeout window serves boxed lunches (order a day ahead) and room-service pizza for pooped hikers (5pm to 9pm).

Mural Room MODERN AMERICAN **$$$**
(✑307-543-1911; Jackson Lake Lodge; mains $22-44, lunch mains $12-20; ⊙7am-9pm) With stirring views of the Tetons, gourmet selections at this classy dining room include game dishes and imaginative takes on trout. Breakfasts are very good; dinner reservations are required.

Peaks AMERICAN **$$$**
(✑307-543-2831; Signal Mountain Lodge; mains $18-38; ⊙5:30-10pm) Dine on selections of cheese and fruit, local free-range beef and organic polenta cakes. Small plates, like wild game sliders, are also available. The indoor ambience is rather drab; hit the patio for sunsets over Jackson Lake and top-notch huckleberry margaritas. If you're here at lunchtime, try the more casual Trapper Grill (mains $11 to $14) or Deadman's Bar (all adjoining).

Jenny Lake Lodge
Dining Room MODERN AMERICAN **$$$**
(✑307-543-3352; Jenny Lake Lodge; breakfast $26, lunch mains $11-15, dinner prix-fixe $88; ⊙7am-9pm) A real splurge, this may be the only five-course wilderness meal of your life, but it's well worth it. For breakfast, try Rocky Mountain trout with eggs. Rotating five-course dinner menus include things like wild-game crepes and buffalo carpaccio. And you can't beat the atmosphere, snuggled in the Tetons. Reservations are required. Dress up in the evening.

❶ Information

Park permits (hiker/vehicle $12/25) are valid for seven days for entry into both Yellowstone and Grand Teton National Parks. It's easy to stay in one park and explore the other in the same day.

Park Headquarters (✑307-739-3600; www. nps.gov/grte; ⊙8am-7pm Jun-Aug, to 5pm Sep-May) Shares a building with the Craig Thomas Discovery & Visitor Center (✑307-739-3399, backcountry permits 307-739-3309; Teton Park Rd; ⊙8am-7pm Jun-Aug, to 5pm Sep-May; 🛜) at Moose Junction.

Jenny Lake Ranger Station (✑307-739-3343; ⊙8am-6pm Jun-Aug) Offers backcountry permits and climbing information.

Laurance S Rockefeller Preserve Center (✑307-739-3654; Moose-Wilson Rd; ⊙8am-6pm Jun-Aug, 9am-5pm Sep-May) Learn about the new and highly recommended Rockefeller Preserve, a less crowded option for hiking. The center is 4 miles south of Moose (road is closed in winter).

MONTANA

Maybe it's the independent frontier spirit, wild and free and oh-so-American, that earned Montana its 'live and let live' state motto. The sky seems bigger and bluer. The air is crisp and pine-scented. From mountains that drop into undulating ranchlands to brick brewhouses and the shaggy grizzly found lapping at an ice-blue glacier lake, Montana brings you to that euphoric place, naturally. And then it remains with you long after you've left its beautiful spaces behind.

❶ Information

Montana Fish, Wildlife & Parks (☑ 406-444-2535; http://fwp.mt.gov) Reservations for camping in Montana's 24 state parks can be made at ☑ 1-855-922-6768 or http://montanastateparks.reserveamerica.com.

Montana Road Conditions (☑ 800-226-7623, within Montana 511; www.mdt.mt.gov/travinfo)

Travel Montana (☑ 800-847-4868; www.visitmt.com)

Bozeman

In a gorgeous locale, surrounded by rolling green hills, pine forests and snowcapped peaks, Bozeman is the defending title holder of Coolest Town in Montana. Brick buildings with brewpubs and boutiques line historic Main St, mashing bohemian style up against cowboy cool and triathlete verve. A prime location up against the Bridger and Gallatin mountains makes it one of the best towns in the West for outdoor activities.

◉ Sights & Activities

★ **Museum of the Rockies** MUSEUM
(☑ 406-994-2251; www.museumoftherockies.org; 600 W Kagy Blvd; adult/child $14.50/9.50; ☺ 8am-8pm Jun-Aug, 9am-5pm Mon-Sat, noon-5pm Sun Sep-May; 🅿 👪) Montana State University's museum is the most entertaining in Montana and shouldn't be missed, with stellar dinosaur exhibits, early Native American art and laser planetarium shows, as well as a living-history outdoors section (closed in winter) and various temporary exhibits. Guided tours happen more or less constantly and are recommended for families with young children, as they let kids get more interactive with some of the displays.

Bridger Bowl Ski Area SNOW SPORTS
(☑ 406-587-2111; www.bridgerbowl.com; 15795 Bridger Canyon Rd; day lift ticket adult/child $54/19;

☺ mid-Dec–Apr) Only in Bozeman would you find a nonprofit ski resort. But this excellent community-owned facility, 16 miles north of Bozeman, is just that. It's known for its fluffy, light powder and unbeatable prices – especially for children under 12. (Kids under six ski free.)

🛏 Sleeping

The full gamut of chain motels lies north of downtown on 7th Ave, near I-90. There are more budget motels east of downtown on Main St.

Bear Canyon Campground CAMPGROUND $
(☑ 800-438-1575; www.bearcanyoncampground.com; I-90 exit 313; tent sites $20, RV sites $30-40; ☺ May–mid-Oct; 🐕🏊) Bear Canyon Campground is on top of a hill 3 miles east of Bozeman, with great views of the surrounding valley. There's even a pool.

Lewis & Clark Motel MOTEL $
(☑ 800-332-7666; www.lewisandclarkmotelbozeman.com; 824 W Main St; r $94-179; ❄@🖥🛜) For a drop of Vegas in your Montana, stay at this flashy, locally owned motel. The large rooms have floor-to-ceiling front windows and the piped 1950s music adds to the retro Rat Pack vibe. With hot tub and steam room. Prices go up on weekends in summer.

Howlers Inn B&B $$
(☑ 406-587-5229; www.howlersinn.com; 3185 Jackson Creek Rd; r $145-160, 2-person cabin $205; 🛜) Wolf-watchers will love this beautiful sanctuary 15 minutes outside of Bozeman. Rescued captive-born wolves live in enclosed natural areas on 4 acres, supported by the profits of the B&B. There are three spacious Western-style rooms in the main lodge and a two-bedroom carriage house. With luck, you will drift off to sleep serenaded by howls. Take exit 319 off I-90.

🍴 Eating & Drinking

As a college town, Bozeman has no shortage of student-oriented cheap eats and enough watering holes to quench a college football team's thirst. Most are on Main St.

Community Co-Op SUPERMARKET $
(www.bozo.coop; 908 W Main St; mains $7-12; ☺ 7am-10pm Mon-Sat, 8am-10pm Sun; 🛜🍴) 🌿 This beloved local market and deli is the best place to stock up on organic and bulk foods, as well as hot meals, salads and soups to eat in or take away. There's another branch at 44 E Main St.

★ **John Bozeman's Bistro**   AMERICAN $$
(☎ 406-587-4100; www.johnbozemansbistro.com; 125 W Main St; mains $12-28; ⊙11:30am-2:30pm, 5-9:30pm Tue-Sat) Bozeman's best restaurant, this pretty blonde-and-gold space offers Thai, Creole and pan-Asian slants on the cowboy dinner steak, plus globally influenced soups and starters and a weekly 'superfood' special ($14.95). Service is classy, friendly and unpretentious. Lunchtime offers an $8 menu of healthy salads and sandwiches. The beer taps are all local; sample five for $8.75.

Plonk   BISTRO $$$
(www.plonkwine.com; 29 E Main St; small plates $5-12, mains $15-30; ⊙11:30am-midnight Tue-Sat, from 4pm Sun & Mon Oct-Apr) Where to go for a drawn-out three-martini, gossipy lunch? Plonk serves a wide-ranging menu from light snacks to full meals, mostly made from local organic products. In summer the entire front opens up and cool breezes enter the long building, which also has a shotgun bar and pressed-tin ceilings.

Zebra Cocktail Lounge   LOUNGE
(☎406-585-8851; 321 E Main St; ⊙9pm-2am) This basement-level nightclub is the epicenter of the local live-music scene, strong on club and hip-hop.

❶ Information

Visitor Center (☎406-586-5421; www.bozemancvb.com; 2000 Commerce Way; ⊙8am-5pm Mon-Fri)

❶ Getting There & Away

Gallatin Field Airport (BZN; ☎406-388-8321; www.bozemanairport.com) Gallatin Field Airport is 8 miles northwest of downtown.

Karst Stage (☎406-556-3540; www.karststage.com) Runs buses daily, December to April, from the airport to Big Sky ($103, one hour) and West Yellowstone ($310, two hours); summer service is by reservation only.

Gallatin & Paradise Valleys

Outdoor enthusiasts could explore the expansive beauty around the Gallatin and Paradise Valleys for days. **Big Sky Resort** (☎800-548-4486; www.bigskyresort.com; Big Sky; lift tickets adult $103, child over/under 10 $83/53), with multiple mountains, 400in of annual powder and Montana's longest vertical drop

---

MONTANA FACTS
....
Nickname Treasure State, Big Sky Country

Population 1,024,000

Area 145,552 sq miles

Capital city Helena (population 29,500)

Other cities Billings (population 109,000), Missoula (population 69,000), Bozeman (population 39,800)

Sales tax No state sales tax

Birthplace of Movie star Gary Cooper (1901–61), motorcycle daredevil Evel Knievel (1938–2007), actress Michelle Williams (1980)

Home of Crow, Blackfeet and Salish Native Americans

Politics Republican ranchers and oil-execs generally edge out the Democratic students and progressives of left-leaning Bozeman and Missoula

Famous for Fly-fishing, cowboys and grizzly bears

Random fact Some Montana highways didn't have a speed limit until the 1990s!

Driving distances Bozeman to Denver 695 miles, Missoula to Whitefish 133 miles

---

(4350ft), is one of the nation's premier downhill and cross-country ski destinations, especially now it has merged with neighboring Moonlight Basin. Lift lines are the shortest in the Rockies, and if you are traveling with kids then Big Sky is too good a deal to pass up – children under 10 ski free if you book lodging through the resort's central reservations system. In summer it offers gondola-served hiking and mountain-biking.

For backpacking and backcountry skiing, head to the Spanish Peaks section of the **Lee Metcalf Wilderness**. It covers 389 sq miles of Gallatin and Beaverhead National Forest land west of US 191. Numerous scenic USFS campgrounds snuggle up to the Gallatin Range on the east side of US 191.

Twenty miles south of Livingston, off US 89 en route to Yellowstone, unpretentious **Chico Hot Springs** (☎406-333-4933; www.chicohotsprings.com; 1 Old Chico Rd, Pray; 2-person cabin $237, main lodge r $61-98; ⊙7am-11pm; 🐾)

DON'T MISS

FLY-FISHING IN BIG SKY

Ever since Robert Redford and Brad Pitt made it look sexy in the 1992 classic *A River Runs Through It*, Montana has been closely tied to fly-fishing cool. Whether you are just learning or you're a world-class trout wrangler, the wide, fast rivers are always spectacularly beautiful and filled with fish. Although the film – and the book it is based on – is set in Missoula and the nearby Blackfoot River, the movie was actually shot around Livingston and the Yellowstone and Gallatin Rivers.

For DIY trout fishing, the Gallatin River, 8 miles southwest of Bozeman along Hwy 191, has the most accessible, consistent angling spots, closely followed by the beautiful Yellowstone River, 25 miles east of Bozeman in the Paradise Valley.

For the scoop on differences between rainbow, brown and cutthroat trout – as well as flies, rods and a Montana fishing license – visit **Bozeman Angler** (☑406-587-9111; www.bozemanangler.com; 23 E Main St; one-day class adult/child $125/75; ☉9am-5:30pm Mon-Sat, to 4pm Sun). Owned by a local couple for nearly two decades, the downtown shop runs a great introduction-to-fly-fishing class ($125 per person, casting lessons $40 per hour) on the second Saturday of the month between May and September.

has garnered quite a following in the last few years, even attracting celebrity residents from Hollywood. Some come to soak in the swimming-pool-sized, open-air hot pools (admission for nonguests is $8.50), others for the lively bar hosting swinging country-and-western dance bands on weekends. The on-site restaurant (mains $20 to $32) is known for fine steak and seafood. You can stay here overnight, too. It's not called Paradise for nothing.

Absaroka Beartooth Wilderness

The fabulous, vista-packed Absaroka Beartooth Wilderness covers more than 943,377 acres and is perfect for a solitary adventure. Thick forests, jagged peaks and marvelous, empty stretches of alpine tundra are all found in this wilderness, saddled between Paradise Valley in the west and Yellowstone National Park in the south. The thickly forested Absaroka Range dominates the area's west half and is most easily reached from Paradise Valley or the Boulder River Corridor. The Beartooth Range's high plateau and alpine lakes are best reached from the Beartooth Hwy south of Red Lodge (closed October to May). Because of its proximity to Yellowstone, the Beartooth portion gets two-thirds of the area's traffic.

A picturesque old mining town with fun bars and restaurants and a good range of places to stay, **Red Lodge** offers great day hikes, backpacking and, in winter, skiing right near town. The **Red Lodge Visitor**

Center (☑406-446-1718; www.redlodge.com; 601 N Broadway Ave; ☉10am-4pm Mon-Fri) has information on accommodations; hikers should seek out the **Yodeler** (☑406-446-1435; www.yodelermotel.com; 601 S Broadway Ave; basement r from $60, upper level from $90; 🛜), whose owners have great intel on local trails. For fancier digs, try the **Pollard** (☑406-446-0001; www.thepollard.net; 2 N Broadway Ave; r $150-195, ste $185-265; 🛜).

Billings

It's hard to believe laid-back little Billings is Montana's largest city. The friendly oil and ranching center is not a must-see but makes for a decent overnight pit stop. The historic downtown has its own unpolished charm.

🛏 Sleeping

Dude Rancher Lodge   MOTEL $
(☑800-221-3302; www.duderancherlodge.com; 415 N 29th St; d from $89; ❋@🛜) Road-weary travelers will appreciate this downtown motor lodge, a fine and friendly motel with groovy oak furniture dating back to the 1940s, Western touches like split-log paneling and cattle-brand carpet, plus flat-screen TVs and in-room coffee. The attached diner is a local breakfast favorite.

🍴 Eating & Drinking

Harper & Madison   CAFE $
(☑406-281-8550; 3115 10th Ave N; mains $7-9; ☉7am-4pm Mon-Fri, to 1pm Sat) With a hefty dose of Martha Stewart, this sweet cafe does some brisk business. It's no wonder with the

excellent coffee, homemade quiches, and gourmet salads and sandwiches. If you're rushing to hit the road, grab some French pastries to go.

Walkers Grill   MODERN AMERICAN $$
(www.walkersgrill.com; 2700 1st Ave N; tapas $5-12, mains $15-36; ⊙5-10pm) Upscale Walkers offers good grill items and fine tapas at the bar (open from 4pm), in a large-windowed, elegant space.

Doc Harper's   BAR
(116 N Broadway; cocktails $7-9; ⊙4pm-midnight Mon-Sat) This long, narrow, pretty martini bar is run by a lawyer who won a (hard-to-get) liquor license in a state lottery and named the place after his dad, a physician who delivered hundreds of babies in the area. Slink up to the mezzanine or sit at the bar and watch the cocktail magic happen.

⊙ Getting There & Away

Logan International Airport (BIL; www. flybillings.com) Logan International Airport, 2 miles north of downtown, has direct flights to Salt Lake City, Denver, Minneapolis, Seattle, Phoenix and destinations within Montana.

Bus Depot (☑406-245-5116; 2502 1st Ave N; ⊙24hr) The bus depot has services to Bozeman ($37, three hours) and Missoula ($77, seven hours) twice daily.

√ Helena

With one foot in cowboy legend (Gary Cooper was born here) and the other in the more hip, less stereotypical lotus land of present-day Montana, diminutive Helena is one of the nation's smallest state capitals (population 29,500), a place where white-collared politicians draft legislation, while white-knuckle adventurers race into the foothills to indulge in that other Montana passion.

Back in town, half hidden among the Gore-Tex and outdoor outfitters, you will find an unexpected Gallic-inspired, neo-Gothic cathedral. Another pleasant surprise is the artsy pedestrian-only shopping quarter along Last Chance Gulch.

⊙ Sights & Activities

State Capitol   LANDMARK
(cnr Montana Ave & 6th St; ⊙7am-6pm Mon-Fri, 9am-3pm Sat & Sun) FREE This grand neoclassical building was completed in 1902 and is

WORTH A TRIP

CUSTER'S LAST STAND

The best detour from Billings is to the **Little Bighorn Battlefield National Monument** (☑406-638-3224; www.nps. gov/libi; US 212; per car $10; ⊙8am-9pm), 65 miles outside town in the arid plains of the Crow (Apsaalooke) Indian Reservation. Home to one of the USA's best-known Native American battlefields, this is where General George Custer made his famous 'last stand.'

Custer, and 272 soldiers, messed one too many times with Native Americans (including Crazy Horse of the Lakota Sioux), who overwhelmed the force in a frequently painted massacre. A visitor center tells the tale or, better, take one of the five daily tours with a Crow guide through **Apsaalooke Tours** (☑406-638-3897; adult/child $10/5; ⊙hourly 10am-3pm Memorial Day-Labor Day). The entrance is a mile east of I-90 on US 212. If you're here for the last weekend of June, the **Custer's Last Stand Re-enactment** (www.littlebighornreenactment.com; adult/child $20/10) is an annual hoot, 6 miles west of Hardin.

known for its beacon-like dome, richly decorated with gold-rimmed paintings inside.

Cathedral of St Helena   CHURCH
(530 N Ewing St; ⊙tours 1pm Tue-Thu) Rising like an apparition from old Europe over the town is this neo-Gothic cathedral completed in 1914. Highlights include the baptistery, organ and intricate stained-glass windows.

Holter Museum of Art   MUSEUM
(www.holtermuseum.org; 12 E Lawrence St; ⊙10am-5:30pm Tue-Sat, noon-4pm Sun) FREE This museum in downtown Helena exhibits contemporary art by Montana artists in a variety of mediums.

Mt Helena City Park   HIKING, CYCLING
Nine hiking and mountain-biking trails wind through Mt Helena City Park, including one that takes you to the 5460ft-high summit of Mt Helena.

🛏 Sleeping & Eating

East of downtown near I-15 is the usual string of chain motels.

Sanders
B&B $$

(☑ 406-442-3309; www.sandersbb.com; 328 N Ewing St; r $130-145; ✴ ☎) A historic B&B with seven elegant guest rooms, a wonderful old parlor and a breezy front porch. Each bedroom is unique and thoughtfully decorated, and it's run by a relative of the Ringling Brothers Circus family, with appropriate memorabilia.

Fire Tower Coffee House
CAFE, BREAKFAST $

(www.firetowercoffee.com; 422 Last Chance Gulch; breakfast $4-9; ⊙ 6am-6pm Mon-Fri, 7am-3pm Sat; ☎) This eclectic space toward the lower end of Last Chance Gulch is a hub for coffee, light meals and live music on Friday evenings. The menu features pastries, granola, breakfast burritos and a wholesome sandwich selection.

ℹ Information

Helena Visitor Center (☑ 406-442-4120; www.helenachamber.com; 225 Cruse Ave; ⊙ 8am-5pm Mon-Fri)

ℹ Getting There & Away

Helena Regional Airport (HNL; www.helenaairport.com) Two miles north of downtown, Helena Regional Airport operates flights to most other airports in Montana, as well as to Salt Lake City, Denver and Minneapolis.

√Missoula

Outsiders in Missoula usually spend the first 30 minutes wondering where they took a wrong turn: Austin, Texas? Portland, Oregon? Canada, perhaps? The confusion is understandable given the city's lack of standard Montana stereotypes. There's no Wild West saloons here and even fewer errant cowboys. Instead, Missoula is a refined university city with ample green space and abundant home pride.

Not surprisingly, its metro-west bounty is contagious. Though it's among the fastest-growing cities in the US, sensible planning means that Missoula rarely feels clamorous. The small traffic-calmed downtown core, with its interesting array of historic buildings, invites exploration by foot or bicycle.

◉ Sights

Missoula is a great city for walking, especially in the spring and summer, when enough people emerge onto its broad streets to give it a definable metro personality.

Missoula Art Museum
MUSEUM

(www.missoulaartmuseum.org; 335 North Pattee; ⊙ 10am-5pm Tue-Sat) FREE All hail a city that encourages free-thinking art and then displays it free of charge in a sleek building that seamlessly grafts a contemporary addition onto a 100-year-old library.

Smokejumper Visitor Center
MUSEUM

(W Broadway; ⊙ 10am-4pm Jun-Aug) FREE Located 7 miles west of downtown, near the airport, is this active base for the heroic men and women who parachute into forests to combat raging wildfires. Its visitor center has thought-provoking displays that do a great job illustrating the life of the Western firefighter.

⊼ Activities

Clark Fork River Trail System
CYCLING, HIKING

Taking advantage of its location astride the Clark Fork River, Missoula has built an attractive riverside trail system punctuated by numerous parks. **Caras Park** is the most central and active green space, with over a dozen annual festivals and a unique hand-carved carousel.

Mount Sentinel
HIKING

A steep switchback trail from behind the football stadium leads up to a concrete whitewashed 'M' (visible for miles around) on 5158ft Mt Sentinel. Tackle it on a warm summer's evening for glistening views of this much-loved city and its spectacular environs.

Adventure Cycling HQ
CYCLING

(www.adventurecycling.org; 150 E Pine St; ⊙ 8am-5pm Mon-Fri year-round, also 9am-1pm Sat Jun-Aug) ✍ The HQ for America's premier nonprofit bicycle travel organization is something of a pilgrimage site for cross-continental cyclists, many of whom plan their route to pass through Missoula. Staff offer a warm welcome and plenty of cycling information.

⛏ Sleeping & Eating

All the usual chain hotels are represented, many along W Broadway within an easy walk of the city center.

Goldsmith's Bed & Breakfast
B&B $$

(☑ 406-728-1585; www.missoulabedandbreakfast. com; 809 E Front St; r $129-164; ✴ @ ☎) This delightful riverside B&B was once a frat house, and before that, home to the university's president. The wraparound deck is the perfect place to kick back with other guests or a good novel. Comfy Victorian-style rooms are simply lovely. Some have private decks, river views, fireplaces and reading nooks.

★Silk Road   INTERNATIONAL $$
(www.silkroadcatering.com; 515 S Higgins; tapas $6-11; ⊙5-10pm Wed-Sat) Spanning global dishes from the Ivory Coast to Piedmont, Silk Road takes on lesser-known world cuisine and, more often than not, nails it. Dishes are tapas-sized, allowing you to mix and match. A warm welcome and an ambience of cushions and candlelit tapestries set the scene.

Caffe Dolce   MODERN AMERICAN $$
(⌨406-830-3055; www.caffedolcemissoula.com; 500 Brooks St; breakfast $6-11, lunch & dinner mains $7-36; ⊙7am-9pm Mon-Thu, 7am-10pm Fri, 8am-9pm Sat, 9am-2pm Sun) In a stately stone building, this chic local favorite is abuzz with well-clad Missoulians getting their fix of gelato, pastries, wine and gorgeous salads. Dinner can be pricey, but exotic pizzas offer a lighter, cheaper option. Coffee is a serious business here; this is your best bet for a good breakfast. Patio seating.

Dolce is located south of the town center on route 12.

🍷 Drinking & Nightlife

★Liquid Planet   COFFEE
(www.liquidplanet.com; 223 N Higgins; ⊙7:30am-9pm) 🖋 Considering how much Missoula loves its beverages, it's no surprise Liquid Planet was born here. Opened by a university professor in 2003, it's a sustainable coffeehouse, cafe and bottle shop selling carefully curated wines and craft beers, loose-leaf tea, coffee beans (with handwritten pedigrees) and sports drinks.

Draught Works   BREWERY
(915 Toole Ave; pints $4; ⊙noon-9pm) This cool brewery in a rehabbed industrial-chic building serves great pints with saucy names (try a 'That's What She Said' cream ale) and free pretzel snacks. There's no menu, but most days you can order from food carts in the parking lot.

The Old Post   BAR
(103 W Spruce St; mains $8-12; ⊙11am-2:30am Mon-Fri, from 9am Sat & Sun) This comfortable, unpretentious Western bar has a lived-in feel, with well-worn booths and bar stools and a cozy little patio out back. Great beer on tap, friendly servers and decer - what's not to love?

ℹ Information

Visitor Center (⌨406-532-3250; http://destinationmissoula.org; 101 E Main St; ⊙8am-5pm Mon-Fri) Destination Missoula has a useful website as well as a walk-in space downtown.

ℹ Getting There & Around

Missoula International Airport (MSO; www.flymissoula.com; 5225 Hwy 10 W) Missoula International Airport is 5 miles west of Missoula on US 10 W (which becomes W Broadway in town).
Depot (1660 W Broadway) Greyhound buses serve most of the state and stop at the depot, 1 mile west of town.

Flathead Lake

The largest natural freshwater lake west of the Mississippi, sitting not an hour's drive from Glacier National Park, completes western Montana's embarrassment of natural lures. The lake's north shore is dominated by the nothing-to-write-home-about city of **Kalispell**; far more interesting is the southern end embellished by the small polished settlement of **Polson**, which sits on the Flathead Indian Reservation.

◉ Sights & Activities

Flathead Lake's eastern shore is kissed by the mysterious Mission Mountains and dotted with apple orchards, cottages and fruit stands, while the west offers patches of evergreen, small farms and grassy hills. To get the best all-round view, hit the water. Soloists can kayak or canoe the conceptual **Flathead Lake Marine Trail** (fwp.mt.gov/recreation/activities/boating) which links various state parks and campsites around the lake.

Miracle of America Museum   MUSEUM
(www.miracleofamericamuseum.org; 58176 Hwy 93, Polson; adult/child $6/3; ⊙8am-8pm Mon-Sat, to 3pm Sun) For a concentrated dose of Americana, visit this museum 2 miles south of Polson on Hwy 93. At turns baffling and fascinating, it consists of 5 acres cluttered with the leftovers of American history. Wander past old motorcycles, a reconstructed soda fountain, chainsaws, old quilts and countless other weird artifacts, including the biggest buffalo (now stuffed) ever recorded in Montana.

.ake Cruises   BOATING

(☑406-883-3636; www.kwataqnuk.com; Polson; family/adult/child $40/15/free, dinner cruise $30) Lake cruises are run out of the Kwataqnuk Resort in Polson. Departure times vary by season; most cruises are one to two hours. Dinner cruises leave at 7pm Thursdays and Sundays.

🛏 Sleeping & Eating

Flathead Lake Marine Trail
Campsites   CAMPGROUND $
(☑855-922-6768, 406-751-4577; http://montanastateparks.reserveamerica.com; tent sites from $10) Montana Fish & Wildlife maintains camp sites along the Flathead Lake Marine Trail. The nearest site to Polson is Finley Point, 5.5 miles away by water.

Kwataqnuk Resort   HOTEL $$
(☑406-883-3636; www.kwataqnuk.com; 49708 US 93, Polson; r from $115; P🖕❄🛜🏊) The lakeside Kwataqnuk Resort, run by the Salish and Kootenai tribes, has a boat dock, indoor pool and a mellow casino-lounge. The spacious rooms have balconies, Keurig coffeemakers, mini-fridges and microwaves; even-numbered rooms have impressive lake views.

Betty's Diner   DINER $
(49779 US 93, Polson; mains $8-15; ⊘7am-8pm Mon-Sat, to 3pm Sun) This lurid-pink diner delivers salt-of-the-earth American food – burgers, steaks and omelets – with customary Montana charm.

ⓘ Information

Visitor Center (www.polsonchamber.com; 418 Main St; ⊘9am-5pm Mon-Fri) The chamber of commerce has visitor information.

Bob Marshall Wilderness Complex

Away from the Pacific coast, America's northwest harbors some of the most lightly populated areas in the lower 48. Case in point: the Bob Marshall Wilderness Complex, an astounding 2344 sq miles of land strafed with 3200 miles of trails including sections that are a 40-mile slog from the nearest road. And you thought the US was car-obsessed.

Running roughly from the southern boundary of Glacier National Park in the north to Rogers Pass (on Hwy 200) in the south, there are actually three designated wilderness areas within the complex: Great Bear, Bob Marshall and Scapegoat. On the periphery the complex is buffered with national-forest lands offering campgrounds, road access to trailheads and quieter country when 'the Bob' (as locals and park rangers call it) hosts hunters in fall.

The main access point to the Bob from the south is from Hwy 200 via the **Monture Guard Station Cabin** (☑406-677-2233; www.recreation.gov; cabins $60; ⊘Dec-Apr), on the wilderness perimeter. To reach it you'll need to drive 7 miles north of Ovando and snowshoe or hike the last mile to your private abode at the edge of the gorgeous Lewis and Clark Range. Contact the forest service about reservations.

Other Bob access points include the Seeley-Swan Valley in the west, Hungry Horse Reservoir in the north and the Rocky Mountain Front in the east. The easiest (and busiest) access routes are from the Benchmark and Gibson Reservoir trailheads in the Rocky Mountain Front.

Trails generally start steep, reaching the wilderness boundary after around 7 miles. It takes another 10 miles or so to really get into the Bob's heart. Good day-hikes run from all sides. Two USFS districts tend to the Bob, **Flathead National Forest Headquarters** (☑406-758-5208; www.fs.fed.us/r1/flathead; 650 Wolfpack Way; ⊘8am-4:30pm Mon-Fri) and **Lewis & Clark National Forest Supervisors** (☑406-791-7700; www.fs.fed.us/r1/lewis-clark; 1101 15th St N, Great Falls; ⊘8am-4:30pm Mon-Fri).

Whitefish

One square mile of rustic Western chic, tiny Whitefish (population 8000) easily charms. Once sold as the main gateway to Glacier National Park, this charismatic and caffeinated New West town merits a visit on its own. Aside from grandiose Glacier (an easy day's cycling distance), Whitefish is home to an attractive stash of restaurants, a historic railway station and an underrated ski resort.

⊙ Sights & Activities

Stumptown Historical
Society Museum   MUSEUM
(www.stumptownhistoricalsociety.org; 500 Depot St; ⊘10am-4pm Mon-Sat; 🎫) **FREE** Whitefish's fine old Tudor Revival Great Northern Railway Depot, built in the 1920s, doubles as a history museum displaying train memorabilia and fascinating photos of early Whitefish.

Whitefish Mountain Resort SNOW SPORTS
(☑406-862-2900; www.bigmtn.com; adult/child $71/37) Whitefish Mountain Resort, known as Big Mountain until 2008, guards 3000 acres of varied ski terrain and offers night skiing on weekends. In the summer there's lift-assisted mountain biking and ziplines.

🛌 Sleeping

**Whitefish Lake
State Park Campground** CAMPGROUND $
(☑406-862-3991; State Park Rd; camp sites $20; ⊙late May-early Oct) On the southwest edge of Whitefish Lake, shady forested grounds hold 25 first-come, first-served sites, including one that is wheelchair-friendly.

Downtowner Inn MOTEL $$
(☑406-862-2535; www.downtownermotel.cc; 224 Spokane Ave; r from $130; ❇@🛜) Cozier than the chain motels that line US 93 south of Whitefish, the cheerful Downtowner has spacious rooms, friendly staff and a morning bagel bar. (There's no longer a Jacuzzi and fitness center, though, despite the signs.)

🍴 Eating & Drinking

★Buffalo Café CAFE $
(www.buffalocafewhitefish.com; 514 3rd St E; breakfast mains $8-10; ⊙7am-2pm & 5-9pm Mon-Sat, from 8am Sun) Hopping with neighborly locals, the Buffalo serves hearty meals a step above standard cafe fare. Try the 'Buffalo pie,' a mountain of poached eggs and various add-ins (cheese, veggies, bacon) piled atop a wedge of hash browns. You won't leave hungry.

Great Northern Brewing Co BREWPUB
(☑406-863-1000; www.greatnorthernbrewing. com; 2 Central Ave; ⊙tours 1pm & 3pm Mon-Thu) Stop in to this high-ceilinged brewpub and tasting room for a pint or sampler anytime, or join a tour to up your beer-nerd game.

ℹ Information

Whitefish Visitor Center (www.whitefishvisit. com; 307 Spokane Ave; ⊙9am-5pm Mon-Fri) Check with the Whitefish Visitor Center for info on activities.

ℹ Getting There & Away

Railroad Depot (☑406-862-2268; 500 Depot St; ⊙6am-1:30pm, 4:30pm-midnight) Amtrak stops daily at Whitefish's railroad depot en route to West Glacier ($7, 30 minutes) and East Glacier ($15, two hours).

Glacier National Park

Few national parks are as magnificent and pristine as Glacier. Created in 1910 during the first flowering of the American conservationist movement, Glacier easily ranks with Yellowstone, Yosemite and the Grand Canyon.

Apart from stunning mountain scenery, it is renowned for its historic 'parkitecture' lodges, the spectacular Going-to-the-Sun Road, and an intact pre-Columbian ecosystem. This is the only place in the lower 48 states where grizzly bears still roam in abundance. Smart park management has kept the place accessible, yet authentically wild (there is no populated town site à la Banff or Jasper). Among a slew of outdoor attractions, the park is particularly noted for its hiking, wildlife-spotting and sparkling lakes, ideal for boating and fishing.

Although Glacier's tourist numbers are relatively high (two million a year), few visitors stray far from the Going-to-the-Sun Road and almost all visit between June and September. Choose your moment and splendid isolation is yours for the taking. The park remains open year-round; however, most services and parts of the Going-to-the-Sun Road are open only from mid-May to September.

Glacier's 1562 sq miles are divided into five regions, each centered on a ranger station: Polebridge (northwest); Lake McDonald (southwest), including the West Entrance and Apgar village; Two Medicine (southeast); St Mary (east); and Many Glacier (northeast). The approximate 50-mile Going-to-the-Sun Road is the only paved road that traverses the park.

🎯 Sights & Activities

Going-to-the-Sun Road OUTDOORS
(⊙mid-Jun-late Sep) A strong contender for the most spectacular road in America, the approximate 50-mile Going-to-the-Sun Road is a national historic landmark, flanked by hiking trails and a mountain pass and served by a free shuttle.

The road skirts near shimmering Lake McDonald before angling sharply to the **Garden Wall** – the main dividing line between the west and east sides of the park. At Logan Pass you can – and should – stroll 1.5 miles to **Hidden Lake Overlook**; heartier hikers can try the one-way, 7.6-mile **Highline Trail**. The shuttle stops on the western side of the road at the trailhead for **Avalanche Lake**, an easy 4-mile return hike to a stunning alpine lake in a cirque beautified with numerous weeping waterfalls.

Many Glacier HIKING

Anchored by the historic 1915 Many Glacier Lodge and sprinkled with more lakes than glaciers, this picturesque valley on the park's east side has some tremendous hikes, some of which link to the Going-to-the-Sun Road. A favorite is the 9.4-mile (return) **Iceberg Lake Trail**, a steep but rewarding jaunt through flower meadows and pine forest to an iceberg-infested lake.

Glacier Park Boat Co BOAT TOUR

(406-257-2426; www.glacierparkboats.com; St Mary Lake cruise adult/child $25.50/12.50) Rents out kayaks and canoes, and runs popular lake cruises, some with guided hikes included in the price, from five locations in Glacier National Park.

🛏 Sleeping

There are 13 **NPS campgrounds** (406-888-7800; www.recreation.gov; tent & RV sites $10-23) and seven historic lodges in the park, dating from the early 1900s, which operate between mid-May and the end of September. Of the camp sites, only Fish Creek and St Mary can be reserved in advance (up to five months). Sites fill by mid-morning, particularly in July and August.

⭐**Many Glacier Hotel** HISTORIC HOTEL $$

(855-733-4522; www.glaciernationalparklodges. com; r US$165-225, ste US$330; mid-Jun–mid-Sep;) Modeled after a Swiss chalet, this national historic landmark on Swiftcurrent Lake is the park's largest hotel, with 215 rooms, many with panoramic views. Evening entertainment, a lounge and fine-dining restaurant specializing in fondue all add to the appeal.

Lake McDonald Lodge HISTORIC HOTEL $$

(855-733-4522; www.glaciernationalparklodges. com; r US$85-190, cabins US$140-205, ste US$329; mid-May–Sep;) 🍽 Built in 1913, this old hunting lodge is adorned with stuffed-animal trophies and exudes relaxation. The 100 rooms are lodge, cabin or motel style. Nightly park-ranger talks and lake cruises add a rustic ambience. There's a restaurant and pizzeria.

Glacier Park Lodge HISTORIC HOTEL $$

(406-226-5600; www.glacierparkinc.com; r $169-256; Jun-Sep; 🍽) 🍽 The park's flagship lodge is a graceful, elegant place featuring interior balconies supported by Douglas fir timbers and a massive stone fireplace in the lobby. It's an aesthetically appealing, historically charming and very comfortable place to stay. Pluses include nine holes of golf and cozy reading nooks.

Rising Sun Motor Inn MOTEL $$

(855-733-4522; www.glaciernationalparklodges. com; r US$135, cabin US$140; Jun–mid-Sep;) One of two classic 1940s-era wooden motels, the Rising Sun lies on the north shore of St Mary Lake in a small complex that includes a store, restaurant and boat launch. The rustic rooms and cabins offer everything an exhausted hiker could hope for.

🍴 Eating

In summer there are grocery stores with limited camping supplies in Apgar, Lake McDonald Lodge, Rising Sun and at the Swiftcurrent Motor Inn. Most lodges have on-site restaurants. Dining options in West Glacier and St Mary offer mainly hearty hiking fare.

Polebridge Mercantile BAKERY, GROCERY $

(406-888-5105; www.polebridgemerc.com; Polebridge Loop Rd, North Fork Valley; pastries from $4; 8am-6pm mid-May–Nov;) An odd little grocery store reached via the scenic dirt road to Bowman Lake, Polebridge Mercantile has all the odds and ends you forgot you needed, plus huge cinnamon buns, known to pump a good couple of hours into tired hiking legs.

Park Café AMERICAN $$

(406-732-9979; www.parkcafe.us; US 89; mains US$12-25; 7:30am-9pm Jun-Sep) Offers hearty breakfasts until noon, and comes recommended for the homemade pies topped in whipped cream or ice cream.

Ptarmigan Dining Room INTERNATIONAL $$$

(Many Glacier Hotel; mains $15-35; 6:30am-9:30pm, mid-Jun–mid-Sep) With its lakeside views, this is the most refined of the lodge restaurants, also serving wine and microbrews.

ℹ Information

Visitor centers and ranger stations in the park sell field guides and hand out hiking maps. Those at Apgar and St Mary are open daily May to October; the visitor center at Logan Pass is open when the Going-to-the-Sun Road is open. The Many Glacier, Two Medicine and Polebridge Ranger Stations close at the end of September. **Park headquarters** (406-888-7800; www.nps.gov/ glac; 8am-4:30pm Mon-Fri year-round) is in West Glacier between US 2 and Apgar.

Entry to the park (hiker/vehicle $12/25) is valid for seven days. Day-hikers don't need permits, but overnight backpackers do (May to October only). Half of the permits are available on a first-come, first-served basis from the **Apgar Backcountry Permit Center** (Apgar Village; permit per person per day $4; ☺ May-Oct), St Mary Visitor Center, and the Many Glacier, Two Medicine and Polebridge ranger stations.

The other half can be reserved at the Apgar Backcountry Permit Center, St Mary and Many Glacier visitor centers and Two Medicine and Polebridge ranger stations.

❶ Getting There & Around

Amtrak's *Empire Builder* train stops daily at West Glacier (year round) and East Glacier Park (April to October) on its route between Seattle and Chicago. **Glacier National Park** (www.nps.gov/glac) runs free shuttles from Apgar Village to St Mary over Going-to-the-Sun Road from July 1 to Labor Day. **Glacier Park, Inc** (www.glacier-parkinc.com) offers the East Side Shuttle ($15 to $45 depending on route) on the eastern side of the park with daily links to Waterton (Canada), Many Glacier, St Mary, Two Medicine and East Glacier; reserve in advance.

IDAHO

Famous for not being particularly famous, the nation's 43rd state is a pristine wilderness of Alaskan proportions, rudely ignored by passing traffic heading west to Seattle or east to Montana. In truth, much of this lightly trodden land is little changed since the days of Lewis and Clark, including a vast 15,000-sq-km 'hole' in the middle of the state and bereft of roads, settlements, or any other form of human interference.

Flatter, dryer southern Idaho is largely dominated by the Snake River, deployed as a transportation artery by early settlers on the Oregon Trail and tracked today by busy Hwy 84. But, outside of this narrow populated strip, the Idaho landscape is refreshingly free of the soulless strip-mall, fast-food infestations so ubiquitous elsewhere in the US.

Boise

Understated, underrated and under-appreciated, Idaho's state capital (and largest city) gets little name recognition from people outside the northwest. The affable downtown impresses unsuspecting visitors with the modest spirit of an underdog. Cool surprises include Basque culture, a grandiose

Idaho capitol building and a fair number of well-heeled bars and Parisian-style bistros. There's also a university campus and enough greenery to make its 'city of trees' moniker more than just a marketing ploy. Boise leaves a lasting impression – primarily because it's not supposed to.

◉ Sights & Activities

Idaho State Capitol   LANDMARK
(700 W Jefferson St; ☺ 6am-10pm Mon-Fri, 9am-5pm Sat & Sun) **FREE** The joy of US state capitol buildings is that visitors can admire some of the nation's best architecture for free. The Boise building, constructed from native sandstone, celebrates the neoclassical style in vogue when it was built in 1920. It was extensively refurbished in 2010 and is now heated with geothermal hot water.

Ridge to Rivers Trail System   HIKING
(www.ridgetorivers.org) ✎ More rugged than Boise's greenbelt are the scrub- and brush-covered foothills above town, offering 75 miles of scenic, sometimes strenuous hiking and mountain-biking routes. The most immediate access from downtown is via Fort Boise Park on E Fort St, five blocks southeast of the state capitol building.

◉ Basque Block

Unbeknownst to many, Boise harbors one of the largest Basque populations outside Spain. European émigrés first arrived in the 1910s to work as Idaho shepherds. Elements of their distinct culture can be glimpsed along Grove St between 6th St and Capitol Blvd.

**Basque Museum &
Cultural Center**   MUSEUM
(www.basquemuseum.com; 611 Grove St; adult/child $5/3; ☺ 10am-4pm Tue-Fri, 11am-3pm Sat) Sandwiched between the ethnic taverns, restaurants and bars is the Basque Museum & Cultural Center, a commendable effort to unveil the intricacies of Basque culture and how it was transposed 6000 miles west to Idaho. Language lessons in Euskara, one of Europe's oldest languages, are held here.

Anduiza Fronton Building   LANDMARK
(619 Grove St) Originally a boarding house from 1912, this building is home to Boise's popular indoor *pala* (Basque racquetball) court – check at the Basque Museum for a schedule of games.

ROCKY MOUNTAINS BOISE

Boise River & Greenbelt

Laid out in the 1960s, the tree-lined river-banks of the Boise River protect 30 miles of vehicle-free trails. It personifies Boise's 'city of trees' credentials, with parks, museums and river fun.

Boise Art Museum   MUSEUM
(www.boiseartmuseum.org; 670 N Julia Davis Dr; adult/child $6/3; ⊙10am-5pm Tue-Sat, noon-5pm Sun) Inside 90-acre Julia Davis Park, this art museum displays contemporary art in all media, including touring exhibitions by some big names (Kara Walker, Nick Cave). On First Thursdays each month, admission is by donation and the museum stays open until 8pm.

Barber Park   PARK
(barber-park.com; Eckert Rd; tube rentals $12) In summer everyone loves to float down the Boise River. Rent tubes or rafts from Epley's Adventures in Barber Park and float 5 or 6 miles downstream. A shuttle bus ($3) runs hourly 1pm to 8pm, to 9pm Friday, from June to August from the take-out point.

IDAHO FACTS

Nickname Gem State

Population 1,596,000

Area 83,570 sq miles

Capital city Boise (population 210,100)

Other cities Idaho Falls (population 57,600)

Sales tax 6%

Birthplace of Lewis and Clark guide Sacagawea (1788–1812); politician Sarah Palin (b 1964); poet Ezra Pound (1885–1972)

Home of Star garnet, Sun Valley ski resort

Politics Reliably Republican with small pockets of Democrats, eg Sun Valley

Famous for Potatoes, wilderness, the world's first chairlift

North America's deepest river gorge Idaho's Hells Canyon (7900ft deep)

Driving distances Boise to Idaho Falls 280 miles, Lewiston to Coeur d'Alene 116 miles

---

🛏 Sleeping

★ Boise Guest House   GUESTHOUSE **$$**
(☑ 208-761-6798; http://boiseguesthouse.com; 614 North 5th St; ste $99-189; 🛜🐾) As close as you can get to a home away from home, this artist-owned guesthouse has a handful of suites with kitchenettes and living areas. Whimsical and well thought-out, it has lovely decor with good books on the shelf and appealing local art. The beach-cruiser bike rentals ($10) encourage further exploration.

Modern Hotel   BOUTIQUE MOTEL **$$**
(☑ 208-424-8244; www.themodernhotel.com; 1314 W Grove St; d from $120, brunch mains $7-12; P🌐🛜) Making an oxymoron (a boutique motel!?) into a fashion statement, the Modern Hotel offers retro-trendy minimalist rooms and a slavishly hip bar in the middle of downtown. The power showers are huge and the service is five-star. On weekends, a fancy brunch menu includes things like truffled eggs and chilled asparagus vichyssoise.

🍴 Eating

Restaurants and nightspots are found downtown in the brick-lined pedestrian plaza of the Grove, and the gentrified former warehouse district between 8th St and Idaho Ave. Seek out some Basque specialties.

Goldy's Breakfast Bistro   BREAKFAST **$**
(http://goldysbreakfastbistro.com; 108 S Capitol Blvd; mains $6-12; ⊙6:30am-2pm Mon-Fri, 7:30am-2pm Sat & Sun) This breakfast joint is a long-standing local favorite – to the point that you want to get here right when it opens or expect a wait. It's cozy and cheerful, with good coffee and a menu built around the many variations of eggs Benedict. Whatever you order, don't skip the Goldy's special potatoes.

Vietnam Pho Nouveau   VIETNAMESE **$$**
(☑ 208-367-1111; www.phonouveau.com; 780 W Idaho St; mains $9-16; ⊙11am-9:30pm Mon-Thu, 11am-10:30pm Fri & Sat, noon-8:30pm Sun) A small, smart cafe oozing understated cool, it's Boise's happy destination for Asian comfort food. Dig into *bun*, a big bowl of noodles with grilled meat and plenty of greens, lily-blossom salad with tender shredded pork, or Saigon crepes.

★ Fork   MODERN AMERICAN **$$**
(☑ 207-287-1700; www.boisefork.com; 199 North 8th St; mains $14-28; ⊙11am-10pm; 🖊) 🍃

Twenty years ago, this kind of upscale green-boosted menu would have been Idaho heresy. No more. Down-home starts with cast-iron fried chicken with waffles and balsamic maple syrup. But there's also creative salads, braised greens, locally and regionally sourced meat and – of course – Idaho potatoes. (Don't even think of skipping the rosemary Parmesan fries.)

Bittercreek Ale House &
Red Feather Lounge INTERNATIONAL **$$**
(www.justeatlocal.com; 246 N 8th St; mains $10-20; ☺11am-late) 🍴 These adjoining restaurants offer lively, intimate environs and lots of personality. They also serve wholesome, usually locally produced food with an emphasis on sustainable growth. The nouveau-American menu features a good selection of vegetarian options. The more polished Red Feather does delicious wood-oven pizza. Order one of the whiskey cocktails made with an old-fashioned pre-Prohibition-era recipe.

🍷 Drinking & Nightlife

⭐**Bar Gernika** PUB
(www.bargernika.com; 202 S Capitol Blvd; mains $8-11; ☺11am-midnight Mon-Thu, to 1am Fri & Sat) *Ongi etorri* (welcome) to the Basque block's most accessible pub-tavern, with a menu that leans heavily on old-country favorites such as lamb kabob, chorizo and beef tongue (Saturdays only). Pair your meal with a 20oz Guinness or a *kalimotxo* (red wine and cola). It's a true only-in-Boise kind of place.

Leku Ona BAR
(☎208-345-6665; www.lekuonaid.com; 117 S 6th St; ☺11am-late Mon-Sat; 🛜) Run by a Basque-born immigrant, this bar and restaurant in the heart of the downtown Basque block is always hopping. Don't miss the chance to try some delicious *pintxos* (Basque tapas). You can also stay at the well-worn little five-room boarding house next-door (singles/doubles $65/85).

Bardenay PUB
(www.bardenay.com; 610 Grove St; cocktails from $7; ☺11am-late) Bardenay was the USA's very first 'distillery-pub,' and remains a one-of-a-kind watering hole. Today it serves its own home-brewed vodka, rum and gin in casual, airy environs.

ℹ️ Information

Visitor Center (☎208-344-7777; www.boise. org; 250 S 5th St, Ste 300; ☺10am-5pm Mon-Fri,

10am-2pm Sat Jun-Aug, 9am-4pm Mon May) The website has a useful events

ℹ️ Getting There & Around

Boise Municipal Airport (BOI; I-84 exit 53) Daily flights to Denver, Las Vegas, Phoenix, Portland, Salt Lake City, and Spokane.
Bus Station (1212 W Bannock St) Greyhound services depart from the bus station with routes fanning out to Spokane, Pendleton and Portland, Twin Falls and Salt Lake City.

Ketchum & Sun Valley

In one of Idaho's most stunning natural locations sits a piece of ski history. Sun Valley was the first purpose-built ski resort in the US, handpicked by Union Pacific Railroad scion William Averell Harriman (after an exhaustive search) in the 1930s and publicized by glitterati Ernest Hemingway, Clark Gable and Gary Cooper. When Sun Valley opened in 1936 it sported the world's first chairlift and a showcase 'parkitecture' lodge that remains its premier resort.

Sun Valley has kept its swanky Hollywood clientele and extended its facilities to include the legendary Bald Mountain, yet it remains a refined and pretty place (no fast-food joints or condo sprawl here). Highly rated nationwide, the resort is revered for its reliably good snow, big elevation drop and almost windless weather. The adjacent village of Ketchum, 1 mile away, holds a rustic beauty despite the skiing deluge. Hemingway made it prime territory for fishing and hunting, though these days fat tires are the summer rage.

🏃 Activities

Main St between 1st and 5th Sts is Ketchum's main drag. Sun Valley is 1 mile north and easily walkable. Twelve miles south of Ketchum, also on Hwy 75, is **Hailey**, another delightful small town with a bar scene.

Wood River Trail HIKING, CYCLING
There are numerous hiking and mountain-biking trails around Ketchum and Sun Valley, as well as excellent fishing spots. The Wood River Trail is the all-connecting artery linking Sun Valley with Ketchum and continuing 32 bucolic miles south down to Bellevue via Hailey. Rent bikes from **Pete Lane's** (☎208-622-2276; petelanes@sunvalley.com; 1 Sun Valley Rd; bike rentals from $35; ☺9am-6pm).

Sun Valley Resort SNOW SPORTS
(www.sunvalley.com; adult/child Bald Mountain $115/69, Dollar Mountain $79/56) Famous for its light, fluffy powder and celebrity guests, this dual-sited resort comprises advanced-terrain **Bald Mountain** and easier-on-the-nerves **Dollar Mountain**, which also has a **tubing hill**. In summer, take the chairlift to the top of either mountain (adult/child $23/19), and hike or cycle down. Facilities are predictably plush.

🛏 Sleeping

In summer, there is free camping on Bureau of Land Management (BLM) land very close to town; see the visitor center for details.

Tamarack Lodge HOTEL $$
(☑208-726-3344; www.tamaracksunvalley.com; 500 E Sun Valley Rd; r $129-169; ✲⊛🖈🏊) Tasteful rooms complete with fireplace, balcony and many amenities are offered at this well-maintained lodge, along with sterling service, a Jacuzzi and an indoor pool. Discounts are often available midweek and off-season.

Sun Valley Lodge HOTEL $$$
(☑208-622-2001; www.sunvalley.com; 1 Sun Valley Rd; r from $289; ✲@🖈🏊) Reopened in June 2015 after a massive renovation that cut the number of rooms in half, this swank 1930s-era beauty – the country's first destination ski resort – is cranking up the luxury and toning down the old woodsy charm. Rooms now feel more like spacious modern apartments, and a new wing contains a 20,000-sq-ft spa.

There's also a pool and poolside cafe, Jacuzzi and downstairs bowling alley (also redone), plus a winter ski-shuttle service and children's program.

🍴 Eating & Drinking

Despo's MEXICAN $
(☑208-726-3068; 211 4th St; mains $6-12; ⊙11:30am-10pm Mon-Sat) Locals dig this healthy Mexican joint. Everything is fresh (if not entirely authentic), salads are huge and homemade salsas (warm, hot and smokin') are worthy.

Glow VEGAN $
(380 Washington #105; mains $6-12; ⊙10am-5pm Mon-Sat; 🖈) An oasis of raw and vegan dining. Sample from its laundry list of smoothies, chia puddings, organic salads, blended soups and (thank god) handmade raw chocolates, and you too might glow.

★Rickshaw ASIAN $$
(www.eat-at-rickshaw.com; 460 N Washington Ave; lunch mains $11-15, dinner small plates $7-15; ⊙from 5:30pm Tue-Sat, lunch 11:30am-2pm Fri) Small and crooked as an actual rickshaw, welcoming and with the vitality of a busy thoroughfare, this restaurant turns out A+ street food from Vietnam, Thailand, Korea and Indonesia. Tender short ribs served with a jalapeno-cilantro glaze are maddeningly wonderful. From green curry to cashew stir fry, the default here is spicy. A must. Opening hours vary; check website for latest.

Pioneer Saloon STEAK $$$
(www.pioneersaloon.com; 320 N Main St; mains $15-35; ⊙5-10pm, bar from 4pm) Around since the 1950s and originally an illicit gambling hall, the Pio is an unashamed Western den decorated with deer heads, antique guns (one being Hemingway's) and bullet boards, and – oh yes – some good food too, as long as you like beef and trout.

Casino Club BAR
(220 N Main St) This dive bar is the oldest thing still standing from days of yore. It has witnessed everything from gambling fistfights, to psychedelic hippies, to the rise and fall of Ernest Hemingway, to tattooed men on Harleys riding through the front door.

ℹ Information

Sun Valley/Ketchum Visitors Center (☑208-726-3423; www.visitsunvalley.com; 491 Sun Valley Rd; ⊙6am-7pm) Staffed only from 9am to 6pm, but you can still come in and get maps and brochures before and after hours.

ℹ Getting There & Around

Friedman Memorial Airport (SUN; http://iflysun.com) The region's airport is in Hailey, 12 miles south of Ketchum.

Sun Valley Express (www.sunvalleyexpress.com) Operates a daily shuttle between Sun Valley and Boise Airport in both directions ($69 one-way).

Stanley

Backed by the ragged Sawtooths, Stanley (population 100), with its gravel roads, log homes and rusted iron sheds, might be the most scenic small town in America. Surrounded by protected wilderness and national-forest land, the remote outpost sits in the crook of the Salmon River, miles from anywhere. Here the high summer twilight stretches past 10pm and the roaring creek lulls you to sleep.

CENTRAL IDAHO'S SCENIC BYWAYS

Goodbye suburban strip malls, hello unblemished wilderness. All three r___
remote Idahoan outpost of Stanley are designated National Scenic Byw___
place in the US where this happens). Considering there are only 125 such road___
country, it means 2.4% of America's prettiest pavement runs through bucolic Stanley___

Sawtooth Scenic Byway

Following the Salmon River along Hwy 75 north from Ketchum to Stanley, this 60-mile drive is gorgeous, winding through a misty, thick ponderosa pine forest – where the air is crisp and fresh and smells like rain and nuts – before ascending the 8701ft **Galena Summit**. From the overlook at the top, there are views of the glacially carved Sawtooth Mountains.

Ponderosa Pine Scenic Byway

Hwy 21, between Stanley and Boise, is so beautiful it will be hard to reach your destination because you'll want to stop so much. From Stanley the trees increase in density, until you find yourself cloaked in pine – more Pacific Northwest than classic Rockies. With frequent bursts of rain, the roadway can feel dangerous. Even in late May the snowfields stretch right down to the highway. Two of the road's many highlights are **Kikham Creek Hot Springs** (208-373-4100; parking per car $5; 6am-10pm), 4 miles east of Lowman, a primitive campground and natural hot spring boiling out of the creek; and the old restored gold rush town of **Idaho City**.

Salmon River Scenic Byway

Northeast of Stanley, Hwy 75 and US 93 make up another scenic road that runs beside the Salmon River for 161 miles to historic **Lost Trail Pass** on the Montana border, the point where Lewis and Clark first crossed the continental divide in 1805. The surrounding scenery has changed little in over 200 years.

🏃 Activities

Middle Fork of the Salmon River RAFTING
(877-444-6777; http://recreation.gov) Stanley is the jumping-off point for rafting the legendary Middle Fork of the Salmon. Billed as the 'last wild river,' it's part of the longest undammed river system in the US, outside Alaska. Permits are required; visit or call the National Recreation Reservation Service for details.

Full trips last six days and allow you to float for 106 miles through 300 or so rapids (class I to IV) in the 2.4-million-acre Frank Church–River of No Return Wilderness, miles from any form of civilization.

Main Fork of the Salmon River RAFTING
(877-444-6777; http://recreation.gov; 🚹) For more affordable, albeit slightly less dramatic, white-water action than Middle Fork, do a DIY float trip down the Main Fork of the Salmon in a raft or inflatable kayak. There are 8 miles of quiet water, starting in Stanley, with views of the Sawtooth Mountains you can't see from the road. Bring fishing gear. Permits are required for certain sections.

Fly Fishing FISHING
(http://stanleycc.org/do/fishing; Mar-Nov) The Salmon River and surrounding mountain lakes have epic trout fishing from March until November, with late June to early October best for dry fly-fishing. The eight species of local trout include the mythical steelhead, which measure up to 40in. These fish travel 900 miles from the Pacific Ocean at winter's end, arriving near Stanley in March and April.

👉 Tours

White Otter RAFTING
(208-788-5005; www.whiteotter.com; 100 Yankee Fork Road & Hwy 75, Sunbeam; full-day float trips per person $300, half-day river rafting adult/child $75/55) The sole rafting outfit that's locally run, White Otter is recommended for fun class III day trips. It also arranges float trips in inflatable kayaks.

Solitude River Trips RAFTING
(800-396-1776; www.rivertrips.com; 6-day trip per person $3140; Jun-Aug) Offers top-notch, multiday trips on the famed Middle Fork of the Salmon. Camping is riverside and guides cook excellent food.

Creek Outfitters FISHING

.?7-622-5282; www.silver-creek.com; 1 Sun Val-
.ßd; full-day drift boat trip $525) Based in Sun
valley, Silver Creek does custom trips to the
Salmon and remote river spots, only accessible via drift boat or float tube.

⨾ Sleeping & Eating

There are about half a dozen hotels in Stanley, all done in traditional pioneer log-cabin
style. During the short summer season a
couple of restaurants open up.

Sawtooth Hotel HOTEL $

(☏ 208-721-2459; www.sawtoothhotel.com; 755
Ace of Diamonds St; d with/without bath $100/70;
⊙ mid-May–mid-Oct; 🛜) Set in a nostalgic 1931
log motel, the Sawtooth updates the slim
comforts of yesteryear, but keeps the hospitality effusively Stanley-esque. Six rooms
are furnished old-country style, two with
private bathrooms. Room No 9 is the fave.
Don't expect TVs or room phones, but count
on homespun dining that is exquisite.

On weekends in peak summer season, a
two-night minimum stay is required.

★ Stanley Baking Co BAKERY, BREAKFAST $

(www.stanleybakingco.com; 250 Wall St; mains
$9-12; ⊙ 7am-2pm May-Oct) This middle-of-
nowhere bakery and brunch spot, from the
same couple that runs the Sawtooth Hotel, is
a godsend. Operating for five months of the
year out of a small log cabin, Stanley Bak-
ing Co is the only place in town where you're
likely to see a queue. The reason: off-the-rat-
ings-scale homemade baked goods and oat-
meal pancakes.

Idaho Panhandle

Idaho grabbed the long skinny spoon-handle
that brushes up against Canada in an 1880s
land dispute with Montana. Yet in both looks
and attitude, the area has more in common
with the Pacific Northwest than the Rockies.
Spokane, a few miles west in Washington,
acts as the regional hub and most of the panhandle observes Pacific Standard Time (one
hour behind the rest of Idaho on mountain
time).

Near the Washington border, fast-growing
Coeur d'Alene (population 46,000) is an extension of the Spokane metro area and the
panhandle's largest town. There's a small
boardwalk and a manicured park in front of
the landmark resort, itself rather anonymous
until the gorgeous evening sunlight makes

it shimmer. The adjacent lake is ideal for
water-based activities like standup paddle-
boarding. Most of the dining-and-drinking
action takes place along a stretch of Sherman
leading uphill from the lake.

Sandpoint, on Lake Pend Oreille, is the
nicest panhandle town, with a cute, walkable core of historic buildings housing cafes,
shops and Pilates studios. Set in a gorgeous
wilderness locale surrounded by mountains, it also sports Idaho's only serviceable
Amtrak train station, an attractive brick
structure dating from 1916. The *Empire
Builder*, running daily between Seattle/Port-
land and Chicago, stops here.

You can soak up Idaho's largest lake from
the Pend Oreille Scenic Byway (US 200),
which hugs the north shore.

⊙ Sights & Activities

Schweitzer Mountain Resort SNOW SPORTS

(www.schweitzer.com; adult/child $72/50) Eleven
miles northwest of Sandpoint is highly rated
Schweitzer Mountain Resort, lauded for its
tree-skiing, with mountain biking in summer.

⨾ Sleeping & Eating

Country Inn MOTEL $

(☏ 208-263-3333; www.countryinnsandpoint.com;
470700 Hwy 95; s/d $80/90; 🛜🅿️) The best
accommodation bargain for miles around is
the clean, friendly, mom-and-pop-run Country Inn, 3 miles south of Sandpoint.

Flamingo Motel MOTEL $$

(☏ 208-664-2159; www.flamingomotelidaho.com;
718 Sherman Ave, Coeur d'Alene; r $102; ❄️🛜)
This fun, friendly place, a retro '50s throw-
back, has rooms elaborately decked out in
various themes – from over-the-top 'Flamingo' to 'Irish' – plus updates like flat-screen
TVs and mini-fridges. For the fanciest digs,
book the Victorian Room.

Java on Sherman CAFE $

(819 Sherman Ave, Coeur d'Alene; mains $7-13,
coffee $2-5; ⊙ 6am-7pm) In a new, roomier
location a little further up the hill, this local favorite serves good coffee and breakfast
along with beer, wine and excellent people-
watching.

ⓘ Information

Coeur d'alene Visitors Center (☏ 208-665-

2350; www.coeurdalene.org; 115 Northwest
Blvd, Coeur d'Alene; ⊙ 10am-3pm Tue-Sat,
to 5pm Jun-Aug) The Coeur d'Alene Visitors
Center is a good regional-info starting point.

Southwest

Best Places to Eat

➜ Elote Cafe (p334)

➜ Hell's Backbone (p368)

➜ Love Apple (p389)

➜ Cafe Roka (p353)

➜ The Curious Kumquat (p393)

Best Places to Stay

➜ Ellis Store Country Inn (p395)

➜ El Tovar Hotel (p341)

➜ La Posada (p346)

➜ Motor Lodge (p331)

➜ Los Poblanos (p375)

Why Go?

The Southwest is America's untamed backyard, where life plays out before a stunning backdrop of red rocks, lofty peaks, shimmering lakes and deserts dotted with saguaro cacti. Reminders of the region's Native American heritage and hardscrabble Wild West heyday dot the landscape, from enigmatic pictographs and abandoned cliff dwellings to crumbling Hispanic missions and rusty mining towns. Today, history making continues, with astronomers and rocket builders peering into star-filled skies while artists and entrepreneurs flock to urban centers and quirky mountain towns.

The best part for travelers? A splendid network of scenic drives linking the most beautiful and iconic sites. But remember: it's not just iconic, larger-than-life landscapes that make a trip through the Southwest memorable. Study that saguaro up close; ask a Hopi artist about their craft; savor some green-chile stew. You may just cherish those moments the most.

When to Go
Las Vegas

Jan Ski near Taos and Flagstaff. In Park City, hit the slopes and the Sundance Film Festival.

Jun–Aug High season for exploring national parks in New Mexico, Utah and northern Arizona.

Sep–Nov Hike to the bottom of the Grand Canyon or gaze at bright leaves in northern New Mexico.

History

By about AD 100, three dominant cultures had emerged in the Southwest: the Hohokam, the Mogollon and the Ancestral Puebloans (previously known as the Anasazi).

The Hohokam lived in the Arizona deserts from 300 BC to AD 1450, and created an incredible canal irrigation system, earthen pyramids and a rich heritage of pottery. A cataclysmic event in the mid-15th century caused a dramatic decrease in the Hohokam population; it's not entirely clear what became of them, but the oral traditions suggest that certain local tribes are their direct descendants.

From 200 BC to AD 1450 the Mogollon lived in the central mountains and valleys of the Southwest; they left behind what are now called the Gila Cliff Dwellings, and many beautifully decorated bowls.

The Ancestral Puebloans left the richest heritage of archaeological sites, such as those at Chaco Culture National Historic Park and Canyon de Chelly National Monument. Their descendants are now found in Pueblo groups throughout New Mexico, as well as the Hopi in Arizona, whose Old Oraibi village may be the oldest continuously inhabited settlement in North America.

In 1540 Francisco Vásquez de Coronado led a Spanish-sponsored expedition from Mexico City to the Southwest. Searching in vain for riches, his party killed or displaced many of the Native Americans they encountered. More than 50 years later, Juan de Oñate established the first capital of New Mexico at San Gabriel; it was moved to Santa Fe around 1610. Great bloodshed resulted from the Spaniards' attempts to impose their religion and way of life, and the Pueblo Revolt of 1680 even briefly expelled them altogether.

Development in the Southwest expanded rapidly during the 19th century, mainly due to railroad and geological surveys. As the US pushed west, the army forcibly removed entire tribes of Native Americans in horrifyingly brutal Indian Wars. Gold and silver mines drew fortune seekers, and the lawless mining towns of the Wild West mushroomed practically overnight. Soon the Santa Fe Railroad was luring a flood of tourists to the West.

Modern settlement is closely linked to water use. Following the Reclamation Act of 1902, huge federally funded dams were built to control rivers and irrigate the desert. Rancorous disagreements over water rights are ongoing, especially with the phenomenal boom in residential development and the extensive recent drought. The other major issue in recent years, especially in southern Arizona, has been illegal immigration across the border from Mexico.

SOUTHWEST IN...

One Week

Museums and a burgeoning arts scene set an inspirational tone in **Phoenix**. In the morning, follow Camelback Rd into **Scottsdale** for top-notch shopping and gallery-hopping in Old Town. Drive north to **Sedona** for spiritual recharging before pondering the immensity of the **Grand Canyon**. From here, choose either bling or buttes. For bling, detour onto **Route 66**, cross the new bridge beside **Hoover Dam** then indulge your fantasies in **Las Vegas**. For buttes, drive east from the Grand Canyon into Navajo country, cruising beneath the giant rock formations in **Monument Valley Navajo Tribal Park** then stepping back in time at stunning **Canyon de Chelly National Monument**.

Two Weeks

Start in glitzy **Las Vegas** before kicking back in funky **Flagstaff** and peering into the abyss at **Grand Canyon National Park**. Check out collegiate **Tucson** or frolic among cacti at **Saguaro National Park**. Watch the gunslingers in **Tombstone** before settling into Victorian **Bisbee**.

Secure your sunglasses for the blinding dunes of **White Sands National Monument** in New Mexico then sink into **Santa Fe**, a magnet for art-lovers. Explore the pueblo in **Taos** and watch the sunrise at awesome **Monument Valley Navajo Tribal Park**. Head into Utah for the red-rock national parks, **Canyonlands** and **Arches**. Do the hoodoos at **Bryce Canyon** then pay your respects at glorious **Zion**.

Local Culture

The peoples of the Southwest encompass a rich mix of Native American, Hispanic and Anglo populations. All have influenced the region's cuisine, architecture and arts, and the Southwest's vast Native American reservations offer exceptional opportunities to learn about Native American culture and history. Visual arts are a strong force as well, from the art colonies dotting New Mexico to the roadside kitsch on view everywhere.

❶ Getting There & Around

Las Vegas' McCarran International Airport and Phoenix' Sky Harbor International Airport are the region's busiest airports, followed by those at Salt Lake City and Albuquerque.

Greyhound stops at major cities, but barely serves national parks or off-the-beaten-path towns such as Moab. Amtrak train service is even more limited, although it too links several Southwestern cities and offers bus connections to others (including Santa Fe and Phoenix). The California Zephyr crosses Utah and Nevada; the Southwest Chief stops in Arizona and New Mexico; and the Sunset Limited traverses southern Arizona and New Mexico.

That means private vehicles are often the only means to reach out-of-the-way towns, trailheads and swimming spots, and to explore the region in any depth.

NEVADA

Nevada has a devil-may-care exuberance that's dangerously intoxicating – and sometimes a little bit wacky. Here, dazzling replicas of the Eiffel Tower, the Statue of Liberty and an Egyptian pyramid rise from the desert. Cowboys gather to recite poetry. Artists build a temporary city on a windswept playa. An Air Force base inspires alien conspiracies. And smack in the middle of it all is a lonely tree, its branches draped in sneakers tossed by mischievous road-trippers.

On the map, the state is a vast and mostly empty stretch of desert, dotted with former mining towns that have traded pickaxes for slot machines. The mother lode is Las Vegas, an over-the-top extravaganza where people still catch gold fever. In the west, adventure outfitters are staking their claims on new treasures: gorgeous scenery and outdoor fun, which beckon from the Sierra Nevada mountains.

The first state to legalize gambling, Nevada is loud with the chime of slot machines

---

NEVADA FACTS

Nickname Silver State

Population 2.84 million

Area 109,800 sq miles

Capital city Carson City (population 54,080)

Other cities Las Vegas (population 606,762), Reno (population 233,300)

Sales tax 6.85%

Birthplace of Andre Agassi (b 1970), Greg LeMond (b 1961)

Home of The slot machine, Burning Man

Politics Nevada has six electoral votes – the state went for Obama in the 2012 presidential election, but it is split evenly in sending elected officials to Washington

Famous for The 1859 Comstock Lode (the country's richest known silver deposit), legalized gambling and prostitution (outlawed in certain counties), and liberal alcohol laws allowing 24-hour bars

Best Las Vegas T-Shirt 'I saw nothing at the Mob Museum.'

Driving distances Las Vegas to Reno 452 miles, Great Basin National Park to Las Vegas 313 miles

---

singing out from gas stations, supermarkets and hotel lobbies. There's no legally mandated closing time for bars, and in rural areas, legalized brothels and hole-in-the-wall casinos sit side by side with Mormon and cowboy culture.

Our advice? Never ask 'Why?' Just embrace the state's go-for-broke joie de vivre.

❶ Information

Prostitution is illegal in Clark County (which includes Las Vegas) and Washoe County (which includes Reno), although there are legal brothels in many of the smaller counties.

Nevada is on Pacific Standard Time.

Nevada Commission on Tourism (☑800-638-2328; www.travelnevada.com) Sends free books, maps and information on accommodations, campgrounds and events.

Nevada Division of State Parks (☑775-684-2770; www.parks.nv.gov; 901 S Stewart St, 5th fl, Carson City; ⊙8am-5pm Mon-Fri) Camping in state parks ($10 to $15 per night) is first-come, first-served.

Southwest Highlights

1 Strolling the Rim Trail at **Grand Canyon National Park** (p337).

2 Living your own John Wayne Western in northeastern Arizona's **Monument Valley** (p346).

3 Practicing your fast draw in dusty **Tombstone** (p352).

4 Gallery-hopping and jewelry-shopping on the stylish streets of **Santa Fe** (p378).

5 Sledding down a shimmering sand dune at **White Sands National Monument** (p394).

6 Wandering a wonderland of stalactites at **Carlsbad Caverns National Park** (p396).

7 Cruising the casinos on the legendary Las Vegas **Strip** (p307).

8 Hiking to flaming-red sandstone formations in **Arches National Park** (p365).

9 Skiing incredible terrain and enjoying chichi nightlife in **Park City** (p359).

10 Exploring a majestic canyon and climbing Angels Landing at **Zion National Park** (p370).

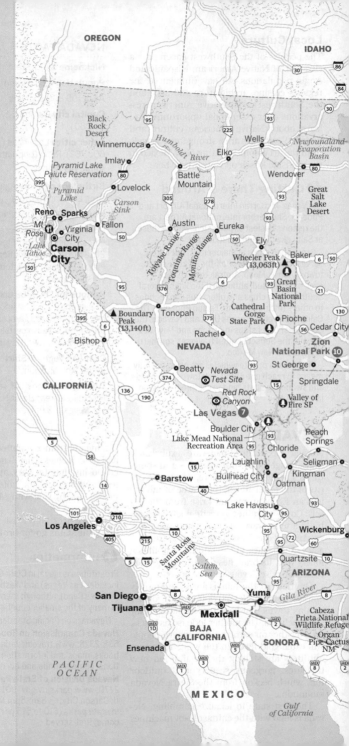

NATIONAL PARKS & MONUMENTS

Holding well more than 60 national parks and monuments, and many stunning state parks, the Southwest is a scenic and cultural jackpot. Arizona's Grand Canyon National Park (p337) surely heads any list, while Arizona's other stupendous parks include Monument Valley (p346), with its towering sandstone pillars and buttes, and Canyon de Chelly (p345), home to magnificent ancient cliff dwellings.

The red-rock Canyon Country of southern Utah holds five national parks – Arches (p365), Canyonlands (p366), Zion (p370), Bryce Canyon (p369) and Capitol Reef (p368) – while New Mexico boasts Carlsbad Caverns (p396) and the mysterious Chaco Culture National Historic Park (p390), and Nevada has Great Basin National Park (p321), a rugged, remote mountain oasis.

Las Vegas

Las Vegas remains the ultimate escape. Where else can you party in ancient Rome, get hitched at midnight, wake up in Egypt and brunch beneath the Eiffel Tower? Double down with the high rollers, browse couture or tacky souvenirs, sip a neon 3ft-high margarita or a frozen vodka martini from a bar made of ice – it's all here for the taking.

Ever notice that there are no clocks inside casinos? Vegas exists outside time, a sequence of never-ending buffets, ever-flowing drinks and adrenaline-fueled gaming tables. In this never-ending desert dreamscape of boom and bust, once-famous signs collect dust in a neon boneyard while the clang of construction echoes over the Strip. After the alarming hiccup of the 2008 recession, the city is once more back on track, attracting well over 40 million visitors per year and bursting with schemes to lure in even more in future.

Las Vegas' largest casinos – each one a gigantic and baffling mélange of theme park, gambling den, shopping and dining destination, hotel and theater district – line up along the legendary Strip. Once you've explored those, head to the city's compact downtown to encounter Vegas' nostalgic beginnings, peppered with indie shops and cocktail bars where local culture thrives. Then detour further afield to find intriguing museums that investigate Vegas' gangster, atomic-fueled past.

History

Contrary to popular legend, there was much more at the dusty crossroads than a gambling parlor and a few tumbleweeds when mobster Ben 'Bugsy' Siegel rolled in in 1946 and erected a glamorous tropical-themed casino, the Flamingo, under the searing sun.

Spawned by the completion of the railroad that linked Salt Lake City to Los Angeles in 1902, Las Vegas boomed in the 1930s thanks to federal construction projects. The legalization of gambling in 1931 carried Vegas through the Depression, WWII brought a huge air-force base and aerospace bucks, plus a paved highway to Los Angeles. During the Cold War, the Nevada Test Site proved to be a textbook case of 'any publicity is good publicity': monthly above-ground atomic blasts shattered casino windows downtown while the city's official Miss Mushroom Cloud mascot promoted atomic everything in tourism campaigns.

Meanwhile, the Flamingo sparked a building spree in which mob-backed tycoons upped the glitz ante at every turn. Big-name entertainers such as Frank Sinatra, Liberace and Sammy Davis Jr arrived at the same time as topless French showgirls.

The high-profile purchase of the Desert Inn in 1966 by eccentric billionaire Howard Hughes gave the gambling industry a much-needed patina of legitimacy, while the debut of the MGM Grand in 1993 signaled the dawn of the corporate megaresort era. These days almost all the major casinos are owned by two rival empires, Caesars Entertainment and Mirage Resorts.

⊙ Sights

Roughly 4 miles long, the Strip, aka Las Vegas Blvd South, is the center of gravity in Sin City, running from around a mile south of downtown to Mandalay Bay near the airport. Whether you're walking or driving, Strip distances are deceiving: a walk to what looks like a nearby casino always takes longer than expected.

Downtown Las Vegas is home to the city's oldest hotels and casinos: expect a retro feel, cheaper drinks and lower table limits. Its main drag is fun-loving Fremont St, a four-block stretch of casinos and restaurants covered by a dazzling canopy that runs a groovy light show every evening. Schemes to 'revitalize' downtown have come and gone with monotonous regularity over the years; the latest, the Downtown Project, spearheaded by Zappo's CEO Tony Hsieh, has yet to make a significant impact on Las Vegas visitors.

Major tourist areas are safe. However, Las Vegas Blvd between downtown and the Strip is shabby, and Fremont St east of downtown can be rather unsavory.

◉ The Strip

★ CityCenter
LANDMARK

(www.citycenter.com; 3780 Las Vegas Blvd S) We've seen this symbiotic relationship before (think giant hotel anchored by a mall 'concept') but the way that this futuristic-feeling complex places a small galaxy of hypermodern, chichi hotels in orbit around the glitzy Crystals (p316) shopping center is a first. The uber-upscale spread includes the subdued, stylish **Vdara** (⏺702-590-2111, 866-745-7767; www.vdara.com; 2600 W Harmon Ave; weekday/weekend ste from $119/179; P⊜✱@⟨wifi⟩☒) ✐, the hush-hush opulent **Mandarin Oriental** (www.mandarinoriental.com; 3752 Las Vegas Blvd S) and the dramatic architectural showpiece **Aria** (⏺702-590-7111; www.aria.com; 3730 Las Vegas Blvd S; ⊘24hr), the sophisticated casino of which provides a fitting backdrop to its many drop-dead-gorgeous restaurants.

Cosmopolitan
CASINO

(⏺702-698-7000; www.cosmopolitanlasvegas. com; 3708 Las Vegas Blvd S; ⊘24hr) Hipsters who thought they were too cool for Vegas finally have a place to go where they don't need irony to endure – or enjoy – the aesthetics of the Strip. Like the new Hollywood 'It' girl, the Cosmopolitan casino looks absolutely fabulous at all times. A steady stream of ingenues and entourages parade through the lobby, along with anyone else who adores contemporary art and design.

Fountains of Bellagio
FOUNTAIN

(www.bellagio.com; Bellagio; ⊘shows every 30min 3-7pm Mon-Fri, noon-7pm Sat & Sun, every 15min 7pm-midnight daily; ♿) **FREE** With a backdrop of Tuscan architecture, the Bellagio's faux Lake Como and dancing fountains are the antithesis of the Mojave Desert – although the resort does use reclaimed water. The fountain show's recorded soundtrack varies, so cross your fingers that it will be Italian opera or Ol' Blue Eyes crooning 'Luck Be a Lady,' instead of country-and-western twang.

Paris Las Vegas
CASINO

(⏺702-946-7000; www.parislasvegas.com; 3655 Las Vegas Blvd S; ⊘24hr) Welcome to the City of Light, Vegas-style. This mini-version of the French capital may not exude the true charm of Paris – it feels like a themed section of Disney World's Epcot – but efforts to emulate the city's great landmarks, including a 34-story Hotel de Ville replica and famous facades from the Paris Opera House and the Louvre, make it a fun stop for families and Francophiles who've yet to see the real thing.

LINQ & High Roller
LANDMARK

(⏺800-223-7277; www.thelinq.com; 3545 Las Vegas Blvd S; High Roller ride before/after 5:50pm $25/35; ⊘High Roller noon-2am daily; monorail Flamingo or Harrah's/Quad) A mammoth open-air dining, entertainment and retail complex, the $550-million LINQ project has transformed what was once a lackluster stretch of the center Strip between the Flamingo and Quad casino hotels. Eclectic shops, buzzing bars, trendy restaurants, live-music venues and even a bowling alley line the pedestrian promenade, where you'll also find the High Roller, a 550ft-tall observation wheel.

Caesars Palace
CASINO

(⏺702-731-7110; www.caesarspalace.com; 3570 Las Vegas Blvd S; ⊘24hr) Despite recent upgrades that have lent the once-gaudy Palace a more sophisticated air, some of the resort's original features from the swinging '60s have survived. Out front are the same spritzing fountains that daredevil Evil Knievel made famous when he jumped them on a motorcycle on December 31, 1967 (and ended up with a shattered pelvis and a fractured skull.; more than two decades later, his son Robby repeated the attempt – more successfully).

Wynn
CASINO

(⏺702-770-7000; www.wynnlasvegas.com; 3131 Las Vegas Blvd S; ⊘24hr) Steve Wynn's signature (literally, his name is written in script across the top, punctuated by a period) casino hotel stands on the site of the imploded 1950s-era Desert Inn. The curvaceous, copper-toned 50-story tower exudes secrecy – the entrance is obscured from the Strip by an artificial mountain of greenery. Inside, the resort comes alive with vibrant colors, inlaid flower mosaics, natural-light windows, lush foliage and waterfalls. The sprawling casino is always crowded, especially the cutthroat poker room.

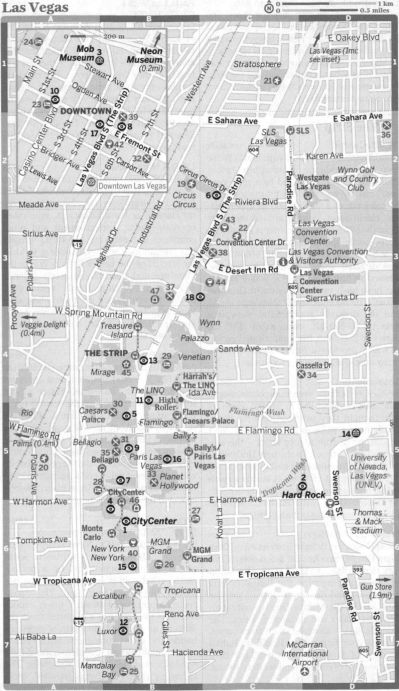

SOUTHWEST LAS VEGAS

Las Vegas

SOUTHWEST LAS VEGAS

New York–New York CASINO
(☎ 702-740-6969; www.newyorknewyork.com; 3790 Las Vegas Blvd S; ☺24hr) Opened in 1997, the mini-megalopolis of New York–New York features scaled-down replicas of the Big Apple's landmarks, such as the **Statue of Liberty** and a miniature **Brooklyn Bridge**, out front. Rising above are perspective-warping replicas of the Chrysler, Empire State and Ziggurat buildings. Wrapped around the hotel's flashy facade is the pièce de résistance: the **Big Apple roller coaster** (1 ride/day pass $14/25; ☺11am-11pm Sun-Thu, 10:30am-midnight Fri & Sat; ⊞), with cars resembling NYC taxicabs.

Luxor CASINO
(☎702-262-4000; www.luxor.com; 3900 Las Vegas Blvd S; ☺24hr) Named after Egypt's splendid ancient city on the east bank of the Nile, the landmark Luxor once had the biggest wow factor on the south Strip. While the theme easily could have produced a pyramid of gaudiness, instead it resulted in a relatively refined shrine to Egyptian art, architecture and antiquities. Some of the more outrageous

kitsch has gone the way of the pharaohs, though – in efforts to modernize, the Luxor was 'de-themed' some years ago.

Mirage Volcano LANDMARK
(Mirage; ☉ shows 8pm-midnight; ⊞) FREE
When the Mirage's trademark artificial volcano erupts with a roar out of a 3-acre lagoon, it inevitably brings traffic on the Strip to a screeching halt. Be on the lookout for wisps of smoke escaping from the top, signaling that the fiery Polynesian-style inferno, with a soundtrack by a Grateful Dead drummer and an Indian tabla musician, is about to begin.

Shark Reef Aquarium AQUARIUM
(☎702-632-4555; www.sharkreef.com; 3950 Las Vegas Blvd S, Mandalay Bay; adult/child 5-12yr $18/12; ☉10am-10pm daily late May-early Sep, 10am-8pm Sun-Thu, to 10pm Fri & Sat early Sep-late May, last admission 1hr before closing; ⊞) M-Bay's unusual walk-through aquarium is home to 2000 submarine beasties, including jellyfish, moray eels, stingrays and, yes, some sharks. Other rare and endangered toothy reptiles on display include some of the world's last remaining golden crocodiles. A staff of scuba-diver caretakers and naturalists are available to chat as you wander around. Better yet, go scuba diving yourself (from $650).

Madame Tussauds MUSEUM
(☎866-841-3739, 702-862-7800; www.madametussauds.com/lasvegas; 3355 Las Vegas Blvd S, Venetian; adult/child 4-12yr $30/20; ☉usually 10am-9pm; ⊞) Outside the Venetian next to the mock Rialto Bridge is this interactive version of the wax museum many love to loathe. Strike a pose with Elvis, pretend to marry George Clooney, go '4D' with Marvel Super Heroes or don Playboy Bunny ears and sit on Hugh Hefner's lap (be sure to touch him, because Hef's made of silicone – how appropriate!)

⊙ Downtown & Off the Strip

★**Mob Museum** MUSEUM
(☎702-229-2734; www.themobmuseum.org; 300 Stewart Ave; adult/child 11-17yr $20/14; ☉10am-7pm Sun-Thu, to 8pm Fri & Sat; ⊞ Deuce) It's hard to say what's more impressive: the museum's physical location in a historic federal courthouse where mobsters sat for federal hearings in 1950–51, the fact that the board of directors is headed up by a former FBI special agent, or the thoughtfully curated exhibits telling the story of organized crime in America. In addition to hands-on FBI equipment and mob-related artifacts, the museum boasts a series of multimedia exhibits featuring interviews with real-life Tony Sopranos.

★**Neon Museum – Neon Boneyard** MUSEUM
(☎702-387-6366; www.neonmuseum.org; 770 Las Vegas Blvd N; 1hr tour adult/child 7-17yr daytime $18/12, after dark $25/22; ☉tours daily, schedules vary; ⊞113) This nonprofit project is doing what almost no one else does: saving Las Vegas' history. Book ahead for a fascinating guided walking tour of the 'neon boneyard,' where irreplaceable vintage neon signs – Las Vegas' original art form – spend their retirement. Start exploring at the visitor center inside the salvaged La Concha Motel lobby, a mid-Century Modern icon designed by African American architect Paul Revere Williams. Tours are usually given throughout the day, special events and weather permitting.

★**Hard Rock** CASINO
(☎702-693-5000; www.hardrockhotel.com; 4455 Paradise Rd; ☉24hr; ⊞108) The world's original rock 'n' roll casino houses what may be

---

LAS VEGAS FOR CHILDREN

With its current focus on adult-oriented fun – 'What happens in Vegas stays in Vegas' – the city isn't a great choice for families. Visitors under 21 can walk through casinos to reach shops, shows and restaurants but they cannot stop, and younger children should always be with an adult for safety reasons. Some casinos prohibit strollers.

If you do land in Sin City with the kids, don't abandon hope. The **Circus Circus** (☎702-734-0410; www.circuscircus.com; 2880 Las Vegas Blvd S; ☉24hr; ⊞) hotel complex is all about kiddie fun, and its **Adventuredome** (www.adventuredome.com; Circus Circus; per ride $5-8, day pass over/under 48in tall $30/17; ☉10am-6pm daily, later on weekends & May-Sep; ⊞) is a 5-acre indoor theme park with rock climbing, bumper cars and, above all (literally) roller coasters. The **Midway** (Circus Circus; ☉11am-midnight; ⊞) features animals, acrobats and magicians performing on center stage.

the most impressive collection of rock-star memorabilia ever assembled under one roof. Priceless items being watched over by security guards suited up like bouncers are concert attire worn by Elvis, Britney Spears and Prince; a display case filled with Beatles mementos; Jim Morrison's handwritten lyrics to one of The Doors' greatest hits; and dozens of leather jackets and guitars formerly owned by everyone from the Ramones to U2.

Fremont Street Experience   LIGHT SHOW
(www.vegasexperience.com; Fremont St, btwn Main St & Las Vegas Blvd; ⊙ hourly dusk-midnight; 🚍 Deuce, SDX) FREE A five-block pedestrian mall topped by an arched steel canopy and filled with computer-controlled lights, the Fremont Street Experience, between Main St and Las Vegas Blvd, has brought life back to downtown. Every evening, the canopy is transformed by hokey six-minute light-and-sound shows enhanced by 550,000 watts of wraparound sound and a larger-than-life screen lit up by 12.5 million synchronized LEDs. Soar through the air on zip-lines strung underneath the canopy from Slotzilla (p312), a 12-story, slot-machine-themed platform.

National Atomic Testing Museum   MUSEUM
(🕿 702-794-5151; www.nationalatomictestingmuseum.org; 755 E Flamingo Rd, Desert Research Institute; adult/child 7-17yr $14/12; ⊙ 10am-5pm Mon-Sat, noon-5pm Sun; 🚌 202) Fascinating multimedia exhibits focus on science, technology and the social history of the 'Atomic Age', which lasted from WWII until atmospheric bomb testing was driven underground in 1961 and a worldwide ban on nuclear testing was declared in 1992. View historical footage of atomic testing and examine southern Nevada's past, present and future, from Native American ways of life to the environmental legacy of atomic testing. Don't miss the cool museum shop near the ticket booth, a replica of a wNevada Test Site guard station replica.

🕺 Activities

★ **Desert Adventures**   KAYAKING
(🕿 702-293-5026; www.kayaklasvegas.com; 1647a Nevada Hwy, Boulder City; full-day Colorado River kayak $169; ⊙ 9am-6pm Apr-Oct, 10am-4pm Nov-Mar) With Lake Mead and the Black Canyon of the Colorado River just a short drive away, would-be river rats should check in here for guided kayaking and stand up paddling (SUP) tours. Experienced paddlers can rent canoes and kayaks for DIY trips.

Escape Adventures   MOUNTAIN BIKING
(🕿 800-596-2953; www.escapeadventures.com; 10575 Discovery Dr; trips incl bike from $129) The source for guided mountain-bike tours of Red Rock Canyon State Park.

Qua Baths & Spa   SPA
(🕿 866-782-0655; 3570 Las Vegas Blvd, Caesars Palace; fitness center day pass $25, incl spa facilities $45; ⊙ 6am-8pm) Qua evokes the ancient Roman rituals of indulgent bathing. Try a signature 'bath liqueur,' a personalized potion of herbs and oils poured into your own private tub. The women's side includes a tea lounge, an herbal steam room and an arctic ice room where artificial snow falls. On the men's side, there's a barber spa and big-screen sports TVs.

🛌 Sleeping

Room rates in Las Vegas rise and fall dramatically each and every day; visiting on weekdays is almost always cheaper than weekends. Note that almost every Strip hotel also charges an additional 'resort fee' of up to $25 per day.

🛏 The Strip

New York–New York   CASINO HOTEL $
(🕿 702-740-6969, 866-815-4365; www.newyork-newyork.com; 3790 Las Vegas Blvd S; weekday/weekend r from $50/110; P ✳ @ 🛜 🏊) A favorite of college students, these decent digs are rather tiny (just what one would expect in NYC).

MGM Grand   CASINO HOTEL $$
(🕿 877-880-0880, 702-891-1111; www.mgmgrand.com; 3799 Las Vegas Blvd S; weekday/weekend r from $70/140; P ✳ @ 🛜 🏊) Vegas' biggest hotel, with high-end **Skylofts** (🕿 877-646-5638, 702-891-3832; www.skyloftsmgmgrand.com; ste from $1000; P ✳ @ 🛜 🏊), apartment-style **Signature** (🕿 877-727-0007, 702-797-6000; www.signaturemgmgrand.com; 145 E Harmon Ave; weekday/weekend ste from $95/170; P ✳ @ 🛜 🏊) suites and the Strip's most mammoth pool complex.

Caesars Palace   CASINO HOTEL $$
(🕿 702-731-7110, 866-227-5938; www.caesarspalace.com; 3570 Las Vegas Blvd S; weekday/weekend r from $90/125; P ✳ @ 🛜 🏊 🏊) Expect towers of oversized rooms with marble bathrooms, Nobu boutique hotel and the Garden of the Gods pool complex.

LAS VEGAS: HIGH-OCTANE THRILLS

➡ **Driving** Hop into a race car at **Richard Petty Driving Experience** (☑ 800-237-3889; www.drivepetty.com; 6975 Speedway Blvd, Las Vegas Motor Speedway, off I-15 exit 54; ridealongs from $99; drives from $449; ☉ hours vary) or career around the track in a souped-up go-kart at **Fast Lap** (☑ 702-736-8113; www.fastlaplv.com; 4288 S Polaris; per race $25; ☉ Mon-Sat 10am-11pm, Sun 10am-10pm).

➡ **Indoor Skydiving** No time to jump from a plane? Enjoy the thrill without the altitude at **Vegas Indoor Skydiving** (☑ 702-731-4768; www.vegasindoorskydiving; 200 Convention Center Dr; single flight $85; ☉ 9.45am-8pm).

➡ **Shooting** If you're dying to fire a sub-machine gun or feel the heft of a Glock in your hot little hands, visit the high-powered **Gun Store** (☑ 702-454-1110; http://thegunstorelasvegas.com; 2900 E Tropicana Ave; packages from $90; ☉ 9am-6:30pm; ☐ 201), with an indoor video training range.

➡ **Stratosphere** Atop this 110-story **casino** (☑ 702-380-7777; www.stratospherehotel.com; Stratosphere, 2000 Las Vegas Blvd S; elevator adult/concession $18/15, incl 3 thrill rides $33, all-day pass $34, SkyJump from $110; monorail Sahara) you can ride a roller coaster, drop 16 stories on the Big Shot, spin above thin air, or plummet 108ft over the edge.

➡ **Ziplining** Swoop above Fremont St's throngs from the world's largest slot machine, the 12-story **Slotzilla** (☑ 844-947-8342; www.vegasexperience.com; Fremont Street Experience; rides from $20; ☉ noon-midnight Sun-Thu, to 2am Fri & Sat).

Paris Las Vegas　CASINO HOTEL $$
(☑ 702-946-7000, 877-796-2096; www.paris-lasvegas.com; 3655 Las Vegas Blvd S; weekday/weekend r from $60/135;　P✳@☎☀) Standard rooms are far from Parisian, but upgraded Red Luxury Rooms, some with lipstick-shaped sofas, evoke Moulin Rouge.

Mandalay Bay　CASINO HOTEL $$
(☑ 877-632-7800, 702-632-7777; www.mandalaybay.com; 3950 Las Vegas Blvd S; weekday/weekend r from $105/130;　P✳@☎☀; ☐Deuce) The upscale Mandalay Bay casino hotel, exclusive **Four Seasons** (☑ 702-632-5000; www.fourseasons.com/lasvegas; weekend r from $229/289; P✳@☎☀) hotel and boutique **Delano** (www.delanolasvegas.com; P✳@☎☀) hotel offer variety at the Strip's southernmost resort.

Venetian　CASINO HOTEL $$
(☑ 866-659-9643, 702-414-1000; www.venetian.com; 3355 Las Vegas Blvd S; weekday/weekend ste from $149/289; P✳@☎☀) Vegas' own 'Most Serene Republic' features huge suites with sunken living rooms and countless luxuries from deep soaking tubs to pillow menus.

Cosmopolitan　CASINO HOTEL $$$
(☑ 855-435-0005, 702-698-7000; www.cosmopolitanlasvegas.com; 3708 Las Vegas Blvd S; r/ste from $160/220; P✳@☎☀; ☐Deuce) Frequented by style-conscious clientele, the arty, cool Cosmo wins the contest for the Strip's hippest hotel rooms.

🛏 Downtown & Off the Strip

Main Street Station　CASINO HOTEL $
(☑ 702-387-1896, 800-713-8933; www.mainstreetcasino.com; 200 N Main St; weekday/weekend r from $35/70; P✳@☎) With tiled foyers, Victorian sconces and marble-trimmed hallways, the hotel has turn-of-the-century charm; bright, cheerful rooms have plantation shutters.

Golden Nugget　CASINO HOTEL $
(☑ 702-385-7111, 800-634-3454; www.goldennugget.com; 129 E Fremont St; weekday/weekend r from $49/89; P✳@☎☀) Pretend to relive the fabulous heyday of Vegas in the 1950s at this swank Fremont St address. Upgrade to a Rush Tower room.

Hard Rock　CASINO HOTEL $
(☑ 702-693-5000, 800-473-7625; www.hardrockhotel.com; 4455 Paradise Rd; weekday/weekend r from $45/89; P✳@☎☀) Sexy, oversized rooms and HRH suites at this shrine to rock 'n' roll pull in the SoCal party crowd. Free Strip shuttles for guests.

🍴 Eating

Sin City is an unmatched eating adventure. Reservations are a must for fancier restaurants.

The Strip

On the Strip itself, cheap eats beyond fast-food joints are hard to find.

Earl of Sandwich DELI $
(www.earlofsandwichusa.com; Planet Hollywood; menu $2-7; ☺ 24hr; ☝) Pennypinchers sing the praises of this super-popular deli next to the casino, which pops out sandwiches on toasted artisan bread, tossed salads, wraps and a kids' menu, all with quick service, unbeatable opening hours and some of the lowest prices on the Strip.

Stripburger BURGERS $
(☎ 702-737-8747; www.stripburger.com; 3200 Las Vegas Blvd S, Fashion Show; menu $4-14; ☺ 11am-11pm Sun-Thu, to midnight Fri & Sat; ☝) This shiny silver, open-air diner in the round serves up all-natural (hormone free etc) beef, chicken, tuna and veggie burgers, atomic cheese fries, thick milkshakes, buckets of beer and fruity cocktails, with elevated patio tables overlooking the Strip.

Tacos El Gordo MEXICAN $
(☎ 702-641-8228; http://tacoselgordobc.com; 3049 Las Vegas Blvd S; menu items $2-10; ☺ 9pm-3am Sun-Thu, to 5am Fri & Sat; ☒ Deuce, SDX) This Tijuana-style taco shop from SoCal is just the ticket when it's way late, you've got almost no money left and you're desperately craving *carne asada* (beef) or *adobada* (chili-marinated pork) tacos in hot, handmade tortillas. Adventurous eaters order the authentic *sesos* (beef brains), *cabeza* (roasted cow's head) or tripe (intestines) variations.

Jean Philippe Patisserie BAKERY, DESSERTS $
(www.jpchocolates.com; Bellagio; snacks & drinks $4-11; ☺ 7am-11pm Mon-Thu, to midnight Fri-Sun; ☝) As certified by the *Guinness Book of World Records,* the world's largest chocolate fountain cascades inside the front windows of this champion pastry-maker's shop, known for its fantastic sorbets, gelati, pastries and chocolate confections. Coffee and espresso are above the Strip's low-bar average.

Social House ASIAN, SUSHI $$$
(☎ 702-736-1122; www.angelmg.com; 3720 Las Vegas Blvd S, Crystals, CityCenter; prix-fixe lunch $20-25, shared plates $5-50, dinner mains $25-50; ☺ noon-5pm & 6-10pm daily) You won't find a sexier sushi bar and pan-Asian grill anywhere on the Strip. Low-slung tatami cushions, faded Japanese woodblock prints and a sky terrace inside Crystals mall add up to a seductively date-worthy atmosphere. Be thrilled by the imported sake list. Dinner reservations recommended.

Bouchon FRENCH $$$
(☎ 702-414-6200; www.bouchonbistro.com; Venezia Tower, 3355 Las Vegas Blvd S, Venetian; mains breakfast & brunch $12-26, dinner $19-51; ☺ 7-10:30am & 5-10pm Mon-Fri, 8am-2pm & 5-10pm Sat & Sun) Napa Valley wunderkind Thomas Keller's rendition of a Lyonnaise bistro features a seasonal menu of French classics. The poolside setting complements the oyster bar (open 3pm to 10:30pm daily) and an extensive raw seafood selection. Decadent breakfasts and brunches, imported cheeses, caviar, foie gras and a superb French and Californian wine list all make appearances. Reservations essential.

Joël Robuchon FRENCH $$$
(☎ 702-891-7925; www.joel-robuchon.com/en; 3799 Las Vegas Blvd S, MGM Grand; tasting menus $120-425; ☺ 5:30-10pm Sun-Thu, to 10:30pm Fri & Sat) The acclaimed 'Chef of the Century' leads the pack in the French culinary invasion of the Strip. Adjacent to the high-rollers' gaming area, Robuchon's plush dining rooms, done up in leather and velvet, feel like a dinner party at a 1930s Paris mansion. Complex seasonal tasting menus promise the meal of a lifetime – and they often deliver.

Gordon Ramsay Steak STEAK $$$
(☎ 877-346-4642, 702-946-4663; www.gordon-ramsay.com; 3655 Las Vegas Blvd S, Paris Las Vegas; mains $32-105, tasting menu without/with wine pairings $145/220; ☺ 4:30-10:30pm daily, bar to midnight Fri & Sat) Carnivores, leave Paris behind and stroll through a miniaturized Chunnel into British chef Gordon Ramsay's

SOUTHWEST LAS VEGAS

WORTHY INDULGENCES: BEST BUFFETS

Extravagant all-you-can-eat buffets are a Sin City tradition. Three of the best:

Bacchanal Buffet (3570 Las Vegas Blvd S, Caesars Palace; buffet per adult $26-54, child 4-10yr $15-27; ☎ ☝; ☒ Deuce)

Wicked Spoon Buffet (3708 Las Vegas Blvd S, Cosmopolitan; per person $26-40; ☺ 8am-2pm & 5-9pm Mon-Fri, 8am-9pm Sat & Sun; ☝)

Buffet at Bellagio (www.bellagio.com; Bellagio; per person $19-40; ☺ 7am-10pm)

steakhouse. Ribboned in red and domed by a jaunty Union Jack, this is one of the top tables in town. Fish, chops and signature beef Wellington round out a menu of Himalayan salt room-aged steaks. No reservation? Sit at the bar instead.

Sage AMERICAN $$$
(☑702-590-8690; Aria, CityCenter; mains $35-54, tastings menus $59-150; ☺5-11pm Mon-Sat) Chef Shawn McClain brings seasonal Midwestern farm-to-table cuisine to the Strip. The backlit mural over the bar almost steals the scene, but creative twists on meat-and-potatoes classics – imagine pork terrine with blue corn succotash and salsa verde – and seafood and pasta also shine. After dinner, sip absinthe poured from a rolling cart. Reservations essential; business casual dress.

✖ Downtown & Off the Strip

As a rule, downtown's restaurants offer better value than those on the Strip.

Container Park FAST FOOD $
(☑702-637-4244; http://downtowncontainerpark.com; 707 E Fremont St; menu $3-9; ☺11am-11pm Sun-Thu, to 1am Fri & Sat; ☐Deuce) With food-truck-style menus, outdoor patio seating and late-night hours, food vendors inside the cutting-edge Container Park sell something to satisfy everyone's appetite. When we last stopped by, the ever-changing line-up included Pinche's Tacos for Mexican flavors, Pork & Beans for piggy goodness, Southern-style Big Ern's BBQ, raw-food and healthy vegan cuisine from Simply Pure and Bin 702 wine bar. After 9pm only over-21s are allowed.

Veggie Delight VEGETARIAN $
(☑702-310-6565; www.veggiedelight.biz; 3504 Wynn Rd; menu $3-10; ☺11am-9pm; ✔) This Buddhist-owned, Vietnamese-flavored vegetarian and vegan kitchen mixes up chakra color-coded Chinese herbal tonics and makes *banh mi*-style sandwiches, hot pots and noodle soups.

Wild PIZZA, AMERICAN $$
(☑702-778-8800; http://eatdrinkwild.com; 150 Las Vegas Blvd S, Ogden; pizzas $9-26, brunch prix-fixe menu $18; ☺7am-7pm Mon-Sat; ✔; ☐Deuce) ✈ At sidewalk level in a high-rise condo complex, this gluten-free pizzeria sources farm-fresh ingredients that are sustainably harvested. Up the feel-good factor with a fruit smoothie from the juice bar or with a side salad of kale and smoked tofu. Pizza flavors

are rule-breaking, from white-truffle ricotta to chicken tikka masala. The unique beer and wine list encourages socializing.

Firefly TAPAS $$
(☑702-369-3971; www.fireflylv.com; 3824 Paradise Rd; shared plates $5-12, mains $15-20; ☺11:30am-midnight; ☐108) Firefly is always packed with a fashionable local crowd, who come for well-prepared Spanish and Latin American tapas, such as *patatas bravas* (potatoes in spicy tomato sauce), chorizo-stuffed empanadas and vegetarian bites like garbanzo beans seasoned with chili, lime and sea salt. A backlit bar dispenses the house specialty sangria – red, white or sparkling – and fruity mojitos. Reservations recommended.

Lotus of Siam THAI $$
(☑702-735-3033; www.saipinchutima.com; 953 E Sahara Ave; mains $9-30; ☺11:30am-2:30pm Mon-Fri, 5:30-10pm daily; ✔; ☐SDX) Saipin Chutima's authentic northern Thai cooking has won almost as many awards as her distinguished European and New World wine cellar. Renowned food critic Jonathan Gold once called it 'the single best Thai restaurant in North America.' Although the strip-mall hole-in-the-wall may not look like much, foodies flock here. Reservations essential.

♟ Drinking & Nightlife

♟ The Strip

Chandelier Bar COCKTAIL BAR
(3708 Las Vagas Blvd S, Cosmopolitan; ☺24hr; ☐Deuce) Towering high in the center of Cosmopolitan, this ethereally designed cocktail bar is inventive yet beautifully simple, with three levels connected by romantic curved staircases, all draped with glowing strands of glass beads. The second level is headquarters for molecular mixology (order a martini made with liquid nitrogen), while the third specializes in floral and fruit infusions.

Double Barrel Roadhouse BAR
(www.sbe.com/doublebarrel; 3770 Las Vegas Blvd S, Monte Carlo; ☺11am-2am) With a Strip-view patio, this double-decker bar and grill anchors the new pedestrian district between the Monte Carlo and New York–New York casino hotels. Staff pour stiff housemade wine coolers into mason jars, cook up Southern comfort food and cheer the live rock bands on stage.

Fireside Lounge　　　　　LOUNGE
(www.peppermilllasvegas.com; 2985 Las Vegas Blvd S, Peppermill; ⊙24hr; 🚌 Deuce) Don't be blinded by the outlandishly bright neon outside. The Strip's most spellbinding retro hideaway awaits at the pint-sized Peppermill casino. Courting couples adore the sunken fire pit, fake tropical foliage and 64oz goblet-sized 'Scorpion' cocktails served by waiters in black evening gowns.

🍷 Downtown & Off the Strip

Want to chill out with the locals? Loads of new and interesting bars and cafes are opening along E Fremont St, making it the number-one alternative to the Strip.

Downtown Cocktail Room　　　LOUNGE
(📱702-880-3696; www.thedowntownlv.com; 111 Las Vegas Blvd S; ⊙4pm-2am Mon-Fri, 7pm-2am Sat; 🚌 Deuce) With a serious list of classic cocktails and housemade inventions, this low-lit speakeasy is undeniably romantic, and it feels decades ahead of downtown's old-school casinos. The entrance is ingeniously disguised: the door looks like just another part of the wall until you discover the sweet spot you have to push to get in. Happy hour runs 4pm to 8pm weekdays.

Double Down Saloon　　　　　BAR
(www.doubledownsaloon.com; 4640 Paradise Rd; ⊙24hr; 🚌108) This dark, psychedelic gin joint appeals to the lunatic fringe. It never closes, there's never a cover charge, the house drink is called 'ass juice' and it claims to be the birthplace of the bacon martini. When live bands aren't terrorizing the crowd, the jukebox vibrates with New Orleans jazz, British punk, Chicago blues and surf-guitar king Dick Dale.

☆ Entertainment

There's always plenty going on in Las Vegas, and **Ticketmaster** (www.ticketmaster.com) sells tickets for pretty much everything. **Tix 4 Tonight** (📱877-849-4868; www.tix4tonight.com; 3200 Las Vegas Blvd S, Fashion Show; ⊙10am-8pm) offers half-price tickets for a limited lineup of same-day shows, plus smaller discounts on 'always sold-out' shows.

Nightclubs & Live Music

In 2015 seven of the 10 highest-earning nightclubs in the US were in Vegas; a couple earned more than $100 million each. Admission prices vary wildly, according to the mood

---

EMERGENCY ARTS

A coffee shop, an art gallery, studios and a de facto community center of sorts, all under one roof and right smack downtown? The **Emergency Arts** (www.emergencyartslv.com; 520 E Fremont St; 🚌 Deuce) FREE building, also home to **Beat Coffeehouse** (📱702-385-2328; www.thebeatlv.com; ⊙7am-midnight Mon-Fri, from 9am Sat, 9am-5pm Sun; 📶; 🚌 Deuce) is a friendly bastion of laid-back cool and strong coffee where vintage vinyl spins on old turntables. If you're aching to meet some savvy locals who know their way around town, this is your hangout spot.

---

of door staff, male-to-female ratio, and how crowded the club may be. Avoid waiting in line by booking ahead with the club VIP host. Most bigger clubs have someone working the door in the late afternoon and early evening. Hotel concierges often have free passes for clubs, or can at least make reservations. Bottle service usually waives cover charges and waiting in line, but is hugely expensive.

XS　　　　　　　　　　CLUB
(📱702-770-0097; www.xslasvegas.com; Encore; cover $20-50; ⊙9:30pm-4am Fri & Sat, from 10:30pm Sun & Mon) XS is *the* hottest nightclub in Vegas – at least for now. Its extravagantly gold-drenched decor and over-the-top design mean you'll be waiting in line for cocktails at a bar towered over by ultra-curvaceous, larger-than-life golden statues of female torsos. Famous-name electronica DJs make the dance floor writhe, while high rollers opt for VIP bottle service at private poolside cabanas.

Marquee　　　　　　　　CLUB
(📱702-333-9000; www.marqueelasvegas.com; 3708 Las Vegas Blvd S, Cosmopolitan; ⊙10pm-5am Thu-Sat & Mon) The Cosmopolitan's glam nightclub cashes in on its multi-million-dollar sound system and a happening dance floor surrounded by towering LED screens displaying light projections that complement EDM tracks handpicked by famous-name DJs. From late spring through early fall, Marquee's mega-popular daytime pool club heads outside to a lively party deck overlooking the Strip, with VIP cabanas and bungalows.

Tao
CLUB

(☑702-388-8588; www.taolasvegas.com; 3355 Las Vegas Blvd S, Grand Canal Shoppes at the Venetian; cover $20-50; ☺nightclub 10pm-5am Thu-Sat, lounge 5pm-1am daily) Like a Top 40 hit that's maxed out on radio play, Tao has reached a been-there, done-that saturation point. Newbies still gush at the decadent details and libidinous vibe, from a giant golden Buddha to nearly naked go-go dancers languidly caressing themselves in rose petal-strewn bathtubs. On the crowded dance floor, Paris Hilton look-alikes bump and grind to hip-hop remixes.

Production Shows

There are hundreds of shows to choose from in Vegas. Any Cirque du Soleil offering tends to be an unforgettable experience.

Beatles LOVE
THEATER

(☑702-792-7777, 800-963-9634; www.cirquedusoleil.com; Mirage; tickets $79-180; ☺7pm & 9:30pm Thu-Mon; ⊞) Another smash hit from Cirque du Soleil, *Beatles LOVE* started as the brainchild of the late George Harrison. Using *Abbey Road* master tapes, the show psychedelically fuses the musical legacy of the Beatles with Cirque's high-energy dancers and signature aerial acrobatics. Come early to photograph the trippy, rainbow-colored entryway and grab drinks at Abbey Road bar, next to Revolution Lounge.

Michael Jackson ONE
THEATER

(☑800-745-3000, 877-632-7400; www.cirquedusoleil.com; 3950 Las Vegas Blvd S, Mandalay Bay; tickets from $69; ☺7pm & 9:30pm Sat-Wed) Cirque du Soleil's musical tribute to the King of Pop blasts onto M-Bay's stage with show-stopping dancers and lissome acrobats and aerialists all moving to a soundtrack of MJ's hits, moon-walking all the way back to his break-out platinum album *Thriller*. No children under five years old allowed.

Le Rêve The Dream
THEATER

(☑888-320-7110, 702-770-9966; http://boxoffice.wynnlasvegas.com; 3131 Las Vegas Blvd S, Wynn; tickets $105-195; ☺7pm & 9:30pm Fri-Tue) Underwater acrobatic feats by scuba-certified performers are the centerpiece of this intimate 'aqua-in-the-round' theater, which holds a 1-million-gallon swimming pool. Critics call it a less-inspiring version of Cirque's *O,* while devoted fans find the romantic underwater tango, thrilling high dives and visually spectacular adventures to be superior. Beware: the cheapest seats are in the 'splash zone.'

House of Blues
LIVE MUSIC

(☑702-632-7600; www.houseofblues.com; 3950 Las Vegas Blvd S, Mandalay Bay; ☺box office 9am-9pm) Live blues is definitely not the only game at this imitation Mississippi Delta juke joint. Big-name touring acts entertain the standing room-only audiences with soul, pop, rock, metal, country, jazz and even burlesque. For some shows, you can skip the long lines to get in by eating dinner in the restaurant beforehand, then showing your same-day receipt.

🛍 Shopping

Fashion Show
MALL

(www.thefashionshow.com; 3200 Las Vegas Blvd S; ☺10am-9pm Mon-Sat, 11am-7pm Sun; ⊞) Nevada's largest shopping mall is an eye-catcher: topped off by 'the Cloud,' a silver multimedia canopy resembling a flamenco hat, Fashion Show harbors more than 250 chain shops and department stores. Hot European additions to the mainstream lineup include British clothier Topshop (and Topman for men). Live runway shows happen hourly from noon to 5pm on Friday, Saturday and Sunday.

Forum Shops
MALL

(www.simon.com; Caesars Palace; ☺10am-11pm Sun-Thu, to midnight Fri & Sat) Caesars' fanciful nod to ancient Roman marketplaces houses 160 designer emporiums, including catwalk wonders Armani, DKNY, Jimmy Choo, John Varvatos and Versace; trendsetting jewelry and accessory stores; and one-of-a-kind specialty boutiques such as Agent Provocateur lingerie, Bettie Page pin-up fashions, MAC cosmetics and Kiehl's bath-and-body shop. Don't miss the spiral escalator, a grand entrance for divas strutting off the Strip.

Crystals
MALL

(www.crystalsatcitycenter.com; 3720 Las Vegas Blvd S; ☺10am-11pm Sun-Thu, to midnight Fri & Sat) Design-conscious Crystals is the most striking shopping center on the Strip. Win big at blackjack? Waltz inside Christian Dior, Dolce & Gabbana, Prada, Hermès, Harry Winston, Paul Smith or Stella McCartney showrooms at CityCenter's shrine to haute couture. For sexy couples with unlimited cash to burn, Kiki de Montparnasse is a one-stop shop for lingerie and bedroom toys.

**Grand Canal Shoppes
at the Venetian** MALL
(www.grandcanalshoppes.com; 3355 Las Vegas Blvd
S, Venetian; ⏰10am-11pm Sun-Thu, to midnight
Fri & Sat) Wandering painted minstrels, jugglers and laughable living statues perform
in Piazza San Marco, while gondolas float
past in the canals and mezzo-sopranos serenade shoppers. In this airy Italianate mall
adorned with frescoes, cobblestone walkways strut past Burberry, Godiva, Sephora
and 85 more luxury shops.

ⓘ Information

EMERGENCY & MEDICAL SERVICES

Police (☑702-828-3111; www.lvmpd.com)
Sunrise Hospital & Medical Center (☑702-731-8000; http://sunrisehospital.com; 3186 S
Maryland Pkwy; ⏰24hr) Specialized children's
trauma services available at a 24-hour emergency room.
University Medical Center (UMC; ☑702-383-2000; www.umcsn.com; 1800 W Charleston
Blvd; ⏰24hr) Southern Nevada's most advanced trauma center has a 24-hour ER.

INTERNET ACCESS & MEDIA

Wi-fi is available in every hotel room (usually
costing $10 to $25 per day, included in the
'resort fee' wherever there is one). The Venetian
and the Tropicana on the Strip, and Main Street
Station downtown, offer free wi-fi throughout the
property. Useful websites include:

Eater Vegas (www.vegas.eater.com) The latest
news about Sin City's chefs and new restaurants. Posts a regularly updated list of the
city's top 38 eateries.
Las Vegas Review-Journal (www.lvrj.com) Daily
paper with a weekend guide, Neon, on Friday.
Las Vegas Weekly (http://lasvegasweekly.
com) Free weekly with good entertainment and
restaurant listings.

POST

Post Office (www.usps.com; 201 Las Vegas
Blvd S; ⏰9am-5pm Mon-Fri) Downtown.

TOURIST INFORMATION

Websites offering travel information and booking
services include www.lasvegas.com and www.
vegas.com.

Las Vegas Convention & Visitors Authority
(LVCVA; ☑702-892-7575, 877-847-4858; www.
lasvegas.com; 3150 Paradise Rd; ⏰8am-5:30pm
Mon-Fri; monorail Las Vegas Convention Center)

ⓘ Getting There & Around

Just southeast of the major Strip casinos and
easily accessible from I-15, **McCarran Inter-**

national Airport (LAS; ☑702-261-5211; www.
mccarran.com; 5757 Wayne Newton Blvd;
🛜) has direct flights from all over the world.
Most domestic flights arrive in Terminal 1, and
international flights in Terminal 3. **Bell Trans**
(☑800-274-7433; www.bell-trans.com) offers
a shuttle service ($8 to $15) to the Strip and
downtown; exit at door 9 near baggage claim to
find the Bell Trans booth.

Most of the attractions in Vegas have free
self-parking and valet parking available (tip $2).
Fast, fun and fully wheelchair accessible, the
Las Vegas Monorail (☑702-699-8299; www.
lvmonorail.com; single-ride $5, 72hr pass $13;
⏰7am-midnight Mon, to 2am Tue-Thu, to 3am
Fri-Sun) connects the SLS Station to the MGM
Grand, stopping at major Strip mega-resorts
along the way, but does not go to the airport or
downtown. The **Deuce** (☑702-228-7433; www.
rtcsnv.com; 2hr/24hr/3-day pass $6/8/20), a
double-decker bus, runs 24 hours daily between
the Strip and downtown.

Around Las Vegas

⊙ Sights

**Red Rock Canyon
National Conservation Area** CANYON
(☑702-515-5350; www.redrockcanyonlv.org; entry
per car/bicycle $7/3; ⏰scenic loop 6am-8pm Apr-Sep, to 7pm Mar & Oct, to 5pm Nov-Feb; visitor center
8am-4:30pm; ♿) The startling contrast between Las Vegas' artificial neon glow and the
awesome natural forces found here can't be
exaggerated. Created about 65 million years
ago, the canyon is more like a valley, with a
steep, rugged red-rock escarpment rising
3000ft on its western edge, dramatic evidence of tectonic-plate collisions. A 13-mile,
one-way scenic drive passes some of the canyon's most striking features, where you can
access hiking trails and rock-climbing routes,
or simply be mesmerized by the vistas.

Lake Mead & Hoover Dam LAKE, HISTORIC SITE
Lake Mead and Hoover Dam are the most
visited sites within the **Lake Mead National
Recreation Area** (☑info desk 702-293-8906,
visitor center 702-293-8990; www.nps.gov/lake;
7-day entry per vehicle $10; ⏰24hr; visitor center
9am-4:30pm Wed-Sun; ♿), which encompasses
110-mile-long Lake Mead, 67-mile-long Lake
Mohave and many miles of desert around
the lakes. The excellent **Alan Bible Visitors Center** (☑702-293-8990; www.nps.gov/
lake; Lakeshore Scenic Dr, off US Hwy 93; ⏰9am-4.30pm), on Hwy 93 halfway between Boulder City and Hoover Dam, has information

VALLEY OF FIRE STATE PARK

A masterpiece of desert scenery filled with psychedelically shaped sandstone outcroppings, **Valley of Fire State Park** (☑702-397-2088; www.parks.nv.gov; per vehicle $10 ; ◔visitor center 8:30am-4:30pm) is a great escape 55 miles northeast of Vegas. Hwy 169 runs past the visitor center, which has hiking and camping (tent/RV sites $20/30) information and excellent desert-life exhibits.

on recreation and desert life. From there, North Shore Rd winds around the lake and makes a great scenic drive.

Straddling the Arizona–Nevada border, the graceful curve and art-deco style of the 726ft **Hoover Dam** (☑702-494-2517, 866-730-9097; www.usbr.gov/lc/hooverdam; off Hwy 93; admission & 30min tour adult/child 4-16yr $15/12; with 1hr tour $30; ◔9am-6pm Apr-Oct, to 5pm Nov-Mar; ◉) contrasts superbly with the stark landscape. Don't miss a stroll over the new **Mike O'Callaghan-Pat Tillman Memorial Bridge** (Hwy 93) which features a pedestrian walkway with perfect views upstream of Hoover Dam. (Not recommended for anyone with vertigo.) Visitors can either take the 30-minute **power plant tour** or the more in-depth, one-hour Hoover Dam tour.

Tickets for both tours are sold at the visitor center. Tickets for the power plant tour only can be purchased online.

For a relaxing lunch or dinner break, head to nearby downtown Boulder City, where **Milo's** (☑702-293-9540; www.miloswinebar.com; 534 Nevada Hwy, Boulder City; mains $9-14; ◔11am-10pm Sun-Thu, to 11pm Fri & Sat) serves fresh sandwiches, salads and gourmet cheese plates at sidewalk tables outside the wine bar.

Western Nevada

A vast and mostly undeveloped sagebrush steppe, Nevada's western corner is carved by mountain ranges and parched valleys. Modern Nevada began here, with the discovery of Virginia City's famous Comstock silver lode. Modern visitors flock here for hiking, biking and skiing adventures on its many mountains. Contrasts are as extreme as the weather: one moment you're driv-

ing through a quaint historic town full of grand homes built by silver barons, and the next you spot a tumbleweed blowing past a homely little bar that turns out to be the local (and legal) brothel.

Reno

In downtown Reno you can gamble at one of two-dozen casinos in the morning then walk down the street and shoot rapids at the Truckee River Whitewater Park. That's what makes 'The Biggest Little City in the World' so interesting – it's holding tight to its gambling roots but also earning kudos as a top-notch base camp for outdoor adventure. The Sierra Nevada Mountains and Lake Tahoe are less than an hour's drive away, and the region teems with lakes, trails and ski resorts. Wedged between the I-80 and the Truckee River, downtown's N Virginia St is casino central; south of the river it continues as S Virginia St.

◉ Sights

National Automobile Museum   MUSEUM
(☑775-333-9300; www.automuseum.org; 10 S Lake St; adult/child 6-18yr $10/4; ◔9:30am-5:30pm Mon-Sat, 10am-4pm Sun; ◉) Stylized street scenes illustrate a century's worth of automobile history at this engaging car museum. The collection is enormous and impressive, with one-of-a-kind vehicles – including James Dean's 1949 Mercury from *Rebel Without a Cause*, a 1938 Phantom Corsair and a 24-karat-gold-plated DeLorean – and rotating exhibits bringing in all kinds of souped-up or fabulously retro rides.

Nevada Museum of Art   MUSEUM
(☑775-329-3333; www.nevadaart.org; 160 W Liberty St; adult/child 6-12yr $10/1; ◔10am-5pm Wed & Fri-Sun, to 8pm Thu) In a sparkling building inspired by the geological formations of the Black Rock Desert north of town, a floating staircase leads to galleries showcasing temporary exhibits and eclectic collections on the American West, labor and contemporary landscape photography.

Circus Circus   CASINO
(www.circusreno.com; 500 N Sierra St; ◔24hr; ◉) The most family friendly of the bunch, Circus Circus has free circus acts to entertain kids beneath a giant, candy-striped big top, which also harbors a gazillion carnival and video games that look awfully similar to slot machines.

Silver Legacy CASINO
(www.silverlegacyreno.com; 407 N Virginia St; ⏲24hr) A Victorian-themed place, the Silver Legacy is easily recognized by its white landmark dome, where a giant mock mining rig periodically erupts into a fairly tame sound-and-light spectacle.

Eldorado CASINO
(www.eldoradoreno.com; 345 N Virginia St; ⏲24hr) The Eldorado has a kitschy Fountain of Fortune that probably has Italian sculptor Bernini spinning in his grave.

Harrah's CASINO
(www.harrahsreno.com; 219 N Center St; ⏲24hr) Founded by Nevada gambling pioneer William Harrah in 1946, it's still one of the biggest and most popular casinos in town.

🏃 Activities

Reno is a 30- to 60-minute drive from Tahoe ski resorts, and many hotels and casinos offer special stay-and-ski packages.

Mere steps from the casinos, the Class II and III rapids at the city-run **Truckee River Whitewater Park** (www.reno.gov) are gentle enough for kids riding inner tubes, yet also sufficiently challenging for professional freestyle kayakers. Two courses wrap around Wingfield Park, a small river island that hosts free concerts in summertime. **Tahoe Whitewater Tours** (☑775-787-5000; www.truckeewhitewaterrafting.com; 400 Island Ave; rafting adult/child $68/58) and **Wild Sierra Adventures** (☑866-323-8928; www.wildsierra.com; 11 N Sierra St; tubing $29) offer kayak trips and lessons.

🛏 Sleeping

Lodging rates vary widely, day by day. Sunday through Thursday are generally the best; Friday is more expensive and Saturday can be as much as triple the midweek rate.

In summer there's gorgeous high-altitude camping at **Mt Rose** (☑877-444-6777; www.recreation.gov; Hwy 431; RV & tent sites $17-50; ⏲mid-Jun–Sep).

Sands Regency HOTEL $
(☑775-348-2200; www.sandsregency.com; 345 N Arlington Ave; r Sun-Thu from $39, Fri & Sat from $85; P❄@🛜♨🐾) With some of the largest standard digs in town, rooms here are decked out in a cheerful tropical palette of upbeat blues, reds and greens – a visual relief from standard-issue motel decor. The 17th-floor gym and Jacuzzi are perfectly

positioned to capture your eyes with drop-dead panoramic mountain views. An outdoor pool opens in summer. Empress Tower rooms are best.

Wildflower Village MOTEL, B&B $
(☑775-747-8848; www.wildflowervillage.com; 4395 W 4th St; dm $34, motel $63, B&B $142; P❄@🛜) Perhaps more of a state of mind than a motel, this artists colony on the west edge of town has a tumbledown yet creative vibe. Individual murals decorate the facade of each room, and you can hear the freight trains rumble on by. Frequent live music and poetry readings at its cafe and pub, and bike rentals available.

Peppermill CASINO HOTEL $$
(☑866-821-9996, 775-826-2121; www.peppermillreno.com; 2707 S Virginia St; r Sun-Thu $59-129, Fri & Sat $79-209, resort fee $16; P❄@🛜♨) 🖋 With a dash of Vegas-style opulence, the ever-popular Peppermill boasts Tuscan-themed suites in its newest 600-room tower, and plush remodeled rooms throughout the rest of the property. The three sparkling pools (one indoor) are dreamy, with a full spa on hand. Geothermal energy powers the resort's hot water and heat.

🍴 Eating

Reno's dining scene goes far beyond the casino buffets.

Peg's Glorified Ham & Eggs DINER $
(www.eatatpegs.com; 420 S Sierra St; mains $7-14; ⏲6:30am-2pm; 🖊) Locally regarded as the best breakfast in town, Peg's offers tasty grill food that's not too greasy.

★ Old Granite Street Eatery NEW AMERICAN $$
(☑775-622-3222; www.oldgranitestreeteatery.com; 243 S Sierra St; dinner mains $12-26; ⏲11am-10pm Mon-Thu, to 11pm Fri, 10am-11pm Sat, to 3pm Sun)

WORTH A TRIP

BURNING MAN

For one week at the end of August, **Burning Man** (www.burningman.com; admission $380) explodes onto the sunbaked Black Rock Desert, and Nevada sprouts a third major population center – Black Rock City. An experiential art party (and alternate universe) that climaxes in the immolation of a towering stick figure, Burning Man is a whirlwind of outlandish theme camps, dust-caked bicycles, bizarre bartering, costume-enhanced nudity and a general relinquishment of inhibitions.

A lovely well-lit place for organic and local comfort food, old-school artisanal cocktails and seasonal craft beers, this antique-strewn hotspot enchants diners with its stately wooden bar, water served in old liquor bottles and lengthy seasonal menu. Forgot to make a reservation? Check out the iconic rooster and pig murals and wait at a communal table fashioned from a barn door.

Silver Peak
Restaurant & Brewery BREWPUB $$
(www.silverpeakrestaurant.com; 124 Wonder St; lunch $8.50-11, dinner $10-23; ⊙restaurant 11am-10pm Sun-Thu, to 11pm Sat & Sun, pub open 1hr later) Casual and pretense free, this place hums with the chatter of happy locals settling in for a night of microbrews and great eats, from pizza with barbecue chicken to shrimp curry and filet mignon.

🍷 Drinking

Jungle CAFE, WINE BAR
(www.thejunglereno.com; 246 W 1st St; ⊙coffee 6am-midnight, wine 3pm-midnight Mon-Thu, 3pm-2am Fri, noon-2am Sat, noon-midnight Sun; 🛜) A side-by-side coffee shop and wine bar with a cool mosaic floor and riverside patio all rolled into one. The wine bar has weekly tastings, while the cafe serves breakfast bagels and lunchtime sandwiches ($6 to $8) and puts on diverse music shows.

☆ Entertainment

The free weekly *Reno News & Review* (www.newsreview.com) is your best source for listings.

Edge CLUB
(www.edgeofreno.com; 2707 S Virginia St, Peppermill; admission $20; ⊙Thu & Sat from 10pm, Fri from 7pm) The Peppermill reels in the nighthounds with a big glitzy dance club, where go-go dancers, smoke machines and laser lights may cause sensory overload. If so, step outside to the lounge patio and relax in front of cozy fire pits.

Knitting Factory LIVE MUSIC
(☑775-323-5648; http://re.knittingfactory.com; 211 N Virginia St) This midsized music venue books mainstream and indie favorites.

ℹ️ Information

Reno-Sparks Convention & Visitors Authority Visitor Center (☑775-682-3800; www.visitrenotahoe.com; 135 N Sierra St; ⊙9am-6pm) Also has an airport desk.

ℹ️ Getting There & Away

About 5 miles southeast of downtown, **Reno-Tahoe International Airport** (RNO; www.renoairport.com; 🛜) is served by most major airlines.

The **North Lake Tahoe Express** (☑866-216-5222; www.northlaketahoeexpress.com) operates a shuttle ($45 one-way, about six to eight daily, 3:30am to midnight) to and from the airport to North Shore Lake Tahoe locations, including Truckee, Squaw Valley and Incline Village. Reserve in advance.

Greyhound (☑775-322-2970; www.greyhound.com; 155 Stevenson St) buses run daily services to Truckee, Sacramento and San Francisco ($12 to $45, five to seven hours), as does the once-daily westbound California Zephyr train route operated by **Amtrak** (☑800-872-7245, 775-329-8638; www.amtrak.com; 280 N Center St). The train is more scenic and comfortable, with a bus connection from Emeryville to San Francisco ($45, seven hours).

ℹ️ Getting Around

The casino hotels offer frequent free airport shuttles for their guests.

Local **RTC Ride buses** (☑775-348-7433; www.rtcwashoe.com; per ride $2) blanket the city. Most routes converge at the RTC 4th St Station downtown; useful options include the RTC Rapid line for Center St and S Virginia St, 11 for Sparks and 19 for the airport. The free Sierra Spirit bus, which has wi-fi, loops around downtown landmarks every 15 minutes from 7am to 7pm.

Carson City

An easy drive from Reno or Lake Tahoe, this underrated town is a perfect stop for lunch and a stroll around the quiet, old-fashioned downtown.

The **Kit Carson Blue Line Trail** passes pretty historic buildings on pleasant tree-lined streets. Pick up a trail map at the **visitor center** (☑800-638-2321, 775-687-7410; www.visitcarsoncity.com; 1900 S Carson St; ☉9am-4pm), a mile south of downtown.

The **1870 Nevada State Capitol** (cnr Musser & Carson; ☉8am-5pm Mon-Fri) FREE anchors downtown; you might spot the governor himself chatting with a constituent. Train buffs shouldn't miss the **Nevada State Railroad Museum** (☑775-687-6953; www.museuems.nevadaculture.org; 2180 S Carson St; adult/child under 18yr $6/free; ☉9am-5pm Thu-Mon), which displays train cars and locomotives from the 1800s to the early 1900s.

Grab lunch at fetching **Comma Coffee** (www.commacoffee.com; 312 S Carson St; breakfast $6-8, lunch $8-10; ☉7am-8pm Mon & Wed-Sat to 10pm Tue; 🛜🍴♿) and eavesdrop on the politicians, or spend the evening in an English-style pub, the **Firkin and Fox** (www.thefirkinandfox.com; 310 S Carson St; mains $10-15; ☉11am-midnight Sun-Thu, to 2am Fri & Sat).

Hwy 395/Carson St is the main drag. For hiking and camping information, stop by the United States Forest Service (USFS) **Carson Ranger District Office** (☑775-882-2766; 1536 S Carson St; ☉8am-4:30pm Mon-Fri).

Virginia City

The discovery of the legendary Comstock Lode in 1859 sparked a silver bonanza in the mountains 25 miles south of Reno. During the 1860s gold rush, Virginia City was a high-flying, rip-roaring Wild West boomtown. Newspaperman Samuel Clemens, alias as Mark Twain, spent time here during its heyday, and described the mining life in his book *Roughing It.*

The high-elevation town is a National Historic Landmark, with a main street of Victorian buildings, wooden sidewalks and some hokey but fun museums. To see how the mining elite lived, stop by the **Mackay Mansion** (☑775-847-0173; 129 South D St; adult/child $5/free; ☉10am-5pm Tue-Sun summer, hours vary winter) and the **Castle** (B St).

Locals agree that **Cafe del Rio** (www.cafedelriovc.com; 394 S C St; mains $11-16; ☉11am--8pm Wed-Sat, 10am-7pm Sun) serves the town's best food – a nice blend of *nuevo* Mexican and good cafe meals, including breakfast. Wet your whistle at the longtime family-run **Bucket of Blood Saloon** (www.bucketofbloodsaloonvc.com; 1 S C St; ☉10am-7pm), which serves up beer and 'bar rules' at its antique wooden bar ('If the bartender doesn't laugh, you are not funny').

The **visitor center** (☑800-718-7587, 775-847-7500; www.visitvirginiacitynv.com; 86 S C St; ☉9am-5pm Mon-Sat, 10am-4pm Sun) is on the main drag, C St.

The Great Basin

A trip across Nevada's Great Basin is a serene, almost haunting experience. Anyone seeking the 'Great American Road Trip' will relish the fascinating historic towns and quirky diversions tucked away along lonely desert highways.

Along I-80

The culture of the American West is diligently cultivated in **Elko**, almost 300 miles along I-80 northeast of Reno. Aspiring cowboys and cowgirls should visit the **Western Folklife Center** (www.westernfolklife.org; 501 Railroad St; adult/child 6-18yr $5/1; ☉10am-5:30pm Mon-Fri, to 5pm Sat), which offers art and history exhibits, musical jams, and dance nights, and hosts the **Cowboy Poetry Gathering** each January. Elko also holds a **National Basque Festival** every July 4, with games, traditional dancing and a 'Running of the Bulls'. If you've never sampled Basque food, the best place for your inaugural experience is the **Star Hotel** (www.elkostarhotel.com; 246 Silver St; lunch $6-12, dinner $15-32; ☉11am-2pm & 5-9pm Mon-Fri, 4:30-9:30pm Sat), a family-style supper club located in a circa-1910 boarding house for Basque sheepherders.

Along Highway 50

The transcontinental Hwy 50 cuts across the heart of Nevada, connecting Carson City in the west to Great Basin National Park in the east. Better known here by its nickname, 'The Loneliest Road in America,' it once formed part of the Lincoln Hwy, and follows the route of the Overland Stagecoach, the Pony Express and the first transcontinental telegraph line. Towns are few, and the only sounds are the hum of the engine or the whisper of wind.

CATHEDRAL GORGE STATE PARK

A hundred miles south of Great Basin National Park, at **Cathedral Gorge State Park** (☏ 775-728-4460; http://parks.nv.gov; Hwy 93; entry $7; ☺ visitor center 9am-4:30pm), it really does feel like you've stepped into a magnificent, many-spired cathedral, albeit one whose dome is a view of the sky. Sleep under the stars at its first-come, first-served tent & RV sites ($17), set amid badlands-style cliffs.

About 25 miles southeast of Fallon, the **Sand Mountain Recreation Area** (☏ 775-885-6000; www.blm.gov/nv; 7-day permit $40, admission free Tue-Wed; ☺ 24hr) is worth a stop for a look at its 600ft sand dune and the ruins of a Pony Express station. Just east, enjoy a juicy burger at an old stagecoach stop, **Middlegate Station** (42500 Austin Hwy) then toss your sneakers onto the new **Shoe Tree** on the north side of Hwy 50 just ahead (the old one was cut down).

A fitting reward for surviving Hwy 50 is the awesome, uncrowded **Great Basin National Park**. Near the Nevada–Utah border, it's home to 13,063ft Wheeler Peak, which rises abruptly from the desert. Hiking trails near the summit take in superb country with glacial lakes, ancient bristlecone pines and even a permanent ice field. Admission is free; in summer, you can get oriented at the **Great Basin Visitor Center** (☏ 775-234-7331; www.nps.gov/grba; ☺ 8am-4:30pm year-round Jun-Aug), just north of Baker.

Along Highway 95

Hwy 95 runs roughly north–south through western Nevada; its starkly scenic southern section passes the Nevada Test Site, where more than 720 nuclear weapons were exploded in the 1950s.

Along Highways 375 & 93

Hwy 375 is dubbed the 'Extraterrestrial Hwy', both for its huge number of UFO sightings and because it intersects Hwy 93 near top-secret **Area 51**, part of Nellis Air Force Base that's a supposed holding area for captured UFOs. Some people may find Hwy 375 more unnerving than the Loneliest Road; it's a desolate stretch of pavement where cars are few and far between. In the tiny town of **Rachel**, on Hwy 375, **Little A'Le' Inn** (☏ 775-729-2515; www.littlealeinn.com; 1 Old Mill Rd, Alamo; RV sites with hookups $15, r $45-150; ☺ restaurant 8am-9pm; ✴ ☎ ✴) accommodates earthlings and aliens alike, and sells extraterrestrial souvenirs. Probings not included.

ARIZONA

The nation's sixth-largest state is dotted with stunning works of nature: the Grand Canyon, Monument Valley, the Chiricahua Mountains and the red rocks of Sedona, to name a few. In the shadows of these icons, a compelling cast of Native Americans, Wild West pioneers and intrepid explorers set out to tame Arizona's wilds, building prehistoric irrigation canals through desert scrub, mapping the labyrinth of canyons and mining the underground riches. Gorgeous back roads link these natural and historic sites, making Arizona a prime destination for road trippers.

Greater Phoenix, ringed by mountains, is a huge metro area with all the sights, restaurants and spas you'd expect in a spot that stakes its claim on rest and renewal. Tucson is the funky, artsy gateway to southern Arizona. Only 60 miles from the Mexican border, it embraces its cross-border heritage.

Up north is Flagstaff, a cool mountain town where locals seek relief from the searing summer heat and people come to play on the nearby San Francisco Peaks all year long. Arizona's star attraction is on its northern edge – the Grand Canyon, carved over aeons by the mighty Colorado River.

History

Native American tribes inhabited Arizona for centuries before Spanish explorer Francisco Vásquez de Coronado led an expedition from Mexico City in 1540. Settlers and missionaries followed in his wake, and by the mid-19th century the US controlled Arizona. The Indian Wars, in which the US Army battled Native Americans to protect settlers and claim land for the government, officially ended in 1886 with the surrender of Apache warrior Geronimo.

Railroad and mining expansion followed, and people arrived in ever larger numbers. After President Theodore Roosevelt visited Arizona in 1903 he supported the damming of its rivers to provide year-round water for irrigation and drinking, thus paving the way to statehood: in 1912 Arizona became the last of the 48 contiguous US states to be admitted to the Union.

The hot-button topic in Arizona these days is immigration. As many as 250,000 illegal immigrants are estimated to cross the state's 250-mile border with Mexico each year, and Arizona's legislature has responded with a wide range of controversial measures.

ℹ Information

Although Arizona is on Mountain Standard Time, it's the only western state that does not observe daylight saving time from spring to early fall – except for on the Navajo Reservation.

Generally speaking, lodging rates in southern Arizona (including Phoenix, Tucson and Yuma) are much higher in winter and spring, considered to be the 'high season', so great deals can be found in the hotter areas in summer.

Arizona Office of Tourism (☑ 602-364-3700; www.arizonaguide.com) Free state information.

Arizona Public Lands Information Center (☑ 602-417-9200; www.publiclands.org) Information about USFS, NPS, Bureau of Land Management (BLM) and state lands and parks.

Phoenix

There's much more to Phoenix than initially meets the eye. Just when you've dismissed the Southwest's largest and most populous urban area as a scorching faux-dobe wasteland of cookie-cutter subdivisions, bland malls and golf courses, you're pulled up short by a golden sunset setting the urban peaks aglow. Or a stubborn desert bloom determined to make a go of it in the dry, scrubby heat, or a busy mom-and-pop breakfast joint thumbing its nose at the ubiquitous chains.

Also known as the Valley of the Sun, Greater Phoenix includes not only Phoenix itself but also the separate communities of Scottsdale, Tempe and Mesa. The whole ensemble is ringed by mountains that range from 2500ft to more than 7000ft high. Central Ave runs north–south through Phoenix, dividing west addresses from east addresses; Washington St runs west–east, dividing north addresses from south addresses.

Above all else, Phoenix is *hot*. In summer when temperatures reach above 110°F (43°C), resort rates drop dramatically. That's great for travelers on a budget, but the most popular seasons to visit are winter and spring, when pleasant days prevail.

⊙ Sights

Greater Phoenix consists of several distinct cities. Phoenix, the largest, combines a businesslike demeanor with top-notch museums, a burgeoning cultural scene and great sports facilities. Southeast of here, lively, student-flavored Tempe (tem-pee), hugs two-mile-long Tempe Town Lake, while ho-hum Mesa, further east, holds a couple of interesting museums. Two ritzy enclaves lie northeast of Phoenix – Scottsdale, known for its cutesy old town, galleries and lavish resorts, and the largely residential Paradise Valley.

⊙ Phoenix

★**Heard Museum** MUSEUM
(☑ 602-252-8848; www.heard.org; 2301 N Central Ave; adult/child 6-12yr & student/senior $18/7.50/13.50; ⊙9:30am-5pm Mon-Sat, 11am-5pm Sun; ▣) This extraordinary museum spotlights the history, life, arts and culture of Native American tribes in the Southwest. Visitors will find art galleries, ethnographic displays, a get-creative kids exhibit and an unrivaled Hopi kachina gallery (many of the pieces were a gift from Barry Goldwater).

SOUTHWEST PHOENIX

ARIZONA FACTS

Nickname Grand Canyon State

Population 6.7 million

Area 113,637 sq miles

Capital city Phoenix (population 1.51 million)

Other cities Tucson (population 526,100), Flagstaff (population 68,700), Sedona (population 10,100)

Sales tax 7.6%

Birthplace of Cesar Chavez (1927–93), singer Linda Ronstadt (b 1946)

Home of The OK Corral, mining towns turned art colonies

Politics Majority vote Republican

Famous for Grand Canyon, saguaro cacti

Best souvenir Pink cactus-shaped neon lamp from roadside stall

Driving distances Phoenix to Grand Canyon Village 235 miles, Tucson to Sedona 230 miles

Phoenix

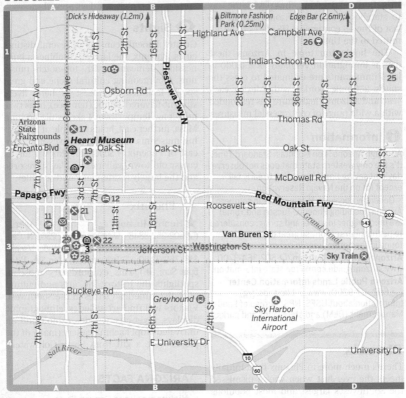

The Heard emphasizes quality over quantity and is one of the best museums of its kind in America.

★ **Musical Instrument Museum** MUSEUM
(📞 480-478-6000; www.themim.org; 4725 E Mayo Blvd; adult/child 13-19yr/under 13yr $18/14/10; ⏰9am-5pm Mon-Sat, 10am-5pm Sun, to 9pm first Fri of the month) From Uganda thumb pianos to Hawaiian ukuleles to Indonesian boat lutes, the ears have it at this lively museum that celebrates the world's musical instruments. More than 200 countries and territories are represented within five regional galleries, where music and video performances begin as you stop beside individual displays. You can also bang a drum in the Experiences Gallery and listen to Taylor Swift rock out in the Artist Gallery.

★ **Desert Botanical Garden** GARDENS
(📞 480-941-1225; www.dbg.org; 1201 N Galvin Pkwy; adult/child 3-12yr/student/senior $22/10/12/20; ⏰8am-8pm Oct-Apr, 7am-8pm May-Sep) Blue bells and Mexican gold poppies are just two of the colorful showstoppers blooming from March to May along the Desert Wildflower Loop Trail at this well-nurtured botanical garden, a lovely place to reconnect with nature while learning about desert plant life. Looping trails lead past an astonishing variety of desert denizens, arranged by theme (including a Sonoran Desert nature loop and an edible desert garden).

Phoenix Art Museum MUSEUM
(📞 602-257-1222; www.phxart.org; 1625 N Central Ave; adult/child 6-17yr/student/senior $15/6/10/12, Wed 3-9pm & 1st Fri of the month 6-10pm free; ⏰10am-9pm Wed, 10am-5pm Thu, Fri & Sat, noon-5pm Sun; 👶) Arizona's premier repository of fine art includes works by Claude Monet, Diego Rivera and Georgia O'Keeffe. The striking landscapes in the Western American gallery will get you in the mind-set for adventure. Got kids? Pick up a

Kidpack at visitor services, examine the ingeniously crafted miniature period Thorne Rooms or visit the PhxArtKids Gallery.

Scottsdale

Scottsdale is best known for its shopping districts, which include Old Town, packed with century-old buildings (amid others built to look old), and the adjacent Arts District. Both are stuffed with art galleries, clothing stores for the modern cowgirl, and some fabulous eating and drinking.

Taliesin West   ARCHITECTURE
(☑ 480-860-2700; www.franklloydwright.org; 12621 Frank Lloyd Wright Blvd; Insights Tour adult/child 4-12yr $36/17; ☉ tours 9am-4pm, closed Tue & Wed Jun-Aug) Frank Lloyd Wright was one of the seminal American architects of the 20th century. Taliesin West was his desert home and studio, built between 1938 and

1940. Still home to an architecture school and open to the public for guided tours, it's a prime example of organic architecture with buildings incorporating elements and structures found in surrounding nature.

⊙ Tempe

Founded in 1885 and home to around 50,000 students, **Arizona State University** (ASU; www.asu.edu) is the heart and soul of Tempe. The **Gammage Auditorium** (☑ box office 480-965-3434, tours 480-965-6912; www.asugammage.com; 1200 S Forest Ave, cnr Mill Ave & Apache Blvd; admission free, performances from $20; ☉ 1-4pm Mon-Fri Oct-May) was Frank Lloyd Wright's last major building.

Easily accessible by light-rail from downtown Phoenix, **Mill Avenue**, Tempe's main drag, is packed with chain restaurants, themed bars and other collegiate hangouts. It's also worth checking out **Tempe Town Lake** (www.tempe.gov/lake), an artificial lake with boat rides and hiking paths.

⊙ Mesa

Founded by Mormons in 1877, low-key Mesa is one of the fastest-growing cities in the nation and is the third-largest city in Arizona, with a population of 458,000.

**★Arizona Museum
of Natural History**   MUSEUM
(☑ 480-644-2230; www.azmnh.org; 53 N MacDonald St; adult/child 3-12yr/student/senior $10/6/8/9; ☉ 10am-5pm Tue-Fri, 11am-5pm Sat, 1-5pm Sun; ⊞) Even if you're not staying in Mesa, this museum is worth a trip, especially if your kids are into dinosaurs (and aren't they all?). In addition to the multi-level Dinosaur Mountain, there are loads of life-size casts of the giant beasts plus a touchable apatosaurus thighbone. Be warned: we saw one small child shrieking in abject terror at it all. Other exhibits highlight Arizona's colorful past, from a prehistoric Hohokam village to an eight-cell territorial jail.

🏃 Activities

Camelback Mountain   HIKING
(☑ 602-261-8318; www.phoenix.gov; ☉ sunrise-sunset) This 2704ft mountain sits smack in the center of the Phoenix action. Two trails, the Cholla Trail (6131 E Cholla Ln) and the Echo Canyon Trail (4925 E McDonald Dr) climb about 1,200ft to the summit. The newly

Phoenix

renovated Echo Canyon Trail is extremely popular and fills very early, even with 135 parking spots.

Piestewa Peak/
Dreamy Draw Recreation Area HIKING
(☑ 602-261-8318; www.phoenix.gov; Squaw Peak Dr, Phoenix; ⊘ trails 5am-11pm, last entry 6:59pm) Dotted with saguaros, ocotillos and other local cacti, this convenient summit was previously known as Squaw Peak. It was renamed for local Native American soldier Lori Piestewa who was killed in Iraq in 2003. Be forewarned: the trek to the 2608ft summit is hugely popular and the park can get jammed on winter weekends. Parking lots northeast of Lincoln Dr between 22nd and 24th Sts fill early. Dogs are allowed on some park trails but not the Summit Trail.

Cactus Adventures MOUNTAIN BIKING
(☑ 480-688-4743; www.cactusadventures.com; half-day rental from $55; ⊘ hours vary) Cactus Adventures rents bikes for use at South Mountain and offers guided hiking and biking tours at various parks. For rentals, they will meet you at the trailhead.

Ponderosa Stables HORSEBACK RIDING
(☑ 602-268-1261; www.arizona-horses.com; 10215 S Central Ave, Phoenix; 1/2/3hr rides $33/55/75,

min 2 riders for 3hr rides; ⊘ 7am-6pm Apr-Aug, 8am-6pm Sep-Mar) This outfitter leads rides through South Mountain Park. Reservations required for most trips.

✯ Festivals & Events

Fiesta Bowl SPORT
(☑ 480-350-0911; www.fiestabowl.org; 1 Cardinals Dr, Glendale) The most popular event in Phoenix is the Fiesta Bowl football game held in early January at the University of Phoenix Stadium. It's preceded by one of the largest parades in the Southwest.

Arizona State Fair FAIR
(www.azstatefair.com; 1826 W McDowell Rd; adult/child 5-13yr $10/5) This fair lures folks to the Arizona State Fairgrounds the last two weeks of October and first week of November with a rodeo, livestock displays, a pie-eating contest and concerts.

⌂ Sleeping

Greater Phoenix is well stocked with hotels and resorts, but you won't find many B&Bs or cozy inns. When prices plummet in the scorching summer, Valley residents take advantage of super-low prices at their favorite resorts.

⛴ Phoenix

HI Phoenix Hostel — HOSTEL $

(☑ 602-254-9803; www.phxhostel.org; 1026 N 9th St; dm from $23, s/d $35/45; ⚕ @ ⛵) Fall back in love with backpacking at this small hostel with fun owners who know Phoenix and want to enjoy it with you. The 22-bed hostel sits in a working-class residential neighborhood and has relaxing garden nooks. Check-in is from 8am to 10am and 5pm to 10pm. Cash or travelers check only.

Budget Lodge Downtown — MOTEL $

(☑ 602-254-7247; www.blphx.com; 402 W Van Buren St; r incl breakfast $63-70; P ⚕ ⛵) The Budget Lodge doesn't have time for sassiness or charisma. It's got a job to do, and it does it well: providing a clean, low-cost place to sleep. Rooms have a microwave and fridge.

La Quinta Inn &
Suites Phoenix I-10 West — HOTEL $

(☑ 602-595-6451; www.lq.com; 4929 W McDowell Rd; r $79-89, ste $119-129; P ⚕ @ ⛵) If you want a no-hassle, low-cost hotel that's easily accessible from the airport and the I-10, try this welcoming La Quinta. For tasty fast food, El Pollo Loco is next door. No pet fee.

Palomar Phoenix — HOTEL $$$

(☑ 877-488-1908, 602-253-6633; www.hotelpalomar-phoenix.com; 2 E Jefferson St; r $309-429, studios & ste $359-369; P ⚕ @ ⛵ ⛱ ⚕) Shaggy pillows, antler-shaped lamps and portraits of blue cows. Yep, whimsy takes a stand at the 242-room Palomar, and we like it. Rooms are larger than average and pop with fresh, modern style. All come with yoga mats, animal-print robes and pillowtop beds with Italian Frette linens. And did we mention the nightly wine reception?

Royal Palms Resort & Spa — RESORT $$$

(☑ 602-840-3610; www.royalpalmshotel.com; 5200 E Camelback Rd; r/stes/casitas from $519/529/559 ste; P ⚕ @ ⛵ ⛱ ⚕) Camelback Mountain is the photogenic backdrop for this posh and intimate resort, which was once the winter retreat of New York industrialist Delos Cook. Today, it's a hushed and elegant place, dotted with Spanish Colonial villas, flower-lined walkways and palms imported from Egypt. Pets can go Pavlovian for soft beds, personalized biscuits and walking services.

⛴ Scottsdale

Sleep Inn — HOTEL $$

(☑ 480-998-9211; www.sleepinnscottsdale.com; 16630 N Scottsdale Rd; r incl breakfast $129-134; P ⚕ @ ⛵) It's part of a national chain, but this Sleep Inn wins points for its extensive complimentary breakfast, afternoon cookies, friendly staff and proximity to Taliesin West. There's also a laundry and free 24hr hotel shuttle that runs within 5 miles of the hotel.

★ Hotel Valley Ho — BOUTIQUE HOTEL $$$

(☑ 480-248-2000; www.hotelvalleyho.com; 6850 E Main St; r $249-299, ste $439-609; P ⚕ @ ⛵ ⛱ ⚕) Everything's swell at the Valley Ho, where mid-Century Modern gets a 21st-century twist. This jazzy joint once bedded Bing Crosby, Natalie Wood and Janet Leigh, and today it's a top pick for movie stars filming on location in Phoenix. Bebop music, upbeat staff and eye-magnets like the 'ice fireplace' recapture the Rat Pack vibe, and the theme travels well to the balconied rooms.

★ Bespoke Inn, Cafe & Bicycles — B&B $$$

(☑ 480-664-0730; www.bespokeinn.com; 3701 N Marshall Way; r incl brunch from $319; P ⚕ ⛵ ⛱ ⚕) Ooh la la. Are we in the English countryside

---

PHOENIX FOR CHILDREN

Wet 'n' Wild Phoenix (☑ 623-201-2000; www.wetnwildphoenix.com; 4243 W Pinnacle Peak Rd, Glendale; over/under 42in tall $40/30, senior $30; ⏲ 10am-6pm Sun-Wed, 10am-10pm Thu-Sat Jun & Jul, varies May, Aug & Sep; ⛨) This water park has pools, tube slides, wave pools, waterfalls and floating rivers. It's in Glendale, 2 miles west of I-17 at exit 217.

Rawhide Western Town & Steakhouse (☑ 480-502-5600; www.rawhide.com; 5700 W N Loop Rd, Chandler; admission free, per attraction or show $5, unlimited day pass $15; ⏲ 5-10pm Thu-Sun Jun & Jul, hr vary rest of year; ⛨) At this re-created 1880s frontier town ,about 20 miles south of Mesa, kids can enjoy all sorts of hokey-but-fun shenanigans. The steakhouse has rattlesnake for adventurous eaters.

Arizona Science Center (☑ 602-716-2000; www.azscience.org; 600 E Washington St; adult/3-17yr/senior $17/12/15; ⏲ 10am-5pm; ⛨) A high-tech temple of discovery; there are more than 300 hands-on exhibits and a planetarium.

or downtown Scottsdale? At this breezy B&B guests can nibble chocolate scones in the chic cafe, loll in the infinity edge pool or pedal the neighborhood on Pashley city bikes. Rooms are plush with handsome touches like handcrafted furniture and nickel bath fixtures. Gourmet brunch served at the onsite restaurant Virtu. Book early.

The Saguaro HOTEL **$$$**
(☑ 480-308-1100; www.jdvhotels.com; 4000 N Drinkwater Blvd; r $169-229, ste 249-669; P✳☂☀☺) Embrace your inner hipster at this candy-bright hideaway beside Old Town Scottsdale. When compared to more established Scottsdale properties there may be less attention to detail here, and the vibe skews young, but the location is great, there's a palm-dotted pool and the Saguaro's rates are lower than its neighborhood competitors.

Tempe

Best Western Inn of Tempe HOTEL **$$**
(☑ 480-784-2233; www.innoftempe.com; 670 N Scottsdale Rd; r incl breakfast from $117; P✳@☂☀☺) This well-kept contender sits right next to the busy 202 freeway but is within walking distance of Tempe Town Lake. ASU and Mill Ave are within staggering distance. The hotel also offers a free airport shuttle. Pets are $10 each per day.

Sheraton Wild Horse Pass Resort & Spa RESORT **$$$**
(☑ 602-225-0100; www.wildhorsepassresort.com; 5594 W Wild Horse Pass Blvd, Chandler; r $259, ste from $334; P✳@☂☀) At sunset, scan the lonely horizon for the eponymous wild horses silhouetted against the South Mountains. Owned by the Gila River tribe and nestled on their sweeping reservation south of Tempe, this 500-room resort is a stunning alchemy of luxury and Native American traditions. The domed lobby is a mural-festooned roundhouse, and rooms reflect the traditions of local tribes.

Eating

Between them, Phoenix and Scottsdale hold the largest selection of restaurants in the Southwest.

Phoenix

★ **Matt's Big Breakfast** BREAKFAST **$**
(☑ 602-254-1074; www.mattsbigbreakfast.com; 825 N 1st St, at Garfield St; breakfast $5-10, lunch $7-10; ☺ 6:30am-2:30pm) First, a warning: even on weekdays lines are often out the door. There are no reservations, so sign your name on the clipboard and expect a 20-minute wait (and bring quarters for the meter). The upside? Best. Breakfast. Ever.

★ **Green New American Vegetarian** VEGAN, VEGETARIAN **$**
(☑ 602-258-1870; www.greenvegetarian.com; 2022 N 7th St; mains $6-9; ☑) Whoa, whoa, whoa. Vegan food isn't supposed to taste this good. Or is it? Your expectations will be forever raised after dining at this hip cafe where vegan chef Damon Brasch stirs up savory vegan and vegetarian dishes. The burgers, po-boys and Asian-style bowls taste as good, if not better, than their carnivorous counterparts. Order at the counter then take a seat in the garage-style digs.

Tee Pee Mexican Food MEXICAN **$**
(☑ 602-956-0178; www.teepeemexicanfood.com; 4144 E Indian School Rd; mains $5-14; ☺ 11am-10pm Mon-Sat, to 9pm Sun) If you're snobby about Mexican food, you will not be happy at Tee Pee. If, however, you like piping-hot plates piled high with cheesy, messy, American-style Mexican food, then grab a booth at this 40-year-old Phoenix fave. George W Bush ate here in 2004 and ordered two enchiladas, rice and beans – now called the Presidential Special. Dig in!

★ **Dick's Hideaway** NEW MEXICAN **$$**
(☑ 602-241-1881; http://richardsonsnm.com; 6008 N 16th St; breakfast $5-20, lunch $12-16, dinner $12-35; ☺ 7am-midnight Sun-Wed, to 1am Thu-Sat) At this pocket-sized ode to New Mexican cuisine, grab a small table beside the bar or settle in at the communal table in the side room and prepare for hearty servings of savory, chili-slathered New Mexican fare, from enchiladas to tamales to *rellenos*. We especially like the Hideaway for breakfast, when the Bloody Marys arrive with a shot of beer.

Pizzeria Bianco PIZZA **$$**
(☑ 602-258-8300; www.pizzeriabianco.com; 623 E Adams St; pizzas $13-18; ☺ 11am-9pm Mon, 11am-10pm Tue-Sat) James Beard–winner Chris Bianco is back in the kitchen at his famous downtown pizza joint after stepping back in 2010 due to allergies. But thanks to new medicine and his love of pizza crafting, Bianco has returned in full force, and his thin-crust gourmet pies are as popular as ever. The tiny restaurant is a convenient stop for

travelers exploring the adjacent Heritage Square.

Durant's
STEAK $$$

(☑ 602-264-5967; www.durantsaz.com; 2611 N Central Ave; lunch $12-26, dinner $22-61; ⊙ 11am-10pm Mon-Fri, 5-11pm Sat, 4:30-10pm Sun) This dark and manly place is a gloriously old-school steak house. You will get steak. It will be big and juicy. There will be a potato. The ambience is awesome too: red velvet cozy booths and the sense that the Rat Pack is going to waltz in at any minute.

Scottsdale

Sugar Bowl
ICE CREAM $

(☑ 480-946-0051; www.sugarbowlscottsdale.com; 4005 N Scottsdale Rd; ice cream $2.25-9, mains $6-12; ⊙ 11am-10pm Sun-Thu, to midnight Fri & Sat; ⏺) Get your ice-cream fix at this pink-and-white Valley institution. Also serves a full menu of sandwiches and salads.

The Mission
MEXICAN $$

(☑ 480-636-5005; www.themissionaz.com; 3815 N Brown Ave; lunch $9-23, dinner $12-36; ⊙ 11am-10pm Sun-Thu, to 11pm Fri & Sat) With its dark interior and glowing votives, we'll call this *nuevo* Latin spot sexy – although our exclamations about the food's deliciousness may ruin the sultry vibe. The *tecate*-marinated steak taco with lime and avocado is superb and makes for a satisfying light lunch. The guacamole is made tableside, and wins raves. Margaritas and mojitos round out the fun.

Herb Box
AMERICAN $$

(☑ 480-289-6160; www.theherbbox.com; 7134 E Stetson Dr; lunch $10-16, dinner $15-28, brunch $7-16; ⊙ 11am-3pm Mon, 11am-9pm Tue-Fri, 9am-10pm Sat, 9am-3pm Sun) It's not just about sparkle and air kisses at this chichi bistro in the heart of Old Town's Southbridge. It's also about fresh regional ingredients, artful presentation and attentive service. For a light, healthy, ever-so-stylish lunch (steak salad, turkey avocado wrap, kale and *capicola* flatbread), settle in on the patio and toast your good fortune with a blackberry mojito.

Tempe

Essence
CAFE $

(☑ 480-966-2745; www.essencebakery.com; 825 W University Dr; breakfast $6-9.25, lunch $8-9; ⊙ 7am-3pm Tue-Sat; ⏺) Look for French toast and egg dishes at breakfast, and salads, gourmet sandwiches and a few Mediterranean specialties at lunch. The eco-minded cafe strives to serve organic, locally grown fare. The popular macaroons are mighty fine.

★ Kai Restaurant
NATIVE AMERICAN $$$

(☑ 602-225-0100; www.wildhorsepassresort.com; 5594 W Wild Horse Pass Blvd, Chandler; mains $42-54, tasting menus $135-$225; ⊙ 5:30-9pm Tue-Sat) Native American cuisine soars to new heights at Kai, enhanced and transformed by traditional crops grown along the Gila River. Dinners strike just the right balance between adventure and comfort. Dress nicely (no shorts or hats). It's at the Sheraton Wild Horse Pass Resort & Spa on the Gila River Indian Reservation.

🍷 Drinking

Scottsdale has the greatest concentration of trendy bars and clubs; Tempe attracts the student crowd.

★ Postino Winecafé Arcadia
WINE BAR

(http://postinowinecafe.com; 3939 E Campbell Ave, at 40th St, Arcadia; ⊙ 11am-11pm Mon-Thu, 11am-midnight Fri, 9am-midnight Sat, 9am-10pm Sun) Your mood will improve the moment you step into this convivial, indoor-outdoor wine bar. It's a perfect gathering spot for friends ready to enjoy the good life – but solos will do fine too. Highlights include the misting patio, rave-worthy bruschetta, and more than 20 wines by the glass for $5 between 11am and 5pm.

Edge Bar
BAR

(5700 E McDonald Dr, Sanctuary on Camelback Mountain, Paradise Valley) This stylish cocktail bar, perched narrowly on the side of Camelback Mountain, is an inviting place to watch the sunset. If it's full, the equally posh, big-windowed Jade Bar next door should do just fine. Both are within the plush confines of Sanctuary on Camelback Mountain. Free valet, but they'll accept a gratuity and a smile.

O.H.S.O. Eatery and nanoBrewery
BREWERY

(www.ohsobrewery.com; 4900 E Indian School Rd, Phoenix) Small-batch brews and Arizona beers are the stars at this bustling nanobrewery in Arcadia. Dog-lovers can bring Fido with them to the patio. Parking is tight, so be prepared to valet (free) when it's busy. And the name? We hear it stands for Outrageous Homebrewers Social Outpost.

Rusty Spur Saloon
BAR

(📞480-425-7787; www.rustyspursaloon.com; 7245 E Main St, Scottsdale; ⊙10am-1am Sun-Thu, to 2am Fri & Sat) Nobody's putting on airs at this fun-lovin', pack-'em-in-tight country bar where the grizzled Budweiser crowd gathers for cheap drinks and twangy bands. It's in an old bank building that closed during the Depression; the vault now holds liquor instead of green-backs – except for the dollar bills hanging from the ceiling. Pardner, we kinda like this place.

☆ Entertainment

The **Phoenix Symphony** (📞administration 602-495-1117, box office 602-495-1999; www.phoe-nixsymphony.org; 75 N 2nd St, box offices 1 N 1st St, 75 N 2nd St) performs at **Symphony Hall** (75 N 2nd St) and other local venues, while the **Arizona Opera** (📞602-266-7464; www.azopera.com; 75 N 2nd St) is now based at a new opera hall across the street from the Phoenix Art Museum.

The Arizona Diamondbacks play baseball at downtown's air-conditioned Chase Field, while the men's basketball team, the **Phoenix Suns** (📞602-379-7867; www.nba.com/suns; 201 E Jefferson St), and the women's team, the **Phoenix Mercury** (📞602-252-9622; www.wnba.com/mercury; 201 E Jefferson St), are also downtown, at the US Airways Center. The **Arizona Cardinals** (📞602-379-0101; www.azcardinals.com; 1 Cardinals Dr, Glendale) play football in Glendale at the new University of Phoenix Stadium, which hosted the Super Bowl in 2015.

Rhythm Room
LIVE MUSIC

(📞602-265-4842; www.rhythmroom.com; 1019 E Indian School Rd, Phoenix; ⊙doors usually open 7:30pm) Some of the Valley's best live acts take the stage at this small venue, where you feel like you're in the front row of every gig. It tends to attract more local and regional talent than big names, which suits us just fine. Check the calendar for show times.

🛍 Shopping

For upscale shopping, visit the **Scottsdale Fashion Square** (www.fashionsquare.com; 7014 E Camelback, at Scottsdale Rd; ⊙10am-9pm Mon-Sat, 11am-6pm Sun) and the even more exclusive **Biltmore Fashion Park** (www.shop-biltmore.com; 2502 E Camelback Rd, at N 24th St, Phoenix; ⊙10am-8pm Mon-Sat, noon-6pm Sun). In northern Scottsdale, the outdoor **Kier-**land Commons (www.kierlandcommons.com; 15205 N Kierland Blvd; ⊙10am-9pm Mon-Sat, noon-6pm Sun) pulls in the crowds.

Heard Museum
Shop & Bookstore
ARTS & CRAFTS

(www.heardmuseumshop.com; 2301 N Central Ave; ⊙shop 9:30am-5pm, from 11am Sun, bookstore 9:30am-5:30pm Mon-Sat, to 5pm Sun) This museum store has a top-notch collection of Native American original arts and crafts. The kachina collection alone is mind-boggling. Jewelry, pottery, Native American books and a broad selection of fine arts are also on offer. The bookstore sells a wide array of books about the Southwest.

ℹ Information

EMERGENCY & MEDICAL SERVICES

Banner Good Samaritan Medical Center (📞602-839-2000; www.bannerhealth.com; 1111 E McDowell Rd, Phoenix)

Police (📞emergency 911, non-emergency 602-262-6151; http://phoenix.gov/police; 620 W Washington St, Phoenix)

INTERNET RESOURCES & MEDIA

Arizona Republic (www.azcentral.com) Arizona's largest newspaper; publishes a free entertainment guide, *Calendar*, every Thursday.

KJZZ 91.5 FM (http://kjzz.org) National Public Radio (NPR).

Phoenix New Times (www.phoenixnewtimes.com) The major free weekly; lots of event and restaurant listings.

POST

Downtown Post Office (📞602-253-9648; 522 N Central Ave, Phoenix; ⊙9am-5pm Mon-Fri)

TOURIST INFORMATION

Downtown Phoenix Visitor Information Center (📞877-225-5749; www.visitphoenix.com; 125 N 2nd St; ⊙8am-5pm Mon-Fri) The Valley's most complete source of tourist information. Located across from the Hyatt Regency.

Mesa Convention & Visitors Bureau (📞480-827-4700, 800-283-6372; www.visitmesa.com; 120 N Center St; ⊙8am-5pm Mon-Fri)

Scottsdale Convention & Visitors Bureau (📞800-782-1117, 480-421-1004; www.experi-encescottsdale.com; 4343 N Scottsdale Rd, Suite 170; ⊙8am-5pm Mon-Fri) Inside the Galleria Corporate Center.

Tempe Convention & Visitors Bureau (📞866-914-1052, 480-894-8158; www.tempetourism.com; 51 W 3rd St, Suite 105; ⊙8:30am-5pm Mon-Fri)

ℹ Getting There & Around

Sky Harbor International Airport (☑ 602-273-3300; http://skyharbor.com; 3400 E Sky Harbor Blvd; 🛜), 3 miles southeast of downtown Phoenix, is served by all major airlines. Its three terminals (Terminals 2, 3 and 4; there's no 1!) and the parking lots are linked by the free 24-hour Airport Shuttle Bus. The free Phoenix Sky Train runs between the economy parking lot, Terminals 3 and 4 and the METRO light-rail station at 44th St and E Washington St.

Greyhound (☑ 602-389-4200; www.greyhound.com; 2115 E Buckeye Rd) runs buses to Tucson ($18, two hours, six daily), Flagstaff ($25, three hours, five daily), Albuquerque ($70 to $87, 9½ hours, three daily) and Los Angeles ($46, 7½ hours, eight daily). Valley Metro's No 13 buses link the airport and the Greyhound station.

Valley Metro (☑ 602-253-5000; www.valleymetro.org) operates daily buses all over the Valley, and a 20-mile light-rail line linking north Phoenix with downtown Phoenix, Tempe/ASU and downtown Mesa. Fares for light-rail and bus are $2 per ride (no transfers) or $4 for a day pass. **Flash buses** (www.tempe.gov) run daily around ASU and downtown Tempe, while the **Scottsdale Trolley** (www.scottsdaleaz.gov/trolley; 🕐11am-6pm Fri-Wed, to 9pm Thu during Artwalk) loops around downtown Scottsdale, both at no charge.

Central Arizona

North of Phoenix, the wooded, mountainous and much cooler Colorado Plateau is draped with scenic sites and attractions. You can channel your inner goddess on a vortex, hike through sweet-smelling canyons, admire ancient Native American dwellings and delve into Old West history. The main hub, Flagstaff, is a lively and delightful college town that's the gateway to the Grand Canyon South Rim. Summer, spring and fall are the best times to visit.

On I-17, you can drive the 145 miles between Phoenix and Flagstaff in just over two hours. Opt for the more leisurely Hwy 89, though, and you'll be rewarded with beautiful landscapes and intriguing diversions.

Prescott

With its historic Victorian-era downtown and colorful Wild West heritage, Prescott feels like the Midwest meets cowboy country. Boasting more than 500 buildings on the National Register of Historic Places, it's the

---

SCENIC DRIVES: ARIZONA'S BEST
....

Oak Creek Canyon A thrilling plunge past swimming holes, rockslides and crimson canyon walls on Hwy 89A between Flagstaff and Sedona.

Hwy 89/89A Wickenburg to Sedona The Old West meets the New West on this lazy drive past dude ranches, mining towns, art galleries and stylish wineries.

Patagonia–Sonoita Scenic Road This one's for the birds, and those who like to track them, in Arizona's southern wine country on Hwys 82 and 83.

Kayenta–Monument Valley Star in your own Western on an iconic loop past cinematic red rocks in Navajo country.

Vermilion Cliffs Scenic Road A solitary drive on Hwy 89A through the Arizona Strip linking condor country, the North Rim and Mormon hideaways.

---

home of the world's oldest rodeo, while the infamous strip of old saloons on Whiskey Row, along the plaza, still ply their patrons with booze.

Just south of downtown, the fun-loving **Motor Lodge** (☑ 928-717-0157; www.themotorlodge.com; 503 S Montezuma St; r $119-139, ste $149, apt $159; 🅿🛜) welcomes guests with 12 snazzy bungalows arranged around a central driveway – it's indie lodging at its best.

For breakfast, mosey into the friendly **Lone Spur Café** (☑ 928-445-8202; www.thelonespur.com; 106 W Gurley St; breakfast $8-18, lunch $8-11, dinner $9-24; 🕐8am-2pm daily, 4:30-8pm Fri), where you always order your breakfast with a biscuit and a side of sausage gravy. Cajun and Southwest specialties spice up the menu at welcoming **Iron Springs Cafe** (☑ 928-443-8848; www.ironspringscafe.com; 1501 Iron Springs Rd; brunch $9-13, lunch $9-12, dinner $9-21; 🕐8am-8pm Wed-Sat, 9am-2pm Sun), which sits inside an old train station 3 miles northwest of downtown.

On Whiskey Row, the **Palace** (☑ 928-541-1996; www.historicpalace.com; 120 S Montezuma St; 🕐11am-9pm Sun-Thu, to 10pm Fri & Sat) is an atmospheric place to drink; you enter through swinging saloon doors into a big room anchored by a Brunswick bar.

The **chamber of commerce** (☑ 800-266-7534, 928-445-2000; www.visit-prescott.com; 117 W Goodwin St; ☺ 9am-5pm Mon-Fri, 10am-2pm Sat & Sun) has tourist information, while **Arizona Shuttle** (☑ 928-776-7433; www.prescotttransit.com; 820 E Sheldon St) runs buses to/from Phoenix airport (one-way adult $32–35, child $25, 2¼ hours, up to 22 daily).

Jerome

The childhood game Chutes and Ladders comes to mind as you stroll up and down the stairways of Jerome, which clings – not always successfully, if the crumbling Sliding Jail is anything to go by – to the side of Cleopatra Hill, between Prescott and Sedona. This resurrected ghost town was known as the 'Wickedest Town in the West' during its late-1800s mining heyday, but its historic buildings have now been restored to hold galleries, restaurants, B&Bs and wine-tasting rooms.

Feeling brave? Stand on the glass platform covering the 1910ft mining shaft at **Audrey Headframe Park** (www.jeromehistoricalsociety.com; 55 Douglas Rd; ☺ 8am-5pm) FREE – it's longer than the Empire State Building by 650ft! Just ahead, the excellent **Jerome State Historic Park** (☑ 928-634-5381; www.azstateparks.com; 100 Douglas Rd; adult/child 7-13yr $5/2; ☺ 8:30am-5pm) preserves the 1916 mansion of mining mogul Jimmy 'Rawhide' Douglas.

A community hospital in the mining era, the **Jerome Grand Hotel** (☑ 928-634-8200; www.jeromegrandhotel.com; 200 Hill St; r $130-190, ste $275-460; ✳ ☏) plays up its past with medical relics in the hallways and an entertaining ghost tour kids will enjoy. The adjoining **Asylum Restaurant** (☑ 928-639-3197; www.asylumrestaurant.com; 200 Hill St; lunch $11-18, dinner $23-35; ☺ 11am-9pm), with its red-rock valley views, is a breathtaking spot for a fine meal and glass of wine. Downtown, the **Spirit Room Bar** (☑ 928-634-8809; www.spiritroom.com; 166 Main St; ☺ 11am-midnight Sun-Thu, until 1am Fri & Sat) is a lively watering hole.

Step into the **Flatiron Café** (☑ 928-634-2733; www.theflatironjerome.com; 416 Main St; breakfast $3-11, lunch $8-10; ☺ 7am-4pm Wed-Mon) at the Y intersection for a savory gourmet breakfast or lunch; the specialty coffees are delicious.

For information, call in at the **chamber of commerce** (☑ 928-634-2900; www.jeromechamber.com; Hull Ave, Hwy 89A north after the Flatiron Café split; ☺ 10am-3pm).

Sedona

Nestled amid majestic red sandstone formations at the southern end of Oak Creek Canyon, Sedona attracts artists, spiritual seekers, hikers and cyclists, and day-trippers from Phoenix fleeing the oppressive heat. Its combination of scenic beauty and mysticism draws throngs of tourists year-round. New Age businesses, fueled by the claim that this

VERDE VALLEY WINE TRAIL

Vineyards, wineries and tasting rooms have opened their doors along Hwy 89A and I-17, bringing a dash of style and energy to Cottonwood, Jerome and Cornville.

In Cottonwood, you can float to Verde River–adjacent **Alcantara Vineyards** (www.alcantaravineyard.com; 3445 S Grapevine Way; wine tasting $10-15; ☺ 11am-5pm daily) then stroll through Old Town where two tasting rooms, **Arizona Stronghold** (www.azstronghold.com; 1023 N Main St; wine tasting $9; ☺ noon-7pm Sun-Thu, to 9pm Fri & Sat) and **Pillsbury Wine Company** (www.pillsburywine.com; 1012 N Main St; wine tasting $10; ☺ 11am-5pm Mon-Thu, 11am-9pm Fri-Sun), sit across from each other on Main St.

Art, views and wine-sipping converge in Jerome, where there's a tasting room on every level of town. Start with **Cellar 433** (www.cellar433.com; 240 Hull Ave; wine tasting $10-12; ☺ 11am-6pm Thu-Sun, 11am-5pm Mon-Wed) near the visitor center, then stroll up to **Caduceus Cellars** (www.caduceus.org; 158 Main St; wine tasting $9-13; ☺ 11am-6pm Sun-Thu, to 8pm Sun).

Three wineries with tasting rooms hug a short stretch of Page Springs Rd east of Cornville: bistro-housing **Page Springs Cellars** (www.pagespringscellars.com; 1500 N Page Springs Rd; wine tasting $10; ☺ 11am-7pm Mon-Wed, to 9pm Thu-Sun), welcoming **Oak Creek Vineyards** (www.oakcreekvineyards.net; 1555 N Page Springs Rd; wine tasting $10; ☺ 10am-6pm) and mellow-rock-playing **Javelina Leap Vineyard** (www.javelinaleapwinery.com; 1565 Page Springs Rd; wine tasting $8; ☺ 11am-5pm).

area stands at the center of vortexes that tap into the earth's power, dot downtown, as do galleries and gourmet restaurants, while the surrounding canyons offer excellent hiking and mountain biking.

In the middle of town, the 'Y' is the landmark junction of Hwys 89A and 179.

◉ Sights & Activities

New Agers believe Sedona's rocks, cliffs and rivers radiate Mother Earth's mojo. The four best-known vortexes are **Bell Rock** near Village of Oak Creek east of Hwy 179; **Cathedral Rock** near Red Rock Crossing; **Airport Mesa** along Airport Rd; and **Boynton Canyon**. Airport Rd is also a great location for watching the Technicolor sunsets.

Red Rock State Park   PARK
(☑928-282-6907; www.azstateparks.com/parks/rero; 4050 Red Rock Loop Rd; adult/child 7-13yr/6yr & under $5/3/free; ◉8am-5pm, visitor center 9am-4.30pm; ♿) Not to be confused with Slide Rock State Park, this low-key 286-acre park includes an environmental education center, a visitor center, picnic areas and 5 miles of well-marked, interconnecting trails in a riparian habitat amid gorgeous scenery. Ranger-led activities include nature walks and bird walks. Popular moonlight hikes are offered April though October; reservations required ($5 reservation fee).

Slide Rock State Park   SWIMMING
(☑928-282-3034; www.azstateparks.com/parks/slro; 6871 N Hwy 89A, Oak Creek Canyon; per car Jun-Sep $20, Sep-May $10; ◉8am-7pm Jun-Aug, shorter hours rest of year; ♿▣) Swoosh down big rocks into cool creek water at Oak Creek Canyon's star attraction, or walk the hiking trails. No entry one hour before closing time.

★Pink Jeep Tours   DRIVING TOUR
(☑928-282-5000; www.pinkjeeptours.com; 204 N Hwy 89A; ♿) At first glance, Pink Jeep may annoy you. It seems like the 50-year-old company's jeeps are everywhere, buzzing around like pink flies. But once you join a tour, well, you just might find yourself laughing, bumping around and having a blast in spite of initial peevishness. We concede to your domination, Pink Jeep!

Bike & Bean   BICYCLE RENTAL
(☑928-284-0210; www.bike-bean.com; 75 Bell Rock Plaza; bike rental 2hr/day from $30/$50)

🛏 Sleeping

Sedona hosts many beautiful B&Bs, creekside cabins, motels and full-service resorts.

Dispersed camping is not permitted in Red Rock Canyon. The **USFS** (☑877-444-6777; http://www.fs.usda.gov/coconino; Hwy 89A; campsites $16-20) runs campgrounds, without hookups, in the woods of Oak Creek Canyon, just off Hwy Alt 89. It costs $18 to camp, and you don't need a Red Rock Pass. All campgrounds except Pine Flat East accept reservations. Six miles north of town, **Manzanita** has 19 sites, showers and is open year-round; 11.5 miles north, **Cave Springs** has 82 sites, and showers; **Pine Flat East** and **Pine Flat West**, 12.5 miles north, together have 58 sites, 18 of which can be reserved.

Star Motel   MOTEL $
(☑928-282-3641; www.starmotelsedona.com; 295 Jordan Rd; r $80-126, ste $176; ☎) This ten-room motel in Uptown is one of Sedona's best deals. Rooms are simple, with a few artsy touches, but what we like most is the hospitality. And hey, the beds in this 1950s-era motel are clean, the shower strong and the refrigerators handy for chilling those sunset beers. Shops, eateries and the visitor center are just a hop, skip and jump away.

Cozy Cactus   B&B $$$
(☑928-284-0082; www.cozycactus.com; 80 Canyon Circle Dr; r incl breakfast $190-340; ▣@☎) This five-room B&B, run by Carrie and Mark, works well for adventure-loving types ready to enjoy the great outdoors. The Southwest-style house bumps up against a

National Forest trail and is just around the bend from cyclist-friendly Bell Rock Pathway. Post-adventuring, get comfy beside the firepit on the back patio for wildlife-watching and stargazing.

✖ Eating & Drinking

Coffee Pot Restaurant   BREAKFAST $
(📞 928-282-6626;   www.coffeepotsedona.com; 2050 W Hwy 89A; breakfast $5-10, lunch $5-14; ⊙ 6am-2pm; 🖼) This has been the go-to breakfast and lunch joint for decades. It's always busy and service can be slow, but it's friendly, the meals are reasonably priced and the selection is huge: 101 types of omelet for starters (peanut butter, jelly and banana perhaps?)

Sedona Memories   DELI $
(📞 928-282-0032; 321 Jordan Rd; sandwiches under $10; ⊙ 10am-2pm Mon-Fri) This tiny local spot assembles gigantic sandwiches on slabs of homemade bread. A great choice for a picnic, they're packed tight to-go, so less mess. You can also nosh on the quiet porch. If you call in your order, they'll toss in a free cookie. Cash only.

Oak Creek Brewery & Grill   AMERICAN $$
(📞 928-282-3300; www.oakcreekpub.com; 336 Hwy 179; mains $10-23; ⊙ 11.30am-8.30pm; 🍺) Fortunately, this spacious brewery at Tlaquepaque Village will satisfy your post-hike drinking needs (although it closes ridiculously early). The menu includes upmarket pub-style dishes like a grilled mahimahi salad and 'fire-kissed' pizza. Oak Creek also runs a low-frills **brewery** (📞 928-204-1300; www.oakcreekbrew.com; 2050 Yavapai Dr; ⊙ 4pm-close Mon-Thu, noon-close Fri-Sun) in West Sedona.

★ Elote Cafe   MEXICAN $$$
(📞 928-203-0105; www.elotecafe.com; Arabella Hotel, 771 Hwy 179; mains $19-26; ⊙ 5pm-late Tue-Sat) Some of the best, most authentic Mexican food in the region. Serves unusual traditional dishes you won't find elsewhere, like the namesake *elote* (fire-roasted corn with spicy mayo, lime and *cotija* cheese) or the tender, smoky pork cheeks.

❶ Information

Sedona Chamber of Commerce Visitor Center (📞 928-282-7722, 800-288-7336; www.visitsedona.com; 331 Forest Rd; ⊙ 8:30am-5pm) Located in Uptown Sedona, pick up free maps and brochures and buy a Red Rock Pass.

❶ Getting There & Around

Ace Xpress (📞 800-336-2239, 928-649-2720; www.acexshuttle.com; one way/round-trip adult $68/109, child $60/40; ⊙ office hours 7am-8pm Mon-Fri, 8am-8pm Sat & Sun) runs door-to-door shuttles between Phoenix Sky Harbor International Airport and Sedona For Jeep rentals, try **Barlow Jeep Rentals** (📞 928-282-8700, 800-928-5337; www.barlows.us; 3009 W Hwy 89A; half-/full-/3-day rental $195/295/589; ⊙ 8am-6pm).

Flagstaff

Flagstaff's laid-back charms are myriad, from its pedestrian-friendly historic downtown crammed with eclectic vernacular architecture and vintage neon to its high-altitude pursuits such as skiing and hiking. Locals are generally a happy, athletic bunch, skewing more toward granola than gunslinger. Northern Arizona University (NAU) gives Flagstaff its college-town flavor, while railroad history still figures firmly in its identity. Throw in a healthy appreciation for craft beer, freshly roasted coffee beans and an all-round good time, and you have the makings of a town you want to slow down and savor.

Flagstaff also makes an ideal gateway for visitors to the Grand Canyon. Hwy 180 is the most direct route northwest to Tusayan and the South Rim (80 miles), while Hwy 89 beelines north to Cameron (59 miles), from where Hwy 64 heads west to the canyon's East Entrance.

◉ Sights

Museum of Northern Arizona   MUSEUM
(📞 928-774-5213; www.musnaz.org; 3101 N Fort Valley Rd; adult/senior/child 10-17y $10/9/6; ⊙ 10am-5pm Mon-Sat, noon-5pm Sun; 🖼) Before venturing across the Colorado Plateau, introduce yourself to the region at this small but excellent museum that spotlights local Native American archaeology, history and culture, as well as geology, biology and the arts. Don't miss the extensive collection of Hopi kachina (also spelled katsina) dolls and a wonderful variety of Native American basketry and ceramics.

Lowell Observatory   OBSERVATORY
(📞 main phone 928-774-3358, recorded information 928-233-3211; www.lowell.edu; 1400 W Mars Hill Rd; adult/child 5-17yr $12/6; ⊙ 9am-10pm Jun-Aug, shorter hours Sep-May; 🖼) Sitting atop a hill just west of downtown, this National Historic Landmark was built by Percival Lowell in

1894. The first sighting of Pluto occurred here in 1930. Weather permitting, visitors can stargaze through on-site telescopes, including the famed Clark Telescope. This 1896 telescope was the impetus behind the now-accepted theory of an expanding universe.

Walnut Canyon RUIN
(☑928-526-3367; www.nps.gov/waca; I-40 exit 204, 8 miles east of Flagstaff; adult/child under 17 $5/free; ⊙8am-5pm May-Oct, from 9am Oct-May; entry to trails close 1hr before park closing; ☒) The Sinagua cliff dwellings here are set in the nearly vertical limestone walls of a small piñon-studded canyon. The mile-long Island Trail steeply descends 185ft (more than 200 stairs), passing 25 rooms built under the natural overhangs and a shorter, wheelchair-accessible Rim Trail affords views of the cliff dwelling from across the canyon.

🏃 Activities

Absolute Bikes BICYCLE RENTAL
(☑928-779-5969; www.absolutebikes.net; 202 E Route 66; bike rentals per day from $39; ⊙9am-7pm Mon-Fri, 9am-6pm Sat, 10am-4pm Sun Apr-Dec, shorter hr Jan-Mar) Visit the super-friendly gearheads for an inside track on the local mountain-biking scene.

Arizona Snowbowl SKIING
(☑928-779-1951; www.arizonasnowbowl.com; 9300 N Snowbowl Rd, Hwy 180 & Snowbowl Rd; lift ticket adult/youth 13-18yr/child 8-12yr $59/55/35; ⊙9am-4pm mid-Dec–mid-Apr) About 14 miles north of downtown, Arizona Snowbowl is small but lofty, with four lifts that service 32 ski runs between 9200ft and 11,500ft.

🛏 Sleeping

Flagstaff provides the widest range of lodging choices you'll find this close to the Grand Canyon. Unlike in southern Arizona, summer is high season.

Dubeau Hostel HOSTEL $
(☑928-774-6731; www.grandcanyonhostel.com; 19 W Phoenix Ave; dm $27, r $50-130; P☒@🛜) This independent hostel offers the same friendly service and clean, well-run accommodations as its sister property, Grand Canyon International Hostel. The basic rooms are like basic hotel rooms, with refrigerators and bathroom with showers, but at half the price. The quieter of the two hostels. Breakfast is included.

Grand Canyon International Hostel HOSTEL $
(☑928-779-9421; www.grandcanyonhostel.com; 19½ S San Francisco St; dm $25, r with shared bath $52-60; ☒@🛜) Housed in a historic building with hardwood floors and Southwestern decor, this bright, homey hostel offers private rooms or dorms with a four-person maximum. Dorms are small but clean. There's also a kitchen and laundry. This hotel gets more traffic than sister property Dubeau Hostel. Breakfast is included.

⭐ Inn at 410 B&B $$
(☑928-774-0088; www.inn410.com; 410 N Leroux St; r $170-220; P☒@🛜) This elegant and fully renovated 1894 house offers nine spacious, beautifully decorated and themed bedrooms, each with a refrigerator and private bathroom. Many rooms have four-poster beds and views of the garden or the San Francisco Peaks. A short stroll from downtown, the inn has a shady garden with fruit trees and a cozy dining room, where the full gourmet breakfast and afternoon snacks are served.

Hotel Monte Vista HISTORIC HOTEL $$
(☑928-779-6971; www.hotelmontevista.com; 100 N San Francisco St; r $85-160, ste $145-180; ☒🛜) A huge, old-fashioned neon sign towers over this allegedly haunted 1926 hotel, hinting at what's inside: feather lampshades, vintage furniture, bold colors and eclectic decor. Rooms are named for the movie stars who slept in them, such as the Humphrey Bogart room, with dramatic black walls, yellow ceiling and gold satin bedding. Several resident ghosts supposedly make regular appearances.

✗ Eating

Macy's
CAFE $

(www.macyscoffee.net; 14 S Beaver St; mains under $8; ⊗6am-8pm; 🖥🍴) The delicious house-roasted coffee at this Flagstaff institution has kept the city buzzing for more than 30 years now. The vegetarian menu includes many vegan choices, along with traditional cafe grub like pastries, steamed eggs, waffles, yogurt and granola, salads and veggie sandwiches.

Diablo Burger
BURGERS $

(✆928-774-3274; www.diabloburger.com; 120 N Leroux St; mains $11-14; ⊗11am-9pm Sun-Wed, to 10pm Thu-Sat) The beef maestros at this gourmet burger joint are so proud of their locally sourced creations that they sear the DB brand onto the English-muffin bun. The cheddar-topped Blake gives a nod to New Mexico with Hatch chile mayo and roasted green chiles. The place is tiny, so come early or plan to sit outside. Beer and wine are also served.

Beaver Street Brewery
BREWPUB $$

(www.beaverstreetbrewery.com; 11 S Beaver St; lunch $8-23, dinner $13-23; ⊗11am-11pm Sun-Thu, to midnight Fri & Sat; 🍴) Families, river guides, ski bums and businesspeople – everybody is here or on the way. The menu is typical brewpub fare, with delicious pizzas, burgers and salads, and there's usually eight hand-crafted beers on tap, like its Railhead Red Ale

or R&R Oatmeal Stout, plus some seasonal brews. Serious drinkers can walk next door to play pool at the 21-and-over Brews & Cues.

★ Brix Restaurant & Wine Bar
MODERN AMERICAN $$$

(✆928-213-1021; www.brixflagstaff.com; 413 N San Francisco St; mains $23-34; ⊗from 5pm Tue-Sat) Are you settled in at the bar? Inhale, look around, relax. This is your vacation reward. Brix brings a breath of fresh, unpretentious sophistication to Flagstaff's dining scene as well as easygoing but polished hospitality. The menu varies seasonally, regularly using what is fresh, ripe, local and organic for dishes like wild mushroom risotto with truffles and grilled rib-eye with red onion jam.

🍷 Drinking & Entertainment

Follow the 1-mile **Flagstaff Ale Trail** (www.flagstaffaletrail.com) to sample craft beer at downtown breweries and a pub or two.

★ Museum Club
BAR

(✆928-526-9434; www.themuseumclub.com; 3404 E Route 66; ⊗11am-2am) This honky-tonk roadhouse on Route 66 has been kicking up its heels since 1936. Inside what looks like a huge log cabin, you'll find a large wooden dance floor, animal mounts and a sumptuous elixir-filled mahogany bar. The origins of the name? In 1931 it housed a taxidermy museum.

ROADSIDE ATTRACTIONS ON ROUTE 66

Route 66 enthusiasts will find 400 miles of pavement stretching across Arizona, including the longest uninterrupted portion of old road left in the country, between Seligman and Topock. The **Mother Road** (www.azrt66.com) connects the dots between gun-slinging Oatman, Kingman's mining settlements, Williams' 1940s-vintage downtown and Winslow's windblown streets, with plenty of kitschy sights, listed here from west to east, along the way.

Wild burros of Oatman Mules beg for treats in the middle of the road.

Grand Canyon Caverns & Inn (✆928-422-3223; www.gccaverns.com; Rte 66, mile 115; 45min tour adult/child $20/13; ⊗9am-5pm Jun-Sep, 10am-5pm Oct-May; 🍴) A guided tour 21 stories underground loops past mummified bobcats, civil-defense supplies and an $800 motel room.

Burma Shave signs Red-and-white ads from a bygone era between Grand Canyon Caverns and Seligman.

Seligman's Snow-Cap Drive In Prankish burger and ice-cream joint open since 1953.

Meteor Crater (✆928-289-5898; www.meteorcrater.com; adult/child 6-17yr/senior $18/9/16; ⊗7am-7pm Jun–mid-Sep, 8am-5pm mid-Sep–May) A 550ft-deep pockmark that's nearly 1 mile across, 38 miles east of Flagstaff.

Wigwam Motel (✆928-524-3048; www.galerie-kokopelli.com/wigwam; 811 W Hopi Dr; r $56-62; ❋) Concrete wigwams with hickory logpole furniture in Holbrook.

Charly's Pub & Grill LIVE MUSIC
(☑928-779-1919; www.weatherfordhotel.com; 23 N Leroux St; ☺8am-2am) This restaurant at the Weatherford Hotel has regular live music. Its fireplace and brick walls provide a cozy setting for the blues, jazz and folk played here. Head upstairs to stroll the wraparound veranda outside the popular third-floor Zane Grey Ballroom, which overlooks the historic district.

❶ Information

Visitor Center (☑928-774-9541, 800-842-7293; www.flagstaffarizona.org; 1 E Route 66; ☺8am-5pm Mon-Sat, 9am-4pm Sun) Inside the Amtrak station, the visitor center has a great Flagstaff Discovery map and tons of information on things to do.

❶ Getting There & Away

Flagstaff Pulliam Airport is 4 miles south of town off I-17. **US Airways** (☑800-428-4322; www.usairways.com) offers several daily flights between Pulliam Airport and Phoenix Sky Harbor International Airport. **Greyhound** (☑800-231-2222, 928-774-4573; www.greyhound.com; 880 E Butler Ave; ☺midnight-6.30am, 10am-midnight Mon-Sun) stops in Flagstaff en route to/from Albuquerque, Las Vegas, Los Angeles and Phoenix. **Arizona Shuttle** (☑928-226-8060, 800-888-2749; www.arizonashuttle.com; ☺year-round) has shuttles that run to the park ($30 one-way), Sedona ($39 one-way) and Phoenix Sky Harbor Airport ($45 one-way).

Operated by **Amtrak** (☑928-774-8679, 800-872-7245; www.amtrak.com; 1 E Route 66; ☺3am-10.45pm), the Southwest Chief stops at Flagstaff on its daily run between Chicago and Los Angeles.

Williams

Affable Williams, 60 miles south of Grand Canyon Village and 35 miles west of Flagstaff, is a gateway town with character. Classic motels and diners line Route 66, and the old-school homes and train station give a nod to simpler times.

Most tourists visit to ride the turn-of-the-19th-century **Grand Canyon Railway** (☑reservations 800-843-8724; www.thetrain.com; Railway Depot, 233 N Grand Canyon Blvd; round-trip adult/child from $65/25; 🚻) to the South Rim, which departs Williams 9:30am and returns at 5:45pm. Even if you're not a train buff, a trip is a scenic stress-free way to visit the Grand Canyon. Characters in period costumes provide historical and regional narration, and banjo folk music sets the tone.

The **Red Garter Inn** (☑928-635-1484; www.redgarter.com; 137 W Railroad Ave; d $150-175; ❋☎) is an 1897 bordello turned B&B where the ladies used to hang out the windows to flag down customers. The four rooms have nice period touches and the downstairs bakery has good coffee. The funky little **Grand Canyon Hotel** (☑928-635-1419; www.thegrandcanyonhotel.com; 145 W Route 66; hostel dm/r $28/32, r with shared bath $70, r with private bath $75-125; ☺Mar-Nov; ❋@☎) has small themed rooms and a six-bed dorm room; no TVs. You can sleep inside a 1929 Santa Fe train caboose or a Pullman railcar at the **Canyon Motel & RV Park** (☑928-635-9371; www.thecanyonmotel.com; 1900 E Rodeo Rd; tent/RV sites $31/43, r $88-94, train cars $94-192; ❋☎❋❋), just east of downtown.

Grand Canyon National Park

No matter how much you read about the Grand Canyon, or how many photographs you've seen, nothing really prepares you for the sight of it. The sheer immensity of the canyon grabs you first, followed by the dramatic layers of rock, which pull you in for a closer look. Next up are the artistic details – rugged plateaus, crumbly spires, maroon ridges – that flirt and catch your eye as shadows flicker across the rock.

Snaking along its floor are 277 miles of the Colorado River, which has carved the canyon over the past six million years and exposed rocks up to two billion years old – half the age of the earth.

The two rims of the Grand Canyon offer quite different experiences; they lie more than 200 miles apart by road and are rarely visited on the same trip. Most visitors choose the South Rim with its easy access, wealth of services and vistas that don't disappoint. The quieter North Rim has its own charms; at 8200ft elevation (1000ft higher than the South Rim), its cooler temperatures support wildflower meadows and tall, thick stands of aspen and spruce.

June is the driest month, July and August the wettest. January has average overnight lows of 13°F (-11°C) to 20°F (-7°C) and daytime highs around 40°F (4°C). Summer temperatures inside the canyon regularly soar above 100°F (38°C). While the South Rim is open year-round, most visitors come between late May and early September.

Grand Canyon National Park

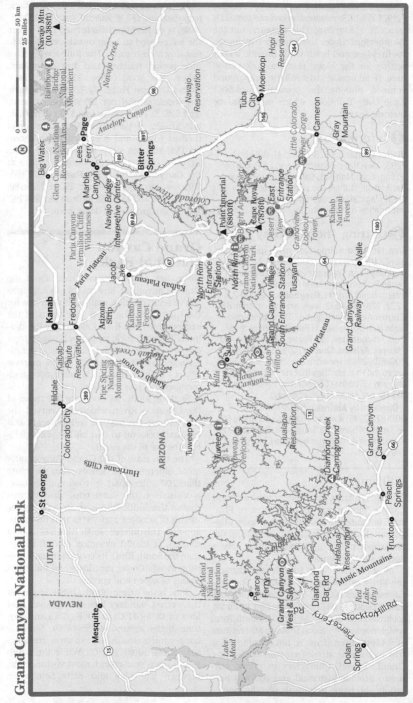

The North Rim is open from mid-May to mid-October.

❶ Information

The most developed area in the **Grand Canyon National Park** (☑ 928-638-7888; www.nps.gov/grca; vehicles/cyclists & pedestrians $25/12) is Grand Canyon Village, 6 miles north of the South Rim Entrance Station. The North Rim has one entrance, which is 30 miles south of Jacob Lake on Hwy 67; continue another 14 miles south to the actual rim. The North and South Rims are 215 miles apart by car, 21 miles on foot through the canyon, or 10 miles as the condor flies.

The park entrance ticket is valid for seven days and can be used at both rims.

All overnight hikes and backcountry camping in the park require a permit. The **Backcountry Information Center** (☑ 928-638-7875; www.nps.gov/grca; Grand Canyon Village; ⊘ 8am-noon & 1-5pm, phone staffed 1-5pm Mon-Fri; ▣ Village) accepts applications for backpacking permits ($10, plus $5 per person per night) starting four months before the proposed month. Your chances are decent if you apply early and provide alternative hiking itineraries. Reservations are accepted in person or by mail or fax, *not* by phone or email. For more information see www.nps.gov/grca/planyourvisit/backcountry-permit.htm.

If you arrive at the South Rim without a permit, head to the backcountry office, by Maswik Lodge, to join the waiting list.

As a conservation measure, the park no longer sells bottled water. Fill your flask at water filling stations along the rim or at Canyon View Marketplace.

SOUTH RIM VISITOR CENTERS

Grand Canyon Visitor Center (☑ 928-638-7888; www.nps.gov/grca; Visitor Center Plaza, Grand Canyon Village; ⊘ 8am-5pm Mar-Nov, 9am-5pm Dec-Feb; ▣ Village, Kaibab/Rim) Three hundred yards behind Mather Point, a large plaza holds the visitor center and the Books & More Store. Outdoor bulletin boards display information about trails, tours, ranger programs and the weather.

National Geographic Visitor Center (☑ 928-638-2468; www.explorethecanyon.com; 450 Hwy 64, Tusayan; adult/child $14/11; ⊘ 8am-10pm Mar-Oct, 10am-8pm Nov-Feb) In Tusayan, 7 miles south of Grand Canyon Village; pay your $25 vehicle entrance fee here to spare yourself a potentially long wait at the park entrance. The IMAX theater screens the terrific film *Grand Canyon – The Hidden Secrets*.

In addition to the visitor centers listed above, information is available inside the park at:

Yavapai Museum of Geology (www.nps.gov/grca; Grand Canyon Village; ⊘ 8am-7pm Mar-May & Sep-Nov, to 6pm Dec-Feb, to 8pm Jun-Aug; ⊞ ; ▣ Kaibab/Rim), **Verkamp's Visitor Center** (www.nps.gov/grca; National Historic Landmark District, Grand Canyon Village; ⊘ 8am-7pm; ⊞ ; ▣ Village), **Kolb Studio** (☑ 928-638-2771; www.nps.gov/grca; National Historic Landmark District, Grand Canyon Village; ⊘ 8am-7pm Mar-May & Sep-Nov, to 6pm Dec-Feb, to 8pm Jun-Aug; ⊞ ; ▣ Village), **Tusayan Ruin & Museum** (www.nps.gov/grca; Desert View Dr; ⊘ 9am-5pm; ⊞) and **Desert View Information Center** (☑ 928-638-7893; ⊘ 8am-5pm Jun-Aug, from 9am rest of year).

South Rim

If you don't mind bumping elbows with other travelers, you'll be fine on the South Rim, where you'll find an entire village worth of lodging, restaurants, bookstores, libraries, a supermarket and a deli. Museums and historic stone buildings illuminate the park's human history, and rangers lead daily programs on subjects from geology to resurgent condors.

In summer, when day-trippers converge en masse, escaping the crowds can be as easy as taking a day hike below the rim or merely tramping a hundred yards away from a scenic overlook.

🏃 Activities

Driving & Hiking

A scenic route follows the rim on the west side of Grand Canyon Village along Hermit Rd. Closed to private vehicles March through November, the 7-mile road is serviced by free park shuttle buses; cycling is encouraged because of the relatively light traffic. Stops offer spectacular views and interpretive signs explain canyon features.

Desert View Drive starts east of Grand Canyon Village and follows the canyon rim for 26 miles to Desert View, the east entrance of the park. Pullouts offer tremendous views.

Hiking trails along the South Rim include options for every skill level. The Rim Trail is the most popular, and easiest, walk in the park. It dips in and out of the scrubby pines of Kaibab National Forest to connect scenic points and historical sights over 13 miles. Portions are paved, and every viewpoint is accessed by one of the three shuttle routes. Along the Trail of Time, bordering the Rim Trail just west of Yavapai Museum of Geology, every meter represents one million years of geologic history.

Hiking down into the canyon itself is a serious undertaking; most visitors content themselves with short day hikes. Bear in mind that the climb back out of the canyon is much harder than the descent into it, and do not attempt to hike all the way to the Colorado River and back in a single day. On the most popular route, the beautiful **Bright Angel Trail**, the scenic 8-mile drop to the river is punctuated with four logical turnaround spots. Summer heat can be crippling; day hikers should either turn around at one of the two resthouses (a 3- or 6-mile round-trip) or hit the trail at dawn to safely make the longer hikes to Indian Garden and Plateau Point (9.2 and 12.2 miles round-trip respectively).

The steeper and much more exposed **South Kaibab Trail** is one of the park's prettiest routes, combining stunning scenery and unobstructed 360-degree views with every step. Hikers overnighting at Phantom Ranch generally descend this way, and return the next day via the Bright Angel. Summer ascents can be dangerous, and during this season rangers advise day hikers to turn around at **Cedar Ridge**, (about 3 miles round-trip), for the park's finest short day hike.

Cycling

Bright Angel Bicycles & Cafe at Mather Point   BICYCLE RENTAL
(☑ 928-814-8704, 928-638-3055; www.bikegrandcanyon.com; Visitor Center Plaza, Grand Canyon Village; 24hr rental adult/child 16yr & under $40/30, 5hr rental $30/20; wheelchair $10; single/double stroller up to 8hrs $18/27; ☺ Apr-Nov; ☐ Village, ☐ Kaibab/Rim) Renting 'comfort cruiser' bikes on the South Rim, the friendly folks here custom-fit each bike to the individual. Rates include helmet; child trailers, strollers and wheelchairs also available. Roads bikes are $45 per day. Three-hour interpretative tours are also offered, with trips on on either Hermit Rd or Yaki Rd (adult/child 15years and under from $48/38).

☞ Tours

Grand Canyon Mule Rides   GUIDED TOUR
(☑ 888-297-2757, same-/next-day reservation 928-638-3283; www.grandcanyonlodges.com; Bright Angel Lodge; 3hr mule ride $120, 1-/2-night mule ride $533/758 incl meals & accommodation; ☺ rides available year-round, hours vary; ♿) Due to erosion concerns, the NPS has limited inner-canyon mule rides to those traveling all the way to Phantom Ranch. Rather than

going below the rim, three-hour day trips now take riders along the rim, through the ponderosa, piñon and juniper forest to the Abyss overlook. Overnight trips and two-night trips follow the Bright Angel Trail to the river, travel east on the River Trail and cross the river on the Kaibab Suspension Bridge. Riders spend the night at Phantom Ranch. If you arrive at the park and want to join a mule trip the following day, ask about availability at the transportation desk at Bright Angel Lodge.

🛏 Sleeping

The South Rim's six lodges are operated by **Xanterra** (☑ 888-297-2757, 303-297-2757, 928-638-3283; www.grandcanyonlodges.com). Contact them to make advance reservations (essential in summer), although it's best to call Phantom Ranch, down beside the Colorado River, directly. For same-day reservations or to reach a guest, call the South Rim switchboard (☑ 928-638-2631). If you can't find accommodations in the national park, try Tusayan (at South Rim Entrance Station), Valle (31 miles south), Cameron (53 miles east), Williams (about 60 miles south) or Flagstaff (80 miles southeast).

All campgrounds and lodges are open year-round except Desert View.

Phantom Ranch   CABIN $
(☑ 888-297-2757, same-/next-day reservation 928-638-3283; www.grandcanyonlodges.com; Grand Canyon National Park, canyon bottom; dm/d cabin $48/135; ✶) Bunks at this camplike complex are spread across cozy private cabins sleeping up to four people and single-sex dorms outfitted for 10 people. Rates include bedding, liquid soap and towels, but meals are extra and must be reserved when booking your bunk. You're free to bring your own food and stove.

Desert View Campground   CAMPGROUND $
(www.nps.gov/grca; Desert View, East Entrance; campsites $12; reservations not accepted; ☺ mid-April–mid-Oct; ✶) In a piñon-juniper forest near the East Entrance, this first-come, first-served campground with 50 sites is quieter than Mather Campground in the Village, with a nicely spread-out design that ensures a bit of privacy. The best time to secure a spot is mid-morning, when people are breaking camp; usually fills by mid-afternoon. Facilities include toilets and drinking water, but no showers or hookups.

Mather Campground
CAMPGROUND **$**

(📞877-444-6777, late arrival 928-638-7851; www.recreation.gov; Market Plaza, Grand Canyon Village; sites $18; ⊙year-round; 🛜🐾; 🖥 Village) Sites are shaded and fairly well dispersed, and the flat ground offers a comfy platform for your tent. You'll find pay showers, laundry facilities, drinking water, toilets, grills and a small general store; a full grocery store is a short walk away. Reservations are accepted from March through November; the rest of the year it's first-come, first-served. No hookups.

Trailer Village
CAMPGROUND **$**

(📞877-404-4611, same-day reservation 928-638-3047; www.visitgrandcanyon.com; Market Plaza, Grand Canyon Village; hook-ups $36; ⊙year-round; 🐾; 🖥 Village) This Xanterra-run campground is basically a trailer park, with RVs lined up tightly at paved pull-through sites amid a rather barren patch of ground. Check for spots with trees on the far north side. You'll find picnic tables, barbecue grills and full hook-ups, but showers are a quarter-mile away at Mather Campground.

Bright Angel Lodge
LODGE **$$**

(📞888-297-2757, front desk & reservations within 48hr 928-638-2631 ext 6285; www.grandcanyonlodges.com; National Historic Landmark District, Grand Canyon Village; r with bath $100, r without bath $77-89, ste $426, cabins $128-197; P 🛜; 🖥 Village) This 1935 log-and-stone lodge on the ledge delivers historic charm by the bucketload as well as nicely appointed rooms. Public spaces, though, are busy and less elegant. If you're economizing, get a basic double (no TV – just a bed, desk and sink) with shared bathrooms down the hall. Cabins are brighter, airier and have tasteful Western character; the most expensive have rim views.

Maswik Lodge
MOTEL **$$**

(📞888-297-2757, front desk & reservations within 48hrs 928-638-2631 ext 6784; www.grandcanyonlodges.com; Grand Canyon Village; r south/north $107/205; P ❄ @ 🛜; 🖥 Village) The Maswik Lodge complex includes 18 modern two-story buildings set in the woods; rooms are of the standard motel variety. Rooms at Maswik North feature private patios, air-con, cable TV, high ceilings and forest views, while those at Maswik South are smaller, with fewer amenities, no air-con and more forgettable views.

Kachina & Thunderbird Lodges
LODGE **$$**

(📞888-297-2757, reservations within 48hr 928-638-2631; www.grandcanyonlodges.com; National Historic Landmark District, Grand Canyon Village; r streetside/rimside $216/232; P ❄ 🛜; 🖥 Village) Beside the Rim Trail between El Tovar and Bright Angel, these institutional-looking lodges, built in the late 1960s, offer standard motel-style rooms with two queen beds, full bath, flat-screen TV, Keurig coffeemaker and a refrigerator. It's worth spending up a little for the rimside rooms, some with partial canyon views.

Yavapai Lodge
MOTEL **$$**

(📞877-404-4611, reservations within 48hr 928-638-6421; www.visitgrandcanyon.com; Market Plaza, Grand Canyon Village; r West/East $140/174; ⊙year-round; P ❄ @ 🛜 🐾; 🖥 Village) The motel-style lodgings are stretched out amid a peaceful piñon and juniper forest. Rooms in Yavapai East are in six two-story buildings with air-conditioning, while rooms in Yavapai West are spread out in 10 single-story buildings, with vault ceilings but no air-conditioning. These are basic, clean motel rooms with tubs, showers and TVs.

★ El Tovar
LODGE **$$$**

(📞888-297-2757, front desk & res within 48hrs 928-638-2631 ext 6380; www.grandcanyonlodges.com; National Historic Landmark District, Grand Canyon Village; r $187-305, ste $381-465; ⊙year-round; P ❄ 🛜; 🖥 Village) Stuffed mounts. Thick pine walls. Sturdy fireplaces. Is this the fanciest hotel on the South Rim or a backcountry hunting lodge? We'd say it's a charismatic mix of both. Despite renovations, this rambling 1905 wooden lodge hasn't lost a lick of its genteel historic patina, or its charm.

🍴 Eating & Drinking

Maswik Food Court
CAFETERIA **$**

(📞928-638-2631; www.grandcanyonlodges.com; Maswik Lodge, Grand Canyon Village; mains $7-13; ⊙6am-10pm May-Aug, varies rest of year; ♿; 🖥 Village) Though fairly predictable, the food encompasses a nice variety and isn't too greasy. The various food stations serve burgers, pasta, Mexican food, chili bowls and hot turkey sandwiches. Deli and grab-and-go sandwiches also available. The adjoining Maswik Pizza Pub serves beer and shows sporting events on TV.

Yavapai Lodge Restaurant   AMERICAN $
(☑928-638-6421; www.visitgrandcanyon.com; Yavapai Lodge, Market Plaza, Grand Canyon Village; breakfast $7-12, lunch & dinner $8-22; ⊙ 6.30am-9pm May-Aug, varies rest of year; ⚿; ☐Village) Next to Yavapai Lodge, this cafe has burgers, salads, hot dogs and pizzas. Closed November through February, except for holidays.

Canyon Village Deli   CAFETERIA $
(☑928-638-2262; Canyon Village Market, Market Plaza, Grand Canyon Village; mains $3-9; ⊙8am-6pm May-Aug, varies rest of year; ⚿; ☐Village) Fresh-made sandwiches, hot dogs and grab-and-go meals inside the grocery store.

★ **El Tovar Dining Room & Lounge**   AMERICAN $$$
(☑928-638-2631; www.grandcanyonlodges.com; El Tovar, National Historic Landmark District, Grand Canyon Village; mains $17-35; ⊙restaurant 6.30-10.45am & 11.15am-2pm & 4.30-10pm, lounge 11am-11pm; ⚿; ☐Village) The setting and the food are equally superb. Dark-wood tables are set with china and white linen, eye-catching murals spotlight Native American tribes and huge windows frame views of the rim and canyon. The service is generally excellent, the menu creative, and the portions big.

Arizona Room   AMERICAN $$$
(www.grandcanyonlodges.com; Bright Angel Lodge, National Historic Landmark District, Grand Canyon Village; mains $12-29; ⊙11.30am-3pm Jan-Oct & 4.30-10pm; ⚿; ☐Village) Antler chandeliers hang from the ceiling and picture windows overlook a small lawn, the rim walk and the canyon. Try to get on the waitlist when doors open at 4:30pm, because by 4:40pm you may have an hour's wait – reservations are not accepted. Mains include steak, chicken and fish dishes, while appetizers include such creative options as pulled-pork quesadillas.

ⓘ Getting There & Around

Most people arrive at the canyon in private vehicles or on a tour. Parking can be a chore in Grand Canyon Village. Once inside the park, free park shuttles operate along three routes: around Grand Canyon Village, west along Hermits Rest Route and east along Kaibab Trail Route. Buses typically run every 15 minutes, from one hour before sunset to one hour afterward.

In summer a free shuttle from Bright Angel Lodge, the Hiker's Express, has early-morning pickups at the Backcountry Information Center and Grand Canyon Visitor Center, and then heads to the South Kaibab trailhead.

North Rim

Solitude reigns supreme on the North Rim. There are no shuttles or bus tours, no museums, shopping centers, schools or garages. In fact, there isn't much of anything here beyond a classic rimside national park lodge, a campground, a motel, a general store and miles of trails carving through sunny meadows thick with wildflowers, willowy aspen and towering ponderosa pines.

The entrance to the North Rim is 24 miles south of Jacob Lake on Hwy 67; Grand Canyon Lodge lies another 20 miles beyond.

RAFTING THE COLORADO RIVER

A boat trip down the Colorado is an epic, adrenaline-pumping adventure, which will take you beyond contact with civilization for several nights. The biggest single drop at Lava Falls plummets 37ft in just 300yd. But the true highlight is experiencing the Grand Canyon by looking up, not down from the rim. Its human history comes alive in ruins, wrecks and rock art. Commercial trips run from three days to three weeks and vary in the type of watercraft used. At night you camp under stars on sandy beaches (gear provided). It takes about two or three weeks to run the entire 279 miles of river through the canyon. Shorter sections of around 100 miles take four to nine days. Space is limited and the trips are popular, so book well in advance.

Arizona Raft Adventures (☑800-786-7238, 928-526-8200; www.azraft.com; 6-day Upper Canyon hybrid/paddle trips $2050/2150, 10-day Full Canyon motor trips $3000) This multigenerational family-run outfit offers paddle, oar, hybrid (with opportunities for both paddling and floating) and motor trips. Music fans can join one of the folk and bluegrass trips, with professional pickers and banjo players providing background music.

Arizona River Runners (☑602-867-4866, 800-477-7238; www.raftarizona.com; 6-day Upper Canyon oar trip $1984, 8-day Full Canyon motor trip $2745) Has been at its game since 1970, offering oar-powered and motorized trips.

At 8000ft, it's about 10°F (6°C) cooler here than the South Rim – even on summer evenings you'll need a sweater. All facilities on the North Rim are closed from mid-October to mid-May, although you can drive into the park and stay at the campground until snow closes the road from Jacob Lake.

Activities

The short and easy paved trail (0.5 miles) to **Bright Angel Point** is a canyon must. Beginning from the back porch of Grand Canyon Lodge, it goes to a narrow finger of an overlook with fabulous views.

The **North Kaibab Trail**, the North Rim's only maintained rim-to-river trail, connects with trails to the South Rim in the Phantom Ranch area. The first 4.7 miles are the steepest, dropping 3050ft to **Roaring Springs** – a popular all-day hike. If you prefer a shorter day hike below the rim, walk just 0.75 miles down to **Coconino Overlook**, or 2 miles to the **Supai Tunnel** to get a taste of steep inner-canyon hiking. The 28-mile round-trip to the Colorado River is a multiday affair.

For a short hike up on the rim, which works well for families, try the 4-mile round-trip **Cape Final** trail, on the Walhalla Plateau east of Grand Canyon Lodge, which leads through ponderosa pines to sweeping views of the eastern Grand Canyon area.

Canyon Trail Rides (☑ 435-679-8665; www. canyonrides.com; North Rim; 1hr/half-day mule ride $40/80; ☉ schedules vary mid-May–mid-Oct) offers mule trips. Of the half-day trips (minimum age 10 years), one is along the rim and the other drops into the Canyon on the North Kaibab Trail.

Sleeping

Accommodations are limited to one lodge and one campground. If these are booked, try your luck 80 miles north in Kanab, UT, or 84 miles northeast in Lees Ferry. There are also campgrounds in the Kaibab National Forest north of the park.

North Rim Campground   CAMPGROUND $
(☑ 928-638-7814, 877-444-6777; www.recreation. gov; tent sites $18, RV sites $18-25; ☉ mid-May–mid-Oct by reservation, first-come, first-served Oct 16-31; ☻) This campground, 1.5 miles north of the lodge, offers shaded sites on level ground blanketed in pine needles. Sites 11, 14, 15, 16 and 18 overlook the Transept (a side canyon) and cost $25. There's water, a store, a snack bar, coin-op showers and laun-

dry facilities, but no hookups. Reservations are accepted up to six months in advance.

Grand Canyon Lodge   HISTORIC HOTEL $$
(☑ advance reservations 877-386-4383, reservations outside USA 480-337-1320, same-day reservations 928-638-2611; www.grandcanyonlodgenorth. com; r $130, cabins per 2 people $138-191; ☉ mid-May–mid-Oct) ☞ Walk through the front door of Grand Canyon Lodge into the lofty sunroom and there, framed by picture windows, is the canyon in all its glory. Rooms are not in the lodge itself, but in rustic cabins sleeping up to five people. The nicest are the bright and spacious Western cabins, made of logs and buffered by trees and grass.

Eating & Drinking

The lodge will prepare sack lunches ($15), ready for pickup as early as 5:30am, for those wanting to picnic on the trail. Place your order the day before. For sandwiches, pizza and breakfast burritos, try **Deli in the Pines** (Grand Canyon Lodge; lunch & dinner $7-15; ☉ 10.30am-9pm mid-May–mid-Oct), also at the Lodge.

★ **Grand Canyon**
Lodge Dining Room   AMERICAN $$
(☑ 928-638-2611, off-season 928-645-6865; www. grandcanyonlodgenorth.com; mains breakfast $6-13, lunch $10-15, dinner $13-33; ☉ 6.30-10am, 11.30am-2.30pm & 4.45-9.45pm mid-May–mid-Oct; ☻) Although seats beside the window are wonderful, views from the dining room are so huge it really doesn't matter where you sit. While the solid dinner menu includes buffalo steak, western trout and several vegetarian options, don't expect culinary memories – the view is the thing. Make reservations in advance of your arrival to guarantee a spot for dinner (reservations are not accepted for breakfast or lunch).

Grand Canyon
Cookout Experience   AMERICAN $$$
(☑ 928-638-2611; Grand Canyon Lodge; adult/child 6-15yr $30/$15; ☉ 5.45pm Jun 1-Sep 30; ☻) Chow down on barbecued meat, roasted chicken, skillet cornbread and beans served buffet-style with a side of Western songs and cheesy jokes. A cute steam train will take you there.

ⓘ Information

North Rim Visitor Center (☑ 928-638-7864; www.nps.gov/grca; North Rim; ☉ 8am-6pm) Beside Grand Canyon Lodge, this is the place to get information on the park, and the starting point for ranger-led nature walks.

ℹ Getting There & Around

The **Transcanyon Shuttle** (☏ 877-638-2820, 928-638-2820; www.trans-canyonshuttle.com; one way rim-to-rim $85, one-way South Rim to Marble Canyon $70; ☺ mid-May–mid-Oct) departs daily from Grand Canyon Lodge for the South Rim (five hours) and is perfect for rim-to-rim hikers. Reserve at least one or two weeks in advance. A complimentary hikers' shuttle to the North Kaibab Trail departs at both 5:45am and 7:10am from Grand Canyon Lodge. You must sign up for it at the front desk 24 hours ahead; if no one signs up, it will not run.

Around the Grand Canyon

Havasu Canyon

In a hidden side canyon off the Colorado River, complete with stunning, spring-fed waterfalls and azure swimming holes, this beautiful spot is hard to reach, but the hike down and back up makes the trip unique – and an amazing adventure.

Located on the Havasupai Indian Reservation, Havasu Canyon is just 35 miles directly west of the South Rim, but it's more like 195 miles by road. The four falls lie 10 miles below the rim, accessed via a moderately challenging hiking trail that starts from Hualapai Hilltop, and is reached by following a 62-mile road that leaves Route 66 7 miles east of Peach Springs.

All trips require an overnight stay, which must be reserved in advance, and there's a $35 entrance fee for all guests. The village of Supai, 8 miles along the trail, is home to the **Havasupai Lodge** (☏ 928-448-2201, 928-448-2111; www.havasuwaterfalls.net; Supai; r for up to 4 people $145; ❀), where the motel-style rooms have canyon views but no phones or TVs. Check in by 5pm, when the lobby closes. A village cafe serves meals and accepts credit cards. The Havasupai Campground, 2 miles beyond, has primitive campsites along a creek; every camper must pay an additional $5 environmental fee. Continue deeper into Havasu Canyon to reach the waterfalls and blue-green swimming holes.

If you don't want to hike to Supai, call the lodge or campground to arrange for a mule or horse (round-trip to lodge/campground $135/197) to carry you there.

Hualapai Nation

Run by the Hualapai Nation, around 215 driving miles west of the South Rim 70 miles northeast of Kingman, the remote site known as Grand Canyon West is not part of Grand Canyon National Park. The rough road out here is partly unpaved, and unsuitable for RVs.

Grand Canyon West
(West Rim)   SCENIC OVERLOOK
(☏ 888-868-9378, 928-769-2636; www.grandcanyonwest.com; Hualapai Reservation; per person $44-81; ☺ 7am-7pm Apr-Sep, 8am-5pm Oct-Mar) Nowadays, the only way to visit Grand Canyon West, the section of the west rim overseen by the Hualapai Nation, is to purchase a package tour. These include a hop-on, hop-off shuttle ride which loops to scenic points along the rim. Tours can include lunch, cowboy activities at an ersatz Western town and informal Native American performances.

All but the cheapest package include admission to the Grand Canyon Skywalk, the horseshoe-shaped glass bridge cantilevered 4000ft above the canyon floor. Jutting out almost 70ft over the canyon, the Skywalk allows visitors to see the canyon through the glass walkway. Another stop, the unfortunately named Guano Point, is good for lunch, shopping and a bit of exploring, with fantastic canyon and river views.

Since would-be visitors to the Skywalk are required to purchase a package tour – and the extra-cost Skywalk is the primary draw – the experience can be a pricey prospect.

Northeastern Arizona

Between the brooding buttes of Monument Valley, the blue waters of Lake Powell and the fossilized logs of the Petrified Forest National Park are photogenic lands locked in ancient history. Inhabited by Native Americans for centuries, this region is dominated by the Navajo reservation – widely known as the Navajo Nation – which spills into surrounding states. The Hopi reservation is here as well, completely surrounded by Navajo land.

Lake Powell

The country's second-largest artificial reservoir, Lake Powell, stretches north from Arizona into Utah. Set amid striking red-rock formations, sharply cut canyon and dramatic desert scenery, and part of the **Glen Canyon National Recreation Area** (☑928-608-6200; www.nps.gov/glca; 7-day pass per vehicle $15, per pedestrian or cyclist $7), it's water-sports heaven.

The lake was created by the construction of Glen Canyon Dam, 2.5 miles north of what's now the region's central town, Page. The Carl Hayden Visitor Center is located beside the dam.

To visit photogenic **Antelope Canyon**, a stunning sandstone slot canyon, you must join a tour. Several tour companies offer trips into **Upper Antelope Canyon**, which is easier to navigate. Expect a bumpy ride and a bit of a cattle call; try **Roger Ekis' Antelope Canyon Tours** (☑928-645-9102; www.antelope-canyon.com; 22 S Lake Powell Blvd; adult/child 5-12yr from $37/27). The more strenuous **Lower Antelope Canyon** sees much smaller crowds.

A deservedly popular hike is the 1.5 mile round-trip trek to **Horseshoe Bend**, where the river wraps around a dramatic stone outcropping to form a perfect U. The trailhead is south of Page off Hwy 89, across from mile marker 541.

Chain hotels line Page's main strip, Hwy 89, with independent alternatives along 8th Ave. The revamped **Lake Powell Motel** (☑928-645-3919; www.powellmotel.com; 750 S Navajo Dr; $69-159; ☉Apr-Oct; ❈🛜) was originally built to house Glen Canyon Dam builders; four of its units have kitchens, and book up quickly, while a fifth, smaller room is usually held for walk-ins.

For breakfast in Page, the **Ranch House Grille** (www.ranchhousegrille.com; 819 N Navajo Dr; mains $7-16; ☉6am-3pm) has good food, huge portions and fast service. The murals of local landcapes are impressive inside **Bonkers** (☑928-645-2706; www.bonkerspageaz.com; 810 N Navajo Dr; mains $9-23; ☉4pm-close Mar-Oct), which serves satisfying steaks, seafood, pasta and a few burgers and sandwiches.

Navajo Nation

Arizona's Navajo lands hold some of North America's most spectacular scenery, including Monument Valley and Canyon de Chelly. Cultural pride remains strong and many speak Navajo as their first language. The Navajo rely heavily on tourism; visitors can help keep Navajo heritage alive by staying on reservation land or purchasing crafts. Stopping at roadside stalls offers a great opportunity for personal interaction and helps to ensure that money goes straight into the artisan's pocket.

HOPI INDIAN RESERVATION

Direct descendants of the Ancestral Puebloans, the Hopi have arguably changed less in the last five centuries than any other Native American group. Their village of Old Oraibi may be the oldest continuously inhabited settlement in North America.

Hopi land is surrounded by the Navajo Nation. Hwy 264 runs past the three mesas (First, Second and Third Mesa) that form the heart of the reservation. On Second Mesa, 8 miles west of First Mesa, the **Hopi Cultural Center Restaurant & Inn** (☑928-734-2401; www.hopiculturalcenter.com; Hwy 264; r $95-105, meals $7-16; ☉restaurant 7am-9pm summer, to 8pm winter) is as visitor-oriented as things get on the Hopi reservation. It provides food and lodging, and holds the small **Hopi Museum** (☑928-734-6650; adult/child 12yr & under $3/1; ☉8am-5pm Mon-Fri, 9am-3pm Sat), filled with historic photographs and cultural exhibits.

Photographs, sketching and recording are not allowed.

Unlike the rest of Arizona, the Navajo Nation observes mountain daylight saving time. During summer, the reservation is one hour ahead of Arizona.

For details about hiking and camping, and required permits, visit www.navajonationparks.org.

CAMERON

Cameron, a historic settlement that serves as the gateway to the east entrance of the Grand Canyon's South Rim, is one of the few worthwhile stops on Hwy 89 between Flagstaff and Page. The **Cameron Trading Post** (☑gift shop 928-679-2231, motel 800-338-7385; www.camerontradingpost.com; Hwy 89; r $109, ste $179; ☉6am-9.30pm summer, 7am-9pm winter; ❈🛜), just north of the Hwy 64 turnoff to the Grand Canyon, offers food, lodging, a gift shop and a post office.

CANYON DE CHELLY NATIONAL MONUMENT

The many-fingered Canyon De Chelly (pronounced *duh-shay*) contains several beautiful Ancestral Puebloan sites, including ancient cliff dwellings. For centuries, though, it has been home to Navajo farmers, who winter on the rims then move to hogans on the canyon floor in spring and summer. The canyon is private Navajo property administered by the NPS. Enter hogans only with a guide and don't photograph people without their permission.

The only lodging in the park is **Sacred Canyon Lodge** (☑ 800-679-2473; www.sacredcanyonlodge.com; r $99-109, ste $169; ✳ @ ⛱ ☷), formerly Thunderbird Lodge, which is just outside the canyon itself. It has comfortable rooms and an inexpensive cafeteria serving Navajo and American meals. The nearby Navajo-run campground has about 90 sites on a first-come, first-served basis ($10), with water but no showers.

The Canyon de Chelly **visitor center** (☑ 928-674-5500; www.nps.gov/cach; ☺ 8am-5pm) is 3 miles off Rte 191, beyond the small village of Chinle, near the mouth of the canyon. Two scenic drives follow the canyon's rim, but you can only explore the canyon floor on a guided tour. Stop by the visitor center, or check the park website, for a list of tour companies. The only unguided hiking trail you can follow in the park is a short but very spectacular round-trip route that descends to the amazing **White House Ruin**.

FOUR CORNERS NAVAJO TRIBAL PARK

Don't be shy: do a spread eagle at the **four corners marker** (☑ 928-871-6647; www.navajonationparks.org; admission $3; ☺ 8am-7pm May-Sep, 8am-5pm Oct-Apr), the middle-of-nowhere landmark that's the only spot in the US where you can straddle four states – Arizona, New Mexico, Colorado, Utah. It makes a good photograph, even if it's not 100% accurate; according to government surveyors, the marker is almost 2000ft east of where it should be, even if it is the legally recognized border point.

MONUMENT VALLEY NAVAJO TRIBAL PARK

With flaming-red buttes and impossibly slender spires bursting to the heavens, the Monument Valley landscape off Hwy 163 has starred in countless Hollywood Westerns and looms large in many a road-trip daydream.

For up-close views of the towering formations, visit the **Monument Valley Navajo Tribal Park** (☑ 435-727-5874; www.navajonationparks.org; per 4-person vehicle $20; ☺ drive 6am-8:30pm May-Sep, 8am-4:30pm Oct-Apr; visitor center 6am-8pm May-Sep, 8am-5pm Oct-Apr), where a rough and unpaved scenic driving loop covers 17 miles of stunning valley views.

You can drive it in your own vehicle, or arrange a tour through one of the kiosks in the parking lot, which will take you to areas where private vehicles can't go (1½ hours $75, 2½ hours $95) .

Inside the tribal park, the sandstone-colored **View Hotel at Monument Valley** (☑ 435-727-5555; www.monumentvalleyview.com; Hwy 163; r/ste from $209/$299; ✳ @ ⛱) blends naturally with its surroundings, and most of the 96 rooms have private balconies facing the monuments. The Navajo-based specialties at the adjoining restaurant (mains $10 to $30, no alcohol) are mediocre, but the red-rock panorama is stunning. The revamped **Monument Valley Campground** (☑ 435-727-5802; www.monumentvalley.com/campground; tent/RV sites $20/40) is located at the other end of the parking lot.

The historic **Goulding's Lodge** (☑ 435-727-3231; www.gouldings.com; r $205-242; ✳ ⛱ ☷ ☷), just across the border in Utah, offers lodge rooms, camping and small cabins. Book early for summer. Kayenta, 20 miles south, holds a handful of okay hotels; try the **Wetherill Inn** (☑ 928-697-3231; www.wetherill-inn.com; 1000 Main St/Hwy 163; r incl breakfast $140; ✳ @ ⛱ ☷) if everything in Monument Valley is booked.

Winslow

'Standing on a corner in Winslow, Arizona, such a fine sight to see...' Sound familiar? Thanks to the Eagles' twangy 1970s tune 'Take It Easy,' otherwise nondescript Winslow has earned its wings in pop-culture heaven. A small **park** (www.standinonthecorner.com; 2nd St & Kinsley Ave) on Route 66 at Kinsley Ave pays homage to the band.

Just 50 miles east of Petrified Forest National Park, Winslow is a good regional base. Old motels border Route 66, and diners sprinkle downtown. The real showpiece here is the irresistible 1929 **La Posada** (☑ 928-289-4366; www.laposada.org; 303 E 2nd St; r $139-169; ✳ ⛱ ☷), a restored hacienda designed by star architect Mary Jane Colter. Elaborate tilework, glass-and-tin chandeliers, Navajo rugs and other details accent its palatial Western-style elegance. The on-site restaurant, the much-lauded **Turquoise Room** (www.theturquoiseroom.net; La Posada; breakfast $8-12, lunch $10-13, dinner $19-42; ☺ 7am-4pm, 5-9pm), serves the best meals between Flagstaff and Albuquerque; dishes have a neo-Southwestern flair.

Petrified Forest National Park

Home not only to an extraordinary array of fossilized ancient logs that predate the dinosaurs but also the multicolored sandscape of the Painted Desert, this **national park** (☑ 928-524-6228; www.nps.gov/pefo; vehicle/walk-in, bicycle & motorcycle $10/5; ☺ scenic drive 7am-8pm Jun & Jul, shorter hr Aug-May) is an unmissable spectacle.

The park straddles I-40 at exit 311, 25 miles east of Holbrook. Its visitor center, just half a mile north of I-40, holds maps and information on guided tours, while the 28-mile paved park road beyond offers a splendid scenic drive. There are no campsites, but a number of short trails, ranging from less than a mile to 2 miles, pass through the stands of petrified rock and ancient Native American dwellings. Those prepared for rugged backcountry camping need to pick up a free permit at the visitor center.

Western Arizona

The Colorado River is alive with sun worshippers at Lake Havasu City, while Route 66 offers well-preserved stretches of classic highway near Kingman. Much further south, beyond I-10 towards Mexico, the wild, empty landscape is among the most barren in the West. If you're already here, there are some worthwhile sites, but there's nothing worth planning an itinerary around unless you're a Route 66 or boating fanatic.

Kingman & Around

Faded motels and gas stations galore grace Kingman's main drag, but several century-old buildings remain. If you're following the Route 66 trail (aka Andy Devine Ave here) or looking for cheap lodging, it's worth a stroll.

Pick up maps and brochures at the historic **Powerhouse Visitor Center** (☑ 866-427-7866, 928-753-6106; www.gokingman.com; 120 W Andy Devine Ave; ☺ 8am-5pm), which has a small but engaging **Route 66 museum** (☑ 928-753-9889; www.gokingman.com; 120 W Andy Devine Ave; adult/senior/child 12yr & under $4/3/free; ☺ 9am-5pm).

A cool neon sign draws road-trippers to the **Hilltop Motel** (☑ 928-753-2198; www.hilltopmotelaz.com; 1901 E Andy Devine Ave; r from $44; ✳@🏠🐾🐕) on Route 66. Rooms are a bit of a throwback, but are well kept, and the views are superb. Pets (dogs only) stay

for $5. There's tasty Southern-style pork at **Redneck's Southern Pit BBQ** (www.redneckssouthernpitbbq.com; 420 E Beale St; mains $5.25-24; ☺ 11am-8pm Tue-Sat; 🏠).

Lake Havasu City

When the city of London auctioned off its 1831 bridge in the late 1960s, developer Robert McCulloch bought it, took it apart, shipped it, and then reassembled it at Lake Havasu City, which sits along a dammed-up portion of the Colorado River. The place now attracts hordes of young spring-breakers and weekend warriors who come to play in the water and party hard. An 'English Village' of pseudo-British pubs and tourist gift shops surrounds the bridge and houses the **visitor center** (☑ 928-855-5655; www.golakehavasu.com; 422 English Village; ☺ 9am-5pm).

The hippest hotel in town is **Heat** (☑ 928-854-2833; www.heathotel.com; 1420 N McCulloch Blvd; r $209-299, ste $249-439; ✳🏠), a slick boutique property where the front desk doubles as a bar, and most of the contemporary-styled rooms have private patios with views of London Bridge. For a hearty, open-air breakfast, rise and shine at the **Red Onion** (☑ 928-505-0302; www.redonionhavasu.com; 2013 N McCulloch Blvd; breakfast & lunch $6.25-12, dinner $10-15; ☺ 7am-8pm Mon-Thu, 7am-9pm Fri & Sat, 7am-2pm Sun), where the menu is loaded with omelets and diet-busting fare. For microbrews and good pub grub, try the **Barley Brothers** (☑ 928-505-7837; www.barleybrothers.com; 1425 N McCulloch Blvd; mains $9-24; ☺ 11am-9pm Sun-Thu, to 10pm Fri & Sat), which has great views of the lake.

Tucson

Arizona's second-largest city is set in the Sonoran Desert, full of rolling, sandy hills and crowds of cacti. The vibe here is ramshackle-cool and cozy compared with the shiny vastness of Phoenix. A college town, Tucson (the 'c' is silent) is home turf to the 40,000-strong University of Arizona (U of A), and was an artsy, dress-down kind of place before that was the cool thing to be. Eclectic shops and scores of funky restaurants and bars flourish in this arid ground. Tucsonans are proud of the city's geographic and cultural proximity to Mexico (65 highway miles south); more than 40% of the population is of Hispanic descent.

◎ Sights & Activities

Downtown Tucson and the historic district lie east of I-10 exit 258. The U of A campus is a mile northeast of downtown; 4th Ave, the main drag here, is packed with cafes, bars and interesting shops.

★ Arizona-Sonora Desert Museum   MUSEUM
(☑ 520-883-2702; www.desertmuseum.org; 2021 N Kinney Rd; adult/child 13-17yr $19.50/15.50; ◎ 8:30am-5pm Oct-Feb, 7:30am-5pm Mar-Sep, to 10pm Sat Jun-Aug) Home to cacti, coyotes and palm-sized hummingbirds, this ode to the Sonoran desert is one part zoo, one part botanical garden and one part museum – a trifecta that'll entertain young and old for easily half a day. Desert denizens, from precocious coatis to playful prairie dogs, inhabit natural enclosures. The grounds are thick with desert plants, and docents give demonstrations.

Old Tucson Studios   FILM LOCATION
(☑ 520-883-0100; www.oldtucson.com; 201 S Kinney Rd; adult/child 4-11yr $18/11; ◎ Oct–late May, hr vary; ▣) Nicknamed 'Hollywood in the Desert,' this old movie set of Tucson in the 1860s was built in 1939 for the filming of *Arizona*. Hundreds of flicks followed, bringing in movie stars from Clint Eastwood to

MINI TIME MACHINE MUSEUM OF MINIATURES
....

'Meddle ye not in the affairs of Dragons, for ye are crunchy and tasteth good with condiments,' reads the sign beside the Pocket Dragons, one of several species of magical creatures that inhabit the Enchanted Realm gallery at this gobsmackingly entertaining **museum** (www.theminitimemachine.org; 4455 E Camp Lowell Dr; adult/child 4-17yr $9/6; ◎ 9am-4pm Tue-Sat, noon-4pm Sun; ▣). Here you can walk over a snowglobe-y Christmas village, peer into intricate mini-homes built in the 1700s and 1800s, and search for the tiny inhabitants of a magical tree. It's great for families and for adults who still have a sense of fun.

To get here from downtown, follow E Broadway Blvd east 3.5 miles. Turn left onto N Alvernon Way and drive 3 miles to E Fort Lowell Rd, which turns into Camp Lowell. Turn right and continue almost 1 mile.

Leonardo DiCaprio. Now a Wild West theme park, it's all about shootouts, stagecoach rides, stunt shows and dancing saloon girls.

Pima Air & Space Museum   MUSEUM
(☑ 520-574-0462; www.pimaair.org; 6000 E Valencia Rd; adult/child 7-12yr/senior & military $16/9/13 Nov-May, $14/8/12 Jun-Oct; ◎ 9am-5pm, last admission 4pm; ▣) An SR-71 Blackbird spy plane and a massive B-52 bomber are among the stars of this extraordinary private aircraft museum. Allow at least two hours to wander through hangars and around the airfield where more than 300 'birds' trace the evolution of civilian and military aviation. A free 50-minute walking tour is offered at 10:30am and 11:30am daily (plus 1:30pm & 2:30pm December through April).

✿ Festivals & Events

Fiesta de los Vaqueros   RODEO
(Rodeo Week; ☑ 520-741-2233; www.tucsonrodeo.com; ◎ Feb) Held the last week of February for 90 years, the Fiesta brings world-famous cowboys to town and features a spectacular parade with Western-themed floats and buggies, historic horse-drawn coaches, folk dancers and marching bands.

🛏 Sleeping

Lodging prices vary considerably, with lower rates in summer and fall. To sleep under stars and saguaros, try **Gilbert Ray Campground** (☑ 520-883-4200; www.pima.gov; Kinney Rd; tent/RV sites $10/20; ▣) near the western district of Saguaro National Park.

Roadrunner Hostel & Inn   HOSTEL $
(☑ 520-940-7280; www.roadrunnerhostelinn.com; 346 E 12th St; dm/r incl breakfast $22/45; ✳@🖝▣) Cultural and language barriers melt faster than snow in the desert at this small and friendly hostel within walking distance of 4th Ave. The guest kitchen and TV lounge are convivial spaces and freebies include coffee, tea and a waffle breakfast. The 1900 adobe building once belonged to the sheriff involved in capturing the Dillinger gang at the Hotel Congress in 1934.

Quality Inn Flamingo Downtown   MOTEL $
(☑ 520-770-1910; www.flamingohoteltucson.com; 1300 N Stone Ave; r incl breakfast $65-80; ✳@🖝🖢▣) Though recently purchased by the Quality Inn chain, the former Flamingo Hotel retains a bit of its great 1950s Rat Pack vibe, and the fact that Elvis slept here doesn't hurt (although the rooms were

renumbered and now no one is sure which room he slept in). Rooms come with chic striped bedding, flat-screen plasma TVs, a good-sized desk and comfy beds.

★**Catalina Park Inn** B&B $$
(☎520-792-4541; www.catalinaparkinn.com; 309 E 1st St; r $145-189; ⊘closed Jul & Aug; ❄@🛜🏊) Style, hospitality and comfort merge seamlessly at this inviting B&B just west of the University of Arizona and 4th Ave. Hosts Mark Hall and Paul Richard have poured their hearts into restoring this 1927 Mediterranean-style villa, and their efforts are on display in each of the six rooms, which vary in style.

Hotel Congress HISTORIC HOTEL $$
(☎520-622-8848; www.hotelcongress.com; 311 E Congress St; r $89-149; P❄@🛜🏊) Charming, confident and occasionally a pain in the ass? Yes. But rest assured, downtown Tucson's most famous lodging is never, ever boring. Beautifully restored, this 1919 hotel feels very modern, mostly because of its popular cafe, bar and club. Many rooms have period furnishings, rotary phones and wooden radios – but no TVs.

Aloft Tucson HOTEL $$
(☎520-908-6800; www.starwoodhotels.com; 1900 E Speedway Blvd; r $169; ❄🛜) Tucson is surprisingly light on trendy boutique hotels. The new Aloft, near the university, isn't an indie property, but it does project a cool, modern vibe that caters to tech-minded, style-conscious travelers. Rooms and common areas pop with bright but spare decor that manages to feel inviting. Beer and cocktails are served at the on-site bar, and there's 24hr grab-n-go food beside the lobby.

Arizona Inn RESORT $$$
(☎800-933-1093, 520-325-1541; www.arizonainn.com; 2200 E Elm St; r $199-259, ste $299-379; ❄@🛜🏊) Our favorite part? High tea in the library, complete with scones and finger sandwiches. Croquet might be a highlight too, if only we could find a teammate. Historic and aristocratic touches such as these provide a definite sense of privilege – and we like it. Mature gardens and old Arizona grace also provide a respite from city life and the 21st century.

 Eating

Mi Nidito MEXICAN $
(☎520-622-5081; www.minidito.net; 1813 S 4th Ave; mains $6-13; ⊘from 11am Wed-Sun) Former president Bill Clinton's order (pre-quadru-

ple bypass) at 'My Little Nest' has become the signature president's plate, a heaping mound of Mexican favorites – tacos, tostadas, burritos, enchiladas and more – groaning under melted cheese. Give the prickly pear cactus chili or the *birria* (spicy, shredded beef) a whirl.

Lovin' Spoonfuls VEGAN $
(☎520-325-7766; 2990 N Campbell Ave; breakfast $6-9, lunch $5.25-8, dinner $7.25-11.25; ⊘9:30am-9pm Mon-Sat, 10am-3pm Sun; 🍴) Burgers, country-fried chicken and club sandwiches – the menu reads like those at your typical diner but there's one big difference: no animal products will ever find their way into this vegan haven. Outstandingly creative choices include the cashew-mushroom pâté and the adzuki-bean burger.

★**Cafe Poca Cosa** SOUTH AMERICAN $$
(☎520-622-6400; www.cafepocacosatucson.com; 110 E Pennington St; lunch $12-15, dinner $18-26; ⊘11am-9pm Tue-Thu, to 10pm Fri & Sat) At this award-winning *nuevo*-Mexican bistro, a Spanish-English blackboard menu circulates between tables because dishes change twice daily. It's all freshly prepared, innovative and beautifully presented. The undecided can't go wrong by ordering the Plato Poca Cosa and letting chef Suzana Davila decide. Great margaritas, too.

Cup Cafe AMERICAN, GLOBAL $$
(☎520-798-1618; www.hotelcongress.com/food; 311 E Congress St; breakfast $7-12, lunch $10-12, dinner $13-25; ⊘7am-10pm Sun-Thu, to 11pm Fri & Sat; 🍴) Cup Cafe, we like your style. Wine-bottle chandeliers. A penny-tiled floor. And 'Up on Cripple Creek' on the speakers. In the morning, choices include a Creole

dish with andouille sausage, eggs, potatoes, buttermilk biscuits and sausage gravy, and cast-iron baked eggs with Gruyère cheese. And the coffee is excellent. There's a global mix of dishes, with a decent selection of vegetarian options.

Hub Restaurant & Creamery AMERICAN $$
(☑ 520-207-8201; www.hubdowntown.com; 266 E Congress Ave; lunch $10-16, dinner $10-24; ☺ 11am-2am; ☷) Exposed-brick walls, a lofty ceiling, sleek booths and, surprisingly, a walk-up ice-cream stand beside the hostess desk – industrial chic takes a Mayberry spin. Upscale comfort food is the name of the game here, from lobster mac & cheese to chicken pot pie, plus a few sandwiches and salads.

🍸 Drinking & Entertainment

Downtown 4th Ave, near 6th St, is the happening bar-hop spot, and there are a number of nightclubs on downtown Congress St.

Che's Lounge BAR
(☑ 520-623-2088; 350 N 4th Ave; ☺ noon-2am) Drinkers unite! If everyone's favorite revolutionary heartthrob was still in our midst, he wouldn't have charged a cover either. A slightly skanky but hugely popular watering hole with $1.50 drafts, a huge wraparound bar and local art gracing the walls, this college hangout rocks with live music most Saturday nights and on the patio on Sunday afternoons (4-7pm) in the summer.

Thunder Canyon Brewery MICROBREWERY
(www.thundercanyonbrewery.com; 220 E Broadway Blvd; ☺ 11am-11pm Sun-Thu, to 2am Fri & Sat) This cavernous microbrewery, within walking distance of Hotel Congress, has more than 40 beers on tap, serving up its own creations as well as handcrafted beers from across the US.

Chocolate Iguana COFFEE SHOP
(www.chocolateiguanaon4th.com; 500 N 4th Ave; ☺ 7am-8pm Mon-Thu, 7am-10pm Fri, 8am-10pm Sat, 9am-6pm Sun) Chocoholics have their pick of sweets and pastries inside this green-and-purple cottage, while coffee-lovers can choose from numerous coffee brews and a long list of specialty drinks. Watching your diet? The delicious Frozen Explosion is a fat-free mocha. Also sells sandwiches ($6-7) and gifts.

Club Congress LIVE MUSIC
(☑ 520-622-8848; www.hotelcongress.com; 311 E Congress St) Skinny jeansters, tousled hipsters, aging folkies, dressed-up hotties – the crowd at Tucson's most-happening club inside the grandly aging Hotel Congress defines the word eclectic. And so does the musical line-up, which usually features the finest local and regional talent. Wanna sit and just drink at a no-fuss bar? Step inside the adjacent Tap Room, open since 1919.

ℹ Information

EMERGENCY & MEDICAL SERVICES
Police (☑ 520-791-4444; www.police.tucsonaz.gov/police; 270 S Stone Ave)
Tucson Medical Center (☑ 520-327-5461; www.tmcaz.com/TucsonMedicalCenter; 5301 E Grant Rd) 24-hour emergency services.

MEDIA
Arizona Daily Star (http://azstarnet.com) The Tucson region's daily newspaper.
Tucson Weekly (www.tucsonweekly.com) A free weekly full of entertainment and restaurant listings.

POST
Post Office (☑ 520-903-1958; 141 S 6th Ave; ☺ 9am-5pm)

TOURIST INFORMATION
Tucson Convention & Visitors Bureau (☑ 800-638-8350, 520-624-1817; www.visittucson.org; 100 S Church Ave; ☺ 9am-5pm Mon-Fri, to 4pm Sat & Sun) Ask for its free Tucson travel guide.

ℹ Getting There & Around

Tucson International Airport (☑ 520-573-8100; www.flytucson.com; 7250 S Tucson Blvd; ☷) is 15 miles south of downtown. **Arizona Stagecoach** (☑ 520-889-1000; www.azstagecoach.com) runs a shared van service with fares for about $25 between downtown and the airport. **Greyhound** (☑ 520-792-3475; www.greyhound.com; 471 W Congress St) runs buses to Phoenix ($21 to $23, two hours, daily) and other destinations. The station is on the western end of Congress St, on the western edge of downtown. **Amtrak** (☑ 800-872-7245, 520-623-4442; www.amtrak.com; 400 E Toole Ave), across from Hotel Congress, is connected to Los Angeles by the Sunset Limited service (from $56, 10 hours, three weekly).

From the **Ronstadt Transit Center** (215 E Congress St, cnr Congress St & 6th Ave), the major downtown transit hub, Sun Tran buses (www.suntran.com) serve metropolitan Tucson (day pass $3.50).

Around Tucson

All the places listed here are less than 1½ hours' drive from Tucson, and make great day trips.

Saguaro National Park

Saguaros are the most iconic symbol of the American Southwest, and an entire army of these majestic ribbed sentinels is protected in this two-part desert playground. **Saguaro National Park** (✔Rincon 520-733-5153, Tucson 520-733-5158, park information 520-733-5100; www.nps.gov/sagu; 7-day pass per vehicle/bicycle $10/5; ☺sunrise to sunset) is divided into two units, 30 miles apart to either side of the city of Tucson, and each filled with trails and desert flora.

The larger section is the **Rincon Mountain District**, about 15 miles east of downtown. The **visitor center** (✔520-733-5153; 3693 S Old Spanish Trail; ☺9am-5pm) has information on day hikes, horseback riding and backcountry camping. The latter requires a permit ($6 per site per day), which must be obtained by noon on the day of your hike. The meandering 8-mile Cactus Forest Scenic Loop Drive, a paved road open to cars and bicycles, provides access to picnic areas, trailheads and viewpoints. Hikers pressed for time should follow the 1-mile round-trip Freeman Homestead Trail to a grove of massive saguaro.

West of town, the **Tucson Mountain District** has its own **visitor center** (✔520-733-5158; 2700 N Kinney Rd; ☺9am-5pm). The Scenic Bajada Loop Drive is a 6-mile graded dirt road through cactus forest that begins 1.5 miles north of the visitor center. Two quick, easy and rewarding hikes are the 0.8-mile Valley View Overlook (awesome at sunset) and the half-mile Signal Hill Trail to scores of ancient petroglyphs.

Trailers longer than 35ft and vehicles wider than 8ft are not permitted on the park's narrow scenic loop roads.

West of Tucson

You want wide solitude? Follow Hwy 86 west from Tucson into some of the emptiest parts of the Sonoran Desert – except for the ubiquitous green-and-white border-patrol trucks.

The lofty **Kitt Peak National Observatory** (✔520-318-8726; www.noao.edu/kpno; Hwy 86; by donation; ☺9am-4pm), west of Sells and about a 75-minute drive from Tucson, features the largest collection of optical telescopes in the world. Guided tours (adult/child $10/3.25, at 10am, 11:30am and 1:30pm) last about an hour. Book two to four weeks in advance for the worthwhile nightly observing program (adult/child $49/45; no programs from mid-July through August). Clear, dry skies equal an awe-inspiring glimpse of the cosmos. Dress warmly, buy gas in Tucson (the nearest gas station is 30 miles from the observatory) and note that children under eight years of age are not allowed at the evening program. The picnic area draws amateur astronomers at night.

If you truly want to get away from it all, you can't get much further off the grid than the huge and exotic **Organ Pipe Cactus National Monument** (✔520-387-6849; www.nps.gov/orpi; Hwy 85; per vehicle $8; ☺visitor center 8:30am-4:30pm) along the Mexican border. It's a gorgeous, forbidding land that supports an astonishing number of animals and plants, including 28 species of cacti, first and foremost its namesake organ-pipe. A giant columnar cactus, it differs from the more prevalent saguaro in that its branches radiate from the base. The 21-mile **Ajo Mountain Drive** takes you through a spectacular landscape of steep-sided, jagged cliffs and rock tinged a faintly hellish red. There are 208 first-come, first-served sites at **Twin Peaks Campground** (www.nps.gov/orpi; tent & RV sites $12) by the visitor center.

South of Tucson

South of Tucson, I-19 is the main route to Nogales and Mexico. Along the way are several interesting stops.

The magnificent **Mission San Xavier del Bac** (✔520-294-2624; www.patronatosanxavier.org; 1950 W San Xavier Rd; donations appreciated; ☺museum 8:30am-5pm, church 7am-5pm), on the San Xavier reservation 9 miles south of downtown Tucson, is Arizona's oldest Hispanic-era building still in use. Complete in 1797, it's a graceful blend of Moorish, Byzantine and late Mexican Renaissance architecture with an unexpectedly ornate interior.

At exit 69, 16 miles south of the mission, the **Titan Missile Museum** (✔520-625-7736; www.titanmissilemuseum.org; 1580 W

Duval Mine Rd, Sahuarita; adult/child 7-12yr/senior $9.50/6/8.50; ☺8:45am-5pm, last tour at 4pm) features an underground launch site for Cold War–era intercontinental ballistic missiles. Tours are chilling and informative.

If history or shopping for crafts interest you, head 48 miles south of Tucson to the small village of **Tubac** (www.tubacaz.com), with more than 100 galleries, studios and shops.

Patagonia & the Mountain Empire

This lovely riparian region, sandwiched between the Mexican border and the Santa Rita and Patagonia Mountains, is one of the shiniest gems in Arizona's jewel box. It's a tranquil destination for bird-watching and wine tasting.

Bird-watchers and nature-lovers wander the gentle trails at the **Patagonia-Sonoita Creek Preserve** (☑520-394-2400; www.nature.org/arizona; 150 Blue Heaven Rd; admission $6; ☺6:30am-4pm Wed-Sun Apr-Sep, 7:30am-4pm Wed-Sun Oct-Mar), an enchanting creekside willow and cottonwood forest managed by the Nature Conservancy. The peak migratory seasons are April through May, and late August to September. For a leisurely afternoon of wine tasting, head to the villages of **Sonoita** and **Elgin** north of Patagonia.

If you stick around for dinner, try the fantastic gourmet pizzas at **Velvet Elvis** (☑520-394-2102; www.velvetelvispizza.com; 292 Naugle Ave, Patagonia; mains $8-24; ☺11:30am-8:30pm Thu-Sat, to 7:30pm Sun). Salute the Old West and its simple charms at the **Stage Stop Inn** (☑520-394-2211; www.stagestophotelpatagonia.com; 303 McKeown, Patagonia; s $79, d $89-109, ste $139; 🏧🐾🏊), where rooms surround a central courtyard and pool. The stage coach did indeed stop here on the Butterfield Trail, and a small **visitor center** (☑888-794-0060; www.patagoniaaz.com; 307 McKeown Ave, Patagonia; ☺10am-4pm Mon-Sat) now provides information.

Southeastern Arizona

Chockablock with places that loom large in Wild West history, southern Arizona is home to the wonderfully preserved mining town of Bisbee, the OK Corral in Tombstone, and a wonderland of stone spires at Chiricahua National Monument.

Kartchner Caverns State Park

The emphasis is on education at **Kartchner Caverns State Park** (☑information 520-586-4100, reservations 520-586-2283; http://azstateparks.com; Hwy 90; park entrance per vehicle/bicycle $6/3, Rotunda Tour adult/child 7-13yr $23/13, Big Room Tour mid-Oct–mid-Apr $23/13; ☺park 7am-6pm, visitor center 8am-6pm Nov-May, shorter hours rest of year), a 2.5-mile wet limestone fantasia of rocks. Two guided tours explore different areas of the caverns, which were discovered in 1974. The Rotunda/Throne Room Tour is open year-round; the Big Room Tour closes in mid-April for five months to protect the migratory bats that roost here. The park is 9 miles south of Benson, off I-10 at exit 302. The $6 entrance fee is waived if you already have a reserved tour ticket.

Tombstone

In Tombstone's 19th-century heyday as a booming mining town, the whiskey flowed and six-shooters blazed over disputes large and small, most famously at the OK Corral. Now a National Historic Landmark, it attracts hordes of tourists to its old Western buildings, stagecoach rides and gunfight reenactments.

And yes, you must visit the **OK Corral** (☑520-457-3456; www.ok-corral.com; Allen St btwn 3rd & 4th Sts; admission $10, without gunfight $6; ☺9am-5pm), site of the legendary gunfight where the Earps and Doc Holliday took on the McLaurys and Billy Clanton on October 26, 1881. The McClaurys and Clanton now rest at the **Boot Hill Graveyard** on Hwy 80 north of town. Also make time for the dusty **Bird Cage Theater** (☑520-457-3421; www.tombstonebirdcage.com; 517 E Allen St; adult/child 8-18yr/senior $10/8/9; ☺8am-6pm), a one-time dance hall and saloon crammed with historic odds and ends. And a merman.

The **Visitor & Information Center** (☑520-457-3929, 888-457-3929; www.tombstonechamber.com; 395 E Allen St, at cnr of 4th St; ☺9am-4pm Mon-Thu, to 5pm Fri-Sun) has walking maps.

Bisbee

Oozing old-fashioned ambience, Bisbee is a former copper-mining town that's now a delightful mix of aging bohemians, elegant buildings, sumptuous restaurants and charming hotels. Most businesses are in the

Historic District (Old Bisbee), along Subway and Main Sts.

To burrow under the earth in a tour led by the retired miners who worked here, take the **Queen Mine Tour** (☑520-432-2071; www.queenminetour.com; 478 Dart Rd, off Hwy 80; adult/child 4-12yr $13/5.50; ☑). The Queen Mine Tour Building, just south of downtown, also holds the local **visitor center** (☑866-224-7233, 520-432-3554; www.discoverbisbee.com; 478 Dart Rd; ☑8am-5pm Mon-Fri, 10am-4pm Sat & Sun), and makes the obvious place to start exploring. Right outside of town, check out the **Lavender Pit**, an ugly yet impressive testament to strip mining.

Rest your head at **Shady Dell RV Park** (☑520-432-3567; www.theshadydell.com; 1 Douglas Rd; rates $87-145, closed early Jul–mid-Sep; ☀), a deliciously retro trailer park extraordinaire where meticulously restored Airstream trailers are neatly fenced off and kitted out with fun furnishings. Swamp coolers provide cold air. You can sleep in a covered wagon at the quirky but fun **Bisbee Grand Hotel** (☑520-432-5900; www.bisbeegrandhotel.com; 61 Main St; r incl breakfast $79-179; ☀☎), which brings the Old West to life (maybe it never died?) with Victorian-era decor and a kick-up-your-spurs saloon.

For good food, stroll up Main St and pick a restaurant – you can't go wrong. For fine American food, try stylish **Cafe Roka** (☑520-432-5153; www.caferoka.com; 35 Main St; dinner $17-24; ☑5-9pm Wed-Sat), where four-course dinners include salad, soup, sorbet and a rotating choice of crowd-pleasing mains. Continue up Main St for wood-fired pizzas and punk-rock style at **Screaming Banshee** (☑520-432-1300; www.screamingbansheepizza.net; 200 Tombstone Canyon Rd; mains $7-15; ☑4-9pm Tue & Wed, 11am-10pm Thu-Sat, 11am-9pm Sun). Bars cluster in Brewery Gulch, at the south end of Main St.

Chiricahua National Monument

The towering rock spires at remote but mesmerizing **Chiricahua National Monument** (☑520-824-3560; www.nps.gov/chir; Hwy 181; adult/child $5/free) in the Chiricahua Mountains sometimes rise hundreds of feet high and often look like they're on the verge of tipping over. The **Bonita Canyon Scenic Drive** takes you 8 miles to Massai Point (6870ft) where you'll see thousands of spires positioned on the slopes like some petrified army. There are numerous hiking trails, but if you're short on time, hike the **Echo**

Canyon Trail at least half a mile to the Grottoes, an amazing 'cathedral' of giant boulders where you can lie still and enjoy the wind-caressed silence. The monument is 36 miles southeast of Willcox off Hwy 186/181.

UTAH

Shhhhh, don't tell. This oft-overlooked state is really one of nature's most perfect playgrounds. Utah's rugged terrain comes ready-made for hiking, biking, rafting, rappelling, rock climbing, skiing, snowboarding, snow riding, horseback riding, four-wheel driving... Need we go on?

More than 65% of the state's lands are public, including 12 national parks and monuments – a dazzling display of geology that leaves visitors awestruck. Southern Utah is a seemingly endless expanse of sculpted sandstone desert, its red-rock country defined by soaring Technicolor cliffs, spindles and spires. The 11,000ft-high forest- and snow-covered peaks of the Wasatch and other mountains and valleys dominate northeastern Utah.

Across the state you'll find well-organized towns with pioneer-era buildings dating to when the first Mormon settlers arrived; church members still make up more than half the impeccably polite population. Rural towns may be quiet and conservative, but the rugged beauty attracts outdoorsy, independent thinkers as well. Salt Lake and Park cities especially have vibrant nightlife and foodie scenes.

So come wonder at the roadside geologic kaleidoscope, hike out into the vast expanses or enjoy a great microbrew. Just don't tell your friends: we'd like to keep this secret to ourselves.

History

Traces of the Ancestral Puebloan and Fremont peoples, this land's earliest human inhabitants, remain in in the rock art and ruins they left behind. But the modern Ute, Paiute and Navajo tribes were living here when settlers of European heritage arrived in large numbers. Led by Brigham Young (second president of the Mormon church), Mormons fled to this territory to escape religious persecution starting in the late 1840s. They set out to settle every inch of their new land, no matter how inhospitable, which resulted

SOUTHWEST SOUTHEASTERN ARIZONA

UTAH FACTS

Nickname Beehive State

Population 2.94 million

Area 82,169 sq miles

Capital city Salt Lake City (population 186,440), metro area (1.2 million)

Other cities St George (population 76,917)

Sales tax 6.85%

Birthplace of Entertainers Donny (b 1957) and Marie (b 1959) Osmond, beloved bandit Butch Cassidy (1866–1908)

Home of 2002 Winter Olympic Games

Politics Mostly conservative

Famous for Mormons, red-rock canyons, polygamy

Best souvenir Wasatch Brewery T-shirt: 'Polygamy Porter – Why Have Just One?'

in skirmishes with Native Americans – and more than one abandoned ghost town.

For nearly 50 years after the United States acquired the Utah Territory from Mexico, petitions for statehood were rejected due to the Mormon practice of polygamy (taking multiple wives). Tension and prosecutions grew until 1890, when Mormon leader Wilford Woodruff had a divine revelation and the church officially discontinued the practice. Utah became the 45th state in 1896. The modern Mormon church, now called the Church of Jesus Christ of Latter-Day Saints (LDS), continues to exert a strong influence.

❶ Information

Utah Office of Tourism (☑ 800-200-1160; www.utah.com) Publishes the free *Utah Travel Guide* and runs several visitor centers statewide. Website has links in six languages.

Utah State Parks & Recreation Department (☑ 801-538-7220; www.stateparks.utah.gov) Produces comprehensive guide to the 40-plus state parks; available online and at visitor centers.

❶ Getting There & Away

Salt Lake City (SLC) has Utah's only international airport. It may be cheaper to fly into Las Vegas (425 miles south) and rent a car.

❶ Getting Around

You will need a private vehicle to get around anywhere besides SLC and Park City. Most Utah towns are laid out in a grid with streets aligned north–south or east–west. Addresses and numerical street names radiate out from a zero point at the central intersection (typically Main St and Center St), rising by 100 with each city block. Thus, 500 South 400 East will be five blocks south and four blocks east of the zero point. It sounds complicated, but it's surprisingly easy to use.

Salt Lake City

Snuggled up against the soaring peaks of the Wasatch Mountains, Salt Lake City is a small town with just enough edge to satisfy city slickers. Yes, it is the Mormon equivalent of the Vatican, but Utah's capital city is surprisingly modern. A redeveloped downtown and local foodie scene balance out the city's charming anachronisms.

◉ Sights & Activities

Top church-related sights cluster near downtown's zero point: the corner of S Temple (east–west) and Main St (north–south). See those 132ft-wide streets? They were originally built so that four oxen pulling a wagon could turn around.

Don't forget that just 45 minutes away, world-class hiking, climbing and snow sports await in the Wasatch Mountains.

◉ Temple Square Area

Temple Square PLAZA
(www.visittemplesquare.com; cnr S Temple & N State Sts; ⊙ grounds 24hr; visitor centers 9am–9pm) **FREE** The city's most famous sight occupies a 10-acre block surrounded by 15ft-high walls. LDS docents give free, 30-minute tours continually, leaving from the visitor centers at the two entrances on South and North Temple Sts. Sisters, brothers and elders are stationed every 20ft or so to answer questions. (Don't worry, no one is going to try to convert you – unless you express interest.) In addition to the noteworthy sights, there are administrative buildings and two theater venues.

Salt Lake Temple RELIGIOUS SITE
(Temple Sq; ⊙ closed to the public) Lording over Temple Sq is the impressive 210ft-tall Salt Lake Temple. Atop the tallest spire stands a statue of the angel Moroni, who appeared

to LDS founder Joseph Smith. Rumor has it that when the place was renovated, cleaners found old bullet marks in one of the gold-plated surfaces. The temple and ceremonies are private, open only to LDS members in good standing.

Tabernacle   RELIGIOUS SITE
(www.mormontabernaclechoir.org; Temple Sq; admission free; ⊙9am-9pm) FREE The domed, 1867 auditorium – with a massive 11,000-pipe organ – has incredible acoustics. A pin dropped in the front can be heard in the back, almost 200ft away. Free daily organ recitals are held at noon Monday through Saturday, and at 2pm Sunday.

Beehive House   HISTORIC SITE
(☑801-240-2671; www.visittemplesquare.com; 67 E South Temple St; admission free; ⊙9am-8:30pm Mon-Sat) FREE Brigham Young lived with one of his wives and families in the Beehive House during much of his tenure as governor and church president in Utah. The required tours vary in the amount of historic house detail provided versus religious education offered, depending on the particular LDS docent. The attached 1855 Lion House, which was home to a number of Young's other wives, has a self-service restaurant (p357) in the basement. Feel free to look around the dining rooms during mealtimes.

◉ Greater Downtown

Utah State Capitol   HISTORIC BUILDING
(www.utahstatecapitol.utah.gov; 350 N State St; ⊙7am-8pm Mon-Fri, 8am-6pm Sat & Sun; visitor center 8:30am-5pm Mon-Fri) FREE The grand 1916 State Capitol is set among 500 cherry trees on a hill north of Temple Sq. Inside, colorful Works Progress Administration (WPA) murals of pioneers, trappers and missionaries adorn part of the building's dome. Free guided tours (hourly, 9am to 5pm, Monday to Friday) start at the 1st-floor visitor center; self-guided tours are available from the visitor center.

City Creek Center   MALL
(www.shopcitycreekcenter.com; Social Hall Ave, btwn Regent & Richards Sts) Inaugurated in 2012, this LDS-funded, 20-acre pedestrian plaza has fountains, restaurants, a creek stocked with trout and retail area with a retractable roof.

◉ University-Foothill District & Beyond

★Natural History Museum of Utah   MUSEUM
(http://nhmu.utah.edu; 301 Wakara Way; adult/child $11/9; ⊙10am-5pm Thu-Tue, to 9pm Wed) The stunning architecture of the Rio Tinto Center forms a multistory indoor 'canyon' that showcases exhibits to great effect. Walk up through the layers as you explore both indigenous peoples' cultures and natural history. Past Worlds paleontological displays are the most impressive – an incredible perspective from beneath, next to and above a vast collection of dinosaur fossils offers the full breadth of pre-history.

This is the Place Heritage Park HISTORIC SITE
(www.thisistheplace.org; 2601 E Sunnyside Ave; adult/child $11/8; ⊙9am-5pm Mon-Sat, 10am-5pm Sun; ⊕) Dedicated to the 1847 arrival of the Mormons, the heritage park covers 450 acres. The centerpiece is a living-history village where, June through August, costumed docents depict mid-19th-century life. Admission includes a tourist-train ride and activities. The rest of the year, access is limited to varying degrees at varyingly reduced prices; you'll at least be able to wander around the exterior of the 41 buildings. Some are replicas, but some are originals, such as Brigham Young's farmhouse.

Red Butte Garden   GARDENS
(www.redbuttegarden.org; 300 Wakara Way; adult/child $10/6; ⊙9am-7:30pm) Both landscaped and natural gardens cover a lovely 150 acres,

SOUTHWEST SALT LAKE CITY

POLYGAMY TODAY

Though the Mormon church eschewed plural marriage in 1890, some unaffiliated offshoot sects still believe it is a divinely decreed practice. Most of the roughly 7000 residents in Hilldale-Colorado City on the Utah–Arizona border are polygamy-practicing members of the Fundamentalist Church of Jesus Christ of Latter-Day Saints (FLDS). Walk into a Walmart in Washington or Hurricane and the shoppers you see in pastel-colored, prairie-style dresses – with lengthy braids or elaborate up-dos – are likely sister wives. Other, less-conspicuous polygamy-practicing sects are active in the southern parts of the state as well.

with access to trails in the Wasatch foothills. Check online to see who's playing at the popular, outdoor summer concert series also held here.

Church Fork Trail HIKING

(Mill Creek Canyon Rd, off Wasatch Blvd; day-use $3) Looking for the nearest workout with big views? Hike the 6-mile round-trip, pet-friendly trail up to Grandeur Peak (8299ft). Mill Creek Canyon is 13.5 miles southwest of downtown.

🛏 Sleeping

Downtown, rates vary greatly depending on local events and occupancy. Cheaper chain motels cluster off I-80 near the airport and south in suburban Midvale. Outside ski season, prices plunge at Wasatch Mountain resorts, 45 minutes from downtown.

Avenues Hostel HOSTEL $

(☑ 801-539-8888, 801-359-3855; www.saltlakehostel.com; 107 F St; dm $19-23, s/d with shared bath $40/47, with private bath $50/57; ❄@🛜) Well-worn hostel; a bit halfway-house-like with long-term residents, but a convenient location.

★ Inn on the Hill INN $$

(☑ 801-328-1466; www.inn-on-the-hill.com; 225 N State St; r incl breakfast $150-189; P❄@🛜) Exquisite woodwork and Maxfield Parrish Tiffany glass adorn this sprawling, 1906 Renaissance Revival mansion-turned-inn. Guest rooms are classically comfortable, not stuffy, with Jacuzzi tubs and some fireplaces and balconies. Great shared spaces include patios, billiard room, library and a dining room where chef-cooked breakfasts are served. The location is high above Temple Sq; expect great views and an uphill hike back from town.

Peery Hotel HOTEL $$

(☑ 801-521-4300, 800-331-0073; www.peeryhotel.com; 110 W 300 South; r $99-130; P❄@🛜) Egyptian-cotton robes and sheets, carved dark-wood furnishings, individually decorated rooms – prepare to be charmed by the 1910 Peery. Small but impeccable bathrooms have pedestal sinks and aromatherapy bath products. This throwback hotel stands smack in the center of the Broadway Ave entertainment district – walking distance to restaurants, bars and theaters. Parking is $12 per day.

Crystal Inn & Suites MOTEL $$

(☑ 800-366-4466, 801-328-4466; www.crystalinnsaltlake.com; 230 W 500 South; r incl breakfast $94-179; P❄@🛜🏊) Restaurants and Temple Sq are within walking distance of the downtown, multistory branch of Crystal Inns, a Utah-owned chain. Smiling staff here are genuinely helpful and there are lots of amenities for this price point (including a huge, hot breakfast).

Grand America HOTEL $$$

(☑ 800-621-4505; www.grandamerica.com; 555 S Main St; r from $260; P❄@🛜🏊) Rooms in SLC's only true luxury hotel are decked out with Italian marble bathrooms, English wool carpeting, tasseled damask draperies and other cushy details. If that's not enough to spoil you, there's always afternoon high tea or the lavish Sunday brunch. Overnight parking is $13.

🍴 Eating

Many of Salt Lake City's bountiful assortment of ethnic and organically minded restaurants are within the downtown core. There's also a good collection (Middle Eastern, a noodle house, upscale new American, a cafe...) at 9th and 9th.

SALT LAKE CITY FOR CHILDREN

Young and old alike appreciate the attractions in the University-Foothill District, but there are also a couple of kid-specific sights to see.

Discovery Gateway (www.childmuseum.org; 444 W 100 South; admission $8.50; ⊘10am-6pm Mon-Thu, to 8pm Fri & Sat, noon-6pm Sun; 🚼) An enthusiastic, hands-on children's museum. The mock network-news desk in the media zone is particularly cool for budding journos.

Hogle Zoo (www.hoglezoo.org; 2600 E Sunnyside Ave; adult/child $15/11; ⊘9am-5pm; 🚼). More than 800 animals inhabit zones like the Asian Highlands on the landscaped 42-acre grounds of this zoo. Daily animal-encounter programs help kids learn more about their favorite species.

Lion House Pantry Restaurant AMERICAN $
(www.templesquarehospitality.com; 63 E South Temple St; meals $8-14; ⊙11am-8pm Mon-Sat) Down-home, carb-rich cookin' just like your Mormon grandmother used to make – only it's served cafeteria-style in the basement of an historic house. Several of Brigham Young's wives used to live here (including a previous author's great-great-great grandmother).

★**Red Iguana** MEXICAN $$
(www.rediguana.com; 736 W North Temple; mains $10-16; ⊙11am-10pm) Mexico at its most authentic, aromatic and delicious – no wonder the line is usually snaking out the door at this family-run restaurant. Ask for samples of the mole to decide on one of seven chile- and chocolate-based sauces. The incredibly tender *conchinita pibil* (shredded roast pork) tastes like it's been roasting for days.

Squatters Pub Brewery AMERICAN $$
(www.squatters.com; 147 W Broadway; dishes $10-22; ⊙11am-midnight Sun-Thu, to 1am Fri & Sat) Come for an Emigration Pale Ale, stay for the blackened tilapia salad. In addition to great microbrews, Squatters does a wide range of American casual dishes as well. The lively pub atmosphere is always fun.

Wild Grape MODERN AMERICAN $$
(www.wildgrapebistro.com; 481 E South Temple; breakfast & lunch $7-15, dinner $13-28; ⊙8am-10pm Mon-Fri, 9am-10pm Sat & Sun) Billing itself as a 'new West' bistro, Wild Grape creates modern versions of country classics. We like the weekend brunch dishes best.

Mazza MIDDLE EASTERN $$
(www.mazzacafe.com; 1515 S 1500 East; sandwiches $8-10, dinner $15-25; ⊙11am-3pm & 5-10pm Mon-Sat; ✐) In an inviting ambience with warm tones and copper highlights, this local favorite consistently delivers well-known fare like kebabs, shawarma and hummus plus wonderful regional specialties, many from Lebanon. We love what they do with lamb and eggplant.

★**Copper Onion** INTERNATIONAL $$$
(☎801-355-3282; www.thecopperonion.com; 111 E Broadway Ave; brunch & small plates $7-15, dinner mains $22-29; ⊙11am-3pm & 5-10pm) Locals keep the Copper Onion bustling at lunch (for $10 specials), at dinner, at weekend brunch, at Happy Hour in the bar... And for good reason: small plates like wagyu beef tartare and pasta carbonara call out to be

CAN I GET A DRINK IN UTAH?

Absolutely. In recent years, laws have relaxed and private club membership bars are no more. Some rules to remember:

➡ Few restaurants have full liquor licenses: most serve beer and wine only. You have to order food to drink.

➡ Minors aren't allowed in bars.

➡ Mixed drinks and wine are available only after midday; 3.2% alcohol beer can be served starting at 10am.

➡ Mixed drinks cannot contain more than 1.5 ounces of a primary liquor, or 2.5 ounces total including secondary alcohol. Sorry, no Long Island Iced Teas or double shots.

➡ Packaged liquor can only be sold at state-run liquor stores; grocery and convenience stores can sell 3.2% alcohol beer and malt beverages. Sales are made from Monday through Saturday only.

shared. Design-driven rustic decor provides a convivial place to enjoy it all.

🍸 **Drinking & Nightlife**

★**Beer Bar** PUB
(161 E 200 South; ⊙11am-2am Mon-Sat, 10am-2am Sun) With shared wooden tables and over 140 beers and 13 sausage styles, Beer Bar is a little slice of Bavaria in Salt Lake City. The crowd is diverse and far more casual than at Bar X next door (a linked venue). A great place to meet friends and make friends, but it gets pretty loud.

Gracie's BAR
(326 S West Temple; ⊙11am-2am) Even with two levels and four bars, Gracie's trendy bar-restaurant still gets crowded. The two sprawling patios are the best place to kick back. Live music or DJs most nights.

Beerhive Pub PUB
(128 S Main St; ⊙noon-1am) More than 200 beer choices, including many Utah-local microbrews, are wedged into this downtown storefront bar. Good for drinking and conversation.

Coffee Garden CAFE
(895 E 900 South; ⊙6am-11pm Sun-Thu, to midnight Fri & Sat; 🛜) Perfection in a coffee shop,

with substance and style, good treats, desserts and ample seating. At the heart of the eclectic 9th and 9th neighborhood.

☆ Entertainment

Music

For a complete list of local music, visit www.cityweekly.net. Orchestra, organ, choir and other LDS-linked performances are listed at www.mormontabernaclechoir.org.

Mormon Tabernacle Choir   LIVE MUSIC
(☑ 801-570-0080; www.mormontabernaclechoir.org) FREE Hearing the world-renowned Mormon Tabernacle Choir is a must-do on any SLC bucket list. A live choir broadcast goes out every Sunday at 9:30am. September through November, and January through May, attend in person at the Tabernacle (p355). Free public rehearsals are held here from 8pm to 9pm Thursday.

From June to August and in December – to accommodate larger crowds – choir broadcasts and rehearsals are held at the 21,000-seat LDS Conference Center. Performance times stay the same, except that an extra organ recital takes place at 2pm, Monday through Saturday.

Theater

The Salt Lake City Arts Council provides a complete cultural events calendar on its website (www.slcgov.com/city-life/ec). Local venues include the **Gallivan Center** (www.thegallivancenter.com; 200 South, btwn State & Main Sts), **Depot** (☑ 801-355-5522; www.smithstix.com; 400 W South Temple), and the **Rose Wagner Performing Arts Center** (www.slccfa.org; 138 W 300 South); you can reserve through **ArtTix** (☑ 888-451-2787, 801-355-2787; www.arttix.org).

Sports

Utah Jazz   BASKETBALL
(☑ 801-325-2500; www.nba.com/jazz) Utah Jazz, the men's professional basketball team, plays at the **Energy Solutions Arena** (☑ 801-355-7328; www.energysolutionsarena.com; 301 W South Temple St), where concerts are also held.

Utah Grizzlies   ICE HOCKEY
(☑ 801-988-7825; www.utahgrizzlies.com) The International Hockey League's Utah Grizzlies plays at the **Maverik Center** (☑ tickets 800-745-3000; www.maverikcenter.com; 3200 S Decker Lake Dr, West Valley City), which hosted most of the men's ice-hockey competitions during the 2002 Winter Olympics.

🔒 Shopping

City Creek (p355) is the indoor-outdoor mall of choice for big-name-brand shopping downtown. A small but interesting array of boutiques line up along Broadway Ave (300 South), between 100 and 300 East. A few crafty shops can be found on the 300 block of W Pierpont Ave.

ℹ Information

EMERGENCY & MEDICAL SERVICES

University Hospital (☑ 801-581-2121; 50 N Medical Dr) For emergencies, 24/7.

MEDIA

City Weekly (www.cityweekly.net) Free alternative weekly with good restaurant and entertainment listings; twice annually it publishes the free City Guide.

Salt Lake Tribune (www.sltrib.com) Utah's largest-circulation daily paper.

TOURIST INFORMATION

Public Lands Information Center (☑ 801-466-6411; www.publiclands.org; REI Store, 3285 E 3300 South; ⏱ 10:30am-5:30pm Mon-Fri, 9am-1pm Sat) Recreation information for nearby public lands (state parks, BLM, USFS), including the Wasatch-Cache National Forest.

Visit Salt Lake (☑ 801-534-4900; www.visitsaltlake.com; 90 S West Temple, Salt Palace Convention Center; ⏱ 9am-6pm Mon-Fri, to 5pm Sat & Sun) Publishes free visitor-guide booklet; large gift shop on site at the visitor center.

THE BOOK OF MORMON, THE MUSICAL

Singing and dancing Mormon missionaries? You betcha...the musical *The Book of Mormon* opened to critical acclaim at the Eugene O'Neill Theatre in New York in 2011. The light-hearted satire about Latter-Day Saints (LDS) missionaries in Uganda came out of the comic minds that also created the musical *Avenue Q* and the animated TV series *South Park*. No wonder people laughed them all the way to nine Tony Awards.

The LDS church's official response? Actually quite measured, avoiding any direct criticism – though it was made clear that their belief is that while 'the Book, the musical' can entertain you, the scriptures of the actual Book of Mormon can change your life. The show has even been staged in Salt Lake City, at the Capitol Theatre in 2015.

WORTH A TRIP

GREAT SALT LAKE

Once part of prehistoric Lake Bonneville, Great Salt Lake today covers 2000 sq miles and is far saltier than the ocean; you can easily float on its surface. The pretty, 15-mile-long **Antelope Island State Park** (☎801-773-2941; http://stateparks.utah.gov; Antelope Dr; day-use per vehicle $10; tent & RV sites without hookups $15; ⏱7am-10pm Jul-Sep, to 7pm Oct-Jun), 40 miles northwest of SLC, has nice hiking and the best beaches for lake swimming (though at low levels they're occasionally smelly). It's also home to one of the largest bison herds in the country. The basic **Bridger Bay Campground** (☎reservations 800-322-3770; http://utahstateparks.reserveamerica.com; tent & RV sites $15) operates year-round.

❶ Getting There & Away

AIR

Five miles northwest of downtown, **Salt Lake City International Airport** (SLC; www.slcairport.com; 776 N Terminal Dr; 🛜) has mostly domestic flights, though you can fly direct to Canada and Mexico. Delta (www.delta.com) is the main SLC carrier.

BUS

Greyhound (☎800-231-2222; www.greyhound.com; 300 S 600 West) connects SLC with Southwestern towns such as Las Vegas, NV ($62, eight hours), and Denver, CO ($86, 10 hours).

TRAIN

Traveling between Chicago and Oakland/Emeryville, the California Zephyr from **Amtrak** (☎800-872-7245; www.amtrak.com) stops daily at **Union Pacific Rail Depot** (340 S 600 West). Schedule delays can be substantial, and trains depart at odd hours, but you can connect with destinations such as Denver (from $79, 15 hours) and Reno, NV (from $70, 10 hours).

❶ Getting Around

TO/FROM THE AIRPORT

Utah Transit Authority (UTA; www.rideuta.com; one-way $2.50; 🛜) With light-rail service to the international airport and free rides within the downtown area. Bus 550 travels downtown from the parking structure between terminals 1 and 2.

Express Shuttle (☎800-397-0773; www.xpressshuttleutah.com) Shared van service; $17 to downtown.

Yellow Cab (☎801-521-2100) Private taxi to Salt Lake, Park City and area destinations.

PUBLIC TRANSPORTATION

UTA (www.rideuta.com) Trax, UTA's light-rail system, runs from Central Station (600 W 250 South) west to the University of Utah and south past Sandy. The center of downtown SLC is a free-fare zone. During ski season UTA buses serve the local ski resorts ($4.50 one-way).

Park City & the Wasatch Mountains

Utah offers some of North America's most awesome skiing, with fabulous low-density, low-moisture snow – between 300in and 500in annually – and thousands of acres of high-altitude terrain. The Wasatch Mountain Range, which towers over SLC, holds numerous ski resorts, abundant hiking, camping and mountain biking – not to mention chichi Park City, with its upscale amenities and famous film festival.

Salt Lake City Resorts

On the western side of the Wasatch mountain range, the four impressive snow-sport resorts in Little Cottonwood and Big Cottonwood Canyons lie within 40 minutes' drive of downtown SLC. All have lodging and dining facilities.

🎿 Activities

Solitude   SNOW SPORTS
(☎801-534-1400; www.skisolitude.com; 12000 Big Cottonwood Canyon Rd; day lift-ticket adult/child $74/46) Exclusive, European-style village surrounded by excellent terrain. The Nordic Center has cross-country skiing in winter and nature trails in summer.

Brighton   SNOW SPORTS
(☎801-532-4731, 800-873-5512; www.brightonresort.com; Big Cottonwood Canyon Rd; day lift-ticket adult/child $68/35) Slackers, truants and badass boarders rule at Brighton. But don't be intimidated: the low-key resort where many Salt Lake residents first learned to ski remains a good first-timers' spot, especially if you want to snowboard. Thick stands of pines line sweeping groomed trails and wide boulevards, and from the top, the views are gorgeous.

SCENIC DRIVE: MIRROR LAKE HIGHWAY

This alpine route, also known as Hwy 150, begins about 12 miles east of Park City in Kamas and climbs to elevations of more than 10,000ft as it winds the 65 miles into Wyoming. The highway provides breathtaking mountain vistas, passing scores of lakes, campgrounds and trail-heads in the **Uinta-Wasatch-Cache National Forest** (www.fs.usda.gov/uwcnf). Sections may be closed to traffic into late spring due to heavy snowfall; check online.

Snowbird   SNOW SPORTS
(☑800-232-9542; www.snowbird.com; Hwy 210, Little Cottonwood Canyon; day lift-ticket adult/child $95/45) The biggest and the busiest of them all, with all-round great snow riding – think steep and deep. Numerous lift-assist summer hiking trails; aerial tramway runs year-round.

Alta   SNOW SPORTS
(☑801-359-1078, 888-782-9258; www.alta.com; Little Cottonwood Canyon; day lift-pass adult/child $79/42) Dyed-in-the-wool skiers make a pilgrimage to Alta, at the top of the valley. No snowboarders are allowed here, which keeps the snow cover from deteriorating, especially on groomers. Locals have grown up with Alta, a resort filled not with see-and-be-seen types, but rather the see-and-say-hello crowd. Wide-open powder fields, gullies, chutes and glades, such as East Greeley, Devil's Castle and High Rustler, have helped make Alta famous. Warning: you may never want to ski anywhere else.

Park City

A mere 35 miles east of SLC via I-80, Park City (elevation 6900ft) boasts two claims to international fame – hosting the downhill, jumping and sledding events at the 2002 Winter Olympics, and being the primary venue for the prestigious annual Sundance Film Festival. The Southwest's most popular ski destination is still home to the US ski team. Come summer, residents (pop 7873) gear up for hiking and mountain biking among the nearby peaks.

The town itself – a silver-mining community during the 19th century – has an attractive main street lined with galleries, shops, hotels, restaurants and bars. Despite the spread of prefab condos, the setting remains relatively charming. Winter is high season.

◉ Sights

Utah Olympic Park   ADVENTURE SPORTS
(☑435-658-4200; www.utaholympiclegacy.com; 3419 Olympic Pkwy; museum admission free, tours adult/child $10/7; ☺10am-6pm, tours 11am-4pm) Visit the site of the 2002 Olympic ski jumping, bobsledding, skeleton, Nordic combined and luge events, which continues to host national competitions. There are 10m, 20m, 40m, 64m, 90m and 120m Nordic ski-jumping hills as well as a bobsled-luge run. The US Ski Team practices here year-round – in summer, the freestyle jumpers land in a bubble-filled jetted pool, and the Nordic jumpers on a hillside covered in plastic. Call for a schedule; it's free to observe.

✦ Activities

In addition to snow sports, each area resort has posh lodging close to the slopes, abundant dining and summer activities including mountain-bike rental and lift-assist hiking. More than 300 miles of interconnecting hiking/biking trails crisscross area mountains; maps are available from the visitor center or online at http://mountaintrails.org. Two trails, **Armstrong** (4 miles; Park City Mountain Resort trailhead) and **Pinecone Ridge** (4 miles), combine for excellent mountain biking.

Park City Mountain Resort ADVENTURE SPORTS
(☑435-649–8111; www.parkcitymountainresort.com; 1310 Lowell Ave; alpine pass adult/child $70/35) We love the **Town Lift**–served hiking and mountain biking (day pass $21 to $23). The alpine pass is priced by size: those over 54" in height pay the adult fare, which includes access to the alpine slide, lifts and base-area activities. Or you can go á la carte: a 3000ft-long **alpine slide** ($12), where a wheeled sled flies down 550ft along a cement track, as well as a super-long **zipline ride** (2300ft long, 550ft vertical; $20).

Deer Valley   ADVENTURE SPORTS
(☑800-424-3337; www.deervalley.com; Deer Valley Dr; scenic chairlift all-day adult/child $23/18) In summer Deer Valley has more than 50 miles of hiking and mountain-biking trails served by its three operating lifts. Horseback riding and free guided hikes are available by request.

Canyons ADVENTURE SPORTS
(☑ 888-226-9667; www.thecanyons.com; 4000 Canyons Resort Dr; adventure pass adult/child $69/59) Adventure passes cover a range of activities. A scenic ride on the **gondola** (round-trip adult/junior $18/13) is great for sightseers, but hiking trails also lead off from here. Mountain bikers should head over to the **Gravity Bike Park** (day pass adult/junior $32/27), which has varied trails accessed by the High Meadow Lift. Other activities include disc golf, miniature golf, lake pedal-boats and hot-air balloon rides. On weekends in summer and winter live-music concerts rock the base area.

✲ Festivals & Events

Sundance Film Festival FILM
(☑ 888-285-7790; www.sundance.org/festival) Independent films and their makers and movie stars and their fans fill the town to bursting for 10 days in late January. Passes, ticket packages and the few individual tickets sell out well in advance – plan ahead.

🛏 Sleeping
More than 100 condos, hotels and resorts rent rooms in Park City; none are dirt cheap. For complete listings, check www.visitparkcity.com. High-season winter rates are quoted below (some require minimum stays); prices drop by half or more out of peak season. Chain motels at the intersection of I-40 and Hwy 248, and in SLC, offer better deals.

Chateau Apres Lodge HOSTEL $
(☑ 800-357-3556, 435-649-9372; www.chateauapres.com; 1299 Norfolk Ave; dm $45, r $130; 🛜) The only budget-oriented accommodation in town is this basic, 1963 lodge – with a 1st-floor dorm – near the town ski lift. Reserve ahead, as it's very popular with groups and seniors.

Park City Peaks HOTEL $$
(☑ 800-333-3333, 435-649-5000; www.parkcitypeaks.com; 2121 Park Ave; r $139-189; ✳@🛜🐾) Comfortable, contemporary rooms include access to heated outdoor pool, hot tub, restaurant and bar. Great deals off season. December through April, breakfast is included.

★ Old Town Guest House B&B $$$
(☑ 800-290-6423, 435-649-2642; www.oldtownguesthouse.com; 1011 Empire Ave; r incl breakfast $219-269; ✳@🛜) Grab the flannel robe, pick a paperback off the shelf and snuggle under a quilt on your lodgepole bed or kick back on the large deck at this comfy in-town B&B. The host will gladly give you the lowdown on the great outdoors, guided ski tours, mountain biking, and the rest.

★ Torchlight Inn B&B $$$
(www.torchlightinn.com; r $225-300; 🅿✳🛜) Right off the traffic circle, this new six-room inn charms with elegant and inviting contemporary spaces, gas fireplaces and flatscreen TVs. There's also a rooftop hot tub, Jeep rentals on-site and two friendly bulldogs to keep you company. With friendly, helpful service, family suites and wheelchair access (including an elevator).

✗ Eating
While not known for cheap eats, Park City has exceptional upscale dining. Pick up Park City Magazine's menu guide (www.parkcitymagazine.com) for more. Between April and November, restaurants reduce hours and may take extended breaks. Reservations are required for all top-end ($$$) establishments.

Uptown Fare CAFE $
(227 Main St; sandwiches $8-11; ⊙11am-3pm) Comforting, house-roasted turkey sandwiches and homemade soups at the hole-in-the-wall hidden below the Treasure Mountain Inn.

DON'T MISS

ROBERT REDFORD'S SUNDANCE RESORT
Wind your way up narrow and twisting Hwy 92, for a truly special experience at Robert Redford's **Sundance Resort** (☑ 800-892-1600, 801-225-4107; www.sundanceresort.com; 9521 Alpine Loop Rd, Provo; r $209-500; 🛜). Even if a night's stay at this elegantly rustic, ecoconscious wilderness getaway is out of reach, you can have a stellar meal at the Treehouse Restaurant or deli, attend an outdoor performance at the amphitheater or watch pottery being made (and sold) at the art shack. Skiing, hiking and spa services are also on site. Just walking the grounds is an experience. The resort is 30 miles south of Park City and 50 miles southeast of SLC.

Good Karma
INDIAN, FUSION $$

(www.goodkarmarestaurants.com; 1782 Prospector Ave; breakfast $7-12, mains $12-22; ⊙7am-10pm; 🖉) 🍃 Whenever possible, local and organic ingredients are used in the Indo-Persian meals at Good Karma. You'll recognize the place by the Tibetan prayer flags flapping out front.

★ Riverhorse on Main
NEW AMERICAN $$$

(🖉435-649-3536; www.riverhorseparkcity.com; 540 Main St; dinner mains $34-49; ⊙5-10pm Mon-Thu, to 11pm Fri & Sat, 11am-2:30pm & 5-10pm Sun; 🖉) A fine mix of the earthy and exotic, with cucumber quinoa salad, polenta fries and Rocky Mountain rack of lamb. There's a separate menu for vegetarians. A wall-sized window and the sleek modern design creates a stylish atmosphere. Reserve ahead: this is a longtime, award-winning restaurant.

★ J&G Grill
AMERICAN $$$

(🖉435-940-5760; www.jggrilldeercrest.com; 2300 Deer Valley Drive E, Deer Valley Resort; breakfast & lunch mains $14-22, dinner mains $26-55; ⊙7am-9pm) A favorite of locals, who love the tempura onion rings and seared scallops with sweet chili sauce. The bold flavors of meat and fish star here at one of celebrity chef Jean-Georges Vongerichten's collaborative projects. The mid-mountain St Regis setting is spectacular.

Wahso
ASIAN $$$

(🖉435-615-0300; www.wahso.com; 577 Main St; mains $30-50; ⊙5:30-10pm Wed-Sun, closed mid-Apr–mid-Jun) Park City's cognoscenti flock to this modern pan-Asian phenomenon, where fine-dining dishes may include lamb vindaloo or Malaysian snapper. Expect to see and be seen.

🍸 Drinking & Nightlife

Main St is where it's at, with half a dozen or more bars, clubs and pubs. In winter, there's action nightly – even restaurants have music. Outside peak season, the scene is weekends-only. For listings, see www.thisweekinparkcity.com.

High West Distillery & Saloon
BAR

(703 Park St; ⊙11am-10pm, tours 3pm & 4pm) A former livery and Model A–era garage is now home to Park City's most happenin' nightspot. You can ski in for homemade rye whiskey at this micro distillery. What could be cooler?

No Name Saloon & Grill
BAR

(447 Main St; ⊙11am-1am) There's a motorcycle hanging from the ceiling and Johnny Cash's 'Jackson' playing on the stereo at this memorabilia-filled bar.

ⓘ Information

Visitor Information Center (🖉435-658-9616, 800-453-1360; www.visitparkcity.com; 1794 Olympic Pkwy; ⊙9am-6pm; 🛜) Vast visitor center with a coffee bar, terrace and incredible views of the mountains at Olympic Park. Visitor guides available online.

ⓘ Getting There & Around

Park City Transportation (🖉800-637-3803, 435-649-8567; www.parkcitytransportation. com) and **Powder For The People** (🖉888-482-7547, 435-649-6648) run shared-van service ($44 one-way) and private-charter vans (from $220 for one to three people) to/from Salt Lake City airport. The latter also has ski shuttles between Park City and Salt Lake City resorts.

PC-SLC Connect (bus 902) takes you from central Salt Lake to the **Park City Transit Center** (www.parkcity.org; 558 Swede Alley). No need for a car once you get to Park City. The excellent transit system covers the town: accessing the historic district, Kimbell Junction and all three ski resorts. The free buses run one to six times an hour from 8am to 11pm (reduced frequency in summer).

Northeastern Utah

Most visitors head northeast to explore Dinosaur National Monument, but this rural, oil-rich area also has some captivating wilderness terrain. All towns are a mile above sea level.

Vernal

As the closest town to Dinosaur National Monument, it's not surprising that Vernal welcomes you with a large pink dino-buddy. The informative film, interactive exhibits, video clips and giant fossils at the **Utah Field House of Natural History State Park Museum** (🖉435-789-3799; http://stateparks.utah. gov; 496 E Main St; adult/child $6/3; ⊙9am-5pm; 👶) make a great all-round introduction to Utah's dinosaurs.

Don Hatch River Expeditions (🖉435-789-4316, 800-342-8243; www.donhatchrivertrips. com; 221 N 400 East; one-day adult/child $99/76) offers rapid-riding and gentler float trips on the nearby Green and Yampa Rivers.

Chain motels are numerous along Main St, but they book up with local workers – so don't expect a price break. **Holiday Inn Express & Suites** (☑800-315-2621, 435-789-4654; www.holidayinn.com/vernal; 1515 W Hwy 40; r incl breakfast $199-222; ❋ 🛜 🛋) has the most amenities, and **Econo Lodge** (☑435-789-2000; www.econolodge.com; 311 E Main St; r $79-119) will do in a bargain pinch.

Backdoor Grille (87 W Main St; mains $5-8; ☺11am-6pm Mon-Sat) makes fresh sandwiches and cookies, which are great to take on a picnic; you can also pick up a hiking guide at the associated bookshop. For dinner, the **Porch** (www.facebook.com/theporchvernal; 251 E Main St; lunches $8-12, dinner mains $14-23; ☺11am-2pm & 5-9pm Mon-Fri, 5-9pm Sat) is the place to go for Southern US favorites.

Dinosaur National Monument

Straddling the Utah-Colorado state line, **Dinosaur National Monument** (www.nps.gov/dino; off Hwy 40, Vernal; 7-day pass per vehicle $10; ☺24hr) protects a huge dinosaur fossil bed, discovered in 1909. Both states' sections are beautiful, but Utah has the bones. Don't miss the **Quarry Exhibit** (☺9am-4pm), an enclosed, partially excavated wall of rock with more than 1600 bones protruding.

In summer, shuttles run to the Quarry itself, 15 miles northeast of Vernal, UT, on Hwy 149, from the **Quarry Visitor Center** (☺8am-6pm mid-May–late Sep, 9am-5pm late Sep–mid-May); out of season you drive there in a ranger-led caravan. Follow the Fossil Discovery Trail from below the parking lot (2.2 miles round-trip) to see a few more giant femurs sticking out of the rock. The rangers' interpretive hikes are highly recommended.

In Colorado, the **Canyon Area** – 30 miles further east, outside Dinosaur, CO, and home to the monument's main **visitor center** (☑970-374-3000; 4545 E Hwy 40; ☺8am-4:30pm daily Jun-Aug, Mon-Fri only Dec-Feb) – holds some stunning overlooks, but thanks to its higher elevation is closed by snow until late spring.

Both sections have numerous hiking trails, interpretive driving tours, Green or Yampa river access and campgrounds ($8 to $15 per tent and RV site).

Flaming Gorge National Recreation Area

Named for its fiery red sandstone formations, this gorge-ous park has 375 miles of reservoir shoreline, part of the Green River system. Resort activities at **Red Canyon Lodge** (☑435-889-3759; www.redcanyonlodge.com; 790 Red Canyon Rd, Dutch John; cabins $115-155) include fly-fishing, rowing, rafting and horseback riding; its pleasantly rustic cabins have no TVs. **Flaming Gorge Resort** (☑435-889-3773; www.flaminggorgeresort.com; 155 Greendale/Hwy 191, Dutch John; r/ste $125/165, RV site $35; ❋ 🛜) has similar water-based offerings and rents motel rooms and suites. Both have decent restaurants.

Contact the **USFS Flaming Gorge Headquarters** (☑435-784-3445; www.fs.usda.gov/ashley; 25 W Hwy 43, Manila; ☺8am-5pm Mon-Fri) for the public camping lowdown. The area's 6040ft elevation ensures pleasant summers.

Moab & Southeastern Utah

Snow-blanketed peaks in the distance provide stark contrast to the red-rock canyons that define this rugged corner of the Colorado Plateau. For 65 million years water has carved serpentine, sheer-walled gorges along the course of the Colorado and Green Rivers. Today these define the borders of expansive Canyonlands National Park (p366). At nearby Arches National Park (p365), erosion sculpted thousands of arches and fin rock formations. Base yourself between the parks in Moab, aka activity central – a town built for mountain biking, river running and four-wheel driving. In Utah's far southeastern corner, Ancestral Puebloan sites are scattered among remote and rocky wilderness areas and parks. Most notable is Monument Valley, which extends into Arizona.

Green River

The 'World's Watermelon Capital,' the town of Green River offers a good base for river running on the Green and Colorado Rivers. The legendary one-armed Civil War veteran, geologist and ethnologist John Wesley Powell first explored these rivers in 1869 and 1871. Learn about his amazing travels at the **John Wesley Powell River History Museum** (☑435-564-3427; www.jwprhm.com; 885 E Main St; adult/child $6/2; ☺8am-7pm Apr-Oct, to 4pm Nov-Mar), which doubles as the local visitor center.

Holiday River Expeditions (☑800-624-6323, 435-564-3273; www.holidayexpeditions.com; 10 Holiday River St; day trip $165) run one-day rafting trips in Westwater Canyon, as well as multiday excursions.

Family-owned, clean and cheerful, **Robbers Roost Motel** (☑ 435-564-3452; www.rrmotel.com; 325 W Main St; r from $38; ❄ ☎ ❄) is a motorcourt budget-motel gem. Otherwise, there are numerous chain motels where W Main St (Business 70) connects with I-70. Residents and rafters alike flock to **Ray's Tavern** (25 S Broadway; dishes $8-27; ⊗ 11am-9:30pm), the local beer joint, for hamburgers and fresh-cut French fries.

Green River is 182 miles southeast of Salt Lake City and 52 miles northwest of Moab, and is a stop on the daily California Zephyr train, run by **Amtrak** (☑ 800-872-7245; www.amtrak.com; 250 S Broadway) to Denver, CO (from $59, 10¾ hours).

Moab

Southeastern Utah's largest community (population 5130) bills itself as the state's recreation capital, and… oh man, does it deliver. Scads of rafting and riding (mountain bike, horse, 4WD…) outfitters here make forays into surrounding public lands. Make this your base, and you can hike Arches or Canyonlands National Parks during the day, then come back to a comfy bed, a hot tub and your selection of surprisingly good restaurants at night. Note, though, that this alfresco adventure gateway is not a secret: Moab is mobbed, especially during spring and fall events. If the traffic irritates you, you can disappear into the vast surrounding desert in no time.

🏃 Activities

Moab's information center carries brochures on near-town rock art, hiking trails, driving tours, etc, and keeps a list of the many outfitters that offer half-day to multiday adventures (from $80 for a sunset 4WD tour to around $175 for a white-water day on the river). Book ahead.

★ Moab Desert Adventures ROCK CLIMBING
(☑ 804-814-3872; www.moabdesertadventures. com; 415 N Main St; half/full day from $165/265) Top-notch climbing tours scale area towers and walls; the 140ft arch rappel is especially exciting. Canyoneering and multisport packages available.

Sheri Griffith Expeditions RAFTING
(☑ 800-332-2439; www.griffithexp.com; 2231 S Hwy 191) Operating since 1971, this rafting

specialist has a great selection of river trips on the Colorado, Green and San Juan Rivers – from family floats to Cataract Canyon rapids, from a couple hours to a couple weeks.

Poison Spider Bicycles MOUNTAIN BIKING
(☑ 435-259-7882, 800-635-1792; www.poisonspiderbicycles.com; 497 N Main St; rental per day $45-75) Friendly staff are always busy helping wheel jockeys map out their routes. Well-maintained road and suspension rigs for rent; private guided trips organized in conjunction with Magpie Adventures.

Farabee's Outlaw Jeep Tours DRIVING TOUR
(☑ 435-259-7494; www.farabeesjeeprentals.com; 35 Grand St) Customized Jeep rental and off-road ride-along or guide-led tours.

🛏 Sleeping

Most lodgings have bike-storage facilities and hot tubs. Despite having an incredible number of motels, Moab does fill up; reservations are highly recommended March through October.

Individual **BLM campsites** (☑ 435-259-2100; www.blm.gov/utah/moab; Hwy 128; tent sites $15; ⊗ year-round) in the area are first-come, first-served. In peak season, check with the Moab Information Center to see which sites are full.

Adventure Inn MOTEL $
(☑ 435-259-6122; www.adventureinnmoab.com; 512 N Main St; r $69-105; ⊗ Mar-Oct; ❄ ☎) A great little indie motel, the Adventure Inn has spotless rooms (some with refrigerators) and decent linens, as well as laundry facilities. There's a picnic area on-site and the owners prove helpful.

Lazy Lizard Hostel HOSTEL $
(☑ 435-259-6057; www.lazylizardhostel.com; 1213 S Hwy 191; dm/s/d $11/30/34, cabins $35-41; ❄ ❄ @ ☎) Hippie hangout with frayed couches, worn bunks and small kitchen.

★ Cali Cochitta B&B $$
(☑ 435-259-4961, 888-429-8112; www.moabdreaminn.com; 110 S 200 East; cottages $140-180; ❄ ☎) Charming and central, these adjoining brick cottages offer snug rooms fitted with smart decor. A long wooden table on the patio makes a welcome setting for community breakfasts. You can also take advantage of the porch chairs, hammock or backyard hot

tub. The vibe is warm but the innkeepers live off-site, leaving you alone to enjoy the house.

Sunflower Hill Inn
INN $$

(☑ 435-259-2974; www.sunflowerhill.com; 185 N 300 East; r $175-250; ✳ 🛜 🌊) A top-shelf B&B, Sunflower Hill offers rooms in two inviting buildings –a cedar-sided early-20th-century home and a 100-year-old farmhouse amid manicured gardens and cottonwoods. Rooms have an elegant country style, with quilt-piled beds and antiques. The staff are eager to please and the hot tub works magic.

Sorrel River Ranch
LODGE $$$

(☑ 877-317-8244; www.sorrelriver.com; Mile 17, Hwy 128; r $429-779; ✳ @ 🌊) Southeast Utah's only full-service luxury resort and gourmet restaurant was originally an 1803 homestead. The lodge and log cabins sit on 240 lush acres, with riding areas and alfalfa fields along the Colorado River. Details strive for rustic perfection, with bedroom fireplaces, handmade log beds, copper-top tables and Jacuzzi tubs.

✖ Eating

Moab holds everything from backpacker coffeehouses to gourmet dining rooms; pick up the *Moab Menu Guide* (www.moabmenuguide.com) at area lodgings.

★ Milt's
BURGERS $

(356 Mill Creek Dr; dishes $4-9; ⏱11am-8pm Mon-Sat) Meet greasy goodness. A triathlete couple bought this classic 1954 burger stand and smartly changed nothing. Heaven is one of their honest burgers, jammed with pickles, fresh lettuce, a side of fresh-cut fries and creamy milkshake. Be patient: the line can get long. It's near the Slickrock Bike Trail.

★ Pantele's Deli
DELI $

(☑ 435-259-0200; 98 E Center St; sandwiches $8-10; ⏱11am-4pm Mon-Sat) Doing a brisk business, this deli makes everything fresh and it shows. Salads come in heaping bowls and high-piled sandwiches are stuffed with fresh roasted turkey or roast beef cooked in-house. The wait is worth it.

Sabaku Sushi
SUSHI $$

(☑ 435-259-4455; www.sabakusushi.com; 90 E Center St; rolls $6-9, mains $13-17; ⏱5pm-midnight Tue-Sun) The ocean is about a million miles away, but you still get a creative selection of fresh rolls, catches of the day and a few Utah originals at this small hole-in-the-wall sushi joint.

Stick with the status quo with traditional sashimi and *nigiri* offerings or get adventurous with the lip-smacking Elk Tataki and Devil's Garden Roll (topped with a pineapple habanero sauce).

★ Desert Bistro
SOUTHWESTERN $$$

(☑ 435-259-0756; www.desertbistro.com; 36 S 100 West; mains $22-42; ⏱5:30-11pm Wed-Sun) Stylized preparations of game and fresh, flown-in seafood are the specialty at this welcoming white-tablecloth restaurant inside an old house. Think smoked elk in a huckleberry glaze, pepper-seared scallops and jicama salad with crisp pears. Everything is made on-site, from freshly baked bread to delicious pastries. Great wine list, too.

ℹ Information

Moab Information Center (www.discovermoab.com; cnr Main & Center Sts; ⏱8am-7pm; 🛜) Excellent source of information on area parks, trails, activities, camping and weather. Extensive bookstore and knowledgeable staff. Walk-in only.

ℹ Getting There & Around

Delta has regularly scheduled flights from **Canyonlands Airport** (CNY; www.moabairport.com; off Hwy 191), 16 miles north of town via Hwy 191, to Salt Lake City.

Moab Luxury Coach (☑ 435-940-4212; www.moabluxurycoach.com) operates a van service to and from SLC ($159 one-way, 4¾ hours) and Grand Junction ($95 one-way, 2 hours). **Roadrunner Shuttle** (☑ 435-259-9402; www.roadrunnershuttle.com) and **Coyote Shuttle** (☑ 435-260-2097; www.coyoteshuttle.com) offer on-demand Canyonlands Airport, hiker-biker and river shuttles.

Moab is 235 miles southeast of Salt Lake City, and 150 miles northeast of Capital Reef National Park.

Arches National Park

Stark, exposed, and unforgettably spectacular, **Arches National Park** (☑ 435-719-2299; www.nps.gov/arch; Hwy 191; 7-day pass per vehicle $10; ⏱24hr; visitor center 7:30am-6:30pm Mar-Oct, 9am-4pm Nov-Feb) boasts the world's greatest concentration of sandstone arches – more than 2000, ranging from 3ft to 300ft wide at last count. Nearly one-million visitors make the pilgrimage here each year; it's just 5 miles north of Moab, and small enough for you to see most of it within a day. Many noteworthy arches are easily reached by paved roads and relatively short hiking trails. To avoid crowds, consider a moonlight exploration, when it's cooler and the rocks feel ghostly.

Highlights along the park's main scenic drive include Balanced Rock, precariously perched beside the main park road, and, for hikers, the moderate-to-strenuous, 3-mile round-trip trail that ascends the slickrock to reach the unofficial state symbol, Delicate Arch (best captured in the late afternoon).

Further along the road, the spectacularly narrow canyons and maze-like fins of the Fiery Furnace are most safely explored on the three-hour, ranger-led hikes, for which advance reservation is usually necessary. This is no walk in the park. (Well, it is, but...) Be prepared to scramble up and over boulders, chimney down between rocks and navigate narrow ledges.

The scenic drive ends 19 miles from the visitor center at Devils Garden. The trailhead marks the start of a 2- to 7.7-mile round-trip hike that passes at least eight arches, though most hikers only go the relatively easy 1.3 miles to Landscape Arch, a gravity-defying, 290ft-long behemoth. For stays between March and October, advance reservations are a must for the Devils Garden Campground (📞877-444-6777; www.recreation.gov; tent & RV sites $20). No showers, no hookups.

Because of water scarcity and heat, few visitors backpack, though it is allowed with free permits (available from the visitor center).

Canyonlands National Park

Red-rock fins, bridges, needles, spires, craters, mesas, buttes – Canyonlands National Park (www.nps.gov/cany; per vehicle 7 days $10; tent & RV sites without hookups $10-15; ⏱24hr) is a crumbling, decaying beauty, a vision of ancient earth. Roads and rivers make inroads into this high-desert wilderness stretching 527 sq miles, but much of it is still untamed. You can hike, raft and 4WD here but be sure that you have plenty of gas, food and water.

The canyons of the Colorado and Green Rivers divide the park into several entirely separate areas. The appropriately named Island in the Sky district, just over 30 miles northwest of Moab, consists of a 6000ft-high flat-topped mesa that provides astonishing long-range vistas. Starting from the visitor center (📞435-259-4712; www.nps.gov/cany; Hwy 313, 1 mile after park entrance; ⏱8am-6pm Mar-Oct, 9am-4:30pm Nov-Feb), a scenic drive leads past numerous overlooks and trailheads, ending after 12 miles at Grand View Point, where a sinuous trail runs for a mile along the very lip of the mesa. Our favorite short hike en route is the half-mile loop to oft-photographed Mesa Arch, a slender, cliff-hugging span that frames a magnificent view of Washer Woman Arch. Seven miles from the visitor center, the first-come, first-served, 12-site Willow Flat Campground (www.nps.gov/cany/planyourvisit/islandinthesky. htm; tent & RV sites $10) has vault toilets but no water, and no hookups.

Named for the spires of orange-and-white sandstone jutting skyward from the desert floor, the wild and remote Needles district is ideal for backpacking and off-roading. To reach the visitor center (📞435-259-4711; Hwy 211; ⏱8am-6pm Mar-Oct, 9am-4:30pm Nov-Feb), follow Hwy 191 south for 40 miles from Moab, then take Hwy 211 west. This area is much more about long, challenging hikes than roadside overlooks. The awesome Chesler Park/Joint Trail Loop is an 11-mile route across desert grasslands, past towering red-and-white-striped pinnacles, and through deep, narrow slot canyons, at times just 2ft across. Elevation changes are mild, but the distance makes it an advanced day hike. The first-come, first-served, 27-site Squaw Flat Campground (www.nps.gov/ cany; tent & RV sites $15), 3 miles west of the visitor center, fills up every day, spring to fall. It has flush toilets and running water, but no showers or hookups.

In addition to normal entrance fees, advance-reservation permits ($10 to $30) are required for backcountry camping, 4WD trips and river trips. Remoter areas west of the rivers, only accessible southwest of the town of Green River, include Horseshoe Canyon, where determined hikers are rewarded with extraordinary ancient rock art, and the Maze.

Dead Horse Point State Park

Tiny but stunning Dead Horse Point State Park (www.stateparks.utah.gov; Hwy 313; park day use per vehicle $10; tent & RV sites $25; ⏱park 6am-10pm, visitor center 8am-6pm Mar-Oct, 9am-4pm Nov-Feb) has been the setting for numerous movies, including the climactic scenes of Thelma & Louise. It's not a hiking destination, but mesmerizing views merit the short detour off Hwy 313 en route to the Island in the Sky in Canyonlands National Park: look out at red-rock canyons rimmed with white cliffs, the Colorado River, Canyonlands and the distant La Sal Mountains. The 21-site campground has limited water (bring your own if possible); no showers, no hookups. Reserve ahead.

Bluff

One hundred miles south of Moab, this little community (population 258) makes a comfortable, laid-back base for exploring Utah's desolately beautiful southeastern corner. Founded by Mormon pioneers in 1880, Bluff sits surrounded by red rock and public lands near the junction of Hwys 191 and 162, along the San Juan River. Other than a trading post and a couple of places to eat or sleep, there's not much town.

For backcountry tours that access rock art and ruins, join **Far Out Expeditions** (☑ 435-672-2294; www.faroutexpeditions.com; day tours $195) on a day or multiday hike into the remote region. A rafting trip along the San Juan with **Wild Rivers Expeditions** (☑ 800-422-7654; www.riversandruins.com; 101 Main St; day trip adult/child $175/133), a history and geology-minded outfitter, also includes ancient site visits.

The hospitable **Recapture Lodge** (☑ 435-672-2281; www.recapturelodge.com; Hwy 191; r incl breakfast $85; ✳ @ 🎅 ⊠) is a rustic, cozy place to stay. Owners sell maps and know the region inside and out. Also nice are the spacious log rooms at the **Desert Rose Inn** (☑ 435-672-2303, 888-475-7673; www.desertroseinn.com; 701 West Main Street; r $140-189, cabins $179-289; ➡ ✳ @ 🎅).

Artsy **Comb Ridge Coffee** (www.combridgecoffee.com; 680 S Hwy 191; dishes $3-10; ☺ 7am-9pm Tue-Sat, to 5pm Sun, varies Nov-Feb; 🎅) serves espresso, muffins and sandwiches inside a timber and adobe cafe, while the Western-themed **Cottonwood Steakhouse** (☑ 435-672-2282; www.cottonwoodsteakhouse.com; Hwy 191, cnr Main & 4th East Sts; mains $18-25; ☺ 5:30-9:30pm Mar-Nov) serves substantial portions of barbecued steak and beans.

Hovenweep National Monument

Beautiful, little-visited Hovenweep (www.nps.gov/hove; Hwy 262; park 7-day per vehicle $6; tent & RV sites $10; ☺ park dusk-dawn, visitor center 8am-6pm Jun-Sep, 9am-5pm Oct-May), meaning 'deserted valley' in the Ute language, showcases several neighboring Ancestral Puebloan sites, where impressive

DON'T MISS

NEWSPAPER ROCK RECREATION AREA

This tiny, free recreation area is really just a parking lot beside a single large sandstone rock panel that's packed with more than 300 **petroglyphs** attributed to Ute and Ancestral Puebloan peoples during a 2000-year period. It's about 12 miles along Hwy 211 from Hwy 191, en route to the Needles section of Canyonlands National Park (8 miles further).

towers and granaries stand in shallow desert canyons. The Square Tower Group is accessed near the visitor center; other sites require long hikes. The campground has 31 basic, first-come, first-served sites (no showers, no hookups). The main access is east of Hwy 191 on Hwy 262 via Hatch Trading Post, more than 40 miles northeast of Bluff.

Monument Valley

Twenty-five miles southwest from Bluff, after the village of **Mexican Hat** (named for an easy-to-spot sombrero-shaped rock), Hwy 163 winds southwest and enters the Navajo Indian reservation. Another 25 miles southwest, the incredible mesas and buttes of Monument Valley rise up. Most of the area, including the tribal park with a 17-mile unpaved driving loop circling the massive formations, is in Arizona (p346).

Natural Bridges National Monument

Fifty-five miles northwest of Bluff, the ultra-remote **Natural Bridges National Monument** (www.nps.gov/nabr; Hwy 275; 7-day pass per vehicle $6; tent & RV sites $10; ☺ 24hr, visitor center 8am-6pm May-Sep, 9am-5pm Oct-Apr) protects a white sandstone canyon (it's not red!) containing three impressive and easily accessible natural bridges. The oldest, Owachomo Bridge, spans 180ft but is only 9ft thick. The flat 9-mile Scenic Drive loop is ideal for overlooking. The campground offers 13 basic sites on a first-come, first-served basis; no showers, no hookups. There is some primitive overflow camping space, but be aware that the nearest services are in Blanding, 40 miles east.

Zion & Southwestern Utah

Local tourist boards call it 'color country,' but the cutesy label hardly does justice to the eye-popping hues that saturate the landscape. The deep-crimson canyons of Zion, the delicate pink-and-orange minarets at Bryce Canyon, the swirling yellow-white domes of Capitol Reef – the region is so spectacular that it holds three national parks and the gigantic Grand Staircase-Escalante National Monument (GSENM).

Capitol Reef National Park

Not as crowded as its fellow parks but equally scenic, **Capitol Reef** (☑435-425-3791, ext 4111; www.nps.gov/care; cnr Hwy 24 & Scenic Dr; admission free, 7-day scenic drive per vehicle $5; tent & RV sites $10; ☉24hr, visitor center & scenic drive 8am-6pm Apr-Oct, to 4:30pm Nov-Mar) contains much of the 100-mile Waterpocket Fold, created 65 million years ago when the earth's surface buckled up and folded, exposing a cross-section of geologic history that is downright painterly in its colorful intensity.

Hwy 24 cuts grandly through the park, but make sure to take the **scenic drive** south, a paved, dead-end 9-mile road that passes through orchards – a legacy of Mormon settlement. In season you can freely pick cherries, peaches and apples, as well as stop by the historic **Gifford Farmhouse** to see an old homestead and buy fruit-filled mini-pies. Great walks en route include the **Grand Wash** and **Capitol Gorge** trails, each following the level floor of a separate slender canyon; if you're in the mood for a more demanding hike, climb the **Golden Throne Trail** instead. The shady, green campground (no showers, no hookups) is first-come, first-served; it fills early spring through fall.

Torrey

Just 15 miles west of Capital Reef, the small pioneer town of Torrey serves as the base for most national-park visitors. In addition to a few Old West–era buildings, there are a dozen or so restaurants and motels.

Western-themed on the outside, **Austin's Chuckwagon Motel** (☑435-425-3335; www.austinschuckwagonmotel.com; 12 W Main St, Torrey; r $61-91, cabins $147; ☉Mar-Oct; ❀❀❀❀) has nice, clean, slightly characterless guest rooms on the inside. Note that budget digs

are over the general store, where you can grab supplies or sandwiches.

Dressed with country elegance, each airy room at the 1914 **Torrey Schoolhouse B&B** (☑435-633-4643; www.torreyschoolhouse.com; 150 N Center St, Torrey; r incl breakfast $115-145; ☉Apr-Oct; ❀❀) has a story to tell. (Butch Cassidy may have attended a town dance here.) After consuming the gourmet breakfast, laze in the garden or the huge 1st-floor lounge.

Thanks to its outstanding, highly stylized Southwestern cooking, **Cafe Diablo** (☑435-425-3070; www.cafediablo.net; 599 W Main St, Torrey; lunch $10-14, dinner mains $22-40; ☉11:30am-10pm mid-Apr–Oct; ❀) ranks high among the finest restaurants in southern Utah.

Boulder

Though the tiny outpost of **Boulder** (www.boulderutah.com; population 227), is just 32 miles south of Torrey on Hwy 12, you have to cross Boulder Mountain to reach it. From here, the attractive **Burr Trail Rd** heads east across the northeastern corner of the Grand Staircase-Escalante National Monument, eventually winding up on a gravel road that leads either up to Capital Reef or down to Bullfrog Marina on Lake Powell.

The small **Anasazi State Park Museum** (www.stateparks.utah.gov; Main St/Hwy 12; admission $5; ☉8am-6pm Mar-Oct, 9am-5pm Nov-Apr) curates artifacts and a Native American site inhabited from AD 1130 to 1175.

Rooms at **Boulder Mountain Lodge** (☑435-335-7460; www.boulder-utah.com; 20 N Hwy 12; r $135-184, ste $310, apt $220; ❀@❀❀❀) are plush, but it's the 15-acre wildlife sanctuary setting that's unsurpassed. An outdoor hot tub with mountain views is a soothing spot to bird-watch. The lodge's destination restaurant, **Hell's Backbone Grill** (☑435-335-7464; www.hellsbackbonegrill.com; 20 N Hwy 12, Boulder Mountain Lodge; breakfast $8-12, lunch $12-18, dinner $18-27; ☉7:30-11:30am & 5-9:30pm Mar-Nov) serves soulful, earthy preparations of regionally inspired and sourced cuisine – book ahead – while the nearby **Burr Trail Grill & Outpost** (www.burrtrailgrill.com; cnr Hwy 12 & Burr Trail Rd; dishes $8-18; ☉grill 11:30am-9:30pm, outpost 8:30am-6pm Mar-Oct; ❀) offers organic vegetable tarts, eclectic burgers and scrumptious homemade desserts.

Grand Staircase-Escalante National Monument

The 2656-sq-mile **Grand Staircase-Escalante National Monument** (GSENM; ☑435-826-5499; www.ut.blm.gov/monument; admission free; ☉24hr) **FREE**, a waterless region so inhospitable that it was the last to be mapped in the continental US, covers more territory than Delaware and Rhode Island combined. The nearest services, and GSENM visitor centers, are in Boulder and Escalante on Hwy 12 in the north, and Kanab on US 89 in the south. Otherwise, infrastructure is minimal, leaving a vast, uninhabited canyon land full of 4WD roads that call to adventurous travelers who have the time, equipment and knowledge to explore.

The most accessible and most used trail in the monument is the 6-mile round-trip hike to the magnificent multicolored waterfall on **Lower Calf Creek** (Mile 75, Hwy 12; day use $5; ☉day use dawn-dusk), between Boulder and Escalante. The 13 creekside campsites, just off Hwy 12, fill fast; no showers, no hookups, and no reservations taken.

Escalante

This national-monument gateway town of 779 people is the closest thing to a metropolis for many a lonely desert mile. Thirty slow and winding miles from Boulder, and 65 from Torrey, it's a good place to base yourself before venturing into the adjacent GSENM. The **Escalante Interagency Office** (☑435-826-5499; www.ut.blm.gov/monument; 775 W Main St; ☉8am-4:30pm daily Apr-Sep, Mon-Fri Oct-Mar) is a superb resource center with complete information on nearby monument and forest-service lands.

Escalante Outfitters & Cafe (☑435-826-4266; www.escalanteoutfitters.com; 310 W Main St; natural history tours $45; ☉7am-9pm) is a traveler's oasis: the bookstore sells maps, guides, camping supplies – and liquor(!) – while the pleasant cafe serves homemade breakfast, pizzas and salads. It also rents out tiny, rustic cabins ($45) and mountain bikes (from $35 per day). Long-time area outfitter **Excursions of Escalante** (☑800-839-7567; www.excursionsofescalante.com; 125 E Main St; full-day from $150; ☉8am-6pm) leads canyoneering, climbing and photo hikes.

Other decent lodgings in town include **Canyons Bed & Breakfast** (☑435-826-4747, 866-526-9667; www.canyonsbnb.com; 120 E Main

Southern Utah is generally warmer than northern Utah. But before you go making any assumptions about weather, check the elevation of your destination. Places less than an hour apart may have several thousand feet of elevation – and 20°F (10°C) temperature – difference.

➡ St George (3000ft)

➡ Zion National Park – Springdale entrance (3900ft)

➡ Cedar Breaks National Monument (10,000ft)

➡ Bryce National Park Lodge (8100ft)

➡ Moab (4026ft)

➡ Salt Lake City (4226ft)

➡ Park City (7100ft)

St; d incl breakfast $140; ☉Mar-Oct; ❋🐾) with upscale cabin-rooms that surround a shady courtyard, and the **Circle D Motel** (☑435-826-4297; www.escalantecircledmotel.com; 475 W Main St; r $74-99, cottage $125; ❋🐾🐾)), an older-but-updated budget motel with a friendly proprietor and a full-service restaurant.

Bryce Canyon National Park

The Grand Staircase, a series of uplifted rock layers that climb in clearly defined 'steps' north from the Grand Canyon, culminates in the Pink Cliffs formation at this deservedly popular **national park** (☑435-834-5322; www.nps.gov/brca; Hwy 63; 7-day pass per vehicle $25; ☉24hr; visitor center 8am-8pm May-Sep, to 4:30pm Oct-Apr). Not actually a 'canyon', but an amphitheater eroded from the cliffs, it's filled with wondrous sorbet-colored pinnacles and points, steeples and spires, and totem-pole-shaped 'hoodoos'. The park is 50 miles southwest of Escalante; from Hwy 12, turn south on Hwy 63.

Rim Road Scenic Drive (8000ft) travels 18 miles, roughly following the canyon rim past the visitor center, the lodge, incredible overlooks (don't miss **Inspiration Point**) and trailheads, ending at **Rainbow Point** (9115ft). From early May through early October, a free shuttle bus runs (8am until at least 5:30pm) from a staging area just north of the park to as far south as **Bryce Amphitheater**.

The park has two camping areas, both of which accept some reservations through the park website. Sunset Campground is bit more wooded, but is not open year-round. Coin-op laundry and showers are available at the general store near North Campground. During summer, remaining first-come sites fill before noon.

The 1920s **Bryce Canyon Lodge** (☑435-834-8700, 877-386-4383; www.brycecanyonforever. com; Hwy 63, Bryce Canyon National Park; r & cabins $208-256; ☺Apr-Oct; @🛜) exudes rustic mountain charm. Rooms are in modern hotel-style units, with up-to-date furnishings, and thin-walled duplex cabins with gas fireplaces and front porches. No TVs. The lodge **restaurant** (☑435-834-8700; breakfasts $6-12, lunch & dinner mains $18-40; ☺7-10am, 11:30am-3pm & 5:30-10pm Apr-Oct) is excellent, if expensive.

Just north of the park boundaries, **Ruby's Inn** (☑866-866-6616, 435-834-5341; www.rubysinn.com; 1000 S Hwy 63; r $135-180; ✳@🛜🏊) is a resort complex with multiple motel lodging options, plus a campground. You can also dine at several restaurants, admire Western art, wash laundry, shop for groceries, fill up with gas, and take a helicopter ride.

Eleven miles east on Hwy 12, the small town of **Tropic** (www.brycecanyoncountry.com) has additional food and lodging.

Kanab

At the southern edge of Grand Staircase-Escalante National Monument, vast expanses of rugged desert surround remote Kanab (population 4468). Western filmmakers made dozens of movies here from the 1920s to the 1970s, and the town still has an Old West feel.

John Wayne and Gregory Peck are among Hollywood notables who slumbered at the somewhat dated **Parry Lodge** (☑888-289-1722, 435-644-2601; www.parrylodge.com; 89 E Center St; r $109-139; ✳🛜🏊🐕).

SCENIC DRIVE: HIGHWAY 12

Arguably Utah's most diverse and stunning route, **Highway 12 Scenic Byway** (www.scenicbyway12.com) winds through rugged canyonland on a 124-mile journey northeast of Bryce Canyon to near Capitol Reef. The section between Escalante and Torrey traverses a moonscape of sculpted slickrock, crosses narrow ridgebacks and climbs over the 11,000ft Boulder Mountain.

The renovated **Canyons Lodge** (☑435-644-3069, 800-644-5094; www.canyonslodge.com; 236 N 300 West; r incl breakfast $89-179; ✳@🛜🏊🐕) 🐾 motel has an art-house Western feel; rooms feature original artwork. Stay there, then eat downtown at **Rocking V Cafe** (www.rockingvcafe.com; 97 W Center St; lunch $8-18, dinner $15-34; ☺11:30am-10pm; ☑), where fresh ingredients star in dishes such as buffalo tenderloin and curried quinoa.

The **Kanab GSENM Visitor Center** (☑435-644-1300; www.ut.blm.gov/monument; 745 E Hwy 89; ☺8am-4:30pm) provides monument information; **Kane County Office of Tourism** (☑435-644-5033, 800-733-5263; www.visitsouthernutah.com; 78 S 100 East; ☺8:30am-6pm Mon-Fri, to 4pm Sat) focuses on town and movie sites.

Zion National Park

Get ready for an overdose of awesome. **Zion National Park** (www.nps.gov/zion; Hwy 9; 7-day pass per vehicle $25; ☺24hr; visitor center Jun-Aug 8am-7:30pm, closes earlier Sep-May) abounds in amazing experiences: gazing up at the red-and-white cliffs of Zion Canyon, soaring high over the Virgin River; peering beyond Angels Landing after a 1400ft ascent; or hiking downriver through the notorious Narrows. But it also holds more delicate beauties: weeping rocks, tiny grottoes, hanging gardens and meadows of mesa-top wildflowers. Lush vegetation and low elevation give the magnificent rock formations a far lusher feel than the barren parks in the east.

Most visitors enter the park along Zion Canyon floor; even the most challenging hikes become congested May through September (shuttle required). If you've time for only one activity, the 6-mile **Scenic Drive**, which pierces the heart of Zion Canyon, is the one. From April through October, you have to take a free shuttle from the visitor center, but you can hop off and on at any of the scenic stops and trailheads along the way.

Of the easy-to-moderate trails, the paved, mile-long **Riverside Walk** at the end of the road is a good place to start. The **Angels Landing Trail** is a much more strenuous, 5.4-mile vertigo-inducer (1400ft elevation gain, with sheer drop-offs), but the canyon views are phenomenal. Allow four hours round-trip.

The most famous backcountry route is the unforgettable **Narrows**, a 16-mile journey into skinny canyons along the Virgin

River's north fork (June through October). Plan on getting wet: at least 50% of the 12-hour hike is in the river. Split the hike into two days, reserving an overnight camping spot in advance, or finish it in time to catch the last park shuttle. A trailhead shuttle is necessary for this one-way trip.

Heading eastwards, Hwy 9 climbs out of Zion Canyon in a series of six tight switchbacks to reach the 1.1-mile Zion-Mt Carmel Tunnel, a 1920s engineering marvel. It then leads quickly into dramatically different terrain – a landscape of etched multicolor slickrock, culminating at the mountainous **Checkerboard Mesa**.

Reserve far ahead and request a riverside site in the canyon's cottonwood-shaded **Watchman Campground** (☑ reservations 877-444-6777; www.recreation.gov; Hwy 9; tent sites $20, RV sites with hookups $30; ☺ year-round; ☻). Adjacent **South Campground** (☑ 435-772-3256; Hwy 9; tent & RV sites $20; ☺ year-round; ☻) is first-come, first-served only.

Smack in the middle of the scenic drive, rustic **Zion Lodge** (☑ 888-297-2757, 435-772-7700; www.zionlodge.com; Zion Canyon Scenic Dr; cabin/r/ste $204/210/270; ☻ @ ☎) has 81 well-appointed motel rooms and 40 cabins with gas fireplaces. All have wooden porches with stellar red-rock cliff views, but no TVs. The lodge's full-service dining room, **Red Rock Grill** (☑ 435-772-7760; Zion Canyon Scenic Dr, Zion Lodge; breakfast & sandwiches $5.85-14.75, dinner $15.75-29.50; ☺ 6:30-10am, 11:30am-2:30pm & 5-9pm Mar-Oct, hours vary Nov-Feb), has similarly amazing views. Just outside the park, the town of Springdale offers many more services.

Note that you must pay the park-entrance fee to drive on public Hwy 9 through the park, even if you are just passing through.

Springdale

Positioned at the main, south entrance to Zion National Park, Springdale is a perfect little park town. Stunning red cliffs form the backdrop to eclectic cafes, restaurants are big on organic ingredients, and artist galleries are interspersed with indie motels and B&Bs.

In addition to hiking trails in the national park, you can take outfitter-led climbing, canyoneering, mountain biking and 4WD trips (from $140 per person, per half-day) on adjacent BLM lands. **Zion Adventure Company** (☑ 435-772-1001; www.zionadventures.com; 36 Lion Blvd; canyoneering day from $177; ☺ 8am-8pm Mar-Oct, 9am-noon & 4-7pm Nov-Feb) offer

excellent excursions, Narrows outfitting, hiker/biker shuttles and river tubing.

The updated rooms at **Canyon Ranch Motel** (☑ 435-772-3357, 866-946-6276; www.canyonranchmotel.com; 668 Zion Park Blvd; r $109-169; ☻ ☎ ☻) ring a shady lawn with picnic tables and swings, while five flower-filled acres spill down to the Virgin River bank at **Cliffrose Lodge** (☑ 435-772-3234, 800-243-8824; www.cliffroselodge.com; 281 Zion Park Blvd; r $200-219, ste from $269; ☻ ☎ ☻).

Zion Canyon B&B (☑ 435-772-9466; www.zioncanyonbandb.com; 101 Kokopelli Circle; r incl breakfast $115-190; ☻ ☎) is the most traditional local B&B, serving a full, sit-down repast. The owners' creative collections of art and artifacts enliven the 1930s bungalow that is **Under the Eaves Inn** (☑ 435-772-3457; www.undertheeaves.com; 980 Zion Park Blvd; r incl breakfast $95-185; ☻ ☎); the morning meal is a gift certificate to a local restaurant.

For a coffee and *trés bonnes* crepes – both sweet and savory – make **MeMe's Cafe** (www.memescafezion.com; 975 Zion Park Blvd; breakfast & lunch $8-13, dinner $11-17; ☺ 7am-9pm) your first stop of the day. It also serves paninis and waffles, and in season has live music and barbecues on the patio. In the evening, the Mexican-tiled patio with twinkly lights at **Oscar's Cafe** (www.cafeoscars.com; 948 Zion Park Blvd; mains $12-18, breakfast $6-12; ☺ 8am-9pm) and the rustic **Bit & Spur Restaurant & Saloon** (www.bitandspur.com; 1212 Zion Park Blvd; mains $13-28; ☺ 5-11pm daily Mar-Oct, 5-10pm Thu-Sat Nov-Feb; ☎) are local-favored places to hang out, eat and drink.

St George

Nicknamed 'Utah's Dixie' for its warm weather and southern location, St George (population 76,917) is popular with retirees. This spacious, ever-growing Mormon town, with an eye-catching temple and pioneer buildings, is a potential stop between Las Vegas (120 miles) and Salt Lake City (304 miles) – or en route to Zion National Park. The 15,000-sq-ft collection of in-situ dino tracks and exhibits at **Dinosaur Discovery Site** (www.dinosite.org; 2180 E Riverside Dr; adult/child under 12yr $6/3; ☺ 10am-6pm Mon-Sat, 11am-5pm Sun, shorter hours Oct-Feb) are worth a detour.

Nearly every chain motel is represented somewhere in St George, at cheaper rates than you'll find 40 miles (one hour) east in Springdale. **Best Western Coral Hills** (☑ 435-673-4844, 800-542-7733; www.coralhills.com;

125 E St George Blvd; r incl breakfast from $130; ✳ @ 🛜 🏊) is walking distance from downtown restaurants and historic buildings. Two lovely, late-1800 houses contain **Seven Wives Inn** (📞435-628-3737, 800-600-3737; www.sevenwivesinn.com; 217 N 100 West; r incl breakfast $99-199; ✳ @ 🛜 🏊), a B&B with a small, central swimming pool.

The **Utah Welcome Center** (📞435-673-4542; http://travel.utah.gov; 1835 S Convention Center Dr, Dixie Convention Center; ⏱8:30am-5:30pm), off I-15, addresses statewide queries.

NEW MEXICO

They call this the 'Land Of Enchantment' for a reason. Maybe it's the drama of sunlight and shadow playing out across juniper-speckled hills; or the Hispanic mountain villages of horse pastures and adobe homes; or the centuries-old towns like soulful Santa Fe and arty Taos on the northern plateaus, overlooked by the magnificent Sangre de Cristos; or the volcanoes, canyons and vast desert plains spread beneath an even vaster sky. The beauty casts a powerful spell. Mud-brick churches filled with sacred art; ancient Indian pueblos; rippling dunes of sheer white sand; real-life cowboys and legendary Wild West characters such as Billy the Kid and Geronimo; chile-smothered enchiladas – all add to the pervasive sense of otherness that often makes New Mexico feel like a foreign country.

Perhaps the state's all-but-indescribable charm is best expressed in the iconic paintings of Georgia O'Keeffe. The artist herself exclaimed, on her very first visit: 'Well! Well! Well!...This is wonderful! No one told me it was like this.'

But seriously, how could they?

History

People have roamed this land for at least 12,000 years. By the time Francisco Vasquez de Coronado got here in the 16th century, Pueblo Indians were the dominant presence. After Santa Fe was established as the Spanish colonial capital, around 1610, Hispanic farmers settled across northern New Mexico, and Catholic missionaries set about converting the Puebloans. Following the Pueblo Revolt of 1680, Native Americans occupied Santa Fe until 1692, when Don Diego de Vargas recaptured the city.

New Mexico became a US Territory in 1850. Native American wars, settlement by cowboys and miners, and trade along the Santa Fe Trail further transformed the region, and the arrival of the railroad in the 1870s prompted an economic boom.

Painters and writers set up art colonies in Santa Fe and Taos in the early 20th century, while a top-secret scientific community developed the atomic bomb in Los Alamos in 1943. Some say aliens crashed outside of Roswell four years later. Maybe that's why New Mexico is now a pioneer in space tourism and commercial space flights.

ⓘ Information

For information on the New Mexico stretch of Route 66, visit www.rt66nm.org.
New Mexico State Parks Division (📞888-667-2757; www.emnrd.state.nm.us/SPD) Info on state parks, with a link to camping reservations.
Public Lands Information Center (📞877-851-8946; www.publiclands.org) Camping and recreation information.

Albuquerque

This bustling desert crossroads has an understated charm, one based more on its locals than on any urban sparkle. In New Mexico's largest city, just west of the Sandia mountains where the east–west Route 66 bridges the north–south Rio Grande, folks are more than happy to share history, highlights and must-try restaurants.

Centuries-old adobes pepper the lively Old Town area, and the shops, restaurants and bars in the hip Nob Hill zone are all within easy walking distance. Good hiking trails abound just outside of town, through evergreen forests or among panels of ancient petroglyphs, while modern museums explore space and nuclear energy. There's a vibrant mix of university students, Native Americans, Hispanics, and gays and lesbians. Flyers for square dances and yoga classes are distributed with equal enthusiasm, while ranch hands and real-estate brokers chow down beside each other at hole-in-the-wall taquerias and retro cafes.

Albuquerque's major boundaries are Paseo del Norte Dr to the north, Central Ave to the south, Rio Grande Blvd to the west and Tramway Blvd to the east. Central Ave, aka old Route 66, is the main artery, passing through Old Town, Downtown, the university and Nob

Hill. The city is divided into four quadrants (NW, NE, SW and SE), with the intersection of Central Ave and the railroad tracks just east of Downtown as the central point.

◉ Sights

◉ Old Town

From its foundation in 1706 until the arrival of the railroad in 1880, the plaza, centering on the diminutive 1793 San Felipe de Neri Church (www.sanfelipedeneri.org; Old Town Plaza; ⊙7am-5:30pm daily, museum 9:30am-5pm Mon-Sat), was the hub of Albuquerque. Today Old Town is the city's most popular tourist area.

★American International
Rattlesnake Museum   MUSEUM
(www.rattlesnakes.com; 202 San Felipe St NW; adult/child $5/3; ⊙10am-6pm Mon-Sat, 1-5pm Sun Jun-Aug; 11:30am-5:30pm Mon-Fri, 10am-6pm Sat, 1-5pm Sun, Sep-May) Anyone charmed by snakes and all things slithery will find this museum fascinating; for ophidiaphobes, it's a complete nightmare, filled with the world's largest collection of different rattlesnake species. You'll also find snake-themed beer bottles and postmarks from every town named 'Rattlesnake' in the US.

Albuquerque Museum
of Art & History   MUSEUM
(☑505-242-4600; www.cabq.gov/museum; 2000 Mountain Rd NW; adult/child $4/1; ⊙9am-5pm Tue-Sun, Old Town walking tours 11am Tue-Sun, Mar-mid-Dec) With revamped history galleries exploring the city's past from Spanish days onward, and a permanent art collection that extends to outsider and vernacular work as well as 20th-century masterpieces from the Taos School, this showpiece museum should not be missed. There's free admission on the first Wednesday of the month and on Sunday until 1pm, and free guided walking tours of Old Town.

◉ Around Town

The University of New Mexico (UNM) area has loads of good restaurants, casual bars, offbeat shops and hip college hangouts. The main drag is Central Ave between University and Carlisle Blvds. Just east is trendy Nob Hill, a pedestrian-friendly neighborhood lined with indie coffee shops, stylish boutiques and patio-wrapped restaurants.

NEW MEXICO FACTS

Nickname Land of Enchantment

Population 2.1 million

Area 121,599 sq miles

Capital city Santa Fe (population 69,00)

Other cities Albuquerque (population 550,000), Las Cruces (population 94,000)

Sales tax 5% to 9%

Birthplace of John Denver (1943–97), Smokey Bear (1950–76)

Home of International UFO Museum & Research Center (Roswell), Julia Roberts

Politics A 'purple' state, with a more liberal north and conservative south

Famous for Ancient pueblos, the first atomic bomb (1945), where Bugs Bunny should have turned left

State question 'Red or green?' (chili sauce, that is)

Highest/Lowest points Wheeler Peak (13,161ft) / Red Bluff Reservoir (2842ft)

Driving distances Albuquerque to Santa Fe 50 miles, Santa Fe to Taos 71 miles

★Indian Pueblo Cultural Center MUSEUM
(IPCC; ☑505-843-7270; www.indianpueblo.org; 2401 12th St NW; adult/child $6/3; ⊙9am-5pm) Collectively run by New Mexico's 19 Pueblos, this cultural center makes an essential stop-off during even the shortest Albuquerque visit. The museum downstairs holds fascinating displays on the Pueblos' collective history and individual artistic traditions, while the galleries above offer changing temporary exhibitions. They're arrayed in a crescent around a plaza that's regularly used for dances and crafts demonstrations, and as well as the recommended Pueblo Harvest Cafe (☑505-724-3510; www.indianpueblo.org; 2401 12th St NW; lunch $9-11, dinner $9-28; ⊙8am-8:30pm Mon-Sat, 8am-4pm Sun; 🅿🖐) there's also a large gift shop and retail gallery.

National Museum
of Nuclear Science & History   MUSEUM
(☑505-245-2137; www.nuclearmuseum.org; 601 Eubank Blvd SE; adult/child & senior $8/7; ⊙9am-5pm; 🖐) Located at the edge of the massive

Kirtland Air Force Base in Albuquerque's southeast corner, and surrounded by an outdoor Heritage Park holding discarded missiles and fighter planes, this lively museum explores the history of nuclear energy in war and peace, from the Manhattan Project and the Cold War up to today. Retired military personnel serve as docents.

Petroglyph National Monument ARCHAEOLOGICAL SITE
(505-899-0205; www.nps.gov/petr; 6001 Unser Blvd NW; ⊙ visitor center 8am-5pm) The lava field preserved in this large desert park, west of the Rio Grande, is adorned with more than 20,000 ancient petroglyphs. Take exit 154 off I-40 to reach the visitor center, 5.5 miles northwest of Old Town, and choose a hiking trail. Boca Negra Canyon is the busiest; Rinconada Canyon – the longest at 2.2 miles round-trip – offers the most solitude; and Piedras Marcadas holds 300 petroglyphs. Smash-and-grab thefts have been reported, so don't leave valuables in your vehicle.

Sandia Peak Tramway CABLE CAR
(505-856-7325; www.sandiapeak.com; 30 Tramway Rd NE; parking $1, adult/youth 13-20/child $20/17/12; ⊙ 9am-9pm Jun-Aug, 9am-8pm Wed-Mon Sep-May, from 5pm Tue) The world's longest aerial tram climbs 2.7 miles from the desert floor in the northeast corner of the city to the summit of 10,378ft Sandia Crest. The views are spectacular at any time, though sunsets are particularly brilliant. The complex at the top holds gift shops and restaurants, while hiking trails lead off through the woods, and there's also a small ski area.

🏃 Activities

The omnipresent Sandia Mountains and the less-crowded Manzano Mountains offer outdoor activities, including hiking, skiing (downhill and cross-country), mountain biking, rock climbing and camping.

Elena Gallegos Open Space HIKING
(www.cabq.gov; Simms Park Rd; weekday/weekend parking $1/2; ⊙ 7am- 9pm Apr–Oct, closes 7pm Nov-Mar) Sandia Crest is Albuquerque's outdoor playground, popular for skiing and hiking. As well as several picnic areas, this foothills park holds trailheads for hiking, running and mountain biking; some routes are wheelchair accessible. Come early, before the sun gets too hot, or late, to enjoy the panoramic views at sunset, as the city lights start to twinkle below. Time evening walks carefully, though; darkness falls quickly and howling coyotes ring the park. They won't bother you, but it can be unnerving.

👉 Tours

Story of New Mexico Program TOUR
(505-277-0077; www.dcereg.com) The UNM Department of Continuing Education offers excellent lectures on all things New Mexico, as well as tours to Santa Fe, Taos and sites throughout the state, including visits to Pueblo feast days and trips to the otherwise inaccessible Lawrence Ranch, home to the ashes of novelist DH Lawrence. Advance registration is required.

🎉 Festivals & Events

Gathering of Nations Powwow CULTURAL
(www.gatheringofnations.com; ⊙ Apr) Dance competitions, displays of Native American arts and crafts, and the 'Miss Indian World' contest. Held in late April.

International Balloon Fiesta BALLOON
(www.balloonfiesta.com; ⊙ early Oct) The largest balloon festival in the world. You simply haven't lived until you've seen a three-story-tall Tony the Tiger land in your hotel courtyard, and that's exactly the sort of thing that

---

ALBUQUERQUE FOR CHILDREN

¡Explora! (www.explora.us; 1701 Mountain Rd NW; adult/child $8/4; ⊙ 10am-6pm Mon-Sat, noon-6pm Sun;) This gung-ho place will captivate kiddies for hours. From the lofty high-wire bike to the mind-boggling Light, Shadow, Color area, there's a hands-on exhibit for every type of child (don't miss the elevator).

New Mexico Museum of Natural History & Science (www.nmnaturalhistory.org; 1801 Mountain Rd NW; adult/child $7/4; ⊙ 9am-5pm;) Across the street, this huge, dinosaur-crazy museum is crammed with ferocious ancient beasts, from the T Rex in the main atrium onwards. The emphasis throughout is on New Mexico, with dramatic displays on the state's geological origins and details of the impact of climate change – and did you know this is where Microsoft first started out?

happens during the festival, which features mass dawn take-offs on each of its nine days, overlapping the first and second weekends in October.

🛏 Sleeping

Route 66 Hostel
HOSTEL $

(☏ 505-247-1813; www.rt66hostel.com; 1012 Central Ave SW; dm $20, r from $25; 🅿 @ 🛜) This pastel-lemon hostel, in a former residence a few blocks west of Downtown, holds male and female dorms plus simple private rooms, some of which share bathrooms. The beds are aging, but there's a welcoming atmosphere, with common facilities including a library and a kitchen offering free self-serve breakfasts. Voluntary chores; no check-ins between 1:30pm and 4:30pm.

Econo Lodge Old Town
MOTEL $

(☏ 505-243-8475; www.econolodge.com; 2321 Central Ave NW; r incl breakfast $69; 🅿 ✳ @ 🛜 ▨) Just five minutes' walk west of the plaza, this bright, clean motel makes a great deal for anyone planning to explore the Old Town or the BioPark, with spacious and well-equipped modern rooms, an indoor pool and free hot breakfasts.

★ Andaluz
BOUTIQUE HOTEL $$

(☏ 505-242-9090; www.hotelandaluz.com; 125 2nd St NW; r $112-279; 🅿 ✳ @ 🛜) Albuquerque's finest historic hotel, built in the heart of Downtown in 1939, has been comprehensively modernized while retaining period details like its stunning central atrium, where cozy arched nooks hold tables and couches. Rooms feature hypoallergenic bedding and carpets, the **Más Tapas Y Vino** (☏ 505-923-9080; www.hotelandaluz.com; 125 2nd St NW; ⊙ 7am-2pm & 5-9:30pm) restaurant is excellent, and there's a rooftop bar. Reserve 30 days in advance for the best rates.

Böttger Mansion
B&B $$

(☏ 505-243-3639; www.bottger.com; 110 San Felipe St NW; r incl breakfast $104-179; 🅿 ✳ @ 🛜 ▨) The friendly proprietor gives this well-appointed B&B, built in 1912 and one minute's walk from the plaza, an edge over tough competition. Three of its seven themed, antique-furnished rooms have pressed-tin ceilings, one has a Jacuzzi tub, and sumptuous breakfasts are served in a honeysuckle-lined courtyard loved by bird-watchers. Past guests include Elvis, Janis Joplin and Machine Gun Kelly.

★ Los Poblanos
B&B $$$

(☏ 505-344-9297; www.lospoblanos.com; 4803 Rio Grande Blvd NW; r $180-330; 🅿 ✳ @ 🛜) This amazing 20-room B&B, on a 1930s rural ranch that's a National Historic Place, is five minutes' drive north of Old Town. Close to the Rio Grande, it's set amid 25 acres of gardens, lavender fields (blooming mid-June through July) and an organic farm. The gorgeous rooms feature kiva fireplaces, while produce from the farm is served for breakfast.

🍴 Eating

★ Frontier
NEW MEXICAN $

(☏ 505-266-0550; www.frontierrestaurant.com; 2400 Central Ave SE; mains $3-12; ⊙ 5am-1am; 🅿 ▨) Get in line for enormous cinnamon rolls (made with something approaching a stick of butter each) and some of the best huevos rancheros in town. The food, people-watching and Western art are all outstanding.

★ Golden Crown Panaderia
BAKERY $

(☏ 505-243-2424; www.goldencrown.biz; 1103 Mountain Rd NW; mains $7-20; ⊙ 7am-8pm Tue-Sat, 10am-8pm Sun) Who doesn't love a friendly neighborhood cafe/bakery? Especially one in a cozy old adobe, with gracious staff, oven-fresh bread and pizza, fruity empanadas, smooth espresso coffees and free cookies all round? Call ahead to reserve a loaf of quick-selling green chili bread – then eat it hot, out on the patio.

Annapurna's World Vegetarian Cafe
INDIAN $

(☏ 505-262-2424; www.chaishoppe.com; 2201 Silver Ave SE; mains $7-11; ⊙ 7am-9pm Mon-Fri, 8am-9pm Sat, 10am-8pm Sun) This awesome vegetarian and vegan cafe, one block south of Route 66 and part of a small local chain, serves fresh, tasty Indian specialties, including delicately spiced Ayurvedic delights that even carnivores love. Dishes are complemented by authentic chai.

Flying Star Cafe
AMERICAN $$

(☏ 505-255-6633; www.flyingstarcafe.com; 3416 Central Ave SE; mains $8-13; ⊙ 6am-11pm, to midnight Fri & Sat; 🛜 ▨ ▨) For visitors, the Nob Hill location of this deservedly popular local chain is the most convenient of outlets throughout Albuquerque and beyond. Locals flock here from early morning onwards, to enjoy an extensive breakfast menu and innovative main courses later on, amid creative, colorful decor. The whole experience is enhanced by the use of organic, free-range and antibiotic-free ingredients.

Artichoke Cafe MODERN AMERICAN $$$
(☑505-243-0200; www.artichokecafe.com; 424 Central Ave SE; lunch mains $10-16, dinner mains $19-39; ☺11am-2:30pm & 5-9pm Mon-Fri, 5-10pm Sat) Elegant and unpretentious, this popular bistro prepares creative gourmet cuisine with panache and is always high on foodies' lists of Albuquerque's best. It's on the eastern edge of Downtown, between the bus station and I-40.

Drinking & Entertainment

Popejoy Hall (www.popejoypresents.com; Central Ave, at Cornell St SE) and the historic **KiMo Theatre** (☑505-768-3544; www.cabq.gov/kimo; 423 Central Ave NW) are the primary venues for big-name national acts, local opera, symphony and theater. To find out what's happening in town, pick up the free weekly *Alibi* (www.alibi.com). Most of Albuquerque's trendy cafes and bars are found in the Nob Hill/UNM Districts.

Satellite Coffee CAFE
(www.satellitecoffee.com; 2300 Central Ave SE; ☺6am-11pm Mon-Fri, from 7am Sat & Sun; ☎) Albuquerque's answer to Starbucks lies in these hip coffee shops – look for the other eight locations around town – luring lots of laptop-toting regulars. Set up and still owned by the same brilliant folks responsible for the Flying Star chain.

Anodyne BAR
(☑505-244-1820; www.theanodyne.com; 409 Central Ave NW; ☺4pm-1:30am Mon-Sat, 7-11:30pm Sun) An excellent spot for a game of pool, Anodyne is a huge space with book-lined walls, wood ceilings, plenty of overstuffed chairs, more than 100 bottled beers and great people-watching on Central Ave.

Launch Pad LIVE MUSIC
(☑505-764-8887; www.launchpadrocks.com; 618 Central Ave SW) This retro-modern place is the hottest stage for local live music.

Shopping

For eclectic gifts, head to Nob Hill, east of the university, and take a stroll past the inviting boutiques and specialty stores.

Palms Trading Post ARTS & CRAFTS
(www.palmstrading.com; 1504 Lomas Blvd NW; ☺9am-5:30pm Mon-Fri, 10am-5:30pm Sat) Large gallery where knowledgeable salespeople sell Native American pottery, jewelery, rugs and crafts.

Silver Sun JEWELRY
(☑505-246-9692; www.silversunalbuquerque.com; 116 San Felipe St NW; ☺9am-4pm) A reputable Old Town store specializing in natural American turquoise, as stones as well as finished jewelry.

Mariposa Gallery ARTS & CRAFTS
(☑505-268-6828; www.mariposa-gallery.com; 3500 Central Ave SE) Beautiful and funky arts, crafts and jewelry, mostly by regional artists.

ℹ Information

EMERGENCY & MEDICAL SERVICES
Police (☑505-242-2677; 400 Roma Ave NW)
Presbyterian Hospital (☑505-841-1234; www.phs.org; 1100 Central Ave SE; ☺24hr emergency)
UNM Hospital (☑505-272-2411; 2211 Lomas Blvd NE; ☺24hr emergency) Head here if you don't have insurance.

POST
Post Office (201 5th St SW; ☺9am-4:30pm Mon-Fri)

TOURIST INFORMATION
Old Town Information Center (☑505-243-3215; www.itsatrip.org; 303 Romero Ave NW; ☺10am-5pm Oct-May, to 6pm Jun-Sep)
Albuquerque Convention & Visitors Bureau (☑505-842-9918; www.itsatrip.org; 20 First Plaza NW, cnr 2nd St & Copper Ave; ☺9am-4pm Mon-Fri) At the corner of 2nd St and Copper Ave.

USEFUL WEBSITE
City of Albuquerque (www.cabq.gov) Public transportation, area attractions and more.

ℹ Getting There & Around

AIR
Albuquerque International Sunport (ABQ; ☑505-244-7700; www.cabq.gov/airport; ☎) is New Mexico's main airport and most major US airlines fly here. Cabs to Downtown cost $20 to $25; try **Albuquerque Cab** (☑505-883-4888; www.albuquerquecab.com).

BUS
The **Alvarado Transportation Center** (100 1st St SW, cnr Central Ave) houses **ABQ RIDE** (☑505-243-7433; www.cabq.gov/transit; 100 1st St SW; adult/child $1/0.35; day pass $2), the public bus system. It covers most of Albuquerque from Monday to Friday and hits the major tourist spots daily. Most lines run until 6pm. ABQ

RIDE Route 50 connects the airport with downtown (last bus at 8pm Monday to Friday; limited service Saturday). Route 36 stops near Old Town and the Indian Pueblo Cultural Center.

Greyhound (☑800-231-2222, 505-243-4435; www.greyhound.com; 320 1st St SW) serves destinations throughout New Mexico. **Sandia Shuttle** (☑888-775-5696; www.sandiashuttle.com; 1-way/round-trip $28/48; ⊗8:45am-11:45pm) runs daily shuttles from the airport to many Santa Fe hotels, while **Twin Hearts Express** (☑575-751-1201; www.twinheartsexpresstransportation.com) runs a shuttle service from the airport to northern New Mexico destinations, including Taos and surrounding communities.

TRAIN
The Southwest Chief stops daily at Albuquerque's **Amtrak station** (☑800-872-7245, 505-842-9650; www.amtrak.com; 320 1st St SW; ⊗9:45am-5pm), heading east to Chicago (from $140, 26 hours) or west through Flagstaff, AZ ($91, five hours), to Los Angeles, CA (from $100, 16½ hours).

A commuter line, the **New Mexico Rail Runner Express** (www.nmrailrunner.com), shares the station, with eight departures for Santa Fe weekdays plus four on Saturday and three on Sunday (one-way/day pass $9/10, 1½ hours).

Along I-40
Although you can zip between Albuquerque and Flagstaff, AZ, in less than five hours, the national monuments and pueblos along the way are well worth a visit. For a scenic loop, take Hwy 53 southwest from Grants, which leads to all the following sights except Acoma. Hwy 602 brings you north to Gallup.

Acoma Pueblo
The dramatic mesa-top 'Sky City' sits 7000ft above sea level and 367ft above the surrounding plateau. One of the oldest continuously inhabited settlements in North America, this place has been home to pottery-making Pueblo peoples since the 11th century. Guided tours leave from the **visitor center** (☑800-747-0181; www.acomaskycity.org; adult/child/camera $23/15/13; ⊗tours 9:30am-3:30pm Mar-Nov) at the foot of the mesa and take two hours, or one hour just to tour the historic mission. From I-40, take exit 102, which is about 60 miles west of Albuquerque, then drive 12 miles south. Check ahead to make sure it's not closed for ceremonial or other reasons.

El Morro National Monument
The 200ft sandstone outcropping at the El Morro National Monument (☑505-783-4226; www.nps.gov/elmo; ⊗9am-6pm Jun-Aug, to 5pm Sep-May) **FREE**, also known as 'Inscription Rock,' has been a travelers' oasis for millennia. Thousands of carvings – from petroglyphs in the pueblo at the top (c 1275) to elaborate inscriptions by Spanish conquistadors and Anglo pioneers – offer a unique historical record. It's about 38 miles southwest of Grants via Hwy 53.

Zuni Pueblo
The Zuni are known for their delicately inlaid silverwork, which is sold in stores lining Hwy 53. Check in at the **visitor center** (☑505-782-7238; www.zunitourism.com; 1239 Hwy 53; tours $10; ⊗8:30am-5:30pm Mon-Fri, 10:30am-

---

SCENIC DRIVES: NEW MEXICO'S BEST

Billy the Kid National Scenic Byway (www.billybyway.com) This mountain-and-valley loop in southeastern New Mexico swoops past Billy the Kid's stomping grounds, Smokey Bear's gravesite and the orchard-lined Hondo Valley. From Roswell, take Hwy 380 west.

High Road to Taos The back road between Santa Fe and Taos passes through sculpted sandstone desert, fresh pine forests and rural villages with historic adobe churches and horse-filled pastures. The 13,000ft Truchas Peaks soar above. From Santa Fe, take Hwy 84/285 to Hwy 513 then follow the signs.

NM Highway 96 From Abiquiu to Cuba, this little road wends through the heart of Georgia O'Keeffe country, beneath the distinctive profile of Cerro Pedernal, then passing Martian-red buttes and sandstone cliffs striped purple, yellow and ivory.

NM Highway 52 Head west from Truth or Consequences into the dramatic foothills of the Black Range, through the old mining towns of Winston and Chloride. Continue north, passing the Monticello Box – where Geronimo finally surrendered – and emerging onto the sweeping Plains of San Augustin before reaching the bizarre Very Large Array.

4pm Sat, noon-4pm Sun) for information, photo permits and tours of the pueblo, which lead you among stone houses and beehive-shaped adobe ovens to the massive **Our Lady of Guadalupe Mission**, featuring impressive kachina murals. The **Ashiwi Awan Museum & Heritage Center** (☑505-782-4403; www.ashiwi-museum.org; Ojo Caliente Rd; admission by donation; ⊘9am-5pm Mon-Fri) displays early photos and other tribal artifacts.

The friendly, eight-room **Inn at Halona** (☑505-782-4547; www.halona.com; 23b Pia Mesa Rd; r from $75; P☎), decorated with local Zuni arts and crafts, is the only place to stay on the pueblo. Its breakfasts rank with the best in the state.

Gallup

Not just a classic Route 66 town, Gallup also serves as the Navajo and Zuni peoples' major trading center, making it a great place to buy top-quality Native American art and crafts at fair prices. The historic district is filled with trading posts, pawnshops, jewelry stores and crafts galleries.

The town's lodging jewel is **El Rancho** (☑505-863-9311; www.elranchohotel.com; 1000 E Hwy 66; r from $102; P❄☎☜). It features a superb Southwestern lobby, a restaurant, a bar and an eclectic selection of simple rooms, in which many of Hollywood's greatest actors once slept. Chain hotels line Route 66, west of the town center.

Santa Fe

Welcome to 'the city different,' a place that makes its own rules without ever forgetting its long and storied past. Walking around the busy Plaza that remains its core, or through its historic neighborhoods, there's no denying that Santa Fe has a timeless, earthy soul. Founded around 1610, this is the second-oldest city and the oldest state capital in the US, its seductive original adobe buildings now standing alongside modern counterparts built in the same style. And yet Santa Fe is also synonymous with contemporary chic, thanks to its thriving art market, gourmet restaurants, great museums, upscale spas and world-class opera.

Santa Fe is also the nation's highest state capital, set over 7000ft above sea level at the foot of the glowing Sangre de Cristo range. A fantastic base for hiking, mountain biking, backpacking and skiing, it's home to a mind-boggling array of characters, taking in artists, New Agers, long-established Hispanic families and recent Mexican immigrants, and more than a few big Hollywood names.

Cerrillos Rd (I-25 exit 278), a 6-mile strip of hotels and fast-food restaurants, enters town from the south; Paseo de Peralta circles the center; and to the west St Francis Dr (I-25 exit 282) turns into Hwy 285 and heads north toward Los Alamos and Taos.

⊙ Sights

★**Georgia O'Keeffe Museum**　MUSEUM
(☑505-946-1000; www.okeeffemuseum.org; 217 Johnson St; adult/child $12/free; ⊘10am-5pm, to 7pm Fri) With 10 beautifully lit galleries in a rambling 20th-century adobe, this museum boasts the world's largest collection of O'Keeffe's work. She's best known for her luminous New Mexican landscapes, but the changing exhibitions here range through her entire career, focusing for example on her years in New York. Major museums worldwide own her most famous canvases, so you may not see familiar paintings, but you're sure to be bowled over by the thick brushwork and transcendent colors on show.

Canyon Road　GALLERY
(www.canyonroadarts.com) The epicenter of the city's upscale art scene. More than 100 galleries, studios, shops and restaurants line the narrow historic road. Look for Santa Fe School masterpieces, rare Native American antiquities and wild contemporary work. The area positively buzzes with activity during the early-evening art openings on Fridays, and especially on Christmas Eve.

Wheelwright Museum of the American Indian　MUSEUM
(☑505-982-4636; www.wheelwright.org; 704 Camino Lejo; ⊘10am-5pm) FREE Mary Cabot established this museum in 1937 to showcase Navajo ceremonial art, and its major strength continues to be exquisite Navajo textiles, displayed under dim lighting to protect the natural dyes. Recent expansion work has added extra space for contemporary Native American art and historical artifacts. The gift store, known as the Case Trading Post, sells museum-quality rugs, vintage jewelry, kachinas and crafts.

St Francis Cathedral　CHURCH
(www.cbsfa.org; 131 Cathedral Pl; ⊘8:30am-4:30pm) Santa Fe's French-born bishop

THE MUSEUM OF NEW MEXICO

The Museum of New Mexico administers four excellent museums in Santa Fe. Two are at the Plaza, two are on Museum Hill, 2 miles southwest. A four-day pass gives adults entry to all four for $20; under-16s get in free.

Palace of the Governors (505-476-5100; www.palaceofthegovernors.org; 105 W Palace Ave; adult/child $9/free; 10am-5pm, closed Mon Oct-May) The oldest public building in the US, this low-slung adobe complex started out as home to New Mexico's first Spanish governor in 1610; was occupied by Pueblo Indians following their Revolt in 1680; and after 1846 became the seat of the US Territory's earliest governors. It now holds fascinating displays on Santa Fe's multi-faceted past, and some superb Hispanic religious artworks, while its modern adjunct alongside, the **New Mexico History Museum**, tells the story of the state as a whole.

New Mexico Museum of Art (505-476-5072; www.museumofnewmexico.org; 107 W Palace Ave; adult/child $9/free; 10am-5pm Tue-Sun, tours 1:30pm) Built in 1917, and a prime early example of Santa Fe's Pueblo Revival architecture, the New Mexico Museum of Art has spent a century collecting and displaying works by regional artists. A treasure trove of works by the great names who put New Mexico on the cultural map, from Georgia O'Keeffe to printmaker Gustave Baumann, it's also a lovely building in which to stroll around, with a cool garden courtyard. Constantly changing temporary exhibitions ensure its continuing relevance.

Museum of International Folk Art (505-827-6344; www.internationalfolkart.org; 706 Camino Lejo; adult/child $9/free; 10am-5pm, closed Mon Sep-May) Santa Fe's most unusual and exhilarating museum centers on the world's largest collection of folk art. Its huge main gallery displays whimsical and mind-blowing objects from more than 100 different countries. Tiny human figures go about their business in fully realized village and city scenes, while dolls, masks, toys and garments spill across the walls. Changing exhibitions in other wings explore vernacular art and culture worldwide.

Try to hit the incredible **International Folk Art Market**, held here in mid-July.

Museum of Indian Arts & Culture (www.indianartsandculture.org; 710 Camino Lejo; adult/child $9/free; 10am-5pm, closed Mon Sep-May) This top-quality museum sets out to trace the origins and history of the various Native American peoples of the entire desert Southwest, and explain and illuminate their widely differing cultural traditions. Pueblo, Navajo and Apache interviewees describe the contemporary realities each group now faces, while a truly superb collection of ceramics, modern and ancient, is complemented by stimulating temporary displays.

Jean-Baptiste Lamy – hero of Willa Cather's *Death Comes for the Archbishop* – set about building this cathedral in 1869. Its Romanesque exterior might seem more suited to Europe than the Wild West, but the Hispanic altarpiece inside lends a real New Mexican flavor. A side chapel holds a diminutive Madonna statue that was taken into exile following the Pueblo Revolt, and has been known since the Spaniards' triumphant return in 1692 as *La Conquistadora*.

Loretto Chapel   HISTORIC BUILDING
(505-982-0092; www.lorettochapel.com; 207 Old Santa Fe Trail; adult/child $3/2.50; 9am-5pm Mon-Sat, 10:30am-5pm Sun) Built in 1878 for the Sisters of Loretto, this tiny Gothic chapel is famous as the site of St Joseph's Miraculous Staircase, a spiraling and apparently unsupported wooden staircase added by a mysterious young carpenter who vanished without giving the astonished nuns his name. The chapel is no longer consecrated, and can be rented for (nondenominational) weddings.

Activities

The **Pecos Wilderness** and **Santa Fe National Forest**, east of town, have more than 1000 miles of hiking and biking trails, several of which lead to 12,000ft peaks. Contact the Public Lands Information Center for maps and details, and check weather reports for advance warnings of frequent summer storms. **Mellow Velo** (505-995-8356; www.mellowvelo.com; 132 E Marcy St; rentals per day

Santa Fe

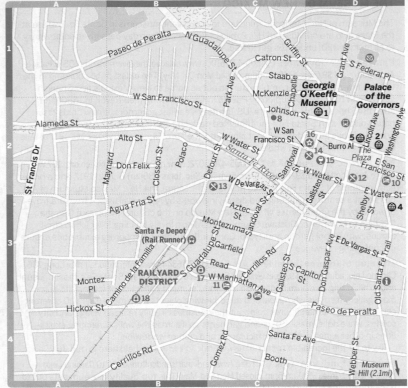

from $35; ⊙10am-6pm Mon-Sat) rents mountain bikes and provides trail information.

Operators including **New Wave Rafting Co** (☏800-984-1444; www.newwaverafting.com) offer white-water rafting adventures through the Rio Grande Gorge (half-day $55), the wild Taos Box (full day $110) and the Rio Chama Wilderness (three days $400).

Dale Ball Trails   MOUNTAIN BIKING
(www.santafenm.gov/trails_1) Over 20 miles of paved and unpaved bike and hiking trails, with fabulous desert and mountain views. The challenging **South Dale Ball Trails** start with a super-long, hard and rocky single-track climb, followed by harrowing switchbacks, while the intermediate **Winsor Trail** (No 254) leads through breathtaking scenery in Hyde State Park and Santa Fe National Forest.

Ski Santa Fe   SKIING
(☏505-982-4429, snow report 505-983-9155; www.skisantafe.com; lift ticket adult/child $69/49;

⊙9am-4pm late Nov-early Apr) Often overlooked for its more famous cousin outside Taos, the Santa Fe ski area boasts the same fluffy powder (though usually a little less), with a higher base elevation (10,350ft) and higher chairlift service (12,075ft). It caters to families and expert skiers, who fly down powder glade shoots, steep bump runs or long groomers, though the length and quality of the season varies wildly from year to year.

🎓 Courses

Santa Fe School of Cooking   COOKING
(☏505-983-4511; www.santafeschoolofcooking. com; 125 N Guadalupe St; 2/3hr class $75/98; ⊙9:30am-5pm Mon-Sat, noon-4pm Sun) If your love for New Mexican cuisine knows no bounds, take a lesson at this Southwestern-style cooking school, where the cost includes the meal at the end.

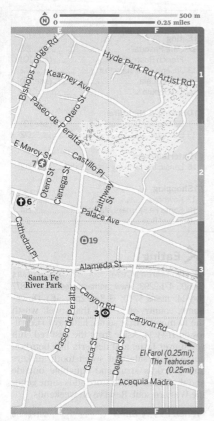

★ **Santa Fe Fiesta** CULTURAL
(☑505-913-1517; www.santafefiesta.org; ☺early Sep) This two-week celebration of the September 4, 1692, resettlement of Santa Fe after the Pueblo Revolt, from Labor Day through early September, includes concerts, a candlelit procession and the much-loved Pet Parade. Everything kicks off with the bizarrely pagan Friday-night torching of Zozobra – a 50-foot-tall effigy of 'Old Man Gloom' – before a baying mob in Fort Marcy Park.

🛏 Sleeping

Cerrillos Rd is lined with chains and independent motels. There's camping in developed sites in Santa Fe National Forest and Hyde State Park on Hwy 475, the road to the ski basin; for more information, go to the Public Lands Information Center.

★ **Silver Saddle Motel** MOTEL $
(☑505-471-7663; www.santafesilversaddlemotel. com; 2810 Cerrillos Rd; r from $62; P❋@🖥🐾) This old-fashioned, even kitschy Route 66 motel compound, 3 miles southwest of the Plaza, offers the best budget value in town. Some rooms have pleasant tiled kitchenettes, while all have shady wooden arcades outside and comfortable cowboy-inspired decor inside – get the Kenny Rogers or Wyatt Earp rooms if you can. Rates include continental breakfast.

Rancheros de Santa Fe Campground CAMPGROUND $
(☑505-466-3482; www.rancheros.com; 736 Old Las Vegas Hwy; tent/RV sites/cabins $25/42/49; ☺mid-Mar–Oct; 🖥🏊🐾) Eight miles southeast of the Plaza, off I-25 exit 290, Rancheros has shady, spacious sites for tents and RVs, plus simple forest cabins, nice views, a convenience store and free wi-fi. Enjoy hot showers, cheap morning coffee and evening movies.

★ **El Paradero** B&B $$
(☑505-988-1177; www.elparadero.com; 220 W Manhattan Ave; r from $130; P❋@🖥) Each room in this 200-year-old adobe B&B, south of the river, is unique and loaded with character. Two have their own bathrooms across the hall, the rest are en-suite; our favorites are rooms 6 and 12. The full breakfasts satisfy, and rates also include afternoon tea. A separate casita holds two kitchenette suites that can be combined into one ($350).

🎊 Festivals & Events

★ **Spanish Market** CULTURAL
(www.spanishcolonial.org; ☺late Jul) Traditional Spanish Colonial arts, from *retablos* and *bultos* (carved wooden religious statues) to handcrafted furniture and metalwork, make this juried show in late July an artistic extravaganza, second only to Indian Market.

★ **Santa Fe Indian Market** CULTURAL
(☑505-983-5220; www.swaia.org; ☺Aug) Over a thousand artists from 100 tribes and Pueblos show work at this world-famous juried show, held the weekend after the third Thursday in August. One hundred thousand visitors converge on the Plaza, at open studios, gallery shows and the Native Cinema Showcase. Come Friday or Saturday to see pieces competing for the top prizes; wait until Sunday before trying to bargain.

Santa Fe

Santa Fe Motel & Inn HOTEL **$$**
(☏505-982-1039; www.santafemotel.com; 510 Cerrillos Rd; r from $149, casitas from $169; ⓟ❋@🌐❄) Even the motel rooms in this downtown option, close to the Railyard and a real bargain in low season, have the flavor of a Southwestern B&B, with colorful tiles, clay sunbursts and tin mirrors. The courtyard casitas cost a little more and come with kiva fireplaces and little patios. Rates include a full hot breakfast, served outdoors in summer.

El Rey Inn HOTEL **$$**
(☏505-982-1931; www.elreyinnsantafe.com; 1862 Cerrillos Rd; r from $105; ⓟ❋@🌐❄) This classic courtyard hotel is highly recommended, thanks to its super, Southwestern-themed rooms and suites, scattered through 5 acres of landscaped gardens. Some rooms have kitchenettes, and the sizable outdoor pool has a hot tub alongside.

⭐**La Fonda** HISTORIC HOTEL **$$$**
(☏800-523-5002; www.lafondasantafe.com; 100 E San Francisco St; r/ste from $219/309; ⓟ❋@🌐❄) Long renowned as the 'Inn at the end of the Santa Fe Trail,' Santa Fe's loveliest historic hotel sprawls through an old adobe just off the Plaza. Recently upgraded while retaining its beautiful folk-art windows and murals, it's both classy and cozy, with some wonderful top-floor luxury suites, and superb sunset views from the rooftop Bell Tower Bar.

✕ Eating

⭐**San Marcos Cafe** NEW MEXICAN **$**
(☏505-471-9298; www.sanmarcosfeed.com; 3877 Hwy 14; mains $7-10; ⊗8am-2pm; 🚼) Down-home, country-style cafe that's well worth the 10-minute drive south, halfway to Cerrillos on Hwy 14. Aside from the best red chili you'll ever taste, and desserts like bourbon apple pie to sate that sweet tooth, turkeys and peacocks strut and squabble outside and the attached feed store adds some genuine Western soul. Reserve on weekends.

French Pastry Shop CREPERIE **$**
(☏505-983-6697; www.thefrenchpastryshop.com; 100 E San Francisco St; mains $6-10; ⊗6:30am-5pm) Charming cafe serving delicious French bistro food inside La Fonda Hotel, including crepes filled with everything from ham and cheese to strawberries and cream – along with a host of quiches, sandwiches, cappuccinos and, of course, pastries.

Tia Sophia's NEW MEXICAN **$**
(☏505-983-9880; 210 W San Francisco St; mains $7-10; ⊗7am-2pm Mon-Sat, 8am-1pm Sun; 🍴🚼) Local artists and visiting celebrities outnumber tourists at this long-standing and always-packed Santa Fe favorite. Breakfast is the meal of choice, with fantastic burritos and other Southwestern dishes, but lunch is pretty damn tasty too; try the perfectly prepared *chile rellenos* (stuffed chile peppers), or the rota of daily specials. The shelf of kids' books helps little ones pass the time.

★**Jambo Cafe** AFRICAN $$
(☑505-473-1269; www.jambocafe.net; 2010 Cerrillos Rd; mains $9-16; ☺11am-9pm Mon-Sat) Despite expanding year on year, this African-flavored cafe is hard to spot from the highway; once inside, though, it's a lovely spot, always busy with locals who love its distinctive goat, chicken and lentil curries, veggie sandwiches and roti flatbreads, not to mention the reggae soundtrack.

★**Cafe Pasqual's** INTERNATIONAL $$$
(☑505-983-9340; www.pasquals.com; 121 Don Gaspar Ave; breakfast & lunch $9-16, dinner $24-43; ☺8am-3pm & 5:30-9:30pm Sun-Thu, to 10pm Fri & Sat; ☑⊞) Whatever time you visit this exuberantly colorful, utterly unpretentious place, the food, most of which has a definite south-of-the-border flavor, is worth every penny of the high prices. The breakfast menu is famous for dishes like *huevos motuleños,* made with sautéed bananas, feta cheese and more; later on, the meat and fish mains are superb. Reservations taken for dinner only.

★**Joseph's Culinary Pub** MEDITERRANEAN $$$
(☑505-982-1272; www.josephsofsantafe.com; 428 Agua Fria St; ☺5:30-10pm Sun-Thu, to 11pm Fri & Sat) This romantic old adobe, open for dinner only, is best seen as a fine-dining restaurant rather than a pub. Order from the shorter, cheaper bar menu if you'd rather, but it's worth lingering in the warm-hued dining room to savor rich, modern Mediterranean dishes like crispy duck with French lentils, or rabbit lasagna with mascarpone cheese.

★**La Plazuela** NEW MEXICAN $$$
(☑505-982-5511; www.lafondasantafe.com; 100 E San Francisco St, La Fonda de Santa Fe; lunch $11-18, dinner $14-32; ☺7am-2pm & 5-10pm Mon-Fri, 7am-3pm & 5-10pm Sat & Sun) One of Santa Fe's greatest pleasures is a meal in the Fonda's irresistible see-and-be-seen central atrium, with its excited bustle, colorful decor and high-class New Mexican food, with contemporary dishes sharing menu space with standards like fajitas and tamales.

Drinking & Entertainment

★**The Teahouse** CAFE
(☑505-992-0972; www.teahousesantafe.com; 821 Canyon Rd; ☺9am-9pm; ☎) This spacious, relaxed indoor/outdoor cafe at the eastern end of Canyon Rd makes the perfect break while gallery-hopping. There are 160 teas from all over the world – with scones – plus a full menu (mains $11 to $16) of eggy brunch items, panini and salads.

Evangelo's BAR
(200 W San Francisco St; ☺noon-1:30am Mon-Sat, to midnight Sun) Everyone is welcome in this casual, rowdy, cash-only joint, owned by the Klonis family since 1971 (ask owner/bartender Nick about his father's unusual fame). Drop in, put on some Patsy Cline and grab a draft beer – it's the perfect escape from Plaza culture. Live Goth and alternative bands perform downstairs in the appropriately named Underground.

Bell Tower Bar BAR
(100 E San Francisco St; ☺3pm-sunset Mon-Thu, 2pm-sunset Fri-Sun May-Oct, closed Nov-Apr) In summer this bar atop La Fonda hotel is the premier spot to catch one of those patented New Mexican sunsets while sipping a killer margarita. After dark, retire to the hotel's lobby Fiesta Bar for live country or folk music.

★**El Farol** DINNER SHOW
(☑505-983-9912; www.elfarolsf.com; 808 Canyon Rd; dinner shows $25; ☺11am-midnight Mon-Sat, 11am-11pm Sun) Aside from its weekly flamenco dinner shows, this popular restaurant-bar programs live entertainment every night, including regular Latin soul shows.

★**Santa Fe Opera** OPERA
(☑505-986-5900; www.santafeopera.org; Hwy 84/285, Tesuque; tickets $32-254; backstage tours adult/child $5/free; ☺Jun-Aug, backstage tours 9am Mon-Fri Jun-Aug) Many visitors flock to Santa Fe for the opera alone: the theater is a marvel, with 360-degree views of sandstone wilderness crowned with sunsets and moonrises, while at center stage the world's finest talent performs magnificent masterworks. It's still the Wild West, though; you can even wear jeans. Shuttles run to and from Santa Fe and Albuquerque; reserve online.

Lensic Performing Arts Center PERFORMING ARTS
(☑505-988-7050; www.lensic.com; 211 W San Francisco St) A beautifully renovated 1930 movie house, the theater hosts touring productions and classic films as well as seven different performance groups, including the Santa Fe Symphony Orchestra & Chorus.

🏠 Shopping

Offering carved howling coyotes, turquoise jewelry and fine art, Santa Fe attracts shoppers of all budgets. Head to the sidewalk outside the Palace of the Governors to buy Indian jewelry direct from the craftspeople who make it.

★ Santa Fe Farmers Market MARKET
(📱 505-983-4098; www.santafefarmersmarket.com; Paseo de Peralta & Guadalupe St, Railyard; ⏰ 8am-1pm Sat, plus Tue May-Nov; 🚻) Local produce, much of it heirloom and organic, is on sale at this spacious indoor/outdoor market, alongside homemade goodies, inexpensive food, natural body products, and arts and crafts.

Pueblo of Tesuque Flea Market MARKET
(📱 505-670-2599; www.pueblooftesuquefleamarket.com; 15 Flea Market Rd; ⏰ 8am-4pm Fri-Sun Mar-Dec) Vendors at this outdoor market, beside the Santa Fe Opera 7 miles north of Santa Fe, sell everything from high-quality rugs, turquoise rings and clothing to the best used (read: broken-in) cowboy boots in the state. Nowadays, most booths are like small shops; a few individuals still turn up to sell funky junk.

Kowboyz CLOTHING
(📱 505-984-1256; www.kowboyz.com; 345 W Manhattan Ave; ⏰ 10am-5:30pm) Secondhand shop selling everything you need to cowboy up. Shirts are a great deal at $12 each; the amazing selection of boots, however, demands top dollar. Movie costumers in search of authentic Western wear often come here.

Travel Bug BOOKS
(📱 505-992-0418; www.mapsofnewmexico.com; 839 Paseo de Peralta; ⏰ 7:30am-5:30pm Mon-Sat, 11am-4pm Sun; 🛜) One of the largest selections of travel books and maps you'll ever find; you can even print topo maps on demand, on waterproof paper. Local travelers, authors and photographers give free talks about their adventures Saturday at 5pm. There's also a coffee bar with wi-fi.

🛈 Information

EMERGENCY & MEDICAL SERVICES
Police (📱 505-428-3710; 2515 Camino Entrada)

St Vincent's Hospital (📱 505-983-3361; www.stvin.org; 455 St Michael's Dr; ⏰ 24hr emergency)

POST
Post Office (120 S Federal Pl; ⏰ 8am-5:30pm Mon-Fri, 9am-4pm Sat)

TOURIST INFORMATION
New Mexico Visitor Information Center (📱 505-827-7336; www.newmexico.org; 491 Old Santa Fe Trail; ⏰ 8am-5pm Mon-Fri, 8am-4pm Sat & Sun) Housed in the historic 1878 Lamy Building, this friendly place offers helpful advice – and free coffee.

Public Lands Information Center (📱 505-954-2002; www.publiclands.org; 301 Dinosaur Trail; ⏰ 8:30am-4pm Mon-Fri) Staff at this hugely helpful office have maps and information on public lands throughout New Mexico, and can talk you through all the hiking options.

🛈 Getting There & Around

A few commercial airlines fly daily between **Santa Fe Municipal Airport** (SAF; 📱 505-955-2900; www.santafenm.gov/airport; 121 Aviation Dr) and Dallas, Denver, and Los Angeles, though these routes are added and cut with surprising frequency. Many more flights arrive at and depart from Albuquerque (one-hour drive south of Santa Fe).

Sandia Shuttle Express (📱 888-775-5696; www.sandiashuttle.com) runs between Santa Fe and the Albuquerque Sunport ($28). **North Central Regional Transit** (📱 505-629-4725; www.ncrtd.org) provides a free shuttle bus service to Espanola on weekdays, where you can transfer to shuttles to Taos, Los Alamos, Ojo Caliente and other northern destinations. Downtown pickup/drop-off is on Sheridan St, northwest of the plaza.

The **Rail Runner** (www.nmrailrunner.com) commuter train has multiple daily departures for Albuquerque, with connections to the airport. The trip takes about 1½ hours. **Amtrak** (📱 800-872-7245; www.amtrak.com) stops at Lamy; buses continue 17 miles to Santa Fe.

Santa Fe Trails (📱 505-955-2001; www.santafenm.gov; 1-way adult/child $1/free, day pass $2) provides local bus services. If you need a taxi, call **Capital City Cab** (📱 505-438-0000; www.capitalcitycab.com).

If driving between Santa Fe and Albuquerque, try to take Hwy 14 – the Turquoise Trail – which passes through the old mining town (now arts colony) of Madrid, 28 miles south of Santa Fe.

DON'T MISS

CHIMAYÓ

The so-called 'Lourdes of America' – the extraordinarily beautiful two-towered adobe chapel of **El Santuario de Chimayó** (☎505-351-9961; www.elsantuariodechimayo.us; ⏱9am-5pm Oct-Apr, to 6pm May-Sep) – nestles amid the hills of the so-called High Road, east of Hwy 84 28 miles north of Santa Fe. It was built in 1826, on a site where the earth was said to have miraculous healing properties. Even today, the faithful come to rub the *tierra bendita* – holy dirt – from a small pit inside the church on whatever hurts. During Holy Week, about 30,000 pilgrims walk to Chimayó from Santa Fe, Albuquerque and beyond, in the largest Catholic pilgrimage in the USA. The artwork in the *santuario* is worth a trip on its own. Stop at **Rancho de Chimayó** (☎505-984-2100; www.ranchodechimayo.com; County Rd 98; mains $8-21; ⏱11:30am-9pm, closed Mon Nov-Apr) afterward for lunch or dinner.

Around Santa Fe

Pueblos

The region north of Santa Fe remains the heartland of New Mexico's Pueblo Indian peoples. Eight miles west of Pojoaque along Hwy 502, the ancient **San Ildefonso Pueblo** (☎505-455-2273; www.sanipueblo.org; per vehicle $10, camera/video/sketching permits $10/20/25; ⏱8am-5pm) was the home of Maria Martinez, who in 1919 revived a distinctive traditional black-on-black pottery style. Stop at the **Maria Poveka Martinez Museum** (⏱8am-4pm Mon-Fri) FREE and browse the shops of the exceptional potters (including Maria's direct descendants) who work in the pueblo today.

Just north of San Ildefonso, on Hwy 30, **Santa Clara Pueblo** is home to the **Puyé Cliff Dwellings** (☎888-320-5008; www.puyecliffs.com; 300 Hwy 30; tour adult/child $20/18; 2 tours $35/33; ⏱hourly tours 9am-5pm May-Sep, 10am-2pm Oct-Apr), where you can visit Ancestral Puebloan cliffside and mesa-top ruins.

Las Vegas

Not to be confused with Nevada's glittery gambling megalopolis, this Las Vegas is one of the loveliest towns in New Mexico, and the largest and oldest community east of the Sangre de Cristo Mountains. Its eminently strollable downtown has a pretty Old Town Plaza and holds some 900 Southwestern and Victorian buildings listed in the National Register of Historic Places.

Built in 1882 and carefully remodeled a century later, the elegant **Plaza Hotel** (☎505-425-3591; www.plazahotel-nm.com; 230 Old Town Plaza; r incl breakfast from $54; P❄@📶🐾) is Las Vegas' most celebrated lodging, as seen in the movie *No Country For Old Men*. Choose between Victorian-style, antique-filled rooms in the original building or bright, modern rooms in a newer adjoining wing.

You can get your caffeine fix at **World Treasures Traveler's Cafe** (☎505-426-8638; 1814 Plaza St; snacks $3-6; ⏱7am-7pm Mon-Sat; 📶), right on the plaza, and substantial Mexican meals at **El Rialto** (☎505-454-0037; 141 Bridge St; mains $7-11; ⏱10:30am-8:30pm Tue-Thu, to 9pm Fri & Sat, closed Sun & Mon) nearby.

Los Alamos

When the top-secret Manhattan Project sprang to life in 1943, it turned the sleepy mesa-top village of Los Alamos into a busy laboratory of secluded brainiacs. Here, in the 'town that didn't exist,' the first atomic bomb was developed in almost total secrecy. Today you'll encounter a fascinating dynamic in which souvenir T-shirts emblazoned with atomic explosions and 'La Bomba' wine are sold next to books on pueblo history and wilderness hiking.

While you can't visit the **Los Alamos National Laboratory**, where classified cutting-edge research still takes place, the interactive **Bradbury Science Museum** (☎505-667-4444; www.lanl.gov/museum; 1350 Central Ave; ⏱10am-5pm Tue-Sat, 1-5pm Sun & Mon) FREE covers atomic history in fascinating detail. The small but interesting **Los Alamos Historical Museum** (☎505-662-6272; www.losalamoshistory.org; 1050 Bathtub Row; ⏱9:30am-4:30pm Mon-Fri, 11am-4pm Sat & Sun) FREE is on the nearby grounds of the former Los Alamos Ranch School – an outdoorsy school for boys that closed when the scientists arrived.

Grab a bite with a boffin at the **Blue Window Bistro** (☏505-662-6305; www.labluewindowbistro.com; 813 Central Ave; lunch $10-12, dinner $10-27; ⊗11am-2:30pm & 5-8:30pm Mon-Fri, 5-9pm Sat).

Bandelier National Monument

Ancestral Puebloans dwelt in the cliffsides of beautiful Frijoles Canyon, now preserved within **Bandelier** (www.nps.gov/band; per vehicle $12; ⊗dawn-dusk; ⊞). The adventurous can climb ladders to reach ancient caves and kivas used until the mid-1500s. Backpacking trails within the park sustained severe damage during recent floods, but there's still camping at **Juniper Campground** (☏877-444-6777; www.recreation.gov; campsites $12), set among the pines near the monument entrance. Note that between 9am and 3pm, from the end of May to late October, you have to take a shuttle bus to Bandelier from the **White Rock Visitor Center** (⊗8am-6pm May-Sep, 10am-2pm Oct-Apr), 11 miles north on Hwy 4.

Abiquiu

The Hispanic village of Abiquiu (sounds like 'barbecue'), on Hwy 84 about 45 minutes' drive northwest of Santa Fe, is famous because artist Georgia O'Keeffe lived and painted here from 1949 until her death in 1986. With the Chama River flowing through farmland and spectacular rock landscape, this ethereal setting continues to attract artists. O'Keeffe's adobe house is open for limited visits, with one-hour **tours** (☏505-685-4539; www.okeeffemuseum.org; tours $35-65; ⊗Tue-Sat Jun-Oct, Tue, Thu & Fri mid-Mar–May & Nov, by private arrangement any other time) offered at least three days per week, but often booked months in advance.

Set amid 21,000 Technicolor acres 15 miles northwest, **Ghost Ranch** (☏505-685-1000; www.ghostranch.org; US Hwy 84; suggested donation $3; Day Pass adult/child $29/14.50; ⊞) is a retreat center where O'Keeffe stayed many times. Besides fabulous hiking trails, it holds a **dinosaur museum** (suggested donation $2; ⊗9am-5pm Mon-Sat, 1-5pm Sun) and offers basic **lodging** (☏505-685-4333; www.ghostranch.org; US Hwy 84; tent/RV sites $23/27, dm incl board $53, r with shared/private bath incl breakfast $118/131; ℗) plus horseback rides (from $50).

The lovely **Abiquiú Inn** (☏505-685-4378; www.abiquiuinn.com; US Hwy 84; r from $120, casitas from $220; ℗☎) is a sprawling collection of shaded faux-adobes. Its spacious casitas have kitchenettes, and the menu at the on-site restaurant, **Cafe Abiquiú** (☏505-685-4378; www.abiquiuinn.com; Abiquiú Inn; breakfast $11, lunch & dinner $12-28; ⊗7am-9pm), includes numerous fish dishes, from chipotle honey-glazed salmon to trout tacos.

Ojo Caliente

At 140 years old, **Ojo Caliente Mineral Springs Resort & Spa** (☏505-583-2233; www.ojospa.com; 50 Los Baños Rd; r $139-169, cottages $179-209, ste $229-349; ⊞☎) is one of the country's oldest health resorts – and Pueblo Indians have used the springs for centuries! Fifty miles north of Santa Fe on Hwy 285, it offers 10 soaking pools with several combinations of minerals (shared/private pools from $12/30). In addition to the pleasant, if nothing special, historic hotel rooms, the resort has several plush, boldly colored suites with kiva fireplaces and private soaking tubs, and New Mexican–style cottages. Its **Artesian Restaurant** (www.ojospa.com; breakfast $7-10, lunch $9-13, dinner $16-29; ⊗7:30am-11am, 11:30am-2:30pm & 5-9pm) prepares organic and local ingredients with aplomb.

Taos

A magical spot even by the standards of this land of enchantment, Taos remains forever under the spell of its elemental surroundings: 12,300ft snowcapped peaks soar behind town, while a sage-speckled plateau unrolls to the west before plunging 800ft into the Rio Grande Gorge.

Taos Pueblo, a marvel of adobe architecture, ranks among the oldest continuously inhabited communities in the US, and stands at the root of a long history that extends from conquistadors to cowboys.

During the 20th century, this little town also became a magnet for artists, writers and creative thinkers, from DH Lawrence to Dennis Hopper. It remains a relaxed and eccentric place, with classic mud-brick buildings, fabulous museums, quirky cafes and excellent restaurants, that's home to 5700 residents including bohemians and hippies, alternative-energy aficionados and old-time Hispanic families.

◉ Sights

The Museum Association of Taos sells a $25 pass, valid for a year, that covers admission to five museums: the Millicent Rogers, Harwood Foundation and Taos Art museums, plus the Blumenschein Home and Martínez Hacienda.

★ Millicent Rogers Museum   MUSEUM

(☑575-758-2462; www.millicentrogers.org; 1504 Millicent Rogers Rd; adult/child $10/2; ⊙10:10am-5pm Apr-Oct, closed Mon Nov-Mar) Rooted in the private collection of model and oil heiress Millicent Rogers, who moved to Taos in 1947, this superb museum, 4 miles northwest of the Plaza, ranges from Hispanic folk art to Navajo weaving, and even modernist jewelry designed by Rogers herself. The principal focus, however, is on Native American ceramics, and especially the beautiful black-on-black pottery created during the 20th century by Maria Martínez from San Ildefonso Pueblo.

Martínez Hacienda   MUSEUM

(☑575-758-1000; www.taoshistoricmuseums.org; 708 Hacienda Way, off Lower Ranchitos Rd; adult/child $8/4; ⊙10am-5pm Mon-Sat, noon-5pm Sun Apr-Oct, Mon-Tue & Thu-Sat 10am-4pm Nov-Mar) Set amid the fields 2 miles southwest of the Plaza, this fortified adobe homestead was built in 1804. It served as a trading post, first for merchants venturing north from Mexico City along the Camino Real, and then west along the Santa Fe Trail. Its 21 rooms, arranged around a double courtyard, are furnished with the few possessions that even a wealthy family of the era would have been able to afford. Cultural events are held here regularly.

Harwood Foundation Museum   MUSEUM

(☑575-758-9826; www.harwoodmuseum.org; 238 Ledoux St; adult/child $10/free; ⊙10am-5pm Mon-Sat, noon-5pm Sun Apr-Oct, closed Mon Nov-Mar) Attractively displayed in a gorgeous and very spacious mid-19th-century adobe compound, the paintings, drawings, prints, sculpture and photographs here are predominantly the work of northern New Mexican artists, both historical and contemporary. Founded in 1923, the Harwood is the second-oldest museum in New Mexico, and is as strong on local Hispanic traditions as it is on Taos' 20th-century school.

Taos Art Museum & Fechin Institute   MUSEUM

(☑575-758-2690; www.taosartmuseum.org; 227 Paseo del Pueblo Norte; adult/child $8/free; ⊙10am-5pm Tue-Sun May-Oct, to 4pm Nov-Apr) Russian artist Nicolai Fechin moved to Taos in 1926, aged 46, and adorned the interior of this adobe home with his own distinctly Russian woodcarvings between 1928 and 1933. Now a museum, it displays Fechin's paintings and sketches along with his private collection and choice works by members of the Taos Society of Artists, and also hosts occasional chamber music performances in summer.

Blumenschein Home & Museum   MUSEUM

(☑575-758-0505; www.taoshistoricmuseums.org; 222 Ledoux St; adult/child $8/4; ⊙10am-5pm Mon-Sat, noon-5pm Sun Apr-Oct, Mon-Tue & Thu-Sat 10am-4pm Nov-Mar) Wonderfully preserved adobe residence, dating originally from 1797, which provides a vivid glimpse of life in Taos' artistic community during the 1920s. Ernest L Blumenschein, founder member of the Taos Society of Artists, lived here with his wife and daughter, Mary and Helen Greene Blumenschein, both also artists, and every room remains alive with their artworks and personal possessions.

San Francisco de Asís Church   CHURCH

(☑575-751-0518; St Francis Plaza, Ranchos de Taos; ⊙9am-4pm Mon-Fri) Just off Hwy 68 in Ranchos de Taos, 4 miles south of Taos Plaza, this iconic church was completed in 1815. Famed for the rounded curves and stark angles of its sturdy adobe walls, it was repeatedly memorialized by Georgia O'Keeffe in paint, and Ansel Adams with his camera. Mass is celebrated at 6pm the first Saturday of the month, and usually at 7am, 9am and 11:30am every Sunday.

Rio Grande Gorge Bridge   BRIDGE, CANYON

Constructed in 1965, this vertigo-inducing steel bridge carries Hwy 64 across the Rio Grande about 12 miles northwest of Taos. It's the seventh-highest bridge in the US, 565ft above the river and measuring 600ft long. The views from the pedestrian walkway, west over the empty Taos Plateau as well as down the jagged walls of the gorge, will surely make you gulp as you gape. Vendors selling jewelry, sage sticks and other souvenirs congregate on the eastern side.

SOUTHWEST TAOS

DON'T MISS

TAOS PUEBLO
····················

New Mexico's most extraordinary – and most beautiful – Native American site, **Taos Pueblo** (☑575-758-1028; www.taospueblo.com; Taos Pueblo Rd; adult/child $16/free; ⊙8am-4pm Mon-Sat, 8:30am-4pm Sun; closed mid-Feb–mid-Apr), stands 3 miles northeast of Taos Plaza. Continuously inhabited for almost a thousand years, Taos Pueblo focuses on twin five-story adobe complexes, thought to have been completed by around 1450 AD. Modern visitors are thus confronted by the same staggering spectacle as New Mexico's earliest Spanish explorers. Guided walking tours explain the Pueblo's history and provide a chance to buy fine jewelry, pottery and other arts and crafts.

The Pueblo closes for 10 weeks around February to April, and at other times for ceremonies and events; check the website for dates.

Earthships　　　　　ARCHITECTURE
(☑575-613-4409; www.earthship.com; US Hwy 64; self-guided tours $7; ⊙9am-6pm Apr-Oct; 10am-4pm Nov-Mar) ✐ Numbering 70 Earthships, with capacity for 60 more, Taos' pioneering community was the brainchild of architect Michael Reynolds. Built with recycled materials like used automobile tires and cans, and buried on three sides, Earthships heat and cool themselves, make their own electricity and catch their own water; dwellers grow their own food. Stay overnight (p388) if possible; the 'tour' is a little disappointing. The visitor center is 1.5 miles west of the Rio Grande Gorge Bridge on US Hwy 64.

🏃 Activities

During summer, **white-water rafting** is popular in the **Taos Box**, the steep-sided cliffs that frame the Rio Grande. There are also plenty of excellent **hiking** and **mountainbiking** trails.

Taos Ski Valley　　　　　SKIING
(www.skitaos.org; half-/full-day lift ticket $64/77; ⊙9am-4pm) With a peak elevation of 11,819ft and a 2612ft vertical drop, Taos Ski Valley offers some of the most challenging skiing in the US and yet remains low-key and relaxed. The resort now allows snowboarders on its slopes.

Los Rios River Runners　　　　　RAFTING
(☑575-776-8854; www.losriosriverrunners.com; 1033 Paseo Del Pueblo Sur; Box trips $105-125, Racecourse trips adult/child $54/44, 3-day Chama trips adult/child $495/375; ⊙8am-6pm) Half-day trips on the Racecourse (in one- and two-person kayaks if you prefer), full-day trips on the Box (minimum age 12), and multinight expeditions on the scenic Chama. On the 'Native Cultures Feast and Float' ($85) you're accompanied by a Native American guide and have lunch homemade by a local Pueblo family. Rates rise slightly at weekends.

🛏 Sleeping

★**Doña Luz Inn**　　　　　B&B $
(☑575-758-9000; www.stayintaos.com; 114 Kit Carson Rd; r $94-229; ✳@🕸) Funky and fun, this central B&B is a labor of love by owner Paul Castillo. Rooms are decorated in colorful themes from Spanish colonial to Native American, with abundant art, murals and artifacts plus adobe fireplaces, kitchenettes and hot tubs. The cozy La Luz room is the best deal in town, and there are also sumptuous larger suites.

Abominable Snowmansion　　　　　HOSTEL $
(☑575-776-8298; www.snowmansion.com; 476 Hwy 150; tent sites/dm/tipi $22/27/55, r without/with bath $50/55; ℗@🕸🐾) Popular and affordable hostel in the heart of Arroyo Seco, which makes a cozy high-country alternative to paying Taos prices. A big round fireplace in the central lodge warms guests in winter, there's a shared kitchen, and you can choose between clean (if a tad threadbare) private rooms, simple dorms, a wonderful campground, and even, in summer, a tipi.

★**Earthship Rentals**　　　　　BOUTIQUE HOTEL $$
(☑575-751-0462; www.earthship.com; US Hwy 64; Earthship $145-350; 🕸🐾) ✐ How about an off-grid night in a boutique-chic, solar-powered dwelling? Part Gaudí-esque visions, part space-age fantasy, these futuristic structures are built using recycled tires and aluminum cans, not that those components are visible. Set on a beautiful mesa across the river 14 miles northwest, they offer a unique experience, albeit rather different to staying in Taos itself. Drop-ins welcome.

★**Historic Taos Inn**　　　　　HISTORIC HOTEL $$
(☑575-758-2233; www.taosinn.com; 125 Paseo del Pueblo Norte; r from $105; ℗✳🕸) Lovely and

always lively old inn, where the 45 characterful rooms have Southwest trimmings like heavy-duty wooden furnishings and adobe fireplaces (some functioning, some for show). The famed Adobe Bar spills into the cozy central atrium, and features live music every night – for a quieter stay, opt for one of the detached separate wings – and there's also a good restaurant.

✗ Eating

Michael's Kitchen NEW MEXICAN $
(☎575-758-4178; www.michaelskitchen.com; 304c Paseo del Pueblo Norte; mains $7-16; ☺7am-2:30pm Mon-Thu, to 8pm Fri-Sun; ☝) Locals and tourists alike converge on this old favorite because the menu is long, the food's reliably good, it's an easy place for kids, and the in-house bakery produces goodies that fly out the door. Plus, it serves the best damn breakfast in town. You just may spot a Hollywood celebrity or two digging into a chile-smothered breakfast burrito.

El Gamal MIDDLE EASTERN $
(☎575-613-0311; 12 Doña Luz St; mains $7-12; ☺9am-5pm Mon-Wed, 9am-9pm Thu-Sat, 11am-3pm Sun; ☝☝☝) Vegetarians rejoice – at this casual Middle Eastern place, there's no meat anywhere. Even if the falafel doesn't quite achieve the stated aim to promote peace through 'evolving people's consciousness and taste buds,' it certainly tastes good. There's a kids playroom in the back with tons of toys, plus a pool table and free wi-fi.

★ Love Apple NEW MEXICAN $$
(☎575-751-0050; www.theloveapple.net; 803 Paseo del Pueblo Norte; mains $14-25; ☺5-9pm Tue-Sun) A real 'only in New Mexico' find, from the setting in the converted 19th-century adobe Placitas Chapel, to the delicious, locally sourced and largely organic food. Everything – from the local beefburger with red chile and blue cheese, via the tamales with mole sauce, to the wild boar tenderloin – is imbued with regional flavors, and the understated rustic-sacred atmosphere enhances the experience. Make reservations.

★ Lambert's MODERN AMERICAN $$$
(☎505-758-1009; www.lambertsoftaos.com; 123 Bent St; lunch $9-19, dinner $18-39; ☺noon-2pm & 5:30-9pm mid-May–mid-Sep, 5:30-9pm Mon-Sat, 10am-2pm Sun mid-Sep–mid-May; ☝☝) Consistently hailed as the 'Best of Taos,' and

now relocated into a charming old adobe just north of the Plaza, Lambert's remains what it's always been – a cozy, romantic local hangout where patrons relax and enjoy sumptuous contemporary cuisine, with mains ranging from lunchtime's barbecue-pork sliders to dinner dishes like chicken mango enchiladas or Colorado rack of lamb.

🍷 Drinking & Entertainment

Adobe Bar BAR
(☎575-758-2233; Historic Taos Inn, 125 Paseo del Pueblo Norte; ☺11am-11pm; music 7-10pm) There's something about the Adobe Bar. All Taos seems to turn up at some point each evening, to kick back in the comfy covered atrium, enjoying no-cover live music from bluegrass to jazz, and drinking the famed 'Cowboy Buddha' margaritas. If you decide to stick around, you can always order food off the well-priced bar menu.

Coffee Spot CAFE
(☎575-758-8556; 900 Paseo del Pueblo Norte; ☺7am-5pm) Large, ramshackle and very popular coffeehouse and bakery, serving all-day breakfasts – try the chile-smothered Taos Benedict – plus espresso, juices, smoothies and salads, and plentiful gluten-free options. Locals lured by the free wi-fi spread out through the copious indoor space and sunny patio.

KTAO Solar Center LIVE MUSIC
(☎575-758-5826; www.ktao.com; 9 Ski Valley Rd; ☺bar 4-9pm Sun-Thu, to 11pm Fri & Sat) Taos' best live-music venue, at the start of Ski Valley Rd, shares its space with much-loved radio station KTAO 101.9FM. Local and touring acts stop by to rock the house; when there's no show, watch the DJs in the booth at the 'world's most powerful solar radio station' while hitting happy hour at the bar.

🔒 Shopping

Taos has historically been a mecca for artists, demonstrated by the huge number of galleries and studios in and around town. Indie stores and galleries line the **John Dunn Shops** (www.johndunnshops.com) pedestrian walkway linking Bent St to Taos Plaza, which is home to the well-stocked **Moby Dickens Bookshop** (☎575-758-3050; www.mobydickens.com; 124a Bent Street; ☺10am-5pm Mon-Wed, 10am-6pm Thu-Sat, noon-5pm Sun).

Just east of the Plaza, pop into El Rincón Trading Post (☑ 575-758-9188; 114 Kit Carson Rd; ⊙ 10am-5pm) for classic Western memorabilia.

ℹ Information

Taos Visitor Center (☑ 575-758-3873; http:// taos.org; 1139 Paseo del Pueblo Sur; ⊙ 9am-5pm; 🛜) This excellent visitor center stocks information of all kinds on northern New Mexico and doles out free coffee; everything, including the comprehensive *Taos Vacation Guide*, is also available online.

ℹ Getting There & Away

From Santa Fe, take either the scenic 'High Road' along Hwys 76 and 518, with galleries, villages and sites worth exploring, or follow the lovely unfolding Rio Grande landscape on Hwy 68.

North Central Regional Transit (☑ 866-206-0754; www.ncrtd.org) provides a free shuttle-bus service to Espanola on weekdays, where you can transfer to Santa Fe and other destinations, while **Taos Express** (☑ 575-751-4459; www. taosexpress.com) can get you to Santa Fe at weekends ($10).

Northwestern New Mexico

Dubbed 'Indian Country' for good reason (huge swaths of land fall under the aegis of the Navajo, Pueblo, Zuni, Apache and Laguna tribes), New Mexico's northwestern quadrant showcases remarkable ancient sites alongside solitary Native American settlements and colorful badlands.

Farmington & Around

The largest town in northwest New Mexico, Farmington makes a convenient base from which to explore the Four Corners area. The **visitors bureau** (☑ 505-326-7602; www.farmingtonnm.org; 3041 E Main St; ⊙ 8am-5pm Mon-Sat) has more information.

Shiprock, a 1700ft-high volcanic plug that rises eerily over the landscape to the west, was a landmark for the Anglo pioneers and is a sacred site to the Navajo.

Fourteen miles northeast of Farmington, the 27-acre **Aztec Ruins National Monument** (☑ 505-334-6174; www.nps.gov/azru; 84 Ruins Rd; adult/child $5/free; ⊙ 8am-5pm Sep-May, to 6pm Jun-Aug) features the largest reconstructed kiva in the country, with an internal diameter of almost 50ft. A few steps away, let your imagination wander as you stoop through low doorways and dark rooms inside the West Ruin.

About 35 miles south of Farmington along Hwy 371, the undeveloped **Bisti Badlands & De-Na-Zin Wilderness** is a trippy, surreal landscape of strange, colorful rock formations, especially spectacular in the hours before sunset; desert enthusiasts shouldn't miss it. The Farmington **BLM office** (☑ 505-564-7600; www.nm.blm.gov; 6251 College Blvd; ⊙ 7:45am-4:30pm Mon-Fri) has information.

The lovely, three-room **Silver River Adobe Inn B&B** (☑ 575-325-8219; www.silveradobe. com; 3151 W Main St; r $115-175; ❄🛜) offers a peaceful respite among the trees along the San Juan River.

Managing to be both trendy *and* kid-friendly, the hippish **Three Rivers Eatery & Brewhouse** (☑ 505-324-2187; www. threeriversbrewery.com; 101 E Main St; mains $9-32; ⊙ 11am-9pm; 🍴) has good steaks, pub grub and its own microbrews. It's the best restaurant in town by a mile.

Chaco Culture National Historic Park

Featuring massive Ancestral Puebloan buildings set in an isolated high-desert environment, intriguing **Chaco** (www.nps.gov/ chcu; per vehicle $8; ⊙ 7am-sunset) contains evidence of 5000 years of human occupation. In its prime, the community at Chaco Canyon was a major trading and ceremonial hub for the region – and the city the Puebloan people created here was masterly in its layout and design. Pueblo Bonito is four stories tall and may have had 600 to 800 rooms and kivas. As well as driving the self-guided loop tour, you can hike various **backcountry trails**. For stargazers, there are evening astronomy presentations in summer.

The park is in a remote area approximately 80 miles south of Farmington, far beyond the reach of any public transport. **Gallo Campground** (☑ 877-444-6777; www.recreation.gov; sites $15) is 1 mile east of the visitor center. No RV hookups.

Chama

Nine miles south of the Colorado border, Chama's **Cumbres & Toltec Scenic Railway** (☑ 888-286-2737; www.cumbrestoltec.com; adult/child 2-12 yr from $95/49; ⊙ late May–mid-

Oct) is the longest (64 miles) and highest (over the 10,015ft-high Cumbres Pass) authentic narrow-gauge steam railroad in the US. It's a beautiful trip (particularly in September and October during the fall foliage) through mountains, canyons and high desert. Lunch is included and on many trips kids ride free. See the website for details.

Northeastern New Mexico

East of Santa Fe, the lush Sangre de Cristo Mountains give way to vast rolling plains. Dusty grasslands stretch to infinity and beyond (well, to Texas, anyway). Cattle and dinosaur prints dot a landscape punctuated with volcanic cones. Ranching is an economic mainstay, and on many roads you'll see more cows than cars.

The Santa Fe Trail, along which pioneer settlers rolled in wagon trains, ran from New Mexico to Missouri. You can still see the wagon ruts in places, off I-25 between Santa Fe and Raton.

Cimarron

Cimarron once ranked among the rowdiest of Wild West towns; its name even means 'wild' in Spanish. According to local lore, murder was such an everyday occurrence in the 1870s that peace and quiet was newsworthy, one paper going so far as to report: 'Everything is quiet in Cimarron. Nobody has been killed in three days.'

Today, the town is quiet, luring nature-minded travelers who want to enjoy the great outdoors. Driving to or from Taos, you'll pass through gorgeous **Cimarron Canyon State Park**, a steep-walled canyon with several hiking trails, excellent trout fishing and camping.

You can stay or dine at what's reputed to be one of the most haunted hotels in the USA, the 1872 **St James** (☏575-376-2664; www.exstjames.com; 617 Collison St; r $85-135; ❄🐾) – one room is so spook-filled that it's never rented out! Many legends of the West stayed here, including Buffalo Bill, Annie Oakley, Wyatt Earp and Jesse James, and the front desk has a long list of who shot whom in the hotel bar.

Capulin Volcano National Monument

Rising 1300ft above the surrounding plains, **Capulin** (☏575-278-2201; www.nps.gov/cavo;

vehicle $5; ◷8am-5pm Jun-Aug, to 4:30pm Sep-May) is the most accessible of several volcanoes hereabouts. A 2-mile road spirals up the mountain to a parking lot at the rim (8182ft), where trails lead around and into the crater. The entrance is 3 miles north of Capulin village, which itself is 30 miles east of Raton on Hwy 87.

Southwestern New Mexico

The Rio Grande Valley unfurls from Albuquerque down to the bubbling hot springs of funky Truth or Consequences and beyond. Before the river hits the Texas line, it feeds one of New Mexico's agricultural treasures: Hatch, the so-called 'chili capital of the world.' The first atomic device was detonated at the Trinity Site, in the bone-dry desert east of the Rio Grande.

To the west, the rugged Gila National Forest is wild with backpacking and fishing adventures. The mountains' southern slopes descend into the Chihuahuan Desert that surrounds Las Cruces, the state's second-largest city.

Truth or Consequences & Around

An offbeat joie de vivre permeates the funky little town of Truth or Consequences ('T or C'), which was built on the site of natural hot springs in the 1880s. Originally, sensibly enough, called Hot Springs, it changed its name in 1950, after a then-popular radio game show called, you guessed it, Truth or Consequences. Publicity these days comes courtesy of Virgin Galactic CEO Richard Branson and other space-travel visionaries driving the development of nearby **Spaceport America**, where wealthy tourists are expected to launch into orbit sometime soon.

About 60 miles north, sandhill cranes and Arctic geese winter in the 90 sq miles of fields and marshes at **Bosque del Apache National Wildlife Refuge** (www.fws.gov/refuge/bosque_del_apache; per vehicle $5; ◷dawn-dusk).

🛏 Sleeping & Eating

⭐**Riverbend Hot Springs** BOUTIQUE HOTEL $ (☏575-894-7625; www.riverbendhotsprings.com; 100 Austin St; r/ste from $70/105; ❄🐾) This delightful place, occupying a fantastic perch beside the Rio Grande, is the only T or C hotel to feature outdoor, riverside hot tubs – tiled, decked and totally irresistible. Accommodations, colorfully decorated by local artists,

WORTH A TRIP

EAVESDROPPING ON OUTER SPACE

Beyond the town of Magdalena on Hwy 60, 130 miles southwest of Albuquerque, the amazing **Very Large Array** (VLA; ☑ 505-835-7243; www.nrao.edu; off Hwy 52; ⊙ 8:30am-sunset) FREE radio telescope consists of 27 huge antenna dishes sprouting like giant mushrooms in the high plains. Watch a short film at the visitor center, then take a self-guided walking tour with a window peek into the control building.

ranges from motel-style rooms to a three-bedroom suite. Guests can use the public pools for free, and private tubs for $10.

Blackstone Hotsprings　　BOUTIQUE HOTEL $
(☑ 575-894-0894; www.blackstonehotsprings.com; 410 Austin St; r $75-135; P ❋ 🤖) Blackstone embraces the T or C spirit with an upscale wink, decorating each of its seven rooms in the style of a classic TV show, from *The Jetsons* to *The Golden Girls* to *I Love Lucy*. Best part? Each room comes with its own over-sized tub or waterfall fed from the hot springs.

Passion Pie Cafe　　CAFE $
(☑ 575-894-0008; http://deepwaterfarm.com; 406 Main St; breakfast & lunch mains $5-10, pizzas $13-18; ⊙ 7am-3pm daily, plus 4-9:30pm Fri & Sat) Watch T or C get its morning groove on through the windows of this espresso cafe, and set yourself up with a breakfast waffle; the Elvis (with peanut butter) or the Fat Elvis (with bacon too) should do the job. Later on there are plenty of healthy salads and sandwiches, plus pizza on Friday and Saturday nights.

Latitude 33　　FUSION $$
(☑ 575-740-7804; 334 S Pershing St; mains $8-16; ⊙ 11am-8pm Mon-Sat) Relaxed, friendly bistro, tucked away downtown between the two main drags, which serves excellent pan-Asian dishes at good prices. Spicy peanut noodles cost $8 at lunch, $10 for dinner.

Las Cruces & Around

The second-largest city in New Mexico, Las Cruces is home to New Mexico State University (NMSU), but there's surprisingly little of real interest for visitors.

◎ Sights

For many, a visit to neighboring **Mesilla** (aka Old Mesilla) is the highlight of their time in Las Cruces. Wander a few blocks off Old Mesilla's plaza to gather the essence of a mid-19th-century Southwestern town of Hispanic heritage.

★ New Mexico Farm & Ranch Heritage Museum　　MUSEUM
(☑ 575-522-4100; www.nmfarmandranchmuseum. org; 4100 Dripping Springs Rd; adult/child $5/2; ⊙ 9am-5pm Mon-Sat, noon-5pm Sun; ♠) This terrific museum doesn't just hold engaging exhibits on the state's agricultural history – it's got livestock too. Enclosures on the working farm alongside hold assorted breeds of cattle, along with horses, donkeys, sheep and goats. The taciturn cowboys who tend the animals proffer little extra information, but they add color, and you can even buy a pony if you have $450 to spare. There are daily milking demonstrations plus weekly displays of blacksmithing, spinning and weaving, and heritage cooking.

White Sands Missile Test Center Museum　　MUSEUM
(☑ 575-678-8800; www.wsmr-history.org; ⊙ 8am-4pm Mon-Fri, 10am-3pm Sat) FREE Explore New Mexico's military technology history with a visit to this museum, 25 miles east of Las Cruces along Hwy 70. It represents the heart of the White Sands Missile Range, a major testing site since 1945. There's a missile garden, a real V-2 rocket and a museum with lots of defense-related artifacts. Visitors have to park outside the Test Center gate and check in at the office before walking in.

🛏 Sleeping

★ Best Western Mission Inn　　MOTEL $
(☑ 575-524-8591; www.bwmissioninn.com; 1765 S Main St; r from $69) A truly out-of-the-ordinary accommodation option; yes it's a roadside chain motel, but the rooms are beautifully kitted out with attractive tiling, stonework and colorful stenciled designs; they're sizeable and comfortable; and the rates are great.

★ Lundeen Inn of the Arts　　B&B $$
(☑ 505-526-3326; www.innofthearts.com; 618 S Alameda Blvd, Las Cruces; r incl breakfast $82, ste from $99; P ❋ 🤖🐾) Each of the 20 guest rooms in this large and very lovely century-old Mexican Territorial-style inn is unique

and named for – and decorated in the style of – a New Mexico artist. Check out the soaring pressed-tin ceilings in the great room. Owners Linda and Jerry offer the kind of genteel hospitality you seldom find these days.

Eating

Nellie's Cafe   MEXICAN $
(☑575-524-9982; 1226 W Hadley Ave; mains $5-9; ⊙8am-2pm Tue-Sat) Cherished by locals, Nellie's has been serving homemade burritos, *chile rellenos* and tamales for decades now, under the slogan 'Chile with an Attitude.' It's small and humble in decor but big in taste, with deliciously spicy food.

★ Double Eagle Restaurant   STEAK $$$
(☑575-523-6700; www.double-eagle-mesilla.com; 308 Calle de Guadalupe; mains $23-49; ⊙11am-10pm Mon-Sat, noon-9pm Sun) A glorious mélange of Wild West opulence, all dark wood and velvet hangings, and featuring a fabulous old bar, this Plaza restaurant is on the National Register of Historic Places. The main dining room offers delicious continental and Southwestern cuisine, especially steaks, while the less formal Peppers in the courtyard claims to serve the world's largest green chili cheeseburger ($25).

ⓘ Information

Las Cruces CVB (☑575-541-2444; www.lascrucescvb.org; 211 N Water St) Helpful office with all sorts of visitor information.

ⓘ Getting There & Away

Greyhound (☑575-524-8518; www.greyhound.com; 800 E Thorpe Rd, Chucky's Convenience Store) buses traverse the two interstate corridors (I-10 and I-25). Daily destinations include Albuquerque ($14, 3½ hours), Roswell ($38, four hours) and El Paso ($10, one hour).

Silver City & Around

The spirit of the Wild West still hangs in the air in Silver City, 113 miles northwest of Las Cruces, as if Billy the Kid himself – who grew up here – might amble past at any moment. But things are changing, as the mountain-man/cowboy vibe succumbs to the charms of art galleries, coffeehouses and gelato.

Silver City is also the gateway to outdoor activities in the **Gila National Forest**, which is rugged country suitable for remote

cross-country skiing, backpacking, camping, and fishing. Two hours north of town, up a winding 42-mile road, is **Gila Cliff Dwellings National Monument** (www.nps.gov/gicl; admission $3; ⊙trail 9am-4pm, visitor center to 4:30pm), occupied in the 13th century by the Mogollon people. Mysterious and relatively isolated, these remarkable cliff dwellings are easily accessed from a 1-mile loop trail and look very much as they would have at the turn of the first millennium. For **pictographs**, stop by the Lower Scorpion Campground and walk a short distance along the marked trail.

Weird rounded monoliths make the **City of Rocks State Park** (☑575-536-2800; www.nmparks.com; Hwy 61; day-use $5, tent/RV sites $8/14) an intriguing playground, with great camping among the formations; there are tables and fire pits. For a rock-lined spot, check out campsite 43, the Lynx. Head 33 miles southeast of Silver City along Hwy 180 and Hwy 61.

For a smattering of Silver City's architectural history, overnight in the 22-room **Palace Hotel** (☑575-388-1811; www.silvercitypalacehotel.com; 106 W Broadway; r from $51; ❉?). Exuding a low-key, turn-of-the-19th-century charm (no air-con, older fixtures), the Palace is a great choice for those tired of cookie-cutter chains.

Downtown eating options range from the comfy, come-as-you-are **Javalina** (☑575-388-1350; 201 N Bullard St; pastries from $2; ⊙6am-6pm Sun-Thu, to 9pm Fri & Sat; ?) coffee shop to the **Curious Kumquat** (☑575-534-0337; http://curiouskumquat.com; 111 E College Ave; lunch mains $7-8, dinner mains $17-23; ⊙11am-4:30pm & 5:30-8:30pm Tue-Sat), an acclaimed gourmet hotspot where many dishes use locally foraged ingredients. For a taste of local culture, head 7 miles north to Pinos Altos and the **Buckhorn Saloon** (☑575-538-9911; www.buckhornsaloonandoperahouse.com; 32 Main St, Pinos Altos; mains $10-39; ⊙3-11pm Mon-Sat), where the specialty is steak and there's live music most nights. Call for reservations.

ⓘ Information

The **visitor center** (☑575-538-5555; www.silvercitytourism.org; 201 N Hudson St; ⊙9am-5pm Mon-Sat, 10am-4pm Sun) and the **Gila National Forest Ranger Station** (☑575-388-8201; www.fs.fed.us/r3/gila; 3005 E Camino Del Bosque; ⊙8am-4:30pm Mon-Fri) have area information.

Southeastern New Mexico

Two of New Mexico's greatest natural wonders are tucked down in the state's arid southeast – mesmerizing White Sands National Monument and magnificent Carlsbad Caverns National Park. This region is also home to some enduring legends: aliens in Roswell, Billy the Kid in Lincoln and Smokey Bear in Capitan. Most of the lowlands are covered by hot, rugged Chihuahuan Desert, but you can escape to cooler climes by driving up to higher altitudes around forested resort towns such as Cloudcroft and Ruidoso.

White Sands National Monument

Slide, roll and slither through brilliant, towering sand hills. Sixteen miles southwest of Alamogordo (15 miles southwest of Hwy 82/70), gypsum covers 275 sq miles to create a dazzling white landscape at this crisp, stark monument (☑575-479-6124; www.nps.gov/whsa; adult/under 16yr $3/free; ☺7am-9pm Jun-Aug, to sunset Sep-May). These captivating windswept dunes, which doubled as space-alien David Bowie's home planet in *The Man Who Fell To Earth*, are a highlight of any trip to New Mexico. Don't forget your sunglasses – the sand is as bright as snow!

Spring for a $15 plastic saucer at the visitor center gift store then sled one of the back dunes. It's fun, and you can sell the disc back for $5 at day's end. Backcountry campsites, with no water or toilet facilities, are a mile from the scenic drive. Pick up a permit ($3, issued first-come, first-served) in person at the visitor center at least one hour before sunset.

Alamogordo & Around

In Alamogordo, a desert outpost famous for its space- and atomic-research programs, the four-story New Mexico Museum of Space History (☑575-437-2840; www.nmspacemuseum.org; 3198 Hwy 2001; adult/child $6/4; ☺9am-5pm; ⊕) has excellent exhibits on space research and flight, and shows outstanding science-themed films in its Tombaugh IMAX Theater & Planetarium (adult/child $6/4.50; ⊕).

Motels stretch along White Sands Blvd, including Best Western Desert Aire Hotel (☑575-437-2110; www.bestwestern.com; 1021 S White Sands Blvd; r from $79; ❈@🛇🛱🐾), with standard-issue rooms and suites (some with kitchenettes), along with a sauna. If you'd

rather camp, hit Oliver Lee State Park (☑575-437-8284; www.nmparks.com; 409 Dog Canyon Rd; day-use $5; tent/RV sites $8/14), 12 miles south of Alamogordo. Grab some grub at the friendly Pizza Patio & Pub (☑575-434-9633; 2203 E 1st St; mains $7-16; ☺11am-8pm Mon-Thu & Sat, to 9pm Fri; ⊕), which serves pizzas, pastas, big salads and pitchers or pints of beer on tap.

Cloudcroft

Situated high in the mountains, little Cloudcroft provides welcome relief from the lowlands heat. With turn-of-the-19th-century buildings, it offers lots of outdoor recreation, is a good base for exploration and has a low-key feel. High Altitude (☑575-682-1229; www.highaltitude.org; 310 Burro Ave; rentals from $30 per day; ☺10am-5:30pm Mon-Thu, to 6pm Fri & Sat, to 5pm Sun) rents mountain bikes and has maps of local fat-tire routes.

The Lodge Resort & Spa (☑800-395-6343; www.thelodgeresort.com; 601 Corona Pl; r from $141; @🛇🛱🐾) is one of the Southwest's finest historic hotels. Rooms in the main Bavarian-style hotel are furnished with period and Victorian pieces, while Rebecca's (☑575-682-3131; Lodge Resort, 601 Corona Pl; mains $8-38; ☺7-10am, 11:30am-2pm & 5:30-9pm), named after the resident ghost, offers by far the best food in town.

Ruidoso

Downright bustling in summer and big with racetrack bettors, resorty Ruidoso (it means 'noisy' in Spanish) has an utterly pleasant climate thanks to its lofty and forested perch near Sierra Blanca (12,000ft). It's spread out along Hwy 48 (known as Mechem Dr or Sudderth Dr), the main drag.

◉ Sights & Activities

To stretch your legs, try the easily accessible forest trails on Cedar Creek Rd just west of Smokey Bear Ranger Station (☑575-257-4095; www.fs.usda.gov/lincoln; 901 Mechem Dr; ☺7:30am-4:30pm Mon-Fri, plus Sat in summer). Choose from the USFS Fitness Trail or the meandering paths at the Cedar Creek Picnic Area. Longer day hikes and backpacking routes abound in the White Mountain Wilderness, north of town. Always check fire restrictions around here – the forest closes during dry spells.

Hubbard Museum of the American West MUSEUM

(☑575-378-4142; www.hubbardmuseum.org; 26301 Hwy 70; adult/child $7/2; ⊙9am-5pm; ▣) This town-run museum focuses on local history, with a wonderful gallery of old photos, and also displays Native American kachinas, war bonnets, weapons and pottery. Traces of its original incarnation as the Museum of the Horse linger in various horse-related exhibits – and be sure to check out the fascinating, if completely irrelevant, history of toilets in the restrooms.

Ski Apache SKIING

(www.skiapache.com; lift ticket adult/child $51/33) Unlikely as it sounds, Ski Apache, 18 miles northwest of Ruidoso on the slopes of Sierra Blanca Peak, really is owned by the Apache. Potentially it's the finest ski area south of Albuquerque, a good choice for affordability and fun – and it's also home to New Mexico's only gondola. Recent seasons, however, have seen poor snowfall – check ahead.

🛏 Sleeping & Eating

Motels, hotels and cute little cabin complexes line the streets. There's plenty of primitive camping along forest roads on the way to the ski area.

Sitzmark Chalet HOTEL $

(☑575-257-4140; www.sitzmark-chalet.com; 627 Sudderth Dr; r from $59; ❉🕙) This ski-themed chalet offers 17 simple but nice rooms. Picnic tables, grills and an eight-person hot tub are welcome perks.

Upper Canyon Inn LODGE $$

(☑575-257-3005; www.uppercanyoninn.com; 215 Main Rd; r/cabins from $89/129; 🕙) Rooms and cabins here range from simple good value to rustic-chic luxury. Bigger doesn't necessarily mean more expensive, so look at a few options. The pricier cabins have some fine interior woodwork and Jacuzzi tubs.

★Cornerstone Bakery CAFE $

(☑575-257-1842; www.cornerstonebakerycafe.com; 359 Sudderth Dr; mains under $10; ⊙7am-2pm; 🖋) Totally irresistible, hugely popular local bakery-cafe, where everything, from the breads, pastries and espresso to the omelets and croissant sandwiches, is just the way it should be. Stick around long enough and the Cornerstone may become your morning touchstone.

☆ Entertainment

Ruidoso Downs Racetrack HORSE RACING

(☑575-378-4431; www.raceruidoso.com; Hwy 70; grandstand seats free; ⊙Fri-Mon late May-early Sep) National attention focuses on the Ruidoso Downs racetrack on Labor Day for the world's richest quarter-horse race, the All American Futurity, which has a purse of $2.4 million. The course is also home to the Racehorse Hall of Fame, and the small Billy the Kid Casino.

Flying J Ranch MUSIC

(☑575-336-4330; www.flyingjranch.com; 1028 Hwy 48; adult/child $27/15; ⊙from 5:30pm Mon-Sat late May-early Sep, Sat only early Sep–mid-Oct; ▣) Families with little ones will love this 'Western village,' 1.5 miles north of Alto, as it delivers a full night of entertainment, with gunfights, pony rides and Western music, to go with its cowboy-style chuckwagon dinner.

ℹ Information

Chamber of commerce (☑575-257-7395; www.ruidosonow.com; 720 Sudderth Dr; ⊙8am-5pm Mon-Fri, 9am-3pm Sat) Has visitor information.

Lincoln & Capitan

Fans of Western history won't want to miss little Lincoln. Twelve miles east of Capitan along the Billy the Kid National Scenic Byway (www.billybyway.com), this is where the gun battle known as the Lincoln County War turned Billy the Kid into a legend. The whole town is beautifully preserved in close to original form, with its unspoiled main street designated as the Lincoln Historic Site (☑575-653-4372; www.nmmonuments.org/lincoln; adult/child $5/free; ⊙hours vary for individual sites).

Buy tickets to the historic town buildings at the Anderson-Freeman Visitors Center, where you'll also find exhibits on Buffalo soldiers, Apaches and the Lincoln County War. Make the fascinating Courthouse Museum, the well-marked site of Billy's most daring – and violent – escape, your last stop. A plaque marks where one of his bullets slammed into the wall.

For overnighters, the Ellis Store Country Inn (☑800-653-6460; www.ellisstore.com; Hwy 380; r incl breakfast $89-129) offers three antique-filled rooms (complete with wood stove) in the main house. Five additional rooms are located in a historic mill on the property, and an amazing six-course dinner

---

DON'T MISS

CARLSBAD CAVERNS NATIONAL PARK

Scores of wondrous caves hide under the hills at this unique **national park** (☑575-785-2232, bat info 505-785-3012; www.nps.gov/cave; adult/child $10/free; ☺ caves 8:30am-5pm late May-early Sep, to 3:30pm early Sep-late May; ♿), which covers 73 sq miles. The cavern formations are an ethereal wonderland of stalactites and fantastical geological features. From the **visitor center** (☺8am-5pm, to 7pm late May-early Sep) you can ride an elevator, which descends the equivalent of the length of the Empire State Building in under a minute, or take a 2-mile subterranean walk from the cave mouth to the Big Room, an underground chamber 1800ft long, 255ft high and more than 800ft below the surface. If you've got kids (or are just feeling goofy), plastic caving helmets with headlamps are sold in the gift shop.

Guided tours (☑877-444-6777; www.recreation.gov; adult $7-20, child $3.50-10) of additional caves are available, and should be reserved well in advance. Wear long sleeves and closed shoes; it gets chilly.

The cave's other claim to fame is the 300,000-plus Mexican free-tailed bat colony that roosts here from mid-May to mid-October. Be here by sunset, when they cyclone out for an all-evening insect feast.

---

is served in the lovely dining room ($75 per person; not Sundays). Perfect for special occasions; reservations recommended.

Like Lincoln, cozy Capitan is surrounded by the beautiful mountains of **Lincoln National Forest**. The main reason to come is so the kids can visit **Smokey Bear Historical State Park** (☑575-354-2748; 118 W Smokey Bear Blvd; adult/child $2/1; ☺9am-5pm), where Smokey (yes, there actually was a real Smokey Bear) is buried.

Roswell

If you believe 'The Truth Is Out There', then the Roswell Incident is already filed away in your memory banks. In 1947 a mysterious object crashed at a nearby ranch. No one would have skipped any sleep over it, but the military made a big to-do of hushing it up, and for a lot of folks, that sealed it: the aliens had landed! International curiosity and local ingenuity have transformed the city into a quirky extraterrestrial-wannabe zone. Bulbous white heads glow atop the downtown streetlamps and busloads of tourists come to find good souvenirs.

Believers and kitsch-seekers must check out the **International UFO Museum & Research Center** (☑575-625-9495; www.roswellufomuseum.com; 114 N Main St; adult/child $5/$2; ☺9am-5pm), displaying documents supporting the cover-up as well as lots of far-out art and exhibitions. The annual **Roswell UFO Festival** (www.roswellufofestival.com) beams down in early July, with an otherworldly costume parade, workshops and concerts.

Ho-hum chain motels line N Main St. About 36 miles south of Roswell, the **Heritage Inn** (☑575-748-2552; www.artesiaheritageinn.com; 209 W Main St, Artesia; r incl breakfast from $119; ❄@🛜🐕) in Artesia offers 11 Old West–style rooms and is the nicest lodging in the area.

For simple, dependable New Mexican fare, try **Martin's Capitol Cafe** (☑575-624-2111; 110 W 4th St; mains $7-15; ☺6am-8:30pm Mon-Sat); for American eats, **Big D's Downtown Dive** (www.bigdsdowntowndive.com; 505 N Main St; $7-10; ☺11am-9pm) has the best salads, sandwiches and burgers in town.

Pick up local information at the **visitors bureau** (☑575-624-6860; www.seeroswell.com; 912 N Main St; ☺8:30am-5:30pm Mon-Fri, 10am-3pm Sat & Sun; 🛜).

The **Greyhound Bus Depot** (☑575-622-2510; www.greyhound.com; 1100 N Virginia Ave) has buses to Las Cruces ($42, four hours).

Carlsbad

Carlsbad is the closest town to Carlsbad Caverns National Park and the Guadalupe Mountains. The **Park Service office** (☑575-785-2232; 3225 National Parks Hwy; ☺8am-4:30pm Mon-Fri) on its southern edge has information on both.

On the northwestern outskirts, off Hwy 285, **Living Desert State Park** (☑575-887-5516; www.nmparks.com; 1504 Miehls Dr N, off Hwy 285; adult/child $5/3; ☺8am-5pm Jun-Aug, 9am-5pm Sep-May, last zoo entry 3:30pm) is a great place to see and learn about desert plants and wildlife. There's a good 1.3-mile trail that showcases different habitats of the Chihuahuan Desert, with live antelopes, wolves, roadrunners and more.

However, a recent boom in the oil industry means that even the most ordinary motel room in Carlsbad is liable to cost well over $200 per night, so it makes much more sense to visit on a *long* day-trip from, say, Roswell or Alamogordo. The best room rates, oddly enough, tend to be at the appealing **Trinity Hotel** (575-234-9891; www.thetrinityhotel.com; 201 S Canal St; r from $189; ❄ 🛜), a historic building that was originally the First National Bank. The sitting room of one suite is inside the old vault, and the restaurant is Carlsbad's classiest.

The perky **Blue House Bakery & Cafe** (575-628-0555; 609 N Canyon St; mains $4-10; 6am-noon Mon-Sat) brews the best coffee in these parts, while the lip-smackin' **Red Chimney Pit Barbecue** (575-885-8744; 817 N Canal St; mains $7-15; 11am-2pm & 4:30-8:30pm Mon-Fri) serves succulent Southern-style meats.

For other in-the-know advice, visit the **chamber of commerce** (575-887-6516; www.carlsbadchamber.com; 302 S Canal St; 9am-5pm Mon, 8am-5pm Tue-Fri).

Greyhound (575-628-0768; www.greyhound.com; 3102 National Parks Hwy) buses depart from the Allsup's gas station a few miles south of town on Hwy 180, heading to El Paso ($57, three hours).

SOUTHWEST SOUTHEASTERN NEW MEXICO

Understand Western USA

Western USA Today

The big news in the West? Drought, marijuana sales, and same-sex marriage. The ongoing drought dominated headlines in California, where the central valley farming region is entering crisis mode. As for pot, the citizens of Colorado and Washington voted to legalize the recreational use of marijuana in 2012 – and sales are booming. In a landmark decision, the US Supreme held in the summer of 2015 that same-sex marriage is a constitutional right.

Best in Print

The Grapes of Wrath (John Steinbeck; 1939) Dust Bowl migrants travel west to California.

Desert Solitaire (Edward Abbey; 1968) Essays about the Southwest and industrial tourism by no-holds-barred eco-curmudgeon.

Bean Trees (Barbara Kingsolver; 1988) Thoughtful look at motherhood and crosscultural adoption in Tucson.

Into the Wild (Jon Krakauer; 1996) Alexander Supertramp wanders across the West in search of meaning.

Wild (Cheryl Strayed; 2013) Author hikes the Pacific Crest Trail solo after the death of her mother.

Best Films

Stagecoach (1939)
Sunset Boulevard (1950)
Butch Cassidy & the Sundance Kid (1969)
Chinatown (1974)
One Flew Over the Cuckoo's Nest (1975)
The Shining (1980)
Thelma & Louise (1991)
Boyz n the Hood (1991)
Sideways (2004)
The Hangover (2009)
127 Hours (2010)

Same-Sex Marriage

In recent years the most high-profile political issue in California has been same-sex marriage. The state Supreme Court struck down a constitutional ban against same-sex marriage in 2008, but later that year the voter-backed Proposition 8 again limited marriage to a union between a man and a woman. In 2013 federal courts ruled that Prop 8 was unconstitutional. A subsequent appeal of this ruling to the US Supreme Court was denied on jurisdictional grounds, and same-sex marriages resumed in the state. The same-sex marriage question was settled in 2015 when the US Supreme court ruled 5-4 that the constitution guarantees a right to same-sex marriage, a right that must now be recognized by all 50 states.

Legalized Marijuana

In the fall of 2012 residents of Colorado and Washington voted to legalize the recreational use of marijuana. Colorado voters passed Amendment 64, which allowed for the limited possession and use of marijuana by anyone 21 years of age and older. Rules for the cultivation and sale of recreational pot in Colorado were adopted in September 2013. A similar initiative was passed in Washington, and by the end of 2014 the state had 160 marijuana shops with total sales estimated at $1.7 million per day. How much in taxes was kept by the state of Washington and its local governments? More than $70 million. In January 2015, Colorado collected $2.3 million in excise taxes, which will be directed to schools. The federal government has indicated that it will not challenge these state laws, which are in conflict with federal laws.

Illegal Immigration

Illegal immigration remains a hot-button issue, and border-patrol agents have a very visible presence in southern Arizona, where their green-and-white SUVs are a common sight on rural roads. In 2010 Arizona lawmakers passed a stringent anti-immigration law requiring police officers to ask for ID from anyone they suspect of being in the country illegally. Sections of the law have been struck down by the courts as unconstitutional, but law-enforcement officers, while enforcing other laws, can still ask people for their papers.

Fire & Water
A 14-year drought has left two major reservoirs along the Colorado River – Lake Powell and Lake Mead – at less than half their capacity. This is troubling because the river supplies drinking water for 40 million people. About 70% of the water is used for agriculture. In California, four years of extreme drought has had a negative economic impact on the Central Valley, an agricultural region producing about 50% of much of the nation's produce, plus 90% of broccoli, grapes and almonds. Farmers here are using 40% to 50% less water than they have in the past. The statewide economic impact of the drought? An estimated $2.2 billion in 2014. Concerned citizens have taken to 'drought shaming' – posting photos of water wasters on social media.

Although the exact causes are unclear – climate change, residential development, government policy – the West has also been hard hit by forest fires. In June 2013, 19 members of the Granite Mountain Hotshots, an elite team of firefighters, were killed during the devastating Yarnell fire in central Arizona. The Rim Fire that same year, in and around Yosemite National Park, ripped across more than 250,000 acres, making it the third-largest fire in California since the 1930s.

Moving Forward
The economy isn't exactly booming, but technological development continues. California's innovations are myriad: PCs, iPods, Google. In Menlo Park, the ever-growing Facebook campus is preparing to open a 433,000-sq-ft office building designed by Frank Gehry. But Northern California holds more than Silicon Valley – it's also the site of a burgeoning biotech industry. In the Pacific Northwest, the Seattle area is headquarters for Microsoft, Nintendo and Amazon.com.

At the Grand Canyon, eco-friendly initiatives are in full-swing, including a park-and-ride shuttle from Tusayan and a bicycle rental service. In Las Vegas, Caesar Entertainment filed for bankruptcy. New casino construction, however, is economically encouraging, most notably with the Chinese-themed Resorts World, which plans to include a replica of the Great Wall of China. Environmentally, Colorado leads the way. Boulder County has passed a Zero Waste Action Plan, with a goal to reduce waste to near zero. Denver International Airport has added solar panels producing about 6% of the airport's power requirements.

POPULATION (US):
318.6 MILLION

AREA (US):
3.79 MILLION SQ MILES

GDP (US): **$17.4 TRILLION**

UNEMPLOYMENT (US): **5.3%**

if USA were 100 people

65 would be white
15 would be Hispanic
13 would be African American
4 would be Asian American
3 would be other

belief systems
(% of population)

51 Protestant
24 Roman Catholic
21 Other
2 Jewish
2 Mormon

population per sq mile

AUSTRALIA USA CANADA

≈ 11 people

History

History is not the stuff of dusty textbooks in the West. It's up-close and willing to be engaged. The downtown plaza in Santa Fe, once the terminus of the Santa Fe Trail, still buzzes. Temple Sq, dating from the mid-1800s, remains a gathering place for Mormons in Salt Lake City. Mining towns share their weathered secrets. A line-up of explorers and settlers – Native American hunters, Spanish conquistadors, East Cast fortune hunters, Mormon pioneers, Asian entrepreneurs – left stubborn reminders of their existence and their dreams.

Between 40,000 and 20,000 years ago the first inhabitants of the region trudged in from the west, crossing the Bering Strait between modern-day Russia and Alaska. These hardy souls flowed south, splitting into diverse communities that adapted as required by the weather and surrounding landscapes. The Spanish arrived in the Southwest in the 1540s, looking for the Seven Cities of Gold. Missions and missionaries followed in the 1700s as the Spanish staked their claim along the California coast.

The Spanish, as well as the British and Americans, were soon searching for the Northwest Passage, an east–west water route, but President Thomas Jefferson eventually scooped this endeavor with the Louisiana Purchase in 1803. His emissaries, Meriwether Lewis and William Clark, marched west from St Louis to explore America's newest holding, opening the door for a wave of pioneers.

Those Who Came Before, by Robert H and Florence C Lister, is an excellent source about the prehistory of the Southwest and the archaeological sites of its national parks and monuments.

An estimated 400,000 people trekked west across America between 1840 and 1860, lured by tales of gold, promises of religious freedom and visions of fertile farmland. The 'Wild West' years soon followed with ranchers, cowboys, miners and entrepreneurs staking claims and raising hell. Law, order and civilization arrived, hastened by the telegraph, the transcontinental railroad and a continual flow of new arrivals who just wanted to settle down and enjoy their piece of the American pie.

This goal became harder to accomplish in the arid West because the lack of water limited expansion. The great dam projects of the early 1900s tempered the water problem and allowed for the development of cities – Los Angeles, Las Vegas, Phoenix – in places where cities didn't necessarily belong.

TIMELINE	20,000–40,000 BC	8000 BC	7000 BC–AD 100
	The first peoples to come to the Americas arrive from Central Asia by migrating over a wide land bridge between Siberia and Alaska (when sea levels were lower than today).	Ice-age mammals, including the woolly mammoth, become extinct due to cooperative hunting by humans and a warming climate. People begin hunting smaller game and gathering native plants.	The 'Archaic period' is marked by nomadic hunter-gatherer lifestyles. By the end of this period, corn, beans and squash, and permanent settlements, are well established.

The West took on a more important economic and technological role during WWII. Scientists developed the atomic bomb in the secret city of Los Alamos. War-related industries, such as timber production and work at naval yards and airplane factories, thrived in the Pacific Northwest and California. After the war, industry took on new forms, with Silicon Valley's dot-com industry drawing talented entrepreneurs to the Bay area in the 1990s. The film industry still holds strong in Los Angeles, but tax incentives have drawn filmmakers to other western enclaves, particularly New Mexico.

Today, the West has been forced to take a closer look at the effects of rapid growth. Immigration, traffic, extended drought conditions, dropping water levels and environmental concerns grab headlines and affect people's way of life. The continuing allure of the West will depend on how these issues are tackled.

In *Finders Keepers: A Tale of Archaeological Plunder and Obsession* (2010), naturalist Craig Childs considers the ethics of collecting prehistoric artifacts – whether for study or for sale – in the Southwest.

The First Americans

When Europeans arrived, two to 18 million Native American people lived north of present-day Mexico and spoke more than 300 languages.

Pacific Northwest

In the Pacific Northwest, early coastal inhabitants went out to sea in pursuit of whales or sea lions, or depended on catching salmon and cod and collecting shellfish. On land they hunted deer and elk while gathering berries and roots. Food was stored for the long winters, when free time could be spent on artistic, religious and cultural pursuits. The construction of ornately carved cedar canoes led to extensive trading networks that stretched along the coast.

Inland, a regional culture based on seasonal migration developed among tribes. During salmon runs, tribes gathered at rapids and waterfalls to net or harpoon fish. In the harsh landscapes of Oregon's southern desert, tribes were nomadic peoples who hunted and scavenged in the northern reaches of the Great Basin desert.

From desert plants and animals to gunslingers and Native Americans to hiking and cycling, www.desertusa.com deals the goods on the allure of the Southwestern desert.

California

By 1500 AD more than 300,000 Native Americans spoke some 100 distinct languages in the California region. Central-coast fishing communities built subterranean roundhouses and saunas, where they held ceremonies, told stories and gambled for fun. Northwest hunting communities constructed big houses and redwood dugout canoes, while the inhabitants of southwest California created sophisticated pottery and developed irrigation systems that made farming in the desert possible. Native Americans in California had no written language but observed oral contracts and zoning laws.

1300	1492	1598	c 1600
The entire civilization of Ancestral Puebloans living in Mesa Verde, CO, abandons the area, possibly due to drought, leaving behind a sophisticated city of cliff dwellings.	Italian explorer Christopher Columbus 'discovers' America, eventually making three voyages to the Caribbean. He names the indigenous inhabitants 'Indians,' mistakenly thinking he'd reached the Indies.	A large force of Spanish explorers, led by Don Juan de Onate, stops near present-day El Paso, TX, and declares the land to the north New Mexico for Spain.	Santa Fe, America's oldest capital city, is founded. The Palace of Governors is the only remaining 17th-century structure; the rest of Santa Fe was destroyed by a 1914 fire.

Within a century of the arrival of Spanish colonists in 1769, California's Native American population was decimated to 20,000 by European diseases, conscripted labor regimes and famine.

The Southwest & Southern Colorado

Archaeologists believe that the Southwest's first inhabitants were hunters. The population grew, however, and wild game became extinct, forcing hunters to augment their diets with berries, seeds, roots and fruits. After 3000 BC, contacts with farmers in what is now central Mexico led to the beginnings of agriculture in the Southwest.

By about AD 100, three dominant cultures were emerging in the Southwest: the Hohokam of the desert, the Mogollon of the central mountains and valleys, and the Ancestral Puebloans – formerly known as the Anasazi.

The Hohokam lived in the deserts of Arizona, adapting to desert life by creating an incredible river-fed irrigation system. They also developed low earthen pyramids and sunken ball courts with earthen walls. By about 1400, the Hohokam had abandoned their villages. There are many theories on this tribe's disappearance, but the most likely involves a combination of factors including drought, overhunting, conflict among groups and disease.

The Mogollon culture settled near the Mexican border from 200 BC to AD 1400. They lived in small communities, often elevated on isolated mesas or ridge tops, and built simple pit dwellings. Although they farmed, they depended more on hunting and foraging for food. By around the 13th or 14th century, the Mogollon had probably been peacefully incorporated by the Ancestral Puebloan groups from the north.

The Ancestral Puebloans inhabited the Colorado Plateau, also called the Four Corners area. This culture left the richest archaeological sites and ancient settlements that are still inhabited in the Southwest. Their descendants live in Pueblo Indian communities in New Mexico. The oldest links with the Ancestral Puebloans are found among the Hopi tribe of northern Arizona. The mesa-top village of Old Oraibi has been inhabited since the 1100s, making it the oldest continuously inhabited settlement in North America.

The Europeans Arrive

Francisco Vasquez de Coronado led the first major expedition into North America in 1540. It included 300 soldiers, hundreds of Native American guides and herds of livestock. It also marked the first major violence between Spanish explorers and the native people.

The expedition's goal was the fabled, immensely rich Seven Cities of Cibola. For two years, it traveled through what is now Arizona, New Mex-

---

Cliff Dwellings

Mesa Verde National Park, NM

Bandelier National Monument, NM

Gila Cliff Dwellings National Monument, NM

Montezuma Castle National Monument, AZ

Walnut Canyon National Monument, AZ

Many modern Pueblo Indians object to the term 'Anasazi', a Navajo word meaning 'enemy ancestors'; it's no longer used.

1787–91	1803	1803–06	1811
The Constitutional Convention in Philadelphia draws up the US Constitution. The Bill of Rights is later adopted as constitutional amendments articulating citizens' rights.	Napoleon sells the Louisiana Territory to the US for $15 million, thereby extending the boundaries of the new nation from the Mississippi River to the Rocky Mountains.	President Jefferson sends Meriwether Lewis and William Clark west. Guided by Shoshone tribeswoman Sacagawea, they trailblaze from St Louis, Missouri, to the Pacific Ocean and back.	Pacific Fur Company mogul John Jacob Astor establishes Fort Astoria, the first permanent US settlement on the Pacific Coast. He later becomes the country's first millionaire.

ico and as far east as Kansas. Instead of gold and precious gems, the expedition found adobe pueblos, which they violently commandeered. During the Spaniards' first few years in northern New Mexico, they tried to subdue the pueblos, with much bloodshed. The Spanish established Santa Fe as the capital around 1610. The city remains the capital of New Mexico today, the oldest capital in what is now the USA.

When 18th-century Russian and English trappers began trading valuable otter pelts from Alta California, Spain concocted a plan for colonization. For the glory of God and the tax coffers of Spain, missions would be built across the state, and within 10 years these would be going concerns run by local converts.

Spain's missionizing plan was approved in 1769, and Franciscan Padre Junípero Serra secured support to set up *presidios* (military posts) alongside several missions in northern and central California in the 1770s and '80s. Clergy relied on soldiers to round up conscripts to build missions. In exchange for their labor, Native Americans were allowed one meal a day (when available) and a place in God's kingdom – which came much sooner than expected due to the smallpox the Spanish brought with them. In the Southwest, more than half of the pueblo populations were decimated by smallpox, measles and typhus.

In 1680, during the Pueblo Revolt, the northern New Mexico Pueblos banded together to drive out the Spanish after the latter's bloody campaign to destroy Puebloan ceremonial objects. The Spanish were pushed south of the Rio Grande and the Pueblo people held Santa Fe until 1682.

Lewis & Clark

After President Thomas Jefferson bought the Louisiana Territory from Napoleon in 1803 for $15 million, he sent his personal secretary, Meriwether Lewis, west to chart North America's western regions. The goal was to find a waterway to the Pacific while exploring the newly acquired Louisiana Purchase and establishing a foothold for American interests. Lewis, who had no training for exploration, convinced his good friend William Clark, an experienced frontiersman and army veteran, to tag along. In 1804, the 40-member party, called the Corps of Discovery, left St Louis.

The expedition fared relatively well, in part because of the presence of Sacagawea, a young Shoshone woman married to a French-Canadian trapper who was part of the entourage. Sacagawea proved invaluable as a guide, translator and ambassador to the area's Native Americans. York, Clark's African American servant, also softened tensions between the group and the Native Americans.

The party traveled some 8000 miles in about two years, documenting everything they came across in their journals. Meticulous notes were made about 122 animals and 178 plants, with some new discoveries being made along the way. In 1805 the party finally reached the mouth of the Columbia River and the Pacific Ocean at Cape Disappointment and bedded down for the winter nearby, thus establishing Fort Clatsop.

Lewis and Clark returned to a hero's welcome in St Louis in 1806.

You can follow the Lewis and Clark expedition on its extraordinary journey west to the Pacific and back again online at www.pbs.org/lewisandclark, featuring historical maps, photo albums and journal excerpts.

1841	1844	1846–48	1847
Wagon trains follow the Oregon Trail, and by 1847 over 6500 emigrants a year are heading west, to Oregon, California and Mormon-dominated Utah.	The first telegraph line is inaugurated with the phrase 'What hath God wrought?'. In 1845, Congress approves a transcontinental railroad, completed in 1869. Together, telegraph and train open the frontier.	The battle for the West is waged with the Mexican-American War. The war ends with the 1848 Guadalupe-Hidalgo treaty that gives most of present-day Arizona and New Mexico to the USA.	Mormons fleeing religious persecution in Illinois start arriving in Salt Lake City; over the next 20 years more than 70,000 Mormons head to Utah via the Mormon Pioneer Trail.

Westward, Ho!

As the 19th century dawned on the young nation, optimism was the mood of the day. With the invention of the cotton gin in 1793 – followed by threshers, reapers, mowers and later combines – agriculture was industrialized, and US commerce surged. The 1803 Louisiana Purchase doubled US territory, and expansion west of the Appalachian Mountains began in earnest.

Exploiting the West's vast resources became a patriotic duty in the 1840s – a key aspect of America's belief in its Manifest Destiny. During the early territorial days, movement of goods and people from the East to the West was very slow. Horses, mule trains and stagecoaches represented state-of-the-art transportation at the time.

One of the major routes was the Oregon Trail. Spanning six states, it sorely tested the families who embarked on this perilous trip. Their belongings were squirreled away under canvas-topped wagons, which often trailed livestock. The journey could take up to eight months, and by the time the settlers reached eastern Oregon their food supplies were running low. Other major routes included the Santa Fe Trail and the Old Spanish Trail, which ran from Santa Fe into central Utah and across Nevada to Los Angeles in California. Regular stagecoach services along the Santa Fe Trail began in 1849; the Mormon Trail reached Salt Lake City in 1847.

The arrival of more people and resources via the railroad led to further land exploration and the frequent discovery of mineral deposits. Many Western mining towns were founded in the 1870s and 1880s; some are now ghost towns like Santa Rita while others like Tombstone and Silver City remain active.

Among the provisions recommended for those traveling the Oregon Trail were coffee (15lb per person), bacon (25lb per person), 1lb of castile soap, citric acid to prevent scurvy and a live cow for milk and emergency meat.

The moving Boarding School Experience exhibit at the Heard Museum in Phoenix traces the forced relocation of Native American children to federally run boarding schools in the 1800s and 1900s for 'Americanization.'

Eureka!

Real estate speculator, lapsed Mormon and tabloid publisher Sam Brannan was looking to unload some California swampland in 1848 when he heard rumors of gold flakes found near Sutter's Mill, 120 miles from San Francisco. Figuring this news should sell some newspapers and raise real estate values, Brannan published the rumor as fact. Initially the story didn't generate excitement. So Brannan ran another story, this time verified by Mormon employees at Sutter's Mill who had sworn him to secrecy. Brannan reportedly kept his word by running through the San Francisco streets, brandishing gold entrusted to him as tithes for the Mormon church, shouting, 'Gold on the American River!'

Other newspapers hastily published stories of 'gold mountains' near San Francisco. By 1850, the year California was fast-tracked for admission as the 31st state, its non-Native population had ballooned from 15,000

1849	1859	1861–65	1864
After the 1848 discovery of gold near Sacramento, an epic cross-country gold rush sees 60,000 'forty-niners' flock to California's Mother Lode. San Francisco's population explodes to 25,000.	The richest vein of silver ever discovered in the USA, the Comstock Lode, is struck in Virginia City, NV, which quickly becomes the most notorious mining town in the Wild West.	American Civil War erupts between North and South. The war's end on April 9, 1865, is marred by President Lincoln's assassination five days later.	Kit Carson forces 9000 Navajo to walk 400 miles to a camp near Fort Sumner. Hundreds of Native Americans die from sickness, starvation and gunshot wounds along 'The Long Walk.'

to 93,000. Most arrivals weren't Americans, but Peruvians, Australians, Chileans and Mexicans, with some Chinese, Irish, native Hawaiian and French prospectors.

The Long Walk & Apache Conflicts

For decades, US forces pushed west across the continent, killing or forcibly moving whole tribes of Native Americans who were in their way. The most widely known incident is the forceful relocation of many Navajo in 1864. US forces, led by Kit Carson, destroyed Navajo fields, orchards and houses, and forced the people into surrendering or withdrawing into remote parts of Canyon de Chelly. Eventually, they were starved out. About 9000 Navajo were rounded up and marched 400 miles east to a camp at Bosque Redondo, near Fort Sumner in New Mexico. Hundreds of Native Americans died from sickness, starvation or gunshot wounds along the way. The Navajo call this 'The Long Walk,' and it remains an important part of their history.

The last serious conflicts were between US troops and the Apache. This was partly because raiding was the essential path to manhood for the Apache. As US forces and settlers moved into Apache land, they became obvious targets for the raids that were part of the Apache way of life. These continued under the leadership of Mangas Coloradas, Cochise, Victorio and, finally, Geronimo, who surrendered in 1886 after being promised that he and the Apache would be imprisoned for two years and then allowed to return to their homeland. As with many promises made during these years, this one, too, was broken.

Even after the wars were over, Native Americans were treated like second-class citizens for many decades. Non-Native Americans used legal loopholes and technicalities to take over reservation land. Many children were removed from reservations and shipped off to boarding schools where they were taught in English and punished for speaking their own languages or behaving 'like Indians' – this practice continued into the 1930s.

The Wild West

Romanticized tales of gunslingers, cattle rustlers, outlaws and train robbers fuel Wild West legends. Good and bad guys were designations in flux – a tough outlaw in one state became a popular sheriff in another. Gunfights were more frequently the result of mundane political struggles in emerging towns than storied blood feuds. New mining towns mushroomed overnight, playing host to rowdy saloons and bordellos where miners would come to brawl, drink and gamble. Riders and swift horses were the backbone of the short-lived but legendary Pony Express (1860–61). They carried letters between Missouri and California in an astounding 10 days!

On November 7, 1893, Colorado became the first US state – and one of the first places in the world – to grant women the right to vote.

HISTORY THE LONG WALK & APACHE CONFLICTS

Best Old West Towns

Bisbee, AZ

Tombstone, AZ

Silverton, CO

Lincoln, NM

Virginia City, NV

1881	1882	1913	1919
In 1881, Wyatt Earp, his brothers Virgil and Morgan, and Doc Holliday, kill Billy Clanton and the McLaury brothers in a blazing gunfight at the OK Corral in Tombstone, AZ.	Racist sentiment, particularly in California (where over 50,000 Chinese immigrants had arrived since 1848) leads to the Chinese Exclusion Act, the only US immigration law to exclude a specific race.	William Mulholland, director of Los Angeles Water & Power, presides over the opening of the 233-mile Owens Valley–Los Angeles Aqueduct.	The Grand Canyon becomes the USA's 15th national park, and a dirt road to the North Rim is built from Kanab. By 2013, the park is visited by 4.5 million people annually.

Legendary figures Billy the Kid and Sheriff Pat Garrett, both involved in the infamous Lincoln County War, were active in the late 1870s. Billy the Kid reputedly shot and killed more than 20 men in a brief career as a gunslinger – he himself was shot and killed by Garrett at the age of 21. In 1881, Wyatt Earp, along with his brothers Virgil and Morgan, and Doc Holliday, shot dead Billy Clanton and the McLaury brothers in a blazing gunfight at the OK Corral in Tombstone – the showdown took less than a minute. Both sides accused the other of cattle rustling, but the real story will never be known.

Water & Western Development

Americans began to think about occupying the area between the coasts. The lingering image of the Great American Desert, a myth propagated by early explorers, had deterred agricultural settlers and urban development. Though the western interior was not a desert, water was a limiting factor as cities such as Denver began to spring up at the base of the Front Range.

The struggle for an adequate supply of water for the growing desert population marked the early years of the 20th century, resulting in federally funded dam projects such as the 1936 Hoover Dam and, in 1963, the Glen Canyon Dam and Lake Powell. Water supply continues to be a key challenge in this region.

Reforming the Wild West

When the great earthquake and fire hit San Francisco in 1906, it signaled change for California. With public funds for citywide water mains and fire hydrants siphoned off by corrupt bosses, there was only one functioning water source in San Francisco. When the smoke lifted, one thing was clear: it was time for the Wild West to change.

While San Francisco was rebuilt at a rate of 15 buildings per day, California's reformers set to work on city, state and national politics, one plank at a time. Californians concerned about public health and trafficking in women pushed for passage of the 1914 statewide Red Light Abatement Act. Mexico's revolution from 1910 to 1921 brought a new wave of migrants and revolutionary ideas, including ethnic pride and worker solidarity. As California's ports grew, longshoremen's unions coordinated a historic 83-day strike in 1934 along the entire West Coast that forced concessions for safer working conditions and fair pay.

At the height of the Depression in 1935, some 200,000 farming families fleeing the drought-stricken Dust Bowl in Texas and Oklahoma arrived in California, where they found scant pay and deplorable working conditions at major farming concerns. California's artists alerted middle America to the migrants' plight, and the nation rallied around Dorothea

For behind-the-scenes stories about Wild West legends, along with their photographs, pick up the monthly magazine *True West* (www.truewestmagazine.com), or visit the website, to see who's in the spotlight.

The Denver Mint struck and minted its first gold and silver coins on February 1, 1906. It is the largest producer of coins in the world. The mint was robbed of $200,000 in broad daylight on 18 December, 1922.

1938	1945	1946	1947
Route 66 becomes the first cross-country highway to be completely paved, including more than 750 miles across Arizona and New Mexico. The Mother Road is officially decommissioned in 1984.	The first atomic bomb is detonated in the ironically named Jornada del Muerto (Journey of Death) Valley in southern New Mexico, which is now part of the White Sands Missile Range.	The opening of the glitzy Flamingo casino in Las Vegas sparks a mob-backed building spree. By the fabulous '50s, Sin City has reached its first golden peak.	An unidentified object falls in the desert near Roswell. The government first calls it a crashed disk, then a day later a weather balloon, and mysteriously closes off the area.

Lange's haunting documentary photos of famine-struck families and John Steinbeck's harrowing fictionalized account in his 1939 novel *The Grapes of Wrath*.

WWII & the Atomic Age
Los Alamos

In 1943, Los Alamos, New Mexico, then home to a boys' school perched on a 7400ft mesa, was chosen as the top-secret headquarters of the Manhattan Project, the code name for the research and development of the atomic bomb. The 772-acre site, accessed by two dirt roads, had no gas or oil lines and only one wire service, and it was surrounded by forest.

Isolation and security marked every aspect of life on 'the hill.' Not only was resident movement restricted and mail censored, but there was also no outside contact by radio or telephone. Perhaps even more unsettling, most residents had no idea why they were living in Los Alamos. Knowledge was on a 'need to know' basis; everyone knew only as much as their job required.

In just under two years, Los Alamos scientists successfully detonated the first atomic bomb at the Trinity site, now White Sands Missile Range.

After the US detonated the atomic bomb in Japan, the secret city of Los Alamos was exposed to the public. The city continued to be cloaked in secrecy, however, until 1957, when restrictions on visiting were lifted.

Changing Workforce & New Industries

California's workforce permanently changed in WWII, when women and African Americans were recruited for wartime industries and Mexican workers were brought in to fill labor shortages. Contracts in military communications and aviation attracted an international elite of engineers, who would launch California's high-tech industry. Within a decade after the war, California's population had grown by 40%, reaching almost 13 million.

The war also brought economic fortune to the Pacific Northwest, when the area became the nation's largest lumber producer and both Oregon's and Washington's naval yards bustled, along with William Boeing's airplane factory. The region continued to prosper through the second half of the 20th century, attracting new migrations of educated, progressively minded settlers from the nation's east and south.

Hollywood & Counterculture

In 1908, California became a convenient movie location for its consistent sunlight and versatile locations, although its role was limited to doubling for more exotic locales and providing backdrops for period-piece

The Oscar-winning There Will Be Blood (2007), adapted from Upton Sinclair's book Oil!, depicts a Californian oil magnate and was based on real-life SoCal tycoon Edward Doheny.

HISTORY WWII & THE ATOMIC AGE

Twenty-year-old artist and vagabond Everett Ruess explored the Four Corners region in the early 1930s. He disappeared under mysterious circumstances outside of Escalante, UT, in November 1934. Read his evocative letters in the book Everett Ruess: A Vagabond for Beauty.

1963	1964	1973	1980
The controversial Glen Canyon Dam is finished and Lake Powell begins, eventually covering up ancestral Native American sites and stunning rock formations but creating 1960 miles of shoreline and a boater fantasyland.	Congress passes the Civil Rights Act, outlawing discrimination on the basis of race, color, religion, sex or national origin. First proposed by Kennedy, it was one of President Johnson's crowning achievements.	The debut of the MGM Grand in 1973 signals the dawn of the corporate-owned 'megaresort,' and sparks a building bonanza along Las Vegas' Strip that's still going strong.	Mt St Helens blows her top, killing 57 people and destroying 250 homes. Her elevation is cut from 9677ft to 8365ft, and where a peak once stood, a mile-wide crater is born.

CALIFORNIA'S CIVIL RIGHTS MOVEMENT

When 110,000 Japanese Americans along the West Coast were ordered into internment camps by President Roosevelt in 1942, the San Francisco–based Japanese American Citizen's League immediately filed suits that advanced all the way to the Supreme Court. These lawsuits established groundbreaking civil-rights legal precedents, and in 1992 internees received reparations and an official letter of apology for internment signed by President George HW Bush.

Adopting the nonviolent resistance practices of Mahatma Gandhi and Martin Luther King Jr, labor leaders César Chávez and Dolores Huerta formed United Farm Workers in 1962 to champion the rights of underrepresented immigrant laborers. While civil-rights leaders marched on Washington, Chávez and Californian grape pickers marched on Sacramento, bringing the issue of fair wages and the health risks of pesticides to the nation's attention. When Bobby Kennedy was sent to investigate, he sided with Chávez, bringing Latinos into the US political fold.

productions. But gradually, California began stealing the scene in movies and iconic TV shows with waving palms and sunny beaches.

Not all Californians saw themselves as extras in *Beach Blanket Bingo,* however. WWII sailors discharged for insubordination and homosexuality in San Francisco found themselves at home in North Beach's bebop jazz clubs, bohemian coffeehouses and City Lights Bookstore. San Francisco became the home of free speech and free spirits, and soon everyone who was anyone was getting arrested: Beat poet Lawrence Ferlinghetti for publishing Allen Ginsberg's epic poem *Howl,* comedian Lenny Bruce for uttering the F-word onstage, and Carol Doda for going topless. When Flower Power faded, other Bay Area rebellions grew in its place: Black Power, gay pride and medical marijuana clubs.

But while Northern California had the more attention-grabbing counterculture from the 1940s to '60s, nonconformity in sunny Southern California shook America to the core. In 1947, when Senator Joseph McCarthy attempted to root out suspected communists in the movie industry, 10 writers and directors who refused to admit communist alliances or to name names were charged with contempt of Congress and barred from working in Hollywood. The Hollywood Ten's impassioned defenses of the Constitution were heard nationwide, and major Hollywood players boldly voiced dissent and hired blacklisted talent until California lawsuits put a legal end to McCarthyism in 1962.

On January 28, 1969, an oil rig dumped 200,000 gallons of oil into Santa Barbara Channel, killing dolphins, seals and some 3600 shore

Chinatown (1974) is the fictionalized yet surprisingly accurate account of the brutal water wars that were waged to build both Los Angeles and San Francisco.

1995	2000	2002	2008
Amazon, one of the first major companies to sell products online, is launched in Seattle. Originally started as a bookseller, it does not become annually profitable until 2003.	Coloradans vote for Amendment 20 in the state election, which provides for dispensing cannabis to registered patients. A proliferation of medical marijuana clinics ensues over the next decade.	Salt Lake City hosts the Winter Olympics, becoming the most populated place to ever hold the games. Women also compete in bobsled racing for the first time.	California voters pass Proposition 8, which bans gay marriage. Federal courts rule the law unconstitutional. In 2013, the US Supreme Court does not take up an appeal; same-sex marriages resume.

birds. The beach community organized a highly effective protest, spurring the establishment of the Environmental Protection Agency.

Geeking Out

When California's Silicon Valley introduced the first personal computer in 1968, Hewlett-Packard's 'light' (40lb) machine cost $4900 (about $29,000 today). Hoping to bring computer power to the people, 21-year-old Steve Jobs and Steve Wozniak introduced the Apple II at the 1977 West Coast Computer Faire with unfathomable memory (4KB of RAM) and microprocessor speed (1MHz).

By the mid-1990s, an entire dot-com industry boomed in Silicon Valley with online start-ups, and suddenly people were getting their mail, news, politics, pet food and, yes, sex online. But when dot-com profits weren't forthcoming, venture funding dried up, and fortunes in stock options disappeared on one nasty Nasdaq-plummeting day: March 10, 2000. Overnight, 26-year-old vice-presidents and Bay Area service-sector employees alike found themselves jobless. But as online users continued to look for useful information and one another in those billions of web pages, search engines and social media websites boomed. Between 2011 and 2015, social media giant Facebook jumped from 2000 employees to 6800.

Meanwhile, California biotech has been making strides. In 1976, an upstart company called Genentech cloned human insulin and introduced the hepatitis B vaccine. California voters approved a $3 billion bond measure in 2004 for stem-cell research, and by 2008 California had become the biggest funder of stem-cell research and the focus of Nasdaq's new Biotech Index.

HISTORY GEEKING OUT

In 2014 the HBO series *Silicon Valley* premiered on HBO. Co-created by Mike Judge, the comedy follows the ups and downs of an internet start-up company and its amusingly quirky founders.

2008	2010	2012	2015
Barack Obama is elected president of the United States, the first African American to hold the office.	Arizona passes controversial legislation requiring police officers to ask for identification from anyone they suspect of being in the US illegally. Immigration rights activists call for a boycott of the state.	New Mexico and Arizona, the 47th and 48th states to join the Union, celebrate their Centennials.	In a landmark five-four decision, the US Supreme Court decides that same-sex marriage is a right guaranteed by the Constitution. Thirteen states banning such unions must comply and issue same-sex marriage licenses.

The Way of Life

If you believe the headlines, Westerners are a quirky bunch, with Arizonans up-in-arms about illegal immigration, hair-pulling housewives in Orange County and pot-smoking deadbeats in Colorado. And, according to *Portlandia* comedy sketches, Portland brims with bike-riding, organic-obsessed hipsters who want to put a bird on everything. Are these accurate depictions? Yes and no. The headlines may reflect some regional attitudes, but most folks are just trying to go about their lives with as little drama as possible.

Key Sports Websites

Baseball
www.mlb.com

Basketball
www.nba.com

Football
www.nfl.com

Hockey
www.nhl.com

NASCAR
www.nascar.com

Soccer
www.mlssoccer.com

Regional Identity

The cowboy has long been a symbol of the West. Brave. Self-reliant. A solitary seeker of truth, justice and a straight shot of whiskey. The truth behind the myth? Those who settled the West were indeed self-reliant and brave. But they had to be. In that harsh and unforgiving landscape, danger was always a few steps behind opportunity. As the dangers dissipated, however, and settlers put down roots, the cowboy stereotype became less accurate. Like the red-rock mesas that have weathered into new and varying forms over the years, the character of the populace has also evolved. Stereotypes today, accurate or not, are regionally based, and the residents of Portland, San Diego, Santa Fe and Phoenix are perceived very differently from one another.

California

Hey dude, don't stick a label on me – that's so uncool. And what's the label? According to the stereotype, Californians are laid-back, self-absorbed, health-conscious, open-minded and eco-aware. The stats behind the stereotype? According to the the National Oceanic and Atmospheric Administration (NOAA), more than 25.5 million Californians lived in a coastal shoreline county in 2010 – the highest number for any coastal state. The state's southern beaches are sunniest and most swim-

THE SPORTING LIFE

Westerners cherish their sports, whether they're players themselves or just watching their favorite teams. Here is a breakdown of the West's professional teams by sport.

National Football League AFC West: Denver Broncos, Oakland Raiders, San Diego Chargers. NFC West: Arizona Cardinals, San Francisco 49ers, Seattle Seahawks.

National Basketball Association Western Conference Pacific: Golden State Warriors, LA Clippers, LA Lakers, Phoenix Suns, Sacramento Kings. Northwest: Denver Nuggets, Portland Trailblazers, Utah Jazz.

Women's National Basketball Association LA Sparks, Phoenix Mercury, Seattle Storm.

Major League Baseball American League: LA Angels, Oakland Athletics, Seattle Mariners. National League: Arizona Diamondbacks, Colorado Rockies, LA Dodgers, San Diego Padres, San Francisco Giants.

mable, thus Southern California's inescapable associations with surf, sun and classic prime-time TV soaps like *Baywatch* and *The OC*.

Self-help, fitness and body modification are major industries throughout California, successfully marketed since the 1970s, while exercise and good food help keep Californians among the fittest in the nation. Politically, the scene is not rosy for Republicans. In 2014, only 28% of registered voters in the state were Republicans while 43% were registered Democrats and 21% were considered independent. Environmentally, Golden Staters have zoomed ahead of the national energy-use curve in their smog-checked cars; more hybrid cars are sold here than in any other state. The Toyota Prius hybrid was the top-selling car in California in 2013.

California's adult prison and jail population was 218,800 in 2014. The state was second only to Texas, which housed 221,800 inmates.

Pacific Northwest

And what about those folks living in Washington and Oregon? Treehugging hipsters with activist tendencies and a penchant for latte? That's pretty accurate, actually. Many locals are proud of their independent spirit, profess a love for nature and, yes, will separate their plastics when it's time to recycle. They're a friendly lot and, despite the common tendency to denigrate Californians, most are transplants themselves. Why did they all come here? Among other things, for the lush scenery, the good quality of life and the lack of pretension that often afflicts bigger, more popular places. Primping up and putting on airs is not a part of Northwestern everyday life, and wearing Gore-Tex outerwear to restaurants, concerts or social functions will rarely raise an eyebrow.

Colorado averages 300 days of sun annually – if you count one hour of sunshine as being a full day. According to the no-fun but more precise National Weather Service, the Front Range averages 115 clear-sky days, 130 partly cloudy days and 120 cloudy days.

Rocky Mountain States

The iconic Western cowboy? You're likely to find the real deal here. Ranching is big business in these parts, and the solitary cowboy – seen riding a bucking bronco on the Wyoming license plate – is an appropriate symbol for the region. It takes a rugged individualist to scratch out a living on the lonely, windswept plains – plains that can leave big-city travelers feeling slightly unmoored.

Politically, the northern Rockies – Wyoming, Montana and Idaho – skew conservative, although you will find pockets of liberalism in the college and resort towns. Wyoming may have been the first territory to give women the right to vote, in 1869, but this nod to liberal thinking has been overshadowed by Wyoming's association with former vice-president Dick Cheney, the divisive Republican who was a six-term congressman from the state. In addition to ranching, the other big industry in Wyoming is energy.

Colorado is the West's most recognizable swing state. For every bastion of liberalism like Boulder there's an equally entrenched conservative counterpart like Colorado Springs.

The Tucson sector of the United States Border Patrol is one of the busiest border sectors in the nation in terms of apprehensions and drug seizures. It oversees 262 miles of borderland between Arizona and Mexico and employs 4200 agents across eight stations.

Southwest

The Southwest has long drawn stout-hearted settlers – Mormons, cattle barons and prospectors – pursuing slightly different agendas from those of the average American. A new generation of idealistic entrepreneurs has transformed former mining towns into New Age art enclaves and Old West tourist attractions. Scientists flocked to the empty spaces to develop and test atomic bombs and soaring rockets. Astronomers built observatories on lonely hills and mountains, making the most of the dark skies and unobstructed views.

In recent years high-profile governmental efforts to stop illegal immigration have impacted the let's-coexist vibe, most vocally in the southern reaches of Arizona. The anti-immigration rhetoric isn't common in day-to-day conversation, but heightened press coverage of the most vitriolic

MARRIAGE: EQUAL RIGHTS FOR ALL

Forty thousand Californians were already registered as domestic partners when, in 2004, San Francisco Mayor Gavin Newsom issued marriage licenses to same-sex couples in defiance of a California same-sex marriage ban. Four thousand same-sex couples promptly got hitched. The state ban was nixed by California courts in June 2008, but then Proposition 8 passed in November 2008 to amend the state's constitution and prohibit same-sex marriage. Civil-rights activists challenged the constitutionality of the proposition, and federal courts eventually ruled that the law unconstitutionally violated the equal protection and due process clauses. In 2013, the US Supreme Court did not take up an appeal and same-sex marriages resumed in the Golden State. In June 2015 the US Supreme Court settled the question across the country by ruling that the Constitution guarantees a right to same-sex marriage.

comments, coupled with a heavy Border Patrol presence, does cast a pall over the otherwise sunny landscape. Other regions of the Southwest, for the most part, have taken a more inclusive approach.

Population & Multiculturalism

California, with 38.8 million residents, is the most populous state in the entire US. California has the country's highest Asian American population, at 6.1 million, and the highest Latino population, currently 14.7 million. In 2014, Hispanics became the state's largest racial or ethnic group. Latino culture is deeply enmeshed with that of California, and most residents see the state as an easygoing multicultural society that gives everyone a chance to live the American Dream. The state had an estimated 2.45 million undocumented immigrants in 2012 – about 6.2% of the state population.

In September 2014, more than 65,900 euphoric souls descended upon the Nevada desert for Burning Man, an annual camping extravaganza, art festival and rave where freedom of expression, costume and libido are all encouraged.

Colorado, Arizona and New Mexico all have large Native American and Hispanic populations. These residents take pride in maintaining their cultural identities through preserved traditions and oral history lessons.

Religion

Although Californians are less churchgoing than the American mainstream, and one in five Californians professes no religion at all, it remains one of the most religiously diverse states. About a third of Californians are Catholic, due in part to the state's large Latino population, while another third are Protestants. About 1% of California's population is Muslim. LA has the third-largest Jewish community in North America behind NYC and southern Florida. About 2% of California's population identifies as Buddhist and another 2% as Hindu.

About a third of Pacific Northwesterners have no religious affiliation. Those who are religious tend to adhere to Christianity and Judaism. Asian Americans have brought Buddhism and Hinduism, and New Age spirituality isn't a stranger here.

The Southwest has its own anomalies. In Utah, 55% of the state's population identifies as Mormon. The church stresses traditional family values, and drinking, smoking and premarital sex are frowned upon. Family and religion are also core values for Native Americans and Hispanics throughout the Southwest. For the Hopi, tribal dances are such sacred events that they are mostly closed to outsiders. And, although many Native Americans and Hispanics are now living in urban areas, working as professionals, large family gatherings and traditional customs are still important facets of daily life.

Native Americans

From the Apache to the Zuni, the indigenous tribes of the West are extremely diverse. Each tribe maintains distinctions of law, language, history and custom, their beliefs molded in part by the landscapes they inhabit. Members within a tribe are linked by common heritage, but follow unique paths as they navigate the legacy of their ancestors and outside cultures. Whether a weaver living on reservation or a web designer living in Phoenix, contemporary Native Americans cannot be slotted into one stereotype.

According to the 2010 census, 5.2 million Native Americans from more than 566 recognized tribes reside in the US, nearly 2% of the total US population. California has the largest Native American population in the country, with Arizona and New Mexico ranking in the top 10. The Navajo tribe is the largest western tribe, second only to the Cherokee nationwide.

Culturally, tribes today grapple with questions about how to prosper in contemporary America while protecting their traditions from erosion and their lands from further exploitation, and how to lift their people from poverty while maintaining their sense of identity and the sacred.

> One of the best museums devoted to Southwest Native American life and culture is Phoenix's Heard Museum.

The Tribes

Most of the major Western tribes are located in the Southwest. Well-known tribes with large reservations in Arizona include the Navajo, the Hopi and the Apache. Two smaller Arizona tribes, the Hualapai and the Havasupai, live on reservations beside the Grand Canyon. New Mexico's tribes are clustered in 19 pueblos located in the north-central region of the state.

Apache

The Southwest has three major Apache reservations: New Mexico's Jicarilla Apache Reservation and Arizona's San Carlos Apache Reservation and Fort Apache Reservation, home to the White Mountain Apache tribe. All the Apache tribes descend from Athabascans who migrated from Canada around 1400. They were nomadic hunter-gatherers who became warlike raiders, particularly of Pueblo tribes and European settlements, and they fiercely resisted relocation to reservations.

The most famous Apache is Geronimo, a Chiricahua Apache who resisted the American takeover of native lands until he was finally subdued by the US Army with the help of White Mountain Apache scouts.

Havasupai

The Havasupai Reservation abuts Arizona's Grand Canyon National Park beneath the canyon's South Rim. The tribe's one village, Supai, can only be reached by an 8-mile hike or a mule or helicopter ride from road's end at Hualapai Hilltop.

> Most (78%) Native Americans live off the reservation. New York City is home to the largest population (111,700) followed by Los Angeles (54,200).

Havasupai (hah-vah-*soo*-pie) means 'people of the blue-green water,' and tribal life has always been dominated by the Havasu Creek tributary of the Colorado River. Reliable water meant the ability to irrigate fields, which led to a season-based village lifestyle. The deep Havasu Canyon

For decades, traditional Navajo and Hopi have thwarted US industry efforts to strip mine sacred Big Mountain. Black Mesa Indigenous Support (www.supportblack mesa.org) tells their story.

also protected them from others; this extremely peaceful people basically avoided Western contact until the 1800s. Today, the tribe relies on tourism, and Havasu Canyon's gorgeous waterfalls draw a steady stream of visitors. The tribe is related to the Hualapai.

Hopi

Surrounded by the Navajo Reservation in northeast Arizona, the Hopi Reservation covers more than 1.5 million acres. Most Hopi live in 12 villages at the base and on top of three mesas jutting from the main Black Mesa; Old Oraibi, on Third Mesa, is considered (along with Acoma Pueblo) the continent's oldest continuously inhabited settlement. Like all Pueblo peoples, the Hopi are descended from the Ancestral Puebloans (formerly known as Anasazi).

Hopi (*ho*-pee) translates as 'peaceful ones' or 'peaceful person,' and perhaps no tribe is more renowned for leading such a humble, traditional and deeply spiritual lifestyle. The Hopi practice an unusual, near-miraculous technique of 'dry farming'; they don't plow, but plant seeds in 'wind breaks' and natural water catchments. Their main crop has always been corn (which is central to their creation story).

The Hopi Arts Trail spotlights artists and galleries on the three mesas that are the heart of the Hopi reservation. For a map, as well as a list of artists and galleries, visit www.hopi artstrail.com.

Hopi ceremonial life is complex and intensely private, and extends into all aspects of daily living. Following the 'Hopi Way' is considered essential to bringing the life-giving rains, but the Hopi also believe it fosters the wellbeing of the entire human race. Each person's role is determined by their clan, which is matrilineal. Even among themselves, the Hopi keep certain traditions of their individual clans private.

The Hopi are skilled artisans; they are famous for pottery, coiled baskets and silverwork, as well as for their ceremonial kachina (spirit) dolls.

ETIQUETTE

When visiting a reservation, ask about and follow any specific rules. Almost all tribes ban alcohol, and some ban pets and restrict cameras. All require permits for camping, fishing and other activities. Tribal rules may be posted at the reservation entrance, or visit the tribal office or the reservation's website.

When you visit a reservation, you are visiting a unique culture with perhaps unfamiliar customs. Be courteous, respectful and open-minded, and don't expect locals to share every detail of their lives.

Ask First, Document Later

Some tribes restrict cameras and sketching entirely; others may charge a fee, or restrict them at ceremonies or in certain areas. *Always ask before taking pictures or drawing.* If you want to photograph a person, ask permission first; a tip is polite and often expected.

Pueblos are not Museums

The incredible adobe structures are homes. Public buildings will be signed; if a building isn't signed, assume it's private. Don't climb around. Kivas are nearly always off limits.

Ceremonies are not Performances

Treat ceremonies like church services; watch silently and respectfully, without talking, clapping or taking pictures, and wear modest clothing. Powwows are more informal, but remember: unless they're billed as theater, they are for the tribe, not you.

Privacy & Communication

Many Native Americans are happy to describe their tribe's general religious beliefs, but not always or to the same degree, and details about rituals and ceremonies are often considered private. Always ask before discussing religion and respect each person's boundaries. Also, Native Americans consider it polite to listen without comment; silent listening, given and received, is another sign of respect.

Hualapai

The Hualapai Reservation occupies around 1 million acres along 108 miles of the Grand Canyon's South Rim. Hualapai (*wah*-lah-pie) means 'people of the tall pines.' Because this section of the Grand Canyon was not readily arable, the Hualapai were originally seminomadic, gathering wild plants and hunting small game.

Today, forestry, cattle ranching, farming and tourism are the economic mainstays. The tribal headquarters are in Peach Springs, AZ, which was the inspiration for 'Radiator Springs' in the animated movie *Cars*. Hunting, fishing, rafting and the lofty Skywalk are prime draws.

Navajo

Nationwide, there are about 330,000 Navajo, making it the USA's second-largest tribe after the Cherokee. The Navajo Reservation (www.discovernavajo.com) is by far the largest and most populous in the US. Also called the Navajo Nation and Navajoland, it covers 17.5 million acres (over 27,000 sq miles) in Arizona and parts of New Mexico and Utah.

The Navajo were feared nomads and warriors who both traded with and raided the Pueblos and who fought settlers and the US military. They also borrowed generously from other traditions: they acquired sheep and horses from the Spanish, learned pottery and weaving from the Pueblos, and picked up silversmithing from Mexico. Today, the Navajo are renowned for their woven rugs, pottery and inlaid silver jewelry, as well as for their intricate sandpainting, which is used in healing ceremonies.

Pueblo

New Mexico contains 19 Pueblo reservations. Four reservations lead west from Albuquerque: Isleta, Laguna, Acoma and Zuni. Fifteen pueblos fill the Rio Grande Valley between Albuquerque and Taos: Sandia, San Felipe, Santa Ana, Zia, Jemez, Santo Domingo, Cochiti, San Ildefonso, Pojoaque, Nambé, Tesuque, Santa Clara, Ohkay Owingeh (or San Juan), Picuris and Taos.

These tribes are as different as they are alike. Nevertheless, the term 'pueblo' (Spanish for 'village') is a convenient shorthand for what these tribes share: all are believed to be descended from the Ancestral Puebloans and to have inherited their architectural style and their agrarian, village-based life – often atop mesas.

Pueblos are unique among Native Americans. These adobe structures can have up to five levels, connected by ladders, and are built with varying combinations of mud bricks, stones, logs and plaster. In the central plaza of each pueblo is a kiva, an underground ceremonial chamber that connects to the spirit world. A legacy of missionaries, Catholic churches are prominent in the pueblos, and many Pueblos now hold both Christian and native religious beliefs.

Arts

Native American art nearly always contains ceremonial purpose and religious significance; the patterns and symbols are woven with spiritual meaning that provides an intimate window into the heart of the people.

In addition to preserving their culture, contemporary Native American artists have used sculpture, painting, textiles, film, literature and performance art to reflect and critique modernity since the mid-20th century, especially after the civil-rights activism of the 1960s and cultural renaissance of the '70s. *Native North American Art* by Janet Berlo and Ruth Phillips offers a superb introduction to North America's varied indigenous art – from pre-contact to postmodernism.

By purchasing arts from Native Americans themselves, visitors have a direct, positive impact on tribal economies, which depend in part on

For a helpful introduction to Navajo culture, stop by the Explore Navajo Interactive Museum (www.explorenavajon.com) in Tuba City, on the way to Monument Valley from Grand Canyon National Park.

In the Pacific Theater during WWII, Navajo 'code talkers' sent and received military messages in the Navajo's Athabascan tongue, which is notoriously complex. Japan never broke the code, and the code talkers were considered essential to US victory.

Not all pueblos have websites, but available links and introductions to all are provided by the Indian Pueblo Cultural Center (www.indianpueblo.org).

NATIVE AMERICANS ARTS

tourist dollars. Many tribes run craft outlets and galleries, usually in the main towns of reservations. The Indian Arts & Crafts Board (www.iacb.doi.gov) lists Native American–owned galleries and shops state-by-state online – click on 'Source Directory of Businesses.'

Pottery & Basketry

Pretty much every Southwest tribe has pottery and/or basketry traditions. Originally each tribe and even individual families maintained distinct styles, but modern potters and basket makers readily mix, borrow and reinterpret classic designs and methods.

Pueblo pottery is perhaps most acclaimed of all. Initially, local clay determined color, so that Zia pottery was red, Acoma white, Hopi yellow, Cochiti black and so on. Santa Clara is famous for its carved relief designs, and San Ildefonso for its black-on-black style, which was revived by world-famous potter Maria Martinez. The Navajo and Ute Mountain Utes also produce well-regarded pottery.

Pottery is nearly always synonymous with village life, while more portable baskets were often preferred by nomadic peoples. Among the tribes who stand out for their exquisite basketry are the Jicarilla Apache (whose name means basket maker), the Kaibab-Paiute, the Hualapai and the Tohono O'odham. Hopi coiled baskets, with their vivid patterns and kachina iconography, are also notable.

Navajo Weaving

Navajo legend says that Spider Woman taught humans how to weave, and she seems embodied today in the iconic sight of Navajo women patiently shuttling handspun wool on weblike looms, creating the Navajo's legendary rugs (originally blankets), which are so tight they hold water. Preparation of the wool and sometimes the dyes is still done by hand, and finishing a rug takes months (occasionally years).

Authentic Navajo rugs are expensive, and justifiably so, ranging from hundreds to thousands of dollars. They are not average souvenirs but artworks that will last a lifetime, whether displayed on the wall or the floor. Take time to research, even a little, so you recognize when quality matches price.

Silver & Turquoise Jewelry

Jewelry using stones and shells has always been a native tradition; silverwork did not arrive until the 1800s, along with Anglo and Mexican contact. In particular, Navajo, Hopi and Zuni became renowned for combining these materials with inlaid-turquoise silver jewelry. In addition to turquoise, jewelry often features lapis, onyx, coral, carnelian and shells.

Authentic jewelry is often stamped or marked by the artisan, and items may come with an Indian Arts & Crafts certificate; always ask. Price may also be an indicator: a high tab doesn't guarantee authenticity, but an absurdly low one probably signals trickery. A crash course can be had at the August Santa Fe Indian Market.

N Scott Momaday's Pulitzer Prize–winning *House Made of Dawn* (1968), about a Pueblo youth, launched a wave of Native American literature.

For a few basic tips about shopping for Native American arts and crafts, check out the relevant articles on the Arizona state tourism website at www.visitarizona.com/experience-and-share.

Western Cuisine

Food served in the western part of the United States can't be slotted into one neat category because regional specialties abound – and they can be very distinct. Half the fun of any trip is digging into a dish that has cultural and agricultural ties to a region, from green chile enchiladas in New Mexico to grilled salmon in the Pacific Northwest to San Diego's delicious fish tacos to sizzlin' steaks in Arizona.

Staples & Specialties
Breakfast

Morning meals in the West, as in the rest of the country, are big business. From a hearty serving of biscuits and gravy at a cowboy diner to a quick Egg McMuffin at the McDonald's drive-thru window or lavish Sunday brunches, Americans love their eggs and bacon, their waffles and hash browns, and their big glasses of orange juice. Most of all, they love that seemingly inalienable American right: a steaming cup of morning coffee with unlimited refills.

Lunch

After a mid-morning coffee break, an American worker's lunch hour (or half-hour these days) affords only a sandwich, quick burger or hearty salad. The formal 'business lunch' is more common in big cities like Los Angeles, where food is not necessarily as important as the conversation.

Dinner

Americans settle in to a more substantial weeknight dinner, usually early in the evening, which, given the workload of so many two-career families, might be takeout (eg pizza or Chinese food) or prepackaged meals cooked in a microwave. Desserts tend toward ice cream, pies and cakes. Some families still cook a traditional Sunday-night dinner, when relatives and friends gather for a big feast, or grill outside and go picnicking on weekends.

Quick Eats

Eating a hot dog from a street cart or a taco from a roadside food truck is a convenient, and increasingly tasty, option in downtown business districts. Don't worry about health risks – these vendors are usually supervised by the local health department. Fast-food restaurants with

---

Must-Try Regional Specialties

Fish tacos (San Diego, CA)

Frito pie (NM)

Green chile cheeseburgers (NM)

Navajo tacos (northeastern AZ)

Sonoran dogs (Tucson, AZ)

Rocky Mountain oysters (CO)

BREAKFAST BURRITOS

There is one Mexican-inspired meal that has been mastered in the West: the breakfast burrito. It's served in diners and delis in Colorado, in coffee shops in Arizona and beach-bum breakfast joints in California. In many ways, it is the perfect breakfast – cheap (usually under $6), packed with protein (eggs, cheese, beans), fresh veggies (or is avocado a fruit?), hot salsa (is that a vegetable?) and rolled to go in paper and foil. Peel it open like a banana and inhale the savory steam.

drive-thru windows are ubiquitous, and you'll usually find at least one beside a major highway exit. At festivals and county fairs, pick from cotton candy, corn dogs, candy apples, funnel cakes, chocolate-covered frozen bananas and plenty of tasty regional specialties. Farmers markets and natural food markets often have more wholesome prepared foods.

California

Owing to its vastness and variety of microclimates, California is truly America's cornucopia for fruits and vegetables, and a gateway to myriad Asian markets. The state's natural resources are overwhelming, with wild salmon, Dungeness crab and oysters from the ocean; robust produce year-round; and artisanal products such as cheese, bread, olive oil, wine and chocolate.

Starting in the 1970s and '80s, star chefs such as Alice Waters and Wolfgang Puck pioneered 'California cuisine' by incorporating the best local ingredients into simple yet delectable preparations. The influx of Asian immigrants, especially after the Vietnam War, enriched the state's urban food cultures with Chinatowns, Koreatowns and Japantowns, along with huge enclaves of Mexican Americans who maintain their own culinary traditions across the state. Global fusion restaurants are another hallmark of California's cuisine scene.

Delicious food-truck fare is no longer a novelty. From crab-cake tacos to red-velvet cupcakes, it's creative, healthy, gourmet, decadent and sometimes downright bizarre. You'll chase down the trucks from Los Angeles to Portland to Las Vegas.

North Coast & the Sierras

San Francisco hippies headed back to the land in the 1970s for a more self-sufficient lifestyle, reviving traditions of making breads and cheeses from scratch and growing their own *everything* (note: farms from Mendocino to Humboldt are serious about No Trespassing signs). Hippie-homesteaders were early adopters of pesticide-free farming, and innovated hearty, organic cuisine that was health-minded yet satisfied the munchies.

On the North Coast, you can taste the influence of wild-crafted Ohlone and Miwok cuisine. In addition to fishing, hunting game and making bread from acorn flour, these Native Northern Californians also tended orchards and carefully cultivated foods along the coast. With such attentive stewardship, nature has been kind to this landscape, yielding bonanzas of wildflower honey and blackberries. Alongside traditional shellfish collection, sustainable caviar and oyster farms have sprung up along the coast. Fearless foragers have identified every edible plant from Sierra's wood sorrel to Mendocino sea vegetables, though key spots for wild mushrooms remain closely guarded local secrets.

San Francisco Bay Area

Based on 2010 census data, San Francisco has nearly 40 restaurants per 10,000 households – the highest number per household in the US. In 2013 there were about 230 licensed food trucks crisscrossing the city.

Some city novelties have had extraordinary staying power, including ever-popular *cioppino* (Dungeness crab stew), chocolate bars invented by the Ghirardelli family, and sourdough bread, with original gold-rush-era mother dough still yielding local loaves with that distinctive tang. Dim

SLOW, LOCAL, ORGANIC

The 'Slow Food' movement, along with renewed enthusiasm for eating local, organically grown fare, is a leading trend in American restaurants. The movement took off in America in 1971 courtesy of chef Alice Waters at Berkeley's Chez Panisse. Farmers markets are great places to meet locals and take a big bite out of America's cornucopia of foods, from heritage fruit and vegetables to fresh, savory and sweet regional delicacies.

sum is Cantonese for what's known in Mandarin as *xiao che* (small eats) or *yum cha* (drink tea), and there are dozens of places in San Francisco where you'll call it lunch.

Mexican, French and Italian food remain perennial local favorites, along with more recent SF ethnic food crazes: *izakaya* (Japanese bars serving small plates), Korean tacos, *banh mi* (Vietnamese sandwiches featuring marinated meats and pickled vegetables on French baguettes) and *alfajores* (Arabic-Argentine crème-filled shortbread cookies).

SoCal

Los Angeles has long been known for its big-name chefs and celebrity restaurant owners. Robert H Cobb, owner of Hollywood's Brown Derby Restaurant, is remembered as the namesake of the Cobb salad (lettuce, tomato, egg, chicken, bacon and Roquefort). Wolfgang Puck launched the celebrity-chef trend with the Sunset Strip's star-spangled Spago in 1982.

For authentic ethnic food in Los Angeles, head to Koreatown for flavor-bursting *kalbi* (marinated barbecued beef short ribs), East LA for tacos *al pastor* (marinated, fried pork) and Little Tokyo for ramen noodles made fresh daily.

Further south, surfers cruise Hwy 1 beach towns from Laguna Beach to La Jolla in search of the ultimate wave and quick-but-hearty eats like breakfast burritos and fish tacos. And everybody stops for a date shake at Ruby's Crystal Cove Shake Shack south of Newport Beach.

Pacific Northwest

The late James Beard (1903–85), an American chef, food writer and Oregon native, believed foods prepared simply, without too many ingredients or complicated cooking techniques, allowed their natural flavors to shine. This philosophy has greatly influenced modern Northwest cuisine. Pacific Northwesterners don't like to think of their food as trendy or fussy, but at the same time they love to be considered innovative, especially when it comes to 'green,' hyper-conscious eating.

Farmland, Wild Foods & Fish

The diverse geography and climate – a mild, damp coastal region with sunny summers and arid farmland in the east – foster all types of farm-grown produce. Farmers grow plenty of fruit, from melons, grapes, apples and pears to strawberries, cherries and blueberries. Veggies thrive here too: potatoes, lentils, corn, asparagus and Walla Walla sweet onions, all of which feed local and overseas populations.

Many wild foods thrive, especially in the damper regions, such as the Coast Range. Foragers seek the same foods once gathered by local Native American tribes – year-round wild mushrooms, as well as summertime fruits and berries.

With hundreds of miles of coastline and an impressive system of rivers, Northwesterners have access to plenty of fresh seafood. Depending on the season, specialties include razor clams, mussels, prawns, albacore tuna, Dungeness crab and sturgeon. Salmon remains one of the region's most recognized foods, whether it's smoked or grilled, or in salads, quiches and sushi.

The Southwest

Moderation is not a virtue when it comes to food in Arizona, New Mexico, Utah, southern Colorado and Las Vegas. These gastronomic wonderlands don't have time for the timid. Sonoran hot dogs, green chile cheeseburgers, huevos rancheros, juicy slabs of steaks and endless buffets – take your Instagram photo then dig in and dine happy.

WESTERN CUISINE PACIFIC NORTHWEST

Dos & Don'ts

Tip 15% of the total bill for standard service; tip 20% (or more) for excellent service.

It's customary to place your napkin on your lap.

Avoid putting your elbows on the table.

Wait until everyone is served to begin eating.

In formal situations, diners customarily wait to eat until the host(ess) has lifted a fork.

Not all chiles are picked – those left on the plant are allowed to mature to a deep ruby red, then strung on the *ristras* which adorn walls and doorways throughout the Southwest.

Two ethnic groups define Southwestern food culture: the Spanish and the Mexicans, who controlled territories from Texas to California until well into the 19th century. While there is little actual Spanish food today, the Spanish brought cattle to Mexico, which the Mexicans adapted to their own corn-and-chile-based gastronomy to make tacos, tortillas, enchiladas, burritos, chimichangas and other dishes made of corn or flour pancakes filled with everything from chopped meat and poultry to beans. In Arizona and New Mexico, a few Native American dishes are served on reservations and at tribal festivals. Steaks and barbecue are always favorites on Southwestern menus, and beer is the drink of choice for dinner and a night out.

For a cosmopolitan foodie scene, visit Las Vegas, where top chefs from New York City, LA and even Paris are sprouting satellite restaurants.

Steak & Potatoes

Have a hankerin' for a juicy hunk of beef with a salad, baked potato and beans? Look no further than the ranch-filled Southwest, home to intimate chophouses, family-friendly steak restaurants and trail-ride cookouts. In Utah, the large Mormon population influences culinary options. Here, good, old-fashioned American food like chicken, steak, potatoes, vegetables, homemade pies and ice cream prevail.

Mexican & New Mexican Food

Mexican food is often hot and spicy. If you're sensitive, test the heat of your salsa before dousing your meal. In Arizona, Mexican food is of the Sonoran type, with specialties such as *carne seca* (dried beef). Meals are usually served with refried beans, rice and flour or corn tortillas; chiles are relatively mild. Tucsonans refer to their city as the 'Mexican food capital of the universe,' which, although hotly contested by a few other places, carries a ring of truth. Colorado restaurants serve Mexican food, but they don't insist on any accolades for it.

New Mexico's food is different from, but reminiscent of, Mexican food. Pinto beans are served whole instead of refried; *posole* (a corn stew) may replace rice. Chiles aren't used so much as a condiment (like salsa) but more as an essential ingredient in almost every dish. *Carne adobada* (marinated pork chunks) is a specialty.

If a menu includes red or green chile dishes and sauces, it probably serves New Mexican–style dishes. The state is famous for its chile-enhanced Mexican standards. The town of Hatch, New Mexico, is particularly known for its green chiles. For both red and green chile on your dish, order it Christmas-style.

Native American Food

Modern Native American cuisine bears little resemblance to that eaten before the Spanish conquest, but it is distinct from Southwestern cuisine. Navajo and Indian tacos – fried bread usually topped with beans, meat, tomatoes, chile and lettuce – are the most readily available. Chewy *horno* bread is baked in the beehive-shaped outdoor adobe ovens *(hornos)* using remnant heat from a fire built inside the oven, then cleared out before cooking.

Most other Native American cooking is game-based and usually involves squash and locally harvested ingredients like berries and piñon nuts. Though becoming better known, it can be difficult to find. Your best bets are festival food stands, powwows, rodeos, Pueblo feast days and casino restaurants.

For LA's most brutally honest foodie opinions, check www.laweekly.com. Read the latest restaurant news at www.la.eater.com.

Some Pacific species have been overfished to near-extinction, disrupting local aquaculture. For best options, good choices, and items to avoid on seafood menus, reference Monterey Bay Aquarium's Seafood Watch (www.seafoodwatch.org).

Favorite Vegetarian Eateries

Green New American Vegetarian, Phoenix, AZ

Lovin' Spoonfuls, Tucson, AZ

Macy's, Flagstaff, AZ

Greens, San Francisco, CA

Drinks

Work-hard, play-hard Americans are far from teetotalers. About 56% of Americans drink alcohol monthly.

Beer

Beer is about as American as Chevrolet, football and apple pie. According to a 2014 Gallup poll, about 41% of Americans who consume alcohol drink beer, while 31% of Americans regularly drink wine. Liquor trails the other two, with only 23% of Americans typically consuming spirits.

Craft & Local Beer

Microbrewery and craft beer production has sky-rocketed in the US over the last 10 years. Craft beer sales now account for 14.3% of the domestic beer market. The term microbrew is used broadly, and tends to include beer produced by large, well-established brands such as Sam Adams and Sierra Nevada. According to the Brewers Association, however, a true craft brewery must produce no more than six million barrels annually. It must also be independently owned and the beer made with traditional ingredients.

In recent years it's become possible to 'drink local' all over the West as microbreweries pop up in urban centers, small towns and unexpected places. They're particularly popular in gateway communities outside national parks, including Moab, Flagstaff and Durango.

Wine

There are more than 8300 wineries in the US, and 2010 marked the first year that the US consumed more wine than France. To the raised eyebrows of European winemakers, who used to regard Californian wines as second class, many American wines are now even (gulp!) winning

In 2008 there were 1521 microbreweries and brewpubs in the US. By 2014 that number had jumped to more than 3200.

California's latest and greatest wines and winemaking trends are covered by the West Coast editor of *Wine Enthusiast*, Steve Heimoff, on his blog: stevehei moff.com.

BEER GOES LOCAL

In outdoorsy communities across the West, the neighborhood microbrewery is the unofficial community center – the place to unwind, swap trail stories, commune with friends and savor seasonal brews. Here are a few of our favorites:

Beaver Street Brewery (www.beaverstreetbrewery.com; 11 S Beaver St; lunch $8-23, dinner $13-23; ⊙11am-11pm Sun-Thu, to midnight Fri & Sat; 🖼) Flagstaff, AZ

O.H.S.O. Eatery and nanoBrewery (www.ohsobrewery.com; 4900 E Indian School Rd) Phoenix, AZ

Great Divide Brewing Company (www.greatdivide.com; 2201 Arapahoe St; ⊙2-8pm Mon & Tue, to 10pm Wed-Sat) Denver, CO

Steamworks Brewing (☑970-259-9200; www.steamworksbrewing.com; 801 E 2nd Ave; ⊙11am-midnight Mon-Thu, 11am-2am Fri-Sun) Durango, CO

Squatters Pub Brewery (www.squatters.com; 147 W Broadway; dishes $10-22; ⊙11am-midnight Sun-Thu, to 1am Fri & Sat) Salt Lake City, UT

Snake River Brewing Co (☑307-739-2337; www.snakeriverbrewing.com; 265 S Millward St; pints $4-5, mains $11-14; ⊙11:30am-midnight) Jackson, WY

North Coast Brewing Company (☑707-964-2739; www.northcoastbrewing.com; 455 N Main St, Fort Bragg; mains $16-25; ⊙restaurant 4pm-10pm Sun-Thu, to 11pm Fri & Sat, bar from 2pm daily) Fort Bragg, CA

Breakside Brewery (☑503-719-6475; www.breakside.com; 820 NE Dekum St; ⊙3-10pm Mon-Thu, noon-11pm Fri & Sat, to 10pm Sun) Portland, OR

Pike Pub & Brewery (☑206-622-6044; www.pikebrewing.com; 1415 1st Ave; ⊙11am-midnight; ℝUniversity St) Seattle, WA

prestigious international awards. In fact, the nation is the world's fourth-largest producer of wine, behind Italy, France and Spain.

Wine isn't cheap in the US, but it's possible to procure a perfectly drinkable bottle of American wine at a liquor or wine shop for around $10 to $12.

Wine Regions

Today almost 90% of US wine comes from California, and Oregon and Washington wines have achieved international status.

Without a doubt, the country's hotbed of wine tourism is in Northern California, just outside of the Bay Area in the Napa and Sonoma Valleys. As other areas – Oregon's Willamette Valley, California's Central Coast and Arizona's Patagonia region – have evolved as wine destinations, they have spawned an entire industry of bed-and-breakfast tourism that goes hand in hand with the quest to find the perfect Pinot Noir.

There are many excellent 'New World' wines that have flourished in the rich American soil. The most popular white varietals made in the US are Chardonnay and Sauvignon Blanc; best-selling reds include Cabernet Sauvignon, Merlot, Pinot Noir and Zinfandel.

Vintage Cocktails

Across the US, it's become decidedly cool to party like it's 1929 by drinking retro cocktails from the days of Prohibition, when alcohol was illegal to consume. While Prohibition isn't likely to be reinstated, you'll find plenty of bars where the spirit of the Roaring Twenties and the illicit 1930s lives on. Inspired by vintage recipes featuring spirits and elixirs, these cocktails, complete with ingredients like small-batch liqueurs, whipped egg whites, hand-chipped ice and fresh fruit, are lovingly concocted by nattily dressed bartenders who regard their profession as something between an art and a craft.

Coffee

America runs on caffeine, and the coffee craze has only intensified in the last 25 years. Blame it on Starbucks. The world's biggest coffee chain was born amid the Northwest's progressive coffee culture in 1971, when Starbucks opened its first location across from Pike Place Market in Seattle. The idea, to offer a variety of roasted beans from around the world in a comfortable cafe, helped start filling the American coffee mug with more refined, complicated (and expensive) drinks compared to the ubiquitous Folgers and diner cups of joe. By the early 1990s, specialty coffee houses were springing up across the country.

Independent coffee shops support a coffee-house culture that encourages lingering; think free wi-fi and comfortable seating. That said, when using free cafe wi-fi, remember: order something every hour, don't leave laptops unattended, and deal with interruptions graciously.

Kim Jordan co-founded Fort Collins–based New Belgium brewery in 1991. Today she is the company's CEO, and New Belgium – maker of Fat Tire beers – is the fourthth-largest craft brewery in the country. The company is regularly named one of the best places to work in the US.

Margaritas, the alcoholic drink of choice in the Southwest, contain tequila, a citrus liquor (Grand Marnier, Triple Sec or Cointreau) and either fresh-squeezed lime or premixed Sweet & Sour. Enjoy them frozen, on the rocks (over ice) or straight up. Most people sip them with salt.

Arts & Architecture

Art created in the American West is often marked by a striking collision of personality, attitude and landscape: the take-it-or-leave-it cow skulls in Georgia O'Keeffe paintings; the prominent shadows in an Ansel Adams' photograph of Half Dome; and the gonzo journalism of Hunter S Thompson in the sun-baked Southwest. Even Nirvana's grunge seems inseparable from its rainy Seattle roots. The landscape is a presence: beautiful yet unforgiving.

Literature

California is the most populous state in a region that has long inspired novelists, poets and storytellers.

Social Realism

Arguably the most influential author to emerge from California was John Steinbeck, who was born in Salinas in 1902. His masterpiece of social realism, *The Grapes of Wrath,* tells of the struggles of migrant farm workers.

Playwright Eugene O'Neill took his 1936 Nobel Prize money and transplanted himself to near San Francisco, where he wrote the autobiographical play *Long Day's Journey into Night.*

Upton Sinclair's *Oil!,* which inspired Paul Thomas Anderson's movie *There Will Be Blood,* was a muckraking work of historical fiction with socialist overtones.

Pulp Noir & Mysteries

In the 1930s, San Francisco and Los Angeles became the capitals of the pulp detective novel. Dashiell Hammett *(The Maltese Falcon)* made San Francisco's fog a sinister character. The king of hard-boiled crime writers was Raymond Chandler, who thinly disguised his hometown of Santa Monica as Bay City.

Since the 1990s, a renaissance of California crime fiction has been masterminded by James Ellroy *(LA Confidential),* Elmore Leonard *(Jackie Brown)* and Walter Mosley *(Devil in a Blue Dress),* whose Easy Rawlins detective novels are set in South Central LA's impoverished neighborhoods.

But not all detectives work in the cities. Tony Hillerman, an enormously popular author from Albuquerque, wrote *Skinwalkers, People of Darkness, Skeleton Man* and *The Sinister Pig.* His award-winning mystery novels take place on the Navajo, Hopi and Zuni Reservations.

Movers & Shakers

After the chaos of WWII, the Beat Generation brought about a provocative new style of writing: short, sharp, spontaneous and alive. Based in San Francisco, the scene revolved around Jack Kerouac *(On the Road),* Allen Ginsberg *(Howl)* and Lawrence Ferlinghetti, the Beats' patron and publisher.

In Northern California, professional hell-raiser Jack London grew up and cut his teeth in Oakland. He turned out a massive volume of influential fiction, including tales of the late-19th-century Klondike Gold Rush.

The National Cowboy Poetry Gathering (www. westernfolklife. org) – the bronco of cowboy poetry events – is held in January in Elko, Nevada. Ropers and wranglers have waxed lyrical here for more than 30 years.

Joan Didion nailed contemporary California culture in *Slouching Towards Bethlehem*, a collection of essays that takes a caustic look at 1960s flower power and the Haight-Ashbury district. Tom Wolfe also put '60s San Francisco in perspective with *The Electric Kool-Aid Acid Test,* which follows Ken Kesey's band of Merry Pranksters.

In the 1970s, Charles Bukowski's semi-autobiographical novel *Post Office* captured down-and-out downtown LA, while Richard Vasquez's *Chicano* took a dramatic look at LA's Latino barrio.

Hunter S Thompson, who committed suicide in early 2005, wrote *Fear and Loathing in Las Vegas,* set in the temple of American excess in the desert; it's the ultimate road-trip novel, in every sense of the word.

Eco-Warriors & Social Commentators

Edward Abbey, noted for his strong environmental and political views, created the thought-provoking and seminal works *Desert Solitaire* and *The Journey Home: Some Words in Defense of the American West*. His classic *Monkey Wrench Gang* is a comic fictional account of real people who plan to blow up Glen Canyon Dam before it floods Glen Canyon.

Wallace Stegner's western-set novel *Angle of Repose* won the Pulitzer Prize in 1972. His book of essays *Where the Bluebird Sings to the Lemonade Springs* discusses the harmful consequences of the mythologizing of the West. Former Tucsonian Barbara Kingsolver published two novels with Southwestern settings, *The Bean Trees* and *Animal Dreams*. She shares her thoughts about day-to-day life in the Southwest in a series of essays in *High Tide in Tucson*.

Music

Much of the American recording industry is based in Los Angeles, and SoCal's film and TV industries have proven powerful talent incubators. Indeed, today's pop princesses and *American Idol* winners are only here thanks to the tuneful revolutions of the decades of innovation that came before, from country folk to urban rap.

Rockin' Out

The first homegrown rock 'n' roll talent to make it big in the 1950s was Richie Valens, whose 'La Bamba' was a rockified version of a Mexican folk song. When Joan Baez and Bob Dylan had their Northern California fling in the early 1960s, Dylan plugged in his guitar and played folk rock. When Janis Joplin and Big Brother & the Holding Company developed their shambling musical stylings in San Francisco, folk rock splintered into psychedelia. Meanwhile, The Doors and The Byrds blew minds on LA's famous Sunset Strip. The epicenter of LA's psychedelic rock scene was the Laurel Canyon neighborhood, just uphill from the Sunset Strip and the legendary Whisky a Go Go nightclub.

Rap & Hip-Hop Rhythms

Since the 1980s, LA has been a hotbed for West Coast rap and hip-hop. Eazy E, Ice Cube and Dr Dre released the seminal NWA (Niggaz With Attitude) album, *Straight Outta Compton,* in 1989. Death Row Records, cofounded by Dr Dre, has launched megawatt rap talents including Long Beach bad boy Snoop Dog and the late Tupac Shakur, who launched his rap career in Marin County and was fatally shot in 1996 in Las Vegas in a suspected East Coast/West Coast rap feud.

Throughout the 1980s and '90s, California maintained a grass-roots hip-hop scene closer to the streets in LA and in the heart of the black-power movement in Oakland. In the late 1990s, the Bay Area birthed underground artists like E-40 and the 'hyphy movement,' a reaction against the increasing commercialization of hip-hop. Also from

Cheryl Strayed's bestselling memoir *Wild* traces her long-distance solo hike on the Pacific Crest Trail after her mother's death. Reese Witherspoon, whose production company bought the movie rights, earned a Best Actress nomination in 2015 for her depiction of Strayed.

For an engaging introduction to a global array of musical instruments, don't miss the Musical Instrument Museum in Phoenix, home to more than 6000 instruments from about 200 countries (www. mim.org).

Oakland, Michael Franti & Spearhead blend hip-hop with funk, reggae, folk, jazz and rock stylings into messages for social justice and peace. Meanwhile, during the late '90s and early 2000s, Korn from Bakersfield and Linkin Park from LA County combined hip-hop with rap and metal to popularize 'nu metal.'

Grunge & Indie Rock

Grunge started in the mid-1980s and was heavily influenced by cult group the Melvins. Distorted guitars, strong riffs, heavy drumming and gritty styles defined the unpolished musical style. Grunge didn't explode until the record label Sub Pop released Nirvana's *Nevermind* in 1991, skyrocketing the 'Seattle Sound' into mainstream music. True purists, however, shunned Nirvana for what they considered selling out to commercialism while overshadowing equally worthy bands like Soundgarden and Alice in Chains. The general popularity of grunge continued through the early 1990s, but the very culture of the genre took part in its downfall. Bands lived hard and fast, never really taking themselves seriously. Many eventually succumbed to internal strife and drug abuse. The final blow was in 1994, when Kurt Cobain – the heart of Nirvana – committed suicide.

A few western cities are especially connected with indie music. Seattle was the original stomping grounds for Modest Mouse, Death Cab for Cutie and The Postal Service. Olympia, WA, has been a hotbed of indie rock and riot grrrls. Portland, OR, has boasted such diverse groups as folktronic hip-hop band Talkdemonic, alt-band The Decemberists and multigenre Pink Martini, not to mention The Shins – originally from Albuquerque, NM – The Dandy Warhols, Blind Pilot and Elliot Smith. Washington-based Sleater-Kinney, with Carrie Brownstein, Corin Tucker and Janet Weiss, hit the road again in 2015 after a nearly 10-year hiatus for their latest album *No Cities to Love*.

Film

From the moment movies – and later TV – became a dominant entertainment medium, California took center stage in the world of popular culture. In 2012, TV and film production and post-production projects generated 107,400 jobs in California, slightly more than half of all such jobs across the United States.

The Industry

The movie-making industry grew out of the humble orchards of Hollywoodland, a residential neighborhood of Los Angeles, where entrepreneurial movie makers, many of whom were European immigrants, established studios in the early 1900s. German-born Carl Laemmle built Universal Studios in 1915, selling lunch to curious guests coming to watch the magic of movie making; Polish immigrant Samuel Goldwyn joined with Cecil B DeMille to form Paramount Studios; and Jack Warner and his brothers, born to Polish parents, arrived a few years later from Canada.

LA's perpetually balmy weather meant that most outdoor scenes could be easily shot there. Fans loved early silent-film stars like Charlie Chaplin and Harold Lloyd, and the first big Hollywood wedding occurred in 1920 when Douglas Fairbanks wed Mary Pickford, becoming Hollywood's first de facto royal couple. The silent-movie era gave way to 'talkies' after 1927's *The Jazz Singer*, a Warner Bros musical starring Al Jolson, premiered in downtown LA, ushering in Hollywood's glamorous Golden Age.

Hollywood & Beyond

From the 1920s, Hollywood became the industry's social and financial hub, but only one major studio, Paramount Pictures, stood in Hollywood proper. Most movies have been shot elsewhere around LA, from Culver

ARTS & ARCHITECTURE FILM

At the Experience Music Project Museum in the Seattle Center, the 'Nirvana: Taking Punk to the Masses' exhibit traces the rise of grunge rockers Nirvana and singer/songwriter Kurt Cobain.

Top Film Festivals

AFI Fest (www.afi. com/afifest)

Outfest (www. outfest.org)

San Francisco International Film Festival (www. sffs.org)

Sundance Film Festival (www. sundance.org/ festival)

Telluride Film Festival (www. telluridefilm festival.com)

Seattle International Film Festival (www.siff.net)

City (at MGM, now Sony Pictures), to Studio City (at Universal Studios) and Burbank (at Warner Bros and later at Disney).

Today's high cost of filming has sent location scouts outside the state. During his two terms as governor of New Mexico (2002–10), Bill Richardson wooed production teams to the state by offering a 25% tax rebate on expenditures. His efforts helped inject more than $3 billion into the economy. Film and TV crews have also moved north to Canada, often shooting in Vancouver, Toronto and Montréal.

In Albuquerque, *Breaking Bad* fans can take a self-guided tour of locations that appeared in the series. Visit www. visitalbuquerque. org/albuquerque/ film-tourism for an interactive map and details about locations.

Western Films

Though many westerns have been shot in SoCal, a few places in Utah and Arizona have doubled as film and TV sets so often that they have come to define the American West. In addition to Utah's Monument Valley, first popularized by director John Ford in *The Stagecoach*, movie-worthy destinations include Moab for *Thelma and Louise* (1991), Dead Horse Point State Park for *Mission Impossible: 2* (2000), Lake Powell for *Planet of the Apes* (1968) and Tombstone for the eponymous *Tombstone* (1993). Scenes in *127 Hours* (2010), the film version of Aron Ralston's harrowing time trapped in Blue John Canyon in Canyonlands National Park, were shot in and around the canyon.

The Small Screen

The first TV station began broadcasting in Los Angeles in 1931. Through the following decades, iconic images of LA were beamed into living rooms across America in shows such as *Dragnet* (1950s), *The Beverly Hillbillies* (1960s), *The Brady Bunch* (1970s), *LA Law* (1980s), *Baywatch*, *Melrose Place* and *The Fresh Prince of Bel-Air* (1990s), through to teen 'dramedies' *Beverly Hills 90210* (1990s) and *The OC* (2000s), the latter set in Newport Beach, Orange County. If you're a fan of reality TV, you'll spot Southern California starring in everything from *Top Chef* to the *Real Housewives of Orange County*.

Southern California has also been a versatile backdrop for edgy cable-TV dramas, from Showtime's *Weeds*, about a pot-growing SoCal widow, to TNT's cop show *The Closer*, about homicide detectives in LA, and FX's *The Shield*, which fictionalized the City of Angels' police corruption.

But SoCal isn't the only TV backdrop. Former *X-Files* writer Vince Gilligan brought more of his off-beat brilliance to the small screen in 2008 with the premiere of *Breaking Bad*, set and shot in sun-baked Albuquerque. Its prequel, *Better Call Saul*, debuted in 2015.

Some exterior shots for David Lynch's quirky *Twin Peaks* were shot in Snoqualmie and North Bend, WA. Because of tax incentives, Vancouver, (British Columbia, Canada) has long been a popular shooting location for television production companies. Many of these shows, from the *X-Files* to *Battlestar Galactica* to *Fringe*, are actually set somewhere else. The *X-Files* reboot returned to Vancouver for shooting in 2015.

Jim Heimann's *California Crazy & Beyond: Roadside Vernacular Architecture* is a romp through the zany, whimsical world of California, where lemonade stands look like giant lemons and motels are shaped like tipis.

Architecture

Westerners have adapted imported styles to the climate and available materials, building cool, adobe-inspired houses in Tucson and fog-resistant redwood-shingle houses in Mendocino.

Spanish Missions & Victorian Queens

The first Spanish missions were built around courtyards, using materials that Native Americans and colonists found on hand: adobe, limestone and grass. Many missions crumbled into disrepair as the church's influence waned, but the style remained practical for the climate. Early California settlers later adapted it into the rancho adobe style, as seen at El Pueblo de Los Angeles and in San Diego's Old Town.

During the mid-19th-century gold rush, California's nouveau riche imported materials to construct grand mansions matching European fashions, and raised the stakes with ornamental excess. Many millionaires favored the gilded Queen Anne style. Outrageous examples of Victorian architecture, including 'Painted Ladies' and 'gingerbread' houses, can be found in such Northern California towns as San Francisco, Ferndale and Eureka.

Many architects rejected frilly Victorian styles in favor of the simple, classical lines of Spanish colonial architecture. Mission revival details are restrained and functional: arched doors and windows, long covered porches, fountains, courtyards, solid walls and red-tiled roofs.

Arts and Crafts & Art Deco

Simplicity was the hallmark of the Arts and Crafts style. Influenced by both Japanese design principles and England's Arts and Crafts movement, its woodwork and handmade touches marked a deliberate departure from the Industrial Revolution. SoCal architects Charles and Henry Greene and Bernard Maybeck in Northern California popularized the versatile one-story bungalow, which became trendy at the turn of the 20th century. Today you'll spot them in Pasadena and Berkeley with their overhanging eaves, terraces and sleeping porches harmonizing indoors and outdoors.

In the 1920s, the international art deco style took elements from the ancient world – Mayan glyphs, Egyptian pillars, Babylonian ziggurats – and flattened them into modern motifs to cap stark facades and outline streamlined skyscrapers, notably in LA and downtown Oakland. Streamline moderne kept decoration to a minimum and mimicked the aerodynamic look of ocean liners and airplanes, as seen at LA's Union Station.

A few years later master architect Frank Lloyd Wright was designing homes in the Romanza style, following the principle that for every indoor space there's an outdoor space, and this flowing design is best exhibited in LA's Hollyhock House, constructed for heiress Alice Barnsdale. His part-time home and studio in Scottsdale, AZ, Taliesin West, complements and showcases the surrounding desert landscape.

Postmodern Evolutions

Architectural styles have veered away from strict high modernism, and unlikely postmodern shapes have been added to the landscape. Richard Meier made his mark on West LA with the Getty Center, a cresting white wave of a building atop a sunburned hilltop. Canadian-born Frank Gehry relocated to Santa Monica. His billowing, sculptural style for LA's Walt Disney Concert Hall winks cheekily at shipshape Californian streamline moderne. Renzo Piano's signature inside-out industrial style can be glimpsed in the sawtooth roof and red-steel veins on the Broad Contemporary Art Museum extension of the Los Angeles County Museum of Art.

San Francisco has lately championed a brand of postmodernism by Pritzker Prize–winning architects that magnifies and mimics California's great outdoors, especially in Golden Gate Park. Swiss architects Herzog & de Meuron clad the MH de Young Memorial Museum in copper, which will eventually oxidize green to match its park setting. Nearby, Renzo Piano literally raised the roof on sustainable design at the LEED platinum-certified California Academy of Sciences, capped by a living garden.

Visual Arts

Although the earliest European artists were trained cartographers accompanying Western explorers, their images of California as an island show more imagination than scientific rigor. This mythologizing tendency continued throughout the gold-rush era, as Western artists alternated between caricatures of Wild West debauchery and manifest-destiny

In 1915 newspaper magnate William Randolph Hearst commissioned California's first licensed female architect Julia Morgan to build his Hearst Castle – a mixed blessing, since the commission would take Morgan decades, and require careful diplomacy through constant changes and a delicate balancing act among Hearst's preferred Spanish, Gothic and Greek styles.

The bestselling novel *Where'd You Go, Bernadette?* by Maria Semple (2012) has fun with Seattle stereotypes while tracing the disappearance of the title character, a feisty but reclusive famous architect.

ART IN NEW MEXICO

Both Taos and Santa Fe have large and active artist communities considered seminal to the development of Southwestern art. Santa Fe, the third-largest art market in the US, is a particularly good stop for those looking to browse and buy art and native crafts. More than 80 of Santa Fe's 200 galleries line the city's Canyon Rd. Native American vendors sell high-quality jewelry and crafts beside the plaza; Friday art walks begin at 5pm. Serious collectors can also take a studio tour or drive the bucolic High Rd, a low-key scenic byway between Santa Fe and Taos that swings by galleries, historic buildings and an art market.

Art in Out-of-the-Way Places

Bisbee, AZ

Jerome, AZ

Aspen, CO

Park City, UT

Bellingham, WA

Photography buffs can plan their California trip around the top-notch SFMOMA in northern California, where the superb collection runs from early Western daguerreotypes to experimental postwar Japanese photography.

propaganda urging pioneers to settle the golden West. The completion of the transcontinental railroad in 1869 brought an influx of romantic painters, who produced epic California wilderness landscapes.

In the early 1900s, homegrown colonies of California impressionist plein-air painters emerged, particularly at Laguna Beach and Carmel-by-the-Sea. In the Southwest, Georgia O'Keeffe (1887–1986) painted stark Southwestern landscapes that are exhibited in museums throughout the world.

Photographer Pirkle Jones saw expressive potential in California landscape photography after WWII, while San Francisco native Ansel Adams' sublime photographs had already started doing justice to Yosemite. Adams founded Group f/64 with Edward Weston from Carmel and Imogen Cunningham in San Francisco. Berkeley-based Dorothea Lange turned her unflinching lens on the plight of Californian migrant workers in the Great Depression and Japanese Americans forced to enter internment camps in WWII.

Glass blowing is a specialty of the Puget Sound area, led by artisans from the Pilchuk School. Washington-born artist Dale Chihuly, acclaimed for his blown-glass creations, can be found in more than 200 galleries worldwide. The Chihuly Garden and Glass Exhibition, a long-term exhibition which opened in 2012 beside the Space Needle, is drawing appreciative crowds.

As the postwar American West became crisscrossed with freeways and divided into planned communities, Californian painters captured the abstract forms of manufactured landscapes. In San Francisco, Richard Diebenkorn and David Park became leading proponents of Bay Area Figurative Art, while San Francisco sculptor Richard Serra captured urban aesthetics in massive, rusting monoliths resembling ship prows and industrial Stonehenges. Pop artists captured the ethos of conspicuous consumerism through Wayne Thiebaud's gumball machines, British émigré David Hockney's LA pools and, above all, Ed Ruscha's studies of SoCal pop culture. In San Francisco, artists showed their love for rough-and-ready-made '50s Beat collage, '60s psychedelic Fillmore posters, earthy '70s funk and beautiful-mess punk, and '80s graffiti and skate culture.

Today's contemporary-art scene brings all these influences together with muralist-led social commentary, an obsessive dedication to craft and a new-media milieu that embraces cutting-edge technology. LA's Museum of Contemporary Art puts on provocative and avant-garde shows, as does LACMA's Broad Contemporary Art Museum and the Museum of Contemporary Art San Diego, which specializes in post-1950s pop and conceptual art. To see California-made art at its most experimental, browse the SoCal gallery scenes in downtown LA and Culver City, then check out independent NorCal art spaces in San Francisco's Mission District and the laboratory-like galleries of SOMA's Yerba Buena Arts District.

The Land & Wildlife

Crashing tectonic plates, mighty floods, spewing volcanoes and frigid ice fields: for millions and millions of years, the American West was an altogether unpleasant place. But from this fire and ice sprang a kaleidoscopic array of stunning landscapes bound by a common modern trait: an undeniable ability to attract explorers, naturalists, artists and outdoor adventurers.

The Land

As Western novelist and essayist Wallace Stegner noted in his book *Where the Bluebird Sings to the Lemonade Springs,* the West is home to a dozen or so distinct and unique subregions. Their one commonality? In Stegner's view it's the aridity. Aridity, he writes, sharpens the brilliance of the light and heightens the clarity of the air in most of the West. It also leads to fights over water rights, a historic and ongoing concern.

Read Marc Reisner's *Cadillac Desert: The American West and Its Disappearing Water* for a thorough account of how exploding populations in the West have utilized every drop of available water.

California

The third-largest state after Alaska and Texas, California covers more than 155,000 sq miles.

Geology & Earthquakes

California is a complex geologic landscape formed from fragments of rock and earth crust scraped together as the North American continent drifted westward over hundreds of millions of years. Crumpled coast ranges, the downward-bowing Central Valley and the still-rising Sierra Nevada are evidence of gigantic forces exerted as the continental and ocean plates crush together.

About 25 million years ago the ocean plates stopped colliding and instead started sliding against each other, creating the massive San Andreas Fault. Because this contact zone doesn't slide smoothly, but catches and slips irregularly, it rattles California with an ongoing succession of tremors and earthquakes.

The state's most famous earthquake in 1906 measured 7.8 on the Richter scale and demolished San Francisco, leaving more than 3000 people dead. The Bay Area made headlines again in 1989 when the Loma Prieta earthquake (7.1) caused a section of the Bay Bridge to collapse. Los Angeles' last 'big one' was in 1994, when the Northridge quake (6.7) caused parts of the Santa Monica Fwy to fall down. With $44 billion in damages, it is the most costly quake in US history – so far.

Many of the Southwest's common flowers can be found in *Canyon Country Wildflowers* by Damian Fagan.

The Coast to the Central Valley

Much of California's coast is fronted by rugged coastal mountains that capture winter's water-laden storms. San Francisco divides the Coast Ranges roughly in half, with the foggy North Coast remaining sparsely populated, while the Central and Southern California coasts have a balmier climate and many more people.

In the northernmost reaches of the Coast Ranges, nutrient-rich soils and abundant moisture foster forests of giant trees. On their eastern flanks, the Coast Ranges subside into gently rolling hills that give way to the 450-mile-long Central Valley, an agricultural powerhouse producing more than 230 different types of crops, from nuts to fruits and vegetables. The region produces one third of all produce grown in the United States.

Mountain Highs

On the eastern side of the Central Valley looms the world-famous Sierra Nevada. At 400 miles long and 50 miles wide, it's one of the largest mountain ranges in the world and is home to 13 peaks over 14,000ft. The vast wilderness of the High Sierra (lying mostly above 9000ft) presents an astounding landscape of glaciers, sculpted granite peaks and remote canyons. The soaring Sierra Nevada captures storm systems and drains

PLANTS OF THE WEST

The presence of many large mountain ranges in the West creates a remarkable diversity of niches for plants. One way to understand the plants of this region is to understand life zones and the ways each plant thrives in its favored zone.

In the Southwest, at the lowest elevations (generally below 4000ft) high temperatures and a lack of water create a desert zone where drought-tolerant plants such as cacti, sagebrush and agave survive. Many of these species have small leaves or minimal leaf surface area to reduce water loss, or hold water like a cactus to survive long hot spells.

At mid-elevations, from 4000ft to 7000ft, conditions cool a bit and more moisture is available for woody shrubs and small trees. In much of Nevada, Utah, northern Arizona and New Mexico, piñon pines and junipers blanket vast areas of low mountain slopes and hills. Both trees are short and stout to help conserve water.

Nearly pure stands of stately, fragrant ponderosa pine are the dominant tree at 7000ft on many of the West's mountain ranges. In fact, this single tree best defines the Western landscape and many animals rely on it for food and shelter; timber companies also consider it their most profitable tree. High mountain, or boreal, forests composed of spruce, fir, quaking aspen and a few other conifers are found on the highest peaks in the Southwest. This is a land of cool, moist forests and lush meadows with brilliant wildflower displays.

Incredibly diverse flowers appear each year in the deserts and mountains of the Southwest. These include desert flowers that start blooming in February, and late-summer flowers that fill mountain meadows after the snow melts or pop out after summer thunderstorms wet the soil. Some of the largest and grandest flowers belong to the Southwest's 100 or so species of cacti.

Southern California's desert areas begin their peak blooming in March, with other lowland areas of the state producing abundant wildflowers in April. As snows melt later at higher elevations in the Sierra Nevada, Yosemite National Park's Tuolumne Meadows is another prime spot for wildflower walks and photography, with peak blooms usually in late June or early July.

In the Pacific Northwest, the wet and wild west side of the Cascade Range captures most rain clouds coming in from the ocean, relieving them of their moisture and creating humid forests full of green life jostling for space. The dry, deserty east side – robbed of rains by the tall Cascades – is mostly home to sagebrush and other semi-arid-loving vegetation, although there are lush pockets here and there, especially along the mountain foothills.

When it comes to trees, California is a land of superlatives: the tallest (coast redwoods approaching 380ft), the largest (giant sequoias of the Sierra Nevada over 36ft across at the base) and the oldest (bristlecone pines of the White Mountains that are almost 5000 years old). The giant sequoia, which is unique to California, survives in isolated groves scattered on the Sierra Nevada's western slopes, including in Yosemite, Sequoia and Kings Canyon National Parks.

them of their water, with most of the precipitation over 3000ft falling as snow. These waters eventually flow into half a dozen major river systems that provide the vast majority of water for San Francisco and LA as well as farms in the Central Valley.

The Deserts & Beyond

With the west slope of the Sierra Nevada capturing the lion's share of water, all lands east of the Sierra crest are dry and desertlike, receiving less than 10 inches of rain a year. Surprisingly, some valleys at the eastern foot of the Sierra Nevada are well watered by creeks and support a vigorous economy of livestock and agriculture.

Areas in the northern half of California, especially on the elevated Modoc Plateau of northeastern California, are a cold desert at the western edge of the Great Basin, blanketed with hardy sagebrush shrubs and pockets of juniper trees. Temperatures increase as you head south, with a prominent transition as you descend from Mono Lake into the Owens Valley east of the Sierra Nevada. This southern hot desert (part of the Mojave Desert) includes Death Valley, one of the hottest places on earth.

The Southwest

Extremely ancient rocks (among the oldest on the planet) exposed in the deep heart of the Grand Canyon show that the region was underwater two billion years ago. Younger layers of rocks in southern Utah reveal that this region was continuously or periodically underwater. About 286 million years ago, near the end of the Paleozoic era, a collision of continents into a massive landmass known as Pangaea deformed the earth's crust and produced pressures that uplifted the ancestral Rocky Mountains. Though this early mountain range lay to the east, it formed rivers and sediment deposits that began to shape the Southwest.

The sequence of oceans and sand ended around 60 million years ago as North America underwent a dramatic separation from Europe, sliding westward over a piece of the earth's crust known as the East Pacific Plate and leaving behind an ever-widening gulf that became the Atlantic Ocean. The East Pacific Plate collided with the North American Plate. This collision, named the Laramide Orogeny, resulted in the birth of the modern Rocky Mountains and uplifted an old basin into a highland known today as the Colorado Plateau. Fragments of the East Pacific Plate also attached themselves to the leading edge of the North American Plate, transforming the Southwest from a coastal area to an interior region increasingly detached from the ocean.

In contrast to the compression and collision that characterized earlier events, the earth's crust began stretching in an east–west direction about 30 million years ago. The thinner, stretched crust of New Mexico and Texas cracked along zones of weakness called faults, resulting in a rift valley where New Mexico's Rio Grande now flows. These same forces created the stepped plateaus of northern Arizona and southern Utah.

During the Pleistocene glacial period, large bodies of water accumulated throughout the Southwest. Utah's Great Salt Lake is the most famous remnant of these mighty ice-age lakes. Basins with now completely dry, salt-crusted lakebeds are especially conspicuous on a drive across Nevada.

For the past several million years the dominant force has probably been erosion. Not only do torrential rainstorms readily tear through soft sedimentary rocks, but the rise of the Rocky Mountains also generates large, powerful rivers that wind throughout the Southwest, carving mighty canyons in their wake. Nearly all of the contemporary features in the Southwest, from arches (Arches National Park has more than 2000 sandstone arches) to hoodoos, are the result of weathering and erosion.

According to recent studies by the US Geological Survey, the southern San Andreas Fault in California has a 19% chance of a 6.7 or larger earthquake in the next 30 years.

A fully hydrated giant saguaro can store more than a ton of water. Saguaros grow slowly, taking 50 years to reach 7ft. Not only is it illegal to shoot them in Arizona, it is also dangerous. In 1982 a vandal shot off the arm off of a 27ft tall saguaro. The arm fell on the shooter and crushed him to death.

Geographic Makeup of the Land

The Colorado Plateau is an impressive and nearly impenetrable 130,000-sq-mile tableland lurking in the corner where Colorado, Utah, Arizona and New Mexico join. Formed in an ancient basin as a remarkably coherent body of neatly layered sedimentary rocks, the plateau has remained relatively unchanged even as the lands around it were compressed, stretched and deformed by powerful forces.

Perhaps the most powerful testament to the plateau's long-term stability is the precise layers of sedimentary rock stretching back two billion years. In fact, the science of stratigraphy – the reading of earth history through its rock layers – stemmed from work at the Grand Canyon, where an astonishing set of layers have been laid bare by the Colorado River cutting across them. Throughout the Southwest, and on the Colorado Plateau in particular, layers of sedimentary rock detail a rich history of ancient oceans, coastal mudflats and arid dunes.

California claims both the highest point in the contiguous US (Mt Whitney; 14,505ft) and the lowest elevation in North America (Badwater, Death Valley; 282ft below sea level) – plus they're only 90 miles apart, as the condor flies.

Landscape Features

The Southwest is jam-packed with remarkable rock formations. One reason for this is that the region's many sedimentary layers are so soft that rain and erosion readily carve them into fantastic shapes. But not any old rain; it has to be hard, fairly sporadic rain, as frequent rain would wash the formations away. Between rains there have to be long arid spells that keep the eroding landmarks intact. The range of colors derives from the unique mineral composition of each rock type.

Geology of the Grand Canyon

Arizona's Grand Canyon is the best-known geologic feature in the Southwest and for good reason: not only is it on a scale so massive it dwarfs the human imagination, but it also records two billion years of geologic history – a huge amount of time considering the earth is just 4.6 billion years old. The canyon itself, however, is young, a mere five to six million years old. Carved by the powerful Colorado River as the land bulged upward, the 277-mile-long canyon reflects the differing hardness of the 10-plus layers of rocks in its walls. Shales, for instance, crumble easily and form slopes, while resistant limestones and sandstones form distinctive cliffs.

The layers making up the bulk of the canyon walls were laid during the Paleozoic era, 542 to 251 million years ago. These formations perch atop a group of one- to two-billion-year-old rocks lying at the bottom of the inner gorge of the canyon. Between these two distinct sets of rock is the Great Unconformity, a several-hundred-million-year gap in the geologic record where erosion erased 12,000ft of rock and left a huge mystery.

Pages of Stone: Geology of the Grand Canyon & Plateau Country National Parks & Monuments by Halka and Lucy Chronic provides an excellent introduction to the Southwest's diverse landscape.

UNIQUE LANDSCAPE FEATURES IN THE SOUTHWEST

Badlands Crumbling, mineral-filled soft rock; found in the Painted Desert at Petrified Forest National Park, at Capitol Reef National Park or in the Bisti Badlands.

Hoodoos Sculptured spires of rock weathered into towering pillars; showcased at Bryce Canyon National Park and Arches National Park.

Natural bridges Formed when streams cut through sandstone layers; three bridges can be seen at Natural Bridges National Monument.

Goosenecks Early-stage natural bridges formed when a stream U-turns across a landscape; visible from Goosenecks Overlook at Capitol Reef National Park.

Mesas Hulking formations of layered sandstone where the surrounding landscape has been stripped away; classic examples can be found at Monument Valley and elsewhere on the Arizona–Utah border.

Pacific Northwest

From 16 to 13 million years ago, eastern Oregon and Washington witnessed one of the premier episodes of volcanic activity in Earth's history. Due to shifting stresses in the earth's crust, much of interior western North America began cracking along thousands of lines and releasing enormous amounts of lava that flooded over the landscape. On multiple occasions, so much lava was produced that it filled the Columbia River channel and reached the Oregon coast, forming prominent headlands like Cape Lookout. Today, the hardened lava flows of eastern Oregon and Washington are easily seen in spectacular rimrock cliffs and flattop mesas.

Not to be outdone, the ice ages of the past two million years created a massive ice field from Washington to British Columbia, Canada – and virtually every mountain range in the rest of the region was blanketed by glaciers.

Wildlife

Although the staggering numbers of animals that greeted the first European settlers are now a thing of the past, it is still possible to see wildlife thriving in the West in the right places and at the right times of year.

Reptiles & Amphibians

On a spring evening, canyons in the Southwest may fairly reverberate with the calls of canyon tree frogs or red-spotted toads. With the rising sun, these are replaced by several dozen species of lizards and snakes that roam among rocks and shrubs. Blue-bellied fence lizards are particularly abundant in the region's parks, but visitors can always hope to encounter a rarity such as the strange and venomous Gila monster. Equally fascinating are the Southwest's many colorful rattlesnakes. Quick to anger and able to deliver a painful or toxic bite, rattlesnakes are placid and retiring if left alone.

Birds

Migrations

There are so many interesting birds in the Southwest – home to 400 species – that it's the foremost reason many people travel to the region. Springtime is a particularly rewarding time for bird-watching here as songbirds arrive from their southern wintering grounds and begin singing from every nook and cranny. In the fall, sandhill cranes and snow geese travel in long skeins down the Rio Grande Valley to winter at the Bosque del Apache National Wildlife Refuge. The Great Salt Lake in Utah is one of North America's premier sites for migrating birds, including millions of ducks and grebes stopping each fall to feed before continuing south.

California lies on major migratory routes for more than 350 species of birds, which either pass through the state or linger through the winter. This is one of the top birding destinations in North America. Witness, for example, the congregation of one million ducks, geese and swans at the Klamath Basin National Wildlife Refuge Complex every November. During winter, these waterbirds head south into the refuges of the Central Valley, another area to observe huge numbers of native and migratory species.

THE LAND & WILDLIFE WILDLIFE

On the evening of July 5, 2011, a mile-high dust storm with an estimated 100-mile width enveloped Phoenix after reaching speeds of more than 50mph. Visibility dropped to between zero and one-quarter of a mile. There were power outages and Phoenix International Airport temporarily closed.

An estimated nine million free-tailed bats once roosted in Carlsbad Caverns. Though reduced in recent years, the evening flight is still one of the premier wildlife spectacles in North America.

California Condors & Bald Eagles

With a 9ft wingspan, the California condor looks more like a prehistoric pterodactyl than any bird you've ever seen. Pushed to the brink of extinction, these unusual birds – which fed on the carcasses of mastodons and saber-toothed cats in prehistoric days – are staging a minor comeback at the Grand Canyon. After several decades in which no condors lived in the wild, a few pairs are now nesting on the canyon rim. The best bet for spotting them is Arizona's Vermilion Cliffs. In California, look skyward as you drive along the Big Sur coast or at Pinnacles National Monument.

The Pacific Northwest is a stronghold for bald eagles, which feast on the annual salmon runs and nest in old-growth forests. With a 7.5ft wingspan, these impressive birds gather in huge numbers in places like Washington's Upper Skagit Bald Eagle Area and the national wildlife refuges in the Klamath Basin region in northern California and southern Oregon. In California, bald eagles have regained a foothold on the Channel Islands, and they sometimes spend winter at Big Bear Lake near LA. At their low point, only two or three breeding pairs nested in Colorado, but that number has increased by eight or nine each year, and in 2014 there were about 115 breeding pairs there. Anywhere from 400 to 1000 bald eagles spend winter in the state.

In 1990, the northern spotted owl was declared a threatened species, barring timber industries from clear-cutting certain old-growth forests. The controversy sparked debate all across the Pacific Northwest, pitting loggers against environmentalists.

Mammals

Many of the West's most charismatic wildlife species – grizzlies, buffalo and prairie dogs – were largely exterminated by the early 1900s. Fortunately, there are plenty of other mammals still wandering the forests and deserts. At the very least, if you keep your eyes open, you'll see some mule deer or a coyote.

Bears

The black bear is probably the most notorious animal in the Rockies. Adult males weigh from 275lb to 450lb; females weigh about 175lb to 250lb. They measure 3ft high on all fours and can be over 5ft when standing on their hind legs.

Black bears also roam the Pacific Northwest, the Southwest and California. They feed on berries, nuts, roots, grasses, insects, eggs, small mammals and fish, but can become a nuisance around campgrounds and mountain cabins where food is not stored properly.

California's mountain forests are home to an estimated 30,000 to 40,000 black bears, whose fur actually ranges in color from black to dark brown, cinnamon and even blond.

The grizzly bear, which can be seen on California's state flag, once roamed California's beaches and grasslands in large numbers, eating everything from whale carcasses to acorns. Grizzlies were particularly abundant in the Central Valley. The grizzly was extirpated in the early 1900s after relentless persecution. Grizzlies are classified as an endangered species in Colorado, but they are almost certainly gone from the state; the last documented grizzly in Colorado was killed in 1979. In 2014, scientists estimated there were more than 700 grizzlies wandering the Yellowstone National Park area. A recent study suggests that the introduction of wolves to Yellowstone may be helping the grizzly population there – wolves eat elk, leaving more berries for the grizzlies.

Elk

More than 3000 elk roam across Rocky Mountain National Park, with a resident winter herd of 600 to 800. Mature elk bulls may reach 1100lb, and cows weigh up to 600lb. Both have dark necks with light tan bodies. Like bighorn sheep, elk were virtually extinct around Estes Park by 1890, wiped out by hunters. In 1913 and 1914, before the establishment of the park, people from Estes Park brought in 49 elk from Yellowstone. The population increase since the establishment of Rocky Mountain National Park is one of the National Park Service's great successes.

Among the Pacific Northwest's signature animals is the Roosevelt elk, whose eerie bugling courtship calls can be heard each September and October in forested areas throughout the region. Full-grown males may reach 1100lb and carry 5ft racks of antlers. During winter, large groups gather in lowland valleys and can be observed along the Spirit Lake Memorial Highway in Mt St Helens National Volcanic Monument. Olympic National Park is home to the largest unmanaged herd of Roosevelt elk in the Pacific Northwest.

THE LAND & WILDLIFE ENVIRONMENTAL ISSUES

Bighorn Sheep

Rocky Mountain National Park is a special place: 'Bighorn Crossing Zone' is a sign you're unlikely to encounter anywhere else. From late spring through summer, groups of up to 60 sheep – typically only ewes and lambs – move from the moraine ridge north of the highway across the road to Sheep Lakes in Horseshoe Park. Unlike the big under-curving horns on mature rams, ewes grow swept-back crescent-shaped horns that reach only about 10in in length. The Sheep Lakes are evaporative ponds ringed with tasty salt deposits that attract the ewes in the morning and early afternoon after lambing in May and June. In August they rejoin the rams in the Mummy Range.

Salmon-conservation efforts include protecting populations around the entire Pacific Rim from the Russian Far East to northern California. Learn more at www.wildsalmoncenter.org.

Pronghorn Antelope

The open plains of eastern Oregon and Washington are the playing grounds of pronghorn antelope, curious-looking deer-like animals with two single black horns instead of antlers. Pronghorns belong to a unique antelope family and are only found in the American West, but they are more famous for being able to run up to 60mph for long stretches – they're the second-fastest land animal in the world.

Environmental Issues

Growth in the West has come with costs. In the Pacific Northwest, the production of cheap hydroelectricity and massive irrigation projects along the Columbia have led to the near-irreversible destruction of the river's ecosystem. Dams have all but eliminated most runs of native salmon and have further disrupted the lives of remaining Native Americans who depend on the river. Logging of old-growth forests has left ugly scars. Washington's Puget Sound area and Portland's extensive suburbs are groaning under the weight of rapidly growing population.

Ongoing controversies in the Southwest include arguments about the locations of nuclear power plants and the transport and disposal of nuclear waste, notably at Yucca Mountain, 90 miles from Las Vegas.

Water distribution and availability continue to be concerns throughout the region. In an arid landscape like the Southwest, many of the region's most important environmental issues revolve around water. Drought has so severely impacted the region that researchers have warned that 110-mile-long Lake Mead has a 50% chance of running dry by 2021, leaving an estimated 12 to 36 million people in cities from Las Vegas to Los Angeles and San Diego in need of alternative water sources.

Construction of dams and human-made water features throughout the Southwest has radically altered the delicate balance of water that sustained life for countless millennia. Dams, for example, halt the flow of warm waters and force them to drop their rich loads of life-giving nutrients. These sediments once rebuilt floodplains, nourished myriad aquatic and riparian food chains, and sustained the life of ancient endemic fish that now flounder on the edge of extinction. In place of rich annual

Visit www.publiclands.org for a one-stop summary of recreational opportunities on government-owned land in the Southwest, regardless of managing agency. The site provides links to relevant books and maps for purchase and includes updates about current fire restrictions and closures.

floods, dams now release cold waters in steady flows that favor the introduced fish and weedy plants that have overtaken the West's rivers.

In July 2014, there were more than 20 large wildfires burning across California, Idaho, Oregon and Washington. By mid-September, fire crews had responded to 4974 wildfires, of varying intensity, in California alone. Evidence indicates that Western fires are occurring more frequently and are more intense than in the past. The reasons? Scientists are looking at three factors. The first is global warming, which may be contributing to the extended Western drought. Drought conditions are exacerbated by low snow packs. Dry vegetation spurs fast-moving fires. A second factor may be increased development, leading more people – and potential fire-starters – to the forest. Finally, the long-running forestry practice of fire suppression may have allowed the build-up of more underbrush, which later ignites and fuels the fire.

Edward Abbey shares his desert philosophy and insights in his classic *Desert Solitaire: A Season in the Wilderness*, a must-read for desert enthusiasts and conservationists.

Survival Guide

Directory A–Z

Accommodations

Rates

➤ Generally, midweek rates are lower except in hotels geared toward weekday business travelers. These hotels lure leisure travelers with weekend deals.

➤ Rates quoted are for high season: June to August everywhere except the deserts and mountain ski areas, where December through April are the busiest months.

➤ Demand and prices spike even higher around major holidays and for festivals, when some properties may impose multiday minimum stays.

Discounts

➤ Discount cards and auto-club membership may get you 10% or more off standard rates at participating hotels and motels.

➤ Look for freebie ad magazines packed with hotel and motel discount coupons at gas stations, travel centers, highway rest areas and tourist offices.

➤ Bargaining may be possible for walk-in guests without reservations, especially during off-peak times.

B&Bs

➤ In the USA, many B&Bs are high-end romantic retreats in restored historic homes that are run by personable, independent innkeepers who serve gourmet breakfasts. These B&Bs often take pains to evoke a theme – Victorian, rustic or Cape Cod – and amenities range from merely comfortable to indulgent. Rates normally top $100, and the best run $200 to $300. Some B&Bs have minimum-stay requirements, some exclude young children and many exclude pets.

➤ European-style B&Bs also exist: these may be rooms in someone's home, with plainer furnishings, simpler breakfasts, shared baths and cheaper rates. These often welcome families.

➤ B&Bs can close out of season and reservations are essential, especially for top-end places. To avoid surprises, always ask about bathrooms (whether shared or private).

B&B agencies are sprinkled throughout this guide. Also check listings online:

Bed & Breakfast Inns Online (www.bbonline.com)

BedandBreakfast.com

BnB Finder (www.bnbfinder.com)

Camping

FEDERAL & STATE PARKS

Most federally managed public lands and many state parks offer camping.

➤ First-come, first-served 'primitive' campsites offer no facilities; overnight fees range from free to under $10.

➤ 'Basic' sites usually provide toilets (flush or pit), drinking water, fire pits and picnic tables; they cost $5 to $15 a night, and some or all may be reserved in advance.

➤ 'Developed' campsites, usually in national or state parks, have nicer facilities and more amenities: showers, barbecue grills, RV sites with hookups etc. These run about $12 to $45 a night, and many can be reserved in advance.

Camping on most federal lands – including national parks, national forests, Bureau of Land Management (BLM) and and so on – can be reserved through **Recreation.gov** (☏877-444-6777, international 518-885-3639; www.recreation.gov). Camping is usually limited to 14 days and can be reserved up to six months in advance. For some state-park campgrounds, you can make bookings through **ReserveAmerica** (✆877-444-6777; www.reserveamerica. com). Both websites let you search for campground locations and amenities, check availability and reserve a site, view maps and get driving directions online.

PRIVATE CAMPGROUNDS

➜ Private campgrounds tend to cater to RVs and families (tent sites may be few and lack atmosphere).

➜ Facilities may include playgrounds, convenience stores, wi-fi access, swimming pools and other activities.

➜ Some rent camping cabins, ranging from canvas-sided wooden platforms to log-frame structures with real beds, heating and private baths.

➜ **Kampgrounds of America** (www.koa.com) is a national network of private campgrounds with a full range of facilities. You can order KOA's free annual directory (shipping fees apply) or browse its comprehensive campground listings and make bookings online.

Dude Ranches

➜ Most visitors to dude ranches today are city-slickers looking for an escape from a fast-paced, high-tech world. These days you can find anything from a working-ranch experience (smelly chores and 5am wake-up calls included) to lavish resorts.

➜ Typical week-long visits start at over $100 per person per day, including accommodations, meals, activities and equipment.

➜ While the centerpiece of dude-ranch vacations is horseback riding, many

> **WHAT'S THE BLM?**
>
> The **Bureau of Land Management** (www.blm.gov) is a Department of Energy agency that oversees more than 245 million surface acres of public land, much of it in the West. It manages its resources for a variety of uses, from energy production to cattle grazing to overseeing recreational opportunities.
>
> What does that mean for you? Outdoor fun, as well as both developed camping and dispersed camping. Generally, when it comes to dispersed camping on BLM land, you can camp wherever you want as long as your campsite is several hundred feet from a water source used by wildlife or livestock (distance varies by region, from 300ft to 900ft). You cannot camp in one spot longer than 14 days. Pack out what you pack in and don't leave campfires unattended. Some regions may have more specific rules, so check the state's camping requirements on the BLM website and call the appropriate district office for specifics.

ranches feature swimming pools and have expanded their activity lists to include fly-fishing, hiking, mountain biking, tennis, golf, skeet-shooting and cross-country skiing.

➜ Accommodations range from rustic log cabins to cushy suites with Jacuzzis and cable TV. Meals range from family-style spaghetti dinners to four-course gourmet feasts.

Arizona Dude Ranch Association (www.azdra.com)

Colorado Dude & Guest Ranch Association (✆866-942-3472; www.coloradoranch. com)

Dude Ranchers' Association (✆307-587-2339, 866-399-2339; www.duderanch.org)

Hostels

➜ In the West, hostels are mainly found in urban areas in the Pacific Northwest, California and the Southwest.

➜ **Hostelling International USA** (✆240-650-2100; www. hiusa.org) runs more than 50 hostels in the US; 18 of them are in California. Most have gender-segregated dorms, a few private rooms, shared baths and

a communal kitchen. Overnight fees for dorm beds range from about $29 to $55. HI-USA members are entitled to small discounts. Reservations are accepted (you can book online) and advised during high season, when there may be a three-night maximum stay.

The USA has many independent hostels not affiliated with HI-USA, particularly in the Southwest. For online listings:

➜ Hostels.com

➜ Hostelworld.com

➜ Hostelz.com

Hotels

➜ Hotels in all categories typically include in-room phones, cable TV, alarm clocks, private baths and a simple continental breakfast.

➜ Many midrange properties provide microwaves, mini-fridges, hairdryers, internet access, air-conditioning and/or heating, swimming pools and writing desks.

➜ Top-end hotels add concierge services, fitness and business centers, spas, restaurants, bars and higher-end furnishings.

➜ Even if hotels advertise that children 'sleep free,' cots

SLEEPING PRICE RANGES

The following price ranges do not include taxes, which average more than 10%, unless otherwise noted.

$ less than $100

$$ $100–$250

$$$ more than $250

or rollaway beds may cost extra.

➲ Always ask about the hotel's policy for telephone calls; all charge an exorbitant amount for long-distance and international calls, but some also charge for dialing local and toll-free numbers.

Lodges

Normally situated within national parks, lodges are often rustic looking but are usually quite comfy inside. Standard rooms start around $100, but can easily be double that in high season. Since they represent the only option if you want to stay inside the park without camping, many are fully booked well in advance. Want a room today? Call anyway – you might be lucky and hit on a cancellation. In addition to on-site restaurants, they often offer touring services.

Motels

➲ Motels – distinguishable from hotels by having rooms that open onto a parking lot – tend to cluster around interstate exits and along main routes into town.

➲ Some remain smaller, less-expensive 'mom and pop' operations. A light continental breakfast is sometimes included and amenities might top out at a phone and a TV (maybe with cable). However, motels often have a few rooms with simple kitchenettes.

➲ Although many motels are of the bland, cookie-cutter variety, these can be good for discount lodging or when other options fall through.

➲ For deals, pick up free coupon books at visitor centers, rest areas and travel centers.

➲ At an independent motel, if the lot isn't full and you're not afraid to move on, try negotiating your rate at the counter.

➲ Don't judge a motel solely on looks. Facades may be faded and tired, but the proprietor may keep rooms spotlessly clean. Of course, the reverse could also be true. Try to see your room before you commit.

Resorts

Luxury resorts really require a stay of several days to be appreciated and are often destinations in themselves. Start the day with a round of golf or a tennis match, then luxuriate with a massage, swimming, sunbathing and drinking. Many are now kid friendly, with extensive children's programs.

Customs Regulations

For a complete and current list of US customs regulations, visit the official portal for US Customs and Border Protection (www.cbp.gov).

Duty-free allowance per person is typically as follows:

➲ 1L of liquor (provided you are at least 21 years old).

➲ 100 cigars and 200 cigarettes (if you are at least 18).

➲ $200 worth of gifts and purchases ($800 if a returning US citizen).

➲ If you arrive with $10,000 or more in US or foreign currency, it must be declared.

There are heavy penalties for attempting to import illegal drugs. Other forbidden items include drug paraphernalia, firearms, lottery tickets, items with fake brand names, and most goods made in Cuba, Iran, Myanmar (Burma), North Korea and parts of Sudan. Any fruit, vegetables or other food or plant material must be declared (whereby you'll undergo a time-consuming search) or left in the bins in the arrival area.

Discount Cards

America the Beautiful Interagency Annual Pass

(www.nps.gov/findapark/passes. htm; store.usgs.gov/pass) This $80 pass admits the driver and all passengers in a single, non-commercial vehicle, or four adults aged 16 or older to all national parks and federal recreational lands (eg USFS, BLM) for one year. Children aged 15 and younger are free. The pass can be purchased online or at any national park entrance station. US citizens and permanent residents 62 years and older are eligible for a lifetime Senior Pass ($10), which grants free entry and 50% off some recreational-use fees like camping, as does the lifetime Access Pass (free to US citizens or permanent residents with a permanent disability). These passes are available in person or by mail. A free annual US Military Pass for current members of the US armed forces and their dependents is available at recreation sites with Common Access card or Military ID (Form 1173).

American Association of Retired Persons (AARP;

☎800-566-0242; www.aarp. org; annual membership $16) Advocacy group for Americans 50 years and older offers member discounts on hotels (usually 10%), car rentals and more. People over the age of 65 (sometimes 55, 60 or 62) often qualify for the same discounts as students; any

ID showing your birth date should suffice as proof of age.

American Automobile Association (AAA; ☑877-428-2277, emergency roadside assistance ☑800-222-4357; www.aaa.com; annual membership from $52) Members of AAA and its foreign affiliates (eg CAA, AA) qualify for small discounts on Amtrak trains, car rentals, motels and hotels (usually 5–15%), chain restaurants, shopping, tours and theme parks.

International Student Identity Card (www.isic.org; $25) Offers savings on airline fares, travel insurance and local attractions for full-time students. For nonstudents under 31 years of age, an International Youth Travel Card ($25) grants similar benefits. Cards are issued by student unions, hostelling organizations and travel agencies.

Student Advantage Card (www.studentadvantage.com) For international and US students, this card offers 10% savings on Amtrak and 20% on Greyhound, plus discounts at some chain shops and car rentals.

Electricity

120V/60Hz

Embassies & Consulates

International travelers who want to contact their home country's embassy while in the US should visit www.embassy.org, which lists contact information for all foreign embassies in Washington, DC. Most countries have an embassy for the UN in New York City. Some countries have consulates in other large cities; look under 'Consulates' in the yellow pages or call local directory assistance.

Food

For details of the cuisine of the Western USA, see p419.

Gay & Lesbian Travelers

LGBTIQ travelers will find lots of places where they can be themselves without thinking twice. Beaches and big cities typically are the most gay-friendly destinations.

Hot Spots

You will have heard of San Francisco, the happiest gay city in America, but what can gays and lesbians do in Los Angeles and Las Vegas? Hmmm, just about anything. In fact, when LA or Vegas gets to be too much, flee to the desert resorts of Palm Springs.

Attitudes

Most major US cities have a visible and open LGBTIQ community.

The level of acceptance varies across the West. In some places, there is absolutely no tolerance whatsoever, and in others acceptance is predicated on LGBTIQ people not 'flaunting' their sexual preference or identity. In rural areas and extremely conservative enclaves, it's unwise to be openly out, as violence and verbal abuse can sometimes occur. When in doubt, assume locals follow a 'don't ask, don't tell' policy.

After a 2015 US Supreme Court decision, same-sex marriage is now legal in all 50 states.

Resources

Advocate (www.advocate.com) Gay-oriented news website reports on business, politics, arts, entertainment and travel.

Gay Travel (www.gaytravel.com) Online guides to US destinations.

GLBT National Help Center (☑888-843-4564; www.glbtnationalhelpcenter.org; ☺1-9pm PST Mon-Fri, 9am-2pm PST Sat) A national hotline for counseling, information and referrals.

National Gay and Lesbian Task Force (www.thetaskforce.org) National activist group's website with news, politics and current issues.

OutTraveler (www.outtraveler.com) Has useful online city guides and travel articles to various US and foreign destinations.

Purple Roofs (www.purple roofs.com) Lists gay-owned and gay-friendly B&Bs and hotels nationwide.

Health

Healthcare & Insurance

➜ Medical treatment in the USA is of the highest caliber, but the expense could kill you. Many healthcare professionals demand payment at the time of service, especially from out-of-towners or international visitors.

➜ Except for medical emergencies (call ☎911 or go to the nearest 24-hour hospital emergency room, or ER), phone around to find a doctor who will accept your insurance.

➜ Keep all receipts and documentation for billing and insurance claims and reimbursement purposes.

➜ Some health-insurance policies require you to get pre-authorization for medical treatment before seeking help.

➜ Overseas visitors with travel health-insurance policies may need to contact a call center for an assessment by phone before getting medical treatment.

➜ Carry any medications you may need in their original containers, clearly labeled. Bring a signed, dated letter from your doctor describing all medical conditions and medications (including generic names).

Environmental Hazards

ALTITUDE SICKNESS

➜ Visitors from lower elevations undergo rather dramatic physiological changes as they adapt to high altitudes.

➜ Symptoms, which tend to manifest during the first day after reaching altitude, may include headache,

fatigue, loss of appetite, nausea, sleeplessness, increased urination and hyperventilation due to overexertion.

➜ Symptoms normally resolve within 24 to 48 hours.

➜ The rule of thumb is, don't ascend until the symptoms descend.

➜ More severe cases may display extreme disorientation, ataxia (loss of coordination and balance), breathing problems (especially a persistent cough) and vomiting. These folks should descend immediately and get to a hospital.

➜ To avoid the discomfort characterizing the milder symptoms, drink plenty of water and take it easy – at 7000ft, a pleasant walk around Santa Fe can wear you out faster than a steep hike at sea level.

DEHYDRATION, HEAT EXHAUSTION & HEATSTROKE

➜ Take it easy as you acclimatize, especially on hot summer days and in Southern California's deserts.

➜ Drink plenty of water. One gallon per person per day minimum is recommended when you're active outdoors.

➜ Dehydration (lack of water) or salt deficiency can cause heat exhaustion, often characterized by heavy sweating, pale skin, fatigue, lethargy, headaches, nausea, vomiting, dizziness, muscle cramps and rapid, shallow breathing.

➜ Long, continuous exposure to high temperatures can lead to possibly fatal heatstroke. Warning signs include altered mental status, hyperventilation and flushed, hot and dry skin (ie sweating stops).

➜ Hospitalization is essential. Meanwhile, get out of the sun, remove clothing that retains heat (cotton is OK),

douse the body with water and fan continuously; ice packs can be applied to the neck, armpits and groin.

HYPOTHERMIA

➜ Skiers and hikers will find that temperatures in the mountains and desert can quickly drop below freezing, especially during winter. Even a sudden spring shower or high winds can lower your body temperature dangerously fast.

➜ Instead of cotton, wear synthetic or woolen clothing that retains warmth even when wet. Carry waterproof layers (eg Gore-Tex jacket, plastic poncho and rain pants) and high-energy, easily digestible snacks like chocolate, nuts and dried fruit.

➜ Symptoms of hypothermia include exhaustion, numbness, shivering, stumbling, slurred speech, dizzy spells, muscle cramps and irrational or even violent behavior.

➜ To treat hypothermia, get out of bad weather and change into dry, warm clothing. Drink hot liquids (no caffeine or alcohol) and snack on high-calorie food.

➜ In advanced stages, carefully put hypothermia sufferers in a warm sleeping bag cocooned inside a wind- and waterproof outer wrapping. Do not rub victims, who must be handled gently.

Insurance

Getting travel insurance to cover theft, loss and medical problems is highly recommended.

➜ Some policies do not cover 'risky' activities such as scuba diving, motorcycling and skiing, so read the fine print. Make sure the policy at least covers hospital stays and an emergency flight home.

➜ Paying for your airline ticket or rental car with a

credit card may provide limited travel accident insurance.

➡ If you already have private health insurance or a homeowner's or renter's policy, find out what those policies cover and only get supplemental insurance.

➡ If you have prepaid a large portion of your vacation, trip cancellation insurance may be a worthwhile expense.

➡ Worldwide travel insurance is available at www.lonelyplanet.com/travel-insurance. You can buy, extend and claim online anytime – even if you're already on the road.

Internet Access

The internet icon (@) indicates a place has a net-connected computer for public use and a wi-fi icon (🛜) indicates it offers wireless internet access, whether free or fee-based.

➡ Most hotels and some motels have either a public computer terminal or wi-fi (sometimes free; sometimes for a surcharge of $10 or more per day).

➡ Wi-fi hot spots (free or fee-based) can be found at major airports; many hotels, motels and coffee shops (eg Starbucks); and some tourist information centers, RV parks (eg KOA), museums, bars, restaurants (including chains such as McDonald's and Panera Bread) and stores (eg Apple).

➡ Free public wi-fi is proliferating and some state parks are now wi-fi enabled.

➡ Public libraries have internet terminals, but online time may be limited, advance sign-up required and a nominal fee charged for out-of-network visitors. Increasingly libraries offer free wi-fi access.

➡ If you're not from the US, remember that you will need an AC adapter for your

> ### PRACTICALITIES
>
> #### Newspapers & Magazines
>
> ➡ National newspapers: *New York Times*, *Wall Street Journal*, *USA Today*
>
> ➡ Western newspapers: *Arizona Republic*, *Denver Post*, *Seattle Times*, *Los Angeles Times*, *San Francisco Chronicle*
>
> ➡ Mainstream news magazines: *Time*, *US News & World Report*
>
> #### Radio & TV
>
> ➡ Radio news: National Public Radio (NPR), lower end of FM dial
>
> ➡ Broadcast TV: ABC, CBS, NBC, FOX, PBS (public broadcasting)
>
> ➡ Major cable channels: CNN (news), ESPN (sports), HBO (movies), Weather Channel
>
> #### Weights & Measures
>
> ➡ Weight: ounces (oz), pounds (lb), tons
>
> ➡ Liquid: ounces (oz), pints, quarts, gallons
>
> ➡ Distance: feet (ft), yards (yd), miles (mi)
>
> #### Video Systems
>
> ➡ DVDs coded for Region 1 (US and Canada only)

laptop, plus a plug adapter for US sockets; both are available at larger electronics shops, such as Best Buy (www.bestbuy.com).

Legal Matters

In everyday matters, if you are stopped by the police, remember that there is no system for paying traffic or other fines on the spot. Attempting to pay a fine to an officer is frowned upon at best and may result in a charge of bribery. For traffic offenses, the police officer or highway patroller will explain the options to you. There is usually a 30-day period to pay a fine. Most matters can be handled by mail.

If you are arrested, you have a legal right to an attorney, and you are allowed to remain silent. There is no legal reason to speak to a police officer if you don't wish, but never walk away from an officer until given permission to do so.

Anyone who is arrested is legally allowed to make one phone call. If you can't afford a lawyer, a public defender will be appointed to you free of charge. Foreign visitors who don't have a lawyer, friend or family member to help should call their embassy; the police will provide the number upon request.

As a matter of principle, the US legal system presumes a person innocent until proven guilty. Each state has its own civil and criminal laws, and what is legal in one state may be illegal in others.

Driving

In all states, driving under the influence of alcohol (the blood-alcohol limit is 0.08%) or drugs is a serious offense, subject to stiff fines and even imprisonment.

Drugs

Recreational drugs are prohibited by federal and most state laws. Washington and Colorado voters recently voted to allow recreational marijuana use, but it is still illegal to smoke in public in either state. Some states, such as California, treat possession of small quantities of marijuana as a misdemeanor, though it is still punishable with fines and/or imprisonment. The federal government recently indicated it won't challenge state laws that have legalized marijuana, but pot use still remains illegal under the federal Controlled Substances Act.

Possession of any illicit drug, including cocaine, ecstasy, LSD, heroin, hashish or more than an ounce of pot, is a felony potentially punishable by lengthy jail sentences. For foreigners, conviction of any drug offense is grounds for deportation.

Money

ATMs

➡ ATMs are available at most banks, shopping malls, airports and grocery and convenience stores.

➡ Expect a minimum surcharge of $2 to $3 per transaction, in addition to any fees charged by your home bank. Some ATMs in Las Vegas may charge more.

➡ Most ATMs are connected to international networks and offer decent foreign-exchange rates.

➡ Withdrawing cash from an ATM using a credit card usually incurs a hefty fee and high interest rates; check with your credit-card company for a PIN number.

Cash

Most people do not carry large amounts of cash for everyday use, relying instead on credit cards, debit cards and ATMs. Some businesses refuse to accept bills over $20.

Credit Cards

Major credit cards are almost universally accepted. In fact, it's almost impossible to rent a car, book a room or buy tickets over the phone without one. A credit card may also be vital in emergencies. Visa, MasterCard and American Express are the most widely accepted.

Moneychangers

➡ You can exchange money at major airports, some banks and all currency-exchange offices such as **American Express**

VISITING NATIONAL & STATE PARKS

Before visiting any national park check out its website, using the navigation search tool on the NPS (www.nps. gov) home page. On the website for the Grand Canyon (www.nps.gov/grca), you can download the seasonal newspaper, *The Guide*, for the latest information on prices, hours and ranger talks. There is a separate edition for both the North and South Rims.

At the entrance of a national or state park, be ready to hand over cash (credit cards may not always be accepted). Costs range from nothing at all to $25 per vehicle for a seven-day pass. If you're visiting several parks in the Southwest, you may save money by purchasing the America the Beautiful annual pass ($80; p442).

Some state parks in Arizona operate on a five-day schedule, closed Tuesdays and Wednesdays. Before visiting a state park, check its website to confirm it's open.

(☎800-528-4800; www. americanexpress.com) or **Travelex** (☎516-300-1622; www.travelex.com). Always inquire about rates and fees.

➡ Outside big cities, exchanging money may be a problem, so make sure you have a credit card and sufficient cash on hand.

Taxes

➡ Sales tax varies by state and county, with state sales taxes ranging from zero in Montana to 7.5% in California.

➡ Hotel taxes vary by city.

Tipping

Tipping is *not* optional. Only withhold tips in cases of outrageously bad service.

Airport skycaps and hotel bellhops $2 per bag, minimum $5 per cart

Bartenders 10% to 15% per round, minimum $1 per drink

Concierges Nothing for simple information, up to $20 for securing last-minute restaurant reservations, sold-out show tickets etc

Housekeeping staff $2 to $4 daily, left under the card provided; more if you're messy

Parking valets At least $2 when handed back your car keys

Restaurant staff and room service 15% to 20%, unless a gratuity is already charged

Taxi drivers 10% to 15% of metered fare, rounded up to the next dollar

Traveler's Checks

➡ Traveler's checks have pretty much fallen out of use.

➡ Larger restaurants, hotels and department stores will often accept traveler's checks (in US dollars only), but small businesses, markets and fast-food chains may refuse them.

➡ Visa and American Express are the most widely accepted issuers of traveler's checks.

Opening Hours

Banks	8:30am-4:30pm Mon-Thu, to 5:30pm Fri (and possibly 9am-noon Sat)
Bars	5pm-midnight Sun-Thu, to 2am Fri & Sat
Nightclubs	10pm-2am Thu-Sat
Post offices	9am-5pm Mon-Fri
Restaurants	11am-2:30pm & 5-9pm. Many Utah restaurants closed Sun
Shopping malls	9am-9pm
Stores	10am-6pm Mon-Sat, noon-5pm Sun
Supermarkets	8am-8pm, some open 24hr

Photography & Video

➜ Print film can be found at specialty camera shops. Digital camera memory cards are widely available at chain retailers such as Best Buy and Target.

➜ Some Native American tribal lands prohibit photography and video completely; when it's allowed, you may be required to purchase a permit. Always ask permission if you want to photograph someone close up; anyone who then agrees to be photographed may expect a small tip.

➜ For more advice on picture-taking, consult Lonely Planet's *Guide to Travel Photography*.

Post

➜ For 24-hour postal information, including post office locations and hours, contact the **US Postal Service** (USPS; ☏800-275-8777; www.usps.com), which is reliable and inexpensive.

➜ For sending urgent or important letters and packages either domestically or overseas, **Federal Express** (☏800-463-3339; www.fedex.com) and **United Parcel Service** (UPS; ☏800-742-5877; www.ups.com) offer more expensive door-to-door delivery services.

Postal Rates

At the time of writing, the postal rates for 1st-class mail within the USA were 49¢ for letters weighing up to 1oz (22¢ for each additional ounce) and 35¢ for postcards. In 2013 the US Post Office introduced the $1.20 Global Forever stamp, which is good for any 1oz letter going anywhere in the world.

Sending Mail

If you have the correct postage, you can drop mail weighing less than 13oz into any blue mailbox. To send a package weighing 13oz or more, go to a post office desk for assistance.

Public Holidays

On the following national public holidays, banks, schools and government offices (including post offices) are closed, and transportation, museums and other services operate on a Sunday schedule. Holidays falling on a weekend are usually observed the following Monday.

New Year's Day January 1

Martin Luther King Jr Day Third Monday in January

Presidents' Day Third Monday in February

TIPS FOR SHUTTERBUGS

➜ If you have a digital camera, bring extra batteries and a charger.

➜ For print film, use 100 ASA film for all but the lowest light situations; it's the slowest film, and will enhance resolution.

➜ A zoom lens is extremely useful; most SLR cameras have one. Use it to isolate the central subject of your photos. A common composition mistake is to include too much landscape around the person or feature that's your main focus.

➜ Morning and evening are the best times to shoot. The same sandstone bluff can turn four or five different hues throughout the day, and the warmest hues will be at sunset. Underexposing the shot slightly (by a half-stop or more) can bring out richer details in red tones.

➜ When shooting red rocks, a warming filter added to an SLR lens can enhance the colors of the rocks and reduce the blues of overcast or flat-light days. Achieve the same effect on any digital camera by adjusting the white balance to the automatic 'cloudy' setting (or by reducing the color temperature).

➜ Don't shoot into the sun or include it in the frame; shoot what the sunlight is hitting. On bright days, move your subjects into shade for close-up portraits.

Memorial Day Last Monday in May

Independence Day July 4

Labor Day First Monday in September

Columbus Day Second Monday in October

Veterans Day November 11

Thanksgiving Fourth Thursday in November

Christmas Day December 25

During spring break (March and April), high school and college students get a week off from school. For students of all ages, summer vacation runs from June to August.

Telephone

Cell Phones

➜ You'll need a multiband GSM phone in order to make calls in the US. Popping in a US prepaid rechargeable SIM card is usually cheaper than using your network.

➜ SIM cards are sold at telecommunications and electronics stores. These stores also sell inexpensive prepaid phones, including some airtime.

➜ If you don't have a compatible phone, you can buy an inexpensive, no-contract (prepaid) phone with a local number and a set number of minutes that can be topped up at will. Electronics stores such as Radio Shack and Best Buy sell these phones.

Dialing Codes

➜ US phone numbers consist of a three-letter area code followed by a seven-digit local number.

➜ When dialing a number within the same area code, you can often use the seven-digit number; however, some places now require you to dial the entire 10-digit number even for a local call.

➜ If you are calling long distance, dial 🖉1 plus the area code plus the phone number.

➜ Toll-free numbers begin with 🖉800, 866, 877 or 888 and must be preceded by 🖉1.

➜ For direct international calls, dial 🖉011 plus the country code plus the area code (usually without the initial '0') plus the local phone number.

➜ For international call assistance, dial 🖉00.

➜ If you're calling from abroad, the country code for the US is 🖉1 (the same as Canada, but international rates apply between the two countries).

Payphones & Phonecards

➜ Where payphones still exist, they are usually coin-operated, although some may only accept credit cards (eg in national parks).

➜ Local calls usually cost 35¢ to 50¢ minimum.

➜ For long-distance calls, you're usually better off buying a prepaid phonecard, sold at convenience stores, supermarkets, newsstands and electronics stores.

Time

➜ Most of Colorado, Wyoming, Montana, Idaho, Utah, New Mexico and Arizona follow Mountain Standard Time (GMT/UTS minus seven hours). California, Nevada, Oregon and Washington generally follow Pacific Standard Time (GMT/UTS minus eight hours). There are some variances within a state, usually based on location or season.

➜ Daylight Saving Time pushes the clocks ahead an hour. It runs from the second Sunday in March to the first Sunday in November.

➜ Arizona does not observe daylight-saving time; during that period it's one hour behind other

Southwestern states. The Navajo Reservation, which lies in Arizona, New Mexico and Utah, does use daylight-saving time. The Hopi Reservation, which is surrounded by the Navajo Reservation in Arizona, follows the rest of Arizona.

➜ The US date system is written as month/day/year. Thus, the 8th of June, 2008, becomes 6/8/08.

Tourist Information

➜ Most tourist offices have a website where you can download free travel guides. They also field phone calls; some local offices maintain daily lists of hotel room availability, but few offer reservation services. All tourist offices have self-service racks of brochures and discount coupons; some also sell maps and books.

➜ State-run 'welcome centers,' usually placed along interstate highways, tend to have materials that cover wider territories, and offices are usually open longer hours, including weekends and holidays.

➜ Many cities have an official convention and visitor bureau (CVB); these sometimes double as tourist bureaus, but since their main focus is drawing the business trade, CVBs can be less useful for independent travelers.

➜ Keep in mind that, in smaller towns, when the local chamber of commerce runs the tourist bureau, their lists of hotels, restaurants and services usually mention only chamber members; the town's cheapest options may be missing.

➜ Similarly, in prime tourist destinations, some private 'tourist bureaus' are really agents who book hotel rooms and tours on commission. They may offer excellent service and deals, but you'll get what they're selling and nothing else.

Travelers with Disabilities

➡ If you have a physical disability, the USA can be an accommodating place. The Americans with Disabilities Act (ADA) requires that all public buildings, private buildings built after 1993 (including hotels, restaurants, theaters and museums) and public transit be wheelchair accessible. However, call ahead to confirm what is available. Some local tourist offices publish detailed accessibility guides.

➡ Telephone companies offer relay operators, available via teletypewriter (TTY) numbers, for the hearing impaired. Most banks provide ATM instructions in Braille, and via earphone jacks for hearing-impaired customers. All major airlines, Greyhound buses and Amtrak trains will assist travelers with disabilities; just describe your needs when making reservations at least 48 hours in advance. Service animals (guide dogs) are allowed to accompany passengers, but bring documentation.

➡ Some car-rental agencies, such as Avis and Hertz, offer hand-controlled vehicles and vans with wheelchair lifts at no extra charge, but you must reserve them well in advance. **Wheelchair Getaways** (☑800-642-2042; www.wheelchairgetaways. com) rents accessible vans throughout the USA. In many cities and towns, public buses are accessible to wheelchair riders; just let the driver know that you need the lift or ramp.

➡ Many national and some state parks and recreation areas have wheelchair-accessible paved, graded

dirt or boardwalk trails. The website for the Rails-to-Trails Conservancy (www.traillink. com) lists wheelchair-accessible trails by state.

➡ US citizens and permanent residents with permanent disabilities are entitled to a free 'America the Beautiful' Access Pass, which gives free entry to all federal recreation lands (eg national parks).

Resources

Some helpful resources for travelers with disabilities:

Access-Able Travel Source (www.access-able. com) General travel website with useful tips and links.

Access Northern California (www.accessnca.com) Extensive links to accessible-travel resources, publications, tours and transportation, including outdoor recreation opportunities, plus a searchable lodgings database and an events calendar.

Arizona Raft Adventures (www.azraft.com) Can accommodate disabled travelers on rafting trips through the Grand Canyon.

Disabled Sports USA (☑301-217-0960; www. disabledsportsusa.org) Offers sport, adventure and recreation programs for those with disabilities. Also publishes *Challenge* magazine.

Mobility International USA (☑541-343-1284; www. miusa.org) Advises travelers with disability about mobility issues, but primarily runs an educational exchange program.

Splore (☑801-484-4128; www.splore.org) Offers accessible outdoor adventure trips in Utah.

Visas

Getting into the US can be complicated and the entry requirements continue to evolve. Plan ahead. For up-to-date information about visas and immigration, start with the **US State Department**

(☑main switchboard 202-647-4000; www.travel.state.gov). For information on Passports, see p449.

Visa Applications

➡ Apart from most Canadian citizens and travelers entering under the Visa Waiver Program (VWP), all foreign visitors to the US need a visa. For more details about visa requirements, visit www.travel.state.gov/content/visas/english.html.

➡ Most visa applicants must schedule a personal interview, to which you must bring all your documentation and proof of fee payment. Wait times for interviews vary, but afterward, barring problems, visa issuance takes from a few days to a few weeks.

➡ You'll need a recent color photo (2in by 2in), and you must pay a nonrefundable $160 processing fee, plus in a few cases an additional visa issuance reciprocity fee. You'll also need to fill out the online DS-160 nonimmigrant visa electronic application.

➡ Depending on the type of visa requested, applicants may have to provide documentation confirming the purpose of their trip, their intent to depart the US after their trip and an ability to cover all costs related to the trip. Visit www.travel.state. gov/content/visas/english/visit/visitor.html for more details.

Visa Waiver Program

➡ Pursuant to the Visa Waiver Program, many travelers visiting the US for sightseeing or for short visits will not need a visa to enter the country.

➡ According to VWP requirements, citizens of certain countries may enter the US for stays of 90 days or fewer without a US visa. This list is subject to continual rejigging. Check www.travel. state.gov/content/visas/english/visit.html to see which countries are included under the waiver and for a summary of current VWP requirements.

➡ If you're a citizen of a VWP country you do not need a visa only if you have a passport that meets current US standards and you get approval from the Electronic System for Travel Authorization (ESTA) in advance. Register online with the Department of Homeland Security at http://esta.cbp.dhs.gov at least 72 hours before arrival. The fee is $14. Canadians are currently exempt from ESTA.

➡ Visitors from VWP countries arriving by air or sea must arrive on an approved air or sea carrier. They must also demonstrate that their trip is for 90 days or less and that they have a round-trip or onward ticket.

➡ Every foreign visitor entering the US from abroad needs a passport. In most cases, your passport must be valid for at least six months after the end of your intended stay in the USA. If your passport doesn't meet current US standards, you'll be turned back at the border. If your passport was issued on or after October 26, 2006 it must be an e-passport with a digital photo and an integrated chip containing biometric data.

➡ For assistance, check out the Visa Wizard on the **State Department** (http://travel.state.gov/content/visas/english/general/visa-wizard.html) website.

Short-Term Departures & Reentry

➡ It's temptingly easy to make trips across the border to Canada or Mexico, but upon return to the USA, non-Americans will be subject to the full immigration procedure.

➡ Always take your passport when you cross the border.

➡ If your immigration card still has plenty of time on it, you will probably be able to reenter using the same one, but if it has nearly expired, you will have to apply for a new card, and border control may want to see your onward air ticket, sufficient funds and so on.

➡ Citizens of most Western countries will not need a visa to visit Canada, so it's really not a problem at all to pass through on the way to Alaska.

➡ Travelers entering the USA by bus from Canada may be closely scrutinized. A round-trip ticket that takes you back to Canada will most likely make US immigration feel less suspicious.

➡ For short visits, Mexico has a visa-free zone along most of its border with the USA, including the Baja Peninsula and most of the border towns, such as Tijuana and Ciudad Juárez. You'll need a Mexican visa or tourist card if you want to go beyond the border zone.

Women Travelers

➡ Women traveling alone or in groups should not expect to encounter any particular problems in the USA. In terms of safety issues, single women just need to practice common sense.

➡ When first meeting someone, don't advertise where you are staying, or that you are traveling alone.

Americans can be eager to help and even take in solo travelers. However, don't take all offers of help at face value. If someone who seems trustworthy invites you to his or her home, let someone (eg hostel or hotel manager) know where you're going.

➡ This advice also applies if you go for a hike by yourself. If something happens and you don't return as expected, you want to know that someone will notice and know where to begin looking for you.

➡ Some women carry a whistle, mace or cayenne-pepper spray in case of assault. If you purchase a spray, contact a police station to find out about local regulations. Laws regarding sprays vary from state to state; federal law prohibits them being carried on planes.

➡ If you are assaulted, consider calling a rape-crisis hotline before calling the police, unless you are in immediate danger, in which case you should call ☎911. But be aware that not all police have as much sensitivity training or experience assisting sexual assault survivors, whereas rape-crisis-center staff will tirelessly advocate on your behalf and act as a link to other community services, including hospitals and the police. Telephone books have listings of local rape-crisis centers, or contact the 24-hour **National Sexual Assault Hotline** (☎800-656-4673). Alternatively, go straight to a hospital emergency room.

Transportation

GETTING THERE & AWAY

Flights and tours can be booked online at www.lonely planet.com/bookings.

Entering the USA

If you are flying into the USA, the first airport where you land is where you must go through immigration and customs, even if you are continuing on the flight to another destination. Fingerprints are taken and biometric information is checked upon entry into the US. For information on visas, see p449.

Passports

➡ Under the Western Hemisphere Travel Initiative (WHTI), all travelers must have a valid machine-readable passport (MRP) when entering the USA by air, land or sea.

➡ The only exceptions are for most US citizens and some Canadian and Mexican citizens traveling by land or sea who can present other WHTI-compliant documents (eg pre-approved 'trusted traveler' cards). For details, check www.getyouhome.gov.

➡ All foreign passports must meet current US standards and be valid for at least six months longer than your intended stay.

➡ MRP passports issued or renewed after October 26, 2006 must be e-passports (ie have a digital photo and integrated chip with biometric data). If your passport was issued before October 26, 2005, it must be 'machine readable' (with two lines of letters, numbers and <<< at the bottom); if it was issued between October 26, 2005, and October 25, 2006, it must be machine readable and include a digital photo.

➡ For more information, consult www.cbp.gov/travel.

Air

Airports

The western USA's primary international airports:

Los Angeles International Airport (www.lawa.org/lax; 1 World Way) California's largest and busiest airport, 20 miles southwest of downtown LA, near the coast.

San Francisco International Airport (www.flysfo. com; S McDonnell Rd) Northern California's major hub, 14 miles south of downtown, on San Francisco Bay.

Seattle-Tacoma International (206-787-5388; www. portseattle.org/Sea-Tac; 17801 International Blvd; 🖧) Known locally as 'Sea-Tac.'

Major regional airports with limited international service (most have wi-fi access – check the website):

Albuquerque International Sunport (505-244-7700; www.cabq.gov/airport; 🖧)

CLIMATE CHANGE & TRAVEL

Every form of transport that relies on carbon-based fuel generates CO_2, the main cause of human-induced climate change. Modern travel is dependent on airplanes, which might use less fuel per kilometer per person than most cars but travel much greater distances. The altitude at which aircraft emit gases (including CO_2) and particles also contributes to their climate change impact. Many websites offer 'carbon calculators' that allow people to estimate the carbon emissions generated by their journey and, for those who wish to do so, to offset the impact of the greenhouse gases emitted with contributions to portfolios of climate-friendly initiatives throughout the world. Lonely Planet offsets the carbon footprint of all staff and author travel.

Serving Albuquerque and all of New Mexico.

Denver International Airport (☎303-342-2000; www.flydenver.com; ☎) Serving southern Colorado; if you rent a car in Denver, you can be in northeastern New Mexico in four hours.

LA/Ontario International Airport (☎909-937-2700; www.lawa.org/ont; 2500 E Airport Dr; ☎) In Riverside County, east of LA.

McCarran International Airport (☎702-261-5211; www.mccarran.com; 5757 Wayne Newton Blvd; ☎) Serves Las Vegas, NV, and southern Utah. Las Vegas is 290 miles from the South Rim of Grand Canyon National Park and 277 miles from the North Rim.

Mineta San José International Airport (www.flysanjose.com; 1701 Airport Blvd, San Jose) In San Francisco's South Bay.

Oakland International Airport (www.oaklandairport.com; 1 Airport Dr; ☎) In San Francisco's East Bay.

Palm Springs International Airport (☎760-318-3800; www.palmspringsairport.com; 3400 E Tahquitz Canyon Way) In the desert, east of LA.

Portland International Airport (☎503-460-4234; www.flypdx.com; 7000 NE Airport Way; ☎) About 12 miles from downtown Portland, OR.

Salt Lake City International Airport (www.slcairport.com; 776 N Terminal Dr; ☎) Serving Salt Lake City and northern Utah; a good choice if you're headed to the North Rim and the Arizona Strip.

San Diego International Airport (www.san.org; 3325 N Harbor Dr; ☎) Four miles northwest of downtown.

Sky Harbor International Airport (☎602-273-3300; http://skyharbor.com; 3400 E Sky Harbor Blvd; ☎) Serving Phoenix and the Grand Canyon, it's one of the 10 busiest airports in the country. Phoenix is 220 miles from the South Rim of

Grand Canyon National Park and 335 miles from the North Rim.

Tucson International Airport (☎520-573-8100; www.flytucson.com; 7250 S Tucson Blvd; ☎) Serving Tucson and southern Arizona.

Vancouver International Airport (☎604-207-7077; www.yvr.ca; ☎) Located six miles south of Vancouver, Canada, on Sea Island; between Vancouver and the municipality of Richmond.

Security

➡ To get through airport security checkpoints (30-minute wait times are standard), you'll need a boarding pass and photo ID.

➡ Some travelers may be required to undergo a secondary screening, involving hand pat-downs and carry-on luggage searches.

➡ Airport security measures restrict many common items (eg pocket knives) from being carried on planes. Check current restrictions with the **Transportation Security Administration** (TSA; www.tsa.gov).

➡ Currently, TSA requires that all carry-on liquids and gels be stored in 3.4oz or smaller bottles placed inside a quart-sized clear plastic zip-top bag. Exceptions, which must be declared to checkpoint security officers, include medications.

➡ All checked luggage is screened for explosives. TSA may open your suitcase for visual confirmation, breaking the lock if necessary. Leave your bags unlocked or use a TSA-approved lock like Travel Sentry (www.travelsentry.org).

Land

Border Crossings

➡ It is relatively easy crossing from the USA into Canada or Mexico; it's crossing back into the USA that can pose

problems if you haven't brought your required documents. Check the ever-changing passport and visa requirements with the US Department of State (www.travel.state.gov) beforehand. US Customs and Border Protection (www.cbp.gov) tracks current wait times at every Mexico border crossing.

➡ Some borders are open 24 hours, but most are not.

➡ Have your papers in order, be polite and don't make jokes or casual conversation with US border officials.

➡ At research time, drug cartel violence and crime were serious dangers along the US–Mexico border.

Bus

➡ Buses can be an inexpensive way to travel between cities and larger towns. They don't serve many national parks or smaller towns.

➡ Bus terminals are often in more dangerous areas of town. US-based **Greyhound** (☎800-231-2222, international customer service ☎214-849-8100; www.greyhound.com) is the main US bus system. In sketchier terminals stay alert and be discreet with valuable personal property.

➡ Greyhound has direct connections between Canada and the Northern US, but you may have to transfer to a different bus at the border. You can also book through Greyhound Canada (www.greyhound.ca).

➡ Northbound buses from Mexico can take some time to cross the US border, as US immigration may insist on checking every person on board.

Car & Motorcycle

➡ If you're driving into the USA from Canada or Mexico, bring your vehicle's registration papers, liability insurance and driver's license; an international driving permit (IDP) is a good supplement, but not required.

→ If you're renting a car or motorcycle, ask if the agency allows its vehicles to be taken across the Mexican or Canadian border; the chances are it doesn't.

TO/FROM CANADA

→ Canadian auto insurance is typically valid in the USA, and vice versa.

→ If your papers are in order, taking your own car across the US–Canada border is usually quick and easy.

→ On weekends and holidays, especially in summer, border-crossing traffic can be heavy and waits long.

→ Occasionally the authorities of either country decide to search a car *thoroughly*. Remain calm and be polite.

TO/FROM MEXICO

→ Very few car-rental companies will let you take a car from the US into Mexico.

→ Unless you're planning an extended stay in Tijuana, taking a car across the Mexican border is more trouble than it's worth. Instead take the trolley from San Diego or leave your car on the US side and walk across.

→ US auto insurance is not valid in Mexico, so even a short trip into Mexico's border region requires you to buy Mexican car insurance, available for around $25 per day at most border crossings, as well as from the **American Automobile Association** (AAA; ☎877-428-2277, emergency roadside assistance ☎800-222-4357; www.aaa.com; annual membership from $52).

→ For a longer driving trip into Mexico beyond the border zone or Baja California, you'll need a Mexican *permiso de importación temporal de vehículos* (temporary vehicle import permit).

CROSSING THE MEXICAN BORDER

The issue of crime-related violence in Mexico has been front and center in the international press in recent years. Nogales, Arizona, for example, is safe for travelers, but Nogales, Mexico is a major locus for the drug trade and its associated violence. Travelers should also exercise extreme caution in Tijuana. We cannot safely recommend crossing the border for an extended period until the security situation changes. You're fine for day trips, but anything past that may be risky.

The **State Department** (www.travel.state.gov/travel/cis_pa_tw/cis/cis_970.html) recommends that travelers visit its website before traveling to Mexico. Here you can check for travel updates and warnings and confirm the latest border-crossing requirements. Before leaving, US Citizens can sign up for the **Smart Traveler Enrollment Program** (https://step.state.gov/step) to receive email updates.

US and Canadian citizens entering the US from Mexico at airports must present a valid passport. To enter by land or sea, US and Canadian citizens are required to present a valid WHTI-compliant document, such as a passport, US passport card, enhanced driver's license or trusted traveler card (NEXUS, SENTRI, Global Entry or FAST).

US and Canadian children under age 16 can also enter using a birth certificate, a consular report of birth abroad, naturalization certificate or Canadian citizenship card. All other nationals must carry a passport and, if needed, visa for entering Mexico and reentering the US. Regulations change frequently, so get the latest scoop at www.cbp.gov.

→ Expect long border-crossing waits, as security has tightened in recent years.

→ See Lonely Planet's *Mexico* guide for further details, or call Mexico's tourist information number (☎800-446-3942) in the USA.

Train

→ **Amtrak** (☎800-872-7245; www.amtrak.com) operates the daily *Cascades* rail service with thruway bus service between Vancouver, BC, in Canada and Seattle, WA.

→ **VIA Rail** (☎888-842-7245; www.viarail.ca) also serves Vancouver, BC, with routes running north and east across Canada.

→ US/Canadian customs and immigration inspections happen at the border, not upon boarding.

→ Currently, no train service connects Arizona or California with Mexico.

GETTING AROUND

Air

The domestic air system is extensive and reliable, with dozens of competing airlines, hundreds of airports and thousands of flights daily. Flying is usually more expensive than traveling by bus, train or car, but it's the best option if you're in a hurry.

Airlines in the Western USA

Overall, air travel in the USA is very safe (much safer than driving on the nation's highways); for comprehensive details by carrier, check out www.airsafe.com.

The main domestic carriers in the West:

Alaska Airlines (☎800-252-7522; www.alaskaair.com) Serves Alaska and the Western US, with flights to the East Coast and Hawaii.

American Airlines (☎800-433-7300; www.aa.com) Nationwide service.

Delta (☎800-221-1212; www.delta.com) Nationwide service.

Frontier Airlines (☎801-401-9000; www.flyfrontier.com) Denver-based airline with service across the continental US.

Hawaiian Airlines (☎800-367-5320; www.hawaiianair.com) Serves the Hawaiian islands and the West Coast, plus Las Vegas and Phoenix.

JetBlue Airways (☎800-538-2583; www.jetblue.com)

TRAVELING TO ALASKA & HAWAII

Alaska

At the northwest tip of North America lies the USA's 49th state, Alaska. It's the biggest state by far, and home to stupendous mountains, massive glaciers and amazing wildlife. Mt McKinley (the continent's highest peak) is here, as are huge numbers of humpback whales and bald eagles. See Lonely Planet's *Alaska* guide for details.

The majority of visitors to Alaska fly into **Ted Stevens Anchorage International Airport** (www.dot.state.ak.us/anc; ☎). **Alaska Airlines** (☎800-252-7522; www.alaskaair.com) has direct flights to Anchorage from Seattle, Portland, Chicago and Los Angeles. It also flies between many towns within Alaska. **Delta** (☎800-221-1212; www.delta.com) offers direct flights from Minneapolis, while **US Airways** (☎800-428-4322; www.usairways.com) flies nonstop from Phoenix and **United** (☎800-864-8331; www.united.com) flies nonstop from Denver. Look for more nonstop flight opportunities with various airlines between Anchorage and cities in the Lower 48 in warmer months.

By ferry it takes almost a week on the **Alaska Marine Highway** (AMHS; ☎800-642-0066; www.dot.state.ak.us/amhs), which connects Bellingham, WA, with more than 12 towns in southeast Alaska. The complete trip (Bellingham to Skagway; $380 one way, 2½ to three days) stops at ports along the way and should be reserved in advance. Alaska Marine Highway ferries are equipped to handle cars (from $500 one way), but space must be reserved months ahead.

The Alaska–Canada Military Hwy is today the Alcan (the Alaska Hwy). This 1387-mile road starts at Dawson Creek in British Columbia and ends at Delta Junction (northeast of Anchorage); in between it winds through the vast wilderness of northwest Canada and Alaska. The driving distance between Seattle and Anchorage is about 2250 miles.

Hawaii

Floating all by itself more than 2500 miles off the California coast, Hawaii enjoys a unique sense of self, separate from the US mainland. On its islands you can hike across ancient lava flows, learn to surf and paddleboard, snorkel with green turtles or kayak to your own deserted island. The primary islands are O'ahu, Hawai'i (the Big Island), Maui, Lana'i, Moloka'i and Kaua'i. No matter the adventure or the island, encounters with nature are infused with the Hawaiian sensibilities of *aloha 'aina* and *malama 'aina* – love and care for the land. See Lonely Planet's *Hawaii* guide for details.

About 99% of visitors to Hawaii arrive by air, and the majority of flights – both international and domestic – arrive at **Honolulu International Airport** (☎808-836-6411; http://hawaii.gov/hnl; 300 Rodgers Blvd, Honolulu; ☎) on O'ahu. In Maui, the **Kahului Airport** (☎808-872-3830; http://hawaii.gov/ogg; 1 Kahului Airport Rd, Kahului) is about 25 minutes from Kihei and 45 minutes from Lahaina.

Most cruises to Hawaii include stopovers in Honolulu and on Maui, Kaua'i and the Big Island. Cruises usually last two weeks, with fares starting at around $100 per person per day. Popular cruise lines include **Holland America** (☎877-932-4259; www.hollandamerica.com), **Princess** (☎800-774-6237; www.princess.com) and **Royal Caribbean** (☎866-562-7625; www.royalcaribbean.com).

Nonstop connections between Eastern and Western US cities, plus Florida, New Orleans and Texas.

Southwest Airlines (☎800-435-9792; www.southwest.com) Service across the continental USA.

Spirit Airlines (☎801-401-2200; www.spiritair.com) Florida-based airline; serves many US gateway cities.

United Airlines (☎800-864-8331; www.united.com) Nationwide service.

US Airways (☎800-428-4322; www.usairways.com) Nationwide service.

Virgin America (☎877-359-8474; www.virginamerica.com) Flights between East and West Coast cities plus Las Vegas, Austin and Dallas.

Bicycle

Regional bicycle touring is popular. It means coasting over winding back roads (because bicycles are often not permitted on freeways), and calculating progress in miles per day, not miles per hour. Cyclists must follow the same rules of the road as automobiles, but don't expect drivers to respect your right of way. Wearing a helmet is mandatory for riders under 18 years of age in California and many Western cities.

Some helpful resources for cyclists:

Adventure Cycling Association (www.adventurecycling.org) Excellent online resource for purchasing bicycle-friendly maps and long-distance route guides.

Better World Club (☎866-238-1137; www.betterworldclub.com) Annual membership ($40, plus $12 enrollment fee) entitles you to two 24-hour emergency roadside pickups with transportation to the nearest bike-repair shop within a 30-mile radius.

Rental & Purchase

➜ You can rent bikes by the hour, the day or the week in most cities and major towns.

➜ Rentals start from around $20 per day for beach cruisers, and up to $39 or more for basic mountain bikes; ask about multiday and weekly discounts.

➜ Most rental companies require a credit-card security deposit of several hundred dollars.

➜ Buy new models from specialty bike shops, sporting-goods stores and discount-warehouse stores, or used bicycles from notice boards at hostels, cafes and universities.

➜ To buy or sell used bikes, check online bulletin boards like Craigslist (www.craigslist.com).

Transporting Bicycles

➜ If you tire of pedaling, some local buses and trains are equipped with bicycle racks.

➜ Greyhound transports bicycles as luggage (surcharge $30 to $40), which must be packed in wood, canvas or a substantial container, and properly secured.

➜ Most of Amtrak's *Cascades*, *Pacific Surfliner*, *Capital Corridor* and *San Joaquin* trains feature onboard racks where you can secure your bike unboxed; try to reserve a spot when making your ticket reservation (surcharge up to $10).

➜ On Amtrak trains without racks, bikes must be put in a box ($15) and checked as luggage (fee $10). Not all stations or trains offer checked-baggage service.

➜ Before flying, you'll need to disassemble your bike and box it as checked baggage; contact the airline directly for details, including applicable surcharges (typically $150 to $200). There may be no surcharge for lighter and smaller bikes (under 50lbs and 62 linear inches).

Boat

There is no river or canal public transportation system in the West, but there are many smaller, often state-run, coastal ferry services. Most larger ferries will transport private cars, motorcycles and bicycles.

Off the coast of Washington, ferries reach the scenic San Juan Islands. Several of California's Channel Islands are accessible by boat, as is Catalina Island, offshore from Los Angeles. On San Francisco Bay, regular ferries operate between San Francisco and Sausalito, Larkspur, Tiburon, Angel Island, Oakland, Alameda and Vallejo.

Bus

➜ **Greyhound** (☎800-231-2222, international customer service ☎214-849-8100; www.greyhound.com) is the major long-distance bus company, with routes throughout the USA and Canada. Greyhound has recently stopped service to many small towns; routes generally trace major highways and stop at larger population centers. To reach country towns on rural roads, you may need to transfer to local or county bus systems; Greyhound can usually provide their contact information.

➜ Most baggage has to be checked in; label it clearly to avoid it getting lost. Larger items, including skis, surfboards and bicycles, can be transported, but there may be an extra charge. Call to check.

➜ Greyhound often has excellent online fares – web-only deals will net you substantial discounts over buying at a ticket counter.

➜ The frequency of bus services varies widely. Despite the elimination of many tiny destinations, nonexpress Greyhound

USEFUL BUS ROUTES

SERVICE	PRICE ($)	DURATION (HR)
Denver–Salt Lake City	89-93	10½-12¼
Las Vegas–Los Angeles	57-66	5¼-7
Los Angeles–San Francisco	59-65	8-11½
Phoenix–Tucson	18-20	2
Seattle–Portland	29-33	4

buses still stop every 50 to 100 miles to pick up passengers. Long-distance buses stop for meal breaks and driver changes.

➡ Greyhound buses are usually clean, comfortable and reliable. The best seats are typically near the front away from the bathroom. Limited onboard amenities include freezing air-con (bring a sweater) and slightly reclining seats; select buses have electrical outlets and wi-fi. Smoking on board is prohibited.

➡ Many bus stations are clean and safe, but some are in dodgy areas.

Costs

➡ For lower fares, purchase tickets seven to 14 days in advance. Price may vary depending on when you're traveling.

➡ Discounts (on unrestricted fares only) are available for veterans (20%), students (20%) with a Student Advantage Card, and up to 50% off for two family members with the purchase of one full-price fare.

➡ Special promotional discounts are often available on the Greyhound website, though they may come with restrictions or blackout periods. The Discovery Pass, which allowed for unlimited travel, has been discontinued.

Reservations

➡ Greyhound bus tickets can be bought over the phone or online. You can print tickets at home or pick them up at the terminal using 'Will Call' service (bring photo ID).

➡ Seating is normally first-come, first-served. Greyhound recommends arriving an hour before departure to get a seat.

➡ Travelers with disabilities who need special assistance should call ☎800-752-4841 (TDD/TTY ☎800-345-3109) at least 48 hours before traveling; there are limited spaces for those in wheelchairs, although wheelchairs are also accepted as checked baggage. Service animals, such as guide dogs, are allowed on board.

Car & Motorcycle

A car allows maximum flexibility and convenience, and it's particularly helpful if you want to explore rural America and its wide-open spaces.

Automobile Associations

For 24-hour emergency roadside assistance, free maps and discounts on lodging, attractions, entertainment, car rentals and more:

American Automobile Association (AAA; ☎877-428-2277, emergency roadside assistance ☎800-222-4357; www.aaa.com; annual membership from $52)

Better World Club (☎866-238-1137; www.betterworldclub.com)

Driver's License

➡ Foreign visitors can legally drive a car in the USA using their home driver's license, but some states may require an international driving permit (IDP); for info see www.usa.gov/visitors-driving.

➡ An IDP will also have more credibility with US traffic police, especially if your home license doesn't have a photo or isn't in English. Your automobile association at home can issue an IDP, valid for one year, for a small fee. Always carry your home license together with the IDP.

➡ To drive a motorcycle in the USA, you will need a valid motorcycle license. International visitors need a drivers' permit from their home country, or an IDP specially endorsed for motorcycles.

Insurance

➡ Liability insurance covers people and property you might hit.

➡ For a rental vehicle, a collision damage waiver (CDW) is available for about $30 per day. Before renting a car, check your auto-insurance policy to see if you're already covered. Your policy probably includes liability protection but check anyway.

➡ Some credit cards offer reimbursement coverage for collision damages when you use the card to rent a car. There may be exceptions for rentals of more than 15 days or for exotic models, Jeeps, vans and 4WD vehicles. If there's an accident you may have to pay the rental-car company first and then seek reimbursement from the credit-card company. Check your credit card's policies carefully before renting.

→ Many rental agencies stipulate that damage a car suffers while being driven on unpaved roads is not covered by the insurance they offer. Check with the agent when you make your reservation.

Car Rental

→ To rent your own wheels, you'll typically need to be at least 25 years old, hold a valid driver's license and have a major credit card, not a check or debit card. A few companies may rent to drivers aged 21 to 25 for a surcharge (around $27 to $30 per day). If you don't have a credit card, you may occasionally be able to make a large cash deposit instead.

→ With advance reservations, you can often get an economy-sized vehicle with unlimited mileage from around $30 per day, plus insurance, taxes and fees. Airport locations may have cheaper rates but higher fees; if you get a fly-drive package, local taxes may be extra when you pick up the car. City-center branches may offer free pick-ups and drop-offs.

→ Rates generally include unlimited mileage (check the mileage cap), but expect surcharges for additional drivers and one-way rentals. Some rental companies let you pay for your last tank of gas upfront; this is rarely a good deal.

→ You might get a better deal by booking through discount-travel websites like Priceline (www.priceline.com) or Hotwire (www.hotwire.com), or by using online travel-booking sites, such as Expedia (www.expedia.com), Orbitz (www.orbitz.com) or Travelocity (www.travelocity.com). You can also compare rates across travel sites at Kayak (www.kayak.com).

→ A few major car-rental companies (including Avis, Budget, Enterprise, and Hertz) offer 'green' fleets of hybrid, clean diesel or electric rental cars, but they're in short supply. Reserve well in advance. Also try **Simply RAC** (☎323-653-0022; www.simplyrac.com) in Los Angeles, which offers free delivery and pick-up from some locations; or **Zipcar** (☎866-494-7227; www.zipcar.com), which is available in California (Los Angeles, San Diego and the San Francisco Bay area) and Denver, Portland and Seattle. This car-sharing club charges usage fees (per hour or daily), and includes free gas, insurance (damage fee of up to $1000 may apply) and limited mileage. Apply online. Monthly memberships run from $7 to $50 and higher, and the application fee is $25. Drivers from outside the US will need to present passport, driver's license and accident history prior to rental.

→ To compare independent car-rental companies, try Car Rental Express (www.carrentalexpress.com), which is especially useful for finding cheaper long-term rentals.

→ Independent companies that may rent to drivers under 25 include **Rent-a-Wreck** (☎877-877-0700; www.rentawreck.com), though minimum rental age and surcharges vary by location; and Super Cheap Car Rental (www.supercheapcar.com) which has no surcharge for drivers aged 21 to 24; daily fee applies for drivers aged 18 to 21.

ROAD DISTANCES (MILES)

	Denver	Grand Canyon National Park (South Rim)	Las Vegas	Los Angeles	Phoenix	Portland	San Francisco	Santa Fe	Seattle
Grand Canyon National Park (South Rim)	68								
Las Vegas	750	270							
Los Angeles	1020	485	270						
Phoenix	825	215	285	375					
Portland	1260	1330	1020	965	1335				
San Francisco	1270	790	570	380	750	635			
Santa Fe	395	455	635	850	530	1450	1145		
Seattle	1330	1365	1165	1135	1500	175	810	1545	
Yellowstone National Park	530	810	670	950	920	795	1000	820	875

458

MAJOR INTERNATIONAL CAR-RENTAL AGENCIES

Alamo (☎877-222-9075; www.alamo.com)

Avis (☎800-633-3469; www.avis.com)

Budget (☎800-218-7992; www.budget.com)

Dollar (☎800-800-3665; www.dollar.com)

Enterprise (☎800-261-7331; www.enterprise.com)

Hertz (☎800-654-3131; www.hertz.com)

National (☎877-222-9058; www.nationalcar.com)

Thrifty (☎800-847-4389; www.thrifty.com)

Motorcycle & Recreational Vehicle (RV) Rental

If you dream of cruising across America on a Harley, **EagleRider** (☎310-321-3180; www.eaglerider.com) has offices in major cities nationwide and rents other kinds of adventure vehicles, too. Motorcycle rental and insurance are expensive.

Companies specializing in RV and camper rentals:

Adventures on Wheels (www.wheels9.com)

Cruise America (☎800-671-8042; www.cruiseamerica.com)

Happy Travel Campers (☎800-370-1262; www.camperusa.com)

Jucy Rentals (☎800-650-4180; www.jucyrentals.com)

Fueling Up

Many gas stations in the West have fuel pumps with automated credit-card pay screens. Most machines ask for your zip code. For foreign travelers, or those with cards issued outside the US, you'll have to pay inside before pumping gas. Tell the clerk how much money you'd like to put on the card. If there's still credit left, go back inside and have the difference refunded to the card.

You cannot pump your own gas in Oregon although the state legislature is considering a bill to allow self-service at rural gas stations.

Road Conditions & Hazards

➡ Road hazards include potholes, city commuter traffic, wandering wildlife and distracted and enraged drivers.

➡ Where winter driving is an issue, many cars are fitted with steel-studded snow tires; snow chains are sometimes required in mountain areas. Driving off-road, or on dirt roads, is often forbidden by rental-car companies, and it can be very dangerous in wet weather.

➡ In deserts and range country, livestock sometimes grazes next to unfenced roads. These areas are signed as 'Open Range' or with the silhouette of a steer. Where deer and other wild animals frequently appear roadside, you'll see signs with the silhouette of a leaping deer. Take these signs seriously, particularly at night.

For nationwide traffic and road-closure information, visit www.fhwa.dot.gov/trafficinfo.

For current road conditions within a state, call ☎511. From outside a state, try the following:

Arizona (☎888-411-7623; www.az511.com)

California (☎800-427-7623; www.dot.ca.gov)

Colorado (☎303-639-1111; www.cotrip.org)

Idaho (☎888-432-7623; 511.idaho.gov)

Montana (☎800-226-7623; www.mdt.mt.gov/travinfo)

Nevada (☎877-687-6237; www.nvroads.com)

New Mexico (☎800-432-4269; nmroads.com)

Oregon (☎503-588-2941; www.tripcheck.com)

Utah (☎866-511-8824; www.commuterlink.utah.gov)

Washington (☎800-695-7623; www.wsdot.com/traffic)

Wyoming (☎888-996-7623; www.wyoroad.info)

Road Rules

➡ Cars drive on the right-hand side of the road.

➡ The use of seat belts and child safety seats is required in every state. Most car-rental agencies rent child safety seats for around $13 per day, but you must reserve them when booking.

➡ In some states, motorcyclists are required to wear helmets.

➡ On interstate highways, the speed limit is sometimes raised to 75mph. Unless otherwise posted, the speed limit is generally 55mph or 65mph on highways, 25mph to 35mph in cities and towns and as low as 15mph in school zones (strictly enforced during school hours). It's forbidden to pass a school bus when its lights are flashing.

➡ When emergency vehicles (ie police, fire or ambulance) approach from either direction, pull over safely and get out of the way. In an increasing number of states, it is illegal to talk on a handheld cell (mobile) phone or text while driving; use a hands-free device or pull over for a call.

➡ The maximum legal blood-alcohol concentration for drivers is 0.08%. Penalties are very severe for 'DUI' – driving under the influence of alcohol and/or drugs. Police can give roadside sobriety checks to assess if you've been drinking or using drugs. If you fail, they'll require you take a breath test, urine test or blood test to determine the level of alcohol or drugs in your body. Refusing to be tested is treated the same as if you'd taken the test and failed.

➡ In some states it is illegal to carry 'open containers' of alcohol in a vehicle, even if they are empty.

Local Transportation

Except in cities, public transport is rarely the most convenient option. Coverage to outlying towns and suburbs can be sparse. However, it is usually cheap, safe and reliable.

Airport Shuttles

Shuttle buses provide inexpensive and convenient transport to/from airports in most cities. Most are 12-seat vans; some have regular routes and stops (which include the main hotels) and some pick up and deliver passengers 'door to door' in their service area. Average costs run from $15 to $22 per person.

Bicycle

Some cities are more amenable to bicycles than others, but most have at least a few dedicated bike lanes and paths. Bikes can usually be carried on public transportation.

Bus

Most cities and larger towns have dependable local bus systems, though they are often designed for commuters and provide limited service in the evening and on weekends. Costs average about $2 per ride. Limited routes in tourist areas may be free.

Subway & Train

The largest systems are in Los Angeles and the San Francisco Bay Area. Other cities may have small, one- or two-line rail systems that mainly serve downtown.

Taxi

➡ Taxis are metered, with average flagfall fees of $2.50 to $3.50, plus $2 to $3 per mile. Credit cards may be accepted.

➡ Taxis may charge extra for baggage and/or airport pick-ups.

➡ Drivers expect a 10% to 15% tip, rounded up to the next dollar.

➡ Taxis cruise the busiest areas in large cities, but elsewhere you may need to call a cab company.

Train

A fairly extensive rail system throughout the USA is operated by **Amtrak** (☎800-872-7245; www.amtrak.com). Fares vary according to the type of train and seating (eg reserved or unreserved coach seats, business class and sleeping compartments). Trains are comfortable, if a bit slow, and are equipped with dining and lounge cars on long-distance routes.

Amtrak routes in the West:

California Zephyr Daily service between Chicago and Emeryville (from $255, 52 hours), near San Francisco, via Denver, Salt Lake City, Reno and Sacramento.

Coast Starlight Travels the West Coast daily from Seattle to LA (from $115, 35½ hours) via Portland, Sacramento, Oakland

---

SCENIC ROUTES

Historic locomotives chug through mountain ranges and other scenic landscapes across the West. Most trains run in the warmer months only, and they can be extremely popular, so book ahead.

Cumbres & Toltec Scenic Railroad (☎888-286-2737; www.cumbrestoltec.com; adult/child 2-12yr from $95/49; ⊙late May–mid-Oct) Living, moving museum from Chama, NM, into Colorado's Rocky Mountains.

Durango & Silverton Narrow Gauge Railroad (☎970-247-2733; www.durangotrain.com; 479 Main Ave; return adult/child 4-11yr from $85/51; ⊙May-Oct) Ends at historic mining town Silverton in Colorado's Rocky Mountains.

Mount Hood Railroad (www.mthoodrr.com) Rolls south from the Columbia River Gorge toward Mount Hood.

Skunk Train (☎707-964-6371; www.skunktrain.com; foot of Laurel St; adult/child 2-12yr $60/34) Runs between Fort Bragg, CA, on the coast, and Willits, further inland, passing through redwoods.

Grand Canyon Railway (☎reservations 800-843-8724; www.thetrain.com; Railway Depot, 233 N Grand Canyon Blvd; round-trip adult/child from $65/25) Vintage steam and diesel locomotives with family-oriented entertainment that runs between Williams, AZ, and Grand Canyon National Park.

Pikes Peak Cog Railway (www.cograilway.com) An 8.9-mile track outside Colorado Springs that climbs from a canyon to above the timberline.

TRANSPORTATION TRAIN

USEFUL TRAIN ROUTES

SERVICE	PRICE ($)	DURATION (HR)
Los Angeles–Flagstaff	88	10½
Los Angeles–Oakland/San Francisco	61	11¼
San Francisco/Emeryville–Salt Lake City	97	17
Seattle–Oakland/San Francisco	104	23

and Santa Barbara; wi-fi may be available.

Southwest Chief Daily departures between Chicago and LA (from $169, 43¼ hours) via Kansas City, Albuquerque, Flagstaff and Barstow.

Sunset Limited Thrice-weekly service between New Orleans and LA (from $256, 46½ hours) via Houston, San Antonio, El Paso, Tucson and Palm Springs.

Costs

➡ Purchase tickets at train stations, by phone or online. Fares depend on the day of travel, the route, the type of seating etc. Fares may be slightly higher during peak travel times such as summer.

➡ Usually seniors over 61 and veterans with a Veterans Advantage Card receive a 15% discount, while students with an ISIC or Student Advantage Card receive a 10% discount. AAA members and US military personnel and families also save 10%. Up to two children aged two to 12 who are accompanied by an adult get 50% off. Special promotions can become available anytime, so check the website or ask.

Reservations

Reservations can be made from 11 months in advance up to the day of departure. Space on most trains is limited, and certain routes can be crowded, especially during summer and holiday periods, so it's a good idea to book as far in advance as you can.

Train Passes

➡ Amtrak's USA Rail Pass (www.amtrak.com) is valid for coach-class travel for 15 ($459), 30 ($689) or 45 ($899) days; children aged two to 12 pay half-price. Actual travel is limited to eight, 12 or 18 one-way 'segments,' respectively. A segment is *not* the same as a one-way trip; if reaching your destination requires riding more than one train, you'll use multiple pass segments.

➡ Purchase rail passes online; make advance reservations for each travel segment.

➡ For travel within California, consider the seven-day California Rail Pass (adult/child $159/$79.50), which must be used within 21 consecutive days.

Behind the Scenes

SEND US YOUR FEEDBACK

We love to hear from travelers – your comments keep us on our toes and help make our books better. Our well-traveled team reads every word on what you loved or loathed about this book. Although we cannot reply individually to your submissions, we always guarantee that your feedback goes straight to the appropriate authors, in time for the next edition. Each person who sends us information is thanked in the next edition – the most useful submissions are rewarded with a selection of digital PDF chapters.

Visit **lonelyplanet.com/contact** to submit your updates and suggestions or to ask for help. Our award-winning website also features inspirational travel stories, news and discussions.

Note: We may edit, reproduce and incorporate your comments in Lonely Planet products such as guidebooks, websites and digital products, so let us know if you don't want your comments reproduced or your name acknowledged. For a copy of our privacy policy visit lonelyplanet.com/privacy.

OUR READERS

Many thanks to the travelers who used the last edition and wrote to us with helpful hints, useful advice and interesting anecdotes:
Brian Penny, Frederique Bergniard, Katrin Brugger, Nicolas Jeanvoine

AUTHOR THANKS

Amy C Balfour

Thanks to my talented co-authors who crisscrossed the West in search of the best adventures. Thanks also to Alex Howard and the Lonely Planet team for putting together an epic guide. Cheers!

Sandra Bao

A big shout-out to those who've made my life much happier while researching the Pacific Northwest: Carolyn Hubbard and Mike Hainsworth in Seattle, Adrienne Robineau in Port Townsend and Celeste Brash in Portland. Special thanks also to my husband, Ben Greensfelder, who has supported my research trips over the years (whether he joins me on my travels or not), and to my parents and brother, who have always been there for me throughout my peripatetic life.

Becky Ohlsen

Thanks to Ryan McCluskey, Joëlle Jones, Mike Russell, Leila del Duca, Michael Byrne, the Admiral 589, Joel and Christina and Karl and Natalie Ohlsen for all the help!

Greg Ward

Thanks to everyone at Lonely Planet, especially Alex Howard and my co-authors; to the many people who helped me on the road, including Steve Lewis and Steve Horak; and, above all, to my wife, Sam.

ACKNOWLEDGMENTS

Climate map data adapted from Peel MC, Finlayson BL & McMahon TA (2007) 'Updated World Map of the Koppen-Geiger Climate Classification', *Hydrology and Earth System Sciences*, 11, 1633-44.

Illustration pp126-7 by Michael Weldon.

Cover photograph: Cowboy boots hanging on barn wall, Oregon; Danita Delimont/AWL.

THIS BOOK

This 3rd edition of Lonely Planet's *Western USA* guidebook was coordinated by Amy C Balfour. The content was researched and written by Amy, along with Sandra Bao, Sara Benson, Becky Ohlsen and Greg Ward. The previous edition was written by Amy C Balfour, along with Sandra Bao, Michael Benanav, Greg

Benchwick, Sara Benson, Alison Bing, Celeste Brash, Lisa Dunford, Carolyn McCarthy, Christopher Pitts and Brendan Sainsbury. This guidebook was produced by the following:

Destination Editor
Alexander Howard

Product Editors
Alison Ridgway, Luna Soo

Regional Senior Cartographer Alison Lyall

Book Designer
Wibowo Rusli

Assisting Editors
Pete Cruttenden, Victoria Harrison, Monique Perrin

Cover Researcher
Naomi Parker

Thanks to Jenna Myers, Kirsten Rawlings, Ellie Simpson, Angela Tinson, Lauren Wellicome

Index

Map Pages **000**
Photo Pages **000**

INDEX G-I

NOTES

Map Legend

Sights
- Beach
- Bird Sanctuary
- Buddhist
- Castle/Palace
- Christian
- Confucian
- Hindu
- Islamic
- Jain
- Jewish
- Monument
- Museum/Gallery/Historic Building
- Ruin
- Shinto
- Sikh
- Taoist
- Winery/Vineyard
- Zoo/Wildlife Sanctuary
- Other Sight

Activities, Courses & Tours
- Bodysurfing
- Diving
- Canoeing/Kayaking
- Course/Tour
- Sento Hot Baths/Onsen
- Skiing
- Snorkeling
- Surfing
- Swimming/Pool
- Walking
- Windsurfing
- Other Activity

Sleeping
- Sleeping
- Camping

Eating
- Eating

Drinking & Nightlife
- Drinking & Nightlife
- Cafe

Entertainment
- Entertainment

Shopping
- Shopping

Information
- Bank
- Embassy/Consulate
- Hospital/Medical
- Internet
- Police
- Post Office
- Telephone
- Toilet
- Tourist Information
- Other Information

Geographic
- Beach
- Gate
- Hut/Shelter
- Lighthouse
- Lookout
- Mountain/Volcano
- Oasis
- Park
- Pass
- Picnic Area
- Waterfall

Population
- Capital (National)
- Capital (State/Province)
- City/Large Town
- Town/Village

Transport
- Airport
- BART station
- Border crossing
- Boston T station
- Bus
- Cable car/Funicular
- Cycling
- Ferry
- Metro/Muni station
- Monorail
- Parking
- Petrol station
- Subway/SkyTrain station
- Taxi
- Train station/Railway
- Tram
- Underground station
- Other Transport

Note: Not all symbols displayed above appear on the maps in this book

Routes
- Tollway
- Freeway
- Primary
- Secondary
- Tertiary
- Lane
- Unsealed road
- Road under construction
- Plaza/Mall
- Steps
- Tunnel
- Pedestrian overpass
- Walking Tour
- Walking Tour detour
- Path/Walking Trail

Boundaries
- International
- State/Province
- Disputed
- Regional/Suburb
- Marine Park
- Cliff
- Wall

Hydrography
- River, Creek
- Intermittent River
- Canal
- Water
- Dry/Salt/Intermittent Lake
- Reef

Areas
- Airport/Runway
- Beach/Desert
- Cemetery (Christian)
- Cemetery (Other)
- Glacier
- Mudflat
- Park/Forest
- Sight (Building)
- Sportsground
- Swamp/Mangrove

Becky Ohlsen

Rocky Mountains Becky Ohlsen grew up in the Rockies and seizes every chance she gets to explore the region. She has a huge crush on the Tetons, believes that jackalopes are real and likes to watch a storm roll in across a far-away horizon.

Greg Ward

Southwest Greg Ward has been exploring the deserts of the Southwest for more than 20 years and has written several guidebooks to the region. He also writes extensively about history, music and European destinations. He lives in London, and his website is gregward.info.

OUR STORY

A beat-up old car, a few dollars in the pocket and a sense of adventure. In 1972 that's all Tony and Maureen Wheeler needed for the trip of a lifetime – across Europe and Asia overland to Australia. It took several months, and at the end – broke but inspired – they sat at their kitchen table writing and stapling together their first travel guide, *Across Asia on the Cheap*. Within a week they'd sold 1500 copies. Lonely Planet was born.

Today, Lonely Planet has offices in Franklin, London, Melbourne, Oakland, Beijing and Delhi, with more than 600 staff and writers. We share Tony's belief that 'a great guidebook should do three things: inform, educate and amuse'.

OUR WRITERS

Amy C Balfour

Coordinating Author, Plan Your Trip, Understand, Survival Guide Amy has hiked, biked and paddled her way across California and the Southwest. She has authored or co-authored 28 guidebooks for Lonely Planet and has written for *Backpacker, Redbook, Southern Living, Women's Health, the Los Angeles Times* and the *Washington Post*.

Read more about Amy at:
http://auth.lonelyplanet.com/profiles/amycbalfour

Sandra Bao

Pacific Northwest Sandra has lived in Buenos Aires, New York and California, but the glorious Pacific Northwest has become her final stop. Researching this region has been a highlight of Sandra's 15-year-long authoring career with Lonely Planet, which has covered four continents and dozens of guidebooks. She's come to appreciate the beauty of this region, how much it has to offer and how friendly people can be in those tiny towns in the middle of nowhere.

Read more about Sandra at:
http://auth.lonelyplanet.com/profiles/sandrabao

Sara Benson

California After graduating from college, Sara jumped on a plane to California with just one suitcase and $100 in her pocket. After driving tens of thousands of miles to every corner of the state, she settled on the sunny side of San Francisco Bay in Oakland. The author of more than 65 travel and nonfiction books, Sara's latest adventures are online at www.indietraveler.blogspot.com, www.indietraveler.net, @indie_traveler on Twitter and indietraveler on Instagram.

Read more about Sara at:
http://auth.lonelyplanet.com/profiles/sara_benson

OVER PAGE MORE WRITERS

Published by Lonely Planet Publications Pty Ltd
ABN 36 005 607 983
3rd edition – April 2016
ISBN 978 1 74321 864 8
© Lonely Planet 2016   Photographs © as indicated 2016
10 9 8 7 6 5 4 3 2 1
Printed in China

Although the authors and Lonely Planet have taken all reasonable care in preparing this book, we make no warranty about the accuracy or completeness of its content and, to the maximum extent permitted, disclaim all liability arising from its use.